# INTERNATIONAL RELATIONS

## Documents and Readings

# INTERNATIONAL

# RELATIONS

*Documents and Readings*

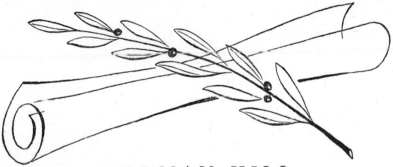

## NORMAN HILL

*Professor of International Law and Relations*
*University of Nebraska*

*New York* · OXFORD UNIVERSITY PRESS · 1950

COPYRIGHT 1950 BY OXFORD UNIVERSITY PRESS, INC.

PRINTED IN THE UNITED STATES OF AMERICA

*To Betsy and Virginia*

# PREFACE

THE COMPILATION of these readings grew out of the conviction that students of international relations are in need of direct contact with documents, speeches, and authoritative articles and books. Out of a long experience in the teaching of international relations, I have found that no single textbook, however excellent it may be, can supply the student with the sense of reality the subject demands, and that no single source can impart the vitality that is to be derived from a variety of sources. From the direct use of treaties, reports, and official statements the student is encouraged to think for himself and to arrive at his own conclusions rather than to rely on those of any one expert.

For the most part the subjects covered by the extracts are those commonly treated by textbooks on international relations. To prepare the student for the extracts that follow and to tie the subject together, each chapter opens with extensive introductory notes. These notes are so organized as to fill any gaps left by the extracts, to summarize historical data, to point out problems, or to offer opinions and points of view.

Among the reading material included is much that will be permanently useful to students: charters and constitutions of important international organizations; classical statements of basic principles of economics, law, or theory; and recent articles or speeches that are unusually illuminating or succinct in the presentation of a subject. Other extracts by the nature of things will become dated, for the relations of nations are never static. I have endeavored to keep the number of extracts of transient value to a minimum.

Included among the extracts are many which properly belong to the field of international organization, if indeed it is possible to separate this field from that of 'international politics' or 'international relations,' as the subject is customarily labeled in college catalogues. The incorporation of this material seemed justified for the reason that courses in international relations generally contain sections on the United Nations and other agencies of international co-operation.

Among those who have given me the benefit of their counsel, special mention should be made of Mr. Grant McClellan of the Department of State.

NORMAN HILL

*November* 1949

# TABLE OF CONTENTS

*Part One · International Relations and Organization*

1. THE STATE IN INTERNATIONAL RELATIONS, 3
    I. Nature of the State in International Relations, 5
    II. What Is the Nation State?, 6
        A. The Future of the Nation State, 7
    III. The Sovereignty of States, 9
        A. Does Sovereignty Apply in International Relations?, 11
    IV. The Equality of States, 13
        A. A Recent View on the Equality of States, 14
        B. An American View on the Equality of States, 15
    V. The Role of Small States, 16
        A. The Communist View of Small States, 22
    VI. The Democratic State, 22
    VII. The Russian Ideal, 24
    VIII. The States of the World, 28

2. THE EARLIER SEARCH FOR SECURITY, 31
    I. A Plan to Abolish War, 33
    II. Non-Aggression Treaties, 35
        A. Treaty between Russia and Italy, 1933, 35
        B. A Definition of Aggression, 36
    III. The Covenant of the League of Nations, 36
    IV. The Geneva Protocol, 44
    V. The Pact of Paris, 47
    VI. Disarmament, 48
    VII. The Failure of Security, 1919-39, 50

3. THE UNITED NATIONS—A NEW SYSTEM OF SECURITY, 59
    I. The Charter of the United Nations, 61
    II. The 'Little Assembly,' 80
    III. The Security Council in Action, 82
    IV. The Problem of the Veto, 86
        A. Assembly Resolution on the Veto, 86

B. The Position of New Zealand, 86
C. The Russian Position, 87
D. Statement by Vishinsky, 88
E. The American Proposal, 89
F. Statement on the American Proposal, 91
V. Military Forces for the United Nations, 92
VI. New Attempts to Regulate Armaments, 100
A. Disarmament and the United Nations, 100
B. The United States Attitude, 102
VII. The Future of the United Nations, 104

4. REGIONALISM AND THE UNITED NATIONS, 106
I. Provisions of the United Nations Charter, 109
II. The Inter-American System, 113
III. Defense of the Western Hemisphere, 116
IV. Unity for Western Europe, 118
V. The Vandenberg Resolution, 121

5. INTERNATIONAL LAW AND COURTS, 123
I. The Place of International Law, 124
II. Order under Law, 125
III. The Reality of International Law, 127
IV. Conditions for the Progress of International Law, 128
V. The Individual and International Law, 133
A. Individual Responsibility for Violations, 133
VI. War Crimes and the Individual, 134
VII. International Law and the United Nations, 135
VIII. International Arbitration, 137
IX. The International Court of Justice, 140
X. Compulsory Jurisdiction, 150

6. THE CONDUCT OF INTERNATIONAL RELATIONS, 151
I. Callières on Diplomacy, 152
II. Diplomatic Rank, 154
III. The Organization of Diplomacy, 155
IV. The Foreign Service of the United States, 155
V. Secret and Open Diplomacy, 158
A. A Criticism of Open Diplomacy, 160
VI. The Publication of Treaties, 161
VII. Diplomacy by Conference, 163
VIII. The United Nations as a Conference System, 166
IX. The Inter-American Conference System, 168

## Part Two · Power Politics and War

7. POWER POLITICS, 177
      I. The Place of Power, 179
     II. The State as Power, 180
    III. The Bases of Power, 182
    IV. The Balance of Power, 185
         A. Vattel's View, 185
         B. The Balance of Power in History, 186
         c. Prussia and the Balance of Power, 1859, 187
         D. Sir Edward Grey on the Balance of Power, 188
     V. Alliances to Gain More Power, 189
         A. The Chinese-Soviet Treaty of Alliance, 189
         B. The Anglo-French Alliance, 1947, 190
    VI. The Great Powers, 191
   VII. Power and Foreign Policy, 196

8. THE GEOGRAPHIC SETTING, 198
      I. The Relation of Geography to Foreign Policy, 199
     II. The State—Its Size and Security, 203
         A. A Finnish Statement, 203
         B. Hitler's Views, 203
    III. Geopolitics, 204
    IV. International Relations and Maps, 210
     V. Geographic Claims to Territory, 217
    VI. Which Hemisphere?, 219

9. NATIONALISM, 226
      I. The Nature of Nationalism, 227
     II. German Racial Doctrines, 231
    III. Chinese Nationalism, 234
    IV. Communism and Nationalism, 236
     V. Self-Determination, 239
         A. Secretary Lansing's Criticism, 239
         B. A More Recent Criticism, 240
    VI. Plebiscites and National Sentiment, 241
         A. A Discussion of Plebiscites, 242
         B. A Plebiscite in Action, 244

10. THE ECONOMIC BASIS, 248
      I. Capitalism and War, 249
     II. Economic Nationalism, 251
    III. The Population Potential, 255

    IV. The Problem of Raw Materials, 256
        A. Geographic Distribution of Raw Materials, 258
        B. List of Strategic and Critical Materials, 258


11. IMPERIALISM, 262
    I. The Economic Side of Imperialism, 265
    II. The Communist Interpretation, 267
    III. Does Imperialism Pay?, 268
    IV. The Military Value of Colonies, 271
    V. The Surplus Population Argument, 272
        A. Colonies as Population Outlets, 273
    VI. Humanitarian Motives, 275
        A. Italy's Mission in Abyssinia, 276
        B. Britain's Claim of Accomplishments, 277
    VII. The British Commonwealth and Empire, 278
        A. Dominion Status, 279
        B. India—The 1947 Independence Act, 280
        C. British Colonial Aims, 282
    VIII. The Trusteeship System, 285
        A. The Mandate or Trusteeship Principle, 286
        B. Trusteeship Agreements, 290
        C. United States Trusteeship for the Pacific Islands, 295


12. THE PROBLEM OF WAR, 299
    I. War in History, 300
    II. Causes of War, 301
        A. A List of Causes, 301
        B. Opinions on the Causes, 302
    III. Human Nature and War, 305
        A. Fear (Prior to World War II), 305
        B. Must Men Fight?, 306
        C. The Biological Aspects of War, 310
    IV. Exponents of War, 311
        A. Machiavelli on War, 311
        B. Von Bernhardi's Views, 312
    V. The Theory of Just Wars, 313
    VI. Pacifism, 314
        A. Jonathan Dymond on War, 314
        B. The Early Church, 315
        C. A Contemporary Christian View, 316
        D. Gandhi's Satyagraha, 317
    VII. The Soviet Philosophy of War, 318
    VIII. The Regulation of War, 321
        A. A Statement by Grotius, 321
        B. The Laws of War and the Atomic Bomb, 322

## Part Three · World Economics and Social Problems

13. TECHNOLOGY IN THE ATOMIC ERA, 327
    I. Science and Man, 328
    II. Transportation and Communication, 329
        A. Some Effects of Technology, 329
        B. Freeing International Travel, 333
    III. The Radio, 336
        A. The Telecommunications Convention (1931), 336
        B. The Political Use of Radio, 338
        C. The 1936 Convention, 341
        D. The 1936 Inter-American Resolution on Radio, 342
    IV. World Aviation, 342
        A. The International Civil Aviation Convention, 343
        B. The Bermuda Plan, 344
        C. Aviation and World Politics, 346
    V. Technology and War, 350
    VI. Atomic Power, 353
        A. President Truman's Announcement—6 August 1945, 354
        B. United States Proposal, 356
        C. The Russian Point of View, 358
        D. Russian Criticism of the United States Plan, 360
        E. Recommendations of the Atomic Energy Commission, 361

14. TRADE AND THE WORLD ECONOMY, 366
    I. Free Trade, 367
        A. Adam Smith on Free Trade, 368
        B. Free Trade and Peace, 369
    II. Economic Co-operation and Peace, 370
        A. Economic or Political Peace?, 370
        B. The Economic Bases of Peace, 372
    III. Restrictions on Trade, 376
    IV. Cartels and Commodity Agreements, 379
        A. An Official American Statement, 379
        B. The Inter-American Coffee Agreement, 381
    V. The International Trade Organization, 384
    VI. The Geneva Trade Agreement, 387
        A. General Nature of the Agreement, 387
        B. Excerpts from State Department Report, 388
    VII. International Investments, 389
        A. Advantages and Problems, 389
    VIII. The International Monetary Fund, 392
    IX. The International Bank, 395
    X. The Marshall Plan, 400

15. SOCIAL PROBLEMS, 403
    I. The Economic and Social Council, 404
        A. An American Statement on the Economic and Social
            Council, 404
        B. The Social Commission, 407
        C. The International Children's Emergency Fund, 408
    II. The Problem of Health, 409
        A. An International Problem, 410
        B. The World Health Organization, 411
        C. World Health Organization Program, 416
    III. Displaced Persons, 419
        A. The Problem, 419
        B. The International Refugee Organization, 421
    IV. Narcotic Control, 423
        A. Past Control Efforts, 423
        B. The United Nations Commission on Narcotic Drugs, 426
    V. Social Principles of the Inter-American System, 427
        A. Declaration of Principles, 427
        B. Child Welfare in the American Republics, 430

16. LABOR AND AGRICULTURE, 432
    I. Labor in World Affairs, 433
        A. The A. F. of L. and International Co-operation, 433
        B. Labor and Foreign Policy, 435
    II. The International Labor Organization, 436
        A. Aims and Purposes of the International Labor Organization,
            441
    III. The Food and Agriculture Organization, 443
        A. Program of the Food and Agriculture Organization, 447
        B. United States Proposals on the Constitution of the Food and
            Agriculture Organization, 450
    IV. The Inter-American Institute of Agricultural Sciences, 452

*Part Four · The Individual and the World of Ideas*

17. HUMAN RIGHTS AND MINORITY RIGHTS, 459
    I. The Four Freedoms, 460
    II. The United Nations and Human Rights, 460
        A. Recommendations on a Bill of Rights, 461
        B. The Commission on Human Rights, 462
        C. Progress Report on Human Rights, 463
        D. Declaration of Human Rights, 469

    III. The Minority Problem, 473
        A. Assembly Resolution on Racial Persecution, 474
        B. Convention Outlawing Genocide, 474
    IV. Minorities in the Soviet Union, 477
        A. Declaration of Rights of the People of Russia, 477
        B. Article 123 of the Russian Constitution, 478
    V. The Transfer of Populations, 478

18. ETHICS AND RELIGION, 481

    I. Morality in International Politics, 483
    II. Chamberlain on Hitlerian Ethics, 486
    III. International Law as a Standard of Conduct, 487
    IV. Hegel's Idea of State Morality, 488
    V. A Catholic Statement on States and Morality, 490
    VI. The Uniting Force in Religion, 491
    VII. Religion and International Affairs, 494
    VIII. A Church Program for Peace, 499
    IX. A Statement by British Church Leaders, 502

19. OPINION, EDUCATION, AND WORLD AFFAIRS, 504

    I. Public Opinion and Power, 505
    II. Foreign Policy and the Democratic Process, 506
    III. Propaganda, 509
    IV. Freedom of Information, 513
        A. Geneva Resolutions, 514
        B. Resolution of the Inter-American Conference, 518
    V. Education, 519
        A. Nazi Education, 519
        B. The Role of Intellectual Co-operation, 522
        C. Intellectual Co-operation in the Americas, 523
        D. The Cinema, 525
        E. The Teaching of History, 526
    VI. The United Nations and Intellectual Co-operation, 527
        A. Constitution of the United Nations Educational, Scientific
           and Cultural Organization, 527
        B. The Program of UNESCO, 1948, 532

# List of Illustrations

The United Nations, 79

Present Inter-American System, 173

'East by North,' 212

Mackinder's Map, 'The Natural Seats of Power,' 213

The Northern Hemisphere, 221

The Map-Maker's Conventional 'Western Hemisphere,' 221

Hemisphere Centered at 28° N., 31° W., 223

Hemisphere with the Northern Limits of the United States at Its Edge, 223

Hemisphere with the Coast of the United States at Its Edge, 224

Hemisphere with the Southern Coast of the United States at Its Edge, 224

Geographic Distribution of Raw Materials, 259

Self-Sufficiency, 259

World Empires, 264

Ratio of European Whites in Ten Overseas Possessions, 274

Trust Areas (1949), 297

Energy Consumed Per Capita for Productive Purposes in 1937, 330

Equal-Cost Distances from St. Louis, Mo., 1804 and 1944, 331

New York to Bombay, 333

Private American Investments Abroad, 391

Structure of the Economic and Social Council, 406

Food and Agriculture Organization, 445

# PART ONE

# INTERNATIONAL RELATIONS AND ORGANIZATION

# THE STATE IN INTERNATIONAL RELATIONS

INTERNATIONAL relations are conducted by states. It is states that engage in diplomacy, make treaties, arbitrate disputes, and go to war. Even when an individual has an interest to promote or protect, such as a financial claim against a foreign state, there is no way to handle it internationally except through the diplomatic machinery of his state. It follows that the state is the basic unit in the world community, much as the individual is the basic unit in national and local communities.

In the circumstances, the student of international relations must understand the state's nature just as the student of sociology must understand human nature. Why do states act as they do? The answer to this question is not simple, but, broadly speaking, the policies of states are reactions to environmental stimuli. Because of the attributes or characteristics of modern states, certain reactions to external stimuli appear to be quite natural. Under given circumstances states find it possible to co-operate with each other, while under other environmental stimuli states are likely to refuse co-operation, become aggressive, or go to war.

The purpose of this chapter is to examine some of the attributes of the modern state that affect its external activities. No attempt is made to deal fully with the nature of the state, or with what is often called the theory of the state. Since the time of Aristotle, philosophers have pondered this subject and many doctrines have been advanced, but none has had general support. Only those theories that help explain the conduct of states *vis-à-vis* other states are examined here. It is commonly asserted, for example, that states are sovereign and that their sovereignty must be respected in international relations. This is a general statement and quite meaningless unless the concept of sovereignty is amplified. Similarly, the idea that states are equal, an idea frequently asserted in the conduct of international relations, requires elaboration.

Reference is also made in this chapter to certain physical characteristics of states and of the community which they constitute, often called the society of nations. The fact that some states are large and others small is a matter of profound importance. Most states today are at the same time nations; they are 'nation states,' being at once political and ethnic entities. This furnishes a striking contrast with conditions during earlier periods of history, when the stage was dominated by city states, feudal principalities, or empires. Indeed a few city states, such as Monaco and San Marino, still exist; but the empires now in the ascendency, unlike the Roman Empire and the Holy Roman Empire of earlier times, are today possessed by nation states.

The trend during the past few centuries has been toward an increase in the total number of states that make up the world community. It was in Europe that the modern state was first created, usually by feudal wars from which the successful chieftains emerged as monarchs. During the Middle Ages, England, France, Sweden, Spain, and other parts of Europe went through this process, so that by 1648 a sizable group of states occupied the European Continent. The Treaty of Westphalia (1648) acknowledged the sovereign independence of those states, recognized their freedom from Church control, and set up boundaries which were expected to be permanent. Thus the European state-system was born, and the modern era of international relations opened.

Since 1648 the state-system has undergone many changes. In the Western Hemisphere the thirteen colonies became free of British control and organized the United States of America. During the early decades of the nineteenth century the peoples of Latin America revolted against Spain and Portugal to establish themselves as independent states—twenty of them. China was opened to the West by the Opium War of 1840-42 and soon took her place among the states of the world. A little later Japan and Siam joined the international state-system.

Many changes, too, were brought about during the nineteenth and twentieth centuries in the European part of the community of nations. The blood-and-iron policies of Bismarck united the three hundred and more sovereignties of Germany into one of the most powerful nation states of the world. At about the same time Cavour led the movement for Italian unification. In the Balkan Peninsula a group of new states—Greece, Bulgaria, Rumania, Serbia, and Albania—took over in place of Turkey, which by 1913 had lost all of her European holdings except a small part of Eastern Thrace. After World War I several new, revived, or remodeled states appeared in central and eastern Europe. In place of the old Hapsburg Empire, Austria and Hungary emerged, while other portions of that empire were awarded to the newly constructed states of Czechoslovakia and Poland; territory was also ceded to the domains of Rumania and Serbia (Yugoslavia) in the Balkans. Finland, Estonia, Latvia, and Lithuania attained their independence from Russia and were recognized as new members of the society of nations, but in World War II all of this latter group except Finland were again brought within the Russian state.

The relations between the seventy or more states that compose the modern world community have constantly grown more and more complex. The industrial revolution increased their dependence on each other for raw materials and other commodities, so that trade, investments, and economic matters generally have become vital subjects of diplomacy. As travel has become easier, the international regulation of such matters as health, passports, citizenship, the sale of opium, and the extradition of criminals has been demanded. Trade and travel have both given a new significance to ports, canals, and rivers of international concern, so that it is necessary to assure free access to them by international action. For the same reason, measures have been undertaken to free the high seas from piracy and to keep them open to the ships of the world. New inventions have added still other items to the list of subjects that now require international regulation: railroads, the radio, aviation, and, more recently, atomic energy. So closely have all these and many other interests knitted the world together that today there are thoughtful persons who believe the modern state is antiquated, that it is inadequate in its treatment of present-day problems and should give way to world government. Popular thinking, however, is so firmly geared to the state and its mechanism that world government does not now appear feasible. It is safe to predict that the state will continue to exist for a long time to come.

## I. Nature of the State in International Relations

Something of the character of states as units of international relations may be seen from the provisions of the following inter-American convention. The convention was signed in 1933 by the twenty-one American republics. Certain of its provisions, notably those relating to state equality, recognition, and intervention, were intended by some of the signatories to impose restraint on the foreign policy of the United States in this hemisphere. Nevertheless, the convention as a whole announces principles in relation to states and their conduct which are widely accepted the world over.

(Inter-American Convention on the Rights and Duties of States, signed 26 December 1933, at Montevideo. *U.S. Treaty Series,* No. 881.)

The Governments represented in the Seventh International Conference of American States . . .

Wishing to conclude a Convention on the Rights and Duties of States, have appointed the following plenipotentiaries . . . [Here follow the names of plenipotentiaries.]

Who, after having exhibited their Full Powers, which were found to be in good and due order, have agreed upon the following:

### Article 1

The State as a person of international law should possess the following qualifications: (a) a permanent population; (b) a defined territory; (c) government; and (d) capacity to enter into relations with other states.

### Article 2

The federal state shall constitute a sole person in the eyes of international law.

### Article 3

The political existence of the state is independent of recognition by other states. Even before recognition the state has the right to defend its integrity and independence, to provide for its conservation and prosperity, and consequently to organize itself as it sees fit, to legislate upon its interests, administer its services, and to define the jurisdiction and competence of its courts.

The exercise of these rights has no other limitation than the exercise of the rights of other states according to international law.

### ARTICLE 4

States are juridically equal, enjoy the same rights, and have equal capacity in their exercise. The rights of each one do not depend upon the power which it possesses to assure its exercise, but upon the simple fact of its existence as a person under international law.

### ARTICLE 5

The fundamental rights of states are not susceptible of being affected in any manner whatsoever.

### ARTICLE 6

The recognition of a state merely signifies that the state which recognizes it accepts the personality of the other with all the rights and duties determined by international law. Recognition is unconditional and irrevocable.

### ARTICLE 7

The recognition of a state may be express or tacit. The latter results from any act which implies the intention of recognizing the new state.

### ARTICLE 8

No state has the right to intervene in the internal or external affairs of another.

### ARTICLE 9

The jurisdiction of states within the limits of national territory applies to all the inhabitants.

Nationals and foreigners are under the same protection of the law and the national authorities and the foreigners may not claim rights other or more extensive than those of the nationals.

### ARTICLE 10

The primary interest of states is in the conservation of peace. Differences of any nature which arise between them should be settled by recognized pacific methods.

### ARTICLE 11

The contracting states definitely establish as the rule of their conduct the precise obligations not to recognize territorial acquisitions or special advantages which have been obtained by force whether this consists in the employment of arms, in threatening diplomatic representations, or in any other effective coercive measures. The territory of a state is inviolable and may not be the object of military occupation nor of other measures of force imposed by another state directly or indirectly or for any motive whatever even temporarily.

### ARTICLE 12

The present convention shall not affect obligations previously entered into by the High Contracting Parties by virtue of international agreements. . .

## II. WHAT IS THE NATION STATE?

The term 'nation state' is, in a purely abstract sense, a good one since it describes very well the entity for which it stands. Most modern states have an ethnic or national basis, unlike the old city states of Athens, Sparta, and the rest, which did not approximate nations. The seventy-odd states today are also different from empires such as the British Empire, which brings many ethnic groups into a single political organization. Both 'state' and 'nation,' however, are words with rather broad meanings, so that the status of a given community either as a state or a nation may not be clear. There is rarely if ever an exact identity between a state and nation because of the presence within many states of minority peoples. Poland is commonly referred to as a nation state, for instance, yet there are within Polish boundaries a considerable number of Russians, Czechs, and other minorities. Other considerations, in addition to the ethnic basis of modern states, are discussed in the following extract.

(Karl Meyer, 'Les Bases historiques de l'état national moderne,' *L'Esprit international*, vol. 13, 1939, pp. 576-7, translation by the compiler. Reprinted by permission of the Carnegie Endowment for International Peace.)

Political history of the nineteenth and twentieth centuries has been dominated by the national state, a distinctly modern phenomenon which appeared first in the countries of the west and which exists today throughout the European and American areas.

An accurate definition of the national state is difficult to give because the words which express the idea are themselves obscure. The term 'national state' was not coined in a work shop as a scientific and unequivocal statement of fact. It is an historical idea, or, if one may use the term, a slogan, created in the course of a battle with the purpose of producing an historical and political effect. It is for that reason that the term is so ambiguous and paradoxical, for a slogan should have those characteristics and thus attract the largest possible number of adherents of all types.

There is one point which all concepts of the national state have in common, a postulate derived from the opposition to the absolute monarchies which preceded it, namely that the unit of politics should not be a conglomerate, formed into a superficial unity, but rather it should be an organic community. But if the question be raised—what is to be the nature of that community—two opposed and totally different answers are given. One is the idea that the national state takes its origin in a common will; the other is more objective and realistic. The former, which had its origin in the philosophic doctrines of the eighteenth century, is today very widely held especially in places where Encyclopedism originated, among the Anglo-Saxon peoples and the French. The latter, the outgrowth of Romanticism, was adopted particularly in the theory and practice of the Germans and the peoples of eastern Europe. According to the first of these concepts, the national state has for its base a community of will and conscience; it is the concrete realization of the subjective right of self-determination; the state includes all who wish to be a part of it, their motives being regarded as unimportant. The second considers that the state has as its base a common 'Kultur,' formed by history and in particular by a common language. . .

## A. *The Future of the Nation State*

Does the nation state effectively serve the interests of mankind, or has it outlived its usefulness? If it has run its course, what is there to take its place? These problems are discussed in the following extract, taken from the author's conclusions to a thoughtful analysis of the present position of the nation state.

(W. Friedmann, *The Crisis of the National State*, London, 1943, pp. 163-4, 167. Reprinted by permission of The Macmillan Company.)

The predominant trend of political, economic, and social forces of today lead away from the national state. The trend is, in many cases, unconscious or contrary to professed ideology. Moreover, the various anti-national movements are not prompted by similar motives and ideals. Indeed, they are, in many cases, violently opposed to each other. The link between them is a negative one: the overcoming of the national state as the determining political unit.

The alliance between nationalism and the state reaches a crisis when both nationalism and the modern state begin to over-reach themselves. An exuberant nationalism, on one hand, leads to a hypertrophy of new states based on the national ideal, but unable to realize it, without suppression of some other national group. The resultant dilemma of national self-determination leads either to the suppression or the incorporation of the smaller national states by the more powerful ones, which themselves turn from nationalism to imperialism. This imperialism develops from a successful national movement that has entered into an alliance with the rulers of the modern state which concentrates an ever-increasing proportion of the forces of society in its hands. This growing power of the state favours the rise of political rulers who use the instruments of power over the masses toward the making of empires which discard and overcome the national state. Their own nation serves merely as the instrument and basis of attack, but its various components are merged in a new international society. . .

The insufficiency of the national state as the principal ordering factor of the political, economic, and social life of man in the world of today is a matter of analysis; the alternative is not a matter of logic or necessity but of decision. It has been the object of this study to demonstrate how the most diverse forces of our time, political ideology as well as strategic planning, dictator power politics as well as monopoly capitalism, the making of empires by conquest as well as the common man's desire for peace and security, are compelled to look beyond the national state. But the irresistible force of this development in no way impedes the necessity for a clear choice of values, for a decision between alternatives. To put the issue as one between nationalism and internationalism means little in terms of ways of life and human happiness. The choice between peace and war, humanitarianism and racialism, freedom and slavery, remains as stark as ever. The only necessary conclusion from the analysis is that the national state, a political institution of relative value, determined by the ideological, economic, and social background of the time, has set on its decline. The alternative is 'necessary' only in the sense that the predominant conditions of modern life would make any but an international solution an anachronism, unable to survive for any length of time. In that sense only the choice is narrowed down. We must not attempt to turn the clock back. But the issue between the highly organized international class of empires of National Socialism or of the Rising Sun and an international society of free peoples remains urgent and uncompromising. Once this fundamental issue is decided, there still remain, within the broad outline of a free, pacific and cosmopolitan society, such issues as those between a loose system of collective security, or a closer constitutional integration of international society, by means of regional or wider federation or an international Charter of the Rights of Man.

### III. THE SOVEREIGNTY OF STATES

The claim that states are sovereign has led to untold complications in contemporary international politics. The idea of sovereignty was presented centuries ago by Jean Bodin, a French writer, and others, to justify the authority of kings against their subjects, but later it came to be applied to the external relations of states, and the view prevailed that a state may not be limited in its policies and actions toward others. The results of such a doctrine are apparent. It prevented international law from possessing full and lasting binding force, made each state its own judge in controversies with others, and reduced the League of Nations to impotency.

For years the doctrine of sovereignty has been under attack as a concept of both constitutional and international law. Some of the views currently held about the doctrine in international law are given in the extracts that follow.

(M. Spahr, 'Sovereignty under Law: A Possible Redefinition of Sovereignty in the Light of Locke's Theory of Liberty,' *The American Political Science Review*, vol. 39, 1945, pp. 350-55. Reprinted by permission of the *American Political Science Review*.)

Does the concept of sovereignty under law necessarily involve a self-contradiction? That it does, has admittedly been held by the great majority of careful thinkers from the time of Hobbes to the present day. Nor has this been inconsequential. The belief that submission to an enforceable law would be a surrender of sovereignty has been a most potent obstacle to the substitution of the law court for the battlefield in the determination of international disputes. On the other hand, it is generally conceded that for the individual the only liberty worth seeking is liberty under law. It is the thesis of this article that sovereignty under law for the state is no more absurd than liberty under law for the individual.

The term 'sovereignty' has been variously and elaborately defined, but for present purposes its essential elements may be listed as authority, equality, and liberty. The first-named attribute—authority—has its great importance in the field of constitutional law, which postulates that in every state there is some agency or combination of agencies possessed of the authority to control everything within the state. However, it is well known that the rise and spread of constitutionalism and federalism have rendered the concept of sovereign authority increasingly mystical. Even in Great Britain, the old simplicity of the sovereignty of 'King in Parliament' has been complicated by the Parliament Act of 1911, and especially by the Statute of Westminster of 1931. To be sure, it is easy enough to visualize sovereign authority in a dictatorial régime, but this arouses no envy on the part of those who enjoy other forms of government. When voices are raised decrying the possible loss of the sovereignty of the United States, there is not the slightest suggestion that the final authority in our sovereign union should be more narrowly localized. (It may be observed in passing that we frequently encounter the opposite demand that the powers now concentrated in the presidency be shared with other organs of government.)

When it comes to the sovereign characteristic of equality, we have an attribute much more popular than that of authority. Especially in the concept of equality cherished by those states which most obviously lack equality with their neighbors in one or more of the factors of population, territorial extent, wealth, and military strength. What kind of equality is claimed by these unequals? In the opinion of the present writer, the 'equality' of a sovereign state is neither more nor less than the privilege of acting and being counted as an individual entity. The small but 'equal' state need not participate in every international conference, but no other state may, without authorization, presume to act as its guardian and spokesman at such conference or elsewhere. In this sense of the word 'equality,' a minor child lacks equality, but a wife in the United States today is the equal of her husband—this latter in striking contrast to the subordination of the wife under the old common law doctrine of coverture. The substitution of representative government for direct democracy does not impair the equality of individual citizens, nor would the establishment of a small representative international council impair the equality of the states electing representatives, even if a few large states should enjoy permanent membership on the council.

It is the third component of sovereignty —liberty—that proves the well-nigh insuperable obstacle in attempts to organize sovereign states into a system of international law and order. Sovereignty is said to necessitate complete freedom from all restrictions, even from that of being judged by an impartial judge on the issue of observance of voluntarily assumed obligations. That is, the sovereignty of liberty of the independent state is the 'natural liberty' that Hobbes describes as 'the liberty each man hath to use his own power as he will himself, for the preservation of his own nature; that is to say, of his own life; and consequently, of doing anything which in his own judgment and reason he shall conceive to be the aptest means thereunto.' The liberty of the sovereign state is the liberty to wage war and to live a life that is 'solitary, poor, nasty, brutish, and short.' To be sure, Hobbes himself hesitates to apply his own characterization of liberty to the international sphere. He declares that 'kings, and persons of sovereign authority, because of their independency, are in continual jealousies, and in the state and posture of gladiators. . . But because they uphold thereby the industry of their subjects, there does not follow from it that misery which accompanies the liberty of particular men.' Yet his argument leads, at least in this day of total war, to the conclusion that 'absolute, unqualified and unchecked sovereignty is a conception of anarchy.'

If anarchy is the substance of liberty, it is clearly profitable to exchange liberty for the security contingent upon subordination to law. So reasoned Hobbes in the middle of the seventeenth century, and so reasons a twentieth-century authority— Professor Corwin—who writes, '*When Total War is the price of Total Sovereignty,* the price is too high.' Similarly, the late Wendell L. Willkie, in one of his very last articles, urged that 'nations must agree to joint responsibilities and to limitation of individual freedom of choice in certain specific situations. . . To be realistic, we should say frankly: "We are exchanging this small measure of our traditional sovereignty for the greater good of preventing wars among men."' . . .

Once it is granted that liberty is subject to limitation even in the state of nature, and that sovereignty is limited even in an unorganized world community, it follows easily that liberty is more effectively enjoyed in a civil state and sovereignty in an international organization. The argument that we should aim at 'sovereignty under law' cannot be better clinched than by asking the reader to adapt to the international sphere the following familiar passages from Locke's 'Second Treatise on Civil Government': 'If man in the state of nature be so free as has been said, if he be absolute lord of his own person and possessions, equal to the greatest and subject to nobody, why will he part with his freedom, why will he give up his empire, and subject himself to the dominion and control of any other power? To which it is obvious to answer, that though in the state of nature he hath such a right, yet the enjoyment of it is very uncertain and constantly exposed to the invasion of others. . . It is not without reason that he seeks out and is willing to join in society with others who are already united, or have a mind to unite for the mutual preservation of their lives, liberties and estates, which I call by the general name —property' . . .

## A. *Does Sovereignty Apply in International Relations?*

An argument that sovereignty has no application in the external relations of nations is given below. The author goes farther than those students and public statesmen who admit sovereignty in foreign affairs and then try to reconcile it with international law and organization.

(J. W. Garner, 'Limitations on National Sovereignty in International Relations,' *American Political Science Review*, vol. 19, 1925, pp. 1-6, 11-24. Reprinted with permission.)

Among the traditional political conceptions which in recent years have become the object of almost irreverent attack, is that which ascribes the quality of absolutism to that often elusive, but ever present, double-faced creation of the jurists which bears the name of sovereignty. Text-writers, sometimes in unqualified terms, still persist in claiming for it the unrestricted supremacy which was attributed to it in an age when its wielders everywhere were absolute monarchs; but an increasing number, less influenced by legal theories than by realities, see in it only the 'ghost of personal monarchy,' as Hobbes characterized it, 'sitting crowned on the grave thereof.'

On the one side the attack is directed by a new school of political writers, who deny its very existence or maintain that it is not an essential constituent attribute of the state. According to them, the notion is useless if not fallacious; the theory is discredited by the facts of modern state life and the term should be abandoned and expunged from the literature of political science.

On the other side, it is attacked by writers on international law who, while affirming that sovereignty is a necessary attribute of the state, and that viewed as the manifestation of a purely internal power it is legally unlimited, maintain that in its external manifestations, that is, when the exercise of the power which flows from it affects the rights or interests of other states or their nationals, the traditional theory as commonly formulated by jurists and expounded by text-writers is an 'archaic,' 'unworkable,' 'misleading,' and even 'dangerous' political dogma—a 'baneful fiction' which no longer corresponds with the facts of international life or practice and is, indeed, incompatible with the existence of a society of states governed by a recognized and generally observed system of international law. The term 'sovereignty,' entirely correct in its purely internal connotation as descriptive of the relation between a superior and an inferior—between the state and its subjects—is inapplicable to the relations between equal and independent states and should, they maintain, either be eliminated from the literature of international law, or the traditional theory should be revised and reformulated so that it will conform to actual international practice.

With the views of the first group of combatants I am not here concerned; those of the second group I fully share and I purpose to examine them briefly in the light of the actual conditions of international life and of international practice. . .

Briefly stated, the theory of sovereignty to which exception is taken attributes to the state absolute and unlimited legal power as over against other states and their nationals, subject to no control except that which is self-imposed—the right to determine its own manner of life, to determine and regulate its own domestic policies, to be the judge of its own international obligations, to set its own standards of national conduct, to choose freely its own form of government and to alter it at will—all this without accountability to anyone. . .

Properly interpreted, sovereignty is a term of constitutional law and political science and not of international law, and it implies nothing more than the legal right of the state to determine its own internal life, regulate its own purely domestic affairs and make law for its own subjects within its own territory. Its power ends at the frontier and even within the national territory it is limited by the rights which international law recognizes as belonging to the subjects of other states domiciled or engaged in business therein. When the manifestation of the will of the state takes effect à l'exterieur it is limited by the rights of other states and of their nationals, to say nothing of the rights of the society of states as a whole. The limitation is enforced through the principle of international responsibility which is one of the foundations of international law, and which all civilized states act upon in practice in their relations with one another.

Vattel, in his day, recognized the limitations when he said a nation is master of its own actions so long as they do not affect the proper and just rights of others. Hall, one of the most respected of modern writers on international law, thus states the limitation: 'A state has a right to live its life in its own way, so long as it keeps itself rigidly to itself and refrains from interfering with the equal rights of other states to live their life in the manner which commends itself to them.'

If we examine in the light of practice the so-called fundamental inherent rights of sovereign states, as they are customarily enumerated in textbooks, we shall find that they are far from being absolute and unlimited. Take the usually asserted right of the state to establish (and alter at will) such form of government as it chooses. Such a right is emphatically denied by authorities of high repute and in practice it has never been admitted. It was denied by the Powers in 1814 when Napoleon invoked it as a right under the law of nations, and on several occasions since then changes in existing forms of government were opposed and sometimes prevented by the action of other states whose safety and the general peace were believed to be menaced by the proposed changes. The establishment of a government which is 'notoriously opposed to the existing order of affairs' is admitted to be a matter of concern to international society, and when recognition is sought for newly-established governments practice shows that other states are not indifferent to the character of those which they are asked to recognize. . .

It is frequently asserted that every state has a right to extend or contract at will its territorial domain by purchase or cession, but its right, like others, is not admitted in practice. If the safety of other states or the general peace is threatened by territorial changes objection will be interposed and instances are by no means lacking in which they have been prevented by the opposition of other states or by the Powers collectively. . .

When we turn from the limitations on the internal sovereignty of the state, that is, its sovereignty over persons and things within its territory, to the consideration of its freedom of action *vis-à-vis* other states we find that this freedom is limited by the body of customary international law—one of the chief objects of which is the imposition of restraint upon the external conduct of states—and by conventions whereby states assume obligations and renounce their liberty of action in respect to certain matters. International law requires states to abstain from certain conduct, to acquiesce in the exercise within their territory of the authority of other states in certain cases, to prevent

their officers and subjects from doing certain acts and to make reparation for the violations by the latter of the law creating these obligations. The acceptance of this law is an essential condition upon which states are admitted to the society of nations; its binding effect is not therefore dependent upon their consent; and it has frequently been asserted by governments that a state which repudiates its authority places itself outside the pale of international intercourse.

It is a striking tribute to its supremacy that never in any official public act, as Rivier remarks, has any state in our time dared to declare that it would not be bound by this law or its precepts. The formal consent of the state is, of course, necessary in the case of conventions enunciating new rules of international law, and it is free to give or withhold that consent, but as regards the generally received customary law—the common law of nations—it is otherwise. In practice states act upon this principle. . .

## IV. THE EQUALITY OF STATES

Closely related to sovereignty is the idea that states are equal. Naturally it follows that if states are sovereign in the sense that they may not be restricted in their relations with one another, then, all being absolute, all are equal. There is no contention, of course, that they are equal physically or in power, for the facts belie this idea so convincingly; rather it is held that they are equal in a legal sense. Many textbooks on international law have made such an assertion, and some of the courts have maintained this thesis. In the case of *The Antelope* (1825), Chief Justice Marshall of the United States Supreme Court stated that 'No principle of international law is more universally acknowledged than the perfect equality of states.' In like manner the Inter-American Convention on the Rights and Duties of States, signed on 26 December 1933, recognized the 'juridical equality' of states.

Although there has been rather general admission of the principle of the equality of states, there is little agreement in regard to its implications. Even the theoretical and legal aspects of the principle are obscure. But it is on the practical rather than the theoretical side that the principle has become an important problem in international affairs. Does it entitle all states, large and small, to equal representation in international bodies and to equal voting power? Such a contention has been made, although with less frequency now-adays than formerly. One of the first writers to advance the idea that states are equal was Emerich de Vattel (1714-67), a Swiss, whose *Law of Nations* has become one of the classics on international law. His views are given below.

(E. de Vattel, *The Law of Nations*, published in 1758, translation by C. G. Fenwick, 1916, pp. 7, 11. Reprinted by permission of the Carnegie Endowment for International Peace.)

Since men are by nature equal, and their individual rights and obligations the same, as coming equally from nature, Nations, which are composed of men and may be regarded as so many free persons living together in a state of nature, are by nature equal and hold from nature the same obligations and the same rights. Strength or weakness, in this case, counts for nothing. A dwarf is as much a man as a giant is; a small Republic is no less a sovereign State than the most powerful Kingdom.

From this equality it necessarily follows that what is lawful or unlawful for one Nation is equally lawful or unlawful for every other Nation.

A Nation is therefore free to act as it pleases, so far as its acts do not affect the perfect rights of another Nation, and so far as the Nation is under merely *internal* obligations without any *perfect external* obligations. If it abuses its liberty it acts wrongfully; but other Nations cannot complain, since they have no right to dictate it.

Since Nations are free, independent, and equal, and since each has the right to decide in its conscience what it must do to fulfill its duties, the effect of this is to produce, before the world at least, a perfect equality of rights among Nations in the conduct of their affairs and in the pursuit of their policies. The intrinsic justice of their conduct is another matter which it is not for others to pass upon finally; so that what one may do another may do, and they must be regarded in the society of mankind as having equal rights. . .

Every Nation which governs itself, under whatever form, and which does not depend on any other Nation, is a *sovereign State*. Its rights are, in the natural order, the same as those of every other State. Such is the character of the moral persons who live together in a society established by nature and subject to the Law of Nations. To give a Nation the right to a definite position in this great society, it need only be truly sovereign and independent; it must govern itself by its own authority and its own laws. . .

## A. *A Recent View on the Equality of States*

(E. D. Dickinson, *The Equality of States in International Law*, pp. 334-5. Copyright 1920 by Harvard University Press.)

The principle of state equality in international law was a creation of publicists. It was derived from the application to nations of theories of natural law, the state of nature, and natural equality. An an- alogy was drawn between nations in international society and men in a state of nature. Thus the natural law became the law of nations, international society was regarded as in a state of nature, and nations were presumed to enjoy a perfect equality of natural rights. The conception of state equality was first developed as part of a coherent theory by the naturalists of the seventeenth and eighteenth centuries. Grotius neither discussed the conception nor based his system upon it. It was not established by the Peace of Westphalia. It had its beginning as a naturalist doctrine in the writing of that school of publicists who acknowledged the leadership of Pufendorf and the inspiration of Thomas Hobbes. The early positivists developed no such conception. It was not until the middle of the eighteenth century, in the period of Burlamaqui, Vattel, Wolff, and Moser, that publicists of all schools included the equality of states among their leading principles. Once established by the process of reasoning summarized above, the principle was reenforced by theories of sovereignty. The absolute equality of sovereign states became one of the primary postulates of *le droit des gens théoretique*.

The principle of equality has an important legal significance in the modern law of nations. It is the expression of two important legal principles. The first of these may be called the equal protection of the law or equality before the law. States are equal before the law when they are equally protected in the enjoyment of their rights and equally compelled to fulfil their obligations. Equality before the law is not inconsistent with the grouping of states into classes and attributing to the members of each class of a status which is the measure of capacity for rights. Neither is it inconsistent with inequalities of representation, voting power, and contribution in international organizations. The second principle is usually described as equality of rights and obligations or more often as equality of rights. The description is a heritage from theories of natural law and natural right. What is really meant is an equal capacity for rights. Equality in this sense is the negation of status. If applied without qualification in international organizations it requires equal representation, voting power, and contribution. Equality before the law is absolutely essential to a stable society of nations. If it is denied the alternatives are universal empire or universal anarchy. Equality of capacity for rights, on the other hand, is not essential to the reign of law. Strictly speaking, it has never been anything more than an ideal in any system of law. Among states, where there is such an utter want of homogeneity in the physical bases for separate existence, there are important limitations upon its utility even as an ideal. . .

## B. *An American View on the Equality of States*

The following statement was made by Secretary of State Cordell Hull in connection with plans for the creation of the United Nations Organization.

(Cordell Hull, Statement, *Department of State Bulletin*, vol. XI, 1944, p. 509.)

. . . The future welfare of each nation depends upon the welfare of all. In view of that common interest and that self-interest in every mutual sense, I doubt whether there could be many nations, large or small, which could have any other purpose than to cooperate in all legiti-

mate and practicable international relationships that could be mutually advantageous and mutually profitable. As far as this government is concerned, whenever I have said anything on this subject, it has always emphasized the all-inclusive nature of the world situation and our disposition and purpose to see that all nations, especially the small nations, are kept on a position of equality with all others and that, in every practicable way, there will be cooperation.

Now, it is not possible at this stage for this government or any government to give anybody a blueprint as to all of the details of how these relationships between all of the different nations will be gradually developed and perfected. . . We have for 150 years preached liberty to all the nations of the earth, to all peoples of the earth, and we have practiced it. We have encouraged all nations to aspire to liberty, and to enjoy it. Our attitude to the Philippines is a striking example. . .

Even back in our earlier days we preached the same spirit of liberty with which we, ourselves, were inspired in acquiring our own liberty, to all nations—especially those that were in chains of despotism, as the South American countries were for centuries under Spanish rule. . .

I have spoken of this often in speeches and at other times before, during and after my trip to Europe. Here is an example from my address to Congress: 'The principle of the sovereign equality of all peace-loving states, irrespective of size and strength, as partners in a future system of general security will be the foundation stone upon which the future international organization will be constructed.' That is our objective. . .

## V. The Role of Small States

During the past few decades there has been much discussion concerning the position of small states in international relations. In both World War I and World War II they were invaded by aggressive countries contemptuous of the rights of these small states and out to destroy them. The argument is advanced by the critics of small countries that they are an element of weakness in the structure of peace because, unable to defend themselves, they invite aggression on the part of powerful neighbors. It is also said that small states add to the economic complications of international relations by setting up a multitude of barriers to trade.

World War I resulted in the creation of additional small states. Several new ones took the place of Austria-Hungary; and Estonia, Latvia, Lithuania, and Finland gained their freedom from Russia. President Woodrow Wilson's stress on self-determination at the Paris Peace Conference after World War I led inevitably to this end. Again in World War II spokesmen of small states —Foreign Minister Carl J. Hambro of Norway and Prime Minister Pierre Bupong of Luxembourg, among others—strongly defended the right of their countries to live. Following the War most of the small states that had been invaded were restored. Today sixty of the seventy-five or more states of the world have less than ten million people each.

(A. Wolfers, 'In Defense of Small Countries,' *Yale Review,* vol. 33, pp. 201-13. Copyright 1943 by Yale University Press.)

If there was ever an age of the great powers it is with us now. In a world where giants of productive and military strength are capable of hurling millions of men and tens of thousands of planes into battle, there would seem to be little future for weak nations. People, therefore, may well ask themselves whether the Allied statesmen are not clinging to outmoded ideas when they proclaim the equality of nations, large and small, or promise restoration of sovereign rights and self-government to small countries, such as Austria.

In the last great war President Wilson was the champion of the weaker states. He heralded the League of Nations as the 'first serious and systematic attempt made in the world to put nations on a footing of equality with each other . . . the smallest as well as the greatest.' His support of the principle of self-determination helped many small nations to emancipate themselves from foreign rule and to establish their independent statehood.

But much has happened since then to bring about a revulsion of feeling towards the small states. Although there was again compassion for the victims of aggression, Germany's attack on her neighbors in this war did not arouse the same instantaneous and warm sympathy which little Belgium enjoyed in 1914. When they were overrun, one by one, without even the chance of successful resistance, many people wondered whether these weak countries had not perhaps constituted a threat both to themselves and to the rest of us. Since another world war had started in the 'balkanized' regions of central Europe it began to look as if self-determination, applauded as a principle of justice in 1918, might have been just another mistake of the peacemakers at Versailles.

A number of writers on post-war problems now appear so convinced of the necessity for doing away with what Mr. Willkie calls an 'outmoded system' of 'small nations, each with its own political, economic, and military sovereignty,' that they do not even bother to give any reasons. Where any argument is offered for doing away with these states, it is frequently of a doubtful nature. Thus it is suggested that since sovereignty is an obstacle to peace, a useful beginning in abolishing it could be made by reducing the number of sovereign small states. Since, however, the major wars have regularly been caused by the conflict and competition of the great powers, it is unlikely that a world of large continental blocs would be particularly peaceful. Frequently, appeal is made to an inexorable 'trend of history' towards ever larger political units, as if there had not been in our time a disintegration of the Ottoman and Austro-Hungarian empires or a decentralization of the British empire in the rise of British Dominions to a level of virtual independence. It is true, however, that the 'shrinking of the earth' brought about by modern technology has created difficulties, both economic and strategic, which are hard to cope with as long as there are so many small, separate units with so many independent and conflicting national policies as existed before the war. If these difficulties were found to be insurmountable, the small states could not hope to be saved by others merely for reasons of sentiment or tradition.

But before even considering any change in the former status of the weaker nations, it is well to remember that no great power could easily afford to advocate policies which would arouse their hostility. Individually, they may seem to count for little. In blocs, linked together by strong feelings of solidarity as soon as their international position is threatened, and covering, as they do, most of Europe, the Near and Middle East, the whole of Central and South America, they represent an impressive force. This country has particular reason for not wanting to break away from a line of policy which with patient effort has done so much in recent years to allay the Latin-American fears of the 'Colossus of the North.' Any sign on our part of disrespect for the rights of small countries would threaten to destroy the valuable assets which have been obtained through the good neighbor policy.

There exists yet another reason for caution. The small states, if they were free to choose, would be unlikely to favor everything that one might wish to do about them or everything which in an ideal world would have to be done about them. What, then, if they could not be persuaded? Would this country, after defeating the ruthless conquerors of weaker countries, wish to undertake the terrifying and thankless task of forcing them into accepting arrangements obnoxious to them? . . .

The economic argument against the small countries is particularly popular in this country. Enjoying the unquestionable benefits of a large internal market and the free movement of men and, for the most part, of goods across their forty-eight States, the American people must look almost with pity upon nations which, as in Europe, run into trade barriers, exchange obstacles, and visa troubles wherever they turn. The smaller a country the more, so it would seem, must it suffer from the strangling effects of these barriers and of independent and conflicting economic policies all around it. Where, as in the case of the Danubian countries, a former large and relatively well-balanced free trade area was suddenly cut into small units, each intent upon erecting protective tariff walls, these disadvantages become even more obvious.

There is, however, a tendency today to exaggerate the evil economic effects of smallness. Even in the most conspicuous and most frequently mentioned Danubian case, it still remains to be shown how much the economic difficulties—for instance, of Austria—can actually be attributed to the trade barriers erected by her small neighbors. It is likely that these difficulties were due far more to the general effects of war and defeat, to internal upheaval, to the world-wide agrarian crisis, and to the trade and financial policies of the great powers. Some groups of the population in all of the Danubian

countries fared better after 1919 than they had done in the days of the empire when conditions for the masses were by no means rosy. While the need for outlets for their agrarian surpluses pressed heavily on the southeastern European states, no union among them could have offered a satisfactory solution since they all needed markets outside of that area. Currency depreciation and default on debt were no specialty of the small Danubian powers—as the case of Germany indicates; in many respects small Czechoslovakia fared better than her large German neighbor.

But even if it were true that the Danubian countries could profit economically by re-establishing a larger free trade area, the same argument cannot be applied indiscriminately to all small countries. The republics of Central or South America might find almost no advantage in economic union. Their natural outlet as food and raw material producers lies overseas or in North America. Trade barriers erected by the great importers of their products hit them hard, but they would also hit hard any large country that happened to live under similar economic conditions. If there is to be improvement in cases like this, it must be sought in a change of the economic policies of the great powers.

Nobody would deny that most small countries are highly vulnerable to protective measures of other countries. They are, as a rule, large per-capita exporters and importers. If policies of self-sufficiency and excessive protection such as Germany applied and advocated should become the rule, the economic existence of small nations might come to be in deadly peril. It is no accident, therefore, that many of them are warm supporters of Mr. Hull's liberal trade policies and were among the first to sign mutually beneficial trade agreements with this country.

Yet even in the Thirties when protectionism flourished as never before, many of the small states managed to pull through with unusual success, while in the preceding period a remarkable number of them ranked high in the list of the most prosperous, most socially advanced, and most contented countries. This was true not only of those little European nations which like Sweden, Switzerland, Denmark, and Holland had enjoyed the advantage of neutrality during the First World War—this particular group had the highest per-capita national income of any country outside of the United States. Belgium and Czechoslovakia, too, had no reason to be envious of their greater neighbors. Turkey's economic progress, following upon the loss of a large empire, has received much favorable comment, while Eire, after obtaining her independence, extricated herself from severe economic troubles. Outside of Europe, small countries like Uruguay or New Zealand compare most favorably with the larger powers.

Many factors including such non-economic matters as good government and social peace—more easily attainable in small cohesive states than in great ones —have helped to compensate for the handicaps of smallness. Then, too, the small countries have not, as a rule, lacked success when bargaining for commercial or financial advantages with the great powers. The explanation may be that, in peacetime, the great powers feel they can afford to be generous with the small ones, or that they are afraid of losing prestige should they fail to come to terms with them. While the absence of a wide internal market has been an obstacle to large-scale and low-cost production, countries like Denmark or Switzerland have compensated for this by excelling in high-quality production.

If the small countries have suffered less from limitations of size than might have been expected, there is also no evidence that their existence has proved harmful to their larger neighbors. Monetary instability was a widespread disease in Europe after the last war, but its roots lay in Germany, France, and Italy as much as, if not more than, in Belgium or Austria. The example of Finland shows that there is no connection between the extent of default on foreign debts and the size of a country. The depression in 1929 started in the great financial centre of New York and not in Holland or Switzerland. The fact that some of the small countries in Germany's neighborhood were not dragged into her financial and monetary disaster in the early Twenties, and did not participate in her 'new' economic policies and maneuvers of more recent years, even made them a stabilizing factor in the economy of the world. It is worth remembering that the clamor for economic *Lebensraum* was raised not in the small countries but in Germany. . .

The whole idea of tying countries together economically solely because of geographical propinquity is fallacious. It makes sense only for war economies and even then only for countries threatened by encirclement or naval blockade. To the Swiss or Czechs it is as little tempting to be locked up with their German competitors in a European customs union as it is to the wheat and beef producers of the United States and the Argentine to be united in a so-called regional economic bloc limited to the Western Hemisphere. There are good reasons why the geographical regional bloc should have appealed so much to the Germans. They were out for political control over the countries of southeastern Europe and at the same time were seeking themselves to become blockade-proof. The sooner other nations recognize that economic regionalism is a part of the ideological arsenal of Nazi war preparations the less will they be misguided in their own economic policies. . .

In general, a return to more liberal trade practices in the world at large will improve the economic situation of the small countries more than any regional arrangement. This does not mean, however, that a more liberal tariff policy will be enough to eliminate all the troubles from which they suffer or that all small countries will sincerely co-operate in bringing about more liberal practices. Some of them may prefer to suffer the disadvantages which accrue to them through the trade barriers of other nations rather than give up protection for their own infant industries or for branches of their economy which they deem essential. The arrangements for world security will determine whether some of the lesser countries will or will not continue to foster the development of their armament industries even though that means depressing their standard of living. . .

While there is reason, then, to believe that the small countries will not prove an obstacle to economic recovery and progress, their military weakness, their fears, and their large number raise some serious issues of security and international organization.

Their military weakness may again tempt strong and aggressive neighbors to expand, as Germany has done. Traditionally, the great nations of Europe have sought to eliminate such temptations by balancing the power of one country against another. Yet paradoxical as it may seem, this policy of the balance of power has resulted frequently not in the elimination but in the establishment of small powers. There are two reasons for this.

In the first place, independent small states may appear as the lesser of two evils. Britain, for instance, was better protected because Holland and Belgium were independent than she would have been if they had been united with Germany. European peace may become more secure if

Poland regains her sovereign independence than if, by incorporating her, the Soviet Union should come to be feared and opposed as a new candidate for European hegemony. It should also not be forgotten that a small well-governed country, Czechoslovakia, for instance, even though weak, might still be a stronger force for peace than a disintegrating Danubian confederation—another 'sick man' in southeastern Europe. Declining empires, like the Austrian or the Turkish of yesterday, tend to arouse predatory desires in their healthier neighbors.

In the second place, small states, as a rule, prove to be *dangerously* weak only if the power of their great neighbors is not sufficiently balanced. If a British-French-Russian alliance, backed by a friendly America, had existed in 1938 and 1939, ready to defend Austria, Czechoslovakia, and Poland, would not the chances of a German attack on these countries have been very slight? Such a set-up and better preparedness on the part of Britain and France would have been sufficient to protect Holland and Belgium; without that, the territory of the two small countries would have been open to invasion whether they were independent or not. As long as weak countries have two strong neighbors instead of only one, as the examples of Spain and Turkey today demonstrate, they can enjoy a high degree of security.

Even so, nothing should be neglected that would help eliminate the dangers which a power vacuum tends to create. This can be done either by giving more strength to the small states or by reducing the power of those of their neighbors which are found to threaten their security. Plans for the unilateral disarmament, if not for the dismemberment, of enemy countries are designed to accomplish the latter. If they are carried out, much of the weakness of their small neighbors will, for a time at least, dis-

appear at the close of this war. But unless unilateral disarmament can be enforced forever, which many doubt, the
change which it creates for a time cannot
be regarded as a solution of the problem. On the contrary, it is likely to arouse
illusions and to induce some, at least, of
the great powers to accept the false notion that they need no longer be worried
about the security of the weaker nations.

To bolster the strength of small countries may prove difficult at times; but there
are several ways in which it can be done.
Their own military preparedness is not
the least important means, even though,
taken by itself, it must necessarily remain
inadequate. If they are to get any help
from outside, the small states must be
expected to make a contribution to their
own defense proportionate to their man
power and resources. Could Australia
hope to be assured of the assistance of
the United States if she neglected her own
defenses? Egypt, one would think, could
hardly expect to preserve her status of
independence in a future crisis if again
she counted wholly on Britain to defend
her territory.

More could be gained if some of the
small countries were willing to merge
their strength. It has been suggested,
therefore, that where there are many of
them in one region they should federate
into larger political units. But federation,
attractive as it may be in theory, is not
a panacea which can be universally applied or even recommended. Whether a
Danubian or a Scandinavian federation
will come into being and, if established,
gain the strength and cohesion necessary
to overcome centrifugal nationalistic
forces will depend in the end not on decisions reached at the council table but
on whether there exists among the peoples concerned a sufficiently broad and
spontaneous desire for union. If countries like Poland and Czechoslovakia were
to seek union with each other, they might

discover that instead of adding to each
other's strength they had merely en-
tangled themselves in each other's conflicts and created for themselves insuperable difficulties in their external and their
domestic affairs.

The great democratic countries would
certainly not want to put obstacles in the
way of any spontaneous process of federation. They would be fooling themselves,
however, if they believed that every successful federation would prove advantageous to them. The Soviet Union is not
alone in questioning the desirability of
federative blocs on its western borders
and in other zones of its special vital interest; an all-Arab federation including
Egypt and Palestine or a Latin American
federation including Panama and Colombia would scarcely make easier the
defense of British and American interests
on the two great inter-ocean canals.

Where the creation of larger political
units is either impractical or undesirable,
the safety of small countries and with it
that of their neighbors must depend on
outside help. The traditional way of
granting such help was in the form of
alliances or pacts of guarantee by which
weak countries assured themselves of military aid from powerful countries. Though
alliances were used again after 1919, as in
the case of the French alliances with Belgium, Poland, and Czechoslovakia, it was
hoped that in time the League of Nations
would prove to offer better protection.
When it failed to do so, some of the small
countries began to feel that the danger
of their commitments to the League more
than offset the advantages which they
might hope to gain. The universal promise of all nations to come to the assistance of every victim of aggression did not
appear a reliable substitute for the specific guarantees which a powerful nation
might give to a weak neighbor in whose
fate it was vitally interested. . .

## A. *The Communist View of Small States*

Communists look upon the modern state as an instrument through which the masses are exploited. Small states are particularly obnoxious, according to official communist statements. The following extract defines the position of the Communist International in 1919 on this question. It should be noted, however, that communist spokesmen following World War II have taken a somewhat more lenient view toward small states. A fuller explanation of the communist view of the state is given in a later extract.

(From the Manifesto of the Third [Communist] International, 1919, *Revolutionary Radicalism—Report of the Joint Legislative Committee Investigating Seditious Activities in the State of New York*, 24 April 1920, pp. 476-85.)

The national state, which has been given a tremendous impulse by capitalistic evolution, has become too narrow for the development of the production forces, and even more untenable has become the position of the small states, distributed among the great powers of the world and in other parts of the world. These small states came into existence at different times as fragments split off the bigger states, as petty currency in payment for services rendered, to serve as strategic buffer states. They, too, have their dynasties, their ruling gangs, their imperialistic pretensions, their diplomatic machinations. Their illusory independence had until the war [1914-18] precisely the same support as the European balance of power, namely, the continuous opposition between the two imperialistic camps. . . After Germany was beaten the bourgeoisie of the small nations, together with their patriotic 'Socialists' turned to the victorious imperialism of the allies and began to seek assurance for their further independent existence in the hypocritical point of the Wilson program. . .

## VI. THE DEMOCRATIC STATE

One of the basic facts in contemporary international politics is the dominance of two philosophies of government—the communist and the democratic, represented, respectively, by Russia and the United States. There are other forms of government in the world, such as fascism in Spain and military dictatorships in some of the Latin-American countries, but in international affairs nations tend to gravitate toward either the Russian or American spheres.

(H. J. Carman, 'An Inventory of American Democracy,' *Vital Speeches of the Day*, vol. 13, No. 21, 1947, pp. 653-4. Reprinted by permission of the City News Publishing Company.)

Today, two ways of life, each resting upon an ideology diametrically opposed to the other, struggle for world domina-tion. Democracy with its emphasis upon the human worth of the individual is pitted in an apparently life and death struggle with authoritarianism or totalitarianism with its emphasis upon the dominance of the state and its appeal to brute force. This struggle is not new; its origin long antedates the twentieth century. Hitlerian fascism and Russian communism are merely the most recent manifestations of the totalitarian ideology. Whenever and wherever found totalitarianism is easily detected; no one has guaranteed rights; secret police may seize anyone, search any home; arbitrary arrests and imprisonment without trial prevail; criticism of the government is taboo; the press and other agencies of communication are not free; the state tells everyone what to believe; religious freedom does not prevail; government is by decrees of dictators, without consent of the people; free elections in the democratic sense are not held. Private enterprise is frowned upon; the state controls all business and wages, and conditions of employment are dictated by bureaucrats; miserable living conditions for the masses usually prevail. We Americans have upon innumerable occasions congratulated ourselves that we were a free people and that our civilization rested upon sound democratic foundations. Yet we must not forget that in America, as elsewhere, democracy means different things to different people. Like liberty or science or progress it is a word with which we are all so familiar that we rarely take the trouble to define its meaning. And even where we do there is no common definition. To some it is a form of government, to others a way of social life broadly conceived. Some have found its essence in the character of the electorate, the relation between government and the people, the absence of wide economic differences between citizens, the refusal to recognize privileges built on birth or wealth, race or creed. Inevitably democracy has changed its substance in terms of time and place. What has seemed democracy to a member of some ruling class has seemed to his less economically fortunate fellow citizens a narrow and indefensible oligarchy. Unquestionably democracy has a context in every sphere of life. Unfor-

tunately, too many Americans view democracy merely as a form of government. As such they may think of it in terms of the ideal, as did Lincoln, as government of the people, by the people, for the people; or more realistically—as do some —as government of the people, by the politicians, for pressure groups. Most Americans who think of democracy as a form of government, in all probability, think of it as government by the many as opposed to government by one or a few. Furthermore, they rightly maintain that the test of a democratic government is whether the source of political authority rests with the majority of the people of a community or in a one-man ruler or in a dictatorial oligarchy.

To me—and in all likelihood to every person in this audience—American democracy is much more than a form of government. It is a way of life—a kind of social philosophy, in which the form of government is incidental, a means and not an end in itself. People may be politically equal without attaining a genuine realization of their personalities. Indeed, that state or society which would lay claim to being really democratic must provide for economic, religious, educational and social democracy as well as for political democracy. Political equality, however profound, as Plato and Aristotle were well aware, does not necessarily mean that real democracy prevails. Equality of economic opportunity must also prevail. It was stressed by many prior to the Eighteenth Century. By the time of the French Revolution this doctrine had become a permanent part of the democratic creed, and from that time to the present, many persons, the world over, have increasingly insisted that in the absence of the equality for economic opportunity no political mechanism will of itself enable the common man to utilize fully his talents for bettering himself and his fellows.

Furthermore, any state wherein social and religious differences are recognized by law stands outside the realm of the really democratic state. Protest against the possession of privilege based on birth goes back to a very early date. So also does the refusal to accept the status of inferiority which slavery implies. Religious equality, educational equality, and the right to equal participation in the results of social discovery and improvement—as health, housing, libraries, museums and the like —must prevail in the really democratic state. So must freedom of speech and press. Equality before the law must be ever present. In the courts of a really democratic state there can be no difference between persons: poor and rich; atheist and Christian, black and white, must in similar circumstances be treated similarly.

Finally, the really democratic state must insist upon the faculty of human, life and human happiness. Life, liberty and pursuit of happiness—beacon lights for millions of Americans living and dead—must not be negatively and conservatively interpreted. Viewed in the light of democracy as a way of life, these concepts mean life, health and leisure not for the few but for the many. They mean freedom from unfair and corrupt methods of business competition, fraud, misrepresentation, racketeering. They mean cheaper and quicker justice. They mean the elimination of abuses on the part of labor.

They mean freedom for the consumer from extortionate and oppressive charges. They mean freedom from overcrowded, unsanitary dwellings, factories and stores. They mean the elimination of human parasitism—of the philosophy of being a leaner and of getting something for nothing. Above all, they mean the fullest opportunity for every person to develop his talents and personality and to share in the higher enjoyments of civilization.

Democracy then is a way of life and, as such, is vastly more than mere extension of the suffrage and participation in political affairs. It is this larger concept of democracy that we associate with the memory of Thomas Jefferson, one of the greatest if not the greatest of Americans. It is not without significance that in devising his own epitaph, Jefferson selected out of all his notable achievements only three for which he wished to be especially remembered: *Here was buried Thomas Jefferson, author of the Declaration of Independence, of the Statute of Virginia for Religious Freedom, and Father of the University of Virginia.* These three taken together with their implications constitute as the late Carl Becker of Cornell University so aptly pointed out, the warp and woof of Jefferson's social philosophy. His was the broader conception of democracy and the one that I have in mind in addressing myself to the main theme of this lecture. . .

## VII. The Russian Ideal

Communist ideology is derived from the writings of Karl Marx (1818-83) and Friedrich Engels (1820-95). It is based upon an economic interpretation of history, which maintains that the political, social, religious, and other institutions of any given period are determined by economic forces, especially by the 'mode of production.' Analyzing capitalism, Marx and Engels concluded that the inner contradictions of the system would lead inevitably to its downfall. They regarded the state as an instrument of oppression. By revolutionary means the proletariat would gain control of the state and manage it until society became classless; then the state would 'wither away.' In practice Russia has not adhered strictly to communist doctrines. The extract below, a pronouncement made in 1919 and altered only in a few minor ways in 1935, explains further some of the aspects of communism in Russia.

(Program of the Communist Party of the U.S.S.R., adopted 18-23 March 1919, *Communist Library*, No. 6.)

### GENERAL POLITICS

A bourgeois republic, even the most democratic, sanctified by such watchwords as 'will of the people,' 'will of the nation,' 'no class privilege,' remains in fact, owing to the existence of private property in land and other means of production, the dictatorship of the bourgeoisie, an instrument for exploitation and oppression of the broad masses of workers by a small group of capitalists. In opposition to this, proletarian or Soviet democracy transformed mass organizations precisely of the classes oppressed by capitalism, of proletarians and poorest peasantry or semi-proletarians, i.e., the vast majority of the population, into a single and permanent basis of the state apparatus, local and central. By this act, the Soviet State realized among other things local and regional autonomy without the appointment of authorities from above, on a much wider scale than is practised anywhere. The aim of the Party is to exert the greatest efforts in order to realize fully this highest type of democracy, which to function accurately requires a continually rising standard of culture, organization and activity on the part of the masses.

In contrast to bourgeois democracy, which concealed the class character of the state, the Soviet authority openly acknowledges that every state must inevitably bear a class character until the division of society into classes has been abolished and all government authority disappears. By its very nature, the Soviet state directs itself to the suppression of the resistance of the exploiters, and the Soviet constitution does not stop at depriving the exploiters of their political rights, bearing in mind that any kind of freedom is a deception if it is opposed to the emancipation of labor from the yoke of capital. The aim of the Party of the proletariat consists in carrying on a determined suppression of the resistance of the exploiters, in struggling against the deeply rooted prejudices concerning the absolute character of bourgeois rights and freedom, and at the same time explaining that deprivation of political rights and any kind of limitation of freedom are necessary as temporary measures in order to defeat the attempts of the exploiters to retain or to re-establish their privileges. With the disappearance of the possibility of the exploitation of one human being by another, the necessity for these measures will also gradually disappear and the Party will aim to reduce and completely abolish them.

Bourgeois democracy has limited itself to formally extending political rights and freedom, such as the right of combination, freedom of speech, freedom of press, equality of citizenship. In practice, however, particularly in view of the economic slavery of the working masses, it was impossible for the workers to enjoy these rights and privileges to any great extent under bourgeois democracy.

Proletarian democracy on the contrary, instead of formally proclaiming those rights and freedoms, actually grants them first of all to those classes which have been oppressed by capitalism, i.e., to the proletariat and to the peasantry. For that purpose the Soviet state expropriates premises, printing offices, supplies of paper, etc., from the bourgeoisie, placing these at the disposal of the working masses and their organizations. The aim of the All-Union Communist Party is to encourage the working masses to enjoy democratic rights and liberties, and to offer them every opportunity for doing so.

Bourgeois democracy through the ages proclaimed equality of persons, irrespective of religion, race or nationality and the equality of the sexes, but capitalism prevented the realization of this equality and in its imperialist stage developed race and national suppression. The Soviet Government, by being the authority of the toilers, for the first time in history could in all spheres of life realize this equality, destroying the last traces of woman's inequality in the sphere of marriage and the family. At the present moment the work of the Party is principally intellectual and educational with the aim of abolishing the last traces of former inequality and prejudices, especially among the backward sections of the proletariat and peasantry.

The Party's aim is not to limit itself to the formal proclamation of woman's equality, but to liberate woman from all the burdens of antiquated methods of housekeeping, by replacing them by house-communes, public kitchens, central laundries, nurseries, etc.

## PUBLIC EDUCATION

The All-Union Communist Party in the field of education sets itself the task of bringing to fulfillment the work begun by the October Revolution of 1917, of transforming the school from an instrument of class domination of the bourgeoisie into an instrument for the abolition of the class divisions of society, into an instrument for a communist regeneration of society.

In the period of the dictatorship of the proletariat, i.e., in the period of prepara-

tion of conditions suitable for the realization of communism, the school must be not only the conductor of communist principles, but it must become the conductor of the intellectual, organizational and educational influences of the proletariat, to the semi-proletariat and non-proletarian sections of the toiling masses, in order to educate a generation capable of establishing communism. The immediate aim in this direction is at the present time the further development of the following principles of school and educational work, already established by the Soviet Government:

The introduction of free and compulsory general and technical education (instruction in the theory and practice of the principal branches of production) for all children of both sexes up to the age of 17. . .

## RELIGION

With reference to religion, the All-Union Communist Party does not content itself with the already decreed separation of church from state, i.e., measures which are one of the items of the programs of bourgeois democracy, which was, however, never fulfilled owing to many and various ties binding capital with religious propaganda.

The All-Union Communist Party is guided by the conviction that only the realization of conscious and systematic social and economic activity of the masses will lead to the disappearance of religious prejudices. The aim of the Party is finally to destroy the ties between the exploiting classes and the organization of religious propaganda, at the same time helping the toiling masses actually to liberate their minds from religious superstitions, and organizing on a wide scale scientific-educational and anti-religious propaganda. It is however necessary carefully to avoid offending the religious susceptibilities of believers, which leads only to the strengthening of religious fanaticism.

## ECONOMICS

Undeviatingly to continue and finally to realize the expropriation of the bourgeoisie which was begun and which has already been largely completed, the transforming of all means of production and exchange into the property of the Soviet republic, i.e., the common property of all toilers.

All possible increase of the productive forces of the country must be considered the fundamental and principal point upon which the economic policy of the Soviet Government is based. In view of the disorganization of the country, everything in other spheres of life must be subordinated to the practical aim immediately and at all costs to increase the quantity of products required by the population. The successful functioning of every Soviet institution connected with public economy must be gauged by the practical results in this direction. . .

The Soviet Government, guaranteeing to the working masses incomparably more opportunities to vote and to recall their delegates in the most easy and accessible manner, than they possessed under bourgeois democracy and parliamentarism, at the same time abolishes all the negative features of parliamentarism, especially the separation of legislative and executive powers, the isolation of the representative institutions from the masses, etc.

In the Soviet state not a territorial district, but a productive unit (factory, mill) forms the electoral unit and the unit of the state. The state apparatus is thus brought near to the masses.

The aim of the Party consists in endeavoring to bring the Government apparatus into still closer contact with the masses, for the purpose of realizing democracy more fully and strictly in practice, by making Government officials responsible to, and placing them under the control of, the masses.

The Soviet state includes in its organs —the Soviets—workmen and soldiers on a basis of complete equality and unity of interests whereas bourgeois democracy, in spite of all its declarations, transformed the army into an instrument of the wealthy classes, separated it from the masses, and set it against them, depriving the soldiers of any opportunity of exercising their political rights. The aim of the Party is to defend and develop this unity of the workmen and soldiers in the Soviets and to strengthen the indissoluble ties between the armed forces and the organizations of the proletariat and semi-proletariat. . .

## RELATIONS OF NATIONALITIES

With reference to the nationality question the All-Union Communist Party is guided by the following theses:

The principal aim is to bring into closer relations the proletarians and semi-proletarians of different nationalities, for the purpose of carrying on a general revolutionary struggle for the overthrow of the landlords and the bourgeoisie.

## MILITARY AFFAIRS

The aims of the Party with reference to military matters are defined by the following fundamental theses:

In the period when imperialism is decaying and civil war is spreading, it is possible neither to retain the old army nor to construct a new one on a so-called national and non-class basis. The Red Army, as the instrument of the proletarian dictatorship, is compelled to have an undisguised class character, i.e., its ranks must be filled exclusively with proletarians. . .

## VIII. The States of the World

The ups and down of international relations—wars, revolutions, and voluntary adjustments—bring frequent changes in the membership of the society of nations. The emergence of new states and the disappearance of old ones will in a few years' time invalidate any list of the states of the world. The list below includes communities generally recognized as states in 1948. It takes into account the major changes brought about by World War II, excluding Estonia, Latvia, and Lithuania, which have been absorbed by Russia, and including the new states of Burma, Ceylon, Pakistan, India, Korea, and the Philippines. For a while, however, the independent status of Korea will be limited by Russian and American military occupation. Germany, Austria, and Japan, too, will be unable during military occupation to act as independent nations. Canada, Australia, New Zealand, South Africa, Pakistan, India, and Ceylon are properly listed as states, for with dominion status they are able to act quite independently in international affairs. Pakistan, a Moslem state, and India, dominated by Hindus, were formed out of the old British dependency of India on 15 August 1947. Burma was granted independence by the British Government on 4 January 1948, and Ceylon became a Dominion of the British Commonwealth on 4 February 1948.

(Data on area and population from League of Nations, *Statistical Yearbook* 1941-42, Geneva, 1943, pp. 13-18. Where changes were brought about by World War II, the figures listed are estimates.)

| Country | Area in Kilometers (000) | Population Estimate (000) | One-time Member of League of Nations | Member of United Nations (1949) | Member of Universal Postal Union |
|---|---|---|---|---|---|
| **I. *Africa*** | | | | | |
| 1. Egypt | 1,000 | 16,550 | x | x | x |
| 2. Ethiopia | 900 | 5,500 | x | x | x |
| 3. Liberia | 120 | 2,500 | x | x | x |
| 4. Union of South Africa | 1,224 | 10,251 | x | x | x |
| **II. *North America*** | | | | | |
| 5. Canada (and Nova Scotia) | 9,680 | 11,662 | x | x | x |
| 6. United States | 7,839 | 131,416 | | x | x |
| 7. Mexico | 1,969 | 19,380 | x | x | x |
| 8. Costa Rica | 50 | 639 | x | x | x |
| 9. Cuba | 114 | 4,253 | x | x | x |
| 10. Dominican Republic | 50 | 1,650 | x | x | x |
| 11. Guatemala | 110 | 3,260 | x | x | x |
| 12. Haiti | 26 | 2,600 | x | x | x |
| 13. Honduras | 154 | 1,090 | x | x | x |
| 14. Nicaragua | 128 | 883 | x | x | x |
| 15. Panama | 74 | 620 | x | x | x |
| 16. Salvador | 34 | 1,745 | x | x | x |

| Country | Area in Kilometers (ooo) | Population Estimate (ooo) | One-time Member of League of Nations | Member of United Nations (1949) | Member of Universal Postal Union |
|---|---|---|---|---|---|
| **III.** *South America* | | | | | |
| 17. Argentina | 2,793 | 13,132 | x | x | x |
| 18. Bolivia | 1,090 | 3,400 | x | x | x |
| 19. Brazil | 8,511 | 40,900 | x | x | x |
| 20. Chile | 742 | 4,940 | x | x | x |
| 21. Colombia | 1,139 | 8,986 | x | x | x |
| 22. Ecuador | 455 | 3,000 | x | x | x |
| 23. Paraguay | 397 | 970 | x | x | x |
| 24. Peru | 1,249 | 7,000 | x | x | x |
| 25. Uruguay | 187 | 2,147 | x | x | x |
| 26. Venezuela | 912 | 3,650 | x | x | x |
| **IV.** *Asia* | | | | | |
| 27. Afghanistan | 650 | 7,000 | x | x | x |
| 28. Arabia | 2,600 | 7,000 | | x | |
| 29. Bhoutan | 50 | 120 | | | |
| 30. Burma | 261,610 sq. miles | 16,823 | | | |
| 31. Ceylon | 25,332 " " | 6,659 | | | |
| 32. China | 11,103 | 450,000 | x | x | x |
| 33. India | 4,096 | 382,000 | x | x | x |
| 34. Irak | 302 | 3,700 | x | x | x |
| 35. Iran | 1,644 | 15,000 | x | x | x |
| 36. Israel | 18[a] | 1,100[a] | | x | x |
| 37. Japan | 386 | 72,520 | x | | x |
| 38. Korea | 220[a] | 27,200 | | | |
| 39. Lebanon | 6.2 | 854[a] | | x | x |
| 40. Nepal | 140 | 5,600 | | | |
| 41. Pakistan | | 65,000 | | x | x |
| 42. Philippines | 296 | 16,300 | | x | x |
| 43. Syria | 58 | 2,224 | | x | x |
| 44. Thailand | 518 | 15,500 | x | x | x |
| 45. Turkey | 767 | 17,620 | x | x | x |
| **V.** *Europe* | | | | | |
| 46. Albania | 28 | 1,064 | x | x | x |
| 47. Austria | 32 | 6,650[a] | x | | x |
| 48. Andorre | 0.5 | 6 | | | |
| 49. Belgium | 30 | 8,396 | x | x | x |
| 50. Bulgaria | 103 | 6,308 | x | | x |
| 51. Czechoslovakia | 140 | 15,239 | x | x | x |
| 52. Denmark | 6.8 | 3,625[a] | x | x | x |
| 53. Finland | 383 | 3,684 | x | | x |
| 54. France | 551 | 41,950 | x | x | x |
| 55. Germany | 480 | 75,000[a] | x | | x |
| 56. Greece | 130 | 7,200 | x | x | x |
| 57. Hungary | 171.8 | 9,129 | x | | x |
| 58. Eire | 69 | 2,946 | x | | x |
| 59. Iceland | 103 | 120 | | x | x |
| 60. Italy | 265 | 41,800[a] | x | | x |
| 61. Liechtenstein | 0.2 | 11 | | | x |
| 62. Luxembourg | 2.6 | 301 | x | x | x |
| 63. Monaco | .002 | 24 | | | x |
| 64. Norway | 523 | 2,937 | x | x | x |
| 65. The Netherlands | 33 | 8,834 | x | x | x |
| 66. Poland | 395 | 31,000[a] | x | x | x |
| 67. Portugal | 92 | 7,620 | x | | x |
| 68. Rumania | 195 | 20,045 | x | | x |
| 69. United Kingdom | 144 | 47,778 | x | x | x |

| Country | Area in Kilometers (ooo) | Population Estimate (ooo) | One-time Member of League of Nations | Member of United Nations (1949) | Member of Universal Postal Union |
|---|---|---|---|---|---|
| V. *Europe—Continued* | | | | | |
| 70. San Marino | 0.1 | 15 | | | x |
| 71. Spain | 505 | 25,600 | x | | x |
| 72. Sweden | 449 | 6,341 | x | x | x |
| 73. Switzerland | 41 | 4,206 | x | | x |
| 74. Vatican City | 108 acres | 1 | | | x |
| 75. Yugoslavia | 265 | 16,700 [a] | x | x | x |
| 76. U.S.S.R. (Europe and Asia) | 22,500 | 182,000 [a] | x | x | x |
| VI. *Oceania* | | | | | |
| 77. Australia | 7,704 | 6,997 | x | x | x |
| 78. New Zealand | 267 | 1,642 | x | x | x |

[a] Estimate.

# The Earlier Search for Security

THE first concern of the state, as of the individual, is its security. In order to live it will face want and hardship in every form. If need be, it will fight. This has been shown on occasion after occasion. It was shown when Poland engaged in a hopeless war against German aggression in 1939, when Finland a little later fought off Russia, when a Czechoslovakian Government was set up in London to take part in the fight against the Axis, and when Great Britain risked extreme poverty and defeat to stay in the war after the collapse of France in 1940. The nation state is hardy and refuses to accept death without a struggle.

The principal reliance of the state for safety has been on its own strength. The state has built armies, navies, and air forces; it has tried to get control of strategic raw materials and to become strong and independent economically; it has used diplomacy to make allies, to weaken the enemy, and to keep the balance of power; and it has sought strategic boundaries to fence off its enemies. Always the aim has been to become so strong that no other nation will dare attack it.

The flaws in this method of security are now well known. It is costly and uneconomic in every respect. Some nations are so small and weak that they are both poor competitors and easy prey for aggressors. Most fatal of all is the temptation on the part of a nation to become aggressive in order to secure itself, to dominate or conquer a small or weak neighbor for the purpose of getting resources or strategic frontiers, to set up spheres of influence all about it which will provide buffer space against a possible enemy, or to get islands useful as naval or air bases. These activities can go only so far before they are challenged by nations fearful lest the balance of power be tipped against them.

Because this system has always failed, the nations have been trying in recent decades to find security by co-operative rather than competitive means. The non-aggression pact is the most elemental form given to this means of keeping the peace. This is a treaty in which each of the parties agrees not to commit aggression against the other. Usually it is bilateral, but there have been a few multilateral non-aggression pacts. It was an instrument much used by Soviet Russia during the 'twenties and 'thirties. While the conclusion of such a treaty may give a momentary feeling of security to its makers, it is by no means a sure preventive of war. Germany and Poland made such a treaty in 1932, only seven years before the German invasion of Poland, and Germany and Russia concluded one in 1939, less than two years before the German attack on Russia.

A more complicated method of providing security by co-operative means is that usually referred to as 'collective security.' It was the method of the League of Nations, set up in 1919 after World War I. Each member of the League agreed to respect and preserve 'the political independence and the territorial integrity' of all the others, to boycott and, if necessary, use military force against a nation going to war in violation of the Covenant. The League also provided peaceful methods of settling disputes, and established procedures of co-operation in social, economic, and other matters.

Much constructive work was done by the League of Nations. Not only did the League carry co-operation in various peace-time interests farther than ever before, it also dealt with a long list of international disputes. When the disputants were not too strong, the League usually was dominant. It contributed to the solution of many controversies, such as the Leticia affair between Colombia and Peru, the boundary dispute between Greece and Bulgaria, and the Aaland Islands case between Sweden and Finland. Only once were the sanctions carried out and that was against Italy when she invaded Ethiopia in 1935. Then an incomplete boycott was attempted, but while it was a handicap to Italy, this action did not prevent her aggression.

With the realization that the League system had weaknesses and loopholes, an effort was made in 1924 to strengthen the Covenant by what was known as the Geneva Protocol. This failed and, two years later, the Locarno Pact was concluded among the western European powers, guaranteeing the boundary located between Germany on the one hand and France and Belgium on the other against attack. The purpose was to stabilize Europe at its weakest point. Then in 1928 the Pact of Paris was concluded, which attempted to outlaw war as an instrument of national policy, but without guarantees in any form.

In the 1930's this whole structure of peace was tested—first by the Japanese invasion of Manchuria in 1931, and in 1935 by the Italian conquest of Ethiopia. The system failed to meet either of these tests of strength, so that it became clear to Nazi Germany that there would be no League action to stop her program of expansion. Thereafter, in 1938, Austria and the Sudetenland were annexed. In 1939 Memel and the rest of Czechoslovakia were taken, and finally came the attack on Poland, which provoked a challenge from Great Britain and France. The League system of security had been found wanting, and World War II had begun.

## I. A Plan to Abolish War

The search for security and peace in the western state system has a long history. As the unity of the medieval world under Christendom fell apart, a call for a supreme ruler to reunite mankind was made by the great poet Dante Alighieri in his *De Monarchia,* written at the opening of the fourteenth century. Dante's scheme, imperial in design, was to remain unheeded by the rising national states in Europe, as later also the plans of Henry IV (King of France from 1593 to 1610) were to come to naught. Other such plans, some in our own day, have been treated with the same indifference. The Abbé Saint-Pierre published his *Project of Perpetual Peace* in the early eighteenth century; Jean-Jacques Rousseau, Jeremy Bentham, Immanuel Kant, and a host of other eminent thinkers have all drafted schemes. Quoted below is the project for peace written by William Penn in 1694, testifying to the Quaker interest in peace.

(William Penn, 'A Plan Towards the Present and Future Peace of Europe by the Establishment of a European Diet, Parliament or Estates,' *The Peace of Europe: The Fruits of Solitude and Other Writings,* New York. Reprinted by permission of E. P. Dutton & Co., Inc.)

To the Reader,—I have undertaken a subject that I am very sensible requires one of more sufficiency than I am master of to treat it as, in truth, it deserves and the groaning state of Europe calls for; but since bunglers may stumble upon the game as well as masters, though it belongs to the skilful to hunt and catch it, I hope this essay will not be charged upon me for a fault if it appear to be neither chimerical nor injurious, and may provoke abler pens to improve and perform the design with better judgment and success. I will say no more in excuse of myself for this undertaking but that it is the fruit of my solicitous thoughts for the peace of Europe, and they must want charity as much as the world needs quiet to be offended with me for so pacific a proposal. Let them censure my management, so they prosecute the advantage of the design; for until the millenary doctrine be accomplished, there is nothing appears to me so beneficial an expedient to the peace and happiness of this quarter of the world.

### 1. Of Peace and Its Advantages

He must not be a man but a statue of brass or stone whose bowels do not melt when he beholds the bloody tragedies of this war, in Hungary, Germany, Flanders, Ireland, and at sea, the mortality of sickly and languishing camps and navies, and the mighty prey the devouring winds and waves have made upon ships and men since '88. And as this with reason ought to affect human nature, and deeply kindred, so there is something very moving that becomes prudent men to consider, and that is the vast charge that has accompanied that blood, and which makes no mean part of these tragedies; especially if they deliberate upon the uncertainty of the war, that they know not how or when it will end, and that the expense cannot be less, and the hazard is as great as before. So that in the contraries of peace we see the beauties and benefits of it; which under it, such is the unhappiness of mankind, we are too apt to nauseate, as the full stomach loathes the honey-comb; and like that unfortunate gentle-man, that having a fine and a good woman to his wife, and searching his pleasure in forbidden and less agreeable company, said, when reproached with his neglect of better enjoyments, that he could love his wife of all women if she were not his wife, though that increased his obligation to prefer her. It is a great mark of the cor-ruption of our natures, and what ought to humble us extremely, and excite the exercise of our reason to a nobler and juster sense, that we cannot see the use and pleasure of our comforts but by the want of them. As if we could not taste the benefit of health but by the help of sick-ness; nor understand the satisfaction of fulness without the instruction of want; nor, finally, know the comfort of peace but by the smart and penance of the vices of war; and without dispute that is not the least reason that God is pleased to chastise us so frequently with it. What can we desire better than peace but the grace to use it? Peace preserves our pos-sessions; we are in no danger of invasions: our trade is free and safe, and we rise and lie down without anxiety. The rich bring out their hoards, and employ poor manu-facturers; buildings and divers projections for profit and pleasure go on: it excites industry, which brings wealth, as that gives the means of charity and hospitality, not the lowest ornaments of a kingdom or commonwealth. But war, like the frost of '83, seizes all these comforts at once, and stops the civil channel of society. The rich draw in their stock, the poor turn sol-diers, or thieves, or starve: no industry, no building, no manufactory, little hos-pitality or charity; but what the peace gave, the war devours. I need say no more upon this head, when the advantages of peace, and mischiefs of war, are so many and sensible to every capacity under all governments, as either of them prevails.

I shall proceed to the next point. What is the best means of Peace which will con-duce much to open my way to what I have to propose. . .

IV. OF A GENERAL PEACE, OR THE PEACE OF EUROPE, AND THE MEANS OF IT

In my first section, I showed the de-sirableness of peace; in my next, the tru-est means of it; to wit, justice not war. And in my last, that this justice was the fruit of government, as government itself was the result of society which first came from a reasonable design in men of peace. Now if the sovereign princes of Europe, who represent that society or independent state of men that was previous to the obligations of society, would, for the same reason that engaged men first into society, viz., love of peace and order, agree to meet by their stated deputies in a general diet, estates, or parliament, and there establish rules of justice for sovereign princes to observe one to another; and thus to meet yearly, or once in two or three years at farthest, or as they shall see cause, and to be styled, the Sovereign or Imperial Diet, Parliament, or State of Europe; before which sovereign assembly should be brought all differences depend-ing between one sovereign and another that cannot be made up by private em-bassies before the sessions begin; and that if any of the sovereignties that constitute these imperial states shall refuse to sub-mit their claim or pretensions to them, or to abide and perform the judgment thereof, and seek their remedy by arms, or delay their compliance beyond the time prefixed in their resolutions, all the other sovereignties, united as one strength, shall compel the submission and perform-ance of the sentence, with damages to the suffering party, and charges to the sov-ereignties that obliged their submission. To be sure, Europe would quietly obtain the so much desired and needed peace to her harassed inhabitants; no sovereignty in Europe having the power and therefore cannot show the will to dispute the conclusion; and, consequently, peace would be procured and continued in Europe.

## II. Non-Aggression Treaties

An example of a non-aggression pact concluded in 1933 is given in extract A below. Like most such treaties it contains no definition of aggression. Extract B is the definition of aggression inserted in another treaty which Russia made in the same year with some of her neighbors.

### A. *Treaty between Russia and Italy, 1933*

(Pact of Friendship, Non-Aggression and Neutrality between Italy and the Union of Soviet Socialist Republics, 1933. League of Nations, *Treaty Series,* no. 3418, vol. 148, pp. 327-9.)

#### ARTICLE 1

Each of the High Contracting Parties undertakes with regard to the other not to resort in any case, whether alone or jointly with one or more third Powers, either to war or to any aggression by land, sea, or air against that other Party, and to respect the inviolability of the territories placed under that Party's sovereignty.

#### ARTICLE 2

Should either High Contracting Party be the object of aggression on the part of one or more third Powers, the other High Contracting Party undertakes to maintain neutrality throughout the duration of the conflict.

Should either High Contracting Party resort to aggression against any Power, the other High Contracting Party may denounce the present Treaty without notice.

#### ARTICLE 3

Each of the High Contracting Parties undertakes, for the duration of the present Treaty, not to become a party to any international agreement of which the effect in practice would be to prevent the purchase of goods from or granting of credits to the other Party, and not to take any measure which would result in the exclusion of the other Party from any participation in its foreign trade.

#### ARTICLE 4

Each of the High Contracting Parties undertakes not to become a party to any agreement of a political or economic character or any combination directed against either Party.

#### ARTICLE 5

The undertakings set forth in the preceding Articles shall not in any way limit or modify the rights and obligations of either High Contracting Party resulting from agreements concluded by that Party prior to the entry into force of the present Treaty, and each Party declares by the present Article that it is not bound by any agreement under which it is obliged to participate in an aggression undertaken by a third state. . .

## B. *A Definition of Aggression*

(Convention for the Definition of Aggression, 4 July 1933, Rumania, Union of Soviet Socialist Republics, Czechoslovakia, Turkey, Yugoslavia, League of Nations, *Treaty Series*, no. 3414, vol. 148, p. 215.)

Being desirous of consolidating the peaceful relations existing between their countries;

Mindful of the fact that the Briand-Kellogg Pact, of which they are signatories, prohibits all aggression . . .

### ARTICLE 2

Accordingly the aggressor in an international conflict shall, subject to the agreements in force between the Parties to the dispute, be considered that State which is the first to commit any of the following actions:

1. Declaration of war upon another State;
2. Invasion by its armed forces, with or without a declaration of war, of the territory of another State;
3. Attack by its land, naval, or air forces, with or without a declaration of war, on the territory, vessels or aircraft of another State;
4. Naval blockade of the coasts or ports of another State;
5. Provision of support to armed bands formed in its territory which have invaded the territory of another State, or refusal, notwithstanding the request of the invaded State, to take, in its territory, all the measures in its power to deprive those bands of all assistance or protection. . .

## III. THE COVENANT OF THE LEAGUE OF NATIONS

The League of Nations came into existence on 10 January 1920, its Covenant forming part of the Treaty of Versailles, which brought World War I to a close. It was the American War-President, Woodrow Wilson, who had been the strongest advocate of the League idea. At the Paris Peace Conference in 1919 Wilson insisted that the League Covenant be included in the Versailles Treaty. With the resurgence of Germany under Adolph Hitler in the inter-war years, the Treaty was attacked because of the onerous terms imposed on the defeated enemy. Thus the Covenant was also berated, but efforts to separate the two documents proved futile. More important, however, the Covenant stands as the first practical attempt to construct a world-wide security system. Both the successes and failures of the League system proved useful guides in the formation of the United Nations after World War II. The League Covenant, therefore, ranks high as one of the leading documents in the study of contemporary international relations. The text of the Covenant follows; the portions printed in italics are the amendments made to the original draft.

*The High Contracting Parties,*
In order to promote international co-operation and to achieve international peace and security

by the acceptance of obligations not to resort to war,

by the prescription of open, just and honorable relations between nations,

by the firm establishment of the understandings of international law as the actual rule of conduct among Governments, and by the maintenance of justice and a scrupulous respect for all treaty obligations in the dealings of organized peoples with one another,

Agree to this Covenant of the League of Nations.

### ARTICLE 1

1. The original Members of the League of Nations shall be those of the Signatories which are named in the Annex to this Covenant and also such of those other States named in the Annex as shall accede without reservation to this Covenant. Such accession shall be effected by a Declaration deposited with the Secretariat within two months of the coming into force of the Covenant. Notice thereof shall be sent to all other Members of the League.

2. Any fully self-governing State, Dominion or Colony not named in the Annex may become a Member of the League if its admission is agreed to by two-thirds of the Assembly, provided that it shall give effective guarantees of its sincere intention to observe its international obligations, and shall accept such regulations as may be prescribed by the League in regard to its military, naval and air forces and armaments.

3. Any Member of the League may, after two years' notice of its intention so to do, withdraw from the League, provided that all its international obligations and all its obligations under this Covenant shall have been fulfilled at the time of its withdrawal.

### ARTICLE 2

The action of the League under this Covenant shall be effected through the instrumentality of an Assembly and of a Council, with a permanent Secretariat.

### ARTICLE 3

1. The Assembly shall consist of Representatives of the Members of the League.

2. The Assembly shall meet at stated intervals and from time to time as occasion may require at the Seat of the League or at such other place as may be decided upon.

3. The Assembly may deal at its meetings with any matter within the sphere of action of the League or affecting the peace of the world.

4. At meetings of the Assembly, each Member of the League shall have one vote, and may have not more than three Representatives.

### ARTICLE 4

1. The Council shall consist of Representatives of the Principal Allied and Associated Powers, together with Representatives of four other Members of the League. These four Members of the League shall be selected by the Assembly from time to time in its discretion. Until the appointment of the Representatives of the four Members of the League first selected by the Assembly, Representatives of Belgium, Brazil, Spain and Greece shall be members of the Council.

2. With the approval of the majority of the Assembly, the Council may name additional Members of the League whose Representatives shall always be Members of the Council; the Council with like approval may increase the number of Members of the League to be selected by the Assembly for representation on the Council.

*2 bis. The Assembly shall fix by a two-thirds majority the rules dealing with the election of the non-permanent Members of the Council, and particularly such regulations as relate to their term of office and the conditions of reeligibility.*

3. The Council shall meet from time to time as occasion may require, and at least once a year, at the Seat of the League, or at such other place as may be decided upon.

4. The Council may deal at its meetings with any matter within the sphere of action of the League or affecting the peace of the world.

5. Any Member of the League not represented on the Council shall be invited to send a Representative to sit as a member at any meeting of the Council during the consideration of matters specially affecting the interests of that Member of the League.

6. At meetings of the Council, each Member of the League represented on the Council shall have one vote, and may have not more than one Representative.

## ARTICLE 5

1. Except where otherwise expressly provided in this Covenant or by the terms of the present Treaty, decisions at any meeting of the Assembly or of the Council, shall require the agreement of all the Members of the League represented at the meeting.

2. All matters of procedure at meetings of the Assembly or of the Council, including the appointment of Committees to investigate particular matters, shall be regulated by the Assembly or by the Council and may be decided by a majority of the Members of the League represented at the meeting.

3. The first meeting of the Assembly and the first meeting of the Council shall be summoned by the President of the United States of America.

## ARTICLE 6

1. The permanent Secretariat shall be established at the Seat of the League. The Secretariat shall comprise a Secretary-General and such secretaries and staff as may be required.

2. The first Secretary-General shall be the person named in the Annex; thereafter the Secretary-General shall be appointed by the Council with the approval of the majority of the Assembly.

3. The Secretaries and the staff of the Secretariat shall be appointed by the Secretary-General with the approval of the Council.

4. The Secretary-General shall act in that capacity at all meetings of the Assembly and of the Council.

5. *The expenses of the League shall be borne by the Members of the League in the proportion decided by the Assembly.*

## ARTICLE 7

1. The Seat of the League is established at Geneva.

2. The Council may at any time decide that the Seat of the League shall be established elsewhere.

3. All positions under or in connection with the League, including the Secretariat, shall be open equally to men and women.

4. Representatives of the Members of the League and officials of the League when engaged on the business of the League shall enjoy diplomatic privileges and immunities.

5. The buildings and other property occupied by the League or its officials or by Representatives attending its meetings shall be inviolable.

## ARTICLE 8

1. The Members of the League recognize that the maintenance of peace requires the reduction of national armaments to the lowest point consistent with

national safety and the enforcement by common action of international obligations.

2. The Council, taking account of the geographical situation and circumstances of each State, shall formulate plans for such reduction for the consideration and action of the several Governments.

3. Such plans shall be subject to reconsideration and revision at least every ten years.

4. After these plans shall have been adopted by the several Governments, the limits of armaments therein fixed shall not be exceeded without the concurrence of the Council.

5. The Members of the League agree that the manufacture by private enterprise of munitions and implements of war is open to grave objections. The Council shall advise how the evil effects attendant upon such manufacture can be prevented, due regard being had to the necessities of those Members of the League which are not able to manufacture the munitions and implements of war necessary for their safety.

6. The Members of the League undertake to interchange full and frank information as to the scale of their armaments, their military, naval and air programs and the condition of such of their industries as are adaptable to warlike purposes.

### ARTICLE 9

A permanent Commission shall be constituted to advise the Council on the execution of the provisions of Articles 1 and 8 and on military, naval and air questions generally.

### ARTICLE 10

The Members of the League undertake to respect and preserve as against external aggression the territorial integrity and existing political independence of all Members of the League. In case of any such aggression or in case of any threat or danger of such aggression the Council shall advise upon the means by which this obligation shall be fulfilled.

### ARTICLE 11

1. Any war or threat of war, whether immediately affecting any of the Members of the League or not, is hereby declared a matter of concern to the whole League, and the League shall take any action that may be deemed wise and effectual to safeguard the peace of nations. In case any such emergency should arise the Secretary-General shall on the request of any Member of the League forthwith summon a meeting of the Council.

2. It is also declared to be the friendly right of each Member of the League to bring to the attention of the Assembly or of the Council any circumstance whatever affecting international relations which threatens to disturb international peace or the good understanding between nations upon which peace depends.

### ARTICLE 12

1. The Members of the League agree that if there should arise between them any dispute likely to lead to a rupture they will submit the matter either to arbitration *or judicial settlement* or to inquiry by the Council, and they agree in no case to resort to war until three months after the award by the arbitrators *or the judicial decision* or the report by the Council.

2. In any case under this Article the award of the arbitrators *or the judicial decision* shall be made within a reasonable time, and the report of the Council shall be made within six months after the submission of the dispute.

### ARTICLE 13

1. The Members of the League agree that whenever any dispute shall arise be-

tween them which they recognize to be suitable for submission to arbitration *or judicial settlement,* and which cannot be satisfactorily settled by diplomacy, they will submit the whole subject-matter to arbitration *or judicial settlement.*

2. Disputes as to the interpretation of a treaty, as to any question of international law, as to the existence of any fact which, if established, would constitute a breach of any international obligation, or as to the extent and nature of the reparation to be made for any such breach, are declared to be among those which are generally suitable for submission to arbitration *or judicial settlement.*

3. *For the consideration of any such dispute, the court to which the case is referred shall be the Permanent Court of International Justice, established in accordance with Article 14, or any tribunal agreed on by the parties to the dispute or stipulated in any convention existing between them.*

4. The Members of the League agree that they will carry out in full good faith any award *or decision* that may be rendered, and that they will not resort to war against a Member of the League which complies therewith. In the event of any failure to carry out such an award *or decision,* the Council shall propose what steps should be taken to give effect thereto.

### ARTICLE 14

The Council shall formulate and submit to the Members of the League for adoption plans for the establishment of a Permanent Court of International Justice. The Court shall be competent to hear and determine any dispute of an international character which the parties thereto submit to it. The Court may also give an advisory opinion upon any dispute or question referred to it by the Council or by the Assembly.

### ARTICLE 15

1. If there should arise between Members of the League any dispute likely to lead to a rupture, which is not submitted to arbitration *or judicial settlement* in accordance with Article 13, the Members of the League agree that they will submit the matter to the Council. Any party to the dispute may effect such submission by giving notice of the existence of the dispute to the Secretary-General, who will make all necessary arrangements for a full investigation and consideration thereof.

2. For this purpose the parties to the dispute will communicate to the Secretary-General, as promptly as possible, statements of their case with all the relevant facts and papers, and the Council may forthwith direct the publication thereof.

3. The Council shall endeavor to effect a settlement of the dispute, and if such efforts are successful, a statement shall be made public giving such facts and explanations regarding the dispute and the terms of settlement thereof as the Council may deem appropriate.

4. If the dispute is not thus settled, the Council either unanimously or by a majority vote shall make and publish a report containing a statement of the facts of the dispute and the recommendations which are deemed just and proper in regard thereto.

5. Any Member of the League represented on the Council may make public a statement of the facts of the dispute and of its conclusions regarding the same.

6. If a report by the Council is unanimously agreed to by the members thereof other than the Representatives of one or more of the parties to the dispute, the Members of the League agree that they will not go to war with any party to the dispute which complies with the recommendations of the report.

7. If the Council fails to reach a report

which is unanimously agreed to by the members thereof, other than the Representatives of one or more of the parties to the dispute, the Members of the League reserve to themselves the right to take such action as they shall consider necessary for the maintenance of right and justice.

8. If the dispute between the parties is claimed by one of them, and is found by the Council, to arise out of a matter which by international law is solely within the domestic jurisdiction of that party, the Council shall so report, and shall make no recommendation as to its settlement.

9. The Council may in any case under this Article refer the dispute to the Assembly. The dispute shall be so referred at the request of either party to the dispute provided that such request be made within fourteen days after the submission of the dispute to the Council.

10. In any case referred to the Assembly, all the provisions of this Article and of Article 12 relating to the action and powers of the Council shall apply to the action and powers of the Assembly, provided that a report made by the Assembly, if concurred in by the Representatives of those Members of the League represented on the Council and of a majority of the other Members of the League, exclusive in each case of the Representatives of the parties to the dispute, shall have the same force as a report by the Council concurred in by all the members thereof other than the Representatives of one or more of the parties to the dispute.

## ARTICLE 16

1. Should any Member of the League resort to war in disregard of its covenants under Articles 12, 13 or 15, it shall *ipso facto* be deemed to have committed an act of war against all other Members of the League, which hereby undertake immediately to subject it to the severance of all trade or financial relations, the pro-

hibition of all intercourse between their nationals and the nationals of the covenant-breaking State, and the prevention of all financial, commercial or personal intercourse between the nationals of the covenant-breaking State and the nationals of any other State, whether a Member of the League or not.

2. It shall be the duty of the Council in such case to recommend to the several Governments concerned what effective military, naval or air force the Members of the League shall severally contribute to the armed forces to be used to protect the covenants of the League.

3. The Members of the League agree, further, that they will mutually support one another in the financial and economic measures which are taken under this Article, in order to minimize the loss and inconvenience resulting from the above measures, and that they will mutually support one another in resisting any special measures aimed at one of their number by the covenant-breaking State, and that they will take the necessary steps to afford passage through their territory to the forces of any of the Members of the League which are cooperating to protect the covenants of the League.

4. Any Member of the League which has violated any covenant of the League may be declared to be no longer a Member of the League by a vote of the Council concurred in by the Representatives of all the other Members of the League represented thereon.

## ARTICLE 17

1. In the event of a dispute between a Member of the League and a State which is not a Member of the League, or between States not Members of the League, the State or States not Members of the League shall be invited to accept the obligations of membership in the League for the purposes of such dispute, upon such conditions as the Council may deem

just. If such invitation is accepted, the provisions of Articles 12 to 16 inclusive shall be applied with such modifications as may be deemed necessary by the Council.

2. Upon such invitation being given, the Council shall immediately institute an inquiry into the circumstances of the dispute and recommend such action as may seem best and most effectual in the circumstances.

3. If a State so invited shall refuse to accept the obligations of membership in the League for the purposes of such dispute, and shall resort to war against a Member of the League, the provisions of Article 16 shall be applicable as against the State taking such action.

4. If both parties to the dispute when so invited refuse to accept the obligations of membership in the League for the purposes of such dispute, the Council may take such measures and make such recommendations as will prevent hostilities and will result in the settlement of the dispute.

## ARTICLE 18

Every treaty or international engagement entered into hereafter by any Member of the League shall be forthwith registered with the Secretariat and shall as soon as possible be published by it. No such treaty or international engagement shall be binding until so registered.

## ARTICLE 19

The Assembly may from time to time advise the reconsideration by Members of the League of treaties which have become inapplicable and the consideration of international conditions whose continuance might endanger the peace of the world.

## ARTICLE 20

1. The Members of the League severally agree that this Covenant is accepted as abrogating all obligations or understandings *inter se* which are inconsistent with the terms thereof, and solemnly undertake that they will not hereafter enter into any engagements inconsistent with the terms thereof.

2. In case any Member of the League shall, before becoming a Member of the League, have undertaken any obligations inconsistent with the terms of this Covenant, it shall be the duty of such Member to take immediate steps to produce its release from such obligations.

## ARTICLE 21

Nothing in this Covenant shall be deemed to affect the validity of international engagements, such as treaties of arbitration or regional understandings like the Monroe doctrine, for securing the maintenance of peace.

## ARTICLE 22

1. To those colonies and territories which as a consequence of the late war have ceased to be under the sovereignty of the States which formerly governed them and which are inhabited by peoples not yet able to stand by themselves under the strenuous conditions of the modern world, there should be applied the principle that the well-being and development of such peoples form a sacred trust of civilization and that securities for the performance of this trust should be embodied in this Covenant.

2. The best method of giving practical effect to this principle is that the tutelage of such peoples should be entrusted to advanced nations who, by reason of their resources, their experience or their geographical position, can best undertake this responsibility, and who are willing to accept it, and that this tutelage should be exercised by them as Mandatories on behalf of the League.

3. The character of the mandate must differ according to the stage of development of the people, the geographical situ-

ation of the territory, its economic conditions and other similar circumstances.

4. Certain communities formerly belonging to the Turkish Empire have reached a stage of development where their existence as independent nations can be provisionally recognized subject to the rendering of administrative advice and assistance by a Mandatory until such time as they are able to stand alone. The wishes of these communities must be a principal consideration in the selection of the Mandatory.

5. Other peoples, especially those of Central Africa, are at such a stage that the Mandatory must be responsible for the administration of the territory under conditions which will guarantee freedom of conscience and religion, subject only to the maintenance of public order and morals, the prohibition of abuses such as the slave trade, the arms traffic and the liquor traffic, and the prevention of the establishment of fortifications or military and naval bases and of military training of the natives for other than police purposes and the defense of territory, and will also secure equal opportunities for the trade and commerce of other Members of the League.

6. There are territories, such as South-West Africa and certain of the South Pacific Islands, which, owing to the sparseness of their population, or their small size, or their remoteness from the centers of civilization, or their geographical contiguity to the territory of the Mandatory, and other circumstances, can be best administered under the laws of the Mandatory as integral portions of its territory, subject to the safeguards above mentioned in the interests of the indigenous population.

7. In every case of mandate, the Mandatory shall render to the Council an annual report in reference to the territory committed to its charge.

8. The degree of authority, control or administration to be exercised by the Mandatory shall, if not previously agreed upon by the Members of the League, be explicitly defined in each case by the Council.

9. A permanent Commission shall be constituted to receive and examine the annual reports of the Mandatories and to advise the Council on all matters relating to the observance of the mandates.

## ARTICLE 23

Subject to and in accordance with the provisions of international conventions existing or hereafter to be agreed upon, the Members of the League:

(a) will endeavor to secure and maintain fair and humane conditions of labor for men, women and children, both in their own countries and in all countries to which their commercial and industrial relations extend, and for that purpose will establish and maintain the necessary international organizations;

(b) undertake to secure just treatment of the native inhabitants of territories under their control;

(c) will entrust the League with the general supervision over the execution of agreements with regard to the traffic in women and children, and the traffic in opium and other dangerous drugs;

(d) will entrust the League with the general supervision of the trade in arms and ammunition with the countries in which the control of this traffic is necessary in the common interest;

(e) will make provision to secure and maintain freedom of communications and of transit and equitable treatment for the commerce of all Members of the League. In this connection, the special necessities of the regions devastated during the war of 1914-1918 shall be borne in mind;

(f) will endeavor to take steps in matters of international concern for the prevention and control of disease.

### ARTICLE 24

1. There shall be placed under the direction of the League all international bureaus already established by general treaties if the parties to such treaties consent. All such international bureaus and all commissions for the regulation of matters of international interest hereafter constituted shall be placed under the direction of the League.

2. In all matters of international interest which are regulated by general conventions but which are not placed under the control of international bureaus or commissions, the Secretariat of the League shall, subject to the consent of the Council and if desired by the parties, collect and distribute all relevant information and shall render any other assistance which may be necessary or desirable.

3. The Council may include as part of the expenses of the Secretariat the expenses of any bureau or commission which is placed under the direction of the League.

### ARTICLE 25

The Members of the League agree to encourage and promote the establishment and cooperation of duly authorized voluntary national Red Cross organizations having as purposes the improvement of health, the prevention of disease and the mitigation of suffering throughout the world.

### ARTICLE 26

1. Amendments to this Covenant will take effect when ratified by the Members of the League whose Representatives compose the Council and by a majority of the Members of the League whose Representatives compose the Assembly.

2. No such amendments shall bind any Member of the League which signifies its dissent therefrom, but in that case it shall cease to be a Member of the League.

## IV. THE GENEVA PROTOCOL

Because the peace machinery of the League of Nations was admittedly weak, a protocol was drafted and adopted by the Assembly on 2 October 1924, for the purpose of strengthening the organization. Shortly after this was accomplished the MacDonald Government in England was replaced by a Conservative cabinet, which refused to sign the protocol. British rejection of the document led to its rejection generally, and consequently it never came into effect. The extract below shows the method by which a strengthening of the Covenant was sought. The definition of aggression in Article 10 is one of the best yet made.

### ARTICLE 1

The signatory States undertake to make every effort in their power to secure the introduction into the Covenant of amendments on the lines of the provisions contained in the following articles. . .

### ARTICLE 2

The signatory States agree in no case to resort to war either with one another or against a State which, if the occasion arises, accepts all the obligations hereinafter set out, except in case of resistance to acts of aggression or when acting in agreement with the Council or the Assembly of the League of Nations in accordance with the Provisions of the Covenant and of the present Protocol.

## ARTICLE 3

The signatory States undertake to recognize as compulsory, *ipso facto* and without special agreement, the jurisdiction of the Permanent Court of International Justice in the cases covered by paragraph 2 of Article 36 of the Statute of the Court, but without prejudice to the right of any State, when acceding to the special protocol provided for in the said Article and opened for signature on December 16th, 1920, to make reservations compatible with the said clause.

Accession to this special protocol, opened for signature on December 16th, 1920, must be given within the month following the coming into force of the present Protocol.

States which accede to the present Protocol, after its coming into force, must carry out the above obligation within the month following their accession.

## ARTICLE 4

With a view to render more complete the provisions of paragraphs 4, 5, 6, and 7 of Article 15 of the Covenant, the signatory States agree to comply with the following procedure:

1. If the dispute submitted to the Council is not settled by it as provided in paragraph 3 of the said Article 15, the Council shall endeavor to persuade the parties to submit the dispute to judicial settlement or arbitration.

2. (a) If the parties cannot agree to do so, there shall, at the request of at least one of the parties, be constituted a Committee of Arbitrators. The Committee shall so far as possible be constituted by agreement between the parties.

(b) If within the period fixed by the Council the parties have failed to agree, in whole or in part, upon the number, the names and the powers of the arbitrators and upon the procedure, the Council shall settle the points remaining in suspense. It shall with the utmost possible dispatch select in consultation with the parties the arbitrators and their President from among persons who by their nationality, their personal character and their experience, appear to it to furnish the highest guaranties of competence and impartiality.

(c) After the claims of the parties have been formulated, the Committee of Arbitrators, on the request of any party, shall through the medium of the Council request an advisory opinion upon any points of law in dispute from the Permanent Court of International Justice, which in such case shall meet with the utmost possible dispatch.

3. If none of the parties ask for arbitration, the Council shall again take the dispute under consideration. If the Council reaches a report which is unanimously agreed to by the members thereof other than the representatives of any of the parties to the dispute, the signatory States agree to comply with the recommendations therein.

4. If the Council fails to reach a report which is concurred in by all its members, other than the representatives of any of the parties to the dispute, it shall submit the dispute to arbitration. It shall itself determine the composition, the powers and the procedure of the Committee of Arbitrators and, in the choice of the arbitrators, shall bear in mind the

guaranties of competence and impartiality referred to in paragraph 2 (b) above.

5. In no case may a solution, upon which there has already been a unanimous recommendation of the Council accepted by one of the parties concerned, be again called in question.

6. The signatory States undertake that they will carry out in full good faith any judicial sentence or arbitral award that may be rendered and that they will comply, as provided in paragraph 3 above, with the Solutions recommended by the Council. In the event of a State failing to carry out the above undertakings, the Council shall exert all its influence to secure compliance therewith. If it fails therein, it shall propose what steps should be taken to give effect thereto, in accordance with the provision contained at the end of Article 13 of the Covenant. Should a State in disregard of the above undertakings resort to war, the sanctions provided for by Article 16 of the Covenant, interpreted in the manner indicated in the present Protocol, shall immediately become applicable to it.

7. The provisions of the present article do not apply to the settlement of disputes which arise as the result of measures of war taken by one or more signatory States in agreement with the Council or the Assembly.

. . .

## ARTICLE 6

If in accordance with paragraph 9 of Article 15 of the Covenant a dispute is referred to the Assembly, that body shall have for the settlement of the dispute all the powers conferred upon the Council as to endeavoring to reconcile the parties in the manner laid down in paragraphs 1, 2 and 3 of Article 15 of the Covenant and in paragraph 1 of Article 4 above.

Should the Assembly fail to achieve an amicable settlement:

If one of the parties asks for arbitration, the Council shall proceed to constitute the Committee of Arbitrators in the manner provided in sub-paragraphs (a), (b) and (c) of paragraph 2 of Article 4 above.

If no party asks for arbitration, the Assembly shall again take the dispute under consideration and shall have in this connection the same powers as the Council. Recommendations embodied in a report of the Assembly, provided that it secures the measure of support stipulated at the end of paragraph 10 of Article 15 of the Covenant, shall have the same value and effect, as regards all matters dealt with in the present Protocol, as recommendations embodied in a report of the Council adopted as provided in paragraph 3 of Article 4 above.

If the necessary majority cannot be obtained, the dispute shall be submitted to arbitration and the Council shall determine the composition, the powers and the procedure of the Committee of Arbitrators as laid down in paragraph 4 of Article 4. . .

## ARTICLE 8

The signatory States undertake to abstain from any act which might constitute a threat of aggression against another State.

If one of the signatory States is of opinion that another State is making preparations for war, it shall have the right to bring the matter to the notice of the Council.

The Council, if it ascertains that the facts are as alleged, shall proceed as provided in paragraphs 2, 4, and 5 of Article 7. . .

### ARTICLE 10

Every State which resorts to war in violation of the undertakings contained in the Covenant or in the present Protocol is an aggressor. Violation of the rules laid down for a demilitarized zone shall be held equivalent to resort to war.

In the event of hostilities having broken out, any State shall be presumed to be an aggressor, unless a decision of the Council, which must be taken unanimously, shall otherwise declare:

1. If it has refused to submit the dispute to the procedure of pacific settlement provided by Articles 13 and 15 of the Covenant as amplified by the present Protocol, or to comply with a judicial sentence or arbitral award or with a unanimous recommendation of the Council, or has disregarded a unanimous report of the Council, a judicial sentence or an arbitral award recognizing that the dispute between it and the other belligerent State arises out of a matter which by international law is solely within the domestic jurisdiction of the latter State; nevertheless,

in the last case the State shall only be presumed to be an aggressor if it has not previously submitted the question to the Council or the Assembly, in accordance with Article 11 of the Covenant.

2. If it has violated provisional measures enjoined by the Council for the period while the proceedings are in progress as contemplated by Article 7 of the present Protocol.

Apart from the cases dealt with in paragraphs 1 and 2 of the present Article, if the Council does not at once succeed in determining the aggressor, it shall be bound to enjoin upon the belligerents an armistice, and shall fix the terms, acting, if need be, by a two-thirds majority and shall supervise its execution.

Any belligerent which has refused to accept the armistice or has violated its terms shall be deemed an aggressor.

The Council shall call upon the signatory States to apply forthwith against the aggressor the sanctions provided by Article 11 of the present Protocol, and any signatory State thus called upon shall thereupon be entitled to exercise the rights of a belligerent. . .

## V. THE PACT OF PARIS

The short but futile renunciation of war contained in the Pact of Paris, sometimes called the Kellogg-Briand Pact, was negotiated in 1928, just before the onset of the Great Depression, the rise of Nazi Germany, and the ten-year-long prelude to World War II. The pact was originally initiated by Aristide Briand, the French Foreign Minister, and Frank B. Kellogg, the United States Secretary of State. Officially called the General Treaty for the Renunciation of War, it was finally adhered to by 62 states. During the negotiations, however, it was clearly set forth that the parties, which were renouncing war as an 'instrument of national policy,' nevertheless retained the right of self-defense. With no definition of self-defense provided, and with no implementation of the Pact by any new procedures for maintaining peace, it was doomed to futility.

### ARTICLE 1

The High Contracting Parties solemnly declare in the names of their respective peoples that they condemn recourse to war for the solution of international controversies, and renounce it as an instrument of national policy in their relations with one another.

### ARTICLE 2

The High Contracting Parties agree that the settlement or solution of all disputes or conflicts of whatever nature or of whatever origin they may be, which may arise between them, shall never be sought except by pacific means.

### ARTICLE 3

The present Treaty shall be ratified by the High Contracting Parties named in the Preamble in accordance with their respective constitutional requirements, and shall take effect as between them as soon as all their several instruments of ratification shall have been deposited at Washington.

This Treaty shall, when it has come into effect as prescribed in the preceding paragraph, remain open as long as may be necessary for adherence by all the other Powers of the world. Every instrument evidencing the adherence of a Power shall be deposited at Washington and the Treaty shall immediately upon such deposit become effective as between the Power thus adhering and the other Powers parties hereto.

It shall be the duty of the Government of the United States to furnish each Government named in the Preamble and every Government subsequently adhering to this Treaty with a certified copy of the Treaty and of every instrument of ratification or adherence. It shall also be the duty of the Government of the United States telegraphically to notify such Governments immediately upon the deposit with it of each instrument of ratification or adherence.

IN FAITH WHEREOF the respective Plenipotentiaries have signed this Treaty in the French and English languages both texts having equal force, and hereunto affix their seals.

DONE at Paris, the twenty-seventh day of August in the year one thousand nine hundred and twenty-eight.

## VI. DISARMAMENT

One of the approaches to security followed between the two World Wars was disarmament. The effort to disarm was begun at the Washington Conference on the Limitation of Armaments (1921-22), where a 5:5:3 ratio was accepted for battleships. This gave 525,000 tons each to Great Britain and the United States, 315,000 tons to Japan, and 175,000 tons each to France and Italy. A conference at Geneva in 1927 dealt with smaller warships, but ended without a treaty because the United States and Great Britain were unable to agree on the number and size of cruisers to be allowed. Three years later in London, however, an agreement was reached on cruisers, destroyers, and submarines. Meanwhile the League of Nations was at work on the subject, and in 1932 convened a world conference on disarmament at Geneva. The whole field was explored, but again no agreement was possible. Because the treaties made at Washington in 1922 and at London in 1930 were about to lapse, a new conference was held in London late in 1935. A new treaty was con-

cluded by the United States, Great Britain, and France, which limited qualitatively the navies of the three states, fixing maximum tonnage figures for
the various types of warships. The author of the extract below explains the
failure of the effort to gain security by disarmament.

(J. T. Shotwell, *On the Rim of the Abyss,*
New York, pp. 264-7, 277-8. Copyright
1936 by The Macmillan Company.)

Only once in history has the peace
movement supplied a drama equal to that
of war. It was at the Washington Conference on the Limitations of Armaments
in 1921-22, when Secretary Charles Evans
Hughes, taking most, if not all, of the
delegates completely by surprise, proposed in the name of the United States
that the great sea Powers should not only
halt the building of battleships but should
actually destroy a percentage of those
already built, and that they should henceforth keep to an agreed ratio. The race in
armaments was due to give way to co-
operation in limiting and lessening the
chief instrument of sea power. Never before had any government taken so bold
a step in this most delicate of all questions of international relations. The
Hague Conferences had failed to produce
any such plan for practical measures of
disarmament. The League had only just
begun to explore the intricacies of the
field. And here, suddenly, from the nation that held aloof from Geneva, came
the leadership that had been lacking. . .

Twelve years of effort to apply and extend the Washington Conference method
ended in Japan's denunciation of the
limitation of its naval armaments that
was then agreed to, and the other sea
Powers, notably Great Britain, followed
suit. Year by year, throughout this period,
armaments have been growing by leaps
and bounds, a sad commentary on the
activities of the Disarmament Conference. Clearly, there has been something
faulty in the method pursued, or the

problem of disarmament is insoluble
under the conditions prevailing in the
world today.

One has not far to go before coming
upon misunderstandings. They begin
with the Washington Conference itself.
The impression, which gained ground,
that Secretary Hughes's dramatic act was
a stroke of genius, planned in the isolation of creative thought without reference
to the preparations of diplomacy, was a
mistake that beclouded most subsequent
negotiations. It looked as if a measuring
rod had been found by which one could
calculate that chief element in sea power,
capital ships, and assign a fitting number
to the nations possessing them. The formula 5:5:3 became a popular slogan. . .

Spurred on by the British, the League
of Nations tried to work out a system of
comparative strengths for the standing
armies of Europe. There was, for instance, the plan of Lord Esher, according
to which the unit in man-power should be
30,000 men for the military and air forces.
France could have 6 units, or 180,000
men; Italy and Poland each 4 units or
120,000 men; Belgium 3 units, or 90,000
men; and others proportionately in a
definitely established ratio. This scheme
was examined by the technical experts,
and while they hesitated to reject a
method which had the high sanction of
the Washington Conference, they found
the practical difficulties insurmountable
in view of both the changing situation in
Europe and the almost insoluble problem
of determining what should be the unit
of measurement as well as the ratio to
be employed. . .

There is no more striking fact in the
history of international relations than

that so serious a question should have been treated with such amateurish simplicity as has been the case in the plans for armament reduction. After fifteen years of history, the nations which have been studying this problem have at last come back to the starting point that national security must be safeguarded in other ways than by armaments, or armaments will continue as its outward and visible sign. The French were right when they insisted, as they have done throughout the long controversy, upon the theory summed up in the phrase, 'security first; disarmament in proportion to security.' But the British and the Americans have also been right in pointing out that while this statement is sound in logic, it lends itself to a mistaken policy, because the accent is placed so strongly upon a word —security—which we are only just beginning to understand. Earlier in this chapter we have pointed out that disarmament is a process that deals with concrete realities—guns, ships, and men; but security is an abstraction, a generalization, which seems to turn false when too much generalized. The security of one country is expressed in different terms than the security of another. It is not a subject commonly studied in the social and political sciences. It is over 150 years since Adam Smith's *Wealth of Nations* laid the basis of the study of economics. There is as yet no parallel manual dealing with the 'security of nations'; in the understanding of the problem of security we are where the eighteenth century was in the field of economics. Indeed, one might carry the analogy still farther and compare the policies at present dominating the field of security with those of the Mercantilist school of protection, which preceded the era of *laissez faire*. . .

## VII. The Failure of Security, 1919-39

The following views on the failure of the peace, 1919-39, were issued by the International Consultative Group of Geneva, Switzerland. The group was made up of citizens of many countries and included those countries that were neutral as well as the belligerents in World War II.

(International Consultative Group of Geneva, 'Causes of the Peace Failure, 1919-1939,' *International Conciliation*, No. 363, October 1940, pp. 335-42, 346-8, 358-61. Reprinted by permission of the Carnegie Endowment for International Peace.)

### The Peace Settlement

Any attempt to assess the main factors in the history of the last twenty years must start from the Peace Conference of Paris. The international institutions that were created by that Conference introduced entirely new standards into the world of international politics. The Covenant implied a new political morality, the substitution of responsibility for power; it predicated a settlement which all were more concerned to preserve than to destroy. But the same Conference that drafted the Covenant was also the Conference that designed the new settlement. That settlement, which is embodied in the Treaties of Versailles, St. Germain, Trianon, and Neuilly, was not wholly, or indeed mainly, an immoral or vindictive settlement; it was none the less a settlement which not all States were equally interested in maintaining.

It was perhaps inevitable that after a world war in which human passions had been aroused in the service of nationalist ends, statesmen should have been unable to control those passions or deflect them into the service of the international community; it was perhaps inevitable that after four years' strain these statesmen should themselves have been too tired to attempt such a task. It was natural that when so many States, old and new, found themselves facing for the first time problems of the magnitude that appeared in 1919, the interests of Europe as a whole, or of the world as a whole, should have gone by default. But none the less the failure to take a European view, or a world view, must be assessed as the heaviest responsibility of 1919. It was a collective failure.

### THE CASE OF GERMANY

The most startling example of the collective failure was the attitude adopted toward Germany, not only in the clauses of the settlement, but still more in the manner of their presentation. General willingness to cooperate in the future obviously presupposed a minimum of common interest in preserving the settlement. The discrepancy between the principles of the settlement and its details brought both the principles and their advocates into disrepute in many States. Germany, Bulgaria, Hungary, and subsequently Italy, rejected them in varying degrees. In particular, the refusal to negotiate with Germany created an attitude of mind in that country that was never subsequently changed.

### ATTITUDE OF THE UNITED STATES AND ITS EFFECT

But the initial mistakes were not irreparable. The Treaty of Versailles had the tremendous advantage that it contained in itself provisions for its own amendment. The damage done might very easily have been remedied had there been an attempt during subsequent years to make the settlement as attractive to the vanquished as it was to the victors. No such attempt was made.

We are forced to conclude that a major factor explaining this failure was the refusal of the United States to ratify the Treaty of Versailles. The nature of the Treaty itself, the unpleasant impression created in the United States by the Paris negotiations, the provision in the Constitution of the United States that a two-thirds vote in the Senate is necessary for the ratification of treaties, all these, and many other factors played their part in leading the United States to withdraw from Europe. This failure of the United States to ratify was certainly the hardest blow to the new institutions. The intervention of the United States had created a military and political situation that might have been stabilized had that country remained; the situation was hopelessly unstable from the moment she withdrew.

### RELATIONS BETWEEN FRANCE AND GREAT BRITAIN

The withdrawal of the United States tended to widen the breach between France and Great Britain that had done so much to vitiate the work of the Peace Conference. On the one hand France sought by all means to preserve the situation that had resulted from the war, and this all the more when the security that she had expected from the Anglo-American guarantee of her territory failed to materialize. Without that guarantee France inevitably saw in the power of Germany a menace to her own independence, and endeavored by all means to circumscribe that power.

On the other hand, Great Britain reverted to her historic policy of preserving a balance of power in Europe. By an extraordinary perverse repetition of the mistake of Metternich in 1815 she continued to see a danger to the security of Europe in France itself. Beset by one of her periodic desires to withdraw from the Continent and fearing that a maintenance of the 1919 situation would give supremacy in Europe to France, she refused to accept security obligations that were the essence of the new system.

The tendency to pull away from Europe, very similar to that shown by the United States, was due only in part to traditional policy. The task of readjustment to a position of lesser power is always both painful and difficult. For Great Britain this task was complicated by developments in the British Commonwealth. The grant of self-government to the various Dominions had not been accompanied by any means of coordinating the foreign policies of the various States that owed allegiance to the British Crown. There was at one and the same time a desire in the Dominions not to be bound by any decisions of the Imperial Government, an intense feeling of being outside Europe (similar to that of the United States), and yet a fervent emotional desire to preserve the unity of the Commonwealth. Unity in these circumstances was best achieved by an all-round agreement to do little or nothing. Traditional reasons, difficulties in the organization of the Commonwealth, problems arising from the changed position of Great Britain in the world, combined to make British policy negative.

## LACK OF LEADERSHIP

But it was positive policy, not negative, that was needed if the new order was to grow. At the outset replacement of anarchy by a system of law in any form of society always works against those members of the society who have been less successful during the period of anarchy. The system of law will survive if those who have in the past been more successful—and it is always they who will endeavor to introduce the rule of law—show themselves prepared both to resist attacks on the system from those whom it benefits least, and to operate the system in such a way that their advantages are shared with the less fortunate. If the League system was to survive, action along three lines was needed. It was necessary that efforts be made by the process of revision or peaceful change to modify the settlement of 1919 so that it would be in the interest of all, rather than in the interest of a group, to preserve it. It was imperative that the specific obligations which the settlement of 1919 imposed upon certain States should be extended so as to limit equally all the members of the League. It was vital that the security of each member of the international community be assured by the society, and that the obligations of various members of that community be enforced. Development of this kind is not obtained unless there is courageous and imaginative leadership. Such leadership did not appear, and it must be accounted as a collective failure of all the States members that it was not forthcoming.

## FAILURE TO 'GENERALIZE' THE OBLIGATIONS OF 1919

It is evident that although in such matters as reparations and the military occupation of Germany the Paris settlement was modified, no considerable effort was made to revise the more questionable of its territorial provisions. Equally striking was the failure to extend to all States the obligations that the settlement imposed on a few.

Society advances more by the development of obligations than by their limitation. But if society is to advance, these obligations must be borne equally by all members of society; if they fall on a few rather than on all, they will become seeds of discord, rather than of concord. In the end they will be enforced rather than accepted, or denounced if not enforced.

Disarmament, mandates, minorities, the

internationalization of rivers, all of these and other provisions of the 1919 treaties contained the germ of fruitful development.

In no case however have those obligations been extended to all the States members of the League, and the States subjected to them have therefore sought to end their inequality by freeing themselves from the obligation. In one case, Turkey adopted the unexceptionable procedure of obtaining international consent for the modification of the Straits Regime. Yet even this case, though in its form it was a perfect example of peaceful change, was a retrograde step in that it abolished an obligation rather than extending its application. In other cases the inequalities were ended not through the mechanisms of society, but in defiance of them. In 1934 Poland denounced the obligations of the minority treaties, though at the same time announcing that she intended to continue to observe them; in 1935 Germany denounced the disarmament clauses of Versailles; in 1936 Germany denounced the demilitarization clauses of Versailles; again in 1936 Germany denounced the clauses of the Treaty of Versailles concerning the internationalization of rivers, and finally in 1939 France ignored the obligations of the mandate in transferring Alexandretta to Turkey. In each case the inequality resulting from a specific obligation imposed on one State was ended not by the constructive method of extending its application to all States, but by the destructive method of releasing the individual State affected from its obligation.

## SECURITY

If in the end, despite moments when a happier fate seemed in store, the States of the League failed to organize justice, no less striking was their failure to organize security. The inexorably linked questions of security and disarmament were almost inextricably complicated by the Versailles settlement. Because it was a dictated, not a negotiated, peace—and this in its outward form to a still greater extent than in its inward content—it was impossible to discuss general disarmament at Paris. In the years that followed the conflict of aims between Great Britain and France prevented a solution of the problem of equality of rights and equality of security. In the end, the States members of the League failed to implement security when the test came in 1935-36.

## GERMANY AND EUROPE

The major problem around which the conflict of aims between Great Britain and France revolved was that of Germany. From the point of view of the historian, the unification of Germany in 1870 created a problem exactly similar to very many of the problems that Europe had had to face during the preceding three hundred years. In the past that problem had been solved by the formation of an alliance of the other European powers against the largest and most powerful of them.

From the point of view of the diplomat, the new system of international organization was an attempt to provide another answer to this problem. 'Collective security' might have replaced the alliance as a method of assuring those States who felt themselves threatened by Germany. The failure to organize the security that the new institutions could have provided led those States that feared Germany to take no steps that, by ending her inequality, would have strengthened her. The absence of such organized security prevented any effective steps being taken to check her when she began to destroy those inequalities in defiance of the international society. Europe was driven back to the alliance system to solve its security problem.

But it was not only the security problem that centered in Germany; it was the State that inevitably stood to lose at least at the inauguration of a system of law and order, because of the lateness of its creation and its consequent limited success in the period of anarchy; it was the State that was affected by almost every one of the specific obligations imposed by the Versailles settlement and that, therefore, was most interested in seeing its equality restored by the extension of those obligations to all States.

### A Joint Responsibility

Countries that benefited from the 1919 settlement showed no alacrity in modifying that settlement, either by accepting its obligations for themselves, or in surrendering advantages it gave to them. But countries that sought revision showed no greater appreciation of their membership of an international society. The positive manifestations of their national egoisms were at least as important as the more negative nationalisms of those who were slow to move toward revision. The responsibility of an aggressor cannot be accounted less than the responsibility of the State that refuses to aid the victim of aggression. The States that sought modification of the settlement of 1919 showed themselves at least as unappreciative of the interests of the wider community as did those States who profited by the maintenance of that settlement.

### Need of a New Spirit

Writing in 1935, Sir Alfred Zimmern said: 'The process of dovetailing or codification or synthesis carried through in the letter of the Covenant assumes a new spirit in the whole field of international politics. It presupposes a transformation of power politics into responsibility politics, or at least a sincere and consistent effort on the part of the Great Powers to

begin to face the innumerable tasks of adjustment which such a transformation would carry with it.'

Today we know that neither of these presuppositions was to be fulfilled. Instead there was unreadiness on the one hand to accept the obligations, positive and negative, of responsibility politics, and on the other a definite attempt to exalt power politics to the dignity of a religion. . .

### Sovereignty

It is customary in modern discussions of the breakdown of the Geneva institutions to direct major criticism against the doctrine of sovereignty. To do so is, in large measure, to mistake cause for effect. A juridical doctrine is seldom more than a decent theoretical garment to cloak current political thought and action. The doctrine serves to justify the essential amorality of States, and thereby brings us nearer to the core of our problem.

It is a truism that the sovereign State, the unit of modern international society, does not feel the same compulsion to honor its obligation as does the socially minded individual in a civilized community. It is equally evident that though the State is amoral in its relations with other States, it is, in its relations with its own citizens a moral agency. It is the difference in the moral outlook, the *mores* within the boundaries of sovereign States, that explains the attitude of those sovereign States to the obligations that they have contracted toward each other. There is an observable difference between the State that accepts an obligation, believing that the burden of its fulfilment will be outweighed by the advantages accruing to it from the obligation imposed simultaneously on its co-signatories, and the State that has no intention of attempting to carry out its obligation after it has reaped the advantage accruing therefrom. Equally evident in all States is the difference in their attitude to positive and negative obligations. An obligation not to go to war is accepted more readily, and indeed more honestly, by most States than is a corollary obligation to take positive action against a State that has gone to war. Yet the doctrine of sovereignty knows no difference between obligations; it allows all to be broken with the same impunity.

It is not the doctrine of sovereignty that has led to the breakdown of the League; it is the passion for independence felt by all peoples. . .

## ECONOMICS OF THE PEACE FAILURE 1919-1939

The rôle of economic factors in the peace failure of 1919-39 was not of first importance. Political and psychological considerations played a more active part. But at every point, interpenetrating the whole complex structure of international relationships during these twenty critical years, economic factors are to be found. They did not pass unnoticed. Repeatedly the League of Nations and the International Labour Organisation brought the nations of the world together in a long series of attempts to deal with the principal social and economic problems of the time. Questions of monetary stabilization, freer trade, the control of raw materials, the prevention of industrial depressions, the improvement of working conditions and of the standard of life have been studied and discussed as never before in the history of mankind. As a result much has been done which would otherwise have been neglected. The net outcome, nevertheless, has been negative, in the sense that peace was not preserved; and unquestionably economic unpreparedness was in part responsible. We cannot afford to make the same mistakes

twice. The main purpose of this paper is to see what lessons may be learned for the future from the experience gained in the course of the last two decades. With this end in view it is necessary to distinguish some of the principal ways in which economic considerations enter into the peace-war calculus.

### A—ECONOMIC FACTORS MAKING FOR WAR

Considered absolutely, economic factors are no longer direct causes of war. In the far-distant past the possession of certain hunting or grazing lands may well have been a matter of life or death for the competing tribes. Today, with modern methods of production, no country is forced to war by sheer economic need; which is fortunate, since otherwise war would probably be unpreventable. But the fact that, under present-day conditions, the economic causes of war are indirect does not deprive them of importance. Their influence has been felt in three main spheres: social, political, and military.

1. Social discontent as a seed-bed for war.

In all probability the principal means by which peace is disturbed and war provoked by economic factors is through their effect on popular feeling. People who are steadily improving their economic position, and realize they have something to lose, do not readily go to war. On the other hand, people who feel they are suffering from economic injustice, people whose economic status is being brought down, people who have lost their means of livelihood or are deprived of their stand-by of savings, are ripe to be worked upon by anyone who can point to a plausible enemy. Partly by inadvertence, partly by design, countries have not used their productive capacity effectively to promote human well-being in the last twenty years. Especially have they fallen short wherever international economic cooperation was involved.

2. Political motives dressed up as economic necessities.

The second major factor in the economic causation of war plays perhaps a larger part in propaganda than in reality. Markets, colonies, protectorates, spheres of influence, control of raw materials, and similar quasi-economic considerations are frequently represented as of vital economic importance to a nation. In certain circumstances they may be. If countries, having secured such controls, follow a dog-in-the-manger policy they can do great damage to the rest of the world. But provided a reasonably liberal policy is pursued, though certain advantages unquestionably accrue to the possessing nation, it is no life or death matter to the others. Food and raw materials in particular have been so freely available over the last ten years that producers have not known what to do with their stocks, and are frequently driven to sell at prices below the costs of production.

Behind this much discussed question the real motives are political rather than economic. The considerations weighing most with the ruling élites of the principal countries are power and prestige. These considerations are of capital importance, since upon them depends the loyalty of the people to the ruling élite. In the game of power politics colonies, control of raw materials, protectorates and the like serve in the nature of a scoring device, indicating who has the upper hand. As genuine economic causes of war they are of relatively little importance, provided always (and it is an essential provision) the liberal and not the dog-in-the-manger policy is followed. At most, their retention or acquisition would represent to the people of the countries concerned some relatively small decrease or increase in the average income: certainly not the difference between starvation and affluence.

3. Fear of economic weakness in case of war.

The third and most actively potent of the economic factors entering into the peace-war calculus is the fear felt by almost every country that, in the event of hostilities, it might find itself cut off from necessary supplies (food or essential war materials) and so be made to yield by sheer economic pressure. This fear may easily lead to aggression. A country so placed will seize upon a favorable occasion of going to war, in the hope that, by reason of the advantages so gained, it may be in a better position to resist economically should it at some time be attacked. Similar considerations apply to the acquisition or retention of fueling stations and fortified points on trade routes.

This dread of economic weakness in the event of war sets up a series of vicious circles. Almost invariably one country's security automatically involves another country's danger. Territorial or economic readjustments which constitute an assurance to one side inevitably appear as a threat to the other. So long as such a situation persists, war is likely to remain a standing menace. This in turn means that a large and increasing proportion of the world's capacity to produce will go in armaments. The higher armaments are piled the more liable they are to explode. And the more liable they are to explode the higher they must be piled. The natural desire of every country to make itself secure places the whole world in peril. . .

## SPIRITUAL FACTORS IN THE PEACE FAILURE 1919-1939

### INTRODUCTORY

A survey of the spiritual factors in the peace failure, the beliefs, ideologies, and fundamental values actuating peoples in the course of the last twenty years, follows naturally on surveys of the political and economic aspects of that failure. It is now widely recognized that the present plight of our civilization is in the last analysis due to our spiritual anarchy and our spiritual impotence. The power which new and in the last resort destructive ideologies exert over the minds of millions of men today has forced us to face in a new way the problem of the basic presuppositions of all common living. It is now clear that no durable international settlement can possibly be arrived at unless the nations accept certain common convictions and common standards as a basis of their own life and of their relations with each other. All schemes for a future international order depend for their realization on this presupposition of a willingness to live together in harmony, which itself depends upon some underlying unity of spirit. It is the absence of any such basis which has brought civilization to the brink of catastrophe. . .

The place which Christianity had occupied as a formative element in society was largely taken by that European movement which began in philosophy as the enlightenment' and then expressed itself politically in the various forms of liberalism and democracy. Its main tenets were the dignity and freedom of men and the power of human reason over social and political conditions. While these tenets were partly borrowed from Christianity, they were soon transformed into a new faith—the faith in the essential goodness of man and the rational character of history. This alternative to the Christian faith became so powerful that even the Christian Churches adapted their teaching to a large extent to the new doctrines, and to that extent gave up their own insights into the life of man and of society.

The result of the new doctrines on the life of the nations was twofold. On the one hand, they succeeded in creating a new equilibrium between society and the individual and elaborated the conception of the State as limited by law in relation to its own citizens and in relation to other States. It is due to the enlightenment acting upon the personal monarchies of the eighteenth century that a modern system of international law was first elaborated. On the other hand, these doctrines led to a loosening of the bonds by which society had been held together. The new individualism undermined the religious and moral convictions which had given society its cohesion. The results of this process became especially evident where and when the old common religious convictions lost ground.

Another important nineteenth century development was the growth of nationalism as an ideological factor. As the spread of democracy led to participation in national affairs by classes which had hitherto remained passive, the consciousness of nationhood became intensified. This new nationalism took different forms, ranging from the nationalism of liberation from foreign domination to the aggressive nationalism which dreams of the world hegemony of one particular nation. In so far as this development was not checked by the concept of international solidarity or of a law binding upon all nations, it became a powerful factor in the breaking up of European unity.

Thus in the early years of this century there was in Western civilization no strong sense of a common heritage or of a common mission. Between the nations of Europe which had adopted the philosophy of liberalism as their national philosophy and the nations which had not, there was no deep bond which could transcend the political and economic conflicts. The World War was the expression of European disintegration rather than its cause.

## The Spirit of the Post-War Settlement

The world of 1918 and of the period immediately following was a world in which extravagant idealism and bitter cynicism, high hopes and utter despair lived side by side. The division between the two moods was not a political-geographical one as between the victorious and the defeated countries. For Germany had at that time not only its embittered nationalists, but also its youth movement and various other movements which believed deeply in social justice and international collaboration. And the Western European nations had not only their League of Nations supporters, but also their headstrong 'realists' who believed only in pure power politics.

It is nevertheless true to say that, in view of the predominance of the Anglo-Saxon nations and the added prestige of democracy, the main note of that period was one of an optimistic liberalism based on faith in progress and in the harmonious outcome of the free interplay of political and economic forces. The war was conceived as an interlude and it was believed that the remarkable nineteenth century advance in political and economic life, under the auspices of liberalism, could now be resumed. Further education would dispel the forces of reaction and inaugurate an era of peace and prosperity for all.

Unfortunately the actual conduct of political affairs was in flagrant contradiction to the professed ideals. This was most easily perceived by those who suffered from these policies, that is the defeated nations and the working classes. Thus there grew up a deep-rooted suspicion that all political idealism was merely a smoke-screen for imperialistic and capitalistic designs.

The curious blend of utopianism and 'realism,' characteristic of this period, found expression in the League of Nations; for the League was conceived by some as the embodiment of a great new ideal, by others as a mere tool in the old game of power politics; and was in fact something of both, according to circumstances and occasions. The tragedy of the League, and indeed of the whole post-war settlement, is that it became the plaything of Utopians who made impossible claims for it and surrounded it with a mystic glamor, and of hard-headed 'realists' who sabotaged its efficacy. Thus public opinion often swung between moods of optimism and cynicism, and the League was constantly diverted from its true object of making slow but real progress toward the ordering of international life.

The post-war settlement has broken down because it reflected rather than transcended the contradictions inherent in Western society. It did not point toward a new spiritual integration, but tried to continue an order of life which was itself in process of disintegration. A fundamental change in international relations proved impossible as long as the nations did not accept corresponding changes in the ideological, political, and economic structure of their national life.

# 3

# The United Nations—A New System of Security

THROUGHOUT World War II the need for a new and better system of security was often expressed, and studies, both private and governmental, were undertaken to produce a plan that would prevent another war. The projects that emerged ranged all the way from a revised League of Nations to a world federation based on the Constitution of the United States. These many plans had the effect of stimulating public discussion, and brought forward ideas that were embodied in the Charter of the United Nations—the world's new system of security.

Like the League of Nations, the United Nations was a creation of the victors of war. The term 'United Nations' was first used in the joint declaration signed at Washington on 1 January 1942 by the nations at war against the Axis, who pledged themselves to continued military and economic co-operation until the enemy should be defeated. From that time on the group set up more and more machinery for co-operation in the war, and meetings were held by the heads of the leading powers at which the question of a post-war peace organization received increasing attention. At the Moscow meeting of the foreign ministers of the United States, Russia, Great Britain, and a representative of China, a joint declaration, dated 30 October 1943, asserted that 'their united action, pledged for the prosecution of the war against their respective enemies, will be continued for the organization and maintenance of peace and security.' The Teheran Declaration of the Three Powers, 1 December 1943, said, 'We express our determination that our nations shall work together in war and in the peace that will follow.'

On 24 August 1944, the representatives of the United States, Great Britain, Russia, and China met at Dumbarton Oaks in Washington and began the preparation of the draft of a constitution for a permanent United Nations organization. When the draft was completed it was announced to the public and became the subject of popular discussion during the months that followed. Some of the problems which had not been treated in the Dumbarton Oaks plan, particularly the voting methods of the Security Council, were taken up at the Crimea Conference of the heads of the Big Three powers early in February 1945.

By the time the San Francisco Conference opened early in April 1945, its members had had the benefit of popular and diplomatic discussions of the problems they were to attempt to solve. It was clear that the main issues would be the voting methods of the Security Council, the relative strength of the large and small states, and the relation of regional organizations to the general organization. Fifty states sent delegates, including the Ukrainian and Byelorussian republics, two of the constituent republics of the Russian federation. The Charter was completed on 26 June 1945, and forthwith submitted to the signatory powers for ratification. It came into effect on 24 October 1945, when the ratifications of China, France, Russia, Great Britain, the United States, and a majority of the other signatories had all been deposited, as required by Article 110 of the Charter. By 27 December 1945, it had been ratified by 51 states, and on the following 10 January the first General Assembly of the United Nations opened.

Besides the security organization set up in accordance with the Charter, the United Nations includes a number of 'specialized agencies,' which are discussed in later chapters. The United Nations Organization on Food and Agriculture, the International Refugee Organization, the Civil Aviation Organization, the World Health Organization, the United Nations Educational, Scientific, and Cultural Organization, the International Bank, the International Monetary Fund, the International Labor Organization, and the International Court of Justice all operate as parts of the main organization, although with separate constitutions of their own. It should be noted also that commissions have been set up by the Economic and Social Council to deal with the status of women, human rights, opium, and other problems. All told, the United Nations system constitutes by far the major part of the world's machinery of co-operation.

The most critical of all of the many duties of the United Nations is to keep the peace. The Security Council is the organ primarily responsible for the performance of this duty, and for the purpose it has been granted special powers. As explained in Chapter vi of the Charter, the Security Council may take the following measures in the treatment of international controversies: (1) call upon the parties to use peaceful means of settlement; (2) investigate in order to determine whether the dispute is a danger to peace; (3) recommend procedures; and (4) recommend terms of settlement if a continuance of the dispute is a threat to peace or if the parties so request. By Chapter vii of the Charter the Security Council is authorized to use sanctions—diplomatic, economic, and military—when there is a 'threat to the peace, a breach of the peace, or act of aggression.' Members of the United Nations are expected to make agreements with the Security Council stating the contributions in the nature of armed forces which they will make for the suppression of aggression. A Military Staff Committee is provided to assist the Security Council when military sanctions are applied.

The 'veto' power is available to any of the 5 permanent members of the Security Council in votes taken on all non-procedural matters. By this rule, as described in Article 27, decisions are always taken by a vote of 7 of the 11 members; when the question does not relate to procedure, it is required that all of the 5 permanent members of the Council must be among the 7. However, when the Council is dealing with the solution of disputes by peaceful means, under Chapter VI of the Charter, the parties to the dispute are not allowed to vote; they may vote when a question of sanctions is before the Council. In effect this means that any one of the 5 permanent members of the Council may by its veto prevent the application of sanctions against itself or against any other nation.

The strength of the Security Council as an agency of peace lies in its powers of discussion and recommendation. There is a great advantage in bringing disputes before an international body. The weakness of the Council is its lack of adequate coercive authority, especially against large powers, the principal disturbers of the peace. In these respects, as in many others, the United Nations bears a striking resemblance to the League of Nations.

## I. THE CHARTER OF THE UNITED NATIONS

*We the peoples of the United Nations determined* to save succeeding generations from the scourge of war, which twice in our lifetime has brought untold sorrow to mankind, and to reaffirm faith in fundamental human rights, in the dignity and worth of the human person, in the equal rights of men and women and of nations large and small, and to establish conditions under which justice and respect for the obligations arising from treaties and other sources of international law can be maintained, and to promote social progress and better standards of life in larger freedom, *and for these ends* to practice tolerance and live together in peace with one another as good neighbors, and to unite our strength to maintain international peace and security, and to ensure, by the acceptance of principles and the institution of methods, that armed force shall not be used, save in the common interest, and to employ international machinery for the promotion of the economic and social advancement of all peoples, *have resolved to combine our efforts to accomplish these aims.* Accordingly, our respective Governments, through representatives assembled in the city of San Francisco, who have exhibited their full powers found to be in good and due form, have agreed to the present Charter of the United Nations and do hereby establish an international organization to be known as the United Nations.

### I. PURPOSES AND PRINCIPLES

#### ARTICLE 1

The Purposes of the United Nations are:

1. To maintain international peace and security, and to that end: to take effective collective measures for the prevention and removal of threats to the peace, and for the suppression of acts of aggression or other breaches of the peace, and to bring about by peaceful means, and in conformity with the principles of justice and international law, adjustment or settlement of international disputes or situations which might lead to a breach of the peace;

2. To develop friendly relations among nations based on respect for the principle of equal rights and self-determination of peoples, and to take other appropriate measures to strengthen universal peace;

3. To achieve international cooperation in solving international problems of an economic, social, cultural, or humanitarian character, and in promoting and encouraging respect for human rights and for fundamental freedoms for all without distinction as to race, sex, language, or religion; and

4. To be a center for harmonizing the actions of nations in the attainment of these common ends.

### ARTICLE 2

The Organization and its Members, in pursuit of the Purposes stated in Article 1, shall act in accordance with the following Principles.

1. The Organization is based on the principle of the sovereign equality of all its Members.

2. All Members, in order to ensure to all of them the rights and benefits resulting from membership, shall fulfil in good faith the obligations assumed by them in accordance with the present Charter.

3. All Members shall settle their international disputes by peaceful means in such a manner that international peace and security, and justice, are not endangered.

4. All Members shall refrain in their international relations from the threat or use of force against the territorial integrity or political independence of any state, or in any other manner inconsistent with the Purposes of the United Nations.

5. All Members shall give the United Nations every assistance in any action it takes in accordance with the present Charter, and shall refrain from giving assistance to any state against which the United Nations is taking preventive or enforcement action.

6. The Organization shall ensure that states which are not Members of the United Nations act in accordance with these Principles so far as may be neces-

sary for the maintenance of international peace and security.

7. Nothing contained in the present Charter shall authorize the United Nations to intervene in matters which are essentially within the domestic jurisdiction of any state or shall require the Members to submit such matters to settlement under the present Charter; but this principle shall not prejudice the application of enforcement measures under Chapter VII.

## II. MEMBERSHIP

### ARTICLE 3

The original Members of the United Nations shall be the states which, having participated in the United Nations Conference on International Organization at San Francisco, or having previously signed the Declaration by United Nations of January 1, 1942, sign the present Charter and ratify it in accordance with Article 110.

### ARTICLE 4

1. Membership in the United Nations is open to all other peace-loving states which accept the obligations contained in the present Charter and, in the judgment of the Organization, are able and willing to carry out these obligations.

2. The admission of any such state to membership in the United Nations will be effected by a decision of the General Assembly upon the recommendation of the Security Council.

### ARTICLE 5

A Member of the United Nations against which preventive or enforcement action has been taken by the Security Council may be suspended from the exercise of the rights and privileges of membership by the General Assembly upon the recommendation of the Security

Council. The exercise of these rights and privileges may be restored by the Security Council.

### ARTICLE 6

A Member of the United Nations which has persistently violated the Principles contained in the present Charter may be expelled from the Organization by the General Assembly upon the recommendation of the Security Council.

## III. ORGANS

### ARTICLE 7

1. There are established as the principal organs of the United Nations: a General Assembly, a Security Council, an Economic and Social Council, a Trusteeship Council, an International Court of Justice, and a Secretariat.

2. Such subsidiary organs as may be found necessary may be established in accordance with the present Charter.

### ARTICLE 8

The United Nations shall place no restrictions on the eligibility of men and women to participate in any capacity and under conditions of equality in its principal and subsidiary organs.

## IV. THE GENERAL ASSEMBLY

### *Composition*

### ARTICLE 9

1. The General Assembly shall consist of all the Members of the United Nations.

2. Each Member shall have not more than five representatives in the General Assembly.

### *Functions and Powers*

### ARTICLE 10

The General Assembly may discuss any questions or any matters within the scope of the present Charter or relating to the powers and functions of any organs provided for in the present Charter, and, except as provided in Article 12, may make recommendations to the Members of the United Nations or to the Security Council or to both on any such questions or matters.

### ARTICLE 11

1. The General Assembly may consider the general principles of cooperation in the maintenance of international peace and security, including the principles of governing disarmament and the regulation of armaments, and may make recommendations with regard to such principles to the Members or to the Security Council or to both.

2. The General Assembly may discuss any questions relating to the maintenance of international peace and security brought before it by any Member of the United Nations, or by the Security Council, or by a state which is not a Member of the United Nations in accordance with Article 35, paragraph 2, and, except as provided in Article 12, may make recommendations with regard to any such questions to the state or states concerned or to the Security Council or to both. Any such question on which action is necessary shall be referred to the Security Council by the General Assembly either before or after discussion.

3. The General Assembly may call the attention of the Security Council to situations which are likely to endanger international peace and security.

4. The powers of the General Assembly set forth in this Article shall not limit the general scope of Article 10.

### ARTICLE 12

1. While the Security Council is exercising in respect of any dispute or situation the functions assigned to it in the present Charter, the General Assembly shall not make any recommendation with regard to

that dispute or situation unless the Security Council so requests.

2. The Secretary-General, with the consent of the Security Council, shall notify the General Assembly at each session of any matters relative to the maintenance of international peace and security which are being dealt with by the Security Council and shall similarly notify the General Assembly, or the Members of the United Nations if the General Assembly is not in session, immediately the Security Council ceases to deal with such matters.

ARTICLE 13

1. The General Assembly shall initiate studies and make recommendations for the purpose of:

a. promoting international cooperation in the political field and encouraging the progressive development of international law and its codification;
b. promoting international cooperation in the economic, social, cultural, educational, and health fields, and assisting in the realization of human rights and fundamental freedoms for all without distinction as to race, sex, language, or religion.

2. The further responsibilities, functions, and powers of the General Assembly with respect to matters mentioned in paragraph 1 (b) above are set forth in Chapters IX and X.

ARTICLE 14

Subject to the provisions of Article 12, the General Assembly may recommend measures for the peaceful adjustment of any situation, regardless of origin, which it deems likely to impair the general welfare or friendly relations among nations, including situations resulting from a violation of the provisions of the present Charter setting forth the Purposes and Principles of the United Nations.

ARTICLE 15

1. The General Assembly shall receive and consider annual and special reports from the Security Council; these reports shall include an account of the measures that the Security Council has decided upon or taken to maintain international peace and security.

2. The General Assembly shall receive and consider reports from the other organs of the United Nations.

ARTICLE 16

The General Assembly shall perform such functions with respect to the international trusteeship system as are assigned to it under Chapters XII and XIII, including the approval of the trusteeship agreements for areas not designated as strategic.

ARTICLE 17

1. The General Assembly shall consider and approve the budget of the Organization.

2. The expenses of the Organization shall be borne by the Members as apportioned by the General Assembly.

3. The General Assembly shall consider and approve any financial and budgetary arrangements with specialized agencies referred to in Article 57 and shall examine the administrative budgets of such specialized agencies with a view to making recommendations to the agencies concerned.

*Voting*

ARTICLE 18

1. Each member of the General Assembly shall have one vote.

2. Decisions of the General Assembly on important questions shall be made by a two-thirds majority of the members present and voting. These questions shall include: recommendations with respect to the maintenance of international peace

and security, the election of the non-permanent members of the Security Council, the election of the members of the Economic and Social Council, the election of members of the Trusteeship Council in accordance with paragraph 1 (c) of Article 86, the admission of new Members to the United Nations, the suspension of the rights and privileges of membership, the expulsion of Members, questions relating to the operation of the trusteeship system, and budgetary questions.

3. Decisions on other questions, including the determination of additional categories of questions to be decided by a two-thirds majority, shall be made by a majority of the members present and voting.

### ARTICLE 19

A Member of the United Nations which is in arrears in the payment of its financial contributions to the Organization shall have no vote in the General Assembly if the amount of its arrears equals or exceeds the amount of the contributions due from it for the preceding two full years. The General Assembly may, nevertheless, permit such a Member to vote if it is satisfied that the failure to pay is due to conditions beyond the control of the Member.

### *Procedure*

### ARTICLE 20

The General Assembly shall meet in regular annual sessions and in such special sessions as occasion may require. Special sessions shall be convoked by the Secretary-General at the request of the Security Council or of a majority of the Members of the United Nations.

### ARTICLE 21

The General Assembly shall adopt its own rules of procedure. It shall elect its President for each session.

### ARTICLE 22

The General Assembly may establish such subsidiary organs as it deems necessary for the performance of its functions.

## V. THE SECURITY COUNCIL

### *Composition*

### ARTICLE 23

1. The Security Council shall consist of eleven Members of the United Nations. The Republic of China, France, the Union of Soviet Socialist Republics, the United Kingdom of Great Britain and Northern Ireland, and the United States of America shall be permanent members of the Security Council. The General Assembly shall elect six other Members of the United Nations to be non-permanent members of the Security Council, due regard being specially paid, in the first instance to the contribution of Members of the United Nations to the maintenance of international peace and security and to the other purposes of the Organization, and also to equitable geographical distribution.

2. The non-permanent members of the Security Council shall be elected for a term of two years. In the first election of the non-permanent members, however, three shall be chosen for a term of one year. A retiring member shall not be eligible for immediate re-election.

3. Each member of the Security Council shall have one representative.

### *Functions and Powers*

### ARTICLE 24

1. In order to ensure prompt and effective action by the United Nations, its Members confer on the Security Council primary responsibility for the maintenance of international peace and security, and agree that in carrying out its duties

under this responsibility the Security Council acts on their behalf.

2. In discharging these duties the Security Council shall act in accordance with the Purposes and Principles of the United Nations. The specific powers granted to the Security Council for the discharge of these duties are laid down in Chapters VI, VII, VIII, and XII.

3. The Security Council shall submit annual and, when necessary, special reports to the General Assembly for its consideration.

### ARTICLE 25

The Members of the United Nations agree to accept and carry out the decisions of the Security Council in accordance with the present Charter.

### ARTICLE 26

In order to promote the establishment and maintenance of international peace and security with the least diversion for armaments of the world's human and economic resources, the Security Council shall be responsible for formulating, with the assistance of the Military Staff Committee referred to in Article 47, plans to be submitted to the Members of the United Nations for the establishment of a system for the regulation of armaments.

### *Voting*

### ARTICLE 27

1. Each member of the Security Council shall have one vote.

2. Decisions of the Security Council on procedural matters shall be made by an affirmative vote of seven members.

3. Decisions of the Security Council on all other matters shall be made by an affirmative vote of seven members including the concurring votes of the permanent members; provided that, in decisions under Chapter VI, and under

paragraph 3 of Article 52, a party to a dispute shall abstain from voting.

### *Procedure*

### ARTICLE 28

1. The Security Council shall be so organized as to be able to function continuously. Each member of the Security Council shall for this purpose be represented at all times at the seat of the Organization.

2. The Security Council shall hold periodic meetings at which each of its members may, if it so desires, be represented by a member of the government or by some other specially designated representative.

3. The Security Council may hold meetings at such places other than the seat of the Organization as in its judgment will best facilitate its work.

### ARTICLE 29

The Security Council may establish such subsidiary organs as it deems necessary for the performance of its functions.

### ARTICLE 30

The Security Council shall adopt its own rules of procedure, including the method of selecting its President.

### ARTICLE 31

Any Member of the United Nations which is not a member of the Security Council may participate, without vote, in the discussion of any question brought before the Security Council whenever the latter considers that the interests of that Member are specially affected.

### ARTICLE 32

Any Member of the United Nations which is not a member of the Security Council or any state which is not a Member of the United Nations, if it is a party to a dispute under consideration by the Security Council, shall be invited to participate, without vote, in the discussion relating to the dispute. The Security Council shall lay down such conditions as it deems just for the participation of a state which is not a Member of the United Nations.

## VI. PACIFIC SETTLEMENT OF DISPUTES

### ARTICLE 33

1. The parties to any dispute, the continuance of which is likely to endanger the maintenance of international peace and security, shall, first of all, seek a solution by negotiation, enquiry, mediation, conciliation, arbitration, judicial settlement, resort to regional agencies or arrangements, or other peaceful means of their own choice.

2. The Security Council shall, when it deems necessary, call upon the parties to settle their dispute by such means.

### ARTICLE 34

The Security Council may investigate any dispute, or any situation which might lead to international friction or give rise to a dispute, in order to determine whether the continuance of the dispute or situation is likely to endanger the maintenance of international peace and security.

### ARTICLE 35

1. Any Member of the United Nations may bring any dispute, or any situation of the nature referred to in Article 34, to the attention of the Security Council or of the General Assembly.

2. A state which is not a Member of the United Nations may bring to the atention of the Security Council or of the General Assembly any dispute to which it is a party if it accepts in advance, for the purposes of the dispute, the obligations of pacific settlement provided in the present Charter.

3. The proceedings of the General Assembly in respect of matters brought to its attention under this Article will be subject to the provisions of Articles 11 and 12.

### ARTICLE 36

1. The Security Council may, at any stage of a dispute of the nature referred to in Article 33 or of a situation of like nature, recommend appropriate procedures or methods of adjustment.

2. The Security Council should take into consideration any procedures for the settlement of the dispute which have already been adopted by the parties.

3. In making recommendations under this Article the Security Council should also take into consideration that legal disputes should as a general rule be referred by the parties to the International Court of Justice in accordance with the provisions of the Statute of the Court.

### ARTICLE 37

1. Should the parties to a dispute of the nature referred to in Article 33 fail to settle it by the means indicated in that Article, they shall refer it to the Security Council.

2. If the Security Council deems that the continuance of the dispute is in fact likely to endanger the maintenance of international peace and security, it shall decide whether to take action under Article 36 or to recommend such terms of settlement as it may consider appropriate.

### ARTICLE 38

Without prejudice to the provisions of Articles 33 to 37, the Security Council may, if all the parties to any dispute so request, make recommendations to the parties with a view to a pacific settlement of the dispute.

## VII. ACTION WITH RESPECT TO THREATS TO THE PEACE, BREACHES OF THE PEACE, AND ACTS OF AGGRESSION

### ARTICLE 39

The Security Council shall determine the existence of any threat to the peace, breach of the peace, or act of aggression and shall make recommendations, or decide what measures shall be taken in accordance with Articles 41 and 42, to maintain or restore international peace and security.

### ARTICLE 40

In order to prevent an aggravation of the situation, the Security Council may, before making the recommendations or deciding upon the measures provided for in Article 39, call upon the parties concerned to comply with such provisional measures as it deems necessary or desirable. Such provisional measures shall be without prejudice to the rights, claims, or position of the parties concerned. The Security Council shall duly take account of failure to comply with such provisional measures.

### ARTICLE 41

The Security Council may decide what measures not involving the use of armed force are to be employed to give effect to its decisions, and it may call upon the Members of the United Nations to apply such measures. These may include complete or partial interruption of economic relations and of rail, sea, air, postal, telegraphic, radio, and other means of communication, and the severance of diplomatic relations.

### ARTICLE 42

Should the Security Council consider that measures provided for in Article 41 would be inadequate or have proved to be inadequate, it may take such action by air, sea, or land forces as may be necessary to maintain or restore international peace and security. Such action may include demonstrations, blockade, and other operations by air, sea, or land forces of Members of the United Nations.

### ARTICLE 43

1. All Members of the United Nations, in order to contribute to the maintenance of international peace and security, undertake to make available to the Security Council, on its call and in accordance with a special agreement or agreements, armed forces, assistance, and facilities, including rights of passage, necessary for the purpose of maintaining international peace and security.

2. Such agreement or agreements shall govern the numbers and types of forces, their degree of readiness and general location, and the nature of the facilities and assistance to be provided.

3. The agreement or agreements shall be negotiated as soon as possible on the initiative of the Security Council. They shall be concluded between the Security Council and Members or between the Security Council and groups of Members and shall be subject to ratification by the signatory states in accordance with their respective constitutional processes.

### ARTICLE 44

When the Security Council has decided to use force it shall, before calling upon a Member not represented on it to provide armed forces in fulfillment of the obligations assumed under Article 43, invite that Member, if the Member so desires, to participate in the decisions of the Security Council concerning the employment of contingents of that Member's armed forces.

### ARTICLE 45

In order to enable the United Nations to take urgent military measures, Members shall hold immediately available national air-force contingents for combined international enforcement action. The strength and degree of readiness of these contingents and plans for their combined action shall be determined, within the limits laid down in the special agreement or agreements referred to in Article 43, by the Security Council with the assistance of the Military Staff Committee.

## ARTICLE 46

Plans for the application of armed force shall be made by the Security Council with the assistance of the Military Staff Committee.

## ARTICLE 47

1. There shall be established a Military Staff Committee to advise and assist the Security Council on all questions relating to the Security Council's military requirements for the maintenance of international peace and security, the employment and command of forces placed at its disposal, the regulation of armaments, and possible disarmament.

2. The Military Staff Committee shall consist of the Chiefs of Staff of the permanent members of the Security Council or their representatives. Any Member of the United Nations not permanently represented on the Committee shall be invited by the Committee to be associated with it when the efficient discharge of the Committee's responsibilities requires the participation of that Member in its work.

3. The Military Staff Committee shall be responsible under the Security Council for the strategic direction of any armed forces placed at the disposal of the Security Council. Questions relating to the command of such forces shall be worked out subsequently.

4. The Military Staff Committee, with the authorization of the Security Council and after consultation with appropriate regional agencies, may establish regional subcommittees.

## ARTICLE 48

1. The action required to carry out the decisions of the Security Council for the maintenance of international peace and security shall be taken by all the Members of the United Nations or by some of them, as the Security Council may determine.

2. Such decisions shall be carried out by the Members of the United Nations directly and through their action in the appropriate international agencies of which they are members.

## ARTICLE 49

The Members of the United Nations shall join in affording mutual assistance in carrying out the measures decided upon by the Security Council.

## ARTICLE 50

If preventive or enforcement measures against any state are taken by the Security Council, any other state, whether a Member of the United Nations or not, which finds itself confronted with special economic problems arising from the carrying out of those measures shall have the right to consult the Security Council with regard to a solution of those problems.

## ARTICLE 51

Nothing in the present Charter shall impair the inherent right of individual or collective self-defense if an armed attack occurs against a Member of the United Nations, until the Security Council has taken the measures necessary to maintain international peace and security. Measures taken by Members in the exercise of this right of self-defense shall be immediately reported to the Security Council and shall not in any way affect the authority and responsibility of the Security Council under the present Charter to take at any time such action as it deems necessary in order to maintain or restore international peace and security.

## VIII. REGIONAL ARRANGEMENTS

### ARTICLE 52

1. Nothing in the present Charter precludes the existence of regional arrangements or agencies for dealing with such matters relating to the maintenance of international peace and security as are appropriate for regional action, provided that such arrangements or agencies and their activities are consistent with the Purposes and Principles of the United Nations.

2. The Members of the United Nations entering into such arrangements or constituting such agencies shall make every effort to achieve pacific settlement of local disputes through such regional arrangements or by such regional agencies before referring them to the Security Council.

3. The Security Council shall encourage the development of pacific settlement of local disputes through such regional arrangements or by such regional agencies either on the initiative of the states concerned or by reference from the Security Council.

4. This Article in no way impairs the application of Articles 34 and 35.

### ARTICLE 53

1. The Security Council shall, where appropriate, utilize such regional arrangements or agencies for enforcement action under its authority. But no enforcement action shall be taken under regional arrangements or by regional agencies without the authorization of the Security Council, with the exception of measures against any enemy state, as defined in paragraph 2 of this Article, provided for pursuant to Article 107 or in regional arrangements directed against renewal of aggressive policy on the part of any such state, until such time as the Organization may, on request of the Governments concerned, be charged with the responsibility for preventing further aggression by such a state.

2. The term enemy state as used in paragraph 1 of this Article applies to any state which during the Second World War has been an enemy of any signatory of the present Charter.

### ARTICLE 54

The Security Council shall at all times be kept fully informed of activities undertaken or in contemplation under regional arrangements or by regional agencies for the maintenance of international peace and security.

## IX. INTERNATIONAL ECONOMIC AND SOCIAL COOPERATION

### ARTICLE 55

With a view to the creation of conditions of stability and well-being which are necessary for peaceful and friendly relations among nations based on respect for the principle of equal rights and self-determination of peoples, the United Nations shall promote:

a. higher standards of living, full employment, and conditions of economic and social progress and development;

b. solutions of international economic, social, health, and related problems; and international cultural and educational cooperation; and

c. universal respect for, and observance of, human rights and fundamental freedoms for all without distinction as to race, sex, language, or religion.

### ARTICLE 56

All Members pledge themselves to take joint and separate action in cooperation with the Organization for the achievement of the purposes set forth in Article 55.

## ARTICLE 57

1. The various specialized agencies, established by intergovernmental agreement and having wide international responsibilities, as defined in their basic instruments, in economic, social, cultural, educational, health, and related fields, shall be brought into relationship with the United Nations in accordance with the provisions of Article 63.

2. Such agencies thus brought into relationship with the United Nations are hereinafter referred to as specialized agencies.

## ARTICLE 58

The Organization shall make recommendations for the coordination of the policies and activities of the specialized agencies.

## ARTICLE 59

The Organization shall, where appropriate, initiate negotiations among the states concerned for the creation of any new specialized agencies required for the accomplishment of the purposes set forth in Article 55.

## ARTICLE 60

Responsibility for the discharge of the functions of the Organization set forth in this Chapter shall be vested in the General Assembly and, under the authority of the General Assembly, in the Economic and Social Council, which shall have for this purpose the powers set forth in Chapter X.

## X. THE ECONOMIC AND SOCIAL COUNCIL

### Composition

## ARTICLE 61

1. The Economic and Social Council shall consist of eighteen Members of the United Nations elected by the General Assembly.

2. Subject to the provisions of paragraph 3, six members of the Economic and Social Council shall be elected each year for a term of three years. A retiring member shall be eligible for immediate re-election.

3. At the first election, eighteen members of the Economic and Social Council shall be chosen. The term of office of six members so chosen shall expire at the end of one year, and of six other members at the end of two years, in accordance with arrangements made by the General Assembly.

4. Each member of the Economic and Social Council shall have one representative.

### Functions and Powers

## ARTICLE 62

1. The Economic and Social Council may make or initiate studies and reports with respect to international economic, social, cultural, educational, health, and related matters and may make recommendations with respect to any such matters to the General Assembly, to the Members of the United Nations, and to the specialized agencies concerned.

2. It may make recommendations for the purpose of promoting respect for, and observance of, human rights and fundamental freedoms for all.

3. It may prepare draft conventions for submission to the General Assembly, with respect to matters falling within its competence.

4. It may call, in accordance with the rules prescribed by the United Nations, international conferences on matters falling within its competence.

## ARTICLE 63

1. The Economic and Social Council may enter into agreements with any of the agencies referred to in Article 57, de-

fining the terms on which the agency concerned shall be brought into relationship with the United Nations. Such agreements shall be subject to approval by the General Assembly.

2. It may coordinate the activities of the specialized agencies through consultation with and recommendations to such agencies and through recommendations to the General Assembly and to the Members of the United Nations.

### ARTICLE 64

1. The Economic and Social Council may take appropriate steps to obtain regular reports from the specialized agencies. It may make arrangements with the Members of the United Nations and with the specialized agencies to obtain reports on the steps taken to give effect to its own recommendations and to recommendations on matters falling within its competence made by the General Assembly.

2. It may communicate its observations on these reports to the General Assembly.

### ARTICLE 65

The Economic and Social Council may furnish information to the Security Council and shall assist the Security Council upon its request.

### ARTICLE 66

1. The Economic and Social Council shall perform such functions as fall within its competence in connection with the carrying out of the recommendations of the General Assembly.

2. It may, with the approval of the General Assembly, perform services at the request of Members of the United Nations and at the request of specialized agencies.

3. It shall perform such other functions as are specified elsewhere in the present Charter or as may be assigned to it by the General Assembly.

### *Voting*

### ARTICLE 67

1. Each member of the Economic and Social Council shall have one vote.

2. Decisions of the Economic and Social Council shall be made by a majority of the members present and voting.

### *Procedure*

### ARTICLE 68

The Economic and Social Council shall set up commissions in economic and social fields and for the promotion of human rights, and such other commissions as may be required for the performance of its functions.

### ARTICLE 69

The Economic and Social Council shall invite any Member of the United Nations to participate, without vote, in its deliberations on any matter of particular concern to that Member.

### ARTICLE 70

The Economic and Social Council may make arrangements for representatives of the specialized agencies to participate, without vote, in its deliberations and in those of the commissions established by it, and for its representatives to participate in the deliberations of the specialized agencies.

### ARTICLE 71

The Economic and Social Council may make suitable arrangements for consultation with non-governmental organizations which are concerned with matters within its competence. Such arrangements may be made with international organizations and, where appropriate, with national organizations after consultation with the Member of the United Nations concerned.

### ARTICLE 72

1. The Economic and Social Council shall adopt its own rules of procedure,

including the method of selecting its President.

2. The Economic and Social Council shall meet as required in accordance with its rules, which shall include provision for the convening of meetings on the request of a majority of its members.

## XI. DECLARATION REGARDING NON-SELF-GOVERNING TERRITORIES

### ARTICLE 73

Members of the United Nations which have or assume responsibilities for the administration of territories whose peoples have not yet attained a full measure of self-government recognize the principle that the interests of the inhabitants of these territories are paramount, and accept as a sacred trust the obligation to promote to the utmost, within the system of international peace and security established by the present Charter, the well-being of the inhabitants of these territories, and, to this end:

a. to insure, with due respect for the culture of the peoples concerned, their political, economic, social, and educational advancement, their just treatment, and their protection against abuses;

b. to develop self-government, to take due account of the political aspirations of the peoples, and to assist them in the progressive development of their free political institutions, according to the particular circumstances of each territory and its peoples and their varying stages of advancement;

c. to further international peace and security;

d. to promote constructive measures of development, to encourage research, and to cooperate with one another

and, when and where appropriate, with specialized international bodies with a view to the practical achievement of the social, economic, and scientific purposes set forth in this Article; and

e. to transmit regularly to the Secretary-General for information purposes, subject to such limitation as security and constitutional considerations may require, statistical and other information of a technical nature relating to economic, social, and educational conditions in the territories for which they are respectively responsible other than those territories to which Chapters XII and XIII apply.

### ARTICLE 74

Members of the United Nations also agree that their policy in respect of the territories to which this Chapter applies, no less than in respect of their metropolitan areas, must be based on the general principle of good-neighborliness, due account being taken of the interests and well-being of the rest of the world, in social, economic, and commercial matters.

## XII. INTERNATIONAL TRUSTEESHIP SYSTEM

### ARTICLE 75

The United Nations shall establish under its authority an international trusteeship system for the administration and supervision of such territories as may be placed thereunder by subsequent individual agreements. These territories are hereinafter referred to as trust territories.

### ARTICLE 76

The basic objectives of the trusteeship system, in accordance with the Purposes of the United Nations laid down in Article 1 of the present Charter, shall be:

a. to further international peace and security;
b. to promote the political, economic, social, and educational advancement of the inhabitants of the trust territories, and their progressive development towards self-government or independence as may be appropriate to the particular circumstances of each territory and its peoples and the freely expressed wishes of the peoples concerned, and as may be provided by the terms of each trusteeship agreement;
c. to encourage respect for human rights and for fundamental freedoms for all without distinction as to race, sex, language, or religion, and to encourage recognition of the interdependence of the peoples of the world; and
d. to ensure equal treatment in social, economic, and commercial matters for all Members of the United Nations and their nationals, and also equal treatment for the latter in the administration of justice, without prejudice to the attainment of the foregoing objectives and subject to the provisions of Article 80.

### ARTICLE 77

1. The trusteeship system shall apply to such territories in the following categories as may be placed thereunder by means of trusteeship agreements:

a. territories now held under mandate;
b. territories which may be detached from enemy states as a result of the Second World War; and
c. territories voluntarily placed under the system by states responsible for their administration.

2. It will be a matter for subsequent agreement as to which territories in the foregoing categories will be brought under the trusteeship system and upon what terms.

### ARTICLE 78

The trusteeship system shall not apply to territories which have become Members of the United Nations, relationship among which shall be based on respect for the principle of sovereign equality.

### ARTICLE 79

The terms of trusteeship for each territory to be placed under the trusteeship system, including any alteration or amendment, shall be agreed upon by the states directly concerned, including the mandatory power in the case of territories held under mandate by a Member of the United Nations, and shall be approved as provided for in Articles 83 and 85.

### ARTICLE 80

1. Except as may be agreed upon in individual trusteeship agreements, made under Articles 77, 79, and 81, placing each territory under the trusteeship system, and until such agreements have been concluded, nothing in this Chapter shall be construed in or of itself to alter in any manner the rights whatsoever of any states or any peoples or the terms of existing international instruments to which Members of the United Nations may respectively be parties.

2. Paragraph 1 of this Article shall not be interpreted as giving grounds for delay or postponement of the negotiation and conclusion of agreements for placing mandated and other territories under the trusteeship system as provided for in Article 77.

### ARTICLE 81

The trusteeship agreement shall in each case include the terms under which the trust territory will be administered and designate the authority which will exercise the administration of the trust territory. Such authority, hereinafter called the administering authority, may be one or more states or the Organization itself.

## ARTICLE 82

There may be designated, in any trusteeship agreement, a strategic area or areas which may include part or all of the trust territory to which the agreement applies, without prejudice to any special agreement or agreements made under Article 43.

## ARTICLE 83

1. All functions of the United Nations relating to strategic areas, including the approval of the terms of the trusteeship agreements and of their alteration or amendment, shall be exercised by the Security Council.

2. The basic objectives set forth in Article 76 shall be applicable to the people of each strategic area.

3. The Security Council shall, subject to the provisions of the trusteeship agreements and without prejudice to security considerations, avail itself of the assistance of the Trusteeship Council to perform those functions of the United Nations under the trusteeship system relating to political, economic, social, and educational matters in the strategic areas.

## ARTICLE 84

It shall be the duty of the administering authority to ensure that the trust territory shall play its part in the maintenance of international peace and security. To this end the administering authority may make use of volunteer forces, facilities, and assistance from the trust territory in carrying out the obligations towards the Security Council undertaken in this regard by the administering authority, as well as for local defense and the maintenance of law and order within the trust territory.

## ARTICLE 85

1. The functions of the United Nations with regard to trusteeship agreements for all areas not designated as strategic, including the approval of the terms of the trusteeship agreements and of their alteration or amendment, shall be exercised by the General Assembly.

2. The Trusteeship Council, operating under the authority of the General Assembly, shall assist the General Assembly in carrying out these functions.

## XIII. THE TRUSTEESHIP COUNCIL

### Composition

#### ARTICLE 86

1. The Trusteeship Council shall consist of the following Members of the United Nations:

a. those Members administering trust territories;
b. such of those Members mentioned by name in Article 23 as are not administering trust territories; and
c. as many other Members elected for three-year terms by the General Assembly as may be necessary to ensure that the total number of members of the Trusteeship Council is equally divided between those Members of the United Nations which administer trust territories and those which do not.

2. Each member of the Trusteeship Council shall designate one specially qualified person to represent it therein.

### Functions and Powers

#### ARTICLE 87

The General Assembly and, under its authority, the Trusteeship Council, in carrying out their functions, may:

a. consider reports submitted by the administering authority;

b. accept petitions and examine them in consultation with the administering authority;

c. provide for periodic visits to the respective trust territories at times agreed upon with the administering authority; and

d. take these and other actions in conformity with the terms of the trusteeship agreements.

### ARTICLE 88

The Trusteeship Council shall formulate a questionnaire on the political, economic, social, and educational advancement of the inhabitants of each trust territory, and the administering authority for each trust territory within the competence of the General Assembly shall make an annual report to the General Assembly upon the basis of such questionnaire.

### *Voting*

### ARTICLE 89

1. Each member of the Trusteeship Council shall have one vote.

2. Decisions of the Trusteeship Council shall be made by a majority of the members present and voting.

### *Procedure*

### ARTICLE 90

1. The Trusteeship Council shall adopt its own rules of procedure, including the method of selecting its President.

2. The Trusteeship Council shall meet as required in accordance with its rules, which shall include provision for the convening of meetings on the request of a majority of its members.

### ARTICLE 91

The Trusteeship Council shall, when appropriate, avail itself of the assistance of the Economic and Social Council and of the specialized agencies in regard to matters with which they are respectively concerned.

## XIV. THE INTERNATIONAL COURT OF JUSTICE

### ARTICLE 92

The International Court of Justice shall be the principal judicial organ of the United Nations. It shall function in accordance with the annexed Statute, which is based upon the Statute of the Permanent Court of International Justice and forms an integral part of the present Charter.

### ARTICLE 93

1. All Members of the United Nations are *ipso facto* parties to the Statute of the International Court of Justice.

2. A state which is not a Member of the United Nations may become a party to the Statute of the International Court of Justice on conditions to be determined in each case by the General Assembly upon the recommendation of the Security Council.

### ARTICLE 94

1. Each Member of the United Nations undertakes to comply with the decision of the International Court of Justice in any case to which it is a party.

2. If any party to a case fails to perform the obligations incumbent upon it under a judgment rendered by the Court, the other party may have recourse to the Security Council, which may, if it deems necessary, make recommendations or decide upon measures to be taken to give effect to the judgment.

### ARTICLE 95

Nothing in the present Charter shall prevent Members of the United Nations from entrusting the solution of their differences to other tribunals by virtue of agreements already in existence or which may be concluded in the future.

## ARTICLE 96

1. The General Assembly or the Security Council may request the International Court of Justice to give an advisory opinion on any legal question.

2. Other organs of the United Nations and specialized agencies, which may at any time be so authorized by the General Assembly, may also request advisory opinions of the Court on legal questions arising within the scope of their activities.

## XV. THE SECRETARIAT

### ARTICLE 97

The Secretariat shall comprise a Secretary-General and such staff as the Organization may require. The Secretary-General shall be appointed by the General Assembly upon the recommendation of the Security Council. He shall be the chief administrative officer of the Organization.

### ARTICLE 98

The Secretary-General shall act in that capacity in all meetings of the General Assembly, of the Security Council, of the Economic and Social Council, and of the Trusteeship Council, and shall perform such other functions as are entrusted to him by these organs. The Secretary-General shall make an annual report to the General Assembly on the work of the Organization.

### ARTICLE 99

The Secretary-General may bring to the attention of the Security Council any matter which in his opinion may threaten the maintenance of international peace and security.

### ARTICLE 100

1. In the performance of their duties the Secretary-General and the staff shall not seek or receive instructions from any government or from any other authority external to the Organization. They shall refrain from any action which might reflect on their position as international officials responsible only to the Organization.

2. Each Member of the United Nations undertakes to respect the exclusively international character of the responsibilities of the Secretary-General and the staff and not to seek to influence them in the discharge of their responsibilities.

### ARTICLE 101

1. The staff shall be appointed by the Secretary-General under regulations established by the General Assembly.

2. Appropriate staffs shall be permanently assigned to the Economic and Social Council, the Trusteeship Council, and, as required, to other organs of the United Nations. These staffs shall form a part of the Secretariat.

3. The paramount consideration in the employment of the staff and in the determination of the conditions of service shall be the necessity of securing the highest standards of efficiency, competence, and integrity. Due regard shall be paid to the importance of recruiting the staff on as wide a geographical basis as possible.

## XVI. MISCELLANEOUS PROVISIONS

### ARTICLE 102

1. Every treaty and every international agreement entered into by any Member of the United Nations after the present Charter comes into force shall as soon as possible be registered with the Secretariat and published by it.

2. No party to any such treaty or international agreement which has not been registered in accordance with the provisions of paragraph 1 of this Article may invoke that treaty or agreement before any organ of the United Nations.

### ARTICLE 103

In the event of a conflict between the obligations of the Members of the United Nations under the present Charter and their obligations under any other international agreement, their obligations under the present Charter shall prevail.

### ARTICLE 104

The Organization shall enjoy in the territory of each of its Members such legal capacity as may be necessary for the exercise of its functions and the fulfillment of its purposes.

### ARTICLE 105

1. The Organization shall enjoy in the territory of each of its Members such privileges and immunities as are necessary for the fulfillment of its purposes.

2. Representatives of the Members of the United Nations and officials of the Organization shall similarly enjoy such privileges and immunities as are necessary for the independent exercise of their functions in connection with the Organization.

3. The General Assembly may make recommendations with a view to determining the details of the application of paragraphs 1 and 2 of this Article or may propose conventions to the Members of the United Nations for this purpose.

## XVII. TRANSITIONAL SECURITY ARRANGEMENTS

### ARTICLE 106

Pending the coming into force of such special agreements referred to in Article 43 as in the opinion of the Security Council enable it to begin the exercise of its responsibilities under Article 42, the parties to the Four-Nation Declaration, signed at Moscow, October 30, 1943, and France, shall, in accordance with the provisions of paragraph 5 of that Declaration, consult with one another and as occasion requires with other Members of the United Nations with a view to such joint action on behalf of the Organization as may be necessary for the purpose of maintaining international peace and security.

### ARTICLE 107

Nothing in the present Charter shall invalidate or preclude action, in relation to any state which during the Second World War has been an enemy of any signatory to the present Charter, taken or authorized as a result of that war by the Governments having responsibility for such action.

## XVIII. AMENDMENTS

### ARTICLE 108

Amendments to the present Charter shall come into force for all Members of the United Nations when they have been adopted by a vote of two thirds of the members of the General Assembly and ratified in accordance with their respective constitutional processes by two thirds of the Members of the United Nations, including all the permanent members of the Security Council.

### ARTICLE 109

1. A General Conference of the Members of the United Nations for the purpose of reviewing the present Charter may be held at a date and place to be fixed by a two-thirds vote of the members of the General Assembly and by a vote of any seven members of the Security Council. Each Member of the United Nations shall have one vote in the conference.

2. Any alteration of the present Charter recommended by a two-thirds vote of the conference shall take effect when ratified in accordance with their respective constitutional processes by two-thirds of the Members of the United Nations in-

# THE UNITED NATIONS

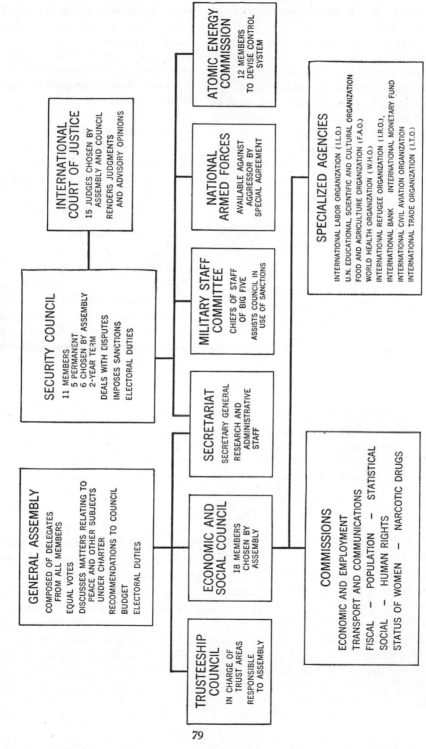

**GENERAL ASSEMBLY**

COMPOSED OF DELEGATES
FROM ALL MEMBERS
EQUAL VOTES
DISCUSSES MATTERS RELATING TO
PEACE AND OTHER SUBJECTS
UNDER CHARTER
RECOMMENDATIONS TO COUNCIL
BUDGET
ELECTORAL DUTIES

**SECURITY COUNCIL**

11 MEMBERS
5 PERMANENT
6 CHOSEN BY ASSEMBLY
2-YEAR TERM
DEALS WITH DISPUTES
IMPOSES SANCTIONS
ELECTORAL DUTIES

**INTERNATIONAL COURT OF JUSTICE**

15 JUDGES CHOSEN BY
ASSEMBLY AND COUNCIL
RENDERS JUDGMENTS
AND ADVISORY OPINIONS

**ATOMIC ENERGY COMMISSION**

12 MEMBERS
TO DEVISE CONTROL
SYSTEM

**TRUSTEESHIP COUNCIL**

IN CHARGE OF
TRUST AREAS
RESPONSIBLE
TO ASSEMBLY

**ECONOMIC AND SOCIAL COUNCIL**

18 MEMBERS
CHOSEN BY
ASSEMBLY

**SECRETARIAT**

SECRETARY GENERAL
RESEARCH AND
ADMINISTRATIVE
STAFF

**MILITARY STAFF COMMITTEE**

CHIEFS OF STAFF
OF BIG FIVE
ASSISTS COUNCIL IN
USE OF SANCTIONS

**NATIONAL ARMED FORCES**

AVAILABLE AGAINST
AGGRESSOR BY
SPECIAL AGREEMENT

**COMMISSIONS**

ECONOMIC AND EMPLOYMENT
TRANSPORT AND COMMUNICATIONS
FISCAL – POPULATION – STATISTICAL
SOCIAL – HUMAN RIGHTS
STATUS OF WOMEN – NARCOTIC DRUGS

**SPECIALIZED AGENCIES**

INTERNATIONAL LABOR ORGANIZATION (I.L.O.)
U.N. EDUCATIONAL, SCIENTIFIC AND CULTURAL ORGANIZATION
FOOD AND AGRICULTURE ORGANIZATION (F.A.O.)
WORLD HEALTH ORGANIZATION (W.H.O.)
INTERNATIONAL REFUGEE ORGANIZATION (I.R.O.).
INTERNATIONAL BANK    INTERNATIONAL MONETARY FUND
INTERNATIONAL CIVIL AVIATION ORGANIZATION
INTERNATIONAL TRADE ORGANIZATION (I.T.O.)

cluding all the permanent members of the Security Council.

3. If such a conference has not been held before the tenth annual session of the General Assembly following the coming into force of the present Charter, the proposal to call such a conference shall be placed on the agenda of that session of the General Assembly, and the conference shall be held if so decided by a majority vote of the members of the General Assembly and by a vote of any seven members of the Security Council.

## XIX. RATIFICATION AND SIGNATURE

### ARTICLE 110

1. The present Charter shall be ratified by the signatory states in accordance with their respective constitutional processes.

2. The ratifications shall be deposited with the Government of the United States of America, which shall notify all the signatory states of each deposit as well as the Secretary-General of the Organization when he has been appointed.

3. The present Charter shall come into force upon the deposit of ratifications by the Republic of China, France, the Union of Soviet Socialist Republics, the United Kingdom of Great Britain and Northern Ireland, and the United States of America, and by a majority of the other signatory states. A protocol of the ratifications deposited shall thereupon be drawn up by the Government of the United States of America which shall communicate copies thereof to all the signatory states.

4. The states signatory to the present Charter which ratify it after it has come into force will become original Members of the United Nations on the date of the deposit of their respective ratifications.

### ARTICLE 111

The present Charter, of which the Chinese, French, Russian, English, and Spanish texts are equally authentic, shall remain deposited in the archives of the Government of the United States of America. Duly certified copies thereof shall be transmitted by that Government to the Governments of the other signatory states.

In faith whereof the representatives of the Governments of the United Nations have signed the present Charter.

Done at the city of San Francisco the twenty-sixth day of June, one thousand nine hundred and forty-five.

## II. THE 'LITTLE ASSEMBLY'

On 17 September 1947, Secretary of State George C. Marshall proposed that the General Assembly create an 'Interim Committee on Peace and Security' to serve between the second and third regular sessions of the Assembly. He suggested that the Committee represent all of the members of the United Nations and that it be available to 'consider situations and disputes impairing friendly relations brought to its attention by member states or by the Security Council pursuant to Articles 11 and 14 of the Charter,' that it be empowered to recommend special sessions of the General Assembly, and that it report at the third regular session of the Assembly on the advisability of making the arrangements permanent. The resolution below, embodying Secretary Marshall's plan for a 'Little Assembly,' was adopted.

(Text from *The New York Times,* 17 November 1947.)

Conscious of the responsibility specifically conferred upon it by the Charter in relation to matters concerning the maintenance of international peace and security (Articles 11 and 35), the promotion of international cooperation in the political field (Article 13) and the peaceful adjustment of any situations likely to impair the general welfare or friendly relations among nations (Article 14);

Deeming it necessary for the effective performance of these duties to establish an Interim Committee to consider and report with its conclusions on such matters to the General Assembly during the period between the closing of the present session and the opening of the next regular session of the General Assembly;

Recognizing fully the primary responsibility of the Security Council for prompt and effective action for the maintenance of international peace and security (Article 14);

Resolves that

1. There shall be established, for the period between the closing of the present session and the opening of the next regular session of the General Assembly, an Interim Committee on which each member of the General Assembly shall have the right to appoint one representative.

2. The Interim Committee, as a subsidiary organ of the General Assembly established in accordance with Article 22 of the Charter, shall assist the General Assembly in the performance of its functions by discharging the following duties:

(A) To consider and report with its conclusions to the General Assembly on such matters as have been referred to it by the General Assembly;

(B) To consider and report with its conclusions to the General Assembly on any dispute or any situation which, in virtue of Articles 11 (2), 14 or 35 of the Charter, has been proposed for inclusion in the agenda of the General Assembly by any member of the United Nations or brought before the General Assembly by the Security Council, provided the committee previously determines the matter to be both important and requiring preliminary study. Such determination shall be made by a majority of two-thirds of those present and voting, unless the matter is one referred by the Security Council under Article 11 (2), in which case a simple majority will suffice;

(C) To consider, as it deems useful and advisable, and report with its conclusions to the General Assembly on methods to be adopted to give effect to that part of Article 11 (1) which deals with the general principles of cooperation in the maintenance of international peace and security, and to that part of Article 13 (1) (A) which deals with the promotion of international cooperation in the political field;

(D) To consider, in connection with any matter under discussion by the Interim Committee, whether occasion may require the summoning of a special session of the General Assembly and, if it deems that such session is required, so to advise the Secretary General in order that he may obtain the views of members thereon;

(E) To conduct investigations and appoint commissions of inquiry within the scope of its duties, as it may deem useful and necessary, provided that decisions to conduct such investigations or inquiries shall be made by a two-thirds majority of the members present and voting. An investigation or inquiry elsewhere than at the headquarters of the United Nations shall not be conducted without the consent of the state or states in whose territory it is to take place;

(F) To report to the next regular session of the General Assembly on the advisability of establishing a permanent committee of the General Assembly to perform the duties of the Interim Committee as stated above with any changes considered desirable in the light of experience.

3. In discharging its duties the Interim Committee shall at all times take into account the responsibilities of the Security Council under the Charter for the maintenance of international peace and security, as well as the duties assigned by the Charter or by the General Assembly or by the Security Council to other councils or to any committee or commission. The Interim Committee shall not consider any matter of which the Security Council is seized.

4. Subject to paragraphs 2 (B) and 2 (E) above, the rules of procedure of the General Assembly shall, so far as they are applicable, govern the proceedings of the Interim Committee and such subcommittees and commissions as it may set up. The Interim Committee shall, however, have authority to adopt such additional rules as it may deem necessary provided that they are not inconsistent with any of the rules of the General Assembly. The Interim Committee shall be convened by the Secretary General not later than six weeks following the close of the second regular session of the General Assembly. It shall meet as and when it deems necessary for the conduct of its business.

5. The Secretary General shall provide the necessary facilities and assign appropriate staff as required for the work of the Interim Committee, its subcommittees and commissions.

## III. The Security Council in Action

The following extract from the first report of the Secretary-General of the United Nations is a statement of the work of the Security Council in dealing with two international controversies.

*(Report of the Secretary-General on the Work of the Organization.* United Nations Document No. A/65. 30 June 1946. pp. 1-4.)

### The Iranian Question

In a letter dated 19 January 1946, the Head of the Iranian delegation to the United Nations stated that, owing to the interferences of the Union of Soviet Socialist Republics, through the medium of its officials and armed forces, in the internal affairs of Iran, a situation had arisen which might lead to international friction. He requested the Executive Secretary, in accordance with the terms of Article 35, of the Charter, to bring the matter to the attention of the Security Council so that the Council might investigate the situation and recommend appropriate terms of settlement.

The application was considered at the Council's third and fifth meetings, the Iranian representative participating in the discussion, and the following resolution was adopted unanimously on 30 January 1946:

The Council . . .
Considering that both parties have affirmed their readiness to seek a solution of the matter at issue by negotiation; and such negotiations will be resumed in the near future,
Requests the parties to inform the Council of any results achieved in such negotiations. The Council in the meanwhile retains the right at any time to request information on the progress of the negotiations.

In a letter dated 18 March 1946, the Iranian Ambassador to the United States of America stated that, pursuant to Article 35, I, of the Charter, Iran brought to the attention of the Security Council a dispute between Iran and the Union of Soviet Socialist Republics, the continuance of which was likely to endanger the maintenace of international peace and security. He also stated that the Union of Soviet Socialist Republics was maintaining Soviet troops in Iranian territory after 2 March 1946, contrary to the express provisions of Article V of the Tripartite Treaty of Alliance of 29 January 1942, and that the Union of Soviet Socialist Republics was continuing to interfere in the internal affairs of Iran through the medium of Soviet agents, officials and armed forces.

The application was considered at the twenty-fifth, twenty-sixth, twenty-seventh, twenty-eighth, twenty-ninth and thirtieth meetings, the Iranian Ambassador participating in the discussions at the twenty-seventh, twenty-eighth, twenty-ninth and thirtieth meetings. After various procedural decisions, the Security Council adopted the following resolution on 4 April 1946 by nine votes, the representative of the Union of Soviet Socialist Republics being absent and the representative of Australia abstaining:

. . . resolved that the Council defer further proceedings on the Iranian appeal until 6 May, at which time the Soviet Government and the Iranian Government are requested to report to the Council whether the withdrawal of all Soviet troops from the whole of Iran has been completed and at which time the Council shall consider what, if any, further proceedings on the Iranian appeal are required. . .

By a letter dated 6 April 1946, the representative of the Union of Soviet Socialist Republics proposed that the Iranian question be removed from the agenda of the Council, on the ground that, under the understanding between the Iranian Government and the Soviet Government, full evacuation of Soviet troops from Iran had been started on 24 March 1946 and

would be completed in five or six weeks. He pointed out that, as was known from the joint Soviet-Iranian communiqué published on 4 April 1946, an understanding on all points had been reached between the Soviet and the Iranian Governments. He submitted that the above resolution of the Council was incorrect and illegal, being in conflict with the Charter.

In a letter dated 9 April 1946, the Iranian Ambassador stated that it was his Government's desire that the question should remain on the agenda of the Council as provided by the above resolution.

By a letter dated 15 April 1946, the Iranian Ambassador communicated the text of a telegram from his Government stating that it had complete confidence in the word and pledge of the Soviet Government and for this reason withdrew its complaint from before the Council.

At the thirty-second meeting, on 15 April, the removal of the Iranian question from the agenda of the Council was discussed.

At the thirty-third meeting, the Secretary-General submitted a memorandum to the President of the Council setting out his views with respect to the legal aspects of the question of the retention of the Iranian question on the agenda. After an analysis of the relevant provisions of the Charter, the Secretary-General concluded that, following withdrawal by the Iranian representative, and since the Council had not chosen to vote an investigation under Article 34, or to invoke Article 36, 1, by deciding that a dispute existed under Article 33 or that there was a situation of like nature, and since no member of the Council had brought the question up as a situation or dispute under Article 35, it might well be that there was no way in which the Council could remain seized of the matter. The

Council referred this memorandum to the Committee of Experts.

At the thirty-sixth meeting, the Council considered the report of the Chairman of the Committee of Experts. The Committee of Experts had been unable to formulate a common opinion concerning the arguments advanced by the Secretary-General, and the report summarized the arguments advanced during its discussion on this subject. The Council continued its discussion of the issues raised in the above letters from the representative of the Union of Soviet Socialist Republics who associated himself with the following resolution proposed by the representative of France at the thirty-third meeting:

. . . that the Security Council request the Secretary-General to collect the necessary information in order to complete the Security Council's report to the Assembly, in accordance with Article 24 of the Charter, on the manner in which it dealt with the case placed on its agenda on 26 March last at the request, not withdrawn of the Government of Iran.

The resolution received three votes (France, Poland and the Union of Soviet Socialist Republics) and was declared lost. Accordingly, the Council remained seized of the Iranian question.

The representative of the Union of Soviet Socialist Republics said that the decision of the Council to retain the Iranian question on its agenda was contrary to the Charter. Accordingly, the Soviet delegation did not consider it possible to take any further part in the discussion of the Iranian question in the Council.

By a letter dated 6 May 1946, the Iranian Ambassador, pursuant to the Council's resolution of 4 April, reported on the withdrawal of Soviet troops. He stated that investigations made by responsible officials of the Government of Iran showed that Soviet troops had been completely evacuated from the Provinces of Khorassan, Gorgan, Mazanderan and

Gilan. Because of the interferences previously complained of, officials of the Government of Iran had been unable to verify by direct observation reports that the evacuation from Azerbaijan had been going forward and would be completed by 7 May 1946.

At the fortieth meeting, on 8 May, the Council adopted by ten votes (the representative of the Union of Soviet Socialist Republics being absent) the following resolution proposed by the representative of the United States of America:

The Security Council resolves,
in view of the statement made by the Iranian Government in its preliminary report of 6 May, submitted in compliance with the resolution of 4 April 1946, that it was not able as of 6 May to state whether the withdrawal of all Soviet troops from the whole of Iran had been completed;
to defer further proceedings on the Iranian matter in order that the Government of Iran may have time in which to ascertain through its official representatives whether all Soviet troops have been withdrawn from the whole of Iran;
that the Iranian Government be requested to submit a complete report on the subject to the Security Council immediately upon the receipt of the information which will enable it so to do; and that in case it is unable to obtain such information by 20 May, it report on that date such information as is available to it at that time;
and that immediately following the receipt from the Iranian Government of the report requested, the Council shall consider whether any further proceedings are required.

In letters dated 20 May and 21 May 1946, the Iranian Ambassador, in compliance with the Council's resolutions of 4 April and 8 May 1946, submitted additional information with respect to the matter brought to the Council's attention by the Iranian Government. In his letter dated 20 May 1946, the Iranian Ambassador stated that, as a consequence of the interferences previously complained of, the

Iranian Government was still being prevented from exercising any effective authority in the Province of Azerbaijan, and that Soviet interferences in the internal affairs of Iran had not ceased. Therefore, it had not been possible to make such investigation as was required to establish that all the Soviet troops had been withdrawn from the whole of Iran. In his letter dated 21 May 1946, the Iranian Ambassador communicated the text of a telegram received by him that afternoon from the Iranian Prime Minister. The telegram stated that the Iranian Prime Minister had dispatched a commission of investigation which in the course of one week had investigated carefully the regions of Azerbaijan surrounding a number of important centres named in the telegram. Telegraphic reports were to the effect that no trace whatever of Soviet troops, equipment or means of transport had been found, and that, according to trustworthy local people who were questioned in the places mentioned, Soviet troops had evacuated Azerbaijan on 6 May 1946.

At the Council's forty-third meeting, on 22 May, the Iranian Ambassador participated in the discussion. The Council adopted the following resolution submitted by the representative of the Netherlands:

The discussion of the Iranian question is adjourned until a date in the near future, the Council to be called together at the request of any of its members.

The Council remains seized of the Iranian question.

· · ·

## THE INDONESIAN QUESTION

By a letter dated 21 January 1946, the representative of the Ukrainian Soviet Socialist Republic, under Articles 34 and 35 of the Charter, drew the attention of the Security Council to the situation which had arisen in Indonesia which, it was alleged, created a threat to the maintenance of international peace and security, and asked the Security Council to carry out the necessary investigations and to take the measures provided for by the Charter.

The letter was placed on the agenda for the twelfth meeting of the Security Council on 7 February 1946. The procedure of hearing various points of view was adopted, and the representative of the Ukrainian Soviet Socialist Republic was invited to participate in the discussions of the Security Council.

After a long discussion, in which the representatives of the United Kingdom, the Ukrainian Soviet Socialist Republic, the Netherlands, China, Egypt, France, Mexico, Poland, Brazil, the United States of America, the Union of Soviet Socialist Republics and Australia participated, a vote was taken, on the proposal of the representative of the Ukraine, on 13 February 1946 at the eighteenth meeting of the Security Council. The Ukrainian representative proposed to set up a Commission consisting of representatives of the United States, the Soviet Union, China, Great Britain and the Netherlands which should carry out an enquiry on the spot, establish peace in Indonesia and report to the Security Council on the result of its work.

The resolution was lost.

Another proposal by the Egyptian representative, with an amendment by the representative of the Union of Soviet Socialist Republics, was made. The Egyptian representative proposed that the British troops should not be used in any circumstances against the National Indonesian Movement and that they should be withdrawn from Indonesia as soon as the surrender of Japanese troops and the liberation of Allied prisoners of war and Allied nationals had been accomplished, and that the Council should express its will to be informed of the result of the negotiations between the Netherlands Government and the chiefs of the Indonesian movement.

The Soviet amendment proposed to despatch a Commission to Indonesia consisting of the representatives of China, the Netherlands, the United Kingdom, the United States of America and the Union of Soviet Socialist Republics.

Neither the Soviet amendment nor the Egyptian proposal obtained the required number of votes, and the matter was closed.

(This problem has remained before the Security Council.)

## IV. The Problem of the Veto

According to the United Nations Charter, votes on non-procedural matters are taken in the Security Council by a concurrence of 7 of the 11 members, provided all 5 of the permanent members of the Council are among the 7. This rule has the effect of granting a veto on action by the United Nations to each of the 5 permanent members—Russia, the United States, Great Britain, France, and China. There has been widespread dissatisfaction with the arrangement; the following extracts give the text of a resolution of the General Assembly on the subject, and the views of small states as well as those of Russia and the United States.

### A. *Assembly Resolution on the Veto*

(Text from *The New York Times*, 14 December 1946.)

The General Assembly,

Mindful of the purposes and principles of the Charter of the United Nations, and having taken notice of the divergencies which have arisen in regard to the application and interpretation of Article 27 of the Charter;

Earnestly requests the permanent members of the Security Council to make every effort, in consultation with one another and with fellow members of the Security Council, to insure that the use of the special voting privilege of its permanent members does not impede the Security Council in reaching decisions promptly;

Recommends to the Security Council the early adoption of practices and procedures, consistent with the Charter, to assist in reducing the difficulties in the application of Article 27 and to insure the prompt and effective exercise by the Security Council of its functions; and

Further recommends that, in developing such practices and procedures, the Security Council take into consideration the views expressed by members of the United Nations during the second part of the first session of the General Assembly.

### B. *The Position of New Zealand*

(Statement by Sir Carl Berendsen to the General Assembly. *Journal of the United Nations*, 29 October 1946.)

Sir Carl Berendsen (New Zealand): . . . the question of voting powers in the Security Council . . . leads inevitably to a consideration of the veto. . . We ask no veto; we ask no predominant or decisive voice. We ask for our proportionate voice in those councils which will influence the affairs of man as far ahead as man can see. . .

. . . We, in New Zealand have never been able to understand . . . why the Great Powers insisted on the right of veto on matters of peaceful settlement; but this with a much larger and more difficult question of the veto on enforcement action, was part of the price that the smaller Powers were called upon by the Great Powers to pay for the very existence of the United Nations. We agreed to pay this price. We thought it was a high price, but even at that, a price worth paying. But we were not without a most earnest hope that in due course of time we should perhaps obtain a refund, that these Powers which had insisted on this privileged position would sooner or later . . .

find themselves able to agree to a modification of those principles.

I very much question whether anybody . . . is satisfied with the transactions of the Security Council. The proceedings of that body have, it must be confessed, offered a humiliating spectacle. The cause of this humiliation lies not only in a failure to come to agreed conclusions on the substance of the difficult international questions brought before the Council, but even more pointedly in the prolonged wrangles of procedure. In taking resolutions on matters of substance, the Council is impeded by the veto. All the more reason why in the field where it is free from this incubus, namely in procedure, it should act with decision, and all the more reason why those Powers which have been granted these extraordinary privileges should see to it that those privileges are utilized with the fullest sense of the high responsibility of those five Powers to mankind.

## C. *The Russian Position*

(V. M. Molotov, head of the Soviet delegation to the United Nations, Speech delivered at the General Assembly, 29 October 1946. Text from *The New York Times*, 30 November 1946.)

Imagine, Gentlemen, that the campaign to repeal the so-called veto were to be crowned with success. What would the political consequences be?

It is quite obvious that the repudiation of the principle of unanimity of the great powers—and this is, in fact, what this proposal for the abolition of the veto amounts to—would mean in practice the liquidation of the United Nations organization because this principle is the cornerstone of this organization. Perhaps not all the members of this noisy campaign sufficiently realize where this is leading to. But, inasmuch as the United

Nations organization is based on the principle of the unanimity of the great powers, the abolition of this principle will result in the collapse of the very edifice of the United Nations.

But this is not the only question at issue.

The success of this campaign would mean victory for the policy aimed at the achievement of domination by one group of states headed by the strongest of powers over other powers which would then find themselves in the minority. The policy that would triumph would not be that of international cooperation in the spirit of democratic principles of the United Nations organization but would be the policy of new claimants to world domination as represented by a corresponding bloc, or, if you wish, by a concert of powers to whom the retention of the principle of unanimity of the great powers already seems to be inconvenient. The disputes and struggle that are going on around the so-called veto testify to the intensification of antagonisms between the two principal policies, one of which consists in the defense of the principles of international cooperation among big and small states recognized by all of us and the other one is prompted by the desire of certain influential groups to have a free hand with a view to waging an unrestrained struggle to gain world domination. An attitude of neutrality towards this question is ambiguous and inappropriate.

The Allies fought against imperialist Germany and imperialist Japan in order to free the people from fascist claimants to world domination. We did not fight to permit any other country or other countries to take their place. Our peoples did not shed their invaluable blood in streams to pave the way for new claimants to world domination. This is exactly what we should now be reminded of. If the great powers which headed the struggle against fascist aggressors keep together and, relying on the support of other nations, will prevent their ranks from being cleft they will be able to do much in counteracting the whetting of insatiable appetites. Otherwise, the new claimants to world domination will be given a free hand for all sorts of adventures until they break their necks.

We know that there are quite a number of methods by which the stronger powers can exert pressure on other states. It is well known that squadrons of warships and military planes appear sometimes in the seas and in places where they were absent before whenever this is considered essential for achieving the greatest possible success in diplomatic negotiations. It is well known, too, that dollars and pounds sterling are not always restricted to home consumption, especially when it is necessary to resort to 'dollar diplomacy' if only, say, for the purpose of securing due respect for 'dollar democracy.' Now, as we know, people also write about 'atomic diplomacy.'

It is an open secret that various combinations of these and other means are frequently resorted to for the purpose of influencing other and small countries in particular. But there are people and whole influential groups who would not rest content with all this. No sooner, therefore, have all the barriers been removed, including the liquidation of the principle of unanimity of the great powers within the United Nations organization, than the way will be fully paved for those persons and groups who will not content themselves with anything less than the submission of all peoples to their dictate and to their money bag.

## D. *Statement by Vishinsky*

(A. Y. Vishinsky, Statement to the General Assembly, 18 September 1947. Text from *The New York Times,* 19 September 1947.)

As far as the Soviet Union is concerned, its policy with regards to the United Nations organization is a policy of strengthening of the organization; it is a policy of broadening and strengthening of international cooperation, a policy of a steady, consistent observance of the Charter and of fulfillment of its principles.

The strengthening of the United Nations organization is only possible on the basis of respectful attitude toward the political and economic independence of the nations, on the basis of respectful attitude toward the sovereign equality of the nations as well as of consistent and unconditional observance of one of the most important principles of the United Nations organization—that is, the principle of unanimity and accord among the Great Powers in taking decisions on the most important problems dealing with maintenance of international peace and security. It is in full accord with the special responsibility of these Powers for the maintenance of universal peace and is a guarantee of the protection of interests of all the members of the United Nations organization, great and small.

The Soviet Union feels it is its duty to resolutely fight against any attempt to shake this principle, no matter under what motives these attempts are made.

. . .

## E. *The American Proposal*

On 21 November 1947, the General Assembly requested its Interim Committee, otherwise known as the 'Little Assembly,' to examine the problem of the veto and report its findings. In this Interim Committee, the United States proposed a list of 31 types of votes to which the veto should not apply. That list is given below. Although the veto has never applied to some of the items listed, it was felt wise to include them in order to avoid future misunderstanding.

(Discussion in the Interim Committee, *Department of State Bulletin,* vol. 18, No. 456, 1948, p. 413.)

1. Decisions with respect to admission of States to membership in the United Nations, pursuant to Article 4 (2).

2. Decisions to bring a question relating to the maintenance of international peace and security before the General Assembly pursuant to Article 11 (2).

3. Decisions to request the recommendation of the General Assembly concerning a matter relating to the maintenance of international peace and security being dealt with by the Security Council pursuant to Article 12 (1).

4. Decisions to cease dealing with a matter relating to the maintenance of international peace and security pursuant to Article 12 (2).

5. Decisions with respect to the consent of the Security Council to the notifications made by the Secretary-General under Article 12 (2).

6. Decisions with respect to the request directed by the Security Council to the Secretary General that he convoke a Special Session of the General Assembly under Article 20.

7. Submission of annual and special reports from the Security Council to the General Assembly pursuant to Article 24 (3).

8. Decisions of the Security Council as to whether a matter is procedural within the meaning of Article 27 (2).

9. Determination of the parties to a dispute and the existence of a dispute for the purpose of deciding whether a Member of the Security Council shall be required to abstain from voting pursuant to Article 27 (3).

10. Decisions concerning the manner of the organization of the Security Council pursuant to Article 28 (1).

11. Decisions concerning the time and place of its regular and periodic meetings pursuant to Article 28 (2) and Article 28 (3).

12. Establishment of subsidiary organs pursuant to Article 29.

13. The election of a President pursuant to Article 30.

14. Adoption of Rules of Procedure pursuant to Article 30.

15. Decisions to permit the participation of Members of the United Nations in the discussion of any question where the Council considers that the interests of the Member are specially affected pursuant to Article 31.

16. Decisions to invite a Member State which is not a Member of the Security Council, or a State not a Member of the United Nations which is a party to a dispute under consideration by the Council, to participate without vote in the discussion relating to the dispute pursuant to Article 32.

17. Decisions with respect to conditions for the participation of a State which is not a Member of the United Nations in the Security Council discussions in accordance with Article 32.

18. Decisions to consider and discuss a matter brought to the attention of the Council.

19. Decisions to call upon the parties to a dispute to settle their disputes by peaceful means of their own choice pursuant to Article 33 (2).

20. Decisions to investigate a dispute or a situation which might lead to international friction or give rise to a dispute, pursuant to Article 34.

21. Decisions to recommend appropriate procedures or methods of adjustment of a dispute or situation endangering the maintenance of international peace and security, pursuant to Article 36 (1).

22. Decisions of the Security Council pursuant to Article 36 (3) to recommend to the parties to a legal dispute that the dispute should be referred by the parties to the International Court of Justice in accordance with provisions of the Statute of the Court.

23. Decisions to make recommendations at the request of all parties to a dispute with a view to its pacific settlement, pursuant to Article 38.

24. Decisions to request assistance from the Economic and Social Council pursuant to Article 65.

25. Reference of a legal question to the International Court of Justice for an advisory opinion pursuant to Article 96 (1).

26. Decision to convoke a conference to review the Charter prior to the Tenth Annual Session of the General Assembly pursuant to Article 109 (1).

27. Decision to convoke a conference to review the Charter subsequent to the Tenth Annual Session of the General Assembly pursuant to Article 109 (3).

28. Election of judges of the International Court of Justice pursuant to Article 4 (1), Article 10 (1) of the Statute of the Court. [Article 10 (2) of the Statute.]

29. Decisions of the Security Council determining the conditions under which a State which is a party to the present Statute of the International Court of Justice, but which is not a Member of the United Nations, may participate in electing the Members of the Court pursuant to Article 4 (3) of the Statute of the Court.

30. Appointment of conferees in connection with election of judges of the International Court of Justice pursuant to Article 12 of the Statute of the Court. [Article 10 (2) of the Statute.]

31. Determination of the date of election of judges of the International Court of Justice pursuant to Article 14 of the Statute of the Court.

## F. *Statement on the American Proposal*

The American deputy representative in the Interim Committee, Philip C. Jessup, has made the following statements in support of the proposals of the United States for a modification of the veto.

(P. C. Jessup, Statement, *Department of State Bulletin*, vol. xviii, No. 456, 1948, pp. 416-17.)

We have submitted a list of Security Council decisions which in our view should as a matter of principle be made by any seven members of the Security Council; in other words, where there should be no veto. I shall not comment in detail at this time on this list. It suffices to say that a number of these decisions are well-established as procedural in the practice of the Security Council and that in other instances a voting procedure not involving the veto is prescribed by the Charter. However, the list of categories of decisions also includes a number of decisions where either no precedent as to voting procedure has as yet been established in the Security Council or where, under existing practice of the Council, a negative vote by a permanent member has been considered a veto. It would perhaps be appropriate to note at this time two or three of the more important of these decisions where we firmly believe that the voting procedure should be liberalized.

In the first place, there is the question of applications for membership. This is item 1 on our list. Ten of the 23 vetoes in the Security Council have related to membership problems. This is not the time nor place for recriminations but I would be less than frank if I failed to point to the most flagrant example of the abuse of the veto, the veto of Italy's membership application by the Soviet Union not once but two times. This was done in the face of overwhelming support for Italy's application in the Security Council and later in the General Assembly. This leads inescapably to the conclusion that the Soviet vetoes of the Italian United Nations membership application can be interpreted only as an expression of lack of friendship of the Soviet Union for the people of Italy. A way must be found to make such an injustice impossible. The Italian people must not be denied the right of United Nations membership which they so richly deserve. It should be noted that one phase of the membership problem has been referred by the General Assembly to the International Court of Justice for an advisory opinion. The Court's opinion, when it is given, should be of assistance in this study.

We have also suggested the elimination of the veto in connection with most of the decisions of the Security Council arising under chapter VI which relates to the pacific settlement of disputes. The Secretary of State in his address to the General Assembly indicated that the United States would be willing to accept the restriction or elimination of the veto in connection with all decisions under chapter VI. We have not, however, at this time, suggested its elimination in connection with the Security Council's authority under article 37 (2) to recommend terms of settlement of disputes. While the United States would be willing to accept the elimination of the veto in connection with the Security Council's recommendations under article 37 (2), nevertheless, as was pointed out by Mr. Dulles to the First Committee of the General Assembly in his statement of November 18, this provision raises certain special problems. Therefore, pending further study, by the Interim Committee, the United States did not include this provision in its list.

We are also suggesting that the veto should never be utilized to prevent the Security Council from obtaining assistance from other organs of the United Nations: the General Assembly, the Economic and Social Council, the International Court of Justice. We believe that the firm establishment of this principle would result in greater coordination of the work of the various organs of the United Nations and would be of great assistance to the Security Council.

It should be emphasized that the list of categories of Security Council decisions which the United States proposes should be made by affirmative vote of seven members, is strictly a provisional list. . .

The second part of the United States proposal relates to consultation among permanent members. The United States suggests that the 'Interim Committee should recommend to the General Assembly that in order to improve the functioning of the Security Council, the General Assembly recommend to the Permanent Members of the Security Council that whenever feasible, consultations should take place among them concerning important decisions to be taken by the Security Council.' Even in the event of substantial liberalization of voting procedures as is contemplated in the first part of the United States proposal, it is still desirable that there should be agreement and there will be many decisions of the Security Council which require agreement among the permanent members. Consultations on such decisions, and also on some important decisions not requiring unanimity, should take place whenever feasible; that is, whenever they are likely to produce constructive results. . .

## V. Military Forces for the United Nations

Chapter VII of the United Nations Charter provides for the application of sanctions—diplomatic, economic, and military—against states committing aggression or breaking the peace. In order to place the military sanctions on a working basis, the Military Staff Committee, described in Article 47, was asked to devise plans that would make force available. After extended deliberation, the Military Staff Committee issued its first report on 3 May 1947. The report showed that the five Great Powers on the Committee had been unable to agree on many important matters, including the following: (1) the size and proportion of ground, naval, and air forces to be provided; (2) the size of the contingents to be furnished by individual nations; (3) the method of choosing a supreme commander; and (4) the provision of military and naval bases by United Nations members. The extract given below is a statement of general principles upon which agreement was reached, together with other statements that had the support of only a part of the Committee.

(Text from *The New York Times*, 4 May 1947.)

## GENERAL PRINCIPLES

### I. PURPOSE OF ARMED FORCES

#### ARTICLE 1

Armed forces made available to the Security Council by member nations of the United Nations are intended for the maintenance of the restoration of international peace and security in cases:

(a) of existence of any threat to international peace;
(b) of any breach of international peace and security;
(c) of any act of aggression,

when measures undertaken by the Security Council in accordance with Article 41 of the United Nations Charter would be inadequate or have proved to be inadequate and when the threat to international peace and security is such that it necessitates the employment of these armed forces.

#### ARTICLE 2

These armed forces may not be employed for purposes inconsistent with the purposes, principles and spirit of the United Nations Charter as defined in its Preamble and Chapter I.

### II. COMPOSITION OF ARMED FORCES

#### ARTICLE 3

Armed forces made available to the Security Council by member nations of the United Nations in accordance with Article 43 of the Charter shall be composed of units (formations) of national armed forces, land, sea and air, which are normally maintained as components of armed forces of member nations of the United Nations.

#### ARTICLE 4

These armed forces shall be made available to the Security Council from the best trained and equipped units (formations) of member nations of the United Nations.

### III. OVER-ALL STRENGTH OF ARMED FORCES

#### ARTICLE 5

The moral weight and the potential power behind any decision to employ the armed forces made available to the Security Council by member nations of the United Nations in enforcement action will be very great, and this fact will directly influence the size of the armed forces required.

#### ARTICLE 6

The armed forces made available to the Security Council by member nations of the United Nations shall be limited to strength sufficient to enable the Security Council to take prompt action in any part of the world for the maintenance or the restoration of international peace and security as envisaged in Article 42 of the Charter.

#### ARTICLE 7

Accepted by the Chinese, French, United Kingdom and United States Delegations: An estimate of the over-all strength of the armed forces and the strength of the services, land, sea and air, constituting those forces will be made by the Security Council with the assistance of the Military Staff Committee, and used as a basis for negotiating the special agreements referred to in Article 43 of the Charter. The final decision regarding the over-all strength required will be made by the Security Council as a result of these negotiations.

The Union of Soviet Socialist Republics delegation accepts Article 7 conditionally. The final acceptance of Article

7 by the U.S.S.R. delegation will depend on the acceptance by the other delegations of the principle of equality regarding strength and composition of armed forces contributed by the five permanent members of the Security Council, as stated in the proposal by the U.S.S.R. delegation for Article 11.

## ARTICLE 8

Accepted by the Chinese, French, United Kingdom and United States Delegations: In order to adapt the over-all strength of the armed forces to international conditions, this over-all strength and the strength of the services constituting these forces may be changed on the initiative of the Security Council by additional agreements between the Security Council and the member nations of the United Nations.

The U.S.S.R. delegation accepts Article 8 conditionally. The final acceptance of Article 8 by the U.S.S.R. delegation will depend on the acceptance by the other delegations of the principle of equality regarding strength and composition of armed forces contributed by the five permanent members of the Security Council, as stated in the proposal by the U.S.S.R. delegation for Article 11.

## IV. CONTRIBUTION OF ARMED FORCES BY MEMBER NATIONS

### ARTICLE 9

All member nations shall have the opportunity as well as the obligation to place armed forces, facilities and other assistance at the disposal of the Security Council on its call and in accordance with their capabilities and the requirements of the Security Council.

### ARTICLE 10

In order to facilitate the early establishment of the armed forces made available to the Security Council, the permanent members of the Security Council shall contribute initially the major portion of these forces. As the contributions of other nations of the United Nations become available, they shall be added to the forces already contributed.

### ARTICLE 11

Accepted by the Chinese, French, United Kingdom and United States delegations: Each of the five permanent members of the Security Council will make a comparable initial over-all contribution to the armed forces made available to the Security Council by member nations of the United Nations. In view of the difference in size and composition of national forces of each permanent member and in order to further the ability of the Security Council to constitute balanced and effective combat forces for operations, these contributions may differ widely as to the strength of the separate components, land, sea and air.

Accepted by the U.S.S.R. delegation: Permanent members of the Security Council shall make available armed forces (land, sea and air) on the principle of equality regarding the over-all strength and the composition of these forces. In individual instances, deviations from this principle are permitted by special decisions of the Security Council, if such a desire is expressed by a permanent member of the Security Council.

### ARTICLE 12

The size and composition of contributions of individual member nations will be determined on the initiative of the Security Council, and on the advice of the Military Staff Committee, in the process of negotiations with each member nation in accordance with Article 43 of the Charter.

### ARTICLE 13

No member nation of the United Nations shall be urged to increase the strength of its armed forces or to create a particular component thereof for the specific purpose of making a contribution to the armed forces made available to the Security Council by member nations of the United Nations.

### ARTICLE 14

Contributions by member nations of the United Nations, other than the permanent members of the Security Council, may not necessarily be represented by armed forces. Such other member nations which may be unable to furnish armed forces may fulfill their obligation to the United Nations by furnishing facilities and other assistance in accordance with agreements reached with the Security Council.

### ARTICLE 15

Proposals for changes in the size or composition of contributions of a member nation or a group of nations may be initiated by the Security Council or by the member nation or group of nations. Any change in contributions will be effected by additional agreements between the Security Council and the respective member nation or group of nations.

### ARTICLE 16

Accepted by the Chinese, French, United Kingdom and United States delegations: The strength and composition of national air force contributions made available to the Security Council shall be determined as set forth in Article 12 above, taking into account the obligations arising from Article 45 of the Charter.

Accepted by the U.S.S.R. delegation: The strength and composition of national air force contingents made available to the Security Council by member nations for action envisaged in Article 45 of the Charter are determined by the Security Council, with the assistance of the Military Staff Committee, within the limits of a special agreement or agreements referred to in Article 43 of the Charter.

### ARTICLE 17

Accepted by the Chinese and French delegations: In case of self-defense (Article 51 of the Charter) and of national emergencies, member nations will have the right to make use of armed forces, which they have made available to the Security Council in conformity with the terms of special agreements. They undertake, however, to assume anew all of their obligations within the shortest possible space of time.

Not accepted by the U.S.S.R., United Kingdom and United States delegations.

## V. EMPLOYMENT OF ARMED FORCES

### ARTICLE 18

The armed forces made available to the Security Council by member nations of the United Nations will be employed, in whole or in part, only by the decision of the Security Council and only for the period necessary for the fulfillment of the tasks envisaged in Article 42 of the Charter.

### ARTICLE 19

In view of the military advantages which would accrue, the employment of the armed forces under Article 42 of the Charter should, whenever possible, be initiated in time to forestall or to suppress promptly a breach of the peace or an act of aggression.

## ARTICLE 20

Accepted by the Chinese, French, United Kingdom and United States delegations: After the armed forces, including line of communication forces, made available to the Security Council have carried out the tasks with which they have been entrusted by the Security Council under Article 42 of the Charter, they shall be withdrawn as soon as possible to the general locations governed by the special agreement or agreements provided for by Article 43 of the Charter. The time for the beginning and completion of the withdrawal shall be fixed by the Security Council.

Accepted by the U.S.S.R. delegation: The armed forces will be withdrawn to their own territories and territorial waters within a time-limit of thirty to ninety days after they have fulfilled the measures envisaged in Article 42 of the Charter, unless otherwise decided by the Security Council. This time-limit should be provided for in agreements concluded under Article 43 of the Charter.

## ARTICLE 21

Not accepted by the Chinese, French, United Kingdom and United States delegations.

Accepted by the U.S.S.R. delegation: If for any reasons these armed forces remain in territories or territorial waters granted for the use of such forces, under agreements between the Security Council and other member nations of the United Nations for the passage, stationing or action of these forces, they should be withdrawn to their own territories or territorial waters not later than thirty days after the expiration of the period indicated in Article 20 (see proposal by the U.S.S.R. delegation), unless otherwise decided by the Security Council. This time-limit should be provided for in agreements

concluded under Article 43 of the Charter.

## VI. DEGREE OF READINESS OF ARMED FORCES

## ARTICLE 22

The degree of readiness of the armed forces made available by individual member nations of the United Nations is fixed by the Security Council, on the advice of the Military Staff Committee, as a result of the negotiations in concluding the special agreements with those member nations under Article 43 of the Charter.

## ARTICLE 23

The degree of readiness of the armed forces should be maintained at a level which will enable these forces to start in good time with the fulfillment of the Security Council measures envisaged in Article 42 of the Charter.

## ARTICLE 24

These armed forces should be either maintained in readiness for combat or brought up to readiness for combat within the time limits to be specified in the special agreements.

## ARTICLE 25

Accepted by the Chinese, French, United Kingdom and United States delegations: The degree of readiness of national air force contingents should be maintained at a level which will enable the United Nations to take urgent military measures in accordance with the provisions of Article 45 of the Charter.

Accepted by the U.S.S.R. delegation: The degree of readiness of national air force contingents made available to the Security Council by member nations for action envisaged in Article 45 of the Charter are determined by the Security Council, with the assistance of the Military Staff Committee, within the limits of a special agreement or agreements referred to in Article 43 of the Charter.

## VII. PROVISION OF ASSISTANCE AND FACILITIES, INCLUDING RIGHTS OF PASSAGE, FOR ARMED FORCES

### ARTICLE 26

Accepted by the Chinese, United Kingdom and United States delegations: The special agreements between the Security Council and member nations under Article 43 of the Charter shall include the following:

(A) A general guarantee of rights of passage and of the use of such of the member nations' available bases as are required by armed forces operating under the Security Council;

(B) Specific provisions covering details of bases and other assistance and facilities, including rights of passage, which member nations agree to make available to the Security Council on its call. Such specific provisions may be contained in the original agreement or in subsequent agreements under Article 43 of the Charter to be concluded at the appropriate time.

Accepted by the French delegation: Special agreements envisaged in Article 43 of the Charter will indicate bases, assistance and facilities, including the right of passage, which the member nations will put at the disposal of the Security Council on its call. In case of necessity, member nations undertake, on call of the Security Council and through additional special agreements, to make available to it, other bases, assistance and facilities which would have proved necessary to the operations undertaken. Specific agree-

ments, concluded at the appropriate time, between the Security Council and the member nation concerned, will indicate the duration and the other conditions involved in the exercise of rights thus extended to the armed forces operating under the direction of the Security Council.

Accepted by the U.S.S.R. delegation: Special agreements envisaged in Article 43 of the Charter will indicate assistance and facilities, including the rights of passage, which the member nations will make available to the Security Council on its call and in accordance with specific agreements concluded between the Security Council and the member nations concerned. Specific agreements, concluded at the appropriate time between the Security Council and the member nation concerned, will indicate the duration and the other conditions involved in the exercise of rights thus extended to the armed forces operating under the direction of the Security Council.

### ARTICLE 27

Accepted by the Chinese, French, United Kingdom and United States delegations: A member nation will retain its national sovereignty, and its control and command over bases and other facilities placed at the disposal of the Security Council.

Not accepted by the U.S.S.R. delegation.

### ARTICLE 28

Accepted by the Chinese, French, United Kingdom and United States delegations.

Not accepted by the U.S.S.R. delegation. If additional contributions from permanent members of the Security Council are requested when enforcement action under Chapter VII of the Charter is under consideration, those contributions should also be of comparable size, taking into account the value of assistance and facilities as well as armed forces which any of the above member nations may provide.

## VIII. LOGISTICAL SUPPORT OF ARMED FORCES

### ARTICLE 29

Member nations of the United Nations which, in accordance with special agreements, have placed armed forces at the disposal of the Security Council on its call for the carrying out of measures envisaged in Article 42 of the Charter, will provide their respective forces with all necessary replacements in personnel and equipment and with all necessary supplies and transport.

### ARTICLE 30

Each member nation will at all times maintain a specified level of reserves to replace initial personnel, transport, equipment, spare parts, ammunition and all other forms of supply for the forces which it has agreed to place at the disposal of the Security Council on its call. This reserve level will be prescribed in the special agreements under Article 43 of the Charter.

### ARTICLE 31

Accepted by the Chinese, United Kingdom and United States delegations: Member nations, in the event of inability to discharge to the full extent their responsibilities under Article 29 above, may invoke the aid of the Security Council, which, on the advice of the Military Staff Committee, will negotiate with other appropriate member nations for the provision of such assistance as it deems necessary. The agreement of member nations concerned must be obtained by the Security Council before the deficiencies in the contribution of one member nation can be made up by transfers from the contribution of another member nation.

Accepted by the French and U.S.S.R. delegations: Deviations from the principle stated in Article 29 above shall be permitted in individual instances at the request of a member nation, by special decisions of the Security Council on the advice of the Military Staff Committee, if this member nation desires to have supplies and transport made available to it for the proper provision of the armed forces placed by this member nation at the disposal of the Security Council.

## IX. GENERAL LOCATION OF ARMED FORCES

### ARTICLE 32

Accepted by the Chinese, United Kingdom and United States delegations: Armed forces made available to the Security Council by member nations when not employed by the Security Council will within the terms of special agreements referred to in Article 43 of the Charter be based at the discretion of member nations in any territories or waters to which they have legal right of access.

Accepted by the French delegation: When they are not employed by the Security Council, the armed forces which the member nation undertakes to make available to the Security Council, on its call, are stationed in the general locations governed by the special agreement or agreements concluded between the Security Council and the member nation under Article 43 of the Charter:

(1) either within the national borders of the member nation or the territories or waters under its jurisdiction;

(2) or within the territory or waters of ex-enemy nations under Article 107

of the Charter or under the terms of the peace treaties;

(3) or within the territory or waters of other nations where armed forces have access under international agreements registered with the United Nations secretariat and published by it in accordance with Article 102 of the Charter;

(4) or in certain strategic areas specified by the Security Council and which have been the subject of specific agreements between the Security Council and the member nation under Articles 82 and 83 of the Charter.

Accepted by the U.S.S.R. delegation: Armed forces made available to the Security Council by member nations of the United Nations shall be garrisoned within the frontiers of the contributing member nations' own territories or territorial waters except in cases envisaged in Article 107 of the Charter.

### ARTICLE 33

Accepted by the Chinese, French, United Kingdom and United States delegations: The locations of these armed forces should be so distributed geographically as to enable the Security Council to take prompt action in any part of the world for the maintenance or restoration of international peace and security.

Not accepted by the U.S.S.R. delegation.

### ARTICLE 34

Accepted by the Chinese, French, United Kingdom and United States delegations.

Not accepted by the U.S.S.R. delegation. Any displacement of forces likely to modify their availability as governed by the special agreement or agreements shall be brought to the notice of the Security Council.

### ARTICLE 35

The armed forces made available to the Security Council by members of the United Nations, on its call, for the fulfillment of measures envisaged in Article 42 of the Charter will be based, during the carrying out of these measures, in areas designated by the Security Council.

## X. STRATEGIC DIRECTION AND COMMAND OF ARMED FORCES

### ARTICLE 36

The armed forces which member nations of the United Nations agree to make available to the Security Council shall be under the exclusive command of the respective contributing nations, except when operating under the Security Council.

### ARTICLE 37

When these forces are called upon for the fulfillment of measures envisaged in Article 42 of the Charter, they shall come under the control of the Security Council.

### ARTICLE 38

During the period these armed forces are employed by the Security Council, the Military Staff Committee shall be responsible, under the Security Council, for their strategic direction. The time and place at which the Military Staff Committee will assume or relinquish strategic direction will be designated by the Security Council.

### ARTICLE 39

The command of national contingents will be exercised by commanders appointed by the respective member nations. These contingents will retain their national character and will be subject at all times to the discipline and regulations in force in their own national armed forces.

## ARTICLE 40

The commanders of national contingencies will be entitled to communicate directly with the authorities of their own country on all matters.

## ARTICLE 41

Accepted by the Chinese, U.S.S.R. and United States delegations. An over-all commander or over-all commanders of armed forces made available to the Security Council may be appointed by the latter, on the advice of the Military Staff Committee, for the period of employment of these forces by the Security Council.

Accepted by the French and United Kingdom delegations: A supreme commander or supreme commanders of armed forces made available to the Security Council may be appointed by the latter, on the advice of the Military Staff Committee, for the period of employment of these forces by the Security Council. Commanders-in-Chief of land, sea or air forces acting under the supreme commander or commanders mentioned above may be appointed by the Security Council on the advice of the Military Staff Committee.

## VI. NEW ATTEMPTS TO REGULATE ARMAMENTS

Several attempts were made between the two World Wars to limit state power by the regulation of armaments. Reference is made to these attempts in Chapter 2. Since World War II there has been a renewal of the disarmament discussion, this time within the United Nations. The first statement that follows is a resolution on disarmament unanimously adopted by the United Nations General Assembly in 1946. The second reveals the attitude of the United States toward the problem.

### A. *Disarmament and the United Nations*

(Principles Governing General Regulation and Reduction of Armaments, a resolution adopted by the United Nations General Assembly on 14 December 1946, *Department of State Bulletin,* vol. xv, No. 390, 1946, pp. 1137-8.)

1. In pursuance of Article 11 of the Charter and with a view to strengthening international peace and security in conformity with the Purposes and Principles of the United Nations,
*The General Assembly recognizes* the necessity of an early general regulation and reduction of armaments and armed forces.

2. Accordingly, *The General Assembly recommends* that the Security Council give prompt consideration to formulating the practical measures, according to their priority, which are essential to provide for the general regulation and reduction of armaments and armed forces and to assure that such regulation and reduction of armaments and armed forces will be generally observed by all participants and not unilaterally by only some of the participants. The plans formulated by the Security Council shall be submitted by the Secretary General to the Members of the United Nations for consideration at a special session of the General Assembly. The treaties or conventions approved by the General Assembly shall be submitted to the signatory States for ratification in accordance with Article 26 of the Charter.

3. As an essential step towards the urgent objective of prohibiting and elimi-

nating from national armaments atomic and all other major weapons adaptable now and in the future to mass destruction, and the early establishment of international control of atomic energy and other modern scientific discoveries and technical developments to ensure their use only for peaceful purposes,

*The General Assembly urges* the expeditious fulfilment by the Atomic Energy Commission of its terms of reference as set forth in Section 5 of the General Assembly Resolution of 24 January 1946.

4. In order to ensure that the general prohibition, regulation and reduction of armaments are directed towards the major weapons of modern warfare and not merely towards the minor weapons,

*The General Assembly recommends* that the Security Council expedite consideration of the reports which the Atomic Energy Commission will make to the Security Council and that it facilitate the work of that Commission, and also that the Security Council expedite consideration of a draft convention or conventions for the creation of an international system of control and inspection, these conventions to include the prohibition of atomic and all other major weapons adaptable now and in the future to mass destruction and the control of atomic energy to the extent necessary to ensure its use only for peaceful purposes.

5. *The General Assembly further recognizes* that essential to the general regulation and reduction of armaments and armed forces is the provision of practical and effective safeguards by way of inspection and other means to protect complying states against the hazards of violations and evasions.

Accordingly,

*The General Assembly recommends* to the Security Council that it give prompt consideration to the working out of proposals to provide such practical and effective safeguards in connection with the control of atomic energy and the regulation and reduction of armaments.

6. To ensure the adoption of measures for the early general regulation and reduction of armaments and armed forces, for the prohibition of the use of atomic energy for military purposes and the elimination from national armaments of atomic and all other major weapons adaptable now or in the future to mass destruction, and for the control of atomic energy to the extent necessary to ensure its use only for peaceful purposes,

*There shall be established* within the framework of the Security Council, which bears the primary responsibility for the maintenance of international peace and security, an international system, as mentioned in paragraph 4, operating through special organs, which organs shall derive their powers and status from the convention or conventions under which they are established.

7. *The General Assembly,* regarding the problem of security as closely connected with that of disarmament, *recommends* the Security Council to accelerate as much as possible the placing at its disposal of the armed forces mentioned in Article 43 of the Charter;

*It recommends* the members to undertake the progressive and balanced withdrawal, taking account of the needs of occupation, of their armed forces stationed in ex-enemy territories, and the withdrawal without delay of armed forces stationed in the territories of Members without their consent freely and publicly expressed in treaties or agreements consistent with the Charter and not contradicting international agreements;

*It further recommends* a corresponding reduction of national armed forces, and a general progressive and balanced reduction of national armed forces.

8. Nothing herein contained shall alter or limit the resolution of the General As-

sembly passed on 24 January 1946, creating the Atomic Energy Commission.

9. *The General Assembly calls* upon all Members of the United Nations to render every possible assistance to the Security Council and the Atomic Energy Commission in order to promote the establishment and maintenance of international peace and collective security with the least diversion for armaments of the world's human and economic resources.

## B. *The United States Attitude*

(*Building the Peace,* No. 13, 1947, State Department Publication No. 2936.)

The development of increasingly powerful weapons of war has resulted in the realization by peoples throughout the world that if civilization is to survive nations must reach effective agreement on the regulation of armaments. With the discovery of atomic energy it became clear that unless there is international control of this most powerful of known forces its use in another war may result in greater destruction than any the world has yet experienced.

At the same time, international security remains only partly organized. Hence not even the prospect of atomic war is sufficient to cause peoples and nations to abandon their reliance on national armaments for security.

In the present uncertain state of world affairs, many nations feel it necessary to their security to maintain large armies and costly armaments. Although there is growing recognition among all nations that security depends upon the maintenance of stable world economic conditions as well as upon adequate armaments and armed forces, the burden of supporting large military forces adds to the difficulties of peoples who are attempting to rebuild economies seriously dislocated by the recent war.

In order to achieve economic stability many nations would like to reduce their present large expenditures for such unproductive purposes as defense forces and armaments programs. The difficulty arises from differences over how best to achieve that objective and still insure the security of each nation. . .

Judging the present and future by the past, the United States takes the position that the creation of adequate international safeguards for its security is an indispensable prerequisite to any program for the regulation and reduction of armaments and armed forces. This policy reflects in large measure past experience in which the United States reduced armaments without obtaining adequate safeguards for our security. In 1922 this country signed the Washington naval agreements, and in fulfilment of our commitments, we sank our battleships and stopped building cruisers. We also subscribed to and faithfully observed the London Naval Conference agreement of 1930. In doing so, we limited the construction of submarines and restricted the elevation and caliber of naval guns.

Both these efforts to regulate armaments, in which we acted in good faith and with what we believed to be the cooperation of other powers, proved to be not only ineffectual but also actually prejudicial to our own security. We learned that Japan, which had signed those agreements, had ignored the naval-gun limitations and, contrary to the letter and spirit of the treaties, had secretly built ships. Germany scrapped the Versailles Treaty; it clandestinely assembled a war machine that was defeated at the sacrifice of American lives and with an enormous expenditure of American dollars for equipment and war materials.

These experiences have convinced the United States of the futility and the peril of attempting to regulate armaments without obtaining the strongest possible security safeguards in return. The United States considers, on the other hand, that its record concerning this problem not only conclusively demonstrates its sincerity of purpose but also justifies insistence upon collective security in the modern world. . .

There are other compelling reasons for a cautious approach to the problem. First, events leading up to our participation in both world wars taught us that insecurity anywhere in the world is a threat to security everywhere. Until the manifestations of unrest apparent in the world today are eliminated, the United States dares not, on a unilateral basis, reduce its national defenses below the present scant margin of safety.

Secondly, the peace treaties with Germany and Japan as well as with Austria, which are essential for tranquillity in the future, have not yet been concluded. Until they are, collective security cannot be regarded as assured.

Thirdly, victory in World War II increased, rather than diminished, the responsibilities and commitments of the United States for world security. We are committed to a major role in the occupation and administration of Japan and Germany for an indefinite period, and to applying policies that will deprive those nations of the means of making war in the future. We must maintain supply lines to our occupation forces abroad and must, of course, meet our own normal defense requirements.

Finally, and as certainly not the least of our international obligations, the United States must exert a stabilizing and constructive influence as one of the founders and foremost members of the United Nations. Article 43 of the Charter provides for the negotiation of agreements by which the members will make available to the United Nations, if need be, armed forces for purposes of enforcing peace by military means. The United States considers the conclusion of these agreements one of the essential requirements for safeguarding collective security. This country expects to hold forces in readiness subject to call by the United Nations under Article 43. American representatives on the Military Staff Committee of the United Nations, in general agreement with those of the United Kingdom, France, and China, have recommended an organization plan for armed forces to be made available to the Security Council, but the representatives of the Soviet Union have disagreed on major issues to such an extent that fulfilment of the terms of Article 43 has thus far been impossible. . .

In the United Nations, this Government has directed its major effort on armament regulation toward obtaining agreement on atomic energy. It believes that once this goal has been reached regulation of conventional armaments and armed forces can also be achieved.

Here too the United States insists upon the establishment of adequate security safeguards before undertaking regulation of conventional armaments. Two other conditions viewed by the United States as necessary prior to actual regulation are the creation of international security forces under the United Nations and the elimination for all time of the ability of our World War II foes to wage war.

## VII. The Future of the United Nations

In his first report, Secretary-General Trygvie Lie made the following observations, which are still valid, in regard to the future development of the United Nations:

(*Report of the Secretary-General on the Work of the Organization*, United Nations Document No. A/65, 30 June 1946, pp. v-vi.)

Has the United Nations succeeded in capturing the imagination and in harnessing the enthusiasm of the peoples of the world? I, for one, do not feel that it has done so in the degree that might be hoped for. What is the explanation, and what measures can, or should, be taken?

Part of the explanation lies no doubt in the inevitable slowness of United Nations proceedings at this stage which, in turn, is due to preoccupation with matters of procedure and organization. Much could be done to 'educate' public opinion to appreciate more fully the significance of the often undramatic but fundamental work that is being performed, and the fact that many of our difficulties are of a temporary character. The world is in the midst of a giant post-war upheaval, its economic life is dislocated, many regions still present a picture of distress and destruction, and many political frontiers and forms of government, as well as the terms of the peace settlement, are still undecided. It is too often overlooked that while such conditions remain, the working of the Charter system will inevitably be affected.

In this educative process, the Secretariat can certainly contribute, and I trust that, with the assistance of Members, the work of the Public Information Services may be substantially expanded in the near future. I should wish it to give attention to bringing home the immense promise of the work already accomplished in the economic and social fields, to which public interest has not yet been fully awakened. I should wish it also to correct certain widespread misunderstandings of the Charter and the functions and limitations of the Organization as laid down in that document. . .

The fact that the Charter gave the right of veto to each of these permanent Members imposes upon them an obligation to seek agreement among themselves. Many of the issues which have come before the Security Council have arisen from inability to reach such agreement.

While the United Nations must take responsibility for its success or failure to fulfil its functions as laid down in the Charter, it cannot properly be held responsible for inability to achieve goals which by the terms of the Charter may not be within its reach.

I should be failing in my duty, in presenting this report, if I did not emphasize the absolute necessity that the Powers should seek agreement among themselves, in a spirit of mutual understanding and a will to compromise, and not abandon their efforts until such agreement has been reached.

Misunderstanding of our problems and discouragement with the results so far achieved may also be attributed, in no small degree, to a lack of historical perspective in surveying the world as we find it today. Without excusing our failure to settle our problems more rapidly, it must be understood that any war on a world-scale is bound to bring vast problems in its wake and that many of these problems demand careful and methodical treatment. It is unquestionably better that time be employed in the proper settlement of controversies when hasty agreement could only lead to future trouble.

We may find some source of encouragement and inspiration for the successful settlement of our difficulties, by recalling that in certain important respects the international situation in 1919 and 1920 was more serious than it is today. And the very existence of the United Nations is now a factor of inestimable value. If anyone doubts this, he has only to ask himself what would now be the state of relationships between peoples and the prospects for the peace of the world if the United Nations were not in being. There is no cause for discouragement, still less for pessimism. But are there not nevertheless very real dangers facing us?

Has not the lively desire of all peoples and governments to establish the authority of the United Nations, and to combine their efforts in achieving the victories of peace, sometimes been impeded by a lack of mutual trust among the Members of the Organization?

The United Nations is no stronger than the collective will of the nations that support it. Of itself it can do nothing. It is a machinery through which the nations can co-operate. It can be used and developed in the light of its activities and experience, to the untold benefit of humanity, or it can be discarded and broken. As in the control of atomic power, the choice is between life and death. The failure of the United Nations would mean the failure of peace, the triumph of destruction. . .

# 4

# REGIONALISM AND THE UNITED NATIONS

R EGIONALISM is based on the assumption that geographic propinquity among a group of states gives rise to a community of interests and problems. Nations often carry on a large volume of trade with their neighbors and they are more concerned with the security problems within their immediate community than with those in other parts of the world. Pan-Americanism is cited as an example of what a group of nations—twenty-one of them in this case, all inhabiting the Western Hemisphere—may do. Admitting the constructive possibilities of regionalism, the United Nations Charter provides in Article 52 that 'Nothing in the present Charter precludes the existence of regional arrangements or agencies for dealing with such matters relating to the maintenance of international peace and security as are appropriate for regional action, provided that such arrangements or agencies and their activities are consistent with the purposes and principles of the United Nations.'

Opponents of the principle look upon regionalism as a form of isolation and contend that all major international problems are world-wide in their bearings. They insist that the British Commonwealth of Nations, one of the most effective co-operative organizations in existence, is in no sense a geographic region. They argue, too, that Pan-Americanism has no geographic basis.

Yet the trend toward regionalism since World War II has been quickened. Later in Chapter 7 almost a score of alliance treaties, concluded during 1942-8 between the Soviet Union and its neighbors in Eastern Europe or among these states themselves, are noted. In effect this new Soviet alliance system constitutes a regional arrangement despite the lack of any formal designation of it as such. It is perhaps only natural that the world-wide struggle between East and West should have given rise to regional groupings of this nature.

The emergence of the Western European Union, created by the Brussels Pact of 17 March 1948, was another indication of this trend. Still more significant is the North Atlantic Pact, signed at Washington, D. C., 4 April 1949, by the representatives of twelve nations—Belgium, Canada, Denmark, France, Iceland, Italy, Luxembourg, the Netherlands, Norway, Portugal, the United Kingdom, and the United States. As stipulated in Article 5, the Pact is designed as a measure of individual and collective self-defense under Article 51 of the Charter. Using the term 'North Atlantic area' in several places and 'regional arrangements' in Article 12, the makers of the Pact imply that it is a regional agreement under Article 52 of the Charter. On the other hand, Russia, charging that the alliance was made against her, contends that there is no need for self-defense and denies that the signatory states constitute a region in the sense of the Charter.

## TEXT OF ATLANTIC DEFENSE TREATY

### PREAMBLE

The parties to this treaty reaffirm their faith in the purposes and principles of the Charter of the United Nations and their desire to live in peace with all peoples and all governments.

They are determined to safeguard the freedom, common heritage and civilization of their peoples, founded on the principles of democracy, individual liberty and the rule of law.

They seek to promote stability and well-being in the North Atlantic area.

They are resolved to unite their efforts for collective defense and for the preservation of peace and security.

They therefore agree to this North Atlantic Treaty:

### ARTICLE 1

The parties undertake, as set forth in the Charter of the United Nations, to settle any international disputes in which they may be involved by peaceful means in such a manner that international peace and security, and justice, are not endangered, and to refrain in their international relations from the threat or use of force in any manner inconsistent with the purposes of the United Nations.

### ARTICLE 2

The parties will contribute toward the further development of peaceful and friendly international relations by strengthening their free institutions, by bringing about a better understanding of the principles upon which these institutions are founded, and by promoting conditions of stability and well-being. They will seek to eliminate conflict in their international economic policies and will encourage economic collaboration between any or all of them.

### ARTICLE 3

In order more effectively to achieve the objectives of this treaty, the parties, separately and jointly, by means of continuous and effective self-help and mutual aid, will maintain and develop their individual and collective capacity to resist armed attack.

### ARTICLE 4

The parties will consult together whenever, in the opinion of any of them, the territorial integrity, political independence or security of any of the parties is threatened.

### ARTICLE 5

The parties agree that an armed attack against one or more of them in Europe or North America shall be considered an attack against them all; and consequently they agree that, if such an armed attack occurs, each of them, in exercise of the right of individual or collective self-defense recognized by Article 51 of the Charter of the United Nations, will assist the party or parties so attacked by taking forthwith, individually and in concert with the other parties, such action as it deems necessary, including the use of armed force, to restore and maintain the security of the North Atlantic area.

Any such armed attack and all measures taken as a result thereof shall immediately be reported to the Security Council. Such measures shall be terminated when the Security Council has taken the measures necessary to restore and maintain international peace and security.

## ARTICLE 6

For the purpose of Article 5 an armed attack on one or more of the parties is deemed to include an armed attack on the territory of any of the parties in Europe or North America, on the Algerian Departments of France, on the occupation forces of any party in Europe, on the islands under the jurisdiction of any party in the North Atlantic area north of the Tropic of Cancer or on the vessels or aircraft in this area of any of the parties.

## ARTICLE 7

This treaty does not affect, and shall not be interpreted as affecting, in any way the rights and obligations under the Charter of the parties which are members of the United Nations, or the primary responsibility of the Security Council for the maintenance of international peace and security.

## ARTICLE 8

Each party declares that none of the international engagements now in force between it and any other of the parties or any third state is in conflict with the provisions of this treaty, and undertakes not to enter into any international engagement in conflict with this treaty.

## ARTICLE 9

The parties hereby establish a Council, on which each of them shall be represented, to consider matters concerning the implementation of this treaty. The Council shall be so organized as to be able to meet promptly at any time. The Council shall set up such subsidiary bodies as may be necessary; in particular it shall establish immediately a defense committee which shall recommend measures for the implementation of Articles 3 and 5.

## ARTICLE 10

The parties may, by unanimous agreement, invite any other European state in a position to further the principles of this treaty and to contribute to the security of the North Atlantic area to accede to this treaty. Any state so invited may become a party to the treaty by depositing its instrument of accession with the Government of the United States of America. The Government of the United States of America will inform each of the parties of the deposit of each such instrument of accession.

## ARTICLE 11

This treaty shall be ratified and its provisions carried out by the parties in accordance with their respective constitutional processes. The instruments of ratification shall be deposited as soon as possible with the Government of the United States of America, which will notify all the other signatories of each deposit. The treaty shall enter into force between the states which have ratified it as soon as the ratifications of the majority of the signatories, including the ratifications of Belgium, Canada, France, Luxembourg, the Netherlands, the United Kingdom and the United States, have been deposited and shall come into effect with respect to other states on the date of the deposit of their ratifications.

## ARTICLE 12

After the treaty has been in force for ten years, or at any time thereafter, the parties shall, if any of them so requests, consult together for the purpose of reviewing the treaty, having regard for the factors then affecting peace and security in the North Atlantic area, including the development of universal as well as regional arrangements under the Charter of the United Nations for the maintenance of international peace and security.

## ARTICLE 13

After the treaty has been in force for twenty years, any party may cease to be a party one year after its notice of denunciation has been given to the Government of the United States of America, which will inform the Governments of the other parties of the deposit of each notice of denunciation.

## ARTICLE 14

This treaty, of which the English and French texts are equally authentic shall be deposited in the archives of the Government of the United States of America. Duly certified copies thereof will be transmitted by that Government to the Governments of the other signatories.

In witness whereof, the undersigned plenipotentiaries have signed this treaty.

## I. PROVISIONS OF THE UNITED NATIONS CHARTER

In the following extract the former attempts of various groups of states to unite along regional lines and the problems inherent in current efforts to do so are examined in light of the provisions on regionalism contained in the United Nations Charter. One of the key problems raised by the existence or future establishment of regional groupings within the United Nations system is that of allocating rights and duties between the United Nations and a region with respect to action to be taken in case of threats to, or breaches of, the peace.

(W. P. Allen, 'Regional Arrangements and the United Nations,' *Department of State Bulletin*, vol. XIV, 1946, pp. 923-7.)

Brief mention of some of the modern tendencies toward development of regional or subregional systems in other geographical areas may provide a setting for the subsequent consideration of the problems of the United Nations Charter.

The Covenant of the League of Nations gave wide latitude to the establishment of regional arrangements by providing in Article 21 that

Nothing in this Covenant shall be deemed to affect the validity of international engagements, such as treaties of arbitration or regional understandings like the Monroe Doctrine, for securing the maintenance of peace.

Thus there was virtually complete freedom for the operation of almost any type of regional arrangement.

With respect to the European region as a whole, the idea of a general European federation, stimulated particularly during the inter-war period by the proposals of M. Briand to the League Assembly in 1929, resulted in the establishment by the League of a 'Commission of Inquiry for European Union' composed of the European members. However, little concrete action emerged from its discussions. At the present time the idea appears again to be gaining some currency.

Within Europe one of the outstanding examples of regionalism following the First World War was the Little Entente. Composed of Czechoslovakia, Yugoslavia, and Rumania and created shortly after the conclusion of the war, it grew out of a series of bilateral mutual assistance treaties among the three countries. It gradually developed into a broader political organization and, after 1933, came to approximate a close diplomatic con-federation with definite organizational structure. The Entente played a signifi-cant role in helping to stabilize condi-tions in Central Europe.

The five Balkan countries and Turkey, despite the differences among them, have exhibited significant tendencies toward close economic collaboration and political understanding as bases for the formation of a regional system. The four Balkan conferences of representatives of these states (1930-32), although semi-official in character, did much to pave the way toward Balkan union along political, so-cial, and economic lines and created or stimulated the establishment of a number of organizations and commissions. The Balkan Entente (Yugoslavia, Rumania, Greece, Turkey) created by the pact of 1934, although not realizing the broader aims toward which the conferences had been working, was an effort at regional security within the Balkan area, later sup-plemented by agreements to give organi-zational structure to the Entente.

With regard to eastern Europe in gen-eral, although in 1942 attempts through agreements between Poland and Czecho-slovakia and between Greece and Yugo-slavia to work toward groupings of small states did not meet with success, a broader regional grouping of the nations of east-ern Europe under leadership of the U.S.S.R. is gradually but effectively evolv-ing through a series of bilateral arrange-ments and agreements. The possibility of a closer union of the Baltic states—Den-mark, Norway, Sweden, Finland, Latvia, Lithuania, and Esthonia—led to a series of conferences of representatives of these states, beginning in 1920 in Helsinki, Riga, and other capitals, but the efforts proved unproductive. Again in 1938-39 Finland and Sweden proposed a limited defensive alliance with Norway and Den-mark, but the arrangement was not com-pleted. As recently as February 1946 an

article in the Soviet publication *Pravda* stated that certain interests were agitat-ing for the formation of a 'Northern Bloc' which presumably would include Sweden, Norway, Denmark, and Finland. Concern was expressed in the article that the proposed bloc might also include 'a reconstructed Germany.' . . .

In the Near East a recent and highly significant development in regional ar-rangements is the creation of the League of Arab States composed of Syria, the Transjordan, Iraq, Saudi-Arabia, Leb-anon, Egypt, and Yemen. It was given formal existence upon the signing of the pact of the League of Arab States at Cairo, on March 22, 1945, as a result of a series of preliminary meetings stimu-lated by war conditions and special prob-lems arising in that area. The constituent states have made full use of this League as a vehicle for common action in the Palestine situation.

In the Far East, the Japanese attempt to create a 'Co-prosperity Sphere,' al-though based on suppression and con-quest and ruthless domination by one power, constituted, nevertheless, an at-tempt to form a regional system.

There have likewise been various moves toward what may be termed 'sub-regional' groupings. The proposal for a union of states of Central America and for the closer association of the Bolivarian countries (Venezuela, Colombia, and Ecuador) are examples within the inter-American field.

The British Commonwealth of Nations, in which the Dominions are free and sov-ereign although closely associated nations, is not a 'regional system' within any defi-nition involving geographical limitations, but is nevertheless, a special groupment of states which share in common with the regional arrangements mentioned a some-what similar status in terms of relation-ship with a world organization. There have been in the past few years a number of semi-official and non-official suggestions for a closer association of the United States with the United Kingdom and the other nations of the Commonwealth which would convert this association into an Anglo-Saxon group. Mr. Winston Churchill's plea to this effect in his Fulton, Missouri, speech on March 5, 1946, brought this issue sharply to the fore.

In addition to all of these developments which in general envisage arrangements involving political, security, economic, social, and cultural collaboration in varying degrees and in most cases a definite organizational structure, there are likewise existing or proposed arrangements, often regional in character, for more limited military and security purposes. They may in some instances be the precursors of broader, regional systems; but they do not necessarily rest upon the same ethnic or cultural bases or the same considerations of geographical proximity as the latter. The present Russo-British treaty of May 26, 1942, the Franco-Russian treaty of December 10, 1944, and the Sino-Russian treaty of August 14, 1945 are, together with similar treaties between Russia and Czechoslovakia, Poland, and Yugoslavia, perhaps the most outstanding examples of this more limited arrangement. That these bilateral agreements between the U.S.S.R. and various states of east-central Europe may be the skeleton for a more extensive network of alliances which would develop into a regional system is indicated by the conclusion of a Yugoslav-Polish Alliance on May 18, 1946 and a Czechoslovak-Yugoslav treaty of friendship on May 9, 1946. These agreements, reminiscent of the beginnings of the Little Entente, may be significant indications of the future pattern of development in this area.

The significance of all such regional and special associations of nations and of the forces manifested by the tendencies toward these regional groupings have been intensified and sharpened by the creation of the new world organization. The establishment of the United Nations has required a consideration of all regional arrangements in the light of the role which the Charter provides for them and their appraisal from the point of view of consistency with its terms. . .

It is, of course, impossible to seek to analyze any major Charter provision in isolation or on the exclusive basis of a particular set of interests, so complex are the factors motivating the positions of the various countries and so interrelated are the provisions of the Charter. At the San Francisco conference, however, the approach of the various countries to the problem of regional arrangements may be said to have been conditioned in part by one or another of five points of view, all of which operated in favor of varying degrees of autonomy for regional or other limited arrangements within the general framework of the United Nations:

1. The desire of the American republics to safeguard the inter-American system;

2. The similar feeling on the part of the states of the Arab League, for whom Egypt acted as spokesman, that the state of that League be preserved;

3. The wish of the U.S.S.R. to except from any restrictive control under the Charter the system of bilateral mutual assistance pacts;

4. France's concern over possible renewal of German aggression, leading her to seek freedom of action against ex-enemy states without the necessity of awaiting prior action by the Security Council;

5. The general uneasiness of the small states over the power granted the Security Council in the light of the Yalta voting formula. . .

The four sponsoring powers (China, United Kingdom, Union of Soviet Socialist Republics, and United States) proposed as an amendment the language finally incorporated into Article 53 of the Charter to the effect that regional or other joint action should be permitted without prior authorization from the Security Council in the case of measures to prevent renewed aggression by the enemy states in the then present war, until responsibility therefor should be transferred to the United Nations by the governments concerned. . .

Articles 33 and 51 to 54, which set forth the relationship of such agencies and arrangements to the world organization in the security field, in conjunction with other pertinent provisions of the Charter, may be summarized as follows:

1. In general, nothing in the Charter 'precludes the existence of regional arrangements or agencies for dealing with such matters relating to the maintenance of international peace and security as are appropriate for regional action, provided that such arrangements or agencies and their activities are consistent with the Purposes and Principles of the United Nations.' (Art. 52, par. 1.)

2. With respect to the *pacific settlement of disputes,* the Charter imposes upon the *members* of regional arrangements or agencies the obligation to 'make every effort to achieve pacific settlement of local disputes' through such institutions before referring them to the Security Council. (Art. 52, par. 2.) This is reinforced by a similar injunction upon 'The *parties* to any dispute, the continuance of which is likely to endanger the maintenance of international peace and security' to seek first of all a solution by peaceful means of their own choice, including 're-sort to regional agencies or arrangements' (Art. 33, par. 1). The obligation is laid upon the *Security Council* to 'encourage the development of pacific settlement of local disputes' through such regional arrangements or agencies (Art. 52, par. 3), and the Council 'shall, when it deems necessary, call upon the parties to settle' a specific dispute by peaceful means of their own choice, including regional arrangements. (Art. 33, par. 2.)

3. Beyond the realm of peaceful measures, the power of the regional system to take action in case of threats to or breaches of the peace or acts of aggression is at the same time both greater and less than its authority in the case of pacific settlement. The Security Council is directed to utilize regional arrangements or agencies for carrying out enforcement measures. But the authorization of the Council is required before measures which may be deemed 'enforcement action' may be taken under regional arrangements or regional agencies (Art. 53, par. 1).

There are, however, two important exceptions to the above rule: one depending upon the state against which action is taken and the other upon the nature of the aggression against which action is sought. Authorization is not necessary if the measures, whatever their nature, are to be taken against any ex-enemy state of the second World War, either as provided for pursuant to Article 107 or in accordance with 'regional arrangements directed against renewal of aggressive policy on the part of any such state.' (Art. 53, par. 1.) This exception ceases to exist only after the organization itself, 'on request of the Governments concerned,' is 'charged with the responsibility for preventing further aggression by such a state.' (Art. 53, par. 1.)

The second exception becomes operative if the breach of the peace or act of aggression takes the form of 'an armed attack.' Article 51 provides that nothing in the Charter 'shall impair the inherent right of individual or collective self-defense if an armed attack occurs against a Member of the United Nations, until the Security Council has taken the measures necessary to maintain international peace and security.'

4. These two exceptions, granting or recognizing the right to take action outside the machinery of the organization, do not refer exclusively to regional systems as does Article 52 concerning pacific settlement. The exception relating to measures against ex-enemy states encompasses as well action pursuant to agreements among the Allied Powers arising out of the war, such as the Franco-Russian Mutual Alliance Treaty. The exception of the right of 'individual or collective self-defense' similarly would include such a collective arrangement as is represented by the British Commonwealth of Nations.

5. However, the Charter makes it equally clear, that while the region may be expected to be the normal theater for the pacific settlement of at least 'local' disputes, while regional agencies will be looked to in an important way in resolving such controversies by peaceful methods, and while Security Council authori-

zation is not always necessary for enforcement action, nevertheless, the rights of the Security Council to take action at any time regarding any dispute remain unimpaired. These include the right of investigation (Art. 34) and of recommending 'at any stage of a dispute' 'appropriate procedures or methods of adjustment' taking into account any procedures adopted by the parties (Art. 36).

In the second place, the existence or functioning of regional arrangements or agencies does not operate to prevent a member state from bringing any situation which might lead to international friction to the attention of the Security Council or the General Assembly (Art. 35). (Indeed Article 52 specifically states that it in no way impairs the application of Articles 34 and 35.)

Thirdly, the right of the General Assembly to discuss and make recommendations concerning any matter relating to the maintenance of international peace and security (Art. 11) is not contingent upon action by regional agencies. . .

## II. The Inter-American System

Regional co-operation among the twenty-one American republics has had its ups and downs. Since 1889, when the first general Pan-American Conference was held, hundreds of conventions and resolutions have been concluded dealing with economic, legal, social, scientific, and political questions. The settlement of disputes by peaceful means has been facilitated and encouraged; and during the last war many constructive measures for mutual defense were adopted. There have been obstacles too, which have stood in the way of co-operation and even yet block effective action. Our own country, the 'Colossus of the North,' has been feared and suspected so widely in this hemisphere that the other nations have sometimes been more interested in opposing than in co-operating with us, and it must be admitted that by interfering in their national affairs and by our haughty attitude we have often merited the treatment that has been given us. Another obstacle has been the distrust that has existed among the other twenty states, which have often been involved in disputes and occasionally in open hostility.

Since World War II efforts have been made to improve the Inter-American system of regionalism. For this purpose an Inter-American Conference on Problems of War and Peace was held from 21 February to 8 March 1945 at Chapultepec Castle in Mexico. Twenty of the American republics, all but Argentina, took part. The agreement given below, known as the Act of Chapultepec, was concluded. It puts forth the measures to be taken to protect the territorial integrity and political independence of the American states against aggression from any quarter. It is understood that the Act does not conflict with the Charter of the United Nations, but is one of the regional organizations specifically approved by the Charter.

(Text in *Toward the Peace* Documents, Department of State Publication, No. 2298, pp. 37-8.)

Whereas: The peoples of the Americas, animated by a profound love of justice, remain sincerely devoted to the principles of international law;

It is their desire that such principles, notwithstanding the present difficult circumstances, may prevail with greater force in future international relations;

The Inter-American Conferences have repeatedly proclaimed certain fundamental principles, but these must be re-affirmed and proclaimed at a time when the juridical bases of the community of nations are being re-established;

The new situation in the world makes more imperative than ever the union and solidarity of the American peoples, for the defense of their rights and the maintenance of international peace;

The American states have been incorporating in their international law, since 1890, by means of conventions, resolutions and declarations, the following principles:

a) The proscription of territorial conquest and the non-recognition of all acquisitions made by force (First International Conference of American States, 1890);

b) The condemnation of intervention by a State in the internal or external affairs of another (Seventh International Conference of American States, 1933, and Inter-American Conference for the Maintenance of Peace, 1936);

c) The recognition that every war or threat of war affects directly or indirectly all civilized peoples, and endangers the great principles of liberty and justice which constitute the American Ideal and the standard of American international policy (Inter-American Conference for the Maintenance of Peace, 1936);

d) The procedure of mutual consultation in order to find means of peaceful cooperation in the event of war or threat of war between American countries (Inter-American Conference for the Maintenance of Peace, 1936);

e) The recognition that every act susceptible of disturbing the peace of America affects each and every one of the American nations and justifies the initiation of the procedure of consultation (Inter-American Conference for the Maintenance of Peace, 1936);

f) That any difference or dispute between the American nations, whatever its nature or origin, shall be settled by the methods of conciliation, or full arbitration, or through international justice (Inter-American Conference for the Maintenance of Peace, 1936);

g) The recognition that respect for the personality, sovereignty and independence of each American State constitutes the essence of international order supported by continental solidarity, which historically has been expressed and sustained by declarations and treaties in force (Eighth International Conference of American States, 1938);

h) The affirmation that respect for and the faithful observance of treaties constitutes the indispensable rule for the development of peaceful relations between States, and that treaties can only be revised by agreement of the contracting parties (Declaration of American Principles, Eighth International Conference of American States, 1938);

i) That in case the peace, security or territorial integrity of any American republic is threatened by acts of any nature that may impair them, they proclaim their common concern and their determination to make effective their solidarity, coordinating their respective sovereign wills by means of the procedure of consultation, using the measures which in each case the circumstances may make advisable (Declaration of Lima, Eighth International Conference of American States, 1938);

j) That any attempt on the part of a non-American State against the integrity or inviolability of the territory, the sovereignty or the political independence of an American State shall be considered as an act of aggression against all the American States (Declaration XV of the Second Meeting of the Ministers of Foreign Affairs, Habana, 1940);

The furtherance of these principles, which the American States have practiced in order to secure peace and solidarity between the nations of the Continent constitutes an effective means of contributing to the general system of world security and of facilitating its establishment;

The security and solidarity of the Continent are affected to the same extent by an act of aggression against any of the American States by a non-American State, as by an act of aggression of an American State against one or more American States;

## PART I. DECLARATION

*The Governments represented at the Inter-American Conference on War and Peace*

Declare:

*First.* That all sovereign States are juridically equal amongst themselves.

*Second.* That every State has the right to the respect of its individuality and independence, on the part of the other members of the international community.

*Third.* That every attack of a State against the integrity or the inviolability of the territory, or against the sovereignty or political independence of an American State, shall, conformably to Part III hereof, be considered as an act of aggression against the other States which sign this Act. In any case invasion by armed forces of one State into the territory of another trespassing boundaries established by treaty and demarcated in accordance therewith shall constitute an act of aggression.

*Fourth.* That in case acts of aggression occur or there may be reasons to believe that an aggression is being prepared by any other State against the integrity and inviolability of the territory, or against the sovereignty or political independence of an American State, the States signatory to this Act will consult amongst themselves in order to agree upon the measures it may be advisable to take.

*Fifth.* That during the war, and until the treaty recommended in Part II hereof is concluded, the signatories of this Act recognize that such threats and acts of aggression, as indicated in paragraphs Third and Fourth above, constitute an interference with the war effort of the United Nations, calling for such procedures, within the scope of their constitutional powers of a general nature and for war, as may be found necessary, including: recall of chiefs of diplomatic missions; breaking of diplomatic relations; breaking of consular relations; breaking of postal, telegraphic, telephonic, radio-telephonic relations; interruption of economic, commercial and financial relations; use of armed force to prevent or repel aggression.

*Sixth.* That the principles and procedure contained in this Declaration shall become effective immediately, inasmuch as any act of aggression or threat of aggression during the present state of war interferes with the war effort of the United Nations to obtain victory. Henceforth, and to the end that the principles and procedures herein stipulated shall conform with the constitutional processes of each Republic, the respective Governments shall take the necessary steps to perfect this instrument in order that it shall be in force at all times.

### Part II. Recommendation

*The Inter-American Conference on Problems of War and Peace*

Recommends:

That for the purpose of meeting threats or acts of aggression against any American Republic following the establishment of peace, the Governments of the American Republics should consider the conclusion, in accordance with their constitutional processes, of a treaty establishing procedures whereby such threats or acts may be met by the use, by all or some of the signatories of said treaty of any one or more of the following measures: recall of chiefs of diplomatic missions; breaking of diplomatic relations; breaking of consular relations; breaking of postal, telegraphic, telephonic, radio-telephonic relations; interruption of economic, commercial and financial relations; use of armed force to prevent or repel aggression.

### Part III

The above Declaration and Recommendation constitute a regional arrangement for dealing with such matters relating to the maintenance of international peace and security as are appropriate for regional action in this Hemisphere. The said arrangement, and the pertinent activities and procedures, shall be consistent with the purposes and principles of the general international organization, when established.

This agreement shall be known as the 'ACT OF CHAPULTEPEC.'

### III. Defense of the Western Hemisphere

To give effect to the declarations of the Act of Chapultepec, a treaty, the text of which is given below, was negotiated and signed on 30 August 1947 at the Inter-American Defense Conference in Rio de Janeiro. It provides for joint action to prevent aggression against an American state.

(Text from *The New York Times,* 31 August 1947.)

#### Article 1

The high contracting parties formally condemn war and undertake in their international relations not to resort to threat or use force in any manner inconsistent with the provisions of the Charter of the United Nations or of this treaty.

#### Article 2

As a consequence of the principle set forth in the preceding article, the high contracting parties undertake to submit every controversy which may arise between them to methods of peaceful settlement and endeavor to settle such controversies among themselves by means of procedures in force in the inter-American system before referring them to the General Assembly or the Security Council of the United Nations.

## ARTICLE 3

(1) The high contracting parties agree that an armed attack by any state against an American state shall be considered as an attack against all the American states and consequently each one of the said contracting parties undertakes to assist in meeting the attack in exercise of the inherent right of individual or collective self-defense recognized by Article 51 of the Charter of the United Nations.

(2) On the request of the state or states directly attacked and until the decision of the organ of consultation of the inter-American system, each one of the contracting parties may determine immediate measures which it may individually adopt in fulfillment of the obligation contained in the preceding paragraph and in accordance with the principle of continental solidarity. The organ of consultation shall meet without delay for the purpose of examining these measures and agreeing upon measures of a collective character that should be adopted.

(3) The provisions of this article shall be applied in case of any armed attack which takes place within the region described in Article 4 or within the territory of an American state. When an attack takes place outside the said areas the provisions of Article 6 shall be applied.

(4) The measures of self-defense provided under this article may be taken until the Security Council of the United Nations has taken measures necessary to maintain international peace and security.

## ARTICLE 4

The region to which this treaty refers is bounded as follows:

Beginning at the North Pole:

Thence due south to a point 74 degrees north latitude 10 degrees west longitude;

Thence by a rhumb line to a point 47 degrees 30 minutes north latitude 50 degrees west longitude;

Thence by a rhumb line to a point 35 degrees north latitude 60 degrees west longitude;

Thence due south to a point in 20 degrees north latitude;

Thence by a rhumb line to a point 5 degrees north latitude 24 degrees west longitude;

Thence due south to the South Pole;

Thence due north to a point 30 degrees south latitude 90 degrees west longitude;

Thence by a rhumb line to a point on the equator at 97 degrees west longitude;

Thence by a rhumb line to a point 15 degrees north latitude 120 degrees west longitude;

Thence by a rhumb line to a point 50 degrees north latitude 170 degrees east longitude;

Thence due north to a point in 54 degrees north latitude;

Thence by a rhumb line to a point 65 degrees 30 minutes north latitude 168 degrees 58 minutes 5 seconds west longitude;

Thence due north to the North Pole.

## ARTICLE 5

The high contracting parties shall immediately send to the Security Council of the United Nations, in conformity with Articles 51 and 54 of the Charter of the United Nations, complete information concerning the activities undertaken or in contemplation in the exercise of the right of self-defense or for the purpose of maintaining inter-American peace and security.

## ARTICLE 6

If the inviolability or the integrity of the territory or the sovereignty or political independence of any American state should be affected by an aggression which is not an armed attack or by an intracontinental or extracontinental conflict, or by any other fact or situation that might endanger the peace of America, the organ of consultation shall meet immediately in order to agree on the measures which must be taken in case of aggression to assist the victim of the aggression or, in any case, the measures which should be taken for the common defense and for the maintenance of the peace and security of the continent.

. . .

### ARTICLE 8

For the purposes of this treaty, the measures on which the organ of consultation may agree will comprise one or more of the following:

Recall of chiefs of diplomatic missions, breaking of diplomatic missions, breaking of diplomatic relations, breaking of consular relations, complete or partial interruption of economic relations or of rail, sea, air, postal, telegraphic, telephonic and radio telephonic or radio-telegraphic communications and the use of armed force.

### ARTICLE 9

In addition to other acts which the organ of consultation may characterize as aggression, the following shall be considered as such:

a. Unprovoked armed attack by a state against the territory, the people or the land, sea or air forces of another state;

b. Invasion by the armed forces of a state or the territory of an American state through the trespassing of boundaries demarcated in accordance with a treaty, judicial decision or arbitral award or, in the absence of frontiers thus demarcated, an invasion affecting a region which is under the effective jurisdiction of another state.

### ARTICLE 10

None of the provisions of this treaty shall be construed as impairing the rights and obligations of the high contracting parties under the Charter of the United Nations.

### ARTICLE 11

The organ of consultation referred to in this treaty shall be, until a different decision is taken, the meeting of the Ministers of Foreign Affairs of the signatory states which have ratified the treaty.

### ARTICLE 12

The Governing Board of the Pan American Union may act provisionally as an organ of consultation until the meeting of the organ of consultation referred to in the preceding article takes place.

. . .

### ARTICLE 17

The organ of consultation shall take its decisions by a vote of two thirds of the signatory states which have ratified the treaty.

### ARTICLE 18

In the case of a situation or dispute between American states the parties directly interested shall be excluded from the voting referred to in the two preceding articles.

. . .

## IV. UNITY FOR WESTERN EUROPE

When the march of communism in Europe reached Czechoslovakia early in 1948, the governments of western Europe became alarmed and began to consider joint defensive measures. Great Britain and France had already agreed to collaborate in matters of international policy, and the Benelux countries

(Belgium, the Netherlands, and Luxembourg) had begun to co-ordinate their economic and, to a lesser extent, their political policies. By 1948, however, the need for wider co-operation for defense was apparent. Consequently the following treaty was negotiated and signed at Brussels on 17 March 1948. Subsequently, on 28 September 1948, the five Defense Ministers of the Brussels treaty powers announced the formation of a common defense organization. The Brussels Pact had the approval of Washington and became the central framework for the North Atlantic Pact, the text of which was given earlier in this chapter.

(Text from *The New York Times*, 18 March 1948.)

### ARTICLE 1

Convinced of the close community of their interests and of the necessity of uniting in order to promote the economic recovery of Europe, the high contracting parties will so organize and coordinate their economic activities as to produce the best possible results, by the elimination of conflict in their economic policies, coordination of production and development of commercial exchanges.

The cooperation provided for in the preceding paragraph, which will be effected through the consultative council referred to in Article 7 as well as through other bodies, shall not involve any duplication of or prejudice to the work of other economic organizations in which the high contracting parties are or may be represented, but shall on the contrary, assist the work of those organizations.

### ARTICLE 2

The high contracting parties will make every effort in common, both by direct consultation and in specialized agencies, to promote the attainment of a higher standard of living by their peoples and to develop on corresponding lines the social and other related services of their countries. The high contracting parties will consult with the object of achieving the earliest possible application of the recommendations of immediate practical interest relating to social matters, adopted with their approval in the specialized agencies. They will endeavor to conclude as soon as possible conventions with others in the sphere of social security.

### ARTICLE 3

The high contracting parties will make every effort in common to lead their peoples toward better understanding of the principles which form the basis of their common civilization and to promote cultural exchanges by conventions between themselves or by other means.

### ARTICLE 4

If any of the high contracting parties should be the object of an armed attack in Europe, the other high contracting parties will, in accordance with the provisions of Article 51 of the Charter of the United Nations, afford the party so attacked all military and other aid and assistance in their power.

### ARTICLE 5

All measures taken as a result of the preceding article shall be immediately reported to the Security Council. They shall be terminated as soon as the Security Council has taken the measures necessary to maintain or restore international peace and security.

The present treaty does not prejudice in any way the obligations of the high contracting parties under the provisions of the Charter of the United Nations. It shall not be interpreted as affecting in any way the authority and responsibility of the Security Council under the Charter to take at any time such action as it deems necessary in order to maintain or restore international peace and security.

### ARTICLE 6

The high contracting parties declare, each so far as he is concerned, that none of the international engagements now in force between him and any other high contracting party or any third state is in conflict with the provisions of the present treaty. None of the high contracting parties will conclude any alliance or participate in any coalition directed against any other of the high contracting parties

### ARTICLE 7

For the purpose of consulting together on all questions dealt with in the present treaty, the high contracting parties will create a consultative council which shall be so organized as to be able to exercise its functions continuously. The Council shall meet at such times as it shall deem fit. At the request of any of the high contracting parties, the Council shall be immediately convened in order to permit the high contracting parties to consult with regard to any situation which may constitute a threat to peace in whatever area this threat should arise, with regard to the attitude to be adopted and the steps to be taken in the case of a renewal by Germany of an aggressive policy, or with regard to any situation constituting a danger to economic stability.

### ARTICLE 8

In pursuance of their determination to settle disputes only by peaceful means, the high contracting parties will apply to disputes between themselves the following provisions:

The high contracting parties will, while the present treaty remains in force, settle all disputes falling within the scope of Article 36, Paragraph 2 of the Statute of the International Court of Justice by referring them to the court, subject only in the case of each of them to any reservation already made by that party when accepting this clause for compulsory jurisdiction to the extent that that party may maintain the reservation.

In addition, the high contracting parties will submit to conciliation all disputes outside the scope of Article 36, Paragraph 2 of the Statute of the International Court of Justice. In the case of a mixed dispute involving both questions for which conciliation is appropriate and other questions for which judicial settlement is appropriate, any party to the dispute shall have the right to insist that the judicial settlement of the legal questions shall precede conciliation. The preceding provisions of this article in no way affect the application of relevant provisions or agreements prescribing some other method of pacific settlement.

### ARTICLE 9

The high contracting parties may, by agreement, invite any other state to accede to the present treaty on conditions to be agreed between them and the state so invited. Any state so invited may become a party to the treaty by depositing an instrument of accession with the Belgian Government. The Belgian Government will inform each of the high contracting parties of the deposit of each instrument of accession.

### ARTICLE 10

The present treaty shall be ratified and the instruments of ratification shall be deposited as soon as possible with the Belgian Government.

It shall enter into force on the date of

deposit of the last instrument of ratification and shall thereafter remain in force for fifty years.

After the expiry of the period of fifty years, each of the high contracting parties shall have the right to cease to be a party thereto provided that he shall have previously given one year's notice of denunciation to the Belgian Government.

The Belgian Government shall inform the governments of the other high contracting parties of the deposit of each instrument of ratification and of each notice of denunciation.

In witness whereof the above mentioned plenipotentiaries have signed the present treaty and have affixed thereto their seals.

Done at Brussels this 17th day of March, 1948, in English and French, each text being equally authentic, in a single copy which shall remain deposited in the archives of the Belgian Government and of which certified copies shall be transmitted by that Government to each of the other signatories.

For Belgium: SPAAK.

For France: BIDAULT.

For Luxembourg: BECH.

For the Netherlands: VAN BOETZELAER.

For the United Kingdom of Great Britain and Northern Ireland: BEVIN.

## V. THE VANDENBERG RESOLUTION

Indicative of the sentiment of the United States Senate toward the United Nations and regional arrangements for defense is the Vandenberg Resolution, passed by the Senate 64 to 4 on 11 June 1948. It was within the terms of the policy here outlined that the United States became a party to the North Atlantic Pact.

(Senate Resolution 239, *Congressional Record*, vol. 94, No. 106, 11 June 1948, p. 7971.)

Whereas peace with justice and the defense of human rights and fundamental freedoms require international cooperation through more effective use of the United Nations: Therefore be it

*Resolved,* That the Senate reaffirm the policy of the United States to achieve international peace and security through the United Nations so that armed force shall not be used except in the common interest, and that the President be advised of the sense of the Senate that this Government, by constitutional process, should particularly pursue the following objectives within the United Nations Charter:

(1) Voluntary agreement to remove the veto from all questions involving pacific settlements of international disputes and situations, and from the admission of new members.

(2) Progressive development of regional and other collective arrangements for individual and collective self-defense in accordance with the purposes, principles, and provisions of the Charter.

(3) Association of the United States, by constitutional process, with such regional and other collective arrangements as are based on continuous and effective self-help and mutual aid, and as affect its national security.

(4) Contributing to the maintenance of peace by making clear its determination to exercise the right of individual or collective self-defense under Article 51 should any armed attack occur affecting its national security.

(5) Maximum efforts to obtain agreements to provide the United Nations with armed forces as provided by the Charter,

and to obtain agreement among member nations upon universal regulation and reduction of armaments under adequate and dependable guaranty against violation.

(6) If necessary, after adequate effort toward strengthening the United Nations, review of the Charter at an appropriate time by a general conference called under Article 109 or by the General Assembly.

# 5

## INTERNATIONAL LAW AND COURTS

IN THEIR dealings with each other, governments frequently refer to rights and duties as established by international law. When in the early 1920's the United States tried to enforce its prohibition laws beyond the three-mile limit, Great Britain maintained that we were violating the law. When Mexico nationalized sub-soil deposits, the United States insisted that international law called for adequate compensation to American owners of oil. Accusations and claims between governments are so numerous that foreign offices in all countries find it necessary to maintain a staff of experts in international law for consultation. When diplomacy fails to adjust differences of a legal nature between nations, they may be taken to international courts.

International law as we know it today is the result of centuries of development. Even in ancient Greece there were primitive rules to regularize the relationships among the city states, and in Rome the *Jus Gentium* was a system of law applicable to the different peoples within the Empire. As the modern state system emerged during the late Middle Ages and permanent diplomatic relations were established, rules were gradually developed which states followed in their dealings with each other. In 1625 Hugo Grotius, a Dutchman, wrote his famous book *The Law of War and Peace,* which systematized and stated the law of his time so well that he is commonly referred to as the founder of modern international law.

Since 1625 the law has been expanded in many ways. For years its exponents relied upon the law of nature (abstract principles of right and justice), but during the last century and a half they have stressed 'positive' sources, basing their deductions more on the practice of nations. During the last half of the nineteenth century the idea of codifying the law gained headway, particularly with relation to the law of war. There are now a considerable number of codes relating to such subjects as the opening of hostilities, land warfare, the treatment of sick and wounded, prisoners of war, and neutrality.

In its present form international law has two divisions. First, there is the law of peace, which deals with states as persons in international law, recognition, claims to territory, boundaries, intervention, treaties, the responsibility of states, jurisdiction over land, sea, and air, and diplomatic and consular representation. The second division of the law, which relates to war, has to do with the beginning of war, the conduct of hostilities, the effect of war upon trade and treaties, the treatment of enemy aliens, and neutrality.

There has been much cynicism toward international law on the part of the layman. He bases his attitude, in part, on the fact that the law has not prevented war. He overlooks the fact that the law is merely a group of rules and, as such, could scarcely be expected, standing alone, to prevent war. It can make contributions to peace but, to be most effective, there must be strong machinery of enforcement and adequate agencies for the settlement of disputes. Even within a nation a code of laws would prove weak as an instrument of peace and order without courts, executive officials, and legislatures.

Another ground for cynicism is the fact that international law is violated, especially the law of war. It is, of course, regrettable that there are violations, but it is not surprising considering that there is no adequate enforcement machinery and that governments are often under great pressure, particularly in war. Municipal law too is violated, very often in fact, as the business of our courts shows; and, while there are penalties available, the culprits do at times go free. In all law, municipal and international, it is the violations that get the publicity. Moreover, many violations that are alleged are groundless; in international relations charges of violations have sometimes been made, especially in war, in order to place the enemy in an unfavorable light.

Arbitration was the first international procedure devised to settle disputes by law. It is an ancient procedure, and was revived as a modern practice by the Jay Treaty of 1794 between the United States and Great Britain. During the nineteenth century there were scores of arbitration cases, and in 1899 a Permanent Court of Arbitration was set up at The Hague. The Court is still in existence, but it has not handled a large number of cases.

In 1919 the Paris Peace Conference agreed to create a Permanent Court of International Justice to settle disputes by a more strictly judicial process. In arbitration the judges are selected by the disputants, and the disputants are able to decide points relating to procedure and the rules to be applied. In judicial settlement proper the court is permanent, with impartial judges applying international law strictly by a fixed procedure.

After World War II the Permanent Court of International Justice was supplanted by a new Court with a new Statute—'The International Court of Justice.' It is a part of the United Nations machinery.

## I. THE PLACE OF INTERNATIONAL LAW

The following extract is from a diplomatic note written in 1864:

(Señor Barrenchia to Señor Herrera, 1864. Translated from the German work *Handbuch der Entscheidungen des Standigen* *Internationalen Gerichtshofs. Repertoire des décisions de la Cour Permanente de Justice Internationale. Digest of the De-*

*cisions of the Permanent Court of International Justice.* Added title page: *Fontes Juris Gentium.* By Abraham Howard Feller, Ernst Schmitz, and Berthold Graf Schenk von Stauffenberg, Joint Editors, Berlin, Carl Heymanns Verlag, 1931. The German interests in the United States copyright in this work were vested in the Attorney General of the United States in 1948, pursuant to law. The use of the following, from Volume I, Part 1, p. 3, is by permission of the Attorney General, in the public interest, under License No. JA-1353.)

The principles of international law form one of the most precious conquests of modern civilization; and all Governments and all peoples have the right and the duty, for the interests of humanity and for their own benefit, to maintain them intact; on this account, whenever the slightest infraction of these principles takes place in Europe, the great European Powers, although proclaiming principles of neutrality and non-intervention, hasten to mark their disapprobation of the overthrow of the guardian principles of Governments and nations.

## II. Order under Law

In an address to the Bar Association in Nashville, Tennessee, on 3 June 1938, Secretary of State Cordell Hull made the following remarks.

(Cordell Hull, 'The Spirit of International Law,' *International Conciliation,* No. 342, September 1938, pp. 297-300. Reprinted by permission of the Carnegie Endowment for International Peace.)

From the dawn of history, human relations have been marked by a constant conflict of two primary principles. One is the principle of untrammeled individual freedom, unrestrained save by the superior force of other equally free individuals—the principle of anarchy. The other is the principle of order under law, which lies at the very foundation of social institutions and which requires the subordination by the individual of a part of his personal freedom in the interest of the maintenance of such institutions.

Each of these two principles, when translated into action, represents a way of life. Through long and bitter experience, mankind has learned the all-important lesson that order under law rather than anarchy affords the more satisfactory way of life and the only assurance of real freedom in the full meaning of that word.

Where every individual is free to follow at will his personal instincts and desires, there is at best only an illusion of freedom. Organized society becomes impossible, and chaos prevails. The efforts of each individual become, of necessity, overwhelmingly devoted to activities of offense or defense. There is little, if any, time or opportunity to engage in constructive processes of life. Oppression of the weak, and challenge and conflict among the strong, become the governing rules of life. Where there is no sense of security there is no real freedom.

An individual may conceivably seek security by isolating himself from his fellowmen and living a hermit life. But by so doing, even if he succeeds in escaping challenge and attack by others, he dooms himself to such a low level of both physical and spiritual existence that his apparently secure freedom becomes slavery to his own limitations.

It is only through the development of social institutions, through the evolution of man as a social being, that humanity has steadily progressed to higher and higher levels of civilized existence and has learned the true meaning of individual freedom. The foundation of such existence and of such freedom is order under law.

The individual who lives in organized society shares in the vast benefits which flow from a properly functioning social organization—by way of security for life and property; by way of the material advancement resulting from organized effort and enterprise; by way of moral, intellectual, and spiritual betterment induced by the contacts and fellowship of community life. But he must make his contribution to the maintenance of such organized society. His first and most direct contribution should be self-restraint, willingness to accept and practice the rules of social conduct which are embodied in law and interpreted by the authorized agencies of government. Of equal importance should be his participation in the functioning of an alert and informed public opinion, which serves, by collective disapproval, to enforce self-restraint upon those individuals who, through anti-social conduct, imperil the safety and progress of organized society.

These two great moral forces—self-restraint on the part of the individual and approval or condemnation by public opinion—constitute the real basis upon which the effectiveness of law rests in organized society. The instrumentality of physical constraint is only a supplement to the basic moral forces. Its use is rendered necessary by the fact that in each community there appear, from time to time, individuals and groups who refuse to abide by the commonly accepted rules of social conduct. But no law which is unacceptable to the great majority of the people can be made effective by police power alone. . .

The primary function of international law is to define and prescribe rules of international conduct. These rules must be such as to represent the maximum practicable reconciliation between the sovereign rights of each nation and the sovereign rights of other nations for the greater benefit of all. In this spirit, international law operates as an incalculably powerful force for human progress.

Rules of conduct must, in themselves, be based upon sound fundamental principles, that breathe the spirit of reasonableness, the spirit of live and let live. On a number of recent occasions, I have set forth some of the principles which, in my opinion, are indispensable to a satisfactory international order. The most important of these are as follows:

Maintenance of peace should be constantly advocated and practiced.

All nations should, through voluntary self-restraint, abstain from use of force in pursuit of policy and from interference in the internal affairs of other nations.

All nations should seek to adjust problems arising in their international relations by processes of peaceful negotiation and agreement.

All nations should uphold the principle of the sanctity of treaties and of faithful observance of international agreements.

Modification of provisions of treaties, when need therefor arises, should be by orderly processes carried out in a spirit of mutual helpfulness and accommodation.

Each nation should respect the rights of others and perform scrupulously its own established obligations.

Steps should be taken toward promotion of economic security and stability the world over through lowering or removal of barriers to international trade, according of effective equality of commercial opportunity, and application of the principle of equality of commercial treatment.

All nations should be prepared to limit and progressively reduce their armaments.

Apart from the question of alliances with others, each nation should be prepared to engage in cooperative effort, by peaceful and practicable means, in support of these principles.

Some of these principles have long been embodied in international law, although at times they have been honored more in the breach than in the observance; there is urgent need today for their revitalization and strengthening. Others of these principles have not as yet acquired the force of law; acceptance and observance of them by all nations is an equally imperative need at the present time.

Definition of rules of conduct is not in itself sufficient for the establishment of a world order based on law. Machinery must be devised for the interpretation and application of the rules.

The world has already made substantial progress in evolving instrumentalities for this purpose. The processes of diplomatic negotiation have been employed from time immemorial. They have been gradually supplemented by the processes of mediation, conciliation, arbitration, and judicial settlement. These methods of composing international differences by pacific means are at our disposal. The task of the nations is to use them and, in the course of using them, to develop and perfect them and to endow them with ever increasing authority and effectiveness. . .

## III. The Reality of International Law

From a purely theoretical point of view it was formerly maintained by John Austin and others that law is the command of a political superior, and because international law does not have such a source, it is not law at all. This point of view is not widely held today. In the case of the *Prometheus*, Chief Justice Sir Henry Berkeley contended that international law is law in the strict sense. The case had to do with a ship chartered by a Norwegian firm to the Japanese Government in the Russo-Japanese War. Contrary to international law, the Russian Government had declared food to be contraband, and the master of the *Prometheus* therefore refused to carry a cargo of rice, sugar, and provisions offered at Kobe, Japan. The charterer brought action for breach of contract. In the opinion given below, the court ruled that the Russian declaration was contrary to international law, and that the food should therefore be carried. In the course of the opinion, the following statements were made on international law:

(Great Britain, Supreme Court of Hong-kong, 1906, 12 *Hong-Kong Law Reports* 207)

It was contended on behalf of the owners of the *Prometheus* that the term 'law' as applied to this recognized system of principles and rules known as international law is an inexact expression, that there is, in other words, no such thing as international law; that there can be no such law binding upon all nations inasmuch as there is no sanction for such law,

that is to say that there is no means by which obedience to such law can be imposed upon any given nation refusing obedience thereto. I do not concur in that contention. In my opinion a law may be established and become international, that is to say binding upon all nations, by the agreement of such nations to be bound thereby, although it may be impossible to enforce obedience thereto by any given nation party to the agreement. The resistance of a nation to a law to which it has agreed does not derogate from the authority of the law because that resistance cannot, perhaps, be overcome. Such resistance merely makes the resisting nation a breaker of the law to which it has given its adherence, but it leaves the law, to the establishment of which the resisting nation was a party, still subsisting. Could it be successfully contended that because any given person or body of persons possessed for the time being power to resist an established municipal law such law had no existence? The answer to such a contention would be that the law still existed, though it might not for the time being be possible to enforce obedience to it.

## IV. CONDITIONS FOR THE PROGRESS OF INTERNATIONAL LAW

(J. L. Brierly, 'International Law: Some Conditions of Its Progress,' *International Affairs*, vol. 22, 1946, pp. 352-7, 358-9. Reprinted by permission of the Royal Institute of International Affairs.)

Some months ago I gave an address at Chatham House on the part that international law is playing in world affairs as things are. I tried to show that it is a working system which fulfils a necessary function in the conduct of international relations and, in confirmation of that view, I would like here to quote some rather striking statistics in which an influential committee estimates that since 1920 international tribunals of one sort or another have decided about 50,000 cases. No doubt most of these cases were quite unimportant in themselves, but then that is true of most of the cases that come before the courts in any system of law. But even if none of them would have disturbed the tranquillity of nations if it had been left unsettled, it was surely a good thing to have them disposed of, and the reason that it was possible to dispose of them was the fact that in international law States had a useful instrument at their service. If we could not rely on its rules being generally accepted and acted upon, on treaties being observed more often than broken, and on awards and judgments being honoured, it is not an exaggeration to say that international relations would become chaotic. Actually we can and we do rely on these things, and it is the exception and not the rule for these expectations to be disappointed.

So I shall assume without further argument that international law is something which is worth maintaining and improving, and I shall address myself to certain conditions which in my view must somehow be satisfied if it is to make further progress. The subject is a big and a controversial one for a short paper, and as my own views on it are not always orthodox I will apologize in advance if I should seem to dogmatize.

I think in the first place that we shall fail to recognize what these conditions of progress are if we do not constantly bear in mind two things—two things which are so obvious in themselves that it would be impertinent to mention them, if it were not for the fact that so much that is said and written about international law even by quite thoughtful people seems sometimes to lose sight of them. The first is that law, any kind of law, is a rather special method of social control, and that its own nature sets limits to its usefulness; and the second is that when we take law out of its familiar milieu in the lives of individual men and women and try to apply it to the behaviour of States, we introduce special considerations which ought to warn us to be very careful how we apply in the changed context analogies suggested by studying its working inside a single State. Most of what I shall have to say is suggested by one or other of these two elementary factors in the problem.

I began by reminding you of the credit side of the international law account, because it is much less well known than the debit side with which I shall be chiefly concerned in this paper. To put this debit side into a sentence, I suppose one may say that it lies in the fact that States have hitherto only been willing to allow law to control their relations in matters, which, though not unimportant in themselves, are of secondary importance, and therefore do not present them with any very strong temptation to set the law at defiance. They do not allow the law, or at any rate it is not their settled practice to allow it, to have the final word in issues which affect their so-called 'vital interests,' and as they reserve the right to decide which of their interests are vital, that means that in the last resort they regard the observance of law as optional, and not as unconditional. It is true that they very rarely repudiate their legal obligations expressly, but there is no need for them to do anything so crude as that; the present state of international organization makes these obligations easy to evade in a more or less gentlemanly way, since a State is not bound to submit its claims to be determined on the basis of law, because, as we commonly say, the law allows a State to be 'a judge in its own cause.'

Now if it is this freedom to evade the law that is at the root of its weakness, it is tempting to say, 'Why not alter this state of things? Establish the compulsory jurisdiction of international courts and you will have established at one stroke the international rule of law.' You can go on to point out that all that stands in the way of this simple solution is the survival of outworn theories of sovereignty which have become anachronisms in the modern world. Unfortunately theories of sovereignty are only formulas which academically-minded people have invented from time to time in order to explain certain facts about the way in which States behave. I think their theories have often exaggerated or distorted the facts; sometimes they still do so. All the same theories of sovereignty are founded on certain facts of which any student of international law will have to take account if his plans for reforming it are not to suffer shipwreck. I do not suggest that the facts can never be changed, though I do not think that can be done in a hurry. I do say that it is essential to look the facts in the face, and not to imagine that it is only a mistaken theory about the nature of the State that has to be corrected.

There is always a temptation to regard international affairs as something remote from ordinary human affairs, except, of course, at times of crisis, when we realize with a shock how closely they do after all affect our daily lives. Then when the crisis has passed we heave a sigh of relief and let them recede again into the hazy distance where, we feel, they properly belong. If it were not for this I think we should recognize more often than we do that this claim of States to be their own final judges, this claim of sovereignty if you prefer the word, is only one special manifestation of an attitude towards law which all powerful groups or associations of men tend to take up on occasion. It is not in any special sense an international phenomenon, though, of course, it takes on special features when it appears in the international field; and it is not something to be explained by any peculiar unreasonableness in the nature of States, or a specially large dose of original sin in those who conduct their affairs. It is a general sociological phenomenon which we can see at work any day if we observe the behaviour of political factions or of organizations of capital and labour inside the State. Like States these bodies do not as a rule avow any claim to be above the law, but they often act as though that were what they are claiming, as though, law or no law, their will must be allowed to prevail. . .

I suppose that fundamentally the explanation of this recalcitrance towards law which powerful groups display is the simple fact that most men like to have their own way at any time, but that when they are acting together with powerful resources behind them, they are often able to brush aside opposition and to take what they want. Obviously the sanctions of the law which normally prevent men from just taking what they want are more easy to apply against individuals than against men associated together, and the difficulty increases in proportion as their association becomes stronger and more cohesive, until in the extreme case of States sanctions are not far from their vanishing point. I am not suggesting for one moment that the fear of sanctions is what normally makes us obey the law; of course, we all know that is not so. But I do suggest that if there are no sanctions to the law, or if they can only be used uncertainly and with great difficulty, then, if obedience to the law is rendered none the less, that obedience can only be a voluntary act, and is likely to be precarious, as in fact it is with States. But I think there is another reason behind the reluctance of groups to submit to law unconditionally besides this superficially evident reason that it is difficult to make them submit if they do not want to, and this other reason is something which provides a certain justification for the attitude and ought to prevent us from condemning it outright as a purely antisocial tendency to which it would be wrong to make any concession. Rules of law are necessarily expressed in general terms; they deal with the subjects of law as instances of types and not as unique individuals; they are, and we rightly require that they should be, impersonal. I am speaking of a characteristic feature of law, and I am aware that there are a number of ways in which in a highly developed system of law this impersonality can be mitigated; judges, for instance, can be given some discretion in administering its rules; but even with these alleviations law neither is, nor ought it to become, a 'respecter of persons.' Now that is all very well so long as the subjects of the law do fall naturally into types, and since individual human beings are very much like one another on the whole in those respects with which law is concerned they can be subjected to general rules with that reasonable approximation to justice which is all that law can ever achieve. But it is far less possible to do this with large and powerful groups even inside the State, for they often have interests and claims which can only be justly treated if they are regarded as special cases and not arbitrarily forced into the general rubrics of the law. The processes of government inside the State recognize this every day as a matter of course; in dealing with groups they inject, so to speak, a political element into the methods of controlling them; they try to resolve difficult situations by persuasion or compromise; they look for a solution which takes into account the special features of the particular case. But of all the social groups into which men form themselves States are the least able to be justly treated as if they were always merely instances of a type; their most important interests are shaped by factors in their individual situations, political, economic, geographical, historical, and so on, which are almost infinitely various, and it seems to me that it is not only impracticable, but that even if it were practicable it would be wrong, to exclude a political approach when we are dealing with the way in which they ought to behave. Professor E. H. Carr has put the point which

I am trying to make in a passage of his *Twenty Years' Crisis* which I should like to quote here:

> The tiny number of states forming the international community creates the same special problem in law as in ethics. The evolution of general rules equally applicable to all, which is the basis of the ethical element in law, becomes extremely difficult. Rules, however general in form, will be constantly found to be aimed at a particular state or group of states; and for this reason, if for no other, the power element is more predominant and more obvious in international than in municipal law, whose subjects are a large body of anonymous individuals. The same consideration makes international law more frankly political than other branches of law.

Now I am aware that this may seem a dangerous line for an international lawyer to take, and that it may be thought to prove too much, that international law is not only difficult, but impossible. I think there are two answers to that. First of all the reasoning does not apply to all the relations of States with one another. It does apply to the most important, to those in which their 'vital interests' are at stake—and by that I mean not *any* interest which the present system allows a State to denominate as vital in a particular controversy, but interests which really are vital. But it does not apply to the issues which are most commonly decided on the basis of law as things are, particularly to questions on the interpretation of treaties, and those arising out of injuries suffered by the nationals of one State in the territory of another. Here are two large groups of topics to which general rules can reasonably be applied and, of course, there are others. But the second answer is that there is no necessary conflict between politics and law, and that politics can be, as within the State they normally are, carried on within a framework of law.

I think this partial inappropriateness of general rules to international relations is an important clue which we shall have to follow up if we are to form a realistic ideal for the progress of international law. Negatively, I think it warns us against supposing that we can get much further by the multiplication of general rules which is the ideal behind schemes for codifying the law, and against concentrating our main efforts on the improvement of the judicial side of international organization, which as a matter of fact is already quite good and certainly far in advance of any of the other sides. But it is more important to consider the positive lessons to which the considerations I have been adducing point, and I think there are two lessons of this kind: first, the absolute necessity, if international law is to advance any further, of a better assurance of international security; and secondly, the need for a better articulated institutional framework for the organization of international cooperation. In short, order and organization are the two pillars on which law rests inside the State, and they are equally vital to law, though, of course, far more difficult to realize, in the field of international relations.

Insecurity is obviously another of the reasons which lie behind the insistence of States on being judges in their own cause. There is a passage in the *Leviathan* —one of those many passages that one would like to disagree with and yet is forced to accept in the end—in which Hobbes explains why a state of anarchy, that is to say, a state of no-law, is the inevitable result of a state of insecurity. 'If there be no power erected,' he says, 'or not great enough for our security, every man will and may lawfully rely on his own strength and art, for causation against all other men'. . .

More than anything else, I suppose, it is the manifest failure of international law to solve the problem of international order, its failure to outlaw war, that makes so many people doubt whether it is any use at all. Here they are inclined to say is the primary, the most necessary and elementary of the purposes for which any system of law is worth having, and yet when international law is confronted with this problem we find that it throws in its hand. It used to profess, in the classical expositions of the system, to lay down rules, as every worth-while system of law does, for distinguishing between the lawful and the unlawful use of physical force, but it has failed to make that distinction good, and in modern times it has come to accept the position that war is simply an event outside the range of legal rules which unfortunately occurs from time to time in the relations of States almost like a cataclysm of nature. If that does not amount to a failure of the system, it may well be asked, what does?

I believe that to state the case in this way, to imply that international law has failed in its function because it has not created international order, is to misrepresent the true relation between order and law. Law never does create order out of disorder; to suppose that it can do that is to put the cart before the horse, for order is a condition on which the very possibility of law depends. The 'rule of law' is a common and convenient phrase, but it becomes misleading if it leads us to think of law, as it may, as an active force in its own right. Law only 'rules' when it is put on the throne and kept there by a power outside itself, for its strength is always derivative and not original. That is not the less true because, as I have already admitted, it is not force that generally makes us obey the law. . .

I pass to the second of the conditions of progress which I referred to. All that an assurance of order can do is to make law possible, to provide a soil in which,

if other conditions are favourable, it can develop. It does not make the growth of law a certainty. To be effective a system of law needs to be a part of a wider system of social organization. I was struck by a phrase that I noticed in a letter to *The Times* some few months ago, in which the writer compared law to a limb of the body politic, and pointed out that a limb can only perform its proper function when it is attached to a body. Unfortunately, he said, there is no body politic for international law to be attached to. This seems to me to be an important truth. Inside a State law is part of a general system of government; it does not stand alone, for government uses many other social instruments besides the law with its appurtenances of courts to interpret, and police to enforce it. Government, modern government especially, comprises, besides machinery for changing the law from time to time, a vast system of administration which becomes ever more complicated and concerned with ever widening functions. To see the necessity of all this if the legal system is to work properly we need only ask ourselves how we should fare in the State if the only public ordering of our affairs consisted of rules of law and courts to apply them. Yet we have been content until recently to assume that international legal relations could function in this sort of political vacuum, that in the international field we needed hardly any organization except a body of rules prescribing how States ought to behave in certain given circumstances. International law has been given a task which the whole history of law shows to be impossible for law, for although the veriest beginner in the study of law knows that law and society are terms, each of which connotes the other, we have assumed that international law could fulfil its function outside a real society. . .

## V. The Individual and International Law

### A. *Individual Responsibility for Violations*

In the past international law has been applicable mainly to states. It is suggested by Hans Kelsen that the individual be held responsible for violations.

(Hans Kelsen, *Peace Through Law*, Chapel Hill, pp. 71-72, 78-79. Copyright 1944 by The University of North Carolina Press.)

One of the most effective means to prevent war and to guarantee international peace is the enactment of rules establishing individual responsibility of the persons who as members of government have violated international law by resorting to or provoking war. It is a fundamental principle of international law that war is permitted only as a reaction against a wrong suffered—that is to say, as a sanction—and that any war which has not this character is a delict, i.e. a violation of international law. This is the substance of the principle of *bellum justum* (just war). Almost all the states are contracting parties to the Briand-Kellogg Pact, by which war as a means of national policy is outlawed. Resorting to war may be a delict not only according to general international law or according to the Briand-Kellogg Pact, but also according to a special treaty concluded between two states, such as a non-aggression pact. . .

To punish the authors of a war means making certain individuals responsible by punishing them for acts committed by themselves, at their command, or with their authorization. This does not mean to punish a state as such, that is, a state as a body corporate. Most writers maintain that the sanctions which international law provides against the states as

such, namely reprisals and war, are not punishments in the sense of criminal law. The difference, however, between the specific sanctions of international law directed against individuals is not clearly manifest. Punishment is forcible deprivation of life, freedom, or property for the purpose of retribution or prevention. This definition applies to the specific sanctions of international law, war and reprisals as well. That the perpetrator must have a guilty mind, that he must have brought about the harmful effect of his conduct willfully and maliciously or with culpable negligence, does not, as is sometimes maintained, exclude 'punishment' of states. . .

It stands to reason that individual responsibility for violations of international law can be established by particular international law, for instance, by an international treaty. An example is the abortive treaty relating to the use of submarines concluded at Washington on February 6, 1922. Article 3 of this treaty states that any person in the service of any state who shall violate any rule of this treaty relative to the attack, capture, or destruction of commercial ships, whether or not he is under order of a governmental superior 'shall be deemed to have violated the laws of war and shall be liable to trial and punishment as if for an act of piracy. . .'

According to general international law, a person who, in the service of a state, has violated a rule of international law is not responsible. But by an international treaty, such persons can be made responsible. . .

The International Convention for the Protection of Submarine Telegraph Cables, signed at Paris on March 14, 1884, is another example of a rule of inter-national law directly obligating individuals and establishing individual responsibility. Article II of the Convention stipulates 'the breaking or injury of a submarine cable, done willfully or through culpable negligence—shall be a punishable offense, . . .'

## VI. War Crimes and the Individual

The Charter of the International Tribunal for War Crimes set up by the United Nations stated the principle of individual responsibility. The following extract is taken from that charter.

(Charter of the International Military Tribunal, *Trial of War Criminals,* Department of State, 1945.)

The following acts, or any of them, are crimes coming within the jurisdiction of the Tribunal for which there shall be individual responsibility:

(a) Crimes against peace: Namely, planning, preparation, initiation or waging of a war of aggression, or a war in violation of international treaties, agreements or assurances, or participation in a common plan or conspiracy for the accomplishment of any of the foregoing;

(b) War Crimes: Namely, violations of the laws or customs of war. Such violations shall include, but not be limited to, murder, ill-treatment or deportation to slave labor or for any other purpose of civilian population of or in occupied territory, murder or ill-treatment of prisoners of war or persons on the seas, killing of hostages, plunder of public or private property, wanton destruction of cities, towns or villages, or devastation not justified by military necessity;

(c) Crimes against humanity: Namely, murder, extermination, enslavement, deportation, and other inhumane acts committed against any civilian population, before or during the war, or persecutions on political, racial or religious grounds

in execution of or in connection with any crime within the jurisdiction of the Tribunal, whether or not in violation of the domestic law of the country where perpetrated.

. . .

Leaders, organizers, instigators and accomplices participating in the formulation or execution of a common plan or conspiracy to commit any of the foregoing crimes are responsible for all acts performed by any persons in execution of such plan.

*Article* 7. The official position of defendants, whether as heads of state or responsible officials in government departments, shall not be considered as freeing them from responsibility or mitigating punishment.

*Article* 8. The fact that the defendant acted pursuant to order of his government or of a superior shall not free him from responsibility, but may be considered in mitigation of punishment if the Tribunal determines that justice so requires.

*Article* 9. At the trial of any individual member of any group or organization the Tribunal may declare (in connection with any act of which the individual may be convicted) that the group or organization of which the individual was a member was a criminal organization.

. . .

## VII. INTERNATIONAL LAW AND THE UNITED NATIONS

Believing that a well-developed system of international law will be an important help in the maintenance of peace, the General Assembly of the United Nations on 11 December 1946 set up a Committee on the Progressive Development of International Law and its Codification. The Committee was composed of the representatives of seventeen states, including all of the five permanent members of the Security Council. After thirty meetings, the last of which was held on 17 June 1947, the Committee published its final report in a series of documents. Some of their conclusions and recommendations are given below in excerpts from the report of the United States representative, Philip C. Jessup.

(P. C. Jessup, Report, *Department of State Bulletin,* vol. XVII, No. 420, 1947, pp. 121-7.)

### A. INTERNATIONAL LAW COMMISSION (ILC)

1. SINGLE COMMISSION. The Committee agreed that, in order to carry out the progressive development of international law and its eventual codification, the General Assembly should establish a single commission composed of persons of recognized competence in international law.

The Committee agreed also that the ILC should deal not only with public international law but with private international law as well as penal international law. Certain delegations had taken the position that more than one commission was needed. Separate commissions for public, for private, and for penal international law were proposed. Other suggestions related to the desirability of having one commission for the development of international law and another for codification. The United States Representative pointed out that, while different procedures might be utilized for codification and for development, the task should be undertaken by a single commission. Separate commissions would render the work unnecessarily complex.

The Committee agreed that the Commission should be called the International Law Commission, hereinafter referred to as the ILC.

2. NUMBER OF MEMBERS. The United States proposed that the ILC should be composed of nine persons. The United Kingdom proposed seven. Several delegations advocated a larger number in order that more systems of law should have an opportunity to be represented.

The Committee first decided to limit the number of members of the ILC to nine. Subsequently, however, during discussion of the rapporteur's report, the Committee reconsidered this decision, and by a vote of 9 to 5, increased the number to fifteen. . .

3. METHOD OF ELECTION. In regard to the method of election of the members of the ILC, a large majority of the Committee preferred, and the Committee adopted, the plan which, with some slight modification, is prescribed by the Statute of the International Court of Justice for the election of the judges of the Court. The recommendation of the Committee is in accord with the position taken by the United States. . .

The proposal for election by the Court was inspired by the belief that under this plan the membership of the ILC would be more likely to represent the best expert talent of the world and that political appointments would be minimized. . .

5. FULL-TIME SERVICE OF MEMBERS. The recommendation that the members of the ILC should be required to render full-time service was warmly debated in the Committee. By a vote of 9 to 5 the Committee thought that this would be necessary.

7. SEAT. The Committee agreed that the seat of the ILC should be at Lake Success, where the headquarters of the United Nations are established. It was pointed out by the Secretariat that any other decision would result in additional heavy expense. . .

9. PROCEDURES FOR THE 'PROGRESSIVE DEVELOPMENT OF INTERNATIONAL LAW' AND THE 'CODIFICATION OF INTERNATIONAL LAW.' . . .

In its recommendations regarding procedure of the work of the ILC, the Committee drew a distinction between (a) progressive development of international law and (b) codification of international law. The ILC might have the task of drafting a convention on a subject not yet regulated by international law or in which the law has not yet been highly developed or formulated in the practice of states. On the other hand, the ILC might have another task, the formulation and systematic arrangement of law in areas where there has been extensive state practice, precedent and doctrine. For purposes of the following procedures the Committee, by a majority vote, referred to the first type of task as 'progressive development' and to the second type as 'codification.' It was realized that the terms employed are not mutually exclusive, that a clear-cut distinction between the law as it is and the law as it ought to be could not be maintained in practice. It was pointed out that codification inevitably has to fill in gaps and amend the law in the light of changing conditions.

Some delegations expressed the view that all the work of the ILC should take the form of draft multipartite conventions which would bind no state unless it ratified the convention. The use of the term 'international legislation' as a synonym for 'multipartite conventions' was strongly objected to by some delegations. The United States Representative agreed that in connection with the regulation of new subjects or of subjects in regard to which the law has not yet been highly developed the only possible procedure for the development of international law is through the ratification of multipartite conventions. However, he pointed out that for work in the field of codification as distinguished from development of international law a different procedure was desirable. While the opposition to scientific restatements of law by the delegations advocating conventions as the only means was quite strong, most of the proposals of the United States which drew a distinction between procedure for development of international law and procedure for codification were accepted. (Doc. A/AC.10/33 introduced jointly with the Representative for China.)

As a compromise, the United States Representative agreed that in connection with codification of international law, ILC should frame its conclusions in the form of draft articles of multipartite conventions. He secured, however, the Committee's approval of a detailed procedure which preserves much of the scientific value of the restatement process. Furthermore, the Committee agreed that for work in the field of codification, the results of the studies of the ILC might be either (a) allowed to rest in the form of a published volume which would have whatever influence its quality warranted, (b) might be adopted in whole or in part by a resolution of the General Assembly, or (c) embodied in a multipartite convention to be submitted to the states for ratification. . .

A majority of the Committee decided to recommend that the ILC should be authorized to consider projects and draft conventions recommended by governments, other United Nations organs, specialized agencies and those official bodies established by intergovernmental agreement to further the progressive development of international law and its codification. . .

## B. Cooperation of the United Nations Organs

With respect to the request of the General Assembly that the Committee study methods of securing the cooperation of the several organs of the United Nations in the task of the development and codification of international law, the Committee recommended:

(a) that the ILC should be authorized to consult with such organs.

(b) that in projects referred to it by an organ of the United Nations, the ILC should be authorized to make an interim report to the organ concerned prior to submitting its final report to the General Assembly. This resolution was carried by a majority of the Committee. A minority of the members dissented from it on the ground that, in their view, it would not be in accordance with the provisions of the United Nations Charter for any organ of the United Nations other than the General Assembly to refer a project to the ILC. Two members of this minority would add 'or the Economic and Social Council under the authority of the General Assembly' at this point. . .

## C. Assistance of National or International Bodies

The General Assembly resolution of December 11, 1946 directed the Committee to study also methods of enlisting the assistance of such national or international bodies as might aid in the attainment of its objective. With respect to this point, the Committee recommended:

(a) that the ILC should be authorized to consult such bodies, official or unofficial. A minority of the Committee was of the opinion that the consultation should be limited to organizations included in the list referred to in the sub-paragraph following.

(b) that, for the purpose of distribution of ILC documents, the Secretary-General, after consultation with the ILC, should draw up a list of national and international organizations dealing with questions of international law. . .

## VIII. International Arbitration

Arbitration may be defined as the settlement of disputes by judges chosen by the parties. Recourse to it is normally by means of a special agreement known as a *compromis*. Because so many disputes were arbitrated during the nineteenth century, and to encourage an even greater use of the procedure, a Permanent Court of Arbitration was set up in 1899 at The Hague. The following extract is from the convention establishing the Court, as revised in 1907:

(Convention for the Pacific Settlement of International Disputes, 1907. *U.S. Statutes at Large*, xxxvi. p. 2199.)

• • •

### Article 37

International arbitration has for its object the settlement of disputes between

States by judges of their own choice and on the basis of respect for law.

Recourse to arbitration implies an engagement to submit in good faith to the award.

### ARTICLE 38

In questions of a legal nature, and especially in the interpretation or application of international conventions, arbitration is recognized by the contracting Powers as the most effective, and, at the same time, the most equitable means of settling disputes which diplomacy has failed to settle.

Consequently, it would be desirable that, in disputes about the above-mentioned questions, the contracting Powers should, if a case arose, have recourse to arbitration, in so far as circumstances permit.

### ARTICLE 39

The arbitration convention is concluded for questions already existing or for questions which may arise eventually.

It may embrace any dispute or only disputes of a certain category.

### ARTICLE 40

Independently of general or private treaties expressly stipulating recourse to arbitration as obligatory on the contracting Powers, the said Powers reserve to themselves the right of concluding new agreements, general or particular, with a view to extending compulsory arbitration to all cases which they may consider it possible to submit to it.

### ARTICLE 41

With the object of facilitating an immediate recourse to arbitration for international differences, which it has not been possible to settle by diplomacy, the contracting Powers undertake to maintain the Permanent Court of Arbitration, as established by the First Peace Confer-

ence, accessible at all times, and operating, unless otherwise stipulated by the parties, in accordance with the rules of procedure inserted in the present Convention.

### ARTICLE 42

The Permanent Court is competent for all arbitration cases, unless the parties agree to institute a special tribunal.

### ARTICLE 43

The Permanent Court sits at The Hague.

An International Bureau serves as registry for the Court. It is the channel for communications relative to the meetings of the Court; it has charge of the archives and conducts all the administrative business.

The contracting Powers undertake to communicate to the Bureau, as soon as possible, a certified copy of any conditions of arbitration arrived at between them and of any award concerning them delivered by a special tribunal.

They likewise undertake to communicate to the Bureau the laws, regulations, and documents eventually showing the execution of the awards given by the Court.

### ARTICLE 44

Each contracting Power selects four persons at the most, of known competency in questions of international law, of the highest moral reputation, and disposed to accept the duties of arbitrator.

The persons thus selected are inscribed, as members of the Court, in a list which shall be notified to all the contracting Powers by the Bureau.

Any alteration in the list of arbitrators is brought by the Bureau to the knowledge of the contracting Powers.

Two or more Powers may agree on the selection in common of one or more members.

The same person can be selected by different Powers.

The members of the Court are appointed for a term of six years. These appointments are renewable.

Should a member of the Court die or resign, the same procedure is followed for filling the vacancy as was followed for appointing him. In this case the appointment is made for a fresh period of six years.

### ARTICLE 45

When the contracting Powers wish to have recourse to the Permanent Court for the settlement of a difference which has arisen between them, the arbitrators called upon to form the tribunal with jurisdiction to decide this difference must be chosen from the general list of members of the Court.

Failing the direct agreement of the parties on the composition of the arbitration tribunal, the following course shall be pursued:

Each party appoints two arbitrators, of whom one only can be its national or chosen from among the persons selected by it as members of the Permanent Court. These arbitrators together choose an umpire.

If the votes are equally divided, the choice of the umpire is intrusted to a third Power, selected by the parties by common accord.

If an agreement is not arrived at on this subject each party selects a different Power, and the choice of the umpire is made in concert by the Powers thus selected.

If, within two months' time, these two Powers cannot come to an agreement, each of them presents two candidates taken from the list of members of the Permanent Court, exclusive of the members selected by the parties and not being nationals of either of them. Drawing lots determines which of the candidates thus presented shall be umpire.

### ARTICLE 46

The tribunal being thus composed, the parties notify to the Bureau their determination to have recourse to the Court, the text of their compromis, and the names of the arbitrators.

The Bureau communicates without delay to each arbitrator the compromis, and the names of the other members of the tribunal.

The tribunal assembles at the date fixed by the parties. The Bureau makes the necessary arrangements for the meeting.

The members of the tribunal, in the exercise of their duties and out of their own country, enjoy diplomatic privileges and immunities.

### ARTICLE 47

The Bureau is authorized to place its offices and staff at the disposal of the contracting Powers for the use of any special board of arbitration.

. . .

### ARTICLE 63

As a general rule, arbitration procedure comprises two distinct phases: pleadings and oral discussions.

The pleadings consist in the communication by the respective agents to the members of the tribunal and the opposite party of cases, counter-cases, and, if necessary, of replies; the parties annex thereto all papers and documents called for in the case. This communication shall be made either directly or through the intermediary of the International Bureau, in the order and within the time fixed by the compromis.

The time fixed by the compromis may

be extended by mutual agreement by the parties, or by the tribunal when the latter considers it necessary for the purpose of reaching a just decision.

The discussions consist in the oral development before the tribunal of the arguments of the parties.

. . .

## IX. THE INTERNATIONAL COURT OF JUSTICE

The International Court of Justice is an integral part of the United Nations organization, and the Statute of the Court below forms an Annex to the Charter of the United Nations. As has been mentioned above, a similar court —the Permanent Court of International Justice—was established after World War I as part of the League of Nations system. The new court is not a continuation of the old, but it was built on the foundations of the Permanent Court. The treaties and declarations relating to the former court, however, are now regarded as applying to the International Court of Justice. One of the reasons for discarding the old court was the fact that some members of the United Nations were not members of that tribunal. Today, all members of the United Nations are also members of the court.

### STATUTE OF THE INTERNATIONAL COURT OF JUSTICE

#### ARTICLE 1

The International Court of Justice established by the Charter of the United Nations as the principal judicial organ of the United Nations shall be constituted and shall function in accordance with the provisions of the present Statute.

### I. ORGANIZATION OF THE COURT

#### ARTICLE 2

The Court shall be composed of a body of independent judges, elected regardless of their nationality from among persons of high moral character, who possess the qualifications required in their respective countries for appointment to the highest judicial offices, or are jurisconsults of recognized competence in international law.

#### ARTICLE 3

1. The Court shall consist of fifteen members, no two of whom may be nationals of the same state.

2. A person who for the purposes of membership in the Court could be regarded as a national of more than one state shall be deemed to be a national of the one in which he ordinarily exercises civil and political rights.

#### ARTICLE 4

1. The members of the Court shall be elected by the General Assembly and by the Security Council from a list of persons nominated by the national groups in the Permanent Court of Arbitration, in accordance with the following provisions.

2. In the case of Members of the United Nations not represented in the Permanent Court of Arbitration, candidates shall be nominated by national groups appointed for this purpose by their governments under the same conditions as those prescribed for members of the Permanent Court of Arbitration by Article 44 of the Convention of The Hague of 1907 for the pacific settlement of international disputes.

3. The conditions under which a state which is a party to the present Statute

but is not a Member of the United Nations may participate in electing the members of the Court shall, in the absence of a special agreement, be laid down by the General Assembly upon recommendation of the Security Council.

### ARTICLE 5

1. At least three months before the date of the election, the Secretary-General of the United Nations shall address a written request to the members of the Permanent Court of Arbitration belonging to the states which are parties to the present Statute, and to the members of the national groups appointed under Article 4, paragraph 2, inviting them to undertake, within a given time, by national groups, the nomination of persons in a position to accept the duties of a member of the Court.

2. No group may nominate more than four persons, not more than two of whom shall be of their own nationality. In no case may the number of candidates nominated by a group be more than double the number of seats to be filled.

### ARTICLE 6

Before making these nominations, each national group is recommended to consult its highest court of justice, its legal faculties and schools of law, and its national academies and national sections of international academies devoted to the study of law.

### ARTICLE 7

1. The Secretary-General shall prepare a list in alphabetical order of all the persons thus nominated. Save as provided in Article 12, paragraph 2, these shall be the only persons eligible.

2. The Secretary-General shall submit his list to the General Assembly and to the Security Council.

### ARTICLE 8

The General Assembly and the Security Council shall proceed independently of one another to elect the members of the Court.

### ARTICLE 9

At every election, the electors shall bear in mind not only that the persons to be elected should individually possess the qualifications required, but also that in the body as a whole the representation of the main forms of civilization and of the principal legal systems of the world should be assured.

### ARTICLE 10

1. Those candidates who obtain an absolute majority of votes in the General Assembly and in the Security Council shall be considered as elected.

2. Any vote of the Security Council, whether for the election of judges or for the appointment of members of the conference envisaged in Article 12, shall be taken without any distinction between permanent and non-permanent members of the Security Council.

3. In the event of more than one national of the same state obtaining an absolute majority of the votes both of the General Assembly and of the Security Council, the eldest of these only shall be considered as elected.

### ARTICLE 11

If, after the first meeting held for the purpose of the election, one or more seats remain to be filled, a second and, if necessary, a third meeting shall take place.

### ARTICLE 12

1. If, after the third meeting, one or more seats still remain unfilled, a joint conference consisting of six members, three appointed by the General Assembly and three by the Security Council, may be formed at any time at the request

of either the General Assembly or the Security Council, for the purpose of choosing by the vote of an absolute majority one name for each seat still vacant, to submit to the General Assembly and the Security Council for their respective acceptance.

2. If the joint conference is unanimously agreed upon any person who fulfils the required conditions, he may be included in its list, even though he was not included in the list of nominations referred to in Article 7.

3. If the joint conference is satisfied that it will not be successful in procuring an election, those members of the Court who have already been elected shall, within a period to be fixed by the Security Council, proceed to fill the vacant seats by selection from among those candidates who have obtained votes either in the General Assembly or in the Security Council.

4. In the event of an equality of votes among the judges, the eldest judge shall have a casting vote.

### ARTICLE 13

1. The members of the Court shall be elected for nine years and may be reelected; provided, however, that of the judges elected at the first election, the terms of five judges shall expire at the end of three years and the terms of five more judges shall expire at the end of six years.

2. The judges whose terms are to expire at the end of the above-mentioned initial periods of three and six years shall be chosen by lot to be drawn by the Secretary-General immediately after the first election has been completed.

3. The members of the Court shall continue to discharge their duties until their places have been filled. Though replaced, they shall finish any cases which they may have begun.

4. In the case of the resignation of a member of the Court, the resignation shall be addressed to the President of the Court for transmission to the Secretary-General. This last notification makes the place vacant.

### ARTICLE 14

Vacancies shall be filled by the same method as that laid down for the first election, subject to the following provision: the Secretary-General shall, within one month of the occurrence of the vacancy, proceed to issue the invitations provided for in Article 5, and the date of the election shall be fixed by the Security Council.

### ARTICLE 15

A member of the Court elected to replace a member whose term of office has not expired shall hold office for the remainder of his predecessor's term.

### ARTICLE 16

1. No member of the Court may exercise any political or administrative function, or engage in any other occupation of a professional nature.

2. Any doubt on this point shall be settled by the decision of the Court.

### ARTICLE 17

1. No member of the Court may act as agent, counsel, or advocate in any case.

2. No member may participate in the decision of any case in which he has previously taken part as agent, counsel, or advocate for one of the parties, or as a member of a national or international court, or of a commission of enquiry, or in any other capacity.

3. Any doubt on this point shall be settled by the decision of the Court.

### ARTICLE 18

1. No member of the Court can be dismissed unless, in the unanimous opinion of the other members, he has ceased to fulfil the required conditions.

2. Formal notification thereof shall be made to the Secretary-General by the Registrar.

3. This notification makes the place vacant.

### ARTICLE 19

The members of the Court, when engaged on the business of the Court, shall enjoy diplomatic privileges and immunities.

### ARTICLE 20

Every member of the Court shall, before taking up his duties, make a solemn declaration in open court that he will exercise his powers impartially and conscientiously.

### ARTICLE 21

1. The Court shall elect its President and Vice-President for three years; they may be re-elected.

2. The Court shall appoint its Registrar and may provide for the appointment of such other officers as may be necessary.

### ARTICLE 22

1. The seat of the Court shall be established at The Hague. This, however, shall not prevent the Court from sitting and exercising its functions elsewhere whenever the Court considers it desirable.

2. The President and the Registrar shall reside at the seat of the Court.

### ARTICLE 23

1. The Court shall remain permanently in session, except during the judicial vacations, the dates and duration of which shall be fixed by the Court.

2. Members of the Court are entitled to periodic leave, the dates and duration of which shall be fixed by the Court, having in mind the distance between The Hague and the home of each judge.

3. Members of the Court shall be bound, unless they are on leave or prevented from attending by illness or other serious reasons duly explained to the President, to hold themselves permanently at the disposal of the Court.

### ARTICLE 24

1. If, for some special reason, a member of the Court considers that he should not take part in the decision of a particular case, he shall so inform the President.

2. If the President considers that for some special reason one of the members of the Court should not sit in a particular case, he shall give him notice accordingly.

3. If in any such case the member of the Court and the President disagree, the matter shall be settled by the decision of the Court.

### ARTICLE 25

1. The full Court shall sit except when it is expressly provided otherwise in the present Statute.

2. Subject to the condition that the number of judges available to constitute the Court is not thereby reduced below eleven, the Rules of the Court may provide for allowing one or more judges, according to circumstances and in rotation, to be dispensed from sitting.

3. A quorum of nine judges shall suffice to constitute the Court.

### ARTICLE 26

1. The Court may from time to time form one or more chambers, composed of three or more judges as the Court may determine, for dealing with particular categories of cases; for example, labor cases and cases relating to transit and communications.

2. The Court may at any time form a chamber for dealing with a particular case. The number of judges to constitute such a chamber shall be determined by the Court with the approval of the parties.

3. Cases shall be heard and determined

by the chambers provided for in this Article if the parties so request.

## ARTICLE 27

A judgment given by any of the chambers provided for in Articles 26 and 29 shall be considered as rendered by the Court.

## ARTICLE 28

The chambers provided for in Articles 26 and 29 may, with the consent of the parties, sit and exercise their functions elsewhere than at The Hague.

## ARTICLE 29

With a view to the speedy despatch of business, the Court shall form annually a chamber composed of five judges which, at the request of the parties, may hear and determine cases by summary procedure. In addition, two judges shall be selected for the purpose of replacing judges who find it impossible to sit.

## ARTICLE 30

1. The Court shall frame rules for carrying out its functions. In particular, it shall lay down rules of procedure.

2. The Rules of the Court may provide for assessors to sit with the Court or with any of its chambers, without the right to vote.

## ARTICLE 31

1. Judges of the nationality of each of the parties shall retain their right to sit in the case before the Court.

2. If the Court includes upon the Bench a judge of the nationality of one of the parties, any other party may choose a person to sit as judge. Such person shall be chosen preferably from among those persons who have been nominated as candidates as provided in Articles 4 and 5.

3. If the Court includes upon the Bench no judge of the nationality of the parties, each of these parties may proceed to choose a judge as provided in paragraph 2 of this Article.

4. The provisions of this Article shall apply to the case of Articles 26 and 29. In such cases, the President shall request one or, if necessary, two of the members of the Court forming the chamber to give place to the members of the Court of the nationality of the parties concerned, and, failing such, or if they are unable to be present, to the judges specially chosen by the parties.

5. Should there be several parties in the same interest, they shall, for the purpose of the preceding provisions, be reckoned as one party only. Any doubt upon this point shall be settled by the decision of the Court.

6. Judges chosen as laid down in paragraphs 2, 3, and 4 of this Article shall fulfil the conditions required by Articles 2, 17 (paragraph 2), 20, and 24 of the present Statute. They shall take part in the decision on terms of complete equality with their colleagues.

## ARTICLE 32

1. Each member of the Court shall receive an annual salary.

2. The President shall receive a special annual allowance.

3. The Vice-President shall receive a special allowance for every day on which he acts as President.

4. The judges chosen under Article 31 other than members of the Court, shall receive compensation for each day on which they exercise their functions.

5. These salaries, allowances, and compensation shall be fixed by the General Assembly. They may not be decreased during the term of office.

6. The salary of the Registrar shall be fixed by the General Assembly on the proposal of the Court.

7. Regulations made by the General Assembly shall fix the conditions under which retirement pensions may be given

to members of the Court and to the Registrar, and the conditions under which members of the Court and the Registrar shall have their traveling expenses refunded.

8. The above salaries, allowances, and compensation shall be free of all taxation.

### ARTICLE 33

The expenses of the Court shall be borne by the United Nations in such a manner as shall be decided by the General Assembly.

## II. COMPETENCE OF THE COURT

### ARTICLE 34

1. Only states may be parties in cases before the Court.

2. The Court, subject to and in conformity with its Rules, may request of public international organizations information relevant to cases before it, and shall receive such information presented by such organizations on their own initiative.

3. Whenever the construction of the constituent instrument of a public international organization or of an international convention adopted thereunder is in question in a case before the Court, the Registrar shall so notify the public international organization concerned and shall communicate to it copies of all the written proceedings.

### ARTICLE 35

1. The Court shall be open to the states parties to the present Statute.

2. The conditions under which the Court shall be open to other states shall, subject to the special provisions contained in treaties in force, be laid down by the Security Council, but in no case shall such conditions place the parties in a position of inequality before the Court.

3. When a state which is not a Member of the United Nations is a party to a case, the Court shall fix the amount which that party is to contribute towards the expenses of the Court. This provision shall not apply if such state is bearing a share of the expenses of the Court.

### ARTICLE 36

1. The jurisdiction of the Court comprises all cases which the parties refer to it and all matters specially provided for in the Charter of the United Nations or in treaties and conventions in force.

2. The states parties to the present Statute may at any time declare that they recognize as compulsory *ipso facto* and without special agreement, in relation to any other state accepting the same obligation, the jurisdiction of the Court in all legal disputes concerning:

    a. the interpretation of a treaty;
    b. any question of international law;
    c. the existence of any fact which, if established, would constitute a breach of an international obligation;
    d. the nature or extent of the reparation to be made for the breach of an international obligation.

3. The declarations referred to above may be made unconditionally or on condition of reciprocity on the part of several or certain states, or for a certain time.

4. Such declarations shall be deposited with the Secretary-General of the United Nations, who shall transmit copies thereof to the parties to the Statute and to the Registrar of the Court.

5. Declarations made under Article 36 of the Statute of the Permanent Court of International Justice and which are still in force shall be deemed, as between the parties to the present Statute, to be acceptances of the compulsory jurisdiction of the International Court of Justice for the period which they still have

to run and in accordance with their terms.

6. In the event of a dispute as to whether the Court has jurisdiction, the matter shall be settled by the decision of the Court.

### ARTICLE 37

Whenever a treaty or convention in force provides for reference of a matter to a tribunal to have been instituted by the League of Nations, or to the Permanent Court of International Justice, the matter shall, as between the parties to the present Statute, be referred to the International Court of Justice.

### ARTICLE 38

1. The Court, whose function is to decide in accordance with international law such disputes as are submitted to it, shall apply:

a. international conventions, whether general or particular, establishing rules expressly recognized by the contesting states;
b. international custom, as evidence of a general practice accepted as law;
c. the general principles of law recognized by civilized nations;
d. subject to the provisions of Article 59, judicial decisions and the teachings of the most highly qualified publicists of the various nations, as subsidiary means for the determination of rules of law.

2. This provision shall not prejudice the power of the Court to decide a case *ex aequo et bono,* if the parties agree thereto.

### III. PROCEDURE

### ARTICLE 39

1. The official languages of the Court shall be French and English. If the par-

ties agree that the case shall be conducted in French, the judgment shall be delivered in French. If the parties agree that the case shall be conducted in English, the judgment shall be delivered in English.

2. In the absence of an agreement as to which language shall be employed, each party may, in the pleadings, use the language which it prefers; the decision of the Court shall be given in French and English. In this case the Court shall at the same time determine which of the two texts shall be considered as authoritative.

3. The Court shall, at the request of any party, authorize a language other than French or English to be used by that party.

### ARTICLE 40

1. Cases are brought before the Court, as the case may be, either by the notification of the special agreement or by a written application addressed to the Registrar. In either case the subject of the dispute and the parties shall be indicated.

2. The Registrar shall forthwith communicate the application to all concerned.

3. He shall also notify the Members of the United Nations through the Secretary-General, and also any other states entitled to appear before the Court.

### ARTICLE 41

1. The Court shall have the power to indicate, if it considers that circumstances so require, any provisional measures which ought to be taken to preserve the respective rights of either party.

2. Pending the final decision, notice of the measures suggested shall forthwith be given to the parties and to the Security Council.

### ARTICLE 42

1. The parties shall be represented by agents.

2. They may have the assistance of counsel or advocates before the Court.

3. The agents, counsel, and advocates of parties before the Court shall enjoy the privileges and immunities necessary to the independent exercise of their duties.

### ARTICLE 43

1. The procedure shall consist of two parts: written and oral.

2. The written proceedings shall consist of the communication to the Court and to the parties of memorials, counter-memorials and, if necessary, replies; also all papers and documents in support.

3. These communications shall be made through the Registrar, in the order and within the time fixed by the Court.

4. A certified copy of every document produced by one party shall be communicated to the other party.

5. The oral proceedings shall consist of the hearing by the Court of witnesses, experts, agents, counsel, and advocates.

### ARTICLE 44

1. For the service of all notices upon persons other than the agents, counsel, and advocates, the Court shall apply direct to the government of the state upon whose territory the notice has to be served.

2. The same provision shall apply whenever steps are to be taken to procure evidence on the spot.

### ARTICLE 45

The hearing shall be under the control of the President or, if he is unable to preside, of the Vice-President; if neither is able to preside, the senior judge present shall preside.

### ARTICLE 46

The hearing in Court shall be public, unless the Court shall decide otherwise, or unless the parties demand that the public be not admitted.

### ARTICLE 47

1. Minutes shall be made at each hearing and signed by the Registrar and the President.

2. These minutes alone shall be authentic.

### ARTICLE 48

The Court shall make orders for the conduct of the case, shall decide the form and time in which each party must conclude its arguments, and make all arrangements connected with the taking of evidence.

### ARTICLE 49

The Court may, even before the hearing begins, call upon the agents to produce any document or to supply any explanations. Formal note shall be taken of any refusal.

### ARTICLE 50

The Court may, at any time, entrust any individual, body, bureau, commission, or other organization that it may select, with the task of carrying out an enquiry or giving an expert opinion.

### ARTICLE 51

During the hearing any relevant questions are to be put to the witnesses and experts under the conditions laid down by the Court in the rules of procedure referred to in Article 30.

### ARTICLE 52

After the Court has received the proofs and evidence within the time specified for the purpose, it may refuse to accept any further oral or written evidence that one party may desire to present unless the other side consents.

### ARTICLE 53

1. Whenever one of the parties does not appear before the Court, or fails to defend its case, the other party may call upon the Court to decide in favor of its claim.

2. The Court must, before doing so, satisfy itself, not only that it has jurisdiction in accordance with Articles 36 and 37, but also that the claim is well founded in fact and law.

### ARTICLE 54

1. When, subject to the control of the Court, the agents, counsel, and advocates have completed their presentation of the case, the President shall declare the hearing closed.

2. The Court shall withdraw to consider the judgment.

3. The deliberations of the Court shall take place in private and remain secret.

### ARTICLE 55

1. All questions shall be decided by a majority of the judges present.

2. In the event of an equality of votes, the President or the judge who acts in his place shall have a casting vote.

### ARTICLE 56

1. The judgment shall state the reasons on which it is based.

2. It shall contain the names of the judges who have taken part in the decision.

### ARTICLE 57

If the judgment does not represent in whole or in part the unanimous opinion of the judges, any judge shall be entitled to deliver a separate opinion.

### ARTICLE 58

The judgment shall be signed by the President and by the Registrar. It shall be read in open court, due notice having been given to the agents.

### ARTICLE 59

The decision of the Court has no binding force except between the parties and in respect of that particular case.

### ARTICLE 60

The judgment is final and without appeal. In the event of dispute as to the meaning or scope of the judgment, the Court shall construe it upon the request of any party.

### ARTICLE 61

1. An application for revision of a judgment may be made only when it is based upon the discovery of some fact of such a nature as to be a decisive factor, which fact was, when the judgment was given, unknown to the Court and also to the party claiming revision, always provided that such ignorance was not due to negligence.

2. The proceedings for revision shall be opened by a judgment of the Court expressly recording the existence of the new fact, recognizing that it has such a character as to lay the case open to revision, and declaring the application admissible on this ground.

3. The Court may require previous compliance with the terms of the judgment before it admits proceedings in revision.

4. The application for revision must be made at latest within six months of the discovery of the new fact.

5. No application for revision may be made after the lapse of ten years from the date of the judgment.

### ARTICLE 62

1. Should a state consider that it has an interest of a legal nature which may be affected by the decision in the case, it may submit a request to the Court to be permitted to intervene.

2. It shall be for the Court to decide upon this request.

### ARTICLE 63

1. Whenever the construction of a convention to which states other than those concerned in the case are parties is in

question, the Registrar shall notify all such states forthwith.

2. Every state so notified has the right to intervene in the proceedings; but if it uses this right, the construction given by the judgment will be equally binding upon it.

### ARTICLE 64

Unless otherwise decided by the Court, each party shall bear its own costs.

## IV. ADVISORY OPINIONS

### ARTICLE 65

1. The Court may give an advisory opinion on any legal question at the request of whatever body may be authorized by or in accordance with the Charter of the United Nations to make such a request.

2. Questions upon which the advisory opinion of the Court is asked shall be laid before the Court by means of a written request containing an exact statement of the question upon which an opinion is required, and accompanied by all documents likely to throw light upon the question.

### ARTICLE 66

1. The Registrar shall forthwith give notice of the request for an advisory opinion to all states entitled to appear before the Court.

2. The Registrar shall also, by means of a special and direct communication, notify any state entitled to appear before the Court or international organization considered by the Court, or, should it not be sitting, by the President, as likely to be able to furnish information on the question, that the Court will be prepared to receive, within a time limit to be fixed by the President, written statements, or to hear, at a public sitting to be held for the purpose, oral statements relating to the question.

3. Should any such state entitled to appear before the Court have failed to receive the special communication referred to in paragraph 2 of this Article, such state may express a desire to submit a written statement or to be heard; and the Court will decide.

4. States and organizations having presented written or oral statements or both shall be permitted to comment on the statements made by other states or organizations in the form, to the extent, and within the time limits which the Court, or, should it not be sitting, the President, shall decide in each particular case. Accordingly, the Registrar shall in due time communicate any such written statements to states and organizations having submitted similar statements.

### ARTICLE 67

The Court shall deliver its advisory opinions in open court, notice having been given to the Secretary-General and to the representatives of Members of the United Nations, of other states and of international organizations immediately concerned.

### ARTICLE 68

In the exercise of its advisory functions the Court shall further be guided by the provisions of the present Statute which apply in contentious cases to the extent to which it recognizes them to be applicable.

## V. AMENDMENT

### ARTICLE 69

Amendments to the present Statute shall be effected by the same procedure as is provided by the Charter of the United Nations for amendments to that Charter, subject however to any provisions which the General Assembly upon recommendation of the Security Council may adopt concerning the participation of states which are parties to the present Statute but are not Members of the United Nations.

ARTICLE 70

The Court shall have power to propose such amendments to the present Statute as it may deem necessary, through written communications to the Secretary-General, for consideration in conformity with the provisions of Article 69.

## X. COMPULSORY JURISDICTION

Article 36 (the 'optional clause') of the Statute of the International Court of Justice permits a member to accept the jurisdiction of the Court as compulsory in disputes of a legal nature. In accordance with a resolution of the Senate, President Harry S. Truman announced on 14 August 1946 the acceptance by the United States Government of compulsory jurisdiction. Over forty members of the Court have now signed the optional clause.

(Declaration of President Truman, *Department of State Bulletin*, 8 September 1948, pp. 452-3.)

I, Harry S. Truman, President of the United States of America, declare on behalf of the United States of America, under Article 36, paragraph 2, of the Statute of the International Court of Justice, and in accordance with the Resolution of August 2, 1946, of the Senate of the United States of America (two-thirds of the Senators present concurring therein), that the United States of America recognizes as compulsory *ipso facto* and without special agreement, in relation to any other state accepting the same obligation, the jurisdiction of the International Court of Justice in all legal disputes hereafter arising concerning

a. the interpretation of a treaty;

b. any question of international law;

c. the existence of any fact which, if established, would constitute a breach of an international obligation;

d. the nature or extent of the reparation to be made for the breach of an international obligation;

*Provided,* that this declaration shall not apply to

a. disputes the solution of which the parties shall entrust to other tribunals by virtue of agreements already in existence or which may be concluded in the future; or

b. disputes with regard to matters which are essentially within the domestic jurisdiction of the United States of America as determined by the United States of America; or

c. disputes arising under a multilateral treaty, unless (1) all parties to the treaty affected by the decision are also parties to the case before the Court, or (2) the United States of America specially agrees to jurisdiction; and

*Provided further,* that this declaration shall remain in force for a period of five years and thereafter until the expiration of six months after notice may be given to terminate this declaration.

Done at Washington this fourteenth day of August 1946.

Harry S. Truman

# 6

# The Conduct of International Relations

THE multifarious interests of the seventy-five or more nation states bring them into constant contact with each other and necessitate machinery and processes by which adjustments can be made. There are trade difficulties to straighten out, and problems of health, immigration, extradition, naturalization, transportation, and so on to solve. Moreover there are national policies to promote and to reconcile with those of other states. The business of states is so voluminous and so vital that it takes the unceasing attention of every participating government.

To look out for its interests abroad, every government appoints diplomatic officers to negotiate with those of other countries. As the representatives of independent nations they are able to arrive at solutions to international problems only by agreement. When these agreements are in the nature of formal treaties, they are signed, subject to ratification. In the United States ratification is effected by the President on the advice and consent of two-thirds of the Senate. Less formal agreements, known as 'executive agreements,' do not require ratification. Today there are many thousands of treaties and agreements in force among the members of the family of nations. These agreements furnish the basis for modern international relations, embodying national policies in some cases, stating rules of international law in others, and sometimes serving as constitutions for international organizations such as the United Nations.

Most diplomatic relations are on a bilateral basis and are conducted by regularly accredited ambassadors and ministers in co-operation with the foreign offices of the country to which they have been sent. For instance, when the United States negotiated with Mexico on the protection of American oil interests against Mexican nationalization, it was done in Washington by the Mexican ambassador and the United States secretary of state, and in Mexico City by the American ambassador and the Mexican foreign secretary.

In contrast with early diplomacy, which was on a temporary or *ad hoc* basis, nations nowadays maintain permanent diplomatic missions at the capital city of every recognized country. In ancient Greece there were so many city states, and relations among them were so occasional, that the dispatch of permanent missions did not seem warranted. Rome also used special representatives and, as a rule, so did the Church, except that in the early fifth century a permanent envoy was sent to the Eastern Empire at Constantinople. The modern practice of maintaining permanent diplomatic missions originated among the city states of northern Italy. It was begun by Genoa in 1455 and was soon adopted by all of the city states of the community. As the nation states of Western Europe emerged, they took over the practice, and from that time on it has been generally followed.

Today the diplomatic agent abroad is expected to interpret to the accrediting country the national ideals of his people and the policies of his government. As 'the eyes and ears' of his government, he sends back his observations on the conditions, trends, and policies of the country in which he is working. It is his duty, too, to see to it that the persons and property of his fellow nationals are protected, to ask for the extradition of criminals, and to perform innumerable other tasks in behalf of his country. Some of this work he shares with consular officials, whose main business, however, is to promote trade and to perform the clerical and routine duties which are incident to it.

Nowadays diplomacy is often on a multilateral basis. This is because modern technological advances have generalized the interests of nations to such an extent that bilateral action is inadequate. The control of the radio, aerial navigation, the promotion of health, postal communication, and citizenship are only a few of the long list of subjects that are of general concern to most, if not all, of the nations of the world. Subjects of this nature can be best treated collectively.

Multilateral diplomacy is conducted in international conferences to which interested governments are invited to send delegates. This idea of 'conference diplomacy' has come to be widely accepted. The United States took part in fifty-three conferences between 1 July 1941 and 30 June 1945. In the absence of a world legislature, these conferences provide a handy means for the formulation of programs for collective international action.

Some conferences are set up *ad hoc* by some one initiating state or by a small group of states. Indeed, this used to be the general practice. During recent decades, however, a number of international organizations have been created which maintain permanent conference systems. The Pan-American organization has set up scores of conferences. Formerly the League of Nations did a great deal of its work by the conference method, and now the United Nations has taken over this procedure, with frequent meetings on health, aviation, trade, and other subjects, besides the regular meetings of the General Assembly, Security Council, and the Economic and Social Council. One of the most important departures in the conduct of international relations is this development of 'institutionalized' diplomacy.

## I. CALLIÈRES ON DIPLOMACY

The extract below is from a book by a French writer, published in the year 1716. It brings out the ethical standards of the diplomacy of that period, as well as the importance attached to the art. Although there have been charges in recent years that diplomats play the role of 'honorable spies,' certainly diplomacy in general is less vicious today.

(F. de Callières, *The Practice of Diplomacy*, 1716, translated by A. F. White, London, 1919, pp. 7, 16, 23, 31. Reprinted by permission of Constable & Co.)

The art of negotiation with princes is so important that the fate of the greatest states often depends upon the good or bad conduct of negotiations and upon the degree of capacity in the negotiations employed. . . Every Christian prince must take as his chief maxim not to employ arms to support or vindicate his rights until he has employed and exhausted the way of reason and of persuasion. It is to his interest also, to add to reason and persuasion the influence of benefits conferred, which indeed is one of the surest ways to make his power secure, and to increase it. . .

It is not necessary to turn far back into the past in order to understand what can be achieved by negotiation. We see daily about us its definite effects in sudden revolutions favourable to this great design of state or that, in the use of sedition in fermenting the hatreds between nations, in causing jealous rivals to arm against one another so that the *tertius gaudens* may profit, in the formation of leagues and other treaties of various kinds between monarchs whose interests might otherwise clash, in the dissolution by crafty means of the closest union between states; in a word, one may say that the art of negotiation, according as its conduct is good or evil, gives form to great affairs and may turn a host of lesser events into a useful influence upon the course of the greater. . .

To maintain the dignity of diplomacy the negotiator must clothe himself in liberality and generosity of heart, even in magnificence, but all with care and a frugality of design so that the trappings of his office do not by their display outshine the sterling merits of his own character and person. Let clean linen and appointments and delicacy reign at his table. Let him frequently give banquets and diversion in honor of the principal persons of the court in which he lives, and even in the honor of the prince himself, if he so cares to take part. Let him also enter into the spirit of the same diversions offered by others, but always in a light, unconstrained, and agreeable manner, and always with an open, good-natured, straight-forward air, and with a continual desire to give pleasure to others. If the custom of the country in which he serves permits freedom of conversation with the ladies of the court, he must on no account neglect any opportunity of placing himself and his master in a favourable light in the eyes of these ladies, for it is well known that the power of feminine charm often extends to cover the weightiest resolutions of state. . .

It frequently happens in negotiation as in war that well-chosen spies contribute more than any other agency to the success of great plans, and indeed it is clear that there is nothing so well adapted to upset the best designs as the sudden and premature revelation of an important secret upon which it depends. And as there is no expense better designed nor more necessary than that which is laid out upon a secret service, it would be inexcusable for a minister of state to neglect it. . .

The ambassador has sometimes been called an honorable spy because one of his principal occupations is to discover great secrets; and he fails in the discharge of his duty if he does not know how to lay out the necessary sums for this purpose. . .

The good negotiator, moreover, will never found the success of his mission on promises which he cannot redeem or on bad faith. It is a capital error, which prevails widely, that a clever negotiator must be a master of deceit. Deceit indeed is but a measure of the smallness of mind of him who employs it. . .

## II. DIPLOMATIC RANK

The ranks of the heads of diplomatic missions are defined by international law. Before 1815 there had been a great deal of rivalry in matters of precedence among diplomatic representatives. To settle the major aspects of the problem, the following agreement was made at Vienna and Aix-la-Chapelle in 1815-18. The ranks listed are still used.

(Regulations of Vienna, 1815, and of Aix-la-Chapelle, 1818, concerning Diplomatic Rank, *United States Diplomatic Instructions*, 1897, paragraph 18.)

In order to prevent in the future the inconveniences which have frequently occurred, and which may still occur, from the claims of Precedence among the different Diplomatic characters, the Plenipotentiaries of the Powers who signed the Treaty of Paris have agreed in the following articles, and think it their duty to invite those of other Crowned Heads to adopt the same regulations:

### ARTICLE 1

Diplomatic characters are divided into three classes:

That of Ambassadors, Legates, or Nuncios.

That of Envoys, Ministers, or other persons accredited to Sovereigns.

That of Chargés d'Affaires to Ministers for Foreign Affairs.

### ARTICLE 2

Ambassadors, Legates, or Nuncios only shall have the representative character.

### ARTICLE 3

Diplomatic characters charged with any special mission shall not, on that account, assume any superiority of rank.

### ARTICLE 4

Diplomatic characters shall rank in their respective classes according to the date of the official notification of their arrival.

The present regulation shall not occasion any change respecting the Representative of the Pope.

### ARTICLE 5

There shall be a regular form adopted by each State for the reception of Diplomatic characters of every class.

### ARTICLE 6

Ties of consanguinity or family alliance between Courts confer no rank on their Diplomatic Agents. The same rule applies to political alliances.

### ARTICLE 7

In Acts or Treaties between several Powers that admit alternity, the order which is to be observed in the signatures of Ministers shall be decided by lot.

### ARTICLE 8

It is agreed between the Five Courts that Ministers Resident accredited to them shall form, with respect to their Precedence, an intermediate class between Ministers of the Second Class and Chargé d'Affaires.

## III. The Organization of Diplomacy

Every country maintains a foreign office, or Department of State as it is called in the United States. This office dispatches diplomatic and consular representatives abroad to each recognized government, the former to capital cities, and the latter to important centers of trade and business. American representation in the British Isles (1946) is given below.

(*Congressional Directory*, 79th Congress, 2nd Session, 29 June 1946, p. 520.)

London—Ambassador Extraordinary and Minister Plenipotentiary
Counselor of Embassy
Counselor of Embassy
Counselor of Embassy for Economic Affairs
Commercial Attaché
Agricultural Attaché
First Secretary; Consul
Belfast—Consul

Birmingham—Consul
Bradford—Consul
Bristol—Consul
Cardiff—Vice Consul; Administrative Assistant
Edinburgh—Consul
Glasgow—Consul General
Hull—Consul
Liverpool—Consul General
Manchester—Consul
Newcastle-on-Tyne—Consul
Plymouth—Vice Consul
Southampton—Consul General

## IV. The Foreign Service of the United States

For some years the United States Government has been endeavoring to make the foreign service an attractive career for young men of ability. As early as 1895 the examination system was adopted on a limited scale for entrance to the consular service. Later the idea was extended to the entire foreign service. The Rogers Act, passed by Congress in 1924, thoroughly overhauled the service, amalgamating the consular and diplomatic branches, providing for promotions and retirement, and in many ways improving its status. From time to time other laws have been enacted and executive orders issued. The present foreign service is described below by Assistant Secretary of State Francis H. Russell, in an address given just before the law of 1946 went into effect.

(F. H. Russell, 'The American Foreign Service of Tomorrow,' *Department of State Bulletin*, vol. xv, No. 386, 1946, pp. 947-9.)

The Foreign Service of the United States is today an organization of some 11,000 persons who serve their country in every foreign land. Although the mem-bers of the Foreign Service are most widely known for the diplomatic aspects of their work, in actual fact they try to be all things to all Americans abroad. The good Foreign Service officer must be a combination of diplomat, attorney, judge, minister, newspaperman, editor, salesman, businessman, farmer, sailor, and economist. He is the man to whom all Americans turn for help in facing the endless problems which arise in foreign lands.

Here at home many governmental and private agencies perform varied services for the American people. Abroad where our citizens must depend much more on our Government's representatives almost all the services are combined in the Foreign Service of the United States. When there is a mutiny on an American ship, when an American citizen runs afoul of foreign laws, when an American is born overseas, or when he wants to get married, it is our Foreign Service that is always ready to protect his rights or to help solve his problems. When a foreign government or its private citizens want to know about our agriculture, our literary development, our latest aircraft, our mines, or our business firms, again the Foreign Service provides the answers. It is this universal quality of the Service which makes it so fascinating but at the same time so complex. The ideal Foreign Service is something we shall aspire to but, with only human material, may never fully achieve.

The Foreign Service of the past has in my opinion done an excellent job. Despite insufficient funds and inadequate personnel it has contributed much to our national welfare.

The Foreign Service of coming years, however, must shoulder a much heavier burden and must do it well if our national heritage is to be preserved. Today, as never before in our history, the fate of our people depends on a solid foreign policy and on efficient execution of that policy abroad.

American foreign policy is not determined by the Foreign Service. Much of the raw material of that policy, however, is provided by the Service in its flow of reports to the various departments of the Government. This flow of intelligence from overseas is the grist for the policy mill of our Government. The policy itself is, of course, basically determined by the American people, but the issues are clarified and the problems resolved in Washington with the help of the reports and evaluations from the Foreign Service.

It is in the execution of our foreign policy that the Foreign Service plays its major role. Our Foreign Service officers serving as Ministers and Ambassadors, Counselors, Secretaries of Embassy, Consuls, Vice Consuls, and Attachés, are largely responsible for the successful application of that policy throughout the world. On high levels such as the Council of Foreign Ministers or the Security Council of the United Nations, the Secretary of State or the members of Congress may participate in policy implementation, but the great bulk of the work in its far-reaching detail is done in the field by the professional Service. If this world-wide Service performs its function well, if it represents our national will and skilfully executes our foreign policy, it may do much to bring us through the anxious years ahead without conflict and with the friendship and support of the nations of the world.

If on the other hand the Foreign Service bungles its job, if we clumsily make enemies in small things as well as large, we may find ourselves again facing a major war.

Fortunately the cost of a fine Foreign Service is not great from a monetary point of view. A single day of the last war cost $245,000,000. One day of such a war could have operated the Foreign Service for years. I do not think I have to emphasize the point that the dollars spent on such a service are an investment if that service can help to make a war unnecessary. Even if it cost a great deal more, I am sure all would agree that it is worth it to have the reality of peace and prosperity in this world brought nearer. The Foreign Service is but one of several major tools to achieve this end but a very important one.

Tomorrow a great change comes over our Service, a change that has been long due and long hoped for. Thanks to the Foreign Service Act of 1946 we will be able to pay our personnel overseas salaries on which they can live and do their jobs. In the past our representatives abroad have often had to pay their own expenses. As a consequence it has sometimes been necessary for us to select men with a view to personal wealth. This has resulted in some instances in the man best fitted for the job not being available. With the salaries now authorized and the allowances which we hope the next Congress will appropriate, this unfortunate situation will largely be a thing of the past. We are still not as generous to our Foreign Service personnel as some other nations, but from tomorrow almost all of our representatives abroad will be able to live and work on their government salaries and allowances.

Tomorrow another anachronism is abolished: a professional Foreign Service officer will be able to accept the job of Minister or Ambassador without withdrawing from the Service. Oddly enough in the past such an appointment required resignation from the Service. It was as if a colonel were required to resign from the Army to become a general. . .

To carry on the development of Foreign Service personnel throughout their careers, a Foreign Service training program is now under way. Here we have borrowed from the sister services, the Army and the Navy, the concept of continuous in-service training throughout a man's career. We visualize our future representative abroad as having the benefit of several tours of duty at a Foreign Service Institute specifically designed to increase that man's value to the Service. We also hope, as part of this program, to enable officers to spend some time at leading universities broadening their backgrounds and expanding their interests. As a climax to the training of the future Ambassador or Minister, attendance at the National War College is envisaged. Already we have 11 officers taking the first course to be given by that highest-level Governmental educational organization.

In a further effort to broaden the base of the Service and to give it flexibility a Foreign Service Reserve Corps is being created. This will be composed of individuals of unusual skills and professions who will serve as officers overseas for short periods of time, and will give to the American representation the benefit of their specialized training and background.

Another basic change that comes over the Service tomorrow lies in the nature of its top direction, the Board of the Foreign Service. In the past the Department of State has had only limited advice and assistance from the other departments of the Government in the supervision of the Service which represents all national interests abroad. The new organization, the Board of Directors, so to speak, is made up of representatives of the Departments of Labor, Agriculture, Commerce, and State, with other governmental agencies sitting in when matters of concern to them are being considered. We feel that this joint supervision will reflect more clearly than in the past the true balance of our varied interests abroad. For in the broad picture our Service represents no one branch of our Government but our entire community of effort, and the broader the base of our guidance the sounder should be our actions. . .

## V. Secret and Open Diplomacy

The opinion has been widely held, especially during recent decades, that secrecy should be eliminated from diplomacy, both for the sake of democratic principle and in the interests of peace. President Woodrow Wilson stated this position very well in the first of his famous Fourteen Points, advocating 'open covenants of peace, openly arrived at, after which there shall be no private international understandings of any kind but diplomacy shall proceed always frankly and in the public view.' Opponents of the idea argue that diplomacy, like business, requires 'deals' or compromises, and that agreements often would not be attainable if diplomats were obliged to defer to public opinion and special pressure groups at every turn. They point out too that openness by any one nation will reveal the secrets of others. A more moderate position admits that agreements once made should be open, but maintains that diplomats should retain the right of secrecy of negotiation. A statement on secret diplomacy by Hugh Gibson, former American diplomat, follows.

(Hugh Gibson, *The Road to Foreign Policy*, New York, pp. 77-81. Copyright 1944 by Hugh Gibson. Reprinted by permission of Doubleday & Company, Inc.)

At the end of the last war, we were told that one of the safeguards of the new order was to be open diplomacy. Secret diplomacy was to be done away with, and international affairs were to be regulated by open covenants openly arrived at.

Probably no group of phrases has led to more muddled thinking on fundamental methods.

People are not always clear in their own minds as to what secret diplomacy is, but it sounds reprehensible and they are against it.

The general assumption has grown up that the negotiations of diplomacy on international affairs ought to be conducted in the glare of pitiless publicity. There are, of course, certain reticences which are permissible for the priest, the lawyer, the doctor, or the father of a family, but governments and their negotiators should, it is held, operate under an entirely different regime.

If the Secretary of State is not forth-coming with public statements as to what he is discussing with this government or what he has said to that Ambassador, or what he has heard from one of our missions abroad, you instantly hear the cry of secret diplomacy. Secret diplomacy is one of those hobgoblins that hover around the idea of democratic control of diplomacy.

As a matter of fact, there is such a thing as secret diplomacy, and it is reprehensible. This might be defined as inter-governmental intrigue for wrongful ends, resulting in obligations for future action of which the people are kept in ignorance until they are called on to pay with their lives and fortunes. There are also secret negotiations between governments to infringe the rights of another.

There is no doubt that every effort should be made to do away with this sort of thing. But we should bear in mind that this brand of diplomacy has the same relation to the real article that smash-and-grab raids have to legitimate business. We must remember that there is a broad margin between hole-and-corner intrigue and diplomatic negotiations in the glare of the floodlights. Perhaps we shall find the best results are to be had by avoiding both extremes.

If the people know the aims of their government and are kept apprised of undertakings and commitments before effective approval is given there is nothing reprehensible in carrying on the day-to-day negotiations in private—in fact, that is the only way negotiations can be carried on, not only governmental negotiations, but private business negotiations or family discussions. The less publicity there is to negotiation the greater the chance of success, but very often the advocates of open diplomacy or democratic control want to sit at the elbow of our negotiator telling him what to say, what not to say, and usually pushing him on to do stunts which have the beauty of being dramatic but don't get him any 'forrader.' This is nothing more or less than backseat driving and is just about as valuable. The sound course is to choose your negotiators for their ability, tell them what they are to seek to obtain, and let them use their own discretion as to their procedure.

Perhaps the greatest proponent of open diplomacy and democratic control was President Wilson, but when he came to grips with the grim realities of international negotiation he forgot all about 'pitiless publicity' and 'open covenants openly arrived at,' and resorted, not only to secrecy in negotiation, but in many cases to secrecy as to his objectives as well. Nobody could say that the Treaty of Versailles was openly arrived at, indeed few professional diplomats have proceeded by means that were so secret. Perhaps if we had had greater public knowledge of policy we should have had a better treaty. . .

Secret diplomacy, if we use the words in their real meaning, is nothing more than the established method of unpublicized negotiation. This method was evolved through centuries of human experience. It is predicated on systematic exploration of a subject in private by trained negotiators. Such exploration involves the exercise of resourcefulness, patience, and good will in order to arrive, perhaps after many failures, at a meeting of minds where conflicting interests are reconciled, at least in principle, under a form of agreement involving the common denominator of understanding.

The problems of diplomacy are often difficult and intricate. If they were not, they would tend to settle themselves and would not call for study by governmental representatives. It is the daily lot of the diplomat to tackle one of these problems and seek, through long and patient negotiation, to reach solutions. It is rare that he succeeds the first time of trying. More often than not he finds that the plan first envisaged cannot be accepted by the other side for reasons which emerge from the discussions. There is no clash about this, and both sides set to work to re-examine the problem in the light of what they have learned. It is the method of trial and error, and the chances are that if all concerned continue the discussions with a desire to meet each other's reasonable difficulties they will one day find an acceptable solution. It is neither showy nor speedy, yet it has a way of succeeding more often than not.

In striking contrast to this we have the method of public conferences as all too generally practiced. Here the negotiators meet in the presence of the public and numerous representatives of the press, to say nothing of microphones and newsreel cameras. At the start, each side states its case. It would not be politic at this stage to divulge how little you could be content with. You are obliged to state your maximum requirements, in order to allow a reasonable margin for future bargaining. But, unfortunately, the other man is obliged to state his case in the same way, and thus at the outset you are entrenched upon your positions—and extreme positions at that. There is an inevitable deadlock. You are obliged to call in the press representatives and make sure that they understand that you are right and the other side wrong. You must make a speech to strengthen your position at home, and incidentally make it harder to reach agreement. The representatives of your national press, being patriotic, rally round to support you. Their dispatches tend to show how sound and reasonable you are in your demands and how exorbitant are the demands of the other side. Editorial comment makes conciliation still more difficult. The press of the other party adopts a similar attitude from their own angle, and you soon find that you have to deal not only with your opposite number in the negotiation but also posite number in the negotiation but also

with a public opinion at home that has been aroused by your speeches and by the well-intentioned efforts of the press. It is often far easier to negotiate with the representative of the other nation than it is to convince the public opinion of your own country of the necessity for making some contribution to agreement. Indeed, the pressure upon any negotiator in a public duel of this sort is almost overwhelming to stand pat and fight vociferously for his original platforms. Thus he becomes a hero in his own country, whereas if he makes any concession, however reasonable he may consider it and however he may have anticipated it in his own mind, he suddenly finds himself charged by the press with being spineless or having been bamboozled by the other side. . .

## A. *A Criticism of Open Diplomacy*

The Paris Peace Conference of 1946 was unusually open in its proceedings. General Jan C. Smuts, former Prime Minister and a delegate from the Union of South Africa, criticized this openness in a speech given at Aberdeen, Scotland, soon after the conference. A portion of that speech is given below.

(From *British Speeches of the Day*, New York, September-October, 1946, vol. 4, No. 8, p. 541. Reprinted by permission of the British Information Services.)

We are still in the aftermath of war. We have still much of the mentality which actuated us in the war. When I say 'we,' I mean all the peoples. That has been a handicap—people have expected too much. You must also remember we have these great difficulties at Paris. There is extreme publicity. We are making an experiment in what our American friends call 'open diplomacy.' You know that real business is never done with open diplomacy. You shrewd business men in Aberdeen do not conduct your business with open diplomacy. You would never get anywhere if you did so. We have sub-

mitted to rules of procedure which mean everything at the Conference. Every sitting of every commission, of every committee, and of every sub-committee has the press there and is fully reported, and what is reported very often is not the things that matter but the things that have news value. You don't blame the press for that. It is their business. . . Under these difficulties you can imagine progress is very difficult. The proceedings are reported out of perspective. You have to be very careful what you say because you are not speaking to the Conference. It is not the give-and-take of a business gathering. Every man there has to speak to the world and to his own country, where his enemies may be lying in wait for him. Under these conditions progress in business is almost impossible. . .

## VI. THE PUBLICATION OF TREATIES

Article 102 of the United Nations Charter requires members to register treaties and agreements, and it places upon the Secretariat the duty of publishing the full texts of those documents. There is thus established the principle that agreements, once made, should not be secret. In accordance with this Article the General Assembly adopted the following resolution on 14 December 1946, providing in detail the procedures to be followed.

*(General Assembly, First Session, Text of Debates,* 15 January 1947, Journal No. 75; Supplement A-64. Add. 1. pp. 946-9.)

### PART ONE—REGISTRATION

#### ARTICLE 1

1. Every treaty or international agreement whatever its form and descriptive name entered into by one or more Members of the United Nations after 24 October 1945, the date of the coming into force of the Charter, shall as soon as possible be registered with the Secretariat in accordance with these regulations.

2. Registration shall not take place until the treaty or international agreement has come into force between two or more of the parties thereto.

3. Such registration may be effected by any party or in accordance with Article 4 of these regulations.

4. The Secretariat shall record the treaties and international agreements so registered in a Register established for that purpose.

#### ARTICLE 2

1. When a treaty or international agreement has been registered with the Secretariat, a certified statement regarding any subsequent action which effects a change in the parties thereto, or the terms, scope or application thereof, shall also be registered with the Secretariat.

2. The Secretariat shall record the certified statement so registered in the Register established under Article 1 of these regulations.

#### ARTICLE 3

1. Registration by a party, in accordance with Article 1 of these regulations, relieves all other parties of the obligation to register.

2. Registration effected in accordance with Article 4 of these regulations relieves all parties of the obligation to register.

#### ARTICLE 4

1. Every treaty or international agreement subject to Article 1 of these regulations shall be registered *ex officio* by the United Nations in the following cases:

(a) Where the United Nations is a party to the treaty or agreement;

(b) Where the United Nations has been authorized by the treaty or agreement to effect registration.

2. A treaty or international agreement subject to Article 1 of these regulations may be registered with the Secretariat by a specialized agency in the following cases:

(a) Where the constituent instrument of the specialized agency provides for such registration;

(b) Where the treaty or agreement has been registered with the specialized agency pursuant to the terms of its constituent instrument;

(c) Where the specialized agency has

been authorized by the treaty or agreement to effect registration.

## ARTICLE 5

A party or specialized agency, registering a treaty or international agreement under Article 1 or 4 of these regulations, shall certify that the text is a true and complete copy thereof and includes all reservations made by parties thereto.

The certified copy shall reproduce the text in all the languages in which the treaty or agreement was concluded and shall be accompanied by two additional copies and by a statement setting forth, in respect of each party:

(a) the date on which the treaty or agreement has come into force;
(b) the method whereby it has come into force (for example: by signature, by ratification or acceptance, by accession, et cetera).

## ARTICLE 6

The date of receipt by the Secretariat of the United Nations of the treaty or international agreement registered shall be deemed to be the date of registration, provided that the date of registration of a treaty or agreement registered *ex officio* by the United Nations shall be the date on which the treaty or agreement first came into force between two or more of the parties thereto.

## ARTICLE 7

A certificate of registration signed by the Secretary-General or his representative shall be issued to the registering party or agency and also to all signatories and parties to the treaty or international agreement registered.

## ARTICLE 8

1. The Register shall be kept in the five official languages of the United Nations. The Register shall comprise, in respect of each treaty or international agreement, a record of:

(a) the serial number given in the order of registration;
(b) the title given to the instrument by the parties;
(c) the names of the parties between whom it was concluded;
(d) the dates of signature, ratification or acceptance, exchange or ratifications, accession, and entry into force;
(e) the duration;
(f) the language or languages in which it was drawn up;
(g) the name of the party or specialized agency which registers the instrument and the date of such registration;
(h) particulars of publication in the treaty series of the United Nations.

2. Such information shall also be included in the Register in regard to the statements registered under Article 2 of these regulations.

3. The texts registered shall be marked *'ne varietur'* by the Secretary-General or his representative, and shall remain in the custody of the Secretariat.

## PART TWO—FILING AND RECORDING

## ARTICLE 10

The Secretariat shall file and record treaties and international agreements, other than those subject to registration under Article 1 of these regulations, if they fall in the following categories:

(a) Treaties or international agreements entered into by the United Nations or by one or more of the specialized agencies;
(b) Treaties or international agreements transmitted by a Member of

the United Nations which were entered into before the coming into
force of the Charter, but which
were not included in the treaty
series of the League of Nations;

(c) Treaties or international agreements transmitted by a party not a
Member of the United Nations
which were entered into before or
after the coming into force of the
Charter which were not included
in the treaty series of the League of
Nations, provided, however, that
this paragraph shall be applied
with full regard to the provisions of
the resolution of the General Assembly of 10 February 1946 set
forth in the Annex of these regulations.

### ARTICLE 11

The provisions of Articles 2, 5, and 8
of these regulations shall apply, *mutatis
mutandis,* to all treaties and international
agreements filed and recorded under
Article 10 of these regulations.

## PART THREE—PUBLICATION

### ARTICLE 12

1. The Secretariat shall publish as soon
as possible in a single series every treaty
or international agreement which is registered, or filed and recorded, in the
original language or languages, followed
by a translation in English and in French.
The certified statements referred to in
Article 2 of these regulations shall be
published in the same manner. . .

## VII. DIPLOMACY BY CONFERENCE

One of the most striking tendencies in diplomacy has been the increasing
resort to the conference method of dealing with international problems. Since
the modern state system was first recognized in the Peace of Westphalia (1648),
conferences have been the usual means of establishing peace at the end of
wars. The Congress at Utrecht (1713), the Congress of Vienna (1815), the Paris
Conference (1856), the Portsmouth Conference (1905), the London Conference (1913), and the Paris Conference (1919) are evidence of this fact. During
the last century and a quarter, starting with the meetings of the Holy Alliance after 1815 and the American Conference at Panama in 1826, the conference method has been extended to the treatment of peacetime problems of
all sorts. During the nineteenth century the Concert of Europe held meetings
to deal with European issues, and there were scores of other gatherings on
such subjects as international law, arbitration, and postal communication.
After World War I the tempo was stepped up and conferences became even
more frequent. Although the conference method is accepted today as a useful method of conducting the affairs of nations, it is nevertheless criticized and
its limitations are recognized. Hugh Gibson, author of the following extract,
has had wide experience both in the diplomatic service and in international
conferences. His criticisms of conference methods are, therefore, unusually
searching.

(Hugh Gibson, *The Road to Foreign Policy*, New York, pp. 81-7. Copyright 1944 by Hugh Gibson. Reprinted by permission of Doubleday & Company, Inc.)

Almost anyone who has followed international conferences since the last war has seen for himself that they have almost uniformly failed to live up to our hopes and expectations. A careful study of them reveals that their failure is largely due to the fact that Pitiless Publicity and the consequent frozen position have made successful negotiations impossible.

Another thing that emerges from a careful study of international conferences is that their success is usually in direct proportion to the amount of confidential and expert spadework which has been done in advance, and to the measure of agreement that was already reached before they were convened. The most successful of all were those convened merely to adjust and ratify agreement in principle already reached.

This does not mean that we should leap to the conclusion that the conference method should be scrapped. That would be jumping from one extreme to the other. But it seems important to draw some lessons from our experience, correct our mistakes, and see if we cannot improve our existing technique.

Common sense is attracted by the apparent advantage of having negotiations conducted by a group of men gathered round a table, rather than by complicated exchange by cable. And it should be possible to get better results.

When we re-examine our earlier work, conferences seem to have suffered from two handicaps. They were conducted under a blaze of publicity. They were given impossible tasks.

If we are capable of learning from our mistakes, it should be possible to reduce and even eliminate the first.

The second calls for common-sense recognition of what conferences can do. They cannot be charged with solving fundamental problems. That is the task of governments, and these solutions must be reached by man-to-man negotiation before calling conferences. Once the general lines of agreement and the will to agree have become clear, the negotiators can be brought together to formulate the actual terms of agreement.

When two corporations seek solution to a conflict on business matters, they do not turn the problem over to their lawyers. The executives find a basis for agreement and then entrust to the lawyers the task of putting the agreement into proper form. Delegates at a conference should have somewhat the same function as the lawyers. People at home are often impatient with our delegates at international conferences for failing to make other people go as far as we should like. They overlook one thing—that in a conference you cannot make anybody do anything. No one can make us do anything, and we labor under the same limitations in imposing our views. Many people assume that the decisions should represent the position of the most enlightened delegation, and that if only we are sufficiently advanced we should have our way. Unfortunately, things do not work out that way. The conference has to content itself with what is accepted by the most backward delegation. You can secure the adoption of only those things agreed to by everybody. The rule of unanimity is the dead hand of this sort of negotiation. . .

The conference method is undoubtedly here to stay, although it is to be hoped that it will be used more discriminatingly, but there are several modifications in present procedures which would tend to secure a larger volume of agreement.

First, it is desirable that the maximum amount of preparatory work be completed by direct and private negotiation before the conference is convened, in order that its work may be narrowed down to the adjustment of minor difficulties and the drafting of the actual terms of the agreement.

Second, the conference itself should be put on a normal, workaday basis and cease to be treated as an emergency with a time limit. There is no real reason for a conference to be carried on differently from any other human activity. What we need most is the application of the laboratory method. If you are seeking a chemical formula, you do not call a meeting, choose sides, and announce to an incredulous press that everything will be tidied up before the end of the week, as Professor Snooks must return to his regular work by that time. Above all, you do not, in agreement with your scientific colleagues, and in order to meet the immediate demands of the situation, dish up a phony formula which you know any scientist with half an eye can see through. On the contrary, you assemble the members of your research staff and send them off to work in their laboratories until they notify you that they have found the answer. It may be days, or weeks, or months, or even years, but the time element is of secondary importance.

There is every reason why conferences should be conducted in the same way. The problems they have to tackle are no less intricate than those entrusted to the scientific research worker. Disarmament, for instance, is so deeply bogged in the soils of human nature that it is folly to expect a quick and simple solution. The only hope is to let men of training and resource and good will disappear into some retreat and work quietly and unhurriedly for as long as may be necessary, many years perhaps, in the hope that they will find ways and means of advancing along the road. Furthermore, conferences should, except for the purpose of stimulating public interest and announcing agreement, be held as private conversa-

tions with a minimum of speeches and publicity in order to lessen the temptation for the negotiators to cavort for the benefit of the press and public opinion. In other words, to make their first concern the solution of the problem and not ephemeral public approval for themselves.

The conference method can hardly be expected to give better results until the conference itself ceases to be regarded as a gladiatorial combat. We must get out of our heads the idea that a conference is like a football game: that we choose sides and that they continue to score until there is victory for one side or the other. That is the mentality that is expressed by the remark attributed to Will Rogers, that the United States never lost a war or won a conference. Will Rogers denied to me on several occasions with some heat that he had ever made this statement, but that is another story.

The fundamental purpose of a conference, or any other form of negotiation, is to secure agreement, not victory. In fact, victory and defeat are the negation of diplomacy. The diplomat should never forget that the problem he is working on is of only relative importance in that it is one of an unending series that must be discussed with the other party through the years, and therefore, while he must get as much as is expedient for his own country, it must be within such limits and under such terms as will obviate resentment and a sense of injustice in future negotiations. It is important to have everybody satisfied, so that they bring to the next meeting a desire for further agreement and not a yearning for revenge—the inevitable result of defeat.

This calls for a radical change in our mental attitude, for there is no doubt that the public in all countries consider international relations in terms of victory and defeat. But we may as well make up our minds that it is only when we have adopted the opposite attitude that we can hope for a larger measure of success.

If the day ever comes when a conference is conducted by these methods, while we cannot of course be sure of success, we can be sure that better machinery has been installed in order to bring that success about. . .

## VIII. The United Nations as a Conference System

A number of international institutions now exist that embody a permanent conference system as a prominent part of their organization. The United Nations and its related special agencies may be said to be the most complex international conference system ever devised. Historically, the Universal Postal Union, created in 1874 to facilitate postal communication of all kinds, first adopted the permanent conference method. In addition to the Bureau located at Berne, Switzerland, the organization of the Union includes conferences held from time to time for the purpose of negotiating special postal conventions to deal with such subjects as parcel post and air mail. The Pan American Union, established on a permanent basis in 1889, is a similar organization.

The League of Nations—before the creation of the United Nations—made extensive use of the conference system. Often the idea of dealing with a subject by conference originated in one of the technical bodies related to the League, or perhaps in the Council or Assembly, which later referred it to a technical organization. If, as a result of preliminary investigations, the subject appeared ready for international action, a commission was set up to prepare for the conference. With the assistance of the Secretariat, this commission issued invitations, sent questionnaires to the invited governments, conducted research, and in other ways set the stage for the meeting of delegates. In 1930, for example, the International Committee of Intellectual Cooperation was advised by its Cinematographic Institute at Rome that an international conference should be called to deal with the international circulation of educational films. After the International Committee of Intellectual Cooperation and the Assembly of the League approved the idea, the Rome Institute was instructed to prepare for the conference. Realizing that information would be needed relating to the laws and customs regulations of the various countries on the importation of films, the director of the Rome Institute sent questionnaires to all of the invited states. Other preparatory measures were undertaken, and later the conference was held and a convention negotiated. By a similar procedure a long list of conventions was negotiated within the League of Nations dealing with matters of international concern: opium, passports, customs formalities, labor, and many other subjects.

This institutionalized form of conference diplomacy is being continued within the organization of the United Nations. Most of it is done by the Economic and Social Council or by technical agencies responsible to it. Within the Secretariat a special division on conferences and general services has been set up 'to make material arrangements for meetings of the General Assembly, the Councils, the Commissions, Committees and special conferences held under the auspices of the United Nations.' Something of the nature of the system may be seen from the following extract.

(*Report of the Secretary-General on the Work of the Organization,* 30 June 1946, pp. 29-30.)

The Economic and Social Council, at its first session, approved a resolution on 18 February 1946 concerning the calling of an International Conference on Trade and Employment in the latter part of 1946.

The preparation of an annotated draft agenda, including a draft convention, for consideration by the conference, taking into account suggestions which may be submitted to it by the Economic and Social Council or by any Members of the United Nations, was entrusted to a Preparatory Committee which the Council set up. The latter considered it essential that the co-operative economic measures already taken be supplemented by further international measures dealing directly with trade barriers and discriminations which stand in the way of an expansion of multilateral trade and by an undertaking on the part of nations to seek full employment. To this end the Council suggested that the agenda of the Preparatory Committee should include the following topics:

1. International agreements relating to:

   (a) the achievement and maintenance of high and stable levels of employment and economic activity;
   (b) regulations, restrictions and discriminations affecting international trade;
   (c) restrictive business practices, and
   (d) inter-governmental commodity arrangements.

2. The establishment of an international trade organization as a specialized agency of the United Nations having responsibilities in the fields of (b), (c) and (d) above.

The Council further requested the Preparatory Committee, when considering the foregoing items, to take into account the special conditions which prevail in countries whose manufacturing industry is still in its initial stages of development, and the questions that arise in connection with commodities which are subject to special problems of adjustment in international markets.

Finally, the Preparatory Committee was requested to make recommendations to a subsequent session of the Council regarding the date and place of the Conference and the agenda (including a draft convention) and also what States, if any, not Members of the United Nations, should be invited to the Conference on Trade and Employment.

In connection with the above resolution, the Council was informed that the Government of the United States had invited the Governments of fifteen countries controlling a substantial portion of world trade to convene for the purpose of negotiating the reduction of specific trade barriers and discriminations in advance of the general Conference.

At the second session of the Economic and Social Council, the Secretary-General made an announcement in which he stated that it would not be possible to hold the International Conference on Trade and Employment until next year in view of the scope and complexity of the preparatory work which will be necessary before the Conference can be held. The Secretary-General announced, however, that arrangements were being made for the Preparatory Committee of the Conference to meet in London on 15 October 1946. . .

## IX. THE INTER-AMERICAN CONFERENCE SYSTEM

The following organization of the Inter-American system of co-operation was agreed upon at the Bogota conference in 1948. The Charter describing this organization takes the place of the convention of 1928. By using the agencies named in Article 32 the American republics may negotiate agreements of all kinds—political, economic, and technical. All six agencies are designed to work together as an integrated whole for the improvement of Inter-American relations.

(Extracts from Charter of the Organization of American States, *Department of State Bulletin,* vol. XVIII, No. 464, 1948, pp. 465-73.)

### ARTICLE 1

The American States establish by this Charter the international organization that they have developed to achieve an order of peace and justice, to promote their solidarity, to strengthen their collaboration, and to defend their sovereignty, their territorial integrity and their independence. Within the United Nations, the Organization of American States is a regional agency.

### ARTICLE 2

All American States that ratify the present Charter are Members of the Organization.

### ARTICLE 3

Any new political entity that arises from the union of several Member States and that, as such, ratifies the present Charter, shall become a Member of the Organization. The entry of the new political entity into the Organization shall result in the loss of membership of each one of the States which constitute it.

### ARTICLE 4

The Organization of American States, in order to put into practice the principles on which it is founded and to fulfill its regional obligations under the Charter of the United Nations, proclaims the following essential purposes:

*a)* To strengthen the peace and security of the continent;

*b)* To prevent possible causes of difficulties and to ensure the pacific settlement of disputes that may arise among the Member States;

*c)* To provide for common action on the part of those States in the event of aggression;

*d)* To seek the solution of political, juridical and economic problems that may arise among them; and

*e)* To promote by cooperative action their economic, social and cultural development.       . . .

### IX—THE ORGANS

### ARTICLE 32

The Organization of American States accomplishes its purposes by means of:

*a)* The Inter-American Conference;

*b)* The Meeting of Consultation of Ministers of Foreign Affairs;

*c)* The Council;

*d)* The Pan American Union;

*e)* The Specialized Conference; and

*f)* The Specialized Organizations.

## X—THE INTER-AMERICAN CONFERENCE

### ARTICLE 33

The Inter-American Conference is the supreme organ of the Organization of American States. It decides the general action and policy of the Organization and determines the structure and functions of its Organs, and has the authority to consider any matter relating to friendly relations among the American States. These functions shall be carried out in accordance with the provisions of this Charter and of other Inter-American treaties.

### ARTICLE 34

All Member States have the right to be represented at the Inter-American Conference. Each State has the right to one vote.

### ARTICLE 35

The Conference shall convene every five years at the time fixed by the Council of the Organization, after consultation with the government of the country where the Conference is to be held.

### ARTICLE 36

In special circumstances and with the approval of two-thirds of the American Governments, a special Inter-American Conference may be held, or the date of the next regular Conference may be changed.

### ARTICLE 37

Each Inter-American Conference shall designate the place of meeting of the next Conference. If for any unforeseen reason the Conference cannot be held at the place designated, the Council of the Organization shall designate a new place.

### ARTICLE 38

The program and regulations of the Inter-American Conference shall be prepared by the Council of the Organization and submitted to the Member State for consideration.

## XI—THE MEETING OF CONSULTATION OF MINISTERS OF FOREIGN AFFAIRS

### ARTICLE 39

The Meeting of Consultation of Ministers of Foreign Affairs shall be held in order to consider problems of an urgent nature and of common interest to the American States, and to serve as the Organ of Consultation.

### ARTICLE 40

Any Member State may request that a Meeting of Consultation be called. The request shall be addressed to the Council of the Organization, which shall decide by an absolute majority whether a meeting should be held.

### ARTICLE 41

The program and regulations of the Meeting of Consultation shall be prepared by the Council of the Organization and submitted to the Member State for consideration.

### ARTICLE 42

If a Minister of Foreign Affairs, for exceptional reasons, is unable to attend the Meeting, he shall be represented by a special delegate.

### ARTICLE 43

In case of an armed attack within the territory of an American State or within the region of security delimited by treaties in force, a Meeting of Consultation shall be held without delay. Such Meeting shall be called immediately by the Chairman of the Council of the Organization, who shall at the same time call a meeting of the Council itself.

### ARTICLE 44

An Advisory Defense Committee shall be established to advise the Organ of Consultation on problems of military co-operation that may arise in connection with the application of existing special treaties on collective security.

### ARTICLE 45

The Advisory Defense Committee shall be composed of the highest military authorities of the American States participating in the Meeting of Consultation. Under exceptional circumstances the Governments may appoint substitutes. Each state shall be entitled to one vote.

### ARTICLE 46

The Advisory Defense Committee shall be convoked under the same conditions as the Organ of Consultation, when the latter deals with matters relating to defense against aggression.

### ARTICLE 47

The Committee shall also meet when the Conference or the Meeting of Consultation or the Governments, by a two-thirds majority of the Member States, assign to it technical studies or reports on specific subjects.

## XII—THE COUNCIL

### ARTICLE 48

The Council of the Organization of American States is composed of one Representative for each Member State of the Organization, especially appointed by the respective Government, with the rank of Ambassador. The appointment may be given to the diplomatic representative accredited to the government of the country in which the Council has its seat. During the absence of the titular Representative, the Government may appoint an interim Representative.

### ARTICLE 49

The Council shall elect a Chairman and a Vice Chairman, who shall serve for one year and shall not be eligible for re-election to either of those positions for the term immediately following.

### ARTICLE 50

The Council takes cognizance, within the limits of the present Charter and of inter-American treaties and agreements, of any matter referred to it by the Inter-American Conference or the Meeting of Consultation of Ministers of Foreign Affairs.

### ARTICLE 51

The Council shall be responsible for the proper discharge by the Pan American Union of the duties assigned to it.

### ARTICLE 52

The Council shall serve provisionally as the Organ of Consultation when the circumstances contemplated in Article 43 of this Charter arise.

### ARTICLE 53

It is also the duty of the Council:

*a*) To draft and submit to the Governments and to the Inter-American Conference proposals for the creation of new Specialized Organizations or for the combination, adaptation or elimination of existing ones, including matters relating to the financing and support thereof;

*b*) To draft recommendations to the Governments, the Inter-American Conference, the Specialized Conferences or the Specialized Organizations, for the coordination of the activities and programs of such organizations, after consultation with them;

*c*) To conclude agreements with the Inter-American Specialized Organizations to determine the relations that shall exist between the respective agency and the Organization;

*d*) To conclude agreements or special arrangements for cooperation with other American organizations of recognized international standing;

*e*) To promote and facilitate collaboration between the Organization of American States and the United Nations, as well as between Inter-American Specialized Organizations and similar international agencies;

*f*) To adopt resolutions that will enable the Secretary General to perform the duties envisaged in Article 84.

*g*) To perform the other duties assigned to it by the present Charter.

### ARTICLE 54

The Council shall establish the bases for fixing the quota that each Government is to contribute to the maintenance of the Pan American Union, taking into account the ability to pay of the respective countries and their determination to contribute in an equitable manner. The budget, after approval by the Council, shall be transmitted to the Governments at least six months before the first day of the fiscal year, with a statement of the annual quota of each country. Decisions on budgetary matters require the approval of two-thirds of the members of the Council.

### ARTICLE 55

The Council shall formulate its own regulations.

### ARTICLE 56

The Council shall function at the seat of the Pan American Union.

### ARTICLE 57

The following are organs of the Council of the Organization of American States:

*a*) The Inter-American Economic and Social Council;

*b*) The Inter-American Council of Jurists; and

*c*) The Inter-American Cultural Council.

. . .

## XIII—THE PAN AMERICAN UNION

### ARTICLE 78

The Pan American Union is the central and permanent organ of the Organization of American States and the General Secretariat of the Organization. It shall perform the duties assigned to it in this Charter and such other duties as may be assigned to it in other Inter-American treaties and agreements.

### ARTICLE 79

There shall be a Secretary General of the Organization, who shall be elected by the Council for a ten-year term and who may not be reelected or be succeeded by a person of the same nationality. In the event of a vacancy in the office of Secretary General, the Council shall, within the next ninety days, elect a successor to fill the office for the remainder of the term, who may be reelected if the vacancy occurs during the second half of the term.

### ARTICLE 80

The Secretary General shall direct the Pan American Union and be the legal representative thereof.

### ARTICLE 81

The Secretary General shall participate with voice, but without vote, in the deliberations of the Inter-American Conference, the Meeting of Consultation of Ministers of Foreign Affairs, the Specialized Conferences, and the Council and its organs.

### ARTICLE 82

The Pan American Union, through its technical and information offices, shall, under the direction of the Council, promote economic, social, juridical and cultural relations among all the Member States of the Organization.

## ARTICLE 83

The Pan American Union shall also perform the following functions:

*a*) Transmit *ex officio* to Member States the convocation to the Inter-American Conference, the Meeting of Consultation of Ministers of Foreign Affairs, and the Specialized Conferences;

*b*) Advise the Council and its organs in the preparation of programs and regulations of the Inter-American Conference, the Meeting of Consultation of Ministers of Foreign Affairs, and the Specialized Conferences;

*c*) Place, to the extent of its ability, at the disposal of the Government of the Country where a conference is to be held the technical aid and personnel which such government may request;

*d*) Serve as custodian of the documents and archives of the Inter-American Conferences, of the Meetings of Consultation of Ministers of Foreign Affairs and, insofar as possible, of the Specialized Conferences;

*e*) Serve as depository of the instruments of ratification of Inter-American agreements;

*f*) Perform the functions entrusted to it by the Inter-American Conference, and the Meeting of Consultation of Ministers of Foreign Affairs;

. . .

## XIV—THE SPECIALIZED CONFERENCES

## ARTICLE 93

The Specialized Conferences shall meet to deal with special technical matters or to develop specific aspects of inter-American cooperation, when it is so decided by the Inter-American Conference or the Meeting of Consultation of Ministers of Foreign Affairs; when inter-American Agreements so provide; or when the Council of the Organization considers it necessary, either on its own initiative or at the request of one of its organs or of one of the Specialized Organizations.

## ARTICLE 94

The program and regulations of the Specialized Conferences shall be prepared by the organs of the Council of the Organization or by the Specialized Organizations concerned; they shall be submitted to the Member Governments for consideration and transmitted to the Council for its information.

## XV—THE SPECIALIZED ORGANIZATIONS

## ARTICLE 95

For the purposes of the present Charter, the Inter-American Specialized Organizations are the inter-governmental organizations established by multilateral agreements and having specific functions with respect to technical matters of common interest to the American States.

. . .

# PRESENT INTER-AMERICAN SYSTEM

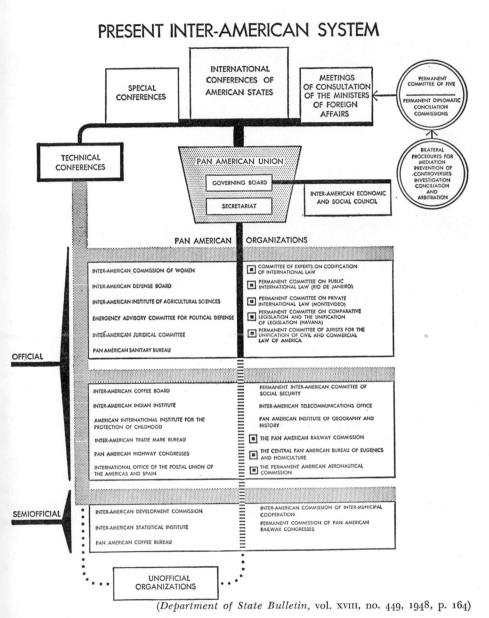

(*Department of State Bulletin,* vol. XVIII, no. 449, 1948, p. 164)

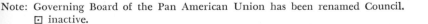

Note: Governing Board of the Pan American Union has been renamed Council.
    ⊡ inactive.

PART TWO

POWER POLITICS AND WAR

# PART TWO

## Power, Politics, and War

# POWER POLITICS

Power is a general term and a difficult one to define. Thomas Hobbes stated in his *Leviathan* (1651) that 'The Power of a man is his present means to obtain some future apparent good.' No doubt he would have used the same idea in defining the power of a nation.

Without going into a scientific discussion of the problem, we can safely say that the term 'power politics' conveys certain very definite ideas when it is applied in international relations. To most people it means the effort of a state to do or get what it desires in the face of opposition from other members of the international community. There is implied a capacity to coerce. This does not mean that governments go about shaking a big stick or that they attach an ultimatum to every diplomatic note. However, the relative ability of nations to bring coercive power to bear on others is usually in the background of any critical diplomatic situation. Where power is fairly evenly divided, a compromise solution may be forthcoming. Where it is not, one or another of the negotiators is likely to come out on top.

In the world of today, states are obviously unequal in power. The terms 'great powers' and 'small powers' are commonly used to express this fact. At one extreme are Russia and the United States, giants in the game of world politics; while at the other are many small and weak states, such as Iran, Albania, and Haiti. This inequality is apparent in the relations between Russia and Iran, or between the United States and Haiti. This does not mean that Russia and the United States are employing force constantly against their neighbors, for in fact such tactics are rare. Rather it means that, as all the parties fully realize, the possibility of force is always in the background.

No doubt it is true, as Professor Carl Becker has pointed out, that the term 'power politics' is a redundancy, for politics is never separable from power. In international politics, however, the presence of power is more obvious than in national politics, probably because its form is so frequently physical might rather than the votes and personal influence characterizing national affairs.

Power can take other forms than physical might. Nowadays it is admitted everywhere that there is power in ideas. Power politics on the world stage may appear to be quite impersonal and connected almost wholly with the policies and pressures of governments, but words and ideas also have power; propaganda techniques are now exploited in what has become a virtual war for the possession of men's minds. A Nazi propaganda barrage ushered in World War II, and soon after its close the war of ideas between East and West began over the relative merits of communism and democracy. This struggle is no less real than that for economic and military power. Perhaps it is ultimately the most significant form of power politics, for it relates directly to the individual and to the individual's social, economic, and political views. This subject is dealt with more fully below in Part Four.

The more traditional manifestations of power politics are reviewed here—geography, nationalism, economic power, imperialism, and war. Little introductory comment is necessary to place geography and war at the very center of the power struggle. The geographic factor was, however, emphasized to a point of absurdity before World War II by 'geopoliticians' in Germany. Whether it is, in fact, deterministic in the formation of foreign policy is discussed below. The extracts included on the subject of war reveal how vast and complex this problem is and the profound concern that men have had toward it. They show, too, that although students have probed it for many years no solution to the problem has yet been found. This is hardly surprising when one considers how deeply rooted war is in our society.

Nationalism, so closely related to geography and war, plays a key role in power politics. The power a nation possesses in the patriotic drive of its people can be formidable. Preceding and during World War II, the world watched with fascinated horror the lengths to which German patriotic fervor was whipped up by the Nazi dictatorship. The call to defend one's country in wartime inevitably produces great sources of energy—fighting morale. The force of nationalism, its nature, and the question whether it has run its course are discussed below.

A state's economy is also of central importance in the contest for power. Combined with nationalism, economic power is a dangerous weapon, as was proved in the autarchic policies of Germany. Economic strength has been used by its possessor to coerce and even to dominate other nations. Thus the Nazi Government placed several of Germany's neighbors in a highly dependent position by the use of one-sided trade agreements. Other ways in which states use their economic power today, both for defense and for cooperation, are dealt with in Part Three, especially Chapter 13.

One of the oldest methods employed by nations to increase their power, economically and otherwise, has been the imperialist drive for colonies overseas where, presumably, manpower, raw materials, and markets have been available. What is important to emphasize here is that the struggle for imperial holdings was, above all else, a contest of power and for power. As a result of the competition for colonies that took place in the eighteenth and nineteenth centuries, most of the 'backward' areas of the world were brought under the domination of one or another European state. Although the greater part of North and South America threw off imperial rule at the turn of the eighteenth century, large portions of the Middle East, Far East, and Africa

still remain under foreign domination. The era of World War II witnessed the
final withdrawal of Great Britain from India—the brightest jewel in the imperial crown—and with Britain's exit from India it can be said that the older
imperialism entered upon its decline. Britain, France, the Netherlands, and
Belgium still retain vast imperial holdings, while a number of dependent
areas, now called trust territories, are administered under the supervision of
the United Nations, much as the mandates, once the possessions of Germany
and Turkey before World War I, were administered under the League of
Nations Mandates Commission. The more technical aspects of trusteeship for
colonial peoples are discussed later.

Various points of view are taken toward the role of power in international
politics. Most pacifists would abolish physical force in every form. To other
critics, power in itself is unmoral. It is only an instrumentality that may be
used to attain ends of all kinds that do have moral qualities. Still other people,
militarists included, are inclined to extol power as an end in itself. Advocates
of strong world organization, on the contrary, argue that power must be
taken from the separate states and placed under an international authority for
the purpose of keeping the peace. Some of these points of view are dealt with
in Part Four. The extracts immediately below discuss the nature of power,
the traditional policy of the balance of power followed by many states, and
some of the methods used to enhance the power of a given state or group of
states.

## I. THE PLACE OF POWER

Power politics, according to the philosopher Bertrand Russell, is founded
on the nature of men and states. Both desire power. However, the relation
between man's will to power, his desire to dominate others, and the drive for
power on the part of states is not as yet clearly understood. Suffice it to say
here that the place of power in international affairs should never be underestimated, for it is everywhere in evidence, everywhere making history.

(Bertrand Russell, *Power*, New York, pp. 11-12. Copyright 1938 by Bertrand Russell. Reprinted by permission of W. W. Norton & Company, Inc.)

While animals are content with ex-istence and reproduction, men desire also to expand, and their desires in this re-spect are limited only by what imagina-tion suggests as possible. Every man would like to be God, if it were possible; some few find it difficult to admit the im-possibility. These are the men framed after the model of Milton's Satan, com-bining, like him, nobility with impiety.

By 'impiety' I mean something not de-pendent upon theological beliefs: I mean refusal to admit the limitations of indi-vidual human power. This Titanic com-bination of nobility with impiety is most notable in the great conquerors, but some element of it is to be found in all men. . .

Of the infinite desires of man, the chief are the desires for power and glory. These are not identical, though closely allied: the Prime Minister has more power than glory, the King has more glory than power. As a rule, however, the easiest way to obtain glory is to obtain power. . .

The orthodox economists, as well as Marx, who in this respect agreed with them, were mistaken in supposing that economic self-interest could be taken as the fundamental motive in the social sciences. The desire for commodities, when separated from power and glory, is finite, and can be fully satisfied by a moderate competence. . .

## II. THE STATE AS POWER

One influential school of thought on the nature of the state holds that it may be equated with power. According to this theory the state is, in essence, power, needed for the maintenance of order at home and for offense or defense abroad. The proponents of the doctrine are able to point to the fact that most states originated through the use of power, as in England and France, where feudal chieftains fought their way to kingship for themselves and unity for the nation, or in the United States and Latin America, where revolution brought independence and statehood. They point out, too, that all states have police and military forces, and that these are used whenever the security of the country is threatened. One of the chief spokesmen of the doctrine was Heinrich von Treitschke, lecturer on history in several German universities from 1857 until 1894, and at one time a member of the German Reichstag. His ideas proved most influential in Germany, and it is obvious from the following extract that they are very much in accord with the concept of international power politics.

(H. von Treitschke, *Politics*, London, vol. I, pp. 302-6, translated by Dugdale and de Bille. Reprinted by permission of Constable and Co.)

The rational task of a legally constituted people, conscious of a destiny, is to assert its rank in the world's hierarchy and in a measure to participate in the great civilizing mission of mankind.

Further, if we examine our definition of the State as 'the people legally united as an independent entity,' we find that it can be more briefly put thus: 'The State is the public force for Offence and Defence.' It is, above all, Power which makes its will to prevail, it is not the totality of the people as Hegel assumes in his deification of it. The nation is not entirely comprised in the State, but the State protects and embraces the people's life, regulating its external aspects on every side. It does not ask primarily for opinion, but demands obedience, and its laws must be obeyed, whether willingly or no.

A step forward has been taken when the mute obedience of the citizens is transformed into a rational inward assent, but it cannot be said that this is absolutely necessary. Powerful, highly developed Empires have stood for centuries without its aid. Submission is what the State primarily requires; it insists upon acquiescence; its very essence is the accomplishment of its will. A State which can no longer carry out its purpose collapses in anarchy.

The State is not an Academy of Arts. If it neglects its strength in order to promote the idealistic aspirations of man, it repudiates its own nature and perishes. This is in truth for the State equivalent to the sin against the Holy Ghost.

We have described the State as an independent force. This pregnant theory of independence implies firstly so absolute a moral supremacy that the State cannot legitimately tolerate any power above its own, and secondly a temporal freedom entailing a variety of material resources adequate to its protection against hostile influences. Legal sovereignty, the State's complete independence of any other earthly power, is so rooted in its nature that it may be said to be its very standard and criterion. . .

It is clear that the international agreements which limit the power of a State are not absolute, but voluntary self-restrictions. Hence, it follows that the establishment of a permanent Arbitration Court is incompatible with the nature of the State, which could at all events only accept the decision of such a tribunal in cases of second- or third-rate importance. When a nation's existence is at stake there is no outside Power whose impartiality can be trusted. Were we to commit the folly of treating the Alsace-Lorraine problem as an open question, by submitting it to arbitration, who would seriously believe that the award could be impartial? It is, moreover, a point of honour for a State to solve such difficulties for itself. International treaties may indeed become more frequent, but a finally decisive tribunal of the nations is an impossibility. The appeal to arms will be valid until the end of history, and therein lies the sacredness of war.

However flexible the conception of Sovereignty may be we are not to infer from that any self-contradiction, but rather a necessity to establish in what its pith and kernel consists. Legally it lies in the competence to define the limits of its own authority, and politically in the appeal to arms. An unarmed State, incapable of drawing the sword when it sees fit, is subject to one which wields the power of declaring war. A defenceless State may still be termed a Kingdom for conventional or courtly reasons, but

science, whose first duty is accuracy, must boldly declare that in point of fact such a country no longer takes rank as a State.

This, then, is the only real criterion. The right of arms distinguishes the State from all other forms of corporate life, and those who cannot take up arms for themselves may not be regarded as States, but only as members of a federated constellation of States. The difference between the Prussian Monarchy and the other German States is here apparent, namely, that the King of Prussia himself wields the supreme command, and therefore Prussia, unlike the others, has not lost its sovereignty.

The other test of sovereignty is the right to determine independently the limits of its power, and herein lies the difference between a federation of States and a Federal State. In the latter the central power is sovereign and can extend its competence according to its judgment, whereas in the former, every individual State is sovereign. The various subordinate countries of Germany are not genuine States; they must at any moment be prepared to see a right, which they possess at present, withdrawn by virtue of Imperial authority. Since Prussia alone has enough votes on the Federal Council to be in a position to prevent an alteration of the Constitution by its veto, it becomes evident that she cannot be outvoted on such decisive questions. She is therefore, in this second respect also, the only truly sovereign State which remains. . .

There are, indeed, States which do not assert themselves positively by virtue of their own strength, but negatively through the exigencies of the balance of power in Europe. Switzerland, Holland, and Belgium are cases in point. They are sustained by the international situation, a foundation which is, however, extremely solid, and so long as the present grouping of the Powers continues Switzerland may look forward to prolonged existence.

The entire development of European polity tends unmistakably to drive the second-rate Powers into the background, and this raises issues of immeasurable gravity for the German nation, in the world outside Europe. Up to the present Germany has always had too small a share of the spoils in the partition of non-European territories among the Powers of Europe, and yet our existence as a State of the first rank is vitally affected by the question whether we can become a power beyond the seas. If not, there remains the appalling prospect of England and Russia dividing the world between them, and in such a case it is hard to say whether the Russian knout or the English money bags would be the worst alternative.

On close examination then, it becomes clear that if the State is power, only that State which has power realizes its own idea, and this accounts for the undeniably ridiculous element which we discern in the existence of a small State. Weakness is not itself ridiculous, except when mas- querading as strength. In small States that puling spirit is hatched, which judges the State by the taxes it levies, and does not perceive that if the State may not en- close and repress like an egg-shell, neither can it protect. Such thinkers fail to under- stand that the moral benefits for which we are indebted to the State are above all price. It is by generating this form of materialism that small States have so deleterious an effect upon their citizens.

Examining closely, we find that culture in general, and in the widest sense of the word, matures more happily in the broader conditions of powerful countries than within the narrow limits of a little State. It must be obvious that the ma- terial resources favourable to Art and Science are more abundant in a large State: and if we inquire of history whether at any time the fairest fruit of human culture has ripened in a genuine petty State, the answer must be that in the normal course of a people's develop- ment the zenith of its political power co- incides with that of its literary excel- lence. . .

### III. THE BASES OF POWER

Why are certain nations referred to as 'great powers' and others as 'small powers'? To answer by saying that it is because the former can place large armies, navies, and air forces in combat only leads to a further query as to why some nations can do this while others cannot. The extract below explains the present bases of national power, stressing three: industrialization, population, and foreign trade. The importance of industrialization may be seen in the capacity of the United States during World War II to invent and produce the atomic bomb, an accomplishment that had the immediate effect of strengthening our power position immeasurably.

(H. F. Rudd, 'A Method of Balanced Representation,' General Extension Serv- ice, University of New Hampshire, pp. 2-4. Reprinted by permission of the Uni- versity of New Hampshire.)

In the past, many factors have com- bined to determine a nation's power to shape world affairs. There are still many factors; but the one new and revolution- ary factor in the twentieth century which far outweighs any other, if not all the others combined, is the degree to which the nation is industrialized. Power among nations, today, belongs to the industrialized states. Without industry no nation can now be much more than a pawn in the game of world politics.

For 30 years great China has been humiliated and robbed by little Japan because Japan had industrial power, which meant financial and military power. Hitler could defy the world and quickly subjugate Europe because he had directed German science and industry to the production of munitions. After Dunkirk, the British, with all their heroic determination, could save themselves only because they had a combination of air defense, first-class sea equipment, and the backing of powerful industrialized allies. The United States could become the 'arsenal of democracy' primarily because we had an industrial plant larger than that of any other three nations combined. Russian defense surprised the world, among other reasons, because that nation's industrial preparation was far better than was generally realized. When the great powers became deeply involved elsewhere, Japan could subjugate her weak neighbors and drive all Western Powers from East Asia because Japan had superior modern fighting equipment throughout that region. Finally, the United Nations are now overwhelming the Axis Powers primarily because the total weight of their industrial production is almost three times as great as that of the Axis nations combined.

Industry is important in war, however, because it is important in peace. It is the modern scientific technique which frees man's productive power and makes him master over the things of earth. It is a tool of man and subordinate to man. It cannot be created in a vacuum. The developing of industry requires the natural resources of the earth, but the real creative power behind industry is human beings and their sciences. In peace time, as in war time, manpower, or population, is a basic item in the strength of nations. The numbers of the people are a primary factor in producing goods and services for home use and for world society. Population also is a prime measure of market or consuming power and of a nation's concern in world affairs. As the mastery of new methods is spread throughout the earth, to bring equality in producing power, the size of population will become increasingly the decisive factor in measuring the power of nations.

A third major factor, fixing the influence of each nation in world affairs is its foreign trade. Imports indicate dependence of the home country on the economy of other nations. Exports in a strong economy represent a home surplus which can be released to supply goods for other peoples. Both are matters of great concern in world affairs. Trade between nations has made possible the growth of science and industry. International exchange of goods is the very foundation of the whole modern pattern of life.

It is no accident that the British Empire was the greatest trading nation before it could lead in the industrial revolution and no accident that, with this background, it is still far ahead of all other nations in the markets of the world. The United States is second in the volume of its foreign trade. Germany, France, Italy, and Japan follow in that order. The progressive smaller nations are even more dependent on outside trade than are the greater states. Only Russia, among the important nations of the world, has had an economic self-sufficiency which could reduce foreign trade to a minimum. That economic self-sufficiency also made possible a relative independence of the Soviet Union in all other international affairs. Only outside aggression forced Russia to become a dominant world power.

Population, industrial development, and foreign trade: these three are the most objective and measurable factors in determining the part which any nation is to play in international processes. If there is to be any sound basis for estimating the prospective power of nations, and for the peaceful control of world affairs, the effort must start with a clear picture of the distribution of these three factors among the peoples of the world. The following table (below) has been prepared

and are as representative of all industry as any simple selection could be.

The historic home of modern industry is in Western Europe and North America. Therefore, it is not strange that industrial power is still centered in these regions. In the tabulation below, the first group, including only 13 nations and dominions and with less than one-third of the world's population, has 92 per cent of the world's industry and 65 per cent of its international trade. Together, they have more than ten times as much industrial capacity as the other two-thirds of the world's peoples.

*Table 1. Basic Elements of World Power*

|  | Population, Millions | Population, Per Cent | Industrialization, Per Cent | International Trade, Per Cent |
|---|---|---|---|---|
| The United States | 131.7 | 6 | 37 | 10 |
| Great Britain and her dominions *a* | 68.4 | 3 | 12 | 22 |
| France | 39.3 | 2 | 5 | 4 |
| Six small nations of Western Europe *b* | 34.7 | 2 | 5 | 13 |
| Russia | 192.7 | 9 | 11 | 1 |
| Germany | 79.4 | 4 | 14 | 9 |
| Japan | 72.9 | 3 | 5 | 3 |
| Italy | 45.3 | 2 | 3 | 3 |
| Totals | (634.4) | (31) | (92) | (65) |
| China | 422.7 | 20 | (Less than 1%) | 1 |
| India | 389. | 19 | 1 | 2 |
| All other peoples | 705.9 | 33 | (Less than 7%) |  |

*a* Including Canada, Australia, New Zealand, and the white population of South Africa.
*b* Including Sweden, Norway, Denmark, Holland, Switzerland, and Belgium-Luxemburg as a combined economic unit.

to show the outstanding facts in that picture. The figures for industrial development are weighted in the direction of heavy industry which is the basis of military power. They are computed by combining the latest pre-war statistics for the production of steel and electricity. These two great industries are basic for many other lines of production. Statistics for these two are most readily available

The table shows also that the United States, the British Commonwealth, the democracies of Western Europe and Germany, with little more than 16 per cent of the world's population, have 73 per cent of the world's industrial power. These countries are leading representatives of the West European type of civilization and, in many ways, a culturally homogeneous section of the world. They have largely created the commercial revolution, political nationalism, the Protestant religion, all modern scientific development, the manifold industrial revolution, liberal individualistic philosophy, and parliamentary democracy. In recent decades, these countries, responding to changed conditions, also have given a new emphasis to social security and economic planning. In spite of the differences and conflicts between them, they still have much to hold them together and much to contribute to the improvement of world society. . .

## IV. The Balance of Power

The politics of power among states has led them, quite naturally, to manipulate power by combining their strength in alliances, by standing ready to throw their weight to one or another of two groups of contending states, or by establishing a condition in which the power of opposing states or groups is in equilibrium. The latter two methods of arranging power are both termed the balance of power, and they are further explained in the four extracts immediately below. Because alliances are often means of balancing power, the texts of two alliances, currently in operation, follow in the next group of extracts. Regional systems of co-operation and defense like those noted in Part One are similar to alliances; at best there is but a technical distinction between a bilateral alliance and one like the Western European Union. The Brussels Pact, creating the Western European Union, backed by the United States, was negotiated to improve the power position of its signatories as a group *vis-à-vis* Russia and the nations within the Soviet sphere of influence. Mention of this regional grouping suggests that the effort to balance power is destined to be carried out on a world-wide basis. In achieving any world balance of power, however, the strongest nations—the super-powers—will play the heaviest roles. The position of the United States, Russia, and Britain, as the present super-powers, is explained in a later extract.

## A. *Vattel's View*

(E. de Vattel, *The Law of Nations*, S. Campbell, 1st American edition, 1796, pp. 379-80.)

Europe forms a political system, a body, where the whole is connected by the relations and different interest of nations inhabiting this part of the world. It is not, as anciently, a confused heap of detached pieces, each of which thought itself very little concerned in the fate of others, and seldom regarded things which did not immediately relate to it. The continual attention of sovereigns to what is on the carpet, the constant residence of ministers, and the perpetual negotiations, make Europe a kind of a republic, the members of which, though independent, unite, through the ties of common interest, for the maintenance of order and liberty. Hence arose that famous scheme of the political equilibrium or balance of power; by which is understood such a disposition of things as no power is able absolutely to predominate, or to prescribe laws to others.

The surest means for preserving this equilibrium would be, that no power should be superior to the others; that all, or at least the greater part, would be nearly equal in force. This project was attributed to Henry IV but there was no executing it without injustice and violence. Besides, had equality been established, how could it be supported by lawful means? Commerce, industry, military virtues could soon put an end to it. The right of inheriting sovereignties could overthrow this system. It is more natural, easy, and just, to have recourse to the means just mentioned, of forming confederacies for making head against the most powerful, and hindering him from dictating law.

This is now observed by the sovereigns of Europe. They consider the two principal powers, which on that very account are naturally rivals, as destined to be checks on each other, and unite with the weakest, like so many weights thrown into the lightest scale, for keeping one in equilibrium with the other. . .

Confederacies would be a sure way of preserving the equilibrium and supporting the liberty of nations, did all Princes thoroughly understand their true interests, and regulate all their steps for the good of the state. . .

## B. *The Balance of Power in History*

(S. B. Fay, 'Balance of Power,' *Encyclopedia of the Social Sciences*, vol. ii, pp. 395-9. Copyright 1930 by The Macmillan Company.)

Balance of power is a phrase current in discussions of international relations. It means such a 'just equilibrium' in power among the members of the family of nations as will prevent any one of them from becoming sufficiently strong to enforce its will upon the others. As an obvious maxim of common sense in politics it was advocated and applied among the ancients and again in modern times during the past four centuries.

As Hume pointed out in his essay 'On the Balance of Power,' the principle was familiar to both the political theorists and practical statesmen among the ancients. It inspired the league which was formed against the growing domination of Athens and which produced the Peloponnesian War. After the decline of Athens, when the Thebians and Lacedaemonians disputed for hegemony; the Athenians in turn always threw themselves into the lighter scale in their endeavour to preserve the balance. . .

With the establishment of overwhelming dominion successively by Macedonia, Rome, Charlemagne and the Holy Roman Empire, balance of power vanished from Europe as a practical principle. It did not reappear until the Renaissance and the rise of modern national states. The Medici and the other Italian princes sought to secure an equilibrium between themselves, and between the Spanish, French, and German kings who attempted to interfere in Italian politics.

In the sixteenth century the enormous territorial possessions of Charles V rendered him so powerful that a natural apprehension was felt by the other states of Europe. Francis I therefore took upon himself the task of adjusting the equilibrium of power in Europe by making a treaty of alliance with the infidel Turk—to the great scandal of Christian Europe —and by constituting himself the friend or protector of the minor German states. In this enterprise he was assisted by Henry VIII of England. . .

During the next half century France in turn was lifted to a position of threatening preponderance through the ruthless ambitions of Louis XIV. There resulted a new series of wars and treaties in which her apprehensive neighbors, led by Holland and England, sought to establish a new balance of power. Many writers, like Fénelon, and practical statesmen generally were becoming more strongly convinced of the need of establishing firmly in Europe a true balance of power (*équilibre européen* or *europäisches Gleichgewicht*). During the next two hundred years, from the Peace of Utrecht until the World War, many of the most important treaties, as has been pointed out at length by Phillimore (vol. I, pt. IV, paragraphs 403-406), were likewise designed to set up or preserve the balance of power against the overwhelming domination of any one state or combination of states.

The prevailing view of this concept was ably set forth by Fénelon in his 'Supplément a'l'examen de conscience sur les devoirs de la royauté,' written toward the close of Louis XIV's reign for the instruction of the king's grandson, the Duke of Burgundy. Neighboring states, in their own interest as well as for the common good, ought to form a kind of family of nations. The strongest will in the long run tend to prevail over the others and overthrow them, unless they unite to establish a balance. 'To hinder one's neighbors from becoming too strong is not to do harm; it is to guarantee one's self and one's neighbors from subjection; in a word it is to work for liberty, tranquillity, and public safety; because the aggrandizement of one nation beyond a certain limit changes the general system of all nations connected with it. . . The excessive aggrandizement of one may mean the ruin and subjugation of all the other neighbors. . . This attention to the maintenance of a kind of equality and equilibrium between neighboring states is what assures peace for all' (*Oeuvres,* vol. III, Paris, 1835, pp. 361.). . .

A balance of power aims primarily to preserve peace and the status quo. It presupposes for its success a static condition in nations. But herein lies its fundamental weakness. Nations are almost never static; some are growing, others declining. Equilibrium between them is therefore unstable and is affected by a great variety of factors.

## C. *Prussia and the Balance of Power,* 1859

The excerpt below, taken from a diplomatic note dispatched in 1859, when France and Sardinia were at war with Austria-Hungary, an ally of Prussia, shows how the balance of power may figure in practical politics. Prussia was concerned in this case lest the balance of power be tilted against her if Austria-Hungary were weakened.

Lord Russell to Lord Bloomfield (Berlin), 1859, from *Fontes Juris Gentium,* Vol. I, Part 1, Berlin, Carl Heymanns Verlag, 1931, p. 22. The German interests in the United States copyright in this work were vested in the Attorney General of the United States in 1948, pursuant to law. The use of the following excerpt is by permission of the Attorney General, in the public interest, under License No. JA-1353.)

Count Bernstorff has read to me two dispatches from Baron Schleinitz, one marked 'very confidential,' upon the subject of the present aspect of affairs, and upon the policy which Prussia is desirous, in conjunction with England and Russia, to pursue with regard to the Italian war and its consequences.

Those dispatches were dated respectively the 24th and the 27th of June (1859).

Baron Schleinitz, in the former of these dispatches, alludes to the state of affairs which has induced Prussia to mobilize part of her army. Not only, he says, has the agitation in Germany caused by the advance of the war towards her frontier rendered necessary armaments not disproportioned to those of her neighbors; but Prussia has considered it necessary at once to place herself in a position to control a course of events which might tend to modify the balance of power in Europe, by enfeebling an empire with which Prussia is confederated, and by affecting the bases of European rights laid down in acts to which Prussia was a party. . .

The Prince Regent of Prussia looks with becoming anxiety to the maintenance of the balance of power in Europe. Let us examine this matter. The balance of power in Europe means, in effect, the independence of its several states. The preponderance of any one Power threatens and destroys this independence.

## D. *Sir Edward Grey on the Balance of Power*

(Sir Edward Grey, Statement on Balance of Power, *British Documents on the Origins of the War, 1898-1914,* vol. III, appendix A., edited by Gooch, G. P., and Temperley, H., London, His Majesty's Stationery Office, 1926.)

[The balance of power is the counterpart to] a policy on the part of the strongest Power in Europe or of the strongest group of powers in Europe, of first of all separating the other Powers outside their own group from each other, taking them in detail, crushing them singly if need be, and forcing each into the orbit of the policy of the strongest Power, or of the strongest group of Powers. Now if any policy of that sort were pursued by any Power, it could only be pursued by the strongest Power, or the strongest group of Powers in Europe at the moment. The moment it was pursued, the moment the weakest Powers in Europe were assailed, either by diplomacy or by force, one by one they would appeal to us to help them. I may say at once that we are not committed by entanglements which tie our hands. Our hands are free, and I have nothing to disclose as to our being bound by any alliance which is not known to all the world at the present time. But I do feel this very strongly, that if such a situation should arise, and there were a risk of any Power, or group of Powers, requiring such a dominating position in Europe that on the continent of Europe it would be the arbiter not only of peace and war, but of the diplomacy of all the other Powers of Europe, and if while that process was going on we were appealed to for help and sat by and looked on and did nothing, then people ought to realize that the result would be one great combination in Europe, outside which we should be left without a friend. If that were the result, then the naval situation would be this, that if we meant to keep command of the sea we should have to estimate as a probable combination against us of fleets in Europe not two Powers but five Powers.

History shows that the danger threatening the independence of this or that nation has generally arisen, at least in part, out of the momentary predominance of a neighboring state at once militarily powerful, economically efficient, and ambitious to extend its frontiers or spread its influence, the danger being directly proportionate to the degree of its power and efficiency, and to the spontaneity or 'inevitableness' of its ambitions. The only check on the abuse of political predominance derived from such a position has always consisted in the op-position of an equally formidable rival, or of a combination of several countries forming a league of defense. The equilibrium established by such a grouping of forces is technically known as the balance of power. . .

## V. ALLIANCES TO GAIN MORE POWER

An alliance is an agreement between two or more states to co-operate, usually by joint military action, for defensive or possibly for offensive action. It is an instrument of power politics by which a nation adds the strength of a friend to its own. Under the Covenant of the League of Nations it was understood that defensive alliances were permissible provided that, like other agreements, they were published and their terms were not in conflict with the League requirements for the peaceful solution of disputes. The provisions of the Charter of the United Nations are quite similar, except for Article 53, which specifically approves such regional agreements as are 'directed against the renewal of aggressive policy' by an enemy state in World War II until the United Nations has developed to the point that it may 'be charged with responsibility for preventing further aggression.'

A number of important alliances are now in force. The two whose texts are given below illustrate some of the main types of agreements. The Chinese-Russian alliance quoted here is but one of a group of similar treaties the Soviet Union has concluded since the war, mainly with neighboring states in Eastern Europe. In turn, the latter countries have negotiated alliances among themselves. Thus what constitutes a very extensive Soviet alliance system, erected between 1942-8, is in effect. This system of alliances has been identified with the regional grouping of powers dealt with in Chapter 4.

### A. The Chinese-Soviet Treaty of Alliance

The Chinese-Soviet alliance was concluded just before World War II came to an end. It is significant that one of the treaty's provisions names Japan specifically as the possible enemy, a second calls for other assistance than military aid, and a third indicates that the alliance is to last for thirty years.

(Chinese-Russian Alliance, 14 August 1945, *United Nations Review*, vol. v, No. 5, 15 September 1945, p. 229.

ARTICLE 1

The high contracting parties have agreed together with the United Nations to wage war against Japan until final vic-tory. The high contracting parties have promised to give each other all indispensable military and other assistance and support in this war.

ARTICLE 2

The high contracting parties have pledged themselves not to enter into separate negotiations with Japan and not to conclude a peace agreement or armistice without mutual agreement with either the present Japanese Government or with any other Government or organ in power in Japan which will not clearly repudiate all aggressive intentions.

### ARTICLE 3

The high contracting powers have pledged themselves after the conclusion of the war against Japan to undertake mutually all existing measures in order to make it impossible to repeat the aggression and breach of peace by Japan. If one of the high contracting powers finds herself involved in military operations against Japan as a result of the aggression and breach of peace by contracting party, the other high contracting party will give the first contracting party involved in the military operations military and other assistance and support with the means at its disposal. This article remains in force until such time as, following the demand of the two high contracting parties, the responsibility shall be laid on the organization of the United Nations for the prevention of further aggression on the part of Japan.

### ARTICLE 4

Each of the high contracting parties pledges itself not to conclude any alli-

ance whatsoever and not to take part in any coalition whatsoever directed against the other contracting party.

### ARTICLE 5

The high contracting parties, taking into consideration the interests of security and economic development of both parties, agree to work together in close and friendly cooperation after the conclusion of peace and to act according to the principles of mutual respect for their sovereignty and territorial entity and non-interference in the internal affairs of both contracting parties.

### ARTICLE 6

The high contracting parties agree to give each other all possible economic assistance in the postwar period in view of the lightening and speeding up of the national rehabilitation of both countries in order to make their contribution to the prosperity of the world.

### ARTICLE 7

Nothing in this treaty should be interpreted in a way which would prejudice the rights and duties of both high contracting parties as members of the organization of the United Nations. . .

## B. *The Anglo-French Alliance,* 1947

On 4 March 1947, the following alliance was concluded by Great Britain and France. Its purpose, as stated, is to prevent German aggression.

(Text from *The New York Times,* 15 March 1947.)

### ARTICLE 1

Without prejudice to any arrangements that may be made under any treaty concluded between all the powers having re-

sponsibility for action in relation to Germany under Article 107 of the Charter of the United Nations, for the purpose of preventing any infringement by Germany of her obligations with regard to disarmament and demilitarization and gen-

THE GREAT POWERS 191

erally of insuring that Germany shall not again become a menace to peace,

The high contracting parties will, in the event of any threat to the security of either of them arising from the adoption by Germany of a policy of aggression, or from action by Germany designed to facilitate such a policy, take, after consulting with each other and where appropriate with the other powers having responsibility for actions in relation to Germany, such agreed action (which, so long as the said Article 107 remains operative, shall be action under that article) as is best calculated to put an end to this threat.

ARTICLE 2

Should either of the high contracting parties become again involved in hostilities with Germany, either in consequence of an armed attack within the meaning of Article 51 of the Charter of the United Nations, by Germany against that party, or as a result of agreed action taken against Germany under Article 1 of this treaty, or as a result of enforcement action taken against Germany by the United Nations Security Council, the other high contracting party will at once give the high contracting party so involved in hostility all the military and other support and assistance in its power.

ARTICLE 3

In the event of either high contracting party being prejudiced by the failure of Germany to fulfill any obligation of an economic character imposed on her as a result of the instrument of surrender, or arising out of any subsequent settlement, the high contracting parties will consult with each other, and where appropriate with the other powers having responsibilities for action in relation to Germany, with a view to taking agreed actions to deal with the situation.

ARTICLE 4

Bearing in mind the interests of the other members of the United Nations, the high contracting parties will, by constant consultation on matters affecting their economic relations with each other, take all possible steps to promote the prosperity and economic security of both countries and thus enable each of them to contribute more effectively to the economic and social objectives of the United Nations.

ARTICLE 5

(1) Nothing in the present treaty should be interpreted as derogating in any way from the obligation devolving upon the high contracting parties from the provisions of the Charter of the United Nations or from any special agreement concluded in virtue of Article 43 of the Charter.

(2) Neither of the high contracting parties will conclude any alliance or take part in any coalition directed against the other high contracting party: nor will they enter into any obligation inconsistent with the provisions of the present treaty.

. . .

VI. THE GREAT POWERS

The author of the extract below explains that the great powers were all European states until the present century. Today, however, the three 'superpowers'—the United States, Russia, and Great Britain—are world rather than European powers. In addition to these three there are France, China, Japan, and Germany, which, he believes, may become important 'regional powers.'

(William T. R. Fox, *The Super Powers,*
New York, pp. 12-17, 18-21. Copyright
1944 by Harcourt, Brace and Co., Inc.)

There is no mystery about which will
be the powers of first rank in the post-
war world. The United States of America,
Great Britain, and the Soviet Union are
the Big Three in war as they will be in
peace. However, to understand the significance of this cardinal political fact
one must know how they got that way,
how their relationships with each other
will differ from the relationships of the
great powers in the past, and what will be
the power position of certain other prominent states which claim great-power status.

Until the twentieth century the great
powers were all European powers. Today,
none of the three greatest powers is
strictly European; nor are any of the
three main centers of power located in
continental Western Europe. Monopoly
in effective use of armed power has certainly passed from the nations of that
continent. Today Europe is an arena
whose internal struggles periodically involve the whole civilized world in organized bloodshed, and whose struggles
end only with the intervention of powers
outside the continent. The transition
from the old, world-dominating Europe
to the new 'problem-Europe' is a central
fact in the international politics of our
time. What are the implications of this
outward dispersion of power for the future of Anglo-Soviet-American relations?

The first of the existing world powers
was Britain. Her domination of the whole
maritime world in the nineteenth century
gave her a unique position in relation to
the other European powers. Britain's
head start in the Industrial Revolution
would have guaranteed her a position of
primacy in any case. But in an era of
water transportation, when overland
movement of goods and men was costly
and slow, and when the discovery of the
New World and the rise of North European trading centers had reoriented Europe toward the Atlantic Ocean, her
earlier marginal position became central.
She had 'the finest site on the Main Street
of the world.' As an island near the European continent, she could with her
mighty navy effectively control the narrow seas through which the men and
goods of other powers must pass. Whether
by design or by good fortune, acquisition
of defensible bases at Gibraltar, Malta,
Suez, Aden, Singapore, Capetown, and
the Falkland Islands—defensible because
they could be supplied most efficiently by
the very sea routes whose security their
possession ensured—reinforced and perfected the British position. From a communications point of view that country
thus controlled both the 'main four-cor-
ners' of Europe and all its seaward approaches.

In the nineteenth century, however,
forces were at work which were to destroy in large part Britain's unique advantages. Her industrial techniques were
adopted first across the Atlantic in the
United States and then with surprising
rapidity in the island empire of Japan.

The United States emerged from its
Civil War a nation whose place among
the great powers could not long be denied. In terms of its capacity to make war
it demonstrated its coming of age by
putting into the field in the 1860's armies
which were tremendous in size and in
striking power. The United States was not
for a generation after the Civil War an
important naval power, but this was at
least partly through choice. Its incomparably bountiful West was a far richer
prize than any European power could win
by military or naval conquest. That the
young giant of the Western Hemisphere
was strong enough to repel any European
intruder, the ever-scheming Napoleon III
came to understand after his fiasco in
Mexico, when he tried without success to

keep the Archduke Maximilian upon the Mexican throne.

Japan, too, experienced large-scale industrialization in the nineteenth century. Although her country lacked rich mineral resources, her statesmen were determined by a total mobilization of her human and mineral resources to make up for this deficiency. Having learned the ways of the Occident, she promptly used her new knowledge to protect herself against the powers of Europe and to assure primacy in the Orient.

With the opening of the twentieth century, therefore, two non-European powers claimed admission to the inner circle of the great powers. By Britain's withdrawal from the Caribbean in the 1890's, symbolized by her reluctant acquiescence in the statement of Secretary of State Olney that 'Today the United States is practically sovereign on this continent, and its fiat is law upon the subjects to which it confines its interposition,' and by her alliance with Japan in 1902, she acknowledged that the Pax Britannica no longer ran to the ends of the earth. Britain was still the only true world power. She had admitted the regional dominance of the United States and Japan; but without a globe-encircling series of bases these powers were still only regional powers, no matter how big their fleets of capital ships. 'Such regional dominance might very well be the most effective means of insuring certain countries—the United States, for example—against blockade or invasion. But . . . no local command of the sea could endow the United States or any other country . . . with a leverage on world politics even approaching that which British statesmen had long derived from their naval ascendancy in Europe's narrow seas.' With the formal acceptance of the transoceanic regional powers into the inner circle of the great powers, the first stage in the outward migration of power from Europe was reached.

These moves were certainly hastened by a trend of events within Europe that was equally unfavorable to the maintenance of British maritime supremacy. Brandenburg-Prussia, in the early eighteenth century 'Europe's biggest little sand-box,' had grown until by 1900 Germany under Kaiser Wilhelm II had won her place as the leading land power of Europe. With the development of the railroad, the strategic position of a centrally located country with an efficient transportation network improved enormously. Bismarck's quick victories against Denmark, Austria, and France gave proof of the new efficiency of overland transport. For Britain this meant a loosening of her former vise-like grip on the main channels of intra-European communication; there were now alternative and speedier routes.

During the mid-nineteenth century, when the Russian bear was the *bête noire* of the British Foreign Office, the further consolidation of North German power under Prussian leadership was watched with friendly interest. But Germany overreached herself. In the words of Sir Eyre Crowe, 'Germany had won her place as one of the leading, if not, in fact, the foremost Power on the European continent. But over and beyond the European Great Powers there seemed to stand the "World Powers." It was at once clear that Germany must become a "World Power." '

This Great Britain was not prepared to admit. Once the German determination to become a world power, by building up a strong fleet, became clear, Britain was necessarily so heavily preoccupied with Europe that her days of unchallenged leadership elsewhere were over. To maintain her physical security at home she was forced to make concessions in America and Asia and to form alliances on the continent of Europe. Her strength after 1900 was still sufficient to make her a valued partner in the alliance system. By forming with France and Russia the Triple Entente the prospects of preserving an equilibrium against the Triple Alliance of the three Central Powers in European politics were somewhat improved, but Britain's days of splendid isolation were over. She was still a power, but only one power in a family of eight. Of these, five were European; two were non-European; and one, Britain, controlled the sea routes between Europe and the outer world.

The First World War saw the complete disintegration of the Austro-Hungarian Empire so that the number of potential candidates for great-power status was permanently reduced by one. Another, Russia, was torn by internal revolution, and, strong or weak, would have been blackballed by the 'respectable' powers if her Bolshevik rules had sought a place for her in the inner circle. A third, Germany, was temporarily so completely disarmed that some of her smaller neighbors, notably Poland, sometimes played a 'great-power' role in their relations with her. A fourth, Italy, had at Caporetto and elsewhere made a very poor showing for a power that claimed to be a great power. However, since Italy was on the side of the victors, for the moment no voice was raised to exclude her from the ranks of the powers. With the return of peace there were therefore only four—or, with Italy, five—functioning great powers.

It was the application of the United States' military strength that broke the stalemate in the European War of 1914-18. The United States could no longer, therefore, be classified merely as a regional great power. The second stage in the outward migration of power had now been reached, for a non-European power inclined this balance in Europe as it chose.

The United States had now become in every sense of the word a world power. Her dominant role in the Washington Conference of 1922 showed that she was quite as influential in the Pacific as in Europe. There were, therefore, two world powers after 1919, the United States and Great Britain. The third great power, France, was essentially a European power; and the fourth, Japan, was exclusively an Asiatic power. The first three dominated the Peace Conference of Paris which established the new order in Europe, while the first, second, and fourth dominated the Washington Conference of 1922 which set the pattern of power politics in the Pacific throughout the interwar period.

The twenty-year 'long armistice' saw the revival of German power and the re-entry of Russia into the European alliance system. With Italy, which was shortly to reveal its true weakness, there were on the eve of the Second World War seven great powers. The spectacular collapse, first of France and then of Italy, has already reduced the list, for the moment, to five. Few can now doubt that Germany and Japan will also taste the bitter ashes of total defeat. The conclusion of the war will therefore see only three of the original seven still functioning as states of the first rank. The final stage in the outward migration of power from Western Europe will then be reached. No great power will remain in non-Russian continental Europe.

The three survivors—Great Britain, the Soviet Union, and the United States—are all world rather than European powers. The demonstrated military efficiency of the Soviet Union in Europe leaves no doubt that it could give a good account of itself in the Far Eastern conflict zone. It, like Britain and the United States, must be classified as a world power. . .

After the final Axis defeat, reconstructed France and victorious China will, in their respective spheres of interest, demand a full share in development of the postwar political order. But France is essentially a European and Mediterranean power; even with Indo-China restored she would not really be a great power in the Far East. China is exclusively an Asiatic power; no one would expect her to assume responsibilities for the enforcement of security in Europe. Both may be rated as 'great' powers in the general international organization which may be set up after the war, but in contrast with the Big Three, they are only regional powers.

It is not merely the geographically restricted interests of France and China which distinguish them from the Big Three. The artificial character of French hegemony on the continent of Europe in the 1920's was demonstrated by its rapid disintegration during the 1930's. Without support from some or all of the Big Three, her long quest for *sécurité* must remain unsatisfied. Only as a regional partner of the powers with global interests and global resources could she achieve this goal. She will be a valued partner because her European territory could constitute a gigantic bridgehead for military operations against a renewed German aggression, and because her North African territory will in an air age be essential to the maintenance of communications between the Eastern and Western Mediterranean. Her trump card in bidding for support from Great Britain or Russia is the alternative possibility of collaborating very closely with the other. Her chief reliance in demanding help from the Big Three acting in concert will be their interest in preventing her collapse before or her collaboration with a resurgent Germany. France will soon be strong again, but her strength will not be comparable to that of Soviet Russia and the United States and she lacks the far-flung bases of Britain. She will be a power, but a power of declining relative strength in a continent of declining relative strength.

China's position will on the other hand be more favorable than before the war with respect to her near neighbors. Will she thereby be able to claim full-rank partnership in the postwar aristocracy of world powers? With more than 400,000,-000 people in a continental area greater than that of the United States, she possesses two of the necessary qualifications. China, however, is not a power which can undertake great international responsibilities beyond her own borders. She has no armed power available for export. Instead, internal political issues are being decided by external intervention. Chiang Kai-shek's primacy at home depends in large measure on his capacity to attract foreign support. With political and social integration achieved, China will become a most important regional power, but her military might is clearly not of the same order as that of Russia, Britain, or America.

The time and circumstances under which Germany or Japan might be permitted to re-enter the circle of great powers depend on the extent to which the present war coalition coheres in the postwar world; but Germany and Japan too will be at most regional powers, and they may not be powers at all. As for Italy, she should never have been rated as more than the least of the great powers. Her performance in two world wars does not suggest an active role for Italy in the high politics of the postwar world. She has lived like a lion for a day; now she will have to lie down like a lamb for a very long time to come.

There will be no fewer than three and no more than seven great powers. Within this group, there will be 'world powers' and 'regional powers.' These world powers we shall call 'super-powers,' in order to distinguish them from the other powers which may enjoy the formal and ceremonial prestige of great-power status but whose interests and influence are great in only a single theater of power conflict. With bases both in the East and in the West and with communications assured between East and West, the bulk of the super-powers' armed force is highly mobile. It can, as in the present emergency, be thrown into whichever of the major theaters of war grand strategy dictates. . .

## VII. POWER AND FOREIGN POLICY

The author of the extract below criticizes the historic position of the United States in international politics on the ground that extensive commitments have been made abroad without the power to fulfil them. He maintains for this reason that the United States heretofore has not had a foreign policy in the proper sense.

(Walter Lippmann, *U.S. Foreign Policy*, Boston, pp. 9-10, 47-8. Copyright 1943 by Walter Lippmann. Reprinted with permission of Little, Brown and Company and the Atlantic Monthly Press.)

Before we examine the history of our insolvent foreign relations, we must be sure that we know what we mean by a foreign commitment and by the power to balance it.

I mean by a *foreign commitment* an obligation, outside the continental limits of the United States, which may in the last analysis have to be met by waging war.

I mean by *power* the force which is necessary to prevent such a war or to win it if it cannot be prevented. In the term *necessary* power I include the military force which can be mobilized effectively within the domestic territory of the United States and also the reinforcements which can be obtained from dependable allies.

The thesis of this book is that a foreign policy consists in bringing into balance, with a comfortable surplus of power in reserve, the nation's commitments and the nation's power. The constant preoccupation of the true statesman is to achieve and maintain this balance. Having determined the foreign commitments which are vitally necessary to his people,

he will never rest until he has mustered the force to cover them. In assaying ideals, interests, and ambitions which are to be asserted abroad, his measure of their validity will be the force he can muster at home combined with the support he can find abroad among other nations which have similar ideals, interests, and ambitions.

For nations, as for families, the level may vary at which a solvent balance is struck. If its expenditures are safely within its assured means, a family is solvent when it is poor, or is well-to-do, or is rich. The same principle holds true of nations. The statesman of a strong country may balance its commitments at a high level or at a low. But whether he is conducting the affairs of Germany, which has had dynamic ambitions, or the affairs of Switzerland which seeks only to hold what it already has, or of the United States, he must still bring his ends and means into balance. If he does not, he will follow a course that leads to disaster.

The habits of a century have fostered prejudices and illusions that vitiate our capacity to think effectively about foreign relations. The elementary means by which all foreign policy must be conducted are the armed forces of the nation, the arrangement of its strategic position, and the choice of its alliances. In the American ideology of our times these things had come to be regarded as militaristic, imperialistic, reactionary, and archaic; the proper concern of right-minded men was held to be peace, disarmament, and a choice between non-intervention and collective security.

We not only ignored the development of the means to achieve our ends: we chose as the ends of our efforts a set of ideals which were incompatible with all the means of achieving any ideals. The ideal of peace diverted our attention from the idea of national security. The ideal of disarmament caused us to be inadequately armed. The apparently opposed ideals of non-intervention on the one hand, and of collective security on the other, had at bottom the same practical result in that they inhibited us from forming our necessary alliances. Thus for nearly half a century after our vast commitments in the Pacific had been superimposed upon our immense commitment in the Western Hemisphere, we have had to conduct our pre-war diplomacy verbally—by promises, threats, and exhortations; we have had to wage war three times without being prepared to fight; and we have twice made peace without knowing what we wanted.

These spendthrift habits have led us to the bankruptcy of a total war in which we have suffered humiliating initial disasters at the hands of the Japanese; and our very independence was for a time in jeopardy. . .

# 8

# The Geographic Setting

IT ᴵˢ often said that national interest, or at least a government's conception of that interest, is what makes foreign policy. Bismarck once remarked, 'For me there is only one compass—only one Polar Star: the well-being of the state.' We are reminded, too, of Lord Palmerston's statement when he was Britain's foreign minister, to the effect that 'England has no eternal friends, no eternal enemies, only eternal interests.' What these assertions do not bring out is that the interests of a nation are themselves the results of many and varied causes—economic, ideological, historic, sociological, and geographic.

Nothing does more to shape a nation's interests and to determine its policies than geography. As the French diplomatist Jules Cambon said, geography is 'the principal factor' in diplomacy. Sir Austin Chamberlain, British Foreign Secretary, stated in the late 1920's that it had been 'most important' in British policy. Frederick the Great of Prussia realized the importance of geography when he complained, 'I am not well favored in this respect.' Certainly he was right, for his country was without defensible frontiers and surrounded by powerful neighbors. Geography fashions a nation's economy by the inescapable facts of climate, raw materials, fertility, and power resources. It helps also to determine the course of a nation's history by providing or withholding easy access to other peoples, and by establishing a location near weak or powerful neighbors. The elemental differences of nations in matters of location, size, boundaries, shape, and natural resources determine their relative power positions, whether they are secure or insecure, whether they can create and maintain large fighting forces, and whether they can get their way by sheer force against other powers.

The basic importance of the facts of geography often stands out strikingly in the behavior of nations. For centuries Russia has sought warm-water ports in the Straits region and in the Persian Gulf because, for a large part of the year, her other ports are ice-bound. The geographic location of the United States has been the principal basis for the policy of isolation which, until recently, has been so frequently asserted. It explains, moreover, the special interest of the United States in Latin America, especially in the Caribbean, and our adherence to the Monroe Doctrine. For years Italy looked for strategic boundaries in the northern Alps and finally obtained them in 1919. At times France has tried to push her frontier up to the Rhine River as a 'natural boundary' in order that she might better secure herself against Germany. Britain's traditional policy of isolating herself from continental affairs as much as possible but, when necessary, of trying to prevent any nation from dominating, of throwing her weight on the weaker side and thereby maintaining a balance of power, was founded on the fact that she is separated from the continent by a narrow channel which provides a measure of security but not enough to allow her to disregard developments on the other side.

There is nothing about geography that is deterministic in the sense that certain foreign policies are inevitable. The German geopoliticians were in error in giving to geography a quality of fatalism. The facts of geography often make certain policies very easy or natural, but other factors in foreign policy must not be ignored, such as nationalism, expansionism, ambition for power, ideology, the personality of the men who make policy, pressure politics, and the internal developments within a nation.

## I. THE RELATION OF GEOGRAPHY TO FOREIGN POLICY

(N. J. Spykman, 'Geography and Foreign Policy,' *American Political Science Review,* vol. 32, 1938, pp. 28-32, 39-43, 213-17, 227-9. Reprinted by permission of the *American Political Science Review.*)

'Le politique de toutes les puissances est dans leur géographie' conceded the man whose famous retort 'Circonstances? Moi, je fais les circonstances,' indicates his contempt for any agency but the human will as the arbiter of human destiny. But since the Red Sea parted for Moses and the sun obligingly paused for Joshua, the human will has been unable to recapture the control over topography and climate exhibited by those forceful gentlemen, and it is probably safe to say that it was by Russian geography rather than by men that the diminutive Corsican was finally defeated. If he is still living, there is at Waterloo even today a loyal guide who asserts with unshakable conviction that neither genius nor skill but a swampy ditch gave that victory to Wellington.

Unfortunately for the political scientist with a fondness for simplification, but fortunately for the statesman striving to overcome the geographic handicaps of his country, neither does the entire foreign policy of a country lie in geography, nor does any part of that policy lie entirely in geography. The factors that condition the policy of states are many; they are permanent and temporary, obvious and hidden; they include, apart from the geographic factor, population density, the economic structure of the country, the ethnic composition of the people, the form of government, and the complexes and pet prejudices of foreign ministers; and it is their simultaneous action and interaction that create the complex phenomenon known as 'foreign policy. . .'

It should be emphasized, however, that geography has been described as a conditioning rather than a determining factor. The word was chosen advisedly. It was not meant to imply that geographic characteristics play a deterministic, causal role in foreign policy. The geographic determinism which explains by geography all things from the fourth symphony to the fourth dimension paints as distorted a picture as does an explanation of policy with no reference to geography. The geography of a country is rather the material for, than the cause of, its policy, and to admit that the garment must ultimately be cut to fit the cloth is not to say that the cloth determines either the garment's style or its adequacy. But the geography of a state cannot be ignored by men who formulate its policy. The nature of the territorial base has influenced them in that formulation in the past and will continue to do so in the future.

The nature of this base exerts a manifold influence on policy. Size affects the relative strength of a state in the struggle for power. Natural resources influence population density and economic structure, which in themselves are factors in the formulation of policy. Location with reference to the equator and to oceans and land masses determines nearness to centers of power, areas of conflict, and established routes of communication, and location with reference to immediate neighbors defines position in regard to potential enemies, thereby determining the basic problems of territorial security.

The significance of size and location as factors in foreign policy cannot be evaluated, however, without a consideration of the modifying effect of topography and climate. Topography affects strength because of its influence on unity and internal coherence. Climate, affecting transportation and setting limits to the possibility of agricultural production, conditions the economic structure of the state, and thus, indirectly but unmistakeably, foreign policy.

## The Factor of Size

The comparative size of states, provided there is an effective political and economic integration of the area, is a rough indication of comparative strength and, as such, an element in foreign policy. Although in its abstract form as total surface area it does not give rise to specific objectives and gives no content to foreign policy, yet it is an indication

of the power to resist pressure from other states and may affect the choice between war and diplomacy as instruments of national policy.

Throughout history, and especially during its earlier periods, an overwhelming majority of the strong states have been large states. Egypt, Babylonia, Assyria, Persia, and Rome were each in their turn the largest existing organized state, and by that token, the strongest. It is true that in certain periods small states like Athens and Venice and Holland, operating as sea-powers, could for a time, by means of the control of sea-routes, extend their sway over large areas of the world, but in land struggles they usually succumbed to the larger units and in sea struggles to units with broader bases, which meant larger territory. . .

Size is of primary importance as an element of defense, particularly if the vital areas of a country are far removed from the border. To reach Moscow, Napoleon forced an exhausted army across a space almost as vast as his own empire, only to find himself confronted by more silent space and his base of supplies hopelessly in the rear. . .

Size and distance as elements of defense have acquired even greater significance since men have flown through the air instead of walking on the ground. The present radius of a bombing squadron is approximately eight hundred miles. Russia is thus the only European country the vital industrial and mining centers of which do not lie within the range of an enemy squadron. Paris is less than two hundred miles from London, and the Ruhr lies less than three hundred miles from Paris. . .

The size of a state at any given time cannot be accounted for in terms of any one conditioning factor. It depends on technical, social, moral, and ideological development, on the dynamic forces within a state, on the political constellation of the past, and on the personality of individuals. But it has undeniably been conditioned by topographical facts. The effect of topography on size is admittedly less since man has learned to tunnel through mountains and throw bridges across great chasms, but until technological conquest is considerably more complete, topography cannot be disregarded.

Greece was divided by nature into small economic units, and she therefore developed small political units. The valleys were self-centered and the most fertile sections of the country were open to the sea but shut off from contact by land with the rest of the peninsula. She therefore exchanged ideas and commodities by sea rather than by land, and the Greek settlements became a string of cities many of which were enemies each with the other. A similar situation prevails in the Balkan peninsula today, where each valley or plain is isolated by a mountain wall, and the various groups preserve their own social, political, and religious characteristics. There is no natural center within the peninsula around which a great state might form and rivalries between the small states are inevitable. . .

Obviously the ideal territorial shape for a state is that of a perfect circle. Given such a configuration, the greatest possible area is enclosed within the shortest possible boundary, facilitating defense, and all parts of the area are equidistant from, and as near as possible to, a government located at the center of the circle. States that are long and narrow in shape—and this is particularly true for land powers —tend inevitably to disintegrate either by losing territory at the periphery where the centralizing influence of government is least felt, or by splitting to reappear as separate states. . .

A factor even more significant than shape in the establishment of centralized control over a given area is topography.

On the height and configuration of mountain ranges, the depth and width of valleys, the direction of rivers, and the modifying effect of climate on all of these features, will depend the ease of communication within a country. . .

### THE FACTOR OF LOCATION

Important as size may be, however, it does not exclusively determine the rank of a state in the hierarchy of world powers and may be less significant than location in determining its importance in international affairs and in defining its problems of foreign policy. The location of a state may be described from the point of view of world-location, that is, with reference to the land masses and oceans of the world as a whole, or from the point of view of regional location, that is, with reference to the territory of the other states and immediate surroundings. The former description will be in terms of latitude, longitude, altitude, and distance from the sea; the latter will be in terms of relations to surrounding areas, distances, lines of communication, and the nature of border territory. . .

The geographic location of a state expressed, then, in terms of the facts and significance of its world and regional location is the most fundamental factor in its foreign policy. It can modify the significance of size and explains the historical importance of many small states. It conditions and influences all other factors for the reason that world location defines climatic zones and thereby economic structure, and regional location defines potential enemies and thereby the problem of territorial security and potential allies, and perhaps even the limits of a state's role as a participant in a system of collective security. If the British were willing to give up Empire, a shift of the Isles a thousand miles to the west might enable them to enjoy the luxury of 'isolationism.' With the present location, Empire or no Empire, they are inevitably enmeshed in the policies of continental Europe.

Since the French dug a ditch near Suez, and the French and Americans blasted a trench near Panama, the great land masses of the world consist of two islands, Eurasia and North America, which, because of navigation problems on the North Polar Sea, function as peninsulas, and three islands, South America, Africa, and Australia. The world location of a state becomes a question of its location with reference to these land masses. The fact that the greater land masses lie in the northern hemisphere, and that the largest land masses that do exist in the southern hemisphere lie in the tropics, has certain implications. Politically and industrially, the northern hemisphere will always be more important than the southern, and relations between various parts of the northern hemisphere will have more influence on the history of the world than relations between the two hemispheres. The location of a state north or south of the equator will therefore play a large part in determining the political significance of that state, the nature of its international relations, and the problems of its foreign policy. . .

Regional location determines whether neighbors will be many or few, strong or weak, and the topography of the region conditions the direction and nature of the contact with those neighbors. The man who once formulated the foreign policy of Manchuria had to do so with one eye on Japan and the other on Russia; every international gesture of Belgium is conditioned by the fact that she lies between France and Germany and across the channel from Great Britain; and the states of Central America can never for a moment forget that the north of them is occupied by one large power and not by several whom they might play off one against the other as their Euro-

pean counterparts, the Balkan states, have been able to do from time to time with their northern neighbors. Two of the traditional and unchanging cornerstones of United States foreign policy have been isolation from all European affairs and that oft-quoted and oftener misquoted principle known as the Monroe Doctrine. Each of these policies is tenable only in view of the fact that the European neighbors of the United States are three thousand miles away. If the United States had been as near to the European continent as is Great Britain, it could never have conceived a policy of isolation, to say nothing of maintaining it; and if most of South America had been as near to Europe as is Africa, the United States could not have prevented European powers from colonizing South America as they have colonized Africa.

A consideration of geographic environment alone suggests three main types of regional location—landlocked states, all of whose frontiers are land frontiers, island states, all of whose frontiers are seacoast, and a third group, much larger than the two preceding states, which have both land and sea frontiers. The significance of such location, however, will vary according to the political constellation of the moment and according to whether a state is situated between states of equal, greater, or less power than its own.

There have always been comparatively few landlocked states. Today there are three in Europe, two in Asia, and two in South America, . . . The outstanding characteristic of the foreign policy of all such states is that their security problem is defined exclusively in terms of land defense, and therefore in terms of immediate neighbors. . .

Until the development of the aëroplane, the defense problem of island states was exclusively a question of the maintenance of a navy. They were strategically secure as long as navigation remained in an undeveloped stage, and, later, as long as they maintained naval supremacy. In comparison with their Continental neighbors, Great Britain and Japan have rarely been invaded. . .

The great majority of the states of the world have both sea and land frontiers. Unless the frontier consists of a wholly insurmountable natural barrier, or the coast is always frozen and hence inaccessible to enemy approach, these states must maintain both land and sea forces. Whether a state's primary defense problem will be military or naval, and whether the contact will be chiefly from overseas or across its land frontiers, will depend on various factors such as the length of its frontiers, its world and regional location, and its topography and climate. . .

A relatively weak state located between two strong states is in the geographic position of a buffer state; whether it will become so in the political sense of the term will depend on various factors. In any case, such a state will be forced to adopt a very special foreign policy. Its own security depends on the security which its neighbors derive from its continued existence. This means that such a state is forced to pursue a precarious policy of neutrality. . .

## II. The State—Its Size and Security

In the statements below, the position is taken that a state with a large territory is more secure than a small state. The first extract, taken from a Finnish communication to the League of Nations in 1939, rejected the Russian claim that she needed the Carelian Isthmus in order to protect the city of Leningrad, which was only a few miles from the border. The second is a statement by Adolf Hitler taken from *Mein Kampf*. The soundness of the doctrine was demonstrated by Hitler's failure to conquer Russia in 1941, and by Japan's futile effort to subdue China.

### A. *A Finnish Statement*

(Aide-Memoire of M. Holsti, delegate of Finland to the League of Nations, 9 December 1939, *The Finnish Blue Book,* 1940, p. 83.)

The principle that its importance or the size of one of its towns entitles a state to require the cession of territory from a smaller state is unknown in the political life of the West. A large country is protected by its very size. To require a small state to renounce its means of defense is tantamount to destroying that state's liberty.

### B. *Hitler's Views*

(Adolf Hitler, *Mein Kampf,* New York, 1940, p. 177. Reprinted by permission of Houghton Mifflin Company.)

The size of a people's living area includes an essential factor for the determination of its outward security. The greater the amount of room a people has at its disposal, the greater is also its natural protection; because military victories over nations crowded in small territories have always been reached more quickly and more completely, than in the case of states which are territorially greater in size. The size of the state territory, therefore, gives a certain protection against frivolous attacks, as success may be gained only after long and severe fighting and, therefore, the risk of an impertinent surprise attack, except for quite unusual reasons, will appear too great. In the greatness of the state territory, therefore, lies a reason for the easier preservation of a nation's liberty and independence, whereas, in the reverse case, the smallness of such a formation simply invites seizure.

## III. Geopolitics

The geopolitician is not content to use geography to explain foreign policy. In a more aggressive mood he makes use of it to give direction and impulse to policy. To him there is something deterministic about geography, especially in fixing the boundaries of a state and in justifying its expansion. The idea of manifest destiny, which was so prominent in the United States during a large part of the nineteenth century, was a form of geopolitics. It took on a much more dynamic and daring character in Nazi Germany. Under General Karl Haushofer, the director of the *Institut für Geopolitik,* the doctrine was developed into what purported to be a science and was given wide publicity as justification for Germany's ruthless policy of expansion. In order to drive their ideas home, maps bringing out particular points were circulated. The extract below, written by an officer of the United States Department of State, describes the historical development and the implications of German geopolitics.

(R. H. Fifield, 'Geopolitics at Munich,' *Department of State Bulletin,* vol. XII, No. 313, 1945, pp. 1154-62.)

The Men of Munich—those who specialized in geopolitics—have defined the subject as follows: 'Geopolitics is the science of the earth's relationship to political developments. It is based on the broad foundations of geography, especially political geography, which is the science of political organisms in space and their structure. . . It guides practical politics to that point where it must take the step into the unknown. Only if inspired by geopolitical knowledge, can this step be successful. Geopolitics will and must become the geographical conscience of the state.' Dr. Karl Haushofer has asserted that the word Politik is not preceded by the prefix geo by accident. The prefix relates politics to the soil.

The Men of Munich have drawn a distinction between geopolitics and political geography. Otto Maull, once a co-editor of the *Zeitschrift für Geopolitik,* has asserted that geopolitics considers the spatial requirements of a state but political geography studies only the space conditions of the country. In other words the German geopoliticians claimed that geopolitics is dynamic in action while political geography is static in scope. The Men of Munich have attempted to apply the principles and methods of geopolitics to 'branch' sciences such as psychology, medicine, and jurisprudence. The category of Geo-Wissenschafte was broadened to include Geo-Psychologie, Geo-Medizin, and Geo-Jurisprudenz.

Geopolitical concepts in Germany centered around a number of subjects. The ideas of the organic state, living space or Lebensraum, and the organic frontier have received considerable attention in German literature. One definition asserted that geopolitics was the scientific basis of the art of political action in the conflict of state organisms for Lebensraum. The political power of the state has been analyzed by the Men of Munich. One definition claimed that geopolitics was really the doctrine of the power of the state on earth. A very important idea back of the political power of the state was its location with reference to a specific concept of the distribution of land masses and ocean spaces. In accordance with relative power, a state was classified as renovating or decadent. The expression of the state in wartime involved the study of *Wehr-Geopolitik* or war geopolitics. The German geopoliticians have used the studies of an American admiral, Alfred T. Mahan, as basic source material on sea power. A Prussian general, Karl von Clausewitz, an authority on land power, inspired subsequent students of military affairs. Dr. Haushofer has quoted the definition of war given by Clausewitz, namely, that war is a continuation of policy with other means. No writer on air power assumed the stature of either Mahan or Clausewitz with the Men of Munich.

## RATZEL, KJELLÉN, MACKINDER

Friedrich Ratzel (1844-1904), a professor of geography at the Polytechnic Institute of Munich and later at the University of Leipzig, developed political geography to a point where geopolitics could easily appear. He was an intimate friend of Max Haushofer, the father of Karl Haushofer. Karl used to accompany the older men on their walks along the Isar River. Friedrich Ratzel was a teacher of Miss Ellen C. Semple, an outstanding geographer of the United States. However, Karl Haushofer accepted many more of Ratzel's ideas than did Ellen Semple. Ratzel himself remained aloof from the problems of German foreign policy.

The German professor taught that the state was a living organism with the biological necessity of growing in order to survive. He began his *Politische Geographie* first published in 1897 with a chapter on 'The State as an Organism Fixed in the Soil.' He asserted on one occasion that a state decayed as the result of a declining conception of space. In 1896 Ratzel published an article in Petermanns Mitteilungen on 'The Laws of the Territorial Growth of States' in which he listed seven laws of state growth. The fourth of these asserted that 'The frontier is the peripheric organ of the state.' Ratzel believed that a frontier was not a drawn line but a changing zone of assimilation. Frontiers were dynamic, reflecting the expansive force of aggressive countries. Boundary questions often led to war because a boundary might be an obstacle to the growth of the state.

The idea of Lebensraum is logically associated with the theory of the organic state. Both Karl Haushofer and Adolf Hitler received many of their ideas regarding Lebensraum from Ratzel. However, Professor Ratzel was only a link in the chain of thought relative to Lebensraum. Friedrich List, a friend of Henry Clay and a leader in the formation of the Zollverein or German customs union, believed that the economic progress of Germany depended upon a large territory of Europe from the North and Baltic Seas to the Black and Adriatic Seas. Von Treitschke was probably the first to use the word Lebensraum in its present political meaning. In the first World War Friedrich Naumann stressed the idea of Mittel-Europa, extending from the North Sea to the Adriatic, from Flanders to the Pripet Marshes, and from the Baltic to the Black Sea. Hitler enlarged the German Lebensraum to include a Euro-African political empire under the 'New Order,' the economic counterpart of which was the concept of Grossraumwirtschaft or continental economy. The idea of German Lebensraum provided camouflage for the imperialistic expansion of the Reich over a large area.

Rudolf Kjellén (1864-1922) expanded the ideas of Ratzel and applied them to world politics. Kjellén was a pro-German Swede of the first World War and a professor of government at the University of Göteborg. Dr. Haushofer and a group of followers enlarged, reedited, and published some of Kjellén's works. The Swedish professor taught in his *Staten som Lifsform* first published in Stockholm in 1916 that the state was not an artificial or accidental conglomeration of human beings united by legalist formulas. On the other hand, the state, deep-rooted in historic and actual realities, had grown organically and had an appearance of the same basic type as an individual man or a living being. He believed that the most important attribute of the state is power. Power was more important in the existence of the state than law because law can be maintained only by power. Kjellén foresaw the emergence of a few giant states in the world with Germany as one of them. The thinking of the Men of Munich was greatly influenced by the works of Kjellén.

Extremely influential in the development of German geopolitics was Sir Halford Mackinder—through no intention of his own. He has been a professor of geography at the University of London, a member of Parliament, a director of the London School of Economics, and vice-president of the Royal Geographical Society. Dr. Haushofer has referred to him as 'the most brilliant English geopolitician.' The Men of Munich have reprinted on a number of occasions the world map

drawn by Mackinder in 1904. Haushofer has acknowledged a debt of gratitude to Mackinder as a geographer. The German geopolitician has even quoted from Ovid: '*fas est et ab hoste doceri.*'

The contribution of Mackinder lies in his political perspective on the geographic distribution of the land masses and the bodies of water on earth. His first important statement on the subject came in a lecture entitled 'The Geographical Pivot of History' delivered to the Royal Geographical Society on January 25, 1904. In 1919 as a warning to the statesmen of the Paris peace conference, Sir Halford Mackinder wrote *Democratic Ideals and Reality*. The Anglo-Saxon world paid little attention to the book but Major General Haushofer saw in the volume many implications. Furthermore, the geostrategy of the Nazis in the second World War took into consideration some of the points stated in *Democratic Ideals and Reality*.

Mackinder visualized the continents of Europe, Asia, and Africa as a World-Island, forming one land mass. He noted that nine-twelfths of the world was water and only three-twelfths land. The World-Island had two-twelfths of this land, and the other land masses—chiefly North America, South America, and Australia —one-twelfth. The World-Island had fourteen-sixteenths of the population, and the other land areas two-sixteenths.

The key to the World-Island was the pivot area or the Heartland. This area extended from the 'broad isthmus between the Baltic and Black Seas' to eastern Siberia with the subsequent exclusion of Lenaland. The Heartland included most of the Iranian Upland in the southwest and much of the Mongolian Upland in the southeast. The pivot area was not vulnerable to sea power from the surrounding water or world ocean. From a political viewpoint the Heartland was largely Russian both in Europe and in

Asia, but Western China, Mongolia, Afghanistan, Baluchistan, and Iran have been included except for a narrow coastal strip in the case of the latter two.

Around the Heartland was an arc of Coastland defined as an area of drainage into navigable seas. The Coastland included all of Europe except the Heartland portion of Russia. The monsoon coastland areas of Asia were also included in the Coastland. The offshore islands were the British and Japanese homelands while the outlying islands were chiefly the Americas and Australia. Africa south of the Sahara Desert was considered a southern but secondary Heartland connected by the bridge of Arabia to the northern or main Heartland. Mackinder stated his thesis in three main points:

'Who rules East Europe commands the Heartland:

'Who rules the Heartland commands the World-Island:

'Who rules the World-Island commands the World.'

The English geographer believed firmly in the primary importance of the Heartland in Eurasia. He recognized the strategic location of Germany in the peninsula of Europe with reference to the Heartland. The north, central, and west areas of the Heartland were a vast plain or Great Lowland broken only by the Ural Mountains. This vast lowland extended into the plains of northern Germany. Although Europe in the past had been frequently invaded from the steppes of Asia, why could not the direction of invasion be reversed? In 1904 Mackinder asserted in his January address before the Royal Geographical Society: 'The oversetting of the balance of power in favour of the pivot state, resulting in its expansion over the marginal lands of Euro-Asia, would permit of the use of vast continental resources for fleet-building, and the empire of the world would then be in sight. This might happen if Germany

were to ally herself with Russia.' In July 1943 in an article in *Foreign Affairs*, Mackinder stated that his Heartland idea was 'more valid and useful today than it was either twenty or forty years ago.' In the same article he also stated that 'All things considered, the conclusion is unavoidable that if the Soviet Union emerges from this war as conqueror of Germany, she must rank as the greatest land Power on the globe. Moreover, she will be the Power in the strategically strongest defensive position. The Heartland is the greatest natural fortress on earth. For the first time in history it is manned by a garrison sufficient both in number and quality.'

### HAUSHOFER

Dr. Karl Haushofer called the attention of many Germans to the political significance of the writings of Ratzel, Kjellén, and Mackinder. Haushofer was born in Munich in 1869. He received a commission in the First Bavarian Artillery Regiment at the age of 19. In 1908 he was sent on a mission to Japan where he served as a military observer for the German General Staff. This period was one of the most formative of his life. He not only studied the language and institutions of Japan but also he became an expert on the Pacific and the Far East. On his trip to Japan he traveled by way of the Mediterranean, the Red Sea, and the Indian Ocean. On his return he traveled across Russia from Vladivostok to the Reich.

In 1913 Haushofer published his first book on Japan entitled *Dai Nihon: Greater Japan's Military Power, World Role, and Future.* He received his doctorate *summa cum laude* from the University of Munich. The title of his dissertation is indicative of his literary style: *The German Share in the Geographical Opening Up of Japan and the Sub-Japanese Earth Space, and Its Advancement Through the Influence of War and De-*

*fense Politics.* By the end of the first World War Haushofer had been promoted to the rank of a major general in the Army of the Kaiser. After the war he laid aside his uniform to teach political geography and military history at the University of Munich.

In 1924 Haushofer founded at Munich the *Zeitschrift für Geopolitik;* Otto Maull and Erich Obts were co-founders of the magazine. The publisher of the *Zeitschrift* from the first was Kurt Vowinckel. Later Dr. Albrecht Haushofer, the elder son of the General, began to write regularly for the *Zeitschrift,* but the other son, Heinz Konrad, did not become so conspicuous in geopolitics as his brother or father. The *Zeitschrift für Geopolitik,* published monthly, was intended chiefly for the lay reader. The magazine was devoted to a discussion of geopolitical matters. The issues contained 'factual' articles and 'dynamic' maps concerning all parts of the world. Albrecht Haushofer specialized in the Atlantic region; his father wrote reports on the Indo-Pacific area. The top organization of geopolitical research was the Institute of Geopolitics (*Institut für Geopolitik*) at Munich under the direction of Karl and Albrecht Haushofer. A large staff of specialists—geographers, demographers, economists, sociologists, biologists, medical men, law professors, and political and military experts—carried on the research. The strength and weaknesses of a certain area (*Raum*) were compared with the location (*Lage*) of the region with reference especially to Germany. . .

### CONTROL OF THE HEARTLAND

A Design for World Conquest has never been written in any one document by the Men of Munich. The published material, however, does present the general ideas of the German geopoliticians on the future of the Reich in the world. The first major objective was the consoli-

dation of the political forces of the Heartland of Mackinder. This objective primarily concerned the Soviet Union; secondary were the control of Middle Europe (*Zwischen-Europa*) and Western Europe and the acquisition of African colonies. The struggle for the Heartland, it was known, might result in war and might become a test of land power. In this respect Haushofer has definitely stated that the infantryman still decides the battle by taking possession of the space. The second major objective was the destruction of the sea power of the maritime states that opposed the Reich. This objective primarily concerned the Anglo-Saxon countries. Haushofer has realized the importance of sea power; he had carefully studied the writings of the American admiral, Alfred T. Mahan, especially the book entitled *The Influence of Sea Power upon History* 1660-1783. The German geopolitican noted that the conflict between oceanic and continental powers is a theme that runs through history. He stated that the most decisive of all political trends in the world is the drive of a country toward the sea. The Men of Munich believed that in the end world power was predicated upon both land and sea power, implemented by air power.

The attitude of Haushofer toward the Soviet Union was motivated by a strong desire to form a combination of powers, consisting of Germany, the Soviet Union, Japan, China and India under German leadership. Although Haushofer believed that the Heartland should be consolidated, he never made a final prescription for German policy toward the Soviet Union. The domination of the Heartland might be effected by 'colonization, amalgamation, or conquest. . .'

The mastery of the marginal lands of western Europe was secondary to the consolidation of the Heartland. The Men of

Munich believed that the small western states like Denmark, Belgium, and the Netherlands were doomed to inevitable disappearance. Haushofer has said that small countries have a constantly smaller chance of independent survival. France was the only real obstacle in the west. The Men of Munich had clearly noted the influence of geography on the foreign policy of France. Wulf Siewert asserted in the *Zeitschrift* in November 1935: 'The conflict between maritime and continental interests runs like a red thread through the whole of French history. . . In the long run, continental politics has always won over maritime interests.' In December 1935 he wrote in the *Zeitschrift:* 'France will defend its position in the Mediterranean as tenaciously as its place in Middle Europe so long as it thinks like Charles de Gaulle: "The sword is the axis of the world, and greatness can bear no subdivision!"' In general the Men of Munich discounted the military threat of France to Germany. France was considered a stagnating country in contrast to the renovating state of Germany. France was alleged to be biologically and politically decaying.

The German geopoliticians also placed little stress on Italy. . .

Meanwhile the Men of Munich emphasized the importance of colonies to the Reich. The German Lebensraum was considered too small without the addition of colonies. Two numbers of the *Zeitschrift* in 1939 were devoted to the colonial question (*Colonialfrage*). A new branch of geopolitics was advocated— Kolonialgeopolitik. The Men of Munich had in mind chiefly the colonial areas of Africa.

INDO-PACIFIC AREA

Karl Haushofer in his *Geopolitik des Pazifschen Ozeans* has declared that the most important geopolitical area in the world is the Pacific. The Men of Munich believed that the realm of the Pacific was the scene of the next great turning point in world history. Dr. Haushofer wrote in the *Zeitschrift* in January 1925: 'A giant space is expanding before our eyes with forces pouring into it which, in cool matter-of-factness, await the dawn of the Pacific age, the successor to the aging Atlantic, the over-age Mediterranean and the European era.' President Theodore Roosevelt of the United States had written in 1905: 'I believe that our future history will be more determined by our position on the Pacific facing China, than by our position on the Atlantic facing Europe.'

The Men of Munich realized that Japanese imperialism would clash with the resisting power of China. They saw the dangers of the Japanese attack on China in 1937. Only an energetic strategy of annihilation could bring success to Japan. Wolf Schenke wrote in the *Zeitschrift* in September 1938 that space permitted China to survive and Japan would do well to make peace. Christian Kröger wrote in January 1939 in the *Zeitschrift* that Japan 'has underestimated the immense spaces of China and she will never understand the spirit of modern China.' The Men of Munich believed that Japan should have struck first against the colonial empires of Great Britain, France, and the Netherlands in the Pacific.

Dr. Haushofer advocated a close relation between Japan and Germany. He based his idea partly on the fact that the Western powers in the first World War had ejected Germany from the Pacific. The Germans in Europe and the '900 million southeast Asiatics' were considered 'comrades of destiny.' In his *Geopolitik des Pazifischen Ozeans* he wrote that the struggle of the Indians and the Chinese for freedom from foreign control and from capitalistic pressure agreed with the secret dreams of central Europe. . .

### ANGLO-SAXONDOM

Since the second major objective of the Men of Munich was the destruction of the sea power of the leading maritime states, the Anglo-American countries were the objects of attention. With the consolidation of the Heartland under the Germans and with the aid of the Japanese, the defeat of the Anglo-Americans could be planned. However, Germany would have to gain sufficient sea power to supplement her land and air power.

The German geopoliticians looked upon the British Isles as the basic representative of sea power. Hitler in *Mein Kampf* advocated an alliance with England in order to pursue an aggressive Eastern policy. Haushofer remarked in his *Weltpolitik von Heute* in 1934 that the Anglo-Saxon statesmen were still able to think in terms of great spaces and times. Until the outbreak of war between Great Britain and Germany in 1939, Haushofer was guarded in his statements about the British. Most of the Men of Munich were convinced that the British Empire was in a state of gradual disintegration. Great Britain was no longer the mistress of the seas; the British Navy could no longer defend the Empire against every foe. The development of air power posed a menace; the home islands did not have a continental base with defense in depth; base areas had become more important than base points like Hong Kong and Gibraltar. The Statute of Westminster, giving the dominions equal status with the mother country, was considered a sign of disintegration; the peoples of Asia were determined to throw off the British rule; the British people did not have 'space mastery' in many areas under the flag. . .

The United States was not given much attention by the Men of Munich. The *Zeitschrift* devoted less time to the Western Hemisphere than to the Old World, with Colin Ross writing much of the material on the New World. He even remarked in March 1935 in the *Zeitschrift* that 'The America of today is tired and old, amazingly old.'

Dr. Haushofer himself was more interested in the World-Island and in the Pacific than in the Western Hemisphere. He studied the 'Pacific face' of the United States more than the Atlantic. In the development of American foreign policy he has praised the Monroe Doctrine as a brilliant application of geopolitical principles. . .

## IV. INTERNATIONAL RELATIONS AND MAPS

The Mercator map, which projects the globe upon a cylinder, gives an erroneous conception of the geographical basis of international relations. It served very well from the sixteenth century, when first devised, up to the twentieth century, but today the airplane has outmoded it. When travel was by wagon, rail, and steamship the distortions of the Mercator map were not important, but now it is necessary to understand that the earth is a globe, not a cylinder unrolled to make a flat surface. Traveling by plane from Chicago across the Arctic region, a person will reach Shanghai as soon as he will from Los Angeles, a fact that does not appear on the Mercator map. The author of the extract below applies the term 'cartohypnosis' to people who accept maps uncritically. He points out that maps are sometimes intended to delude people.

(S. W. Boggs, 'Cartohypnosis,' *Department of State Bulletin*, vol. xv, No. 390, 1946, pp. 1119-24.)

Many primitive societies are quite unaccustomed to maps. For them, territorial and boundary questions are relatively simple and radically different from those of map-conscious nations. For example, when two tribes in a certain region near the Indian-Afghan frontier find difficulty in agreeing upon a common tribal boundary they sometimes have recourse, as recounted by Col. A. H. McMahon, to laying down a boundary by oath. A leading man of one side is prevailed upon to undergo the ordeal and is accepted by both sides. Holding the Koran firmly on his bare head, the soles of his feet being bare and cleansed of every particle of his own tribal soil, and having taken every precaution to save his soul from perjury, he steps out, amid a scene of excited tribesmen, and the course he follows becomes the unquestioned boundary line. It may unexpectedly diverge widely from both claims, but salient points are sometimes found to be marked by crumbling rock cairns of great age whose existence had long been forgotten. Boundary makers of many nations wish their tasks were as simple and as easy!

Map-conscious people, however, usually accept subconsciously and uncritically the ideas that are suggested to them by maps. This is true in part because maps appear to represent facts pertaining to mother earth herself; veracity and authority beyond their deserts are frequently attributed to them. In what may be called 'cartohypnosis' or 'hypnotism by cartography,' the map user or the audience exhibits a high degree of suggestibility in respect to stimuli aroused by the map and its explanatory text.

Sometimes self-hypnotism and illusion occur quite innocently. Frequently, however, a sort of mass hypnotism is practiced by men who attempt to delude the public. Maps may also be used effectively to dehypnotize people; we should therefore consider what maps may be made, and how they may be used, to awaken people to an intelligent understanding of the world and the problems of our times.

ILLUSION AND CONFUSION

The innocence of some people's illusions when they look at maps uncritically reminds one of a four-year-old child's question, 'Why do I see things when I shut my eyes that aren't there when I open them?' People often suppose that maps reveal facts which, if they were wide awake to maps, they would realize are not shown at all. An example of illusion and confusion, arising from use of the overfamiliar Mercator projection, is shown on the accompanying map (fig. 1a) on which there is added a long straight line indicating the true compass course known to mariners as 'east by north.' On the Mercator map every continuous true compass direction is a straight line,[1] whereas on the earth all such lines are spirals—except the meridians (great circles) and the parallels (small circles). The 'E x N' line in figure 1b illustrates how such a spiral goes around the earth an infinite number of times without actually reaching the North Pole.

Illusion may occur when men use world maps instead of globes in seeking to understand some of the world relation-

[1] The Mercator map projection is one in which the parallels of latitude, represented by straight lines, are mathematically spaced in such a way that, at any point on the map, the north-south and east-west scales are identical. In consequence, every true compass direction or course is a straight line of indefinite extension; this property makes the map especially useful to navigators in plotting courses at sea. The projection is *not* projected onto a cylinder from the center of the globe, as is often depicted—a very different and quite useless map,

ships of our times. Observe, for example, a world map (fig. 2a) prepared by a brilliant geographer, Professor Halford Mackinder (now Sir Halford), to illustrate his famous paper on 'The Geographical Pivot shown on the map as being bordered by an inner or marginal crescent of land accessible to ships, paralleled by an outer crescent of continents and islands festooned across the map. That is how it

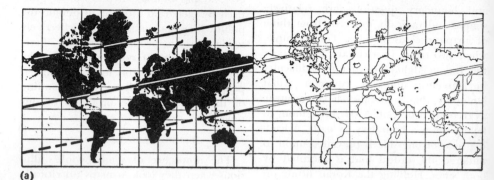

(a)

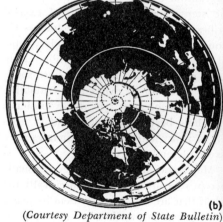

(b)

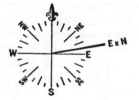

'EAST BY NORTH' (Fig. 1)

*(Courtesy Department of State Bulletin)*

of History,' which he read in 1904. The map was made on the Mercator projection; its limiting border is an ellipse; and parts of North and South America are repeated at the left and right sides of the map. The 'pivot area' or 'heartland' in north central Asia (which was for many centuries a region of horse and camel mobility insulated from the continental margins in large degree by deserts) is appears on a particular map. When the Mackinder map is traced on a transparency and wrapped around a cylinder (and the Mercator map is, of course, developed mathematically as on a cylinder), the repeated areas will overlap (fig. 2b). But what is it like on the earth itself? As seen on the globe (approximated by the circular world map, fig. 2c), the left and right portions of the elliptical Mackinder world map correspond to a single lens-shaped area embracing that portion of the Americas which appears twice. To the called 'outer crescent,' whose ends overlap in the Americas, and which traverses Australia and southern Africa, is seen on

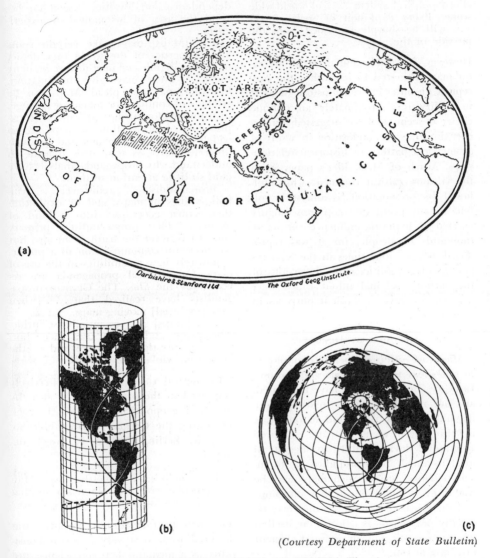

MACKINDER'S MAP, 'THE NATURAL SEATS OF POWER' (Fig. 2)

*(Courtesy Department of State Bulletin)*

north and south there are loops enclosing the polar regions which are altogether missing from the map. The remainder of the earth's surface appears on the Mackinder map once and once only. The so- the globe as a belt obliquely encircling the earth; also, the Arctic area is seen in its spherical compactness in normal relationships to Eurasia and North America. Professor Mackinder's own concept of 'global realities' was clearly revealed in these words:

'. . . we shall . . . have to deal with a closed political system . . . of world-wide scope. Every explosion of social forces . . . will be sharply re-echoed from the far side of the globe.'

However, it would seem that the Mercator map suggested to its author the concept of an outer crescent, instead of what in reality is approximately an oblique circle; it seems to have suggested also an over-simplified generalization in a sort of geometrical pattern of historical relationships. Much of Mackinder's paper, with the salutary critical comment which followed its presentation, is almost forgotten. In any event the map subsequently exerted a hypnotic influence on many thousands of people, for it was reproduced at least four times in the Nazi literature of geopolitics with perversions of the author's original intent which were destined to serve malevolent purposes in propaganda.

## Delusion by Design

Maps are often deliberately employed to sell ideas to individuals and nations. In every continent maps have been used, and are now being used, to disseminate mischievous half-truths and to obfuscate the thinking of men. They are employed as graphic devices—subtly to suggest an idea, to inculcate a prejudice, or to instill patriotic fervor. Such maps may be true in every detail, but in their omissions and their perverse emphases they may be socially poisonous—as chlorine by itself is a poisonous gas, but an essential element in common salt.

In an article entitled 'Magic Cartography,' relating to the uses of maps in propaganda, Hans Speier observes:

'The use of maps in propaganda is dependent upon highly developed techniques of map making and reproduction, a certain minimum of mass education in reading cartographic symbols and a specific organization of society. This organization may be characterized briefly as one in which the individual's functional dependence and loyalties extend far beyond the area of his immediate experiences.

'. . . [Maps] may make certain traits and properties of the world they depict more intelligible—or may distort or deny them. . . They may give information, but they may also plead. Maps can be symbols of conquest or tokens of revenge, instruments for airing grievances or expressions of pride. Indeed, maps are so widely used in propaganda and for such different purposes that it is difficult to understand why propaganda analysts have paid so little attention to them.

'Propagandists . . . rediscover . . . symbolic values in maps, and by exploiting them, turn geography into a kind of magic. . . The propagandist's primary concern is never the truth of an idea but its successful communication to a public.

'Entirely new possibilities in the use of maps for political propaganda are revealed by the film. The German propagandists have realized that . . . [when they produced] moving maps.

'. . . [Maps] are essentially scientific. The propagandist who uses them borrows the prestige of science and at the same time violates its spirit.'

Chimerical cartography was effectively employed in the propagation of ideas by the Nazi geopoliticians. Dr. K. Frenzel, addressing the German Cartographic Society in Berlin, October 22, 1938, declared:

'Every map has a suggestive force! Man is an ocular creature. He reacts to that which he sees and can take in at a glance.'

The private cartographic industry was declared to bear a very heavy responsibility as a mediator between science and the people, and between the policies of the government and the people. Every map had to be submitted before publication to all government departments that might have an interest in it. An obligatory organization of several large publishers of school atlases was created in order that unified school atlases would be published for the whole Reich.

Special symbols and devices, adapted to a minimum of mass education in reading maps, were developed and standardized by frenetic propagandists, in order to convey ideas of threatening forces, attack and resistance to attack, hostile encirclement, and the like. Posters in railway stations and other public places utilized maps that had a powerful effect upon the uncritical mass of the population.

In Italy cartography was employed by Mussolini to stimulate an urge for territorial expansion. Most striking, perhaps, was the series of maps on a wall in Rome, erected on the Via Imperiale, a new boulevard cut through from the National Monument to the restored Forum. On these maps, which were executed in choice marbles of selected colors, the growth of Rome from a city state to the empires of Augustus and Trajan was artistically depicted. The purpose was obvious; the method artful. The dominion of Rome once encircled the Mediterranean. Modern Italy's destiny seemed manifest; *mare nostrum* was again used with the present tense. No critical appraisal of the lack of pertinence of the extent of Trajan's conquests to the role that can or should be played by Italians in the twentieth century world was ever tolerated.

The map of Hungary, in a park in Budapest, delineated in a pattern of flowers and foliage which portrayed Hungary's former and current territorial extent, was for years a striking example of cartographic propaganda. Surrounded by stirring words of a famous Magyar poetess, spelled out in the foliage, and with the national flag near by always at half-staff in perpetual mourning for territories lost after the first World War, people were never to be allowed to accept the imposed territorial changes.

## INTELLIGENT USE OF MAPS

In a distraught world whose teeming millions sometimes hesitatingly follow their leaders and would-be leaders as they pick their way among the rubble of shattered cities and ideas, honest and critical thinking about maps is important. Men, women, and even children should all be more critical of the maps they see in daily papers and periodical publications, in books and atlases, and on the screen. They need to be taught to *read* maps (an art in itself), and not merely to *consult* maps (frequently only for location of a single city or point, or regarding a route of travel). Economists, historians, political scientists, and others need to cultivate a keener sense of earth distributions of resources and of peoples and their activities—which necessitates development of ability to read distributional maps.

Cartohypnosis is no more common, however, than delusion and confusion of the mind by subtle uses of words and phrases —but it is perhaps more difficult for the average man to protect himself against the use of mischievous maps. Even the phrases of the most honest men are sometimes inadequate, for as Whitehead remarked, 'the success of language in conveying information is vastly overrated, especially in learned circles.'

The map user who desires to guard against becoming the victim of cartohypnosis should keep in mind three things:

(a) That it is the actual situation on the earth that is significant;

(b) That maps have definite limitations as well as certain unique capabilities; and

(c) That map makers are human.

(a) It is what one would find on the ground, in all its complexity, and not simply what one finds on a map, that is significant. In looking at a map one may well ask, 'What the map shows may be perfectly true, but what is the whole truth? What is on the ground—including peoples, and their customs, their ideas and prejudices? What other types of information are pertinent to the subject?'

A small-scale map in a newspaper, designed to indicate territorial transfers and boundary changes, cannot reveal the bilingual populations and the economic and cultural ties between peoples throughout the region. Men could not be so sanguine of solving some of the present perplexing political problems by means of shifting international boundaries in areas in which boundary changes are ardently advocated (always in other people's territory), if some of the mappable data regarding economic interdependence and cultural transition zones were adequately visualized on maps.

(b) Like an aerial photograph that reveals a pattern, perhaps of archeological origin, almost erased by time and imperceptible on the ground—or like an X-ray photograph—a map may disclose patterns of great significance which are not discernible on surface inspection. Many maps based on statistical data thus reveal pertinent invisible transitions which, if even suspected, would be only vaguely perceived on visiting the area.

A map is unique in its capacity to represent with fidelity literally millions of observed facts, accurately generalized and artistically presented, conveying to the mind a vivid, true picture of the distribution of certain phenomena on the earth's surface that could not be obtained in any other manner. Large-scale topographic maps, for example, if they are highly accurate, belong to this category.

But the limitations of a map should be borne in mind. One of the most important is that a map cannot be more accurate and reliable than the data upon which it is based. A map printed in beautiful colors may be of little value and may mislead the uncritical if it is a work of art. On the other hand, a crudely executed map compilation may be highly accurate and of the greatest importance.

People seldom consider that a map is like a single chapter in an encyclopedic compendium; one map cannot present the results of an inventory of geology, natural vegetation, and water resources. Any map that attempts to show too much is of little use.

Use of the Mercator projection for world maps should be abjured by authors and publishers for all purposes. The world is round. No man ever saw or will ever see a world that has much resemblance to the Mercator world map; and the misconceptions it has engendered have done infinite harm. A map that makes Greenland look larger than all South America, instead of smaller than Argentina, is not suited to portray world relationships. The Mercator is ideal only for navigation, each chart covering a relatively small area. Discrimination should always be exercised in selecting map bases for world maps, the choice depending upon the data or the relationships to be represented.

In this so-called 'air age' in which men glibly talk of global relations—which are misleadingly visualized on *all* world maps, polar and otherwise—one ventures to suggest that the phrase *global geography* should be restricted to those aspects of world relations which can be rationally comprehended, without geometrical acrobatics, only with the aid of globes. The writer finds that transparent plastic hemispheres, some with geographical patterns and others with geometrical patterns imprinted, which can be moved into any position upon a globe resting only in a cup or ring, provide the best means of comparisons between one part of the globe and another. Map projection distortions and differences of scale are completely eliminated. After a situation is clearly seen on the globe itself, a map projection may be selected which is adapted to the special requirements of visualizing that particular set of data. There are, to be sure, many types of data which may be grasped even better when presented on maps than on globes. But there are other categories of highly significant relationships, notably the longer ocean trade routes, air routes and distances, radio and other wave propagations in the field of electronics, and problems relating to the peaceful development of atomic energy for the benefit of all mankind, which require the use of globes and certain types of accessories, and actually deserve the appellation *global geography*. . .

## V. GEOGRAPHIC CLAIMS TO TERRITORY

At no point does international rivalry become keener than in the acquisition of territory. In making claims to territory it is customary for nations to attempt to justify themselves by a variety of arguments. They use the facts of geography, economics, history, and ethnography in support of their claims, and not always with accuracy. When geography is used, one of the points most commonly asserted is that the territory will bring a natural or a strategic boundary. Italy for many years asked for the Tyrol in order to have a good defensible frontier in the Alps, and France has long looked upon the Rhine River as a natural boundary. Another geographic argument is that the coveted area forms a geographic unit with the territory of the claimant. Greece claimed Western Turkey on this ground in 1919. Still another argument is that the area asked for will provide access to the sea. President Wilson argued for the Polish acquisition of the corridor area in 1919 in order to assure 'a free and secure access to the sea.' Some of these arguments, along with others, appear in the following extracts from statements made by Yugoslav spokesmen before the Council of Foreign Ministers in 1945 in connection with the claim of their Government to the Julian March (including Trieste). The settlement finally made gave all of the area to Yugoslavia except Trieste, which was set up as a free city under the protection of the United Nations.

(Ljubo Leontic, Statement to the Council of Foreign Ministers, September 1945, *Trieste,* published by the Yugoslav Embassy in Washington, 1946, pp. 46-7.)

From the economic point of view, the Julian March is of primary importance for Yugoslavia as, and vice versa, Yugoslavia is to the Julian March. The one is directed towards the other by fate, by reason of a geographical fact of great importance. On its territory lies the most favorable, if not the only, route from the Sava basin and the Pannonian Plains, to the Adriatic. This is the route through Hrusice. To the north of this passage there are the first Alpine mountain chains and to the south the system of the Dinaric mountains. This latter system runs parallel with the Adriatic coast, ascending abruptly from the coastline and penetrating deeply, almost to the heart of Bosnia and Herzegovina, so as to create an almost unsurmountable barrier to communications from the interior to the Adriatic ports. Therefore all through history all the important lines of communication from the sea to the East have run through the Julian March. Here was built the first Roman route in the direction of Pannonia. Here passed the Argonauts and the Roman Legions; and here also passed the peoples in the Great Migration.

In more recent times, in the time of the development of world commerce, this route began to play a very important economic role. Along it went the basic trade-route from the Sava Plains and from Central Europe to the Adriatic Sea. Here also was constructed the first modern highway and later the first railway line. Because of all this there developed in the last two centuries, in the most favorable place of the northern Adriatic, the greatest port of the then Austro-Hungarian Empire—Trieste.

The economic role of Trieste is therefore most precisely defined by its natural situation. Trieste originated as a port for its northeastern hinterland. As such it has remained until today.

A great deal of the natural hinterland of the port of Trieste belongs to Yugoslavia. Therefore Trieste is the main and the most natural port of Yugoslavia.

How strong is this geographical fact, is best demonstrated by the maps of the railway network on Yugoslav territory and in the more distant hinterland, in the time before the first World War and the time after it. Before the first World War, no political frontiers existed between the northern Yugoslav territory and Trieste. After that war, Trieste was divided from its hinterland by the Italo-Yugoslav frontier of Rapallo, but none the less the railway system on the Yugoslav territory retained the same characteristic lines. The main line goes along the river Sava which at Zidini Most joins the line Vienna-Maribor-Trieste, and all the other railway networks incline towards the line of the Sava.

Despite the political frontier, this whole system gravitates towards Trieste. The only effect of the frontier has been that, in the period from 1918 to 1941, the traffic was diverted from its natural route to the sea to the very unfavorable line Zagrab-Karalovac-Susak.

All the other lines of northern and central Yugoslavia connecting with the sea remained, so far as world trade is concerned, unimportant because of their inadequacy, for they run through the very rugged Dinaric mountain system, which practically shuts off Central Yugoslavia from the Adriatic.

The frontier of Rapallo was, therefore, from the economic point of view detrimental to Yugoslavia and to Trieste alike. This frontier separated Yugoslavia from her natural port and also separated the port from its natural Yugoslav hinterland.

Moreover, this frontier was not detrimental to Yugoslavia alone; it was also an unnatural, artificially-created frontier, drawn against all reason, between Trieste and its Central European hinterland. This frontier is an imposed frontier which cannot be justified, either ethnographically or historically; and even less for economic reasons or the interests of other countries of its hinterland. All the basic connections of Trieste with its hinterland, i.e. the main highway and the main railway lines, run through the place already mentioned, Hrusice, which is situated in the center of the Slovene ethnical territory, within the very frontier-line of Rapallo. Passing Hrusice, the highway and also the railway line runs further upon the Slovene ethnical territory, through Ljubljana and Maribor to St. Ilj —a distance of over 300 km. Furthermore, Trieste is connected with Austria, Hungary and Czechoslovakia only through Yugoslav territory.

All this means that Yugoslavia holds the key to the connections of Trieste with Central Europe. Yet, despite these undeniable facts, Trieste was assigned to another country—Italy—and was thus cut off from Central Europe.

All these circumstances had very serious consequences, which were especially grave for Trieste itself.

Yugoslavia was compelled to use as her main port Susak, which was for her far from favorable. This poor, artificially-constructed seaport did not possess the conditions necessary for its development into a port which could handle the traffic of Yugoslavia. The Central European countries also began to direct their traffic to other ports, such as Venice and Hamburg, while Trieste was left to decline.

The seaborne tonnage alone, passing through Trieste, dropped from 2,314,000 tons in 1913 to 1,312,580 tons in 1932. Later, especially since 1937, the tonnage increased, however, but this occurred primarily with a view to war preparations.

The only rational solution for Trieste as a port would be that it should belong to that country which forms its hinterland, that is, to Yugoslavia. Trieste is necessary to her as her natural outlet to the sea and Yugoslavia alone, while possessing all the connections with the hinterland, is capable of raising Trieste to its former prosperity as an outlet to the sea for the whole of Central Europe.

Furthermore, Trieste is linked with its natural hinterland not only as a port but also as an industrial center. Since it has no waterway leading to its hinterland, but only railway and road connections, it has followed that in the city itself and around it, as well as along the railway line leading towards Ljubljana and Maribor, there have developed various industries which manufacture from the raw materials brought in by sea. . .

## VI. Which Hemisphere?

Although Americans habitually think in terms of the 'western hemisphere,' the author of the following article shows how misleading it is to consider international relationships from a hemisphere point of view.

(S. W. Boggs, 'This Hemisphere,' *Department of State Bulletin*, vol. XII, No. 306, 6 May 1945, pp. 845-50.)

. . .

Hemispheres are infinite in number. Rest a transparent glass or plastic geographical globe on its south pole, half fill it with water exactly to the line of the equator, and seal it shut. Roll it into any position whatever; the bottom hemisphere will be filled with water and the top with air. The water level will always be a plane passing through the center of the globe. The visible waterline will invariably be a 'great circle'—a circle greater than any that can be described on the globe with a radius either less or more than the interval between one of the poles and the equator. Any two points on the earth's surface lie on one of these great circles—which constitutes the shortest route between them. Therefore, with surface features and weather permitting, great-circle routes between ports are naturally preferred by both steamships and airplanes.

### The Northern Hemisphere

Any hemisphere may be identified and distinguished from all other hemispheres by its center point. Conversely, any point on the earth's surface is the center of a hemisphere which somewhat differs from all other hemispheres.

The United States is in the northern hemisphere, nearly half way between the equator and the North Pole, the 45th parallel of latitude coinciding with the northern boundary of New York State and with the Montana-Wyoming boundary.

The northern and southern hemispheres are the only hemispheres whose common boundary has any geographic significance. The seasons on opposite sides of the equator are antipodal, since it is summer in one when it is winter in the other.

Approximately 37,570,000 square miles (74 percent of the world's 50,973,000 square miles of land area, exclusive of the icecaps in Greenland and Antarctica), with a population of approximately 1,968,577,000 (constituting 91 percent of the world's population of approximately 2,166,879,000), are to be found in the northern hemisphere. This hemisphere includes all of North America, Europe, and continental Asia, part of South America (17 percent of its area and 15 percent of its population), and part of Africa (67 percent of its area and 68 percent of its population).

## THE SO-CALLED 'WESTERN HEMISPHERE'

The concept of the 'western hemisphere' or New World, comprising the American continents and islands, is very important, both historically and politically. But this so-called 'western hemisphere' is inadvisedly called 'western' and does not deserve the appellation 'hemisphere.'

Because the Americas are west of Europe, Europeans and their descendants on this side of the Atlantic frequently call them 'the western hemisphere.' The American continents are, however, east of Asia and of the whole of the so-called 'eastern hemisphere' quite as much as they are west of it. This is shown on figure 3. If the Chinese or Japanese had crossed the broad Pacific and had discovered the Americas they might have called these continents the 'eastern hemisphere.'

The Americas comprise only about 30 percent of the world's land area and contain about 13 percent of its population. As may be seen in figure 4, the American continents and islands, including Greenland, lie wholly within one half of a certain hemisphere, and in that quartersphere there is twice as much water as land. The Americas therefore scarcely deserve to be called a 'hemisphere.'

'Western' hemisphere suggests limiting lines running due north and south, namely meridians. Now it happens that map-makers make many maps of the Americas within circular limits which embrace, therefore, a hemisphere. Merely for convenience and economy, they utilize limiting lines, a pair of meridians 180° apart, that would appear on the map anyway. So they take a meridian between Africa and South America, usually 20° west of Greenwich (if that is used as the prime meridian for the map), and then necessarily employ its anti-meridian, 160° east longitude.

The center of this conventional hemisphere is in the Pacific Ocean, on the equator, in 110° W. longitude. It is about 1,250 statute miles from the nearest point on the American mainland, west of Acapulco, Mexico, and 1,850 miles from the nearest point in the United States, near Brownsville, Texas. Clearly this center point is without geographic significance.

The limiting meridians of this so-called 'western hemisphere' have no political, historic, geographic, or economic significance. If we were to follow the ancient custom of 'beating the bounds' (easily, in an airplane today) we would traverse open ocean most of the time. Going north on the 20th meridian we would cross part of Antarctica, Iceland, and a mere northeastern tip of Greenland; going south on the 160th meridian we would cross the eastern tip of Siberia including the Kamchatka peninsula, the island of Guadalcanal in the Solomons, and part of Antarctica. Within this hemi-

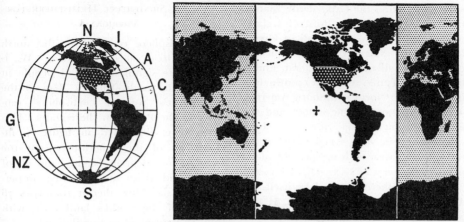

*(Courtesy Department of State Bulletin)*

**THE MAP-MAKER'S CONVENTIONAL 'WESTERN HEMISPHERE'** (Fig. 3)

The meridians 20° W. and 160° E. of Greenwich constitute the conventional limit of this hemisphere. The center is a point in the Pacific Ocean, on the equator, in 110° W. longitude, about 1250 statute miles from the nearest point on the American continents, near Acapulco, Mexico, and more than 2000 miles from the Panama Canal. The unshaded portion of the world map comprises this conventional 'western hemisphere': the shaded portion is the 'eastern hemisphere.' The letters around the circular hemisphere map signify: N, North Pole; I, Iceland; A, Azores; C, Canary Islands; S, South Pole; NZ, New Zealand; and G, Guadalcanal Island in the Solomon group.

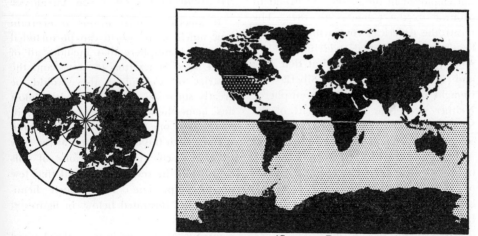

*(Courtesy Department of State Bulletin)*

**THE NORTHERN HEMISPHERE** (Fig. 4)

The center is the North Pole, and the limiting great circle is the equator. The unshaded portion of the world map on the Miller projection corresponds to the hemisphere map at the left.

sphere are found the Cape Verde Islands, the Azores, the western third of Iceland with its capital city, almost all of Greenland, eastern Siberia, thousands of Pacific islands, all of New Zealand, and a large part of the Antarctic continent—in addition to North and South America. The Atlantic and Pacific islands and the eastern portion of Asia within this hemisphere comprise only 1.1 percent of the world's land area, with 0.5 percent of its population.

This hemisphere, mapped by itself, induces complacency in Americans. It embraces almost the maximum area of ocean in any hemisphere which contains all of North and South America. Like an ostrich with its head in the sand, we avoid seeing the other half of the world, much of it surprisingly near.

People in the United States sometimes identify this so-called 'western hemisphere' with the Monroe Doctrine. The term 'western hemisphere,' however, was not employed in the message of President Monroe to the Congress in 1823. The terms 'the American continents' and 'this hemisphere' were used, evidently synonymously; Russia was in mind at that time and certainly no part of Siberia was thought of as part of 'this hemisphere.' Neither were New Zealand, part of the Solomon Islands, Samoa, the Fijis, and other Pacific islands, nor was any part of Antarctica (of which they knew almost nothing) contemplated when men spoke of 'the American continents' and 'this hemisphere' in 1823. Would it not be fatuous, indeed, to regard the meridians of 20° W. and 160° E. longitude as significant in relation to American policy, and therefore to have one policy with reference to the eastern portion of the island of Guadalcanal and another toward the western portion? Surely, a saner and more realistic understanding of geography than that is needed!

## A More Significant Hemisphere for Americans

A hemisphere centered in the north Atlantic Ocean, at 28° N. and 31° W., is much more significant for all people in North and South America than is the map-maker's 'western hemisphere' centered in the Pacific on the equator. This hemisphere, illustrated in figure 5, includes all of the Americas except the westernmost Aleutian Islands, and all of Europe and Africa and more than 40 percent of Asia. Altogether it comprises 76 percent of the world's land area, with fully 50 percent of its population.

This might be called a 'western-civilization hemisphere,' since it embraces Europe and the Americas (but with all of Africa and much of Asia besides). Only Australia and New Zealand are outside its bounds. Both history and geography make this hemisphere important to peoples on both sides of the Atlantic. . .

## Hemispheres à la Carte for Americans

If Americans were curious to ascertain how much of the world can be included in some hemisphere that includes all of the United States (the 48 States and the District of Columbia) they would be greatly surprised. They can order almost any hemisphere they like à la carte in more than one sense. A series of hemispheres, with the United States at the very edge of each, reveals relations of this country to the rest of the world that few people appreciate. Three such hemispheres are illustrated below, in figures 7, 8, and 9.

(a) Northern boundary of the United States at hemisphere's edge. If the northern edge of a hemisphere is placed on the northwestern corner and the northeastern tip of the United States there will be included, in addition to all of the United States and a narrow strip of Canada, all of Mexico, Central America, the Carib-

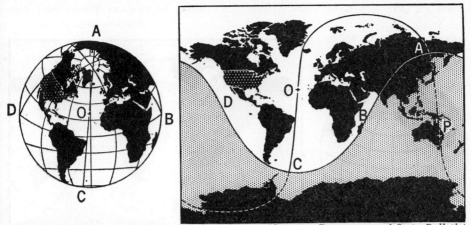

*(Courtesy Department of State Bulletin)*

HEMISPHERE CENTERED AT 28° N., 31° W. (Fig. 5)

The straight line AOC through the center divides the hemisphere into quarter-spheres. The western quarter-sphere contains all of North and South America, including Greenland and a portion of Siberia. The eastern quarter-sphere comprises all of Europe and Africa (except a small part of Madagascar) and about 42 per cent of the area of Asia. The limit of the hemisphere, ABCDA on both maps, is a complete great circle (like the equator or any meridian circle), while the line AOC, which divides it into halves, is half of such a great circle, the other half being APC, as shown in a dotted line on the world map.

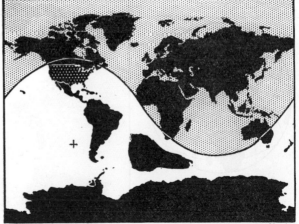

*(Courtesy Department of State Bulletin)*

HEMISPHERE WITH THE NORTHERN LIMITS OF THE UNITED STATES AT ITS EDGE (Fig. 7)

The center of this hemisphere is in the South Pacific, near 38° S. latitude and 98° W. longitude.

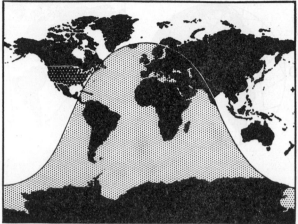

(*Courtesy Department of State Bulletin*)

**HEMISPHERE WITH THE COAST OF THE UNITED STATES AT ITS EDGE** (Fig. 8)

The center of this hemisphere is in the North Pacific, near 24° N. latitude and 177° E. longitude.

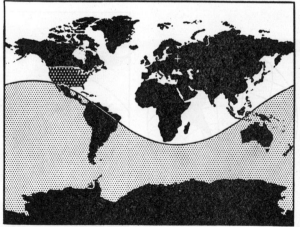

(*Courtesy Department of State Bulletin*)

**HEMISPHERE WITH THE SOUTHERN COAST OF THE UNITED STATES AT ITS EDGE** (Fig. 9)

The center of this hemisphere is west of Moscow near 55° N. latitude and 35° E. longitude.

bean, South America, Antarctica, New Zealand, a portion of Australia, and the tip of South Africa, still larger areas of the Atlantic and Pacific Oceans, and a portion of the Indian Ocean near the Antarctic continent.

(b) Atlantic coast of the United States at hemisphere's edge. If the northeastern and southeastern extremities of the United States are placed at the edge of a hemisphere, almost all of Canada, Labrador, and Greenland, all of Mexico and part of Central America, a very great part of Asia and the northern tip of Europe,

all of Australia and New Zealand, all of the Arctic, most of the Pacific, and the eastern edge of the Indian Ocean will be included.

(c) Southern boundary of the United States at hemisphere's edge. A hemisphere which has Brownsville, Texas, and San Diego, California, on its southern edge will include not only all of Canada, Alaska, and Greenland but also all of Europe, Africa, and Asia, except a small portion of the Netherlands Indies and large parts of the Atlantic, Pacific, and Indian Oceans.

# 9

## NATIONALISM

NATIONALISM is a loyalty which people feel toward their national group. It is a psychological attitude or sentiment, at times approaching fanaticism. Although we commonly think of it as identical with patriotism, nationalism is patriotism toward the national group, not patriotism toward cities, feudal principalities, and empires. Historically, nations came into being before nationalism. In the Middle Ages national groups began to form nation states —England, France, Spain, Portugal, and Poland were among the earliest to come into existence. During the fifteenth, sixteenth, and seventeenth centuries the development of national consciousness was stimulated by mercantilism, the rise of vernacular literatures, strong monarchs, religious differentiation, and wars. It was the French Revolution, with its stress upon self-determination and democracy, that fanned to a flame these earlier sparks of nationalism.

The nineteenth century was a century of nationalism. It saw the unification of the German and Italian peoples and the overthrow of Turkish rule in most of the Balkan Peninsula as the new states of Greece, Rumania, Bulgaria, Montenegro, and Serbia were set up. The twentieth century has seen the destruction of Austria-Hungary in the name of nationalism, the revival of Poland, the establishment of Czechoslovakia, the independence of Finland from Russia, and the independence from 1917 to 1940 of Latvia, Lithuania, and Estonia.

The nationalist movement, moreover, has not spent itself. Strong national tendencies are asserting themselves in China, India, Burma, Indo-China, and the East Indies. The Arabs of the Near East and North Africa have also fallen in line. Thus, while nationalism was European in origin, it has since spread to all continents. The peak of its strength has not yet been reached and must, doubtless, be reckoned with for many years to come.

So long as the world is dominated by nationalism, difficult problems will be projected in the field of international relations. A loyalty that calls upon a man to lay down his life in war, and that in peace requires him to sacrifice butter for bullets so that his nation may be strong, is an important ingredient of national power. Because nationalism is a basic factor in national strength, it is an essential aspect of contemporary power politics and of the war system generally. It is not surprising that the German, Italian, and Japanese Govern-

226

ments resorted to extreme measures to whip up patriotic feeling to a fanatical pitch during the 1930's, when they were getting ready for war.

Egocentric in outlook, nationalism leads a people to seek special advantages in trade and in matters of security, completely oblivious to the welfare of other groups. While striving to outdo all competitors, each group is in a mood to suspect others of skullduggery of some kind. As a people magnify in their minds their own deeds and virtues, they come to regard others as inferior, the Germans looking down upon the Poles, and the Japanese upon the Chinese.

There are more specific problems, too, which nationalism raises in international affairs. National groups aspire to political independence, and claim the right of self-determination. Recently the people of India have sought freedom from Britain, the Indonesians from the Netherlands, the Indo-Chinese from the French, as in 1919 the Czechs, Slovaks, Slovenes, and Rumanians wanted to be free from Hapsburg control. Is there in any sense a 'right' of self-determination? If so, is it unlimited? Should the answer to these questions be affirmative, there may well be two or three times the number of states in the world than there are at present, with a multiplication of tariff barriers and boundary disputes.

Another problem is that caused by national minority groups, especially in Europe, where they are so numerous. There have been many instances of real and extreme persecution of minorities, as of alien groups in Russia before 1917 and of the Jews in Germany under the Nazis. Is there any international action that may be taken to prevent such persecution? Many of these problems relating to nationalism are treated in the readings which follow in this chapter. The problem of minority groups, however, is discussed in Chapter 17 under Human Rights and Minority Rights.

## I. THE NATURE OF NATIONALISM

The extract below discusses some of the causes of nationalism, its nature and significance.

(Hans Kohn, 'The Nature of Nationalism,' *American Political Science Review,* vol. 33, 1939, pp. 1001-10, 1016-17. Reprinted by permission of the *American Political Science Review*.)

Nationalism as we understand it is not older than the second half of the eighteenth century. Its first great manifestation was the French Revolution, which gave the new movement an increased dynamic force. Nationalism had, however, become manifest at the end of the eighteenth century almost simultaneously in a number of widely separated European countries. Its time in the evolution of mankind had arrived, and although the French Revolution was one of the most powerful factors in its intensification and spread, it was not its date of birth. Like all historical movements, nationalism has its roots deep in the past. The conditions which made its emergence possible had matured during the centuries before they converged at its formation. These political, economic, and intellectual developments took a long time for their growth and proceeded in the various European countries at different pace. It is impossible to grade them according to their importance or to make one dependent upon the other. All are closely interconnected, each reacting upon the other; and although their growth can be traced separately, their effects and consequences cannot be separated otherwise than in the analysis of the scholar; in life, they are indissolubly intertwined. . .

The growth of nationalism is the process of integration of the masses of the people into a common political form. Nationalism therefore presupposes the existence, in fact or as an ideal, of centralized form of government over a distinct and large territory. This form was created by the absolute monarchies, who were the pace-makers of modern nationalism; the French Revolution inherited and continued the centralizing tendencies of the kings, but at the same time it filled the central organization with a new spirit and gave it a power of cohesion unknown before. Nationalism is unthinkable before the emergence of the modern state in the period from the sixteenth to the eighteenth centuries. Nationalism accepted this form, but changed it by animating it with a new feeling of life and with a new religious fervor.

For its composite texture, nationalism used, in its growth, some of the oldest and most primitive feelings of man which throughout history we find as important factors in the formation of social groups. There is a natural tendency in man—and we mean by 'natural tendency' a tendency which, having been produced by social circumstances since time practically immemorial, appears to us as natural—to love his birthplace or the place of his childhood sojourn, its surroundings, its climate, the contours of hills and valleys, of rivers and trees—he prefers native customs and native food to alien ones, which appear to him unintelligible and undigestible. Should he travel, he will return to his chair and his table with a feeling of relaxation and will be elated by the joy of finding himself again at home, away from the strain of a sojourn in foreign lands and contact with foreign peoples.

Small wonder that he will take pride in his native characteristics, and that he will easily believe in their superiority! As they are the only ones in which civilized people like himself can apparently feel at home, are they not the only ones fit for human beings? On the other hand, contact with alien men and alien customs, which appear to him strange, unfamiliar, and therefore threatening, will arouse in him a feeling of distrust of everything foreign. This feeling of strangeness will again develop in him sentiments of superiority, and sometimes even of open hostility. The more primitive men are, the stronger will be their distrust of strangers, and therefore the intensity of their group feeling. Rudyard Kipling, in his poem, 'The Stranger,' * gives forceful expression to this general feeling.

The Stranger within my gate,
  He may be true or kind,
But he does not talk my talk—
  I cannot feel his mind.
I see the face and the eyes and the mouth,
  But not the soul behind.

The men of my own stock
  They may do ill or well,
But they tell the lies I am wonted to,
  They are used to the lies I tell.
We do not need interpreters
  When we go to buy or sell.

* 'The Stranger' from *Songs from Books* by Rudyard Kipling. Copyright 1912 by Rudyard Kipling. Reprinted by permission of Doubleday & Co., Inc., and Mrs. George Bambridge.

The Stranger within my gates,
    He may be evil or good,
But I cannot tell what powers control—
    What reasons sway his mood;
Nor when the Gods of his far-off land
    May repossess his blood.

These feelings always existed. They do not form nationalism. They correspond to certain facts—territory, language, common descent—which we also find in nationalism. But here they are entirely transformed, charged with new and different emotions, and embedded in a broader context. They are the natural elements out of which nationalism is formed. But nationalism is not a natural phenomenon, not a product of 'eternal' or 'natural' laws; it is a product of the growth of social intellectual factors at a certain stage of history. It may be said that some feeling of nationality existed before the birth of modern nationalism, a feeling varying in strength and in frequency from time to time, at some epochs almost completely extinguished, at others more or less clearly discernible. But it was largely unconscious and inarticulate. It did not influence the thought and actions of men in a deep and all-pervading way. It found a clear expression only occasionally in individuals, and in groups only at times of stress or provocation. It did not permanently or in the long run determine their aims or actions. It was no purposeful will welding together all the individuals into a unity of emotions, thoughts, and actions.

Before the age of nationalism, the masses very rarely became conscious of the fact that the same language was spoken over a large territory. In fact, it was not even the same language; the several dialects existed side by side, sometimes even incomprehensible to the man of a neighboring province. The spoken language was accepted as a natural fact. It was in no way regarded as a political or cultural factor, still less as an object of political or cultural struggle. During the Middle Ages, people deduced from the Bible that as mankind was one, it should have one common language, and that the diversity of languages was the result of the sinfulness of man, and God's punishment at the time of the building of the Tower of Babel. Consciousness of language was aroused only at times of expeditions and travel or in frontier districts. There, the alien character of the group speaking the alien language was felt, and many names of what we today call national groups derive from the fact that they were first recognized as different groups by those of alien tongue. Some of these national groups even received their names from outside, because they were felt to be a distinct group by an outsider sooner than by a member of the group. The Greek word barbaros, which means 'strange' or 'foreign,' and in consequence 'rude' and 'ignorant,' probably has its source in the idea of stammering or inability to speak in a comprehensible way—a word akin to the Sanskrit expression barbara, which meant stammering or non-Aryan.

Nationalism is not, as some scholars under the influence of Aristotle suggest, a harmonious natural growth qualitatively identical with love for family and home. It is frequently assumed that man loves in widening circles—his family, his village, his tribe or clan, the nation, and finally humanity and the supreme good. But love of home and family is a concrete feeling, accessible to everyone in daily experience. Nationalism, and in an even higher degree cosmopolitanism, is a highly complex and originally abstract feeling which gains the emotional warmth of concreteness only through the effects of an historical development which, by education, economic interdependence, and corresponding political and social institutions, brings about the integration of the masses and their identification

with a body far too great for any concrete experience. Nationalism—our identification with the life and aspirations of
uncounted millions whom we shall never
know, with a territory which we shall
never visit in its entirety—is qualitatively
different from the love of family or of
home surroundings. It is qualitatively
akin to the love of humanity or of the
whole earth.

Nationalism is first and foremost a
state of mind, an act of consciousness,
which since the French Revolution is
becoming more and more common to
mankind. The mental life of a man is
as much dominated by an ego-conscious-
ness as it is by a group-consciousness.
Both are complex states of mind at which
we arrive by experiences of differentiation and opposition, of the ego and the
surrounding world, of the we-group and
those outside the group. The collective
or group consciousness can center around
entirely different groups, of which some
have a more permanent character, like
the family, the class, the clan, the caste,
the village, the sect, the religion, etc.,
whereas others are of a more or less
passing character, e.g., schoolmates, a
football team, or passengers of a ship.
In each case, varying with its permanence,
this group-consciousness will strive toward creating homogeneity within the
group, a conformity and likemindedness
which will lead to and facilitate concerted
action. In that sense, we may speak of a
group-mind and a group-action. We may
speak of a Catholic mind and Catholic
action, of an English mind and English
action, but we may also speak of a rural
mind or an urban mind, and of action
of rural groups or urban groups. All
these groups develop their group character. The character of an occupational
group, as peasants, soldiers, civil servants,
may be as clearly defined and stable as,
or even more than, any character of a
national group. Each group creates its

own symbols and social conventions, is
dominated by social traditions, which
find their expression in the public opinion of the group.

In different periods of history, and in
different civilizations, we find different
groups to which this supreme loyalty is
given. The modern period of history,
which started with the French Revolution, is characterized by the fact that in
this period, and in this period alone, the
nation demands the supreme loyalty of
man, that all men, not only certain individuals or classes, are drawn into this
common loyalty, and that all civilizations which up to this modern period
have followed their own, and frequently
widely different, ways are now dominated
more and more by this one supreme
group-consciousness, nationalism.

Nationalism as a group-consciousness
is therefore a psychological and a sociological fact, but any psychological or sociological explanation is insufficient. An
American psychologist defined a nation
as 'a group of individuals that feels itself one, is ready within limits to sacrifice
the individual for the group advantage,
that prospers as a whole, that has groups
of emotions experienced as a whole, each
of whom rejoices with the advancement
and suffers with the losses of the group. . .
Nationality is a mental state or community in behavior.' This definition is
valid, as far as it goes, not only for the
nation, but for any other supreme group
to which man owes loyalty and with which
he identifies himself. It is therefore not
sufficient to distinguish the national group
from other groups of similar importance
and prominence.

Nationalities come into existence only
when certain objective bonds delimit a
social group. These bonds are most frequently used for the definition of nationality. None, however, is essential for
the existence of a nationality. A nation

ality generally possesses several of these attributes; very few possess all of them. Usually, the following attributes are enumerated: common descent, language, territory, political entity, customs and traditions, and religion. A short discussion will suffice to show that none of these attributes is essential for the existence or definition of nationality.

Nationalism is a state of mind. The process of history can be analyzed as a succession of changes in communal psychology, in the attitude of man toward all manifestations of individual and social life. Such factors as language, territory, traditions—such sentiments as attachment to the native soil, the Heimat, and to one's kin and kind—assume different positions in the scale of values as communal psychology changes. Nationalism is an idea, an idea-force, which fills man's brain and heart with new thoughts and new sentiments, and drives him to translate his consciousness into deeds of organized action. Nationality is therefore not only a group held together and animated by common consciousness; it also seeks to find its expression in what it regards as the highest form of organized activity, a sovereign state. As long as nationality is not able to attain this consummation, it satisfies itself with some form of autonomy or pre-state organization, which, however, always tends at a given moment, the moment of 'liberation,' to develop into a sovereign state. Nationalism demands the nation-state; the creation of the nation-state strengthens nationalism; here, as elsewhere in history, we find a continuous interdependence and interaction.

'Nationality is a state of mind corresponding to a political fact,' or striving to correspond to a political fact. This definition reflects the genesis of nationalism and of modern nationality. . .

## II. GERMAN RACIAL DOCTRINES

It is characteristic of nationalism that the people who are under its spell think of themselves as superior to others. The Nazi spokesmen in Germany tried to give scientific proof of the superiority of the Aryan people, particularly their own branch of Aryans. They enacted laws to protect and promote the 'racial purity' of the Germans, and persecuted the Jews. The nature of the Aryan doctrine and its historical background are given below. Serious scholars, both in Germany and elsewhere, have not supported the doctrine in any way. Anthropologists have shown beyond question that there is no pure race, for every national group is a mixture of many peoples completed after many centuries of time.

(Julian Huxley, *Race in Europe,* Oxford Pamphlets on World Affairs, No. 5, 1939, pp. 19-29. Reprinted by permission of the Clarendon Press, Oxford.)

In 1848 the young German scholar Friedrich Max Müller (1823-1900) settled in Oxford, where he remained for the rest of his life. The high character and great literary and philological gifts of Max Müller are well known. About 1853 he introduced into English usage the unlucky term Aryan, as applied to a large group of languages. His use of this Sanskrit word contains in itself two assumptions—one linguistic, that the Indo-Persian sub-group of language is older or more primitive than any of its relatives; the other geographical, that the cradle of the common ancestor of these languages was the Ariana of the ancients, in Central Asia. Of these the first is now known to be certainly erroneous and the second now regarded as probably erroneous. Nevertheless, around each of these two assumptions a whole library of literature has arisen.

Moreover, Max Müller threw another apple of discord. He introduced a proposition which is demonstrably false. He spoke not only of a definite Aryan language and its descendants, but also of a corresponding 'Aryan race.' The idea was rapidly taken up both in Germany and in England.

In England and America the phrase 'Aryan race' has quite ceased to be used by writers with scientific knowledge, though it appears occasionally in political and propagandist literature. A foreign secretary recently blundered into using it. In Germany the idea of an 'Aryan' race received no more scientific support than in England. Nevertheless, it found able and very persistent literary advocates who made it appear very flattering to local vanity. It therefore steadily spread, fostered by special conditions.

Max Müller himself was later convinced by scientific friends of the enormity of his error and he did his very best to make amends. Thus in 1888 he wrote:

I have declared again and again that if I say Aryans, I mean neither blood nor bones, nor hair, nor skull; I mean simply those who speak an Aryan language. . . When I speak of them I commit myself to no anatomical characteristics. The blue-eyed and fair-haired Scandinavians may have been conquerors or conquered. They may have adopted the language of their darker lords or vice-versa. . . To me an ethnologist who speaks of Aryan race, Aryan blood, Aryan eyes and hair, is as great a sinner as a linguist who speaks of a dolichocephalic dictionary or a brachycephalic grammar.

Max Müller frequently repeated his protest, but alas! 'the evil that men do lives after them, the good is oft interred with their bones'! Who does not wish to have had noble ancestors? The belief in an 'Aryan' race had become accepted by philologists, who knew nothing of science —and the word was freely used by writers who claimed to treat of science though they had no technical training and no clear idea of the biological meaning to be attached to the word 'race.' The influence of the untenable idea of an 'Aryan race' vitiates all German writings on anthropology which are now allowed to appear. If the term 'Aryan' is given a racial meaning at all, it should be applied to that tribal unit, whatever it was, that first spoke a language distinguishable as Aryan. Of the physical characters of that hypothetical unit it is the simple truth to say that we know nothing whatever. As regards the locality where this language was first spoken, the only tolerably certain statement that can be made is that it was somewhere in Asia and was not in Europe. It is thus absurd to distinguish between 'non-Aryans' and 'Europeans.'

There is no need to trace in detail the history of the Aryan controversy. It will be enough to say that while the Germans claimed that these mythical Aryans were tall, fair, and long-headed—the hypothetical ancestors of hypothetical early Teutons—the French claimed that the Aryan language and the Aryan civilization came into Europe with the Alpines (Eurasiatics), who are of medium build rather dark, and broad-headed. The decipherment of the language of the very 'Jewish'-looking Hittites—which was certainly Aryan—and the discovery of certain Aryan languages in North-West India throws a new complexion on the whole question of the origin of the Aryan languages.

A consideration of this 'Aryan fallacy' leads us to two so-called 'race problems' which are of immediate political importance—the Nordic and the Jewish. Beginning with the latter, we find that the Jewish problem is far less a 'racial' than a cultural one. Jews are no more a distinct sharply marked 'race' than are German or English. The Jews of the Bible were of mixed descent. During their dispersal they have interbred with the surrounding populations, so that a number of hereditary elements derived from the immigrant Jews are scattered through the general population, and the Jewish communities have come to resemble the local population in many particulars. In this way Jews of Africa, of eastern Europe, of Spain and Portugal, and so on, have become markedly different from each other in physical type. What they have preserved and transmitted is not 'racial qualities' but religious and social traditions. Jews do not constitute a race, but a society with a strong religious basis and peculiar historic traditions, parts of which society have been forced by segregation and external pressure into forming a pseudo-national group. Biologically it is almost as illegitimate to speak of a 'Jewish race' as of an 'Aryan race.'

The Nordic theory, which is a development of the 'Aryan fallacy,' is in another category. Instead of ascribing racial qualities to a group which is today held together on a cultural basis, it takes an hypothetical past 'race,' ascribes to it a number of valuable qualities, notably initiative and leadership, and then, whenever it finds such qualities in the mixed national groups, ascribes them to the Nordic elements in the population. It then proceeds farther and sets up, as a national ideal, a return to purity of stock of a Nordic 'race' the very existence of which is unproved and probably unprovable.

The real source of all these modern ideas of the innate inferiority of certain races' is the work of the French Count Joseph de Gobineau (1816-82), *Essai sur l'inégalité des races humaines* (1853-5). It is essentially a plea for 'national' history. He advocated especially the superiority of the so-called 'Aryan races.' The idea was carried to the most ridiculous lengths in the work of his countryman Lapouge, *L'Aryen* (1899), in which the 'Aryans' were identified with the 'Nordic race.' This ridiculous Nordic-Aryan theory, launched by French writers, was eagerly developed in Germany and linked with anti-Jewish propaganda. In the beginning of the present century the East Prussian Gustav Kossinna took up the idea, applied it to prehistoric archaeology, and claimed to make German prehistory—to use his own words—'a preeminently national science.' His naive object was to show that throughout the prehistoric ages advances in culture had been entirely due to peoples whom he identified with the Nordic, Germanic, or 'Aryan' peoples, these terms being regarded as interchangeable, though including not merely Germans but also Scandinavians. The 'Aryan' cradle was conveniently located in the north-European forest about the Baltic and North Sea coasts.

This theory is scientifically quite untenable on many grounds. Thus, to take a single point, the earliest of the rough stone monuments (of which Stonehenge is a late and highly developed example, *c.*1700-1600 B.C.) go back, even in England, at least as far as 3000 B.C. The culture that they represent spread from the Mediterranean to the Iberian peninsula and thence through France into Britain and beyond to north Germany and Scandinavia. Yet these monuments, involving high enterprise, considered design, and complex social organization, were produced by a people devoid of metal implements and quite certainly not of 'Nordic' origin. The skulls from the early English burials associated with these monuments are, in fact, usually stated to be of 'Mediterranean' type.

Nevertheless, the Nordic theory speedily became very popular in Germany. It made a special appeal to national vanity and was made the basis of propaganda in the pseudo-scientific writings of the Germanized Englishman Houston Stewart Chamberlain and others in Germany, and of Madison Grant and others in America. Hitler—himself anything but Nordic—is completely obsessed by this fantastic theory. Among the absurdities connected with the development of the theory it is perhaps sufficient to mention that Jesus Christ and Dante have been turned into 'good Teutons' by German writers. The 'Nordic theory' has had a very great effect, not only in serving as a basis for the 'Aryan' and anti-Jewish doctrines upon which the Nazi regime is now being conducted, but also as the inspiring influence in a great deal of political agitation which claimed superiority for the 'Nordic' in the discussion of legislation determining the recent revision of the immigration laws in the United States.

The facts of the case are as follows. The 'Nordic race,' like other human races, has no present existence. Its former existence, like that of all 'pure races,' is hypothetical. . .

### III. CHINESE NATIONALISM

One of the most striking facts in the Far East today is the growing strength of Chinese nationalism. Dr. Sun Yat-sen, the founder of the Kuomintang, advocated it to the Chinese people along with democracy and economic development as the principles that must be adopted if China is to become modern and strong. He pointed out that nationalism would be necessary if China is to be united and if she is to be free from foreign interference in her affairs. He gave a series of six lectures on the subject from which the extract below is taken. Under the stimulus of Japanese aggression in 1931 and again in 1937, Chinese nationalism developed rapidly. It has already added much to the power position of China in world affairs, and it will add more if all of the 450 million people of the country come under its influence in a unified land.

(Sun Yat-sen, *San Min Chu I,* translated by F. W. Price, Shanghai, 1928, from lectures I, III, pp. 4-5, 72-6. Reprinted by permission of the translator and of the Commercial Press.)

To-day I shall begin the discussion of the Principle of Nationalism. When the recent reorganization of the Kuomintang took place, the plans for national salvation laid stress upon propaganda. Widespread propaganda among the people needs, first of all, a clear exposition of the Principles. During the last ten or more years, thoughtful people have be- come accustomed to hearing about the Three Principles of the People, but many are still unable to comprehend them fully. So I shall first discuss with you in some detail the Principle of Nationalism

What is the Principle of Nationalism? Looking back over the history of China's social life and customs, I would say briefly that the Principle of Nationalism is equivalent to the 'doctrine of the state.' The Chinese people have shown the greatest loyalty to family and clan with the result that in China there have been family-ism and clan-ism but no real nationalism. Foreign observers say that the Chinese are like a sheet of loose sand. Why? Simply because our people have shown loyalty to family and clan but not to the nation—there has been no nationalism. The family and the clan have been powerful unifying forces; again and again Chinese have sacrificed themselves, their families, their lives in defense of their clan. For example, in the Kwangtung feuds between two clans, neither one will yield, no matter what the struggle costs in life or property, all because of the clan idea which is so deeply imbedded in the minds of the people that they are willing to sacrifice anything for their fellow clansmen. But for the nation there has never been an instance of the supreme spirit of sacrifice. The unity of the Chinese people has stopped short at the clan and has not extended to the nation.

It is difficult to explain just how we have lost our nationalism. To illustrate I will tell a story which may seem off the point and unrelated to our thesis, but perhaps it will make clearer the causes of which we are speaking. It is an incident which I personally witnessed in Hongkong. There was a coolie who worked daily at the steamer jetty carrying passengers' baggage with his bamboo pole and two ropes. Each day's load was his means of livelihood for that day, but he finally managed to save more than ten dollars. The Luzon lotteries were flourishing at that time and this coolie used his savings to buy a Luzon lottery ticket. He had no home and no place to keep his things or the lottery ticket which he had bought. All his tool of trade was his bamboo pole and two ropes which he carried about with him everywhere he went. So he hid the lottery ticket inside of his bamboo pole, and since he could not always be pulling out the ticket to be looking at it, he fixed the number indelibly on his mind and thought about

it all the time. When the day for the drawing came, he went to the lottery shop to match this number, and as soon as he saw the list of numbers he knew that he had won first prize, acquiring a wealth of $100,000. He was in ecstasy, almost insane with joy. Thinking he would no longer have to be a coolie and use his bamboo pole and ropes, that he would be a rich man forever, he gleefully took the pole and ropes and threw them into the sea!

The coolie's bamboo pole may represent nationalism—a means of existence; the winning of the first prize may represent the time when China's flourishing imperialism was evolving into cosmopolitanism and when our forefathers, believing that China was the world's great state —that 'Heaven has but one sun, people but one king'; that 'gentry of all nations bow before the crown and pearls'; that universal peace would henceforth prevail and that the only thing necessary was world harmony in which the world would bring its tribute to China—threw away nationalism as the coolie threw his bamboo pole into the sea. Then when China was overcome by the Manchus, she not only failed to become the master of the world, but even failed to keep her small family property intact. The national spirit of the people was destroyed, just as the bamboo pole was thrown into the sea.

If we Chinese can in the future find some way to revive our nationalism, can discover another bamboo pole, then no matter what foreign political and economic forces oppress us, we will survive through the ages. We can overcome the forces of natural selection; Heaven's preservation of our four hundred millions of Chinese till now shows that it has not wanted to destroy us; if China perishes, the guilt will be on our own heads and we shall be the world's great sinners. Heaven has placed great responsibilities upon us Chinese. If we do not love ourselves, we are rebels against Heaven. China has come to the time when each one of us has a great responsibility to shoulder. If Heaven does not want to eliminate us, it evidently wants to further the world's progress. If China perishes, she will perish at the hands of the Great Powers; those Powers will thus be obstructing the world's progress. Yesterday a Russian said to me: 'Why has Lenin been attacked by all the Powers? Because he dared to say that the people of the world were divided into two classes—the twelve hundred fifty millions and the two hundred fifty millions; the twelve hundred fifty millions are being oppressed by the two hundred fifty millions, and the oppressors are moving not in harmony with but in defiance of Nature.' If we want to resist Might we must unite our four hundred millions and join the twelve hundred fifty millions of the world. We must espouse nationalism and in the first instance attain our own unity, then we can consider others and help the weaker, smaller peoples to unite in a common struggle against the two hundred fifty millions. Together we shall use Right to fight Might, and when Might is overthrown and the selfishly ambitious have disappeared, then we may talk about cosmopolitanism.

## IV. COMMUNISM AND NATIONALISM

Most socialist groups, although not the Communists, accept nationalism. It will be recalled that in both World War I and World War II British and French socialist parties rallied to the support of their respective national states. This was also true of the German socialist parties in World War I. Nationalistic action of this nature was not inconsistent with the essential doctrines of such groups. They stress the universal brotherhood of mankind, but do not go as far as the Communists, who proclaim that the workers have no country. Communists vehemently denounce nationalism just as they energetically advocate international working-class solidarity.

In the famous Communist Manifesto of 1848 the opposition of theoretical communism to national loyalty was clearly outlined. In the Manifesto, Karl Marx (1818-83) and Friedrich Engels (1820-1895), founders of theoretical communism, declared, 'The working men have no country. We cannot take from them what they have not got.' Only because the proletariat must first rise and acquire political supremacy in the nation could workers be called national, Marx and Engels continued. National differences were already vanishing, these writers believed, and with the supremacy of the proletariat the hostility of one nation to another would come to an end.

In contrast to the theoretical view held by Communists on nationalism is their practice. In Russia nationalism has been steadily increasing since 1917. It reached a high peak during World War II when the Russians displayed great unity and patriotism against the German invader. It may be noted also that the Communists of China, who adhere even less in practice to pure Marxian doctrines than do the Russians, patriotically supported the national cause of China against Japan in the war that began in 1937. A discussion of Soviet nationalism in contrast to the older nationalism of Czarist Russia is given below.

(H. H. F. Eulau, 'The New Soviet Nationalism,' *Annals of the American Academy of Political and Social Science,* vol. 232, 1944, pp. 25-30. Reprinted by permission of the *Annals of the American Academy of Political and Social Science.*)

While noting the accelerated crystallization of Soviet nationalism during the war, writers treating the subject have not as yet inquired into its social purposes. Nationalism, like power, contains constructive and destructive elements. The nationalism of the czarist regime was eminently destructive. Its main ingredients were the Russification of the national minorities within the Empire for the purpose of perpetuating the absolutism of the czars, and an aggressive imperialism, often disguised as benevolent Pan-Slavism, which ended in the disasters of 1905 and 1917. It is folly, therefore, to equate the new Soviet nationalism with czarist nationalism, or even to seek for an organic relationship between the former and the latter.

It is impossible, of course, to differentiate czarist from Soviet nationalism without emphasizing their totally different social objectives. Omission to do so can only result in confusion remindful of the failure to distinguish between the social purposes of Nazism and the Soviet system. . .

There is overwhelming evidence that while the new Soviet nationalism has to a large extent expressed itself in the *form* of a revival of traditionalism in historical writing and classicism in literature and culture generally, its social purpose remains in harmony with the *ultimate ideals* of the Communist Revolution as well as the achievements of Soviet Socialist construction. Nor is there any evidence, as will appear later, that it is anti-international or counterrevolutionary. It

is not the past that gives meaning to the present renaissance of the Soviet Union's historical heritage, but on the contrary it is the success of the Soviet experiment, no longer an experiment, that renders possible historical re-evaluation. The immediate social purpose of the present war is the defeat of the foreign aggressor. Czarist Russia, much as it differed from the Soviet Union politically, economically, and socially, periodically had the same social task of driving out an invader. But this is the only point of connection between past and present as far as social purpose is concerned. On the other hand, the limitation imposed upon the past in terms of social values does not preclude the adaptation of traditional and classical *forms* to the social needs of the present.

These considerations should be kept in mind lest new disillusionment sweep the Soviet Union's present allies, culminating in fresh vituperations, when the war is over. For nationalism will persist in the Soviet Union after the war. . .

Soviet nationalism is not a product of the present war. It came into being with the announcement of the policy of 'socialism in one country' and its institutionalization in the successive five-year plans. In foreign policy it manifested itself in the disappearance of international revolutionary Communism from Soviet policy with the ouster of Leon Trotsky from power, in isolationism until the advent of Hitler, in collective security and popular front policies until 1939, and finally in the ephemeral Soviet-German pact of that year. The social purpose of this national policy within and without the Soviet Union was identical. The Soviet Union's economic objectives after 1928 were the industrialization of the country and the collectivization of agriculture. Her political objectives were the firm establishment of the proletarian-revolutionary regime and the gradual introduction of democratic processes. The corollary of this internal policy was a foreign policy directed toward the maintenance of peace at any price.

In spite of the intensified expression of Soviet nationalism under the conditions of war, there is no indication that its social goals have been changed. No better source to document this can be cited than Stalin's speech of November 6, 1943, commemorating the twenty-sixth anniversary of the October Revolution. 'The present war,' he stated, 'has forcefully confirmed the well-known words of Lenin to the effect that war is an all-around test of a nation's material and spiritual forces.' What are these 'material and spiritual forces' which made possible the Soviet Union's strength in withstanding foreign aggression? Stalin finds the answer in the social purposes of the Soviet system as they emerged after 'war Communism' and the subsequent 'new economic policy' had been replaced by the policy of 'socialism in one country': the development of a socialist industry, the collectivization of agriculture, and the multinational solution of the nationality problem. There is nothing mythical or illusory in the social objectives of Soviet nationalism if the latter is identified with 'socialism in one country.' Stalin emphasized:

The Soviet State was never so stable and unshakable as now, in the third year of the Patriotic War. The lessons of the war show that the Soviet system is not only the best form of organizing the economic and cultural development of the country in the years of peaceful construction, but also the best form of mobilizing all the forces of the people for resistance to the enemy in wartime.

If by Soviet nationalism is meant the constructive policy of building socialism in one country as pursued in the Soviet Union before and during the present war, it is quite clear that it has nothing to do with the destructive Russifying, Pan-Slavic, and imperialistic nationalism of the czarist past, and is the very opposite of the aggressive, tribal, and pathological nationalism of modern fascism. The foreign policy of Soviet nationalism has been predicated on the maintenance of peace, and there is little likelihood that this basic aim will be changed in the future. . .

The reason for the eastward orientation of the European peoples lies to a large degree in the successful solution of the nationality problem in the Soviet Union. It is the solution of the nationality question that gives Soviet nationalism its unique flavor. Whether it is called 'multinationalism' or 'supernationalism,' it differs so blatantly from czarist or western nationalism that the very word 'nationalism' seems a terminological miscarriage. Too great an emphasis has been laid, perhaps, on the cultural aspects of Soviet nationality policy, which, in conformity with the trend of the time after the First World War, promoted and helped to awaken the national consciousness of the numerous ethnic and national minorities of the former Russian Empire

This aspect of Soviet nationality policy stands out because it differs so conspicuously from the czarist policy of forced Russification, which had precisely the opposite effect from what was intended In reality, the Russification program alienated the subject nationalities and made them sympathetic to the revolution. But what is more important, though less spectacular, is the fact that Soviet nationality policy gave the non-Russian nationalities an economic base which colonial peoples rarely acquire. By acknowledging the centrifugal cultural tendencies of modern nationalism and simultaneously integrating the nationalities in one common economic process, Soviet nationality policy molded the new Soviet nationalism and inextricably linked it with socialist control of the means of production. . .

The nationality policy of the Soviet Union is also a clue to an understanding of two companion features of Soviet nationalism—its All-Slav orientation and its territorial dimensions. If the Soviet Union as a multinational and classless state appeals to all the peoples of Europe, she may be expected to be particularly attractive to the peoples of central and southeastern Europe, where the element of Slavic kinship makes for even closer relations. Obviously, no question affecting all Slavs can be solved without taking account of the attitude of the Soviet

Union as the greatest of all Slav nations. But a sincere effort at Slav unity must give equal consideration to the wishes, opinions, and traditions of all Slavic peoples. Czarist-sponsored Pan-Slavism failed for precisely the same reasons as the policy of Russification within the old empire. Being built on a purely Russian and Orthodox basis, it was doomed as an integrating force of all Slavs. For instance, its unwillingness to reach an understanding with the Poles, and its disregard for the fact that five Slavic nationalities—Poles, Czechs, Slovaks, Croats, and Slovenes—were overwhelmingly Catholic, betrayed its character as an autocratic tool of czarist imperialism. . .

## V. SELF-DETERMINATION

The doctrine of self-determination holds that a people should be allowed to decide their own political allegiance, whether they shall belong to one nation or another, or, if they choose, set up an independent state of their own. Although the idea is an old one, it attained the height of its popularity during World War I, with President Wilson its main proponent. He advocated independence for the Poles who had been living as minorities in Germany, Russia, and Austria-Hungary, and to the many restless peoples within the Austro-Hungarian Empire. In his address to Congress on 11 February 1918, President Wilson asserted that 'Peoples are not to be handed about from one sovereignty to another by an international conference or an understanding between rivals and antagonists.' Self-determination, he said, is 'not a mere phrase,' but rather 'an imperative principle of action which statesmen will henceforth ignore at their own peril.' On the other hand, President Wilson's Secretary of State, Robert Lansing, denounced the doctrine as divisive and disruptive in its effects. Is the doctrine sound? If so, how far can it be carried? For instance, should the Baltic States of Estonia, Latvia, and Lithuania be free from Russia if that is their wish, and should Puerto Rico be allowed to choose freedom from the United States?

## A. *Secretary Lansing's Criticism*

Robert Lansing, *The Peace Negotiations,* New York, 1921, pp. 96-8. Reprinted by permission of Houghton Mifflin Company and the Lansing estate.)

'Self-determination' is as right in theory as the more famous phrase 'the consent of the governed,' which has for three centuries been repeatedly declared to be sound by political philosophers and has been generally accepted as just by civilized peoples, but which has been for three centuries commonly ignored by statesmen because the right could not be practically applied without imperiling national safety, always the paramount consideration in international and national affairs. The two phrases mean substantially the same thing and have to an extent been used interchangeably by those who advocate the principle as a standard of right. 'Self-determination' was not a new thought. It was a restatement of the old one.

Under the present political organization of the world, based as it is on the idea of nationality, the new phrase is as unsusceptible of universal application as the old one was found to be. Fixity of national boundaries and of national allegiance, and political stability would disappear if this principle was uniformly applied. Impelled by new social conditions, by economic interests, by racial prejudices, and by the various forces which affect society, change and uncertainty would result from an attempt to follow the principle in every case to which it is possible to apply it.

Among my notes I find one of December 20, 1918—that is, one week after the American Commission landed in France —in which I recorded my thoughts concerning certain phrases or epigrams of the President, which he had declared to be bases of peace, and which I considered to contain the seeds of future trouble. In regard to the asserted right of 'self-determination' I wrote:

When the President talks of 'self-determination,' what unit has he in mind? Does he mean a race, a territorial area, or a community? Without a definite unit which is practical, application of this principle is dangerous to peace and stability.

Ten days later (Dec. 30) the frequent repetition of the phrase in the press and by members of certain groups and unofficial delegations, who were in Paris seeking to obtain hearings before the Conference, caused me to write the following:

The more I think about the President's declaration as to the rights of 'self-determination,' the more convinced I am of the danger of putting such ideas into the minds of certain races. . . What effect will it have on the Irish, the Indians, the Egyptians, and the nationalists among the Boers? Will it not breed discontent, disorder, and rebellion? . . .

The phrase is simply loaded with dynamite. It will raise hopes which can never be realized. It will, I fear, cost thousands of lives. In the end it is bound to be discredited, to be called the dream of an idealist who failed to realize the danger until too late to check those who attempt to put the principle in force. What a calamity that phrase was ever uttered! What misery it will cause. . .

## B. *A More Recent Criticism*

(Vera Micheles Dean, *On the Threshold of World Order*, Headline Series, No. 44, New York, January 1944, pp. 43-5. Reprinted by permission of the Foreign Policy Association.)

The idea of self-determination of nations, which played so important a part in the Paris peace settlement of 1919, when the allies recognized a reunited Poland, the new state of Czechoslovakia and an enlarged Yugoslavia and Roumania, was correct in that it tried to give each national group an opportunity to express its preference as to the way of life it would like to pursue. But it was a mistake to assume that this could be done only within the confines of a national state, and that therefore any people, no matter how small its numbers, must be fenced off from its neighbors by territorial boundaries. Within these boundaries each of the peoples, in turn, tried to act as a sovereign state, with its own army, tariffs, and attempts to create a self-sufficient economy. This proved, in the long run, a self-defeating policy. For it broke up eastern Europe and the Balkans, where populations have so intermingled for centuries that it is well-nigh impossible to draw a frontier satisfactory to all concerned, into tiny units which could neither defend themselves nor thrive economically. And it led still other peoples within the borders of new states who had not achieved self-determination to demand it, thus multiplying the problem indefinitely.

Instead of splitting up Europe further, and reducing it to political and economic atoms which would only facilitate the expansion of great powers like Germany, the United Nations should seek to reintegrate the peoples of Europe into a common framework, where they could have both national identity and security. But it would not be enough for this purpose, as some people recommend, that small countries should join in federations such as a Scandinavian or Balkan bloc. That would be merely to pool the weak, and would not create sufficient strength to hold an expansionist power at bay.

In the formation of a federation the experience of Russia, as well as the British Commonwealth, would be most helpful. . . Within Russia are living today 150 nationalities, stemming from several races, which differ profoundly in economic, social, and political development, from White Russia in the west to Siberia and Turkestan in Asia. All these peoples enjoy cultural autonomy, but are joined together under the aegis of a strong political and economic dictatorship.

That does not mean that the peoples of Europe want to subject themselves to any kind of dictatorship, no matter how benevolent. Many of the European nations, especially in the west and north, have had a long tradition of democracy, and if they do develop a federation, it will be more likely to be on democratic than on any other lines. But a purely European federation would still not be able to achieve political security and economic stability through its own efforts—especially if it does not include the two European powers on the periphery of the continent, Britain and Russia. It is toward a world, rather than a continental, organization that many of the conquered nations would like to look for their security in the future. . .

## VI. PLEBISCITES AND NATIONAL SENTIMENT

Where the principle of self-determination is to be applied and some doubt exists in regard to the wishes of the majority of the people of an area, the plebiscite is a useful tool. It was used in many European areas after World War I, notably in Allenstein, Marienwerder, Schleswig, Klagenfurt, Upper Silesia, and Burgenland. The first extract below was written by an eminent authority on plebiscites, Sarah Wambaugh, who has actively participated in the administration of several of them. Extract B is on the Saar Basin plebiscite held on 13 January 1935, after the area had been governed for fifteen years by a commission appointed by the Council of the League of Nations. It was probably the most satisfactory plebiscite ever held. Over 90 per cent of the votes favored Germany, and the territory was therefore given to that country.

## A. *A Discussion of Plebiscites*

(S. Wambaugh, *Plebiscites Since the World War*, 1933, vol. 1, pp. 485-7. Reprinted by permission of the Carnegie Endowment for International Peace.)

Careful consideration of the evidence must lead to the conclusion that the plebiscite is a device of great potential usefulness in the allocation of certain areas where there is no obvious line of cleavage in national sentiment. In spite of the contentions which have surrounded the plebiscite held under the Paris treaties, they represent a real and, on the whole, a successful attempt to apply the principle of self-determination to a limited number of such areas. Specific, and occasionally trenchant, criticism may be brought against the conduct of all of the individual plebiscites except that in Schleswig, but even in the case of the most faulty it is apparent that the result of the voting gave a fairly accurate picture of the wishes of the inhabitants. True it is that in every instance the vote was more or less affected by particular circumstances, yet on no occasion can one say that the result was radically modified by them. Except for the disturbances in Upper Silesia, the worst of which took place after the plebiscite, there was no occurrence of serious violence in the areas where the vote was actually held. In every one of the plebiscites the abuses were far less numerous and far less flagrant than the partisan journals contended. Such abuses as existed in no sense show that the method of the plebiscite is wrongly conceived but merely that the technique employed has been faulty and should be studied and improved. . .

That the plebiscite has proved itself a useful tool for securing a stable settlement becomes increasingly clear. . . In spite of the fact that the pre-war German maps show that the majority of the population of the 'Polish Corridor' was Polish-speaking, there are many who remain unconvinced that the majority wished to be parts of Poland. Similar uncertainty exists about the new Hungarian frontiers. . .

On the other hand, wherever a formal plebiscite has been held with local administration internationally controlled, the question as to the popular will has been settled and the dispute has been removed from the international docket, except in so far as policies of European capitals create many local issues. . .

As the agitation for revision of the territorial provisions of the treaties centers precisely in those areas where no plebiscites have been held, the conclusion appears to be sound that the plebiscite, if held under approximately fair conditions, is more authoritative as a method of determination than are linguistic, historical, religious, strategic, economic, or other criteria. It is authoritative for two reasons: not only does it ascertain the actual desires of the inhabitants but it effectually weakens the appeal of the losing party to liberals in other countries. . .

The most important objection to the plebiscite is that the officials and other public office-holders in the area have been appointed by the state enjoying sovereignty, and that while the highest ones can easily be removed, some at least of the local officials must be retained by the plebiscite commission to carry on the ordinary administrative duties. This means that the inhabitants belonging to the other party will have a justifiable feeling of inequality, based on the fact, and it is a fact, that such local officials have infinite power, under the guise of law, of favoring one party against the other in countless ways, petty often to the outsider but serious indeed to the men and women whose welfare is so completely in their hands under a bureaucratic system.

The greatest danger accompanying a plebiscite is that it will mean the rousing of national feelings of an acute pitch by chauvinists and extremists. The residuum of bitterness, however, depends on how great has been the feeling of lack of fair play during the plebiscitary period. As the plebiscite becomes more scientific, bitterness due to it will tend to diminish, for what is blamed on the plebiscite in the abstract is largely due to the lack of adequate measures of neutralization in some particular area.

The charges, true or false, brought in the past regarding plebiscites, formal and informal, held and not held, neutralized and not neutralized, are numerous and varied. Those most familiar to the general public concern patriotic organizations, often called 'bands,' which in some plebiscites have spread terror, in country districts especially, threatening those showing sympathy for the other party, preventing free speech, breaking up public meetings, organizing boycotts, extorting written statements from terrified peasants that they will vote according to the wishes of the 'band,' compelling them to take part in public processions, and threatening, perhaps with death, any who should vote for the opposite party. Against this the secrecy of the ballot is no remedy, for in small communities a man's sympathies are well known, and the 'bands' may threaten those known to be of the opposite party if they merely present themselves for voting or for registration.

Actuated by a misguided sense of patriotism the local officials can play into the hands of the 'bands' if they will in many ways. . .

In determining the organization of the plebiscite of the future there are several conclusions which may appear to be axiomatic. First, the plebiscite must be a formal one, that is, it must be based on some form of agreement to which both of the contending countries are party, or on an arbitral award accepted by both states. Second, to avoid later disagreement it is absolutely essential that in the basic instrument the conditions of the plebiscite should be clearly set forth, and particularly with regard to the removal of partisan troops and officials, for the dispositions regarding these are as much a part of the conditions of the plebiscite as are the composition and powers of the plebiscite commission and the voting qualifications. . .

For future plebiscites experience dictates further measures of neutralization. First, immediately on the signature of the agreement to hold a plebiscite, the area should be put under neutral control or supervision. Secondly, the make-up of the plebiscite commission should be more scientific than in the past. We have found that a balance of partisans on a commission secures only an approximate and unstable form of neutrality and opens the door to constant friction. . .

Although it would be desirable, whenever possible, to do without troops, especially on account of expense, experience has shown that in an area of any considerable size, and also in an industrial area, no matter how small, the commission should have at its disposal a sufficient number of neutral troops to police not only the towns but the country region. . .

Experience has shown that the powers of the commission over the political administration of the area must be absolute. It is certain that hereafter no plebiscite, even if held under an agreement between two states, can command serious consideration if it is held under the control of one of them. Such a plebiscite could be considered valid only should the party in control be defeated. This is a remote contingency. It is essential that the com mission should have the right to assume the government should it decide this to be necessary, and in any case it should exercise effective control over all the public services which might in any war affect plebiscitary atmosphere. For this purpose an adequate personnel is imperative. . .

To take care of arrangements for registration and voting, it would be well to set up a subcommittee of the plebiscite commission. This would relieve the commission of a good deal of detail and routine work in connection with the lower boards.

The suffrage qualifications should be clearly stated in the original agreement for the plebiscite, as experience has shown that they can be settled with far less difficulty at that time than if they are left to a later agreement. . .

Necessarily the vote will be taken by small units. In Europe, the commune of *Gemeinde* is the recognized administrative entity for this. Whether the vote shall be counted by communes and the final line drawn according to the vote in each commune or whether the vote of the whole area shall be counted as a unit, is a question of the first importance which must be determined by the local history and the situation of the precise area to be consulted. . .

## B. *A Plebiscite in Action*

(*The Saar Plebiscite,* League of Nations Information Section, Geneva, 1935.)

### ORGANISATION OF THE PLEBISCITE

The Treaty of Versailles provided that, at the termination of a period of fifteen years from its coming into force, the population of the Saar Territory was to state in the following manner the sovereignty under which it wished to be placed:

A vote will take place by communes or districts on the three following alternatives: (a) maintenance of the regime established by the present Treaty and by this Annexes; (b) union with France; (c) union with Germany.

All persons without distinction of sex, more than twenty years old at the date of voting, resident in the territory at the date of signature of the present Treaty, will have the right to vote. The other conditions, methods and the date of voting shall be fixed by the Council of the League of Nations in such a way as to secure the freedom, secrecy and trustworthiness of the voting.

The Treaty of Versailles having come into force on January 10, 1920, the measures to be taken with a view to the plebiscite in 1935 were an item on the Council's agenda for January 1934. . .

The Council noted first the declarations made on June 2nd by the German and French Governments in an exchange of letters during the negotiations with the Council Committee. In these documents, the two Governments undertook:

(a) To abstain from pressure of any kind, whether direct or indirect, likely to affect the freedom and trustworthiness of the voting;

(b) Likewise to abstain from taking any proceedings or making any reprisals or discriminations against persons having the right to vote, as a result of their political attitude in connection with the purpose of the plebiscite during the administration by the League of Nations;

(c) To take the necessary steps to prevent or punish any action by their nationals contrary to these undertakings.

The German and French Governments at the same time agreed that any difference concerning the application or interpretation of these undertakings should be submitted to the Permanent Court of Arbitration at The Hague, without prejudice to the rights of the Council of the League.

It was further agreed that, for a transitional period of one year from the establishment of the final regime, a Supreme Plebiscite Court should have jurisdiction as regards any complaint submitted by a person having the right to vote in the Saar, of pressure, prosecution, reprisals or discrimination as a result of his political attitude in connection with the purpose of the plebiscite during the administration of the territory by the League. The competence of the Court was to extend to cases in which penal or administrative proceedings were taken outside the territory against any person having the right to vote in the Saar. No decision, even of a judicial nature, was to prevail against the decision of the Plebiscite Court.

In taking note of these declarations, the Council added that it would reserve the right to examine in due course the conditions under which the benefit of the undertakings given by the two Governments in the above-mentioned declarations as regards voters could be extended to inhabitants of the Saar Territory who did not possess the right to vote.

Sunday, January 13th, 1935, was fixed as the voting-day.

The following decisions were taken as to the organisation and carrying-out of the plebiscite:

## THE PLEBISCITE COMMISSION

The government of the territory was still to be carried on by the Governing Commission during the plebiscite; but a special body, the Plebiscite Commission, was constituted under the authority of the Council for the organisation, direction and supervision of the plebiscite. This Commission consisted of three members and an expert (who might act as deputy member): M. Victor Henry (Swiss), M. Daniel De Jongh (Dutch) and M. Alan Rodhe (Swedish), with Miss Sarah Wambaugh (United States) as technical adviser.

The chairmanship of the Commission was held in turn by members; the Commission entered on its duties on July 1st, 1934. During its labours, it submitted to the Council a series of progress reports.

## REGULATIONS FOR THE PLEBISCITE

These regulations related to the following points: the right to vote, the status of residents, the voting divisions, the local bodies to be established in connection with the plebiscite, the compilation of the voting-lists, the presentation of claims in connection with the voting-lists, voting procedure and the treatment of persons committing offences against the Regulations.

It was at the same time laid down that, in the provision that 'a vote will take place by communes or districts,' the Treaty was referring to already existing areas. The results of the voting were to be determined by unions of communes (*Bürgermeistereien*) or, in the case of communes not forming part of any union, by communes. Each union of communes and each commune which did not form part of a union was to constitute a voting area. In each of the 83 areas thus formed, the voting was to be calculated separately.

## PLEBISCITE TRIBUNALS

A Supreme Plebiscite Court and eight district tribunals were set up, with jurisdiction in disputes concerning the entries in the registers of persons entitled to vote and the validity of the voting, offences covered by the plebiscite regulations and breaches of ordinary criminal law (in so far as they were connected with the purpose of the plebiscite) committed before, during and after the plebiscite proceedings.

The President of the Supreme Court was M. Bindo Galli (Italian), and the Vice-President Mr. James Creed Meredith (Irish); there were six other judges and an examining magistrate, a public prosecutor and his assistants, the registrars and the district judges. All these were appointed by the President of the Council, after consulting his colleagues, and on the proposal of the Council Committee. The judges of all these courts were required to know German, were strangers to the territory and were not nationals of either of the States interested in the plebiscite.

The Supreme Court and the eight district tribunals began their duties at the beginning of October 1934.

### FINANCING OF THE PLEBISCITE

It was agreed that the cost of the plebiscite should be borne by the German and French Governments and by the Governing Commission. Each of these Governments provided five million French francs and the Commission one million. As this amount proved insufficient, the Council subsequently asked for a further advance from the two Governments. The total cost, including that of the 'International Force,' was more than 22 million French francs. . .

### MAINTENANCE OF ORDER

As the date of the plebiscite approached, the political situation in the territory became more strained. On several occasions, the Governing Commission was obliged to take exceptional measures to maintain order.

In June 1934, the Council of the League authorised the Commission to increase the police and local gendarmerie during the plebiscite period, so far as possible by local recruitment; but if necessary the Commission considered that it would be well for foreigners to be enrolled, and an appeal made by the President of the Council to the States Members of the League was favourably re-

ceived by a certain number of Governments.

At the December meeting, the French representative asked the Council to entrust the maintenance of order to international contingents, among which neither France nor Germany would be represented.

The representatives of the United Kingdom and Italy accepted this suggestion. They added, however, that other countries should also contribute and that Germany must give her consent to the despatch of such forces.

Germany having meanwhile given a favourable reply, the Council asked the Governments of the United Kingdom, Italy, the Netherlands and Sweden to participate in the forming of an international force, which would, under the authority of the Governing Commission, provide for the maintenance of order in the territory before, during and after the plebiscite.

On December 11th, the four Governments having replied favourably, the Council decided that such a force should be created. The costs of transport and maintenance due to service abroad, in so far as they were not covered by credits existing in the budgets of the respective Governments, would be borne by the funds for plebiscite expenses.

The contingent was placed under the command of Major-General Brind (United Kingdom). Its strength was fixed as follows:

| United Kingdom | 1,500 |
| Italy | 1,300 |
| Netherlands | 250 |
| Sweden | 250 |

. . . On January 13th, after the electoral bureaux had been opened, the voting began at 7.30 A.M. Each bureau had received from the Communal Committee three certified copies of the extract from the voters' lists. Each holder of an electoral certificate entered the building of his voting-section and submitted his certificate to the chairman, who read out the name of the voter and the number allotted to him in the extract from the register. He then handed the voter an envelope and a ballot with three sections relating to the three possible alternatives: maintenance of the regime established by the Treaty; union with France; union with Germany.

As evidence of the delivery of a ballot and of the due identification of the voter, a teller placed his initials against the voter's name on the identification list. The voter then withdrew into a voting-booth and put a cross to indicate his choice in the appropriate section on the ballot with a black pencil to be found in the voting-booth. He then placed the ballot in the envelope, which he closed before handing it to the chairman, who placed it in the ballot-box.

The voting ended at 8 P.M. Immediately afterwards, the boxes containing the ballots were collected from the electoral bureaux by military or police lorries and conveyed to the headquarters of the voting-districts; thence, they were forwarded by special trains to the capital of the territory. Throughout their journey, as far as the Wartburg Hall in Saarbruck, where the count took place, the boxes were accompanied by a military escort and by a neutral representative of the Commission and two witnesses. At the Wartburg, the boxes were received by officials of the Plebiscite Commission, who signed the records of receipt. These various operations were marked by no incident.

The count began on Monday, January 14th, at 5 P.M., under the direct and exclusive supervision of the Plebiscite Commission. The votes were counted by voting-districts; there were 300 neutral tellers selected from the chairmen of the electoral bureaux. All decisions concerning the validity of ballots were taken by the Plebiscite Commission. Seats had been reserved in the hall for representatives of the Saar population, the French and German Governments and the Press.

On Tuesday, January 15th, between 6 and 7 A.M., the results of the plebiscite were communicated by telephone to the Secretariat of the League of Nations. At 8.15 A.M., they were announced in the Wartburg Hall.

# 10

# THE ECONOMIC BASIS

RANKING high among the bases of national power is the economic strength of a nation. Modern states that lack sufficient manpower or essential raw materials, and do not have a highly developed technology will not rank as great powers. The relative importance of these three economic factors is difficult to measure, however, and their importance has varied for different periods of history. Manpower was once more significant than technology. In the contemporary scene it is only the right combination of economic factors that produces a powerful state. That country which does not have the raw materials of modern industrial life may, if it can maintain access to them, retain its power. For many decades those countries with a high productivity in steel have ranked at the top of the power scale. This is still true, but the factor of technological 'know-how'—again in the right combination with other factors—will increasingly determine a state's power status in the future. The release of atomic energy is proof of this.

Since economic strength is basic to a state's power, it is hardly surprising that the power struggle in international politics has so often revolved about the attempts of nations to improve their economic status. As has already been noted in Part One, the Marxian analysts, who look upon economic motives as the most fundamental in all social-political affairs, claim that economic drives determine a state's action both at home and abroad. It follows on the Marxist assumptions that economic motives furnish the basis for all international relations, war included. There is danger here of over-simplification. Yet there can be no doubt that the economic aspects of international politics are vital. Any understanding of world power conflicts would be wholly unbalanced were the economic basis overlooked.

In general, economic conflict is not caused by an insufficiency of the world's supply of food and other commodities, nor by an inability to bring production up to the level of a high standard of consumption. It is the division of the world into seventy or more independent states which is basic to international economic competition. Were these states intent only on prosperity for all, the problem would not be beyond solution. But governments are more interested in a power economy than in a welfare economy. The states of the world are distrustful, nationalistic groups, each trying to attain security, some of them at any cost. To many of them a managed national economy appears an instrument of power by which they may get and conserve important raw materials, particularly strategic materials, and stimulate the home production of goods to avoid dependence on foreign markets. By economic policy a government may undermine the economic position of a potential enemy and strengthen an ally. Indeed, economic policy can be used as an instrument of warfare, which suspicious and ambitious states could not be expected to overlook either before a war or as belligerents after war has begun; just as during the 1930's, economic warfare preceded the outbreak of military hostilities.

A full review of the many problems related to the underlying economic forces affecting world politics is impossible here. The extracts in this chapter can only briefly note the Marxist view on the relation between capitalism and war, the place of economic nationalism, raw materials, and population in the world power struggle. Thereafter Chapter 11 deals with the closely related issue of imperialism, so generally conceded to be based on the economic drive for more power.

## I. CAPITALISM AND WAR

Must those states which have an economy based on the principles of capitalism inevitably follow a path that leads to war? That they must is the contention of communists, and most Marxists, socialists as well as communists, adhere in greater or lesser degree to this analysis. Other motives than economic ones have led to war, however. Moreover, this is an age when the capitalist structure of many modern states has either been swept away entirely, as in Russia and some Eastern European countries, or has been appreciably altered, as in many nations of Western Europe. Yet war persists and threatens today as before, when most nations of the western state system could be said to have been capitalist states in so far as their economic status was concerned. Today, therefore, it is fair to ask also—Is socialism incompatible with peace? The extract below is a forceful statement of the Marxian case by Professor Harold J. Laski, political theorist and one-time Secretary of the British Labour Party.

(Harold J. Laski, *The State in Theory and Practice,* London, Copyright 1935, by Harold J. Laski, pp. 228-35. Reprinted by permission of The Viking Press, Inc., New York.)

If what it demands is something that war alone can secure, no doubt the state will exhaust all the resources of diplomacy before it employs that terrible expedient; but when they are exhausted, it will make war. It will do so, no doubt, for the sake of 'national honor,' or its 'civilising mission,' or to 'make the world safe for democracy,' or some other verbally noble end; and no one who examines the psychology of peoples engaged in war but must admit how much of sincerity there is in these protestations. But when each of them is soberly examined in concrete terms they always appear as the attempt to achieve some tangible economic good for the class which dominates the belligerent state at the time of making war. It is always this tangible economic good which is the basis upon which the ideological superstructure is erected. . .

The view, therefore, that I take is in essence a simple one, even though its expression in a complex world is intricate. It is the view that the state in a capitalist society needs to remain sovereign in order to protect the interests of capitalism. In the last resort, these interests have to be protected by war, which is the supreme expression of sovereignty in international relations. So long, therefore, as the effective purpose of the state, internally regarded, is to protect the principles of capitalism, so long, in its external aspect, will it require to retain the use of war as an instrument of national policy. If sovereignty and an effective world-order are incompatible ways of life, then, also, capitalism and a world-order are incompatible; for war is rooted in the capitalist system in our experience of its necessary functioning.

This is, of course, stoutly denied by the protagonists of capitalism; and it is well to examine, at the outset, the burden of the argument they make. 'There is not a tittle of evidence to show,' writes Professor Gregory, 'that capitalism necessarily leads to war—it was not the era of capitalist supremacy in the nineteenth century which is richest in armed conflict, and, in any case, were there no wars before the middle of the eighteenth century?' Or we are asked to remember that the strongest opponents of war in the nineteenth century were exactly these statesmen who, like Cobden and Bright, were most concerned to develop the full assumptions of capitalist democracy. . .

But we have to analyse not the pure theory of a conceptual capitalism, but the habits of the capitalists we know. It is obvious that a capitalist society in which, alike, the capitalist refrains from asking the state for assistance, and the state refrains from assisting the capitalist, the operations of the economic system will not result in war. If the capitalism we know had been a capitalism of this kind,

thinkers of Professor Gregory's school would be entitled to say that war is not necessarily inherent in capitalism at all. But the capitalism of which they speak has never existed outside of economic literature; it is a creature of their conceptual imagination. The capitalism we know has at every stage of its history sought the protection of the state for its operations. It has demanded and secured, tariffs, subsidies, quotas, the influence of the Foreign Office for its trading agents abroad, the use of the state's prestige (a pseudonym for the right to call upon its armed forces) to protect the claims it has thought fit to make in foreign countries. The history of Egypt since the British occupation, the history of Africa in the last two generations, of China, of Mexico, of the central American States, are quite unintelligible except upon the basis of a capitalism which has been able to put the force of the state behind its enterprises. . .

There were, no doubt, many wars before the nineteenth century in which noneconomic motives, dynastic, religious, political, were of great significance. But, even in those wars, a careful scrutiny of their purpose always leaves the economic contest a relevant one. The drive to war is never divorced from the search by the state after economic power. The search may be indirect, as when a state seeks for a strategic frontier; or it may be mixed, as in the French desire to recover Alsace-Lorraine, where sentiment born of historic tradition and the interest of French heavy industry were united in perhaps fairly equal proportions. But the explanation of war is never adequate where it fails to find an economic perspective to its occurrence. . .

The capitalism we know is a system in which the instruments of production are privately owned, and in which the effective motive to production is the profit made possible by such ownership. This system implies, as I have sought to show, a special system of class relations, and the essence of its habits lies in the fact that the power of the state is used to maintain the implications of these class-relations. The whole effort of the state, therefore, is directed to securing the owner's right to profit. Given the postulates of the system, it could not, as I have argued, be otherwise. Whatever interferes with the making of profit the power of the state will be used to repress, if it can be repressed; for there is always a struggle in society between the classes which own, and the classes which do not own, the instruments of production, for a larger share in the product of the industrial process. In a capitalist society, the internal function of the state is to safeguard these ultimate principles of law which assure to the owner of property a predominant share in that production. And, again as I have argued, from this fundamental fact, all social activities take their shape and complexion. . .

Now what the state is in its internal, that, also, in my view, it is in its external relations. Exactly as it uses its force to protect the interests of the capitalist at home, so it uses force to protect his interest abroad. The value to it of its sovereignty in the international field is precisely that, in extreme cases, it can bring force into play against any rival which seeks to interfere with the expression of its will. If it surrendered that sovereignty it would be subject to rules; and, so long as it observed them, it would not be able to make the might at its disposal the measure of the right it may seek to enforce. . .

## II. ECONOMIC NATIONALISM

The doctrine that a state should be economically self-sufficient is called economic nationalism, or autarchy. In its methods and purposes it is much the same as the system of mercantilism that flourished during the sixteenth and seventeenth centuries. This system came under severe criticism late in the eighteenth century, and by the middle of the nineteenth century was generally discarded. Like mercantilism, autarchy involves intricate trade regulations designed to increase the power of the state. Thus the policy of Fascist Italy and Nazi Germany was intended to improve the fighting strength of those nations, by providing necessary resources for war and a high immunity against a blockade. Because a nation with a well-rounded economic system is stronger than a country with a more specialized and dependent economy, autarchy has great appeal when war appears likely. No doubt it is also true that economic policies designed to produce self-sufficiency are injurious to other nations and help bring on war. The article below discusses selected aspects of economic nationalism.

(F. C. James, 'Economic Nationalism and War,' *Annals of the American Academy of Political and Social Science*, vol. 175, 1934, pp. 65-71. Reprinted by permission of the *Annals of the American Academy of Political and Social Science*.)

Exactly a century ago, during the depressed thirties and the hungry forties that were the aftermath of the Napoleonic war, a small group of men headed by John Bright and Richard Cobden were urging the voters of England to establish as a political reality the ideal of an international economy that had already been well portrayed in the writings of economists from Adam Smith and the Physiocrats up to Ricardo. The England that this small band of idealists set out to convert was still wearing the protectionist mantle woven during the imperialistic era that began with the War of the Spanish Succession and the Seven Years' War; and the repeal of the Corn Laws, with its promise of cheap bread for the large and hungry population of the industrial cities, marked the beginning of a new era. That legislative decision was the foundation stone on which the economic fabric of the nineteenth-century world was reared.

From the material economic viewpoint, the latter half of the nineteenth century constituted a phenomenal period of enlarged wealth and growing prosperity. For the first time in human history it could be said with truth that man 'held the world in fee,' and the income derived from that vassalage was staggering, both in its aggregate size and in the diversity of the goods and services that it comprised. . .

In these troubled days of the twentieth century, when the world follows after more refined psychological concepts, like Aryanism and the self-determination of small peoples (ideals so refined that their rarefaction defies simple definition or facile application), the straightforward and selfish materialism that underlies the laissez-faire economy of the nineteenth century appears crude and primitive. Yet, if one takes the trouble to read those monumental Victorian biographies of Richard Cobden, Lord Morley, or John Bright—the apostles of economic internationalism—the men do not appear to be of cruder clay than our modern knights in shining armor who preside over the destinies of nations.

Moreover, it must be frankly acknowl-edged that, despite the inequalities in the distribution of wealth which marred the perfection of the nineteenth-century picture, the leaders of that age did, through the economic development of the whole world, succeed in their ambition of enlarging the real income of prince and pauper alike. Even though we consider the ideal to have been a low one—an intellectual criticism with which many victims of the present depression would find it hard to agree—we must admit that it was capable of attainment, and that the goal was pleasant when attained.

We are, however, considering the relationship between economic nationalism and war, and it has been suggested by some writers that the prewar ideals of an international economy contained the seeds of the holocaust that raged from 1914 to 1918 and has continued to smolder right up to the present time. Admittedly the World War followed the development of international economic ideals, but the above argument will not hold water even in the weak sense of a *post hoc ergo propter hoc*. Between the fifties and sixties, when the ideals of Cobden were being most widely practiced, and the dark days of 1914, there intervened another period. From the time of the war between Austria and Prussia until the assassination of an almost unknown man at an unheard-of-place called Sarajevo, political nationalism was resurgent.

The bases of political nationalism, and the proximate causes of its eruption at different periods, have been the subject of a good many books, and it is impossible to attempt analysis of them within the confines of this article. We can readily admit, however, that political nationalism and economic internationalism are fundamentally opposed to each other. Economic internationalism cares nothing about the color of the flag that flies over a farm or a factory as long as the produce of that farm or factory can be freely obtained in exchange for goods produced in other areas. It is crassly material, it is concerned only about the problem of getting the largest quantity and the greatest variety of goods in return for the expenditure of a given amount of productive effort. Probably it would admit the benefits of a single world-wide political empire, since the existence of national frontiers, even in a world devoted to laissez faire, do impose some minor inconveniences upon international trade; but apart from that refinement it would care little whether the world were sleeping under twenty flags or two thousand, nor would it pay much attention to their color or design. They would, in fact, be no more important than the emblems of the several states comprised in the Union, very few of which we ever remember.

Such an attitude of mind is heresy to the disciple of political nationalism—to the imperialist as he came to be called toward the end of the nineteenth century. To him the flag that flies over his home is sacred. He will speak of it with bated breath and he will rise to salute it when called upon to do so in public places. He is the embodiment of patriotism, which Dr. Johnson was not entirely wrong in defining as 'the last resort of scoundrels.'

Perhaps sentimental flag waving is not dangerous in itself, but it soon grows into a desire to see that flag flying from as many poles as possible in all parts of the world. England fought the Boers for that ideal, and Mr. Kipling hymned the praises of a flag that was always in the sunshine. But England did nothing more than demonstrate, rather inefficiently on the whole, the spirit that was moving every important nation on the face of the earth with the single, sensible, exception of China.

When flag waving has reached that stage, it begins to cut at the roots of economic internationalism. It replaces the materialistic idea of a full belly by the higher psychology of sacrifice to intangible ideals. If new poles are to be set up around the world, on which to fly the flag, an army and a navy are necessary to deal with unappreciative natives who do not immediately acquire a full perception of the honor thus conferred upon them. Armies and navies cost money, and leave less of the national income free for the purchase of other luxuries. Moreover, since the partition of Africa and the peaceful penetration of China, all the available flagposts of the world are defended by fairly strong armies and navies, so that any further attempt by a single country to enlarge the area over which its emblem flies would involve a rather serious war.

At that point imperialism kills economic internationalism. A country that fears a war (because every war is always forced upon each of the reluctant contenders, who merely defend what they think they are equitably entitled to) will naturally wish to produce under its own flag as large a part as possible of the goods and services that it consumes. Economic self-sufficiency, the ability to grow all the food needed to maintain the population in a state of sacrificial satisfaction and to produce all the munitions considered essential to the successful prosecution of a war, is the logical goal of imperialism and the absolute contradiction of international economic ideals. Economic self-sufficiency had gone far to destroy the ideals of Cobden long before it precipitated the World War.

Despite the political idealism of President Wilson and the machinery of the League of Nations that it inspired, the great nations of the world have frankly espoused the doctrines of economic nationalism since the war, and, in many cases, set as their goal a condition of economic self-sufficiency. Whether this development is to be regarded as a re-action from the strain of international cooperation among the belligerents during the war, or as the product of an intense fear of future wars, does not immediately concern us. These are problems for the psychologist, perhaps even for the neurologist, and there are enough problems in the field of economics to occupy our attention. Let us therefore confine our analysis to the weapons of economic nationalism as they have been used since 1920, and to the effects of that usage upon the present and future peace of the world.

First of all, we are confronted at the present time by a variety of obstacles to trade more numerous and more complicated in their nature than anything experienced in any previous era of human history. All the new countries that emerged from the war with a flag and a frontier of their own have set out to erect along that frontier a tariff barrier high enough to compel most of their nationals to purchase goods produced under the cover of the revered flag. Nor have the older countries been slow to follow suit; so that the economic world is today intersected by innumerable tariff walls that prevent the flow of goods from one country to another, and therefore enable the citizens of the countries concerned to console themselves for the material lowering of their standard of living by the spiritual satisfaction of knowing that almost all the articles that they consume have been produced by the labor of their fellow countrymen. . .

· Those people who believe that indirect taxation is less painful than a direct levy of equal size have sometimes suggested that the scientific weapons of modern economic nationalism are less dangerous to the peace of the world than the older, cruder habits of mercantilism. Centuries of human experience have taught us that the monopolizing of markets and the at-

tempts to control important sources of vital raw materials are prolific of much international discord. The bellicose desire for Eastern spices and American gold in the sixteenth and seventeenth centuries does not differ very much from the prewar German theory that she was being hemmed in by England and other great commercial powers who would not allow that degree of expansion to Germany to which she considered herself entitled. Nor, parenthetically, does it differ greatly from the popular sentiment current today in countries that find themselves suffering from the tariff experiments of their neighbors.

But as a matter of fact it can well be contended that the scientific protectionist devices of the twentieth century cause a larger amount of friction than the cruder methods that preceded them. Although the diminution, through tariffs, of the markets of an exporting nation presents a serious problem, it is much less serious than the situation created in a growing debtor nation by the sudden cessation of the flow of new capital funds. Economic depression results in the first case, but in the second, depression leads rapidly, through default and economic bankruptcy into chaos. It would be interesting, to cite but one example, to discover by a careful study of the recent history of Germany and Austria how large a share of responsibility for the present situation rests upon those who supplied capital in uneconomically large amounts for a short period and then cut off the flow entirely!

Again, there can be no doubt that the present habit of negotiating specific trade agreements between countries, with its necessity for haggling and bargaining to exclude other nations from the advantages bestowed upon the favored parties, causes a great deal more friction among commercial nations than was ever produced by the cruder use of increased tariff rates tempered only by an almost universal most-favored-nation clause.

The most insidious device is, however, the most dangerous in its effects upon international harmony and good will. Foreign exchange regulation, together with the standstill agreements, moratoria, and manipulative devices that accompany it, is probably responsible for a larger share of the present international ill will than any other single weapon in the armory of economic nationalism. . .

But if continuous friction increases the possibility of war, it tends to be re-enforced by a growing realization of the cost of economic nationalism. The very need for tariffs and other protective devices, so pathetically and emphatically declared by the business men of every country, is clearly an indication of the fact that many commodities could be purchased more cheaply abroad than they can be produced at home. To exclude foreign goods and concentrate upon domestic production, therefore, implies higher costs and a reduced annual output of goods and services in return for a given expenditure of human energy. Economic nationalism reduces the size of the real national income, and the sanctifying touch of the national flag on the goods consumed must compensate for the absence of the variety that can be achieved only as a result of active international intercourse.

Naturally, the cost of such policies is in reverse proportion to the size of the country adopting them. The United States might well bear the burden for several years without undue discomfort, whereas Belgium or Luxembourg—to say nothing of Latvia or Monaco—could not long survive such an imposition.

But in every case there is a burden of increased cost to be borne, and it is undertaken only with the desire to render the country self-sufficient in time of war. Despite all the ingenious political slogans that are used to hide this fact, it stands out clearly in its naked ruggedness as soon as one probes below the surface. How long, therefore, can the enthusiasm of false patriotism inspire the people of the world to a continuing sacrifice that bears no fruit? How long will they be content to propitiate the gods without invoking them? How long can we expect that statesmen, harassed by economic problems to which economic nationalism offers no solution, will be strong enough to refuse the specious popularity of wartime leadership? . . .

### III. THE POPULATION POTENTIAL

Every great power—as well as some states that do not hold that rank at the moment—is seriously concerned about the size and rate of growth of its population. Numbers count in the military and economic calculations of power politics, although in an industrial world skilled manpower counts for more than mere numbers. It is important to note, however, that in the last decade an annual average of 17 million persons has been added to the world's total population. Thus the pressure of population on land and food resources has created crucial problems for statesmen and students of world affairs.

Although in recent years statisticians have greatly improved their ability to predict the probable growth of different population groups, forecasts are still open to grave questions. Some of these figures are given on page 256; despite

possible error, they show that the greatest population increases are to be expected in non-industrialized areas, principally in Asian countries. For example,
the population in India increased virtually 50 million in the decade between
1936-46. At about 400 million, her population now equals that of all Europe
west of the Soviet Union. The query naturally arises, are the older countries
of the Far East destined to become great powers along with the United States,
Russia, and Britain?

*World Population Figures and Forecasts*

(ooo)

| Area | 1936 | 1946 | 1955 | 2000 |
|---|---|---|---|---|
| World Totals | 2,076 | 2,251 | 2,438 | 3,300 |
| Europe | 371 [a] | 382 [a] | 404 [a] | 417 [a] |
| North America | 140 | 155 | 166 | 176 |
| U.S.S.R. | 187 | 193 | 210 | 298 |
| Central and South America | 124 | 149 | 175 | 283 |
| Oceania | 10 | 12 | 12 | 21 |
| Africa | 151 | 173 | 191 | 250 |
| Asia | 1,093 | 1,187 | 1,280 | 1,900 |

[a] Excluding U.S.S.R.
  (Sources for figures in chart: 'World Population Estimates,' Department of State, 1947, and
Notestein, F. W., 'Food for the World,' Harris Foundation Lectures, 1945.)

## IV. The Problem of Raw Materials

There have been complaints from some nations that they lack raw materials and have encountered great difficulty in attempting to purchase them
from other countries. Nazi Germany and Fascist Italy made such statements
in justification of their conquest of territories whose natural resources would
supplement their own. It is true that the world's resources are unevenly
distributed and that Germany and Italy do stand in a more dependent position than other countries, notably the United States and Russia. To some
extent, however, all countries are dependent for raw materials on exterior
sources. The world's supply of asbestos is located in two places, Canada and
Eastern Africa. The supply of tin is concentrated in the Malay States, the
East Indies, and Bolivia. Because of the complaints made by the poorer
states that they lacked access to raw materials generally, a commission was set
up by the League of Nations to study the subject. The extract below is from
a report submitted in 1937.

(Report of the Committee for the Study
of the Problem of Raw Materials, *League
of Nations Official Journal,* December
1937, p. 1229.)

. . . It is obvious that there would be
no 'raw material problem' in the form in
which it has presented itself to the Committee if the distribution of raw ma-

terials was not uneven. For countries poor in raw materials the difficulties experienced as regards access to such materials vary according to the general economic conditions of each country. No doubt, in principle, all of them are in the same situation *vis-à-vis* countries which produce raw materials if the latter hinder the development and export of any one of these materials. . .

It will be remembered that in the discussions of the raw material problem in the period preceding the examination of this question at the Assembly, a great deal of attention was devoted to colonial raw materials; indeed, some part of public opinion appeared to consider that the problem was predominantly a colonial one. In fact, some countries have exhibited a lively interest in the question of commercial access to raw materials produced in colonial and Mandated Territories. The Committee reached the conclusion that most raw materials are produced wholly, or to a great extent, in sovereign countries. In fact, the raw materials which are typically colonial, i.e. those which colonial territories alone produce or are in a position to produce, number only three, vis. palm oil, rubber, and copra. Of these, rubber is a raw material of major importance for all industrial countries. The other two, palm oil and copra, form part of the large group of vegetable oils and fats (which are used both for human consumption and for industrial purposes) some of which are produced in many countries. These two commodities have no special uses for which other articles in the group are not equally suitable. A fourth product is found in abundance, but not exclusively, in the colonies, viz. tin. As for the other products of the colonies, they have to compete with similar products of sovereign countries, from which the great part of the supply is derived.

A calculation, which necessarily can only be a rough one, seems to indicate that, including production both for domestic consumption and for export, the total present production of all commercially important raw materials in all colonial territories is no more than about 3 per cent. of world production, a substantially smaller percentage than is the proportion (12½ per cent.) of the population of these territories to world population. Nor is the share of colonial territories in international trade much more important. In 1936 these territories provided 9.7 per cent. of world exports and took 8.1 per cent. of world imports. Of course, Dominions and other self-governing territories have not been included in these calculations. . .

It has been pointed out above that the Committee's particular duty was to examine, and, if possible, to pronounce upon the complaints regarding difficulties in respect of raw materials which had come to its notice, and a preliminary examination of them soon disclosed the fact that these difficulties fall into two quite different classes. 'On the one hand difficulties were felt regarding the *supply* of raw materials, that is, certain countries considered that, even when they were in a position to pay for all the raw materials they required, they either could not obtain them at all, or were compelled to pay what was in their view an excessively high price for them. On the other hand, certain countries experienced principally difficulties in regard to *payment*, that is, they felt that, even when ample supplies were available, they themselves were, for reasons beyond their own control, unable to obtain the necessary foreign exchange to pay for their requirements.'

Hence the Report to the Committee is divided into two main chapters dealing with these two classes of difficulties. . .

The foregoing analysis shows that the solution of the present difficulties in regard to the payment for raw materials is in large part bound up with the solution of wider economic problems which requires concerted action to restore freer circulation of capital, goods, and labour. Any progress realized in this direction should help to meet certain countries' complaints in regard to payments for raw materials. It should be borne in mind, however, that such action can only be effective:

(a) if the countries which at present restrict foreign exchange transactions find means to modify their financial and economic policies so as to re-establish confidence, and if they succeed in re-establishing the free negotiability of their currencies;

(b) if measures can be taken which will protect the countries which have imposed foreign exchange control, and now desire to abolish this system, against the very dangers in which it had its origin, and which they have reason to fear might again arise if it were abolished;

(c) if the impediments to trade, such as high or preferential tariffs; quotas, clearings, &c., can be diminished so as to give the debtor countries the possibility of meeting their obligations;

(d) and lastly if there is a movement towards an international standard which will facilitate the settlement of the balances arising from mutual exchanges between nations, a matter which to-day presents so many complications. . .

There is no doubt that there is an inequality in the distribution of raw materials and that certain countries have particularly serious difficulties in supplying their requirements. The Report mentions certain measures for alleviating these difficulties. But the only general and permanent solution of the problem of commercial access is to be found in a restoration of international exchanges on the widest basis.

### A. *Geographic Distribution of Raw Materials*

The geographic distribution of some of the basic raw materials is shown in the following chart. The unequal productive position of various nations is apparent. The relative pre-eminence of the United States and Russia stands out in all cases except in rice production, which is unimportant to America and the Soviet Union in view of their wheat and corn production. Of the three great powers today, only Britain appears vitally deficient in most of the six products listed.

The raw materials shown here are not the only key commodities needed by powerful states. Others are shown in the chart on Self-Sufficiency. The complete list of strategic and critical materials as set forth by the United States Army and Navy Munitions Board is given in extract B.

### B. *List of Strategic and Critical Materials*

No better index of a nation's power exists than its possession of, or ability to command, what may be called strategic and critical materials. The list of such commodities is exhaustive and reveals the wide industrial base on which modern power is built. The following list is that prepared by the United

# WORLD PRODUCTION

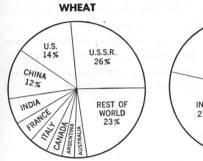

**WHEAT**

U.S. 14%
CHINA 12%
INDIA
FRANCE
ITALY
CANADA
ARGENTINA
AUSTRALIA
U.S.S.R. 26%
REST OF WORLD 23%

**RICE**

CHINA 46%
INDIA 27%
JAPAN 12%
BURMA
INDO-CHINA
NETH. INDIA
REST OF WORLD

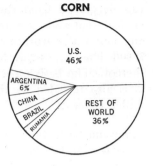

**CORN**

U.S. 46%
ARGENTINA 6%
CHINA
BRAZIL
RUMANIA
REST OF WORLD 36%

**IRON ORE**

U.S. 33%
FRANCE 17%
U.S.S.R. 14%
GERMANY 7%
GREAT BRITAIN 6%
REST OF WORLD 23%

**COAL**

U.S. 35%
GREAT BRITAIN 19%
GERMANY 15%
U.S.S.R. 10%
FRANCE 4%
REST OF WORLD 17%

**OIL**

U.S. 63%
U.S.S.R. 9%
VENEZUELA 9%
PERSIA 4%
NETH. INDIES 3%
REST OF WORLD 12%

GEOGRAPHIC DISTRIBUTION OF RAW MATERIALS

# SELF — SUFFICIENCY

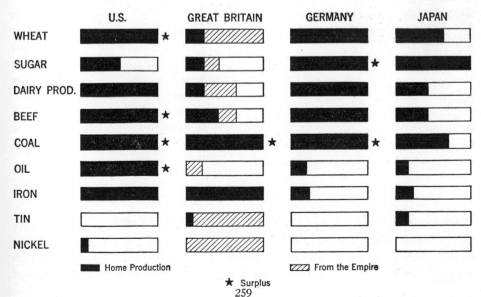

|  | U.S. | GREAT BRITAIN | GERMANY | JAPAN |
|---|---|---|---|---|
| WHEAT | ★ | | | |
| SUGAR | | | ★ | |
| DAIRY PROD. | | | | |
| BEEF | ★ | | | |
| COAL | ★ | ★ | ★ | |
| OIL | ★ | | | |
| IRON | | | | |
| TIN | | | | |
| NICKEL | | | | |

■ Home Production    ▨ From the Empire

★ Surplus

259

States Army and Navy Munitions Board. The basis on which it was made up can be gained from the very definitions used by the Board. 'Strategic and critical materials are those materials required for essential uses in a war emergency, the procurement of which in adequate quantities, quality and time is sufficiently uncertain for any reason to require prior provision for the supply thereof.' The basis on which the materials are classified in Groups A, B, and C is also revealed by this definition. Note the explanation about uranium under Group C.

(Army and Navy Munitions Board List of Strategic and Critical Materials, Washington, ANMB, 14 January 1946, Circular 4.)

## GROUP A

Materials for which stock piling is deemed the only satisfactory means of insuring an adequate supply for a future emergency.

Agar
Antimony
Asbestos:
 Rhodesian chrysotile
 South African amosite
Bauxite
Beryl
Bismuth
Cadmium
Castor oil
Celestite
Chromite:
 Metallurgical grade
 Refractory grade:
  Rhodesian origin
  Other origin
Cobalt
Coconut oil
Columbite
Copper
Cordage fibers:
 Manila
 Sisal
Corundum
Diamonds, industrial
Emetine
Graphite:
 Amorphous lump
 Flake

Hyoscine
Iodine
Jewel bearings:
 Instrument jewels, except V jewels
 Sapphire and ruby V jewels
 Watch and timekeeping device jewels
Kapok
Kyanite, Indian
Lead
Manganese ore:
 Battery grade
 Metallurgical grade
Mercury
Mica:
 Muscovite block and film, food stained
  and better
 Muscovite splittings
 Phlogopite splittings
Monazite
Nickel
Opium
Palm oil
Pepper
Platinum group metals:
 Iridium
 Platinum
Pyrethrum
Quartz crystals
Quebracho
Quinine
Rapeseed oil
Rubber:
 Crude rubber
 Natural rubber latex
Rutile
Sapphire, and ruby
Shellac
Sperm oil

Talc, steatite, block or lava
Tantalite
Tin
Tung oil
Tungsten
Vanadium
Zinc
Zirconium ores:
　Baddeleyite
　Zircon

### GROUP B

Materials practicable for stock piling, but recommended for acquisition only to the extent available for transfer from Government agencies because adequacy of supply can be insured either by stimulation of existing North American production or by partial or complete use of available substitutes.

Aluminum
Barite
Chalk, English
Chromite:
　Chemical grade
Cryolite, natural
Diamond dies
Emery
Fluorspar:
　Acid grade
　Metallurgical grade
Graphite:
　Crystalline fines
Magnesium
Mica:
　Muscovite block, stained and lower
　Phlogopite block
Molybdenum
Platinum group metals:
　Osmium
　Palladium
　Rhodium
　Ruthenium

Selenium
Talc, steatite, ground
Wool

### GROUP C

Materials which are not now recommended for stock piling.

Asbestos:
　Canadian chrysotile
Bristles, pig and hog
Burlap, jute
Cordage fibers:
　Hemp, true American
　Henequen
　Jute
Cork
Glass, optical
Iron ore
Leather:
　Cattle hides:
　　Heavy
　　Light
　Calf and kip skins
Loofa sponges
Lumber:
　Balsa
　Mahogany
Petroleum and petroleum products
Radium
Scrap, iron and steel
Sesame oil
Uranium (Uranium has been omitted previously from the List of Strategic and Critical Materials for reasons of security. It is added to Group C rather than Group A for the reason that the U.S. Government has not determined yet the agency to have control and cognizance of Uranium, together with the responsibility for stockpiling.)

# 11

# IMPERIALISM

IMPERIALISM is a much abused term. People apply it carelessly to any nation whose policies they disapprove as endangering peace, much as they apply the word 'communist' to any man whose ideas they denounce as threatening internal order. When a strong power takes advantage in any way of a small one the cry of 'imperialism' is usually raised. It is also common to speak of any aggressive action, whether it be economic, military, or diplomatic, as 'imperialism.' One of the main abuses of the term is in the phrase 'economic imperialism' as applied to the economic penetration of a weak or backward country.

In its most exact meaning, imperialism is the political domination by one people of another. An aggressive or unethical foreign policy does not necessarily lead to such domination. While economic penetration by means of investments and concessions may lead to political domination, this is not necessarily the case. Certainly there is no imperialism in the economic development of a country by the nationals of another. There are large American investments in Canada, but no political control. The most extreme form of domination occurs when an alien people has been given the status of a colony, a protectorate, or a protected state. For instance, Puerto Rico is a dependency of the United States, and the Belgian Congo is one of Belgium. In such cases the imperialist state has very substantial if not complete political control over the area in question.

In some instances political control is exerted in a less direct manner. Japan in 1931 set up the state of Manchukuo in conquered Manchuria and recognized its independence, but saw to it that the personnel of the government was friendly to Japanese interests. Later Japan tried to establish permanent 'puppet' regimes of this nature in parts of China conquered after 1937, but the defeat of Japan in 1945 brought a complete collapse of the structure both in China proper and in Manchuria. The United States has often refused recognition to unfriendly governments in Latin America and hastily recognized friendly regimes. This amounts in fact to political control over such countries, for Latin American states find it difficult to remain in office without recognition by the United States. A still more subtle form of control exercised by the United States in Latin America has been the shipment of arms to revolutionists or to governments in power that are friendly to our interests.

No doubt such actions are imperialistic in the strict sense. Because the control exerted is less direct than that employed in dependencies, the domination exercised through puppet regimes, recognition policies, shipment of arms, and the like has been referred to as 'indirect imperialism.'

In all recorded history there have been subject peoples governed by imperialist powers. Empires were built by Babylon, Egypt, Persia, Carthage, and Rome, but the groundwork for modern empires was laid in the fifteenth and sixteenth centuries by the Great European explorers. Exploration was soon followed by colonization for purposes of trade, religious freedom, or missionary work. The kings of England, France, Spain, and Portugal often encouraged the movement. All came under the spell of mercantilism during the seventeenth and eighteenth centuries. Stressing gold and silver as wealth, export markets for manufactured goods, and the importation of cheap raw materials, mercantilism placed a high evaluation upon colonies whose economic life could be regulated toward these ends. Rivalry for colonies in the New World, Asia, and the numerous islands that spot oceans became intense as substantial empires were laid out.

Then, as four of the largest empires met with discouraging experiences, there came a period of relative indifference to colonies. Much of the French Empire was lost to Britain in 1763 at the end of a series of wars. Great Britain lost the thirteen American colonies. Between 1810 and 1825 the Spanish colonies in the New World also became free, and in 1822 Portugal lost her large colony of Brazil. It was no wonder that Turgot, French Finance Minister to Louis XVI, stated that 'colonies are like fruit which cling to the tree only till they ripen.' By this time the doctrine of mercantilism had been discredited, and in the middle of the nineteenth century Britain's restrictive trade and navigation laws were repealed and free trade became the rule. Benjamin Disraeli wrote in 1852 that 'these colonies . . . are a millstone around our necks,' though, as Britain's Prime Minister after 1874, Disraeli was an avid champion of Empire. William Gladstone, also one-time Prime Minister, expressed the opinion in the middle years of the nineteenth century that colonies should be liberated.

During the closing decades of the nineteenth century, Europe changed its mind again and the competition for colonies was renewed. Some of the big business groups born of the industrial revolution believed that colonies would bring them sure markets for their products and ready access to raw materials. Investors in backward areas often pressed for annexation so that their investments would be more secure. More than ever as power politics became worldwide in scope, it seemed to statesmen that colonial possessions would add to the fighting strength of a nation, giving it naval and military bases, buffer territory, and greater economic self-sufficiency. Consequently the quest for colonies was renewed, particularly in Africa. By 1914 the only independent areas in Africa were Abyssinia and Liberia.

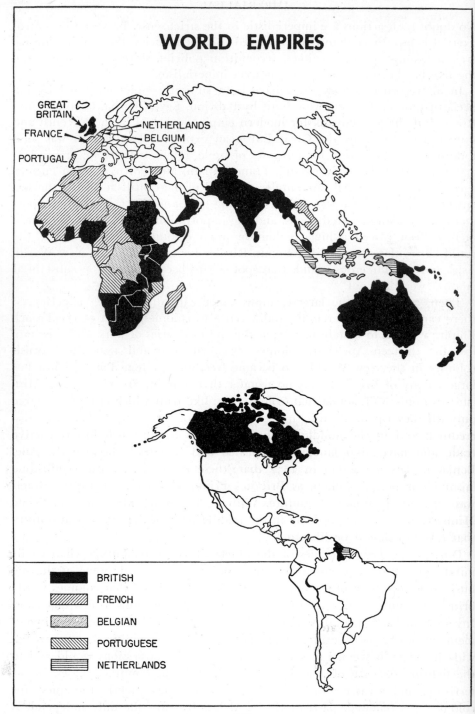

# WORLD EMPIRES

GREAT
BRITAIN
FRANCE
PORTUGAL
NETHERLANDS
BELGIUM

BRITISH

FRENCH

BELGIAN

PORTUGUESE

NETHERLANDS

Nations seeking empires try to justify themselves by an imposing array of arguments. They say that they need colonies to take care of surplus populations, to provide import and export markets, and to secure themselves against attack. The enterprise, so they say, will be beneficial to the backward peoples as well as to themselves, for the advantages of civilization will be carried to the remote parts of the world. Peoples everywhere will profit, according to them, from the resources that are made available.

These arguments for imperialism have always met with criticism, but in recent decades the logic against them has piled high. The increased feeling against imperialism in 1919 was one of the main reasons for the establishment of the mandate system for the territories liberated from Germany and Turkey. With some revision, this became the trusteeship system of the United Nations. Neither could be regarded as a substitute generally for imperialism, for each was too limited in application. The basic theory of both—that the world at large should be responsible for the development of backward areas—has a strong appeal.

Native opposition to alien rule is an old story. There are always strong centrifugal forces in an empire, but as a rule they are held in check. Any weakening of the metropolitan country sets them in motion. This is the principal explanation of the present challenge to imperialism. World War II left Great Britain, France, and the Netherlands weakened and unable to suppress colonial rebellions without great effort. After nineteen months of war against the Indonesians, the Dutch promised the East Indies independence in 1947, but in the light of subsequent hostilities it is not impossible that withdrawal will be indefinitely postponed. Great Britain has withdrawn from India, recognizing the two dominions of Pakistan and India. She has granted independence to Burma and has relinquished her mandate over Palestine, while her position in the Sudan has been raised in question by Egypt. French rule in Indo-China and in Madagascar has been fiercely opposed by the natives. Do these challenges imply that imperialism as a system is decadent, and that independence or trusteeship must take its place? Is imperialism doomed?

## I. The Economic Side of Imperialism

One of the explanations given for imperialism is economic—the argument that, because of over-production, nations are led to seek areas that will offer new markets for their products. This is the point of view held by J. A. Hobson, one of the first writers to deal critically with the subject. It is also the attitude of socialists and communists. According to communist doctrine, imperialism is a final phase in the decay of capitalism. These views are given below, together with some analyses of the economic value of empire.

(J. A. Hobson, *Imperialism*, New York, 1902, pp. 76-9, 85. Reprinted by permission of The Macmillan Company.)

. . . It is open to Imperialists to argue thus: We must have markets for our growing manufactures, we must have new outlets for the investment of our surplus capital and for the energies of the adventurous surplus of our population: such expansion is a necessity of life to a nation with our great and growing powers of production. An ever larger share of our population is devoted to the manufactures and commerce of towns, and is thus dependent for life and work upon food and raw materials from foreign lands. In order to buy and pay for these things we must sell our goods abroad. During the first three-quarters of the century we could do so without difficulty by a natural expansion of commerce with continental nations and our colonies, all of which were far behind us in the main arts of manufacture and the carrying trades. . . These new markets must lie in hitherto undeveloped countries, chiefly in the tropics, where vast populations live capable of growing economic needs which our manufacturers and merchants can supply. Our rivals are seizing and annexing territories for similar purposes, and when they have annexed them close them to our trade. . .

Far larger and more important is the pressure of capital for external fields of investment. Moreover, while the manufacturer and trader are well content to trade with foreign nations, the tendency for investors to work towards the political annexation of countries which contain their more speculative investments is very powerful. Of the fact of this pressure of capital there can be no question. Large savings are made which cannot find any profitable investment in this country; they must find employment elsewhere, and it is to the advantage of·the nation that they should be employed as largely as possible in lands where they can be utilised in opening up markets for British trade and employment for British enterprise.

However costly, however perilous, this process of imperial expansion may be, it is necessary to the continued existence and progress of our nation; if we abandon it we must be content to leave the development of the world to other nations, who will everywhere cut into our trade, and even impair our means of securing the food and raw materials we require to support our population. Imperialism is thus seen to be, not a choice, but a necessity.

The practical force of this economic argument in politics is strikingly illustrated by the recent history of the United States. Here is a country which suddenly breaks through a conservative policy, strongly held by both political parties, bound up with every popular instinct and tradition and flings itself into a rapid imperial career for which it possesses neither the material nor the moral equipment, risking the principles and practices of liberty and equality by the establishment of militarism and the forcible subjugation of peoples which it cannot safely admit to the condition of American citizenship.

Is this a mere wild freak of spread-eagleism, a burst of political ambition on the part of a nation coming to a sudden realisation of its destiny? Not at all. The spirit of adventure, the American 'mission of civilisation,' are, as forces making for Imperialism, clearly subordinate to the driving force of the economic factor. The dramatic character of the change is due to the unprecedented rapidity of the industrial revolution in the United States during the last two decades. . .

The same needs exist in European countries, and, as is admitted, drive Governments along the same path. Overproduction in the sense of an excessive manufacturing plant, and surplus capital which cannot find sound investments within the country, force Great Britain, Germany, Holland, and France to place larger and larger portions of their economic resources outside the area of their present political domain, and then stimulate a policy of political expansion so as to take in the new areas.

## II. THE COMMUNIST INTERPRETATION

Imperialism is an anathema to communists, and much communist literature is devoted to attacking it in all its manifestations. It was not Karl Marx, the founder of the communist movement, however, who fully explained what might be called the communist interpretation of imperialism. This was done by Nicolai (Vladimir Il'ich) Lenin (1870-1924)—the brilliant polemicist, organizer of the Russian Revolution, and first dictator of the Soviet Union. Among his many books none is more important for an understanding of communist ideas than that on imperialism. In the following extract, taken from this work, Lenin explains imperialism as 'capitalism in transition, or more precisely as dying capitalism.'

(V. I. Lenin, *Imperialism*, New York, 1916, pp. 103-4. Reprinted by permission of International Publishers.)

We have seen that imperialism is, in its economic essence, monopolist capitalism. Its historic place is determined by this fact, for monopoly born out of free competition, and precisely out of free competition, is the transition of the capitalist social order to a higher order. We must notice especially four chief aspects of monopolies, or four chief manifestations of capitalist monopoly, which are characteristic of the period under review.

(1) Monopoly has grown up out of the concentration of production at a very advanced step in the latter's development. This is illustrated in the case of monopolist capitalist unions: combines, syndicates and trusts. We have seen the large part that it plays in modern economic life. At the beginning of the 20th century, monopolies have acquired complete supremacy in advanced countries. . .

(2) Monopolies have led to the intensive seizure of the most important sources of raw materials, especially for

the coal and iron industry, which is the principal industry of the capitalist society. . .

(3) Monopoly has sprung from the banks. These have developed into the monopolists of finance-capital out of modest intermediaries. . .

(4) Monopoly has grown out of colonial policy. To the numerous 'old' motives of colonial policy the capitalist financier has added the struggle for the purpose of raw materials, for the exportation of capital, for 'spheres of influence,' i.e., for spheres of good business, concessions, monopolies, profits, and so on; in fine, for economic territory in general. When the European powers did not as yet occupy with their colonies a tenth part of Africa (as was the case in 1876) colonial policy was able to develop otherwise than by the methods of monopoly— by 'free-grabbing' of territories, so to speak. But when nine-tenths of Africa had been seized (towards 1900), when the whole world had been shared out, the period of colonial monopoly opened and as a result the period of bitterest struggle for the partition or the repartition of the world.

Monopolies, oligarchy, the tendency towards domination instead of the tendency towards liberty, the exploitation of an increasing number of small or weak nations by an extremely small minority of the richest and most powerful nations —all these have given birth to those distinctive characteristics of imperialism which oblige us to define it as decaying capitalism. More and more there emerges as one of the tendencies of imperialism, the creation of the 'Bond-holding (Rentier) State,' the usurer state, in which the bourgeoisie lives on the exploitation of capital and on the 'clipping of coupons.' It would be a mistake to believe that this tendency to decay excludes the possibility of the rapid growth of capitalism.

It does not. Separate branches of production, different strata of the bourgeoisie and individual countries display with more or less strength in the imperialist period one or another of these tendencies. In a general way capitalism is growing far more rapidly than before, but this growth is becoming more and more irregular, and the irregularity is showing itself, in particular, in the decay of the countries which are richest in capital (such as England). . .

From all that has been said in this book on the economic nature of imperialism, it follows that we must define it as capitalism in transition, or more precisely as dying capitalism.

## III. Does Imperialism Pay?

Before World War II the question was hotly discussed—Do colonies pay? This discussion was prompted most insistently by the German demand for return of the colonies lost in 1919. Many able students also undertook an investigation of the question. An extract from the report of one study of the problem is given below.

(Report by a Study Group of the Royal Institute of International Affairs, *The Colonial Problem,* London, 1937, pp. 40-45. Reprinted by permission of the Royal Institute of International Affairs.)

The simple inquiry 'Do colonies pay?' involves more complicated considerations than is generally realized. Not only are there almost insuperable practical difficulties in the way of isolating all the items of profit and loss to the various participants in the development of a colony, but there is also a problem of definition. The form in which the query is put assumes that the beneficiary of colonial development is the metropolitan Power itself. But even if a colony were unprofitable to the metropolitan country it might be a source of revenue to other countries trading with

it. It is conceivable that, under conditions of free access secured by an Open Door policy, the metropolitan country might bear all the expense of administration and acquisition, while other countries derived all the profits from mineral and agricultural exploitation; and it has been maintained on behalf of Great Britain that, while the labor and expense incurred in building up the colonial empire fell upon Great Britain, the benefits to be derived from pacification and good administration have been open for all to share. It is possible, too, that the development of colonies—particularly in the more backward areas of the world—may be a source of profit neither to the metropolitan nor to any other advanced country; but that in itself would not prove that the enterprise was not worth while, for the increase in material well-being of the colonial population might, in terms of real wealth, more than offset the slight decline caused elsewhere by subsidizing the colony. While conscious disinterested action of this kind may be regarded as the exception rather than the rule, it may well be implied in the phrase 'trusteeship' or the 'mission civilisatrice de la France.'

Whether a colony is of value to countries other than the metropolitan Power is, however, not the question in the minds of those who ask, 'Do colonies pay?'

If, therefore, an attempt were made to assess the economic value of a colony to the metropolitan Power, the value to be measured would not be the whole of the economic benefits derived from the relations between the colony and the metropolitan country; but only that part of them derived from the particular relationship between the colony and the possessing Power. For some, at least, of these benefits might still be obtainable if the colony were independent or were administered by another Power. What has to be computed is the value in economic terms which the metropolitan country derives from the special advantages conferred upon it by sovereignty over the colony. In practice, this means that benefits derived from preferential export and import duties or from partial or total exclusion of foreign goods, making the trade of the metropolitan Power with the colony more profitable than that of other countries; the value of the special opportunities to the investors of the metropolitan country, either in being first in the field and reaping the initial profits, if any, in reselling their claims at enhanced prices or in excluding foreigners completely from participation; and the value to metropolitan nationals of special opportunities for settlement. Against the additional value so obtained must be set the expenses incurred in administration and, where colonial defence can be sep-

arated from national defence in general, the cost of naval and military establishments.

If it were merely a question of finding out how much total benefit the metropolitan Power derived from the colony, the question would be easier to answer; and in most cases the answer would be that the benefits were less than those which could be derived from trade with and investment in independent countries, as in the latter there would be no cost of administration and defence to set off against profits. If equality of opportunity in every respect could be secured, there would be scant support from business men for the possession of colonies, though perhaps an increased support from humanitarians. It is the special advantages derived from possessions that make a colony an asset; without them, the objections raised by the Manchester school in the last century against the cost of maintaining colonies once more become valid.

But the value of these advantages to the metropolitan Power is for many reasons hard to estimate. In the first place, many colonies have been annexed not so much to obtain special advantages for the metropolitan country as to prevent another country from obtaining even greater advantages for itself. Colonies, that is to say, are sometimes acquired and maintained more in order to ensure against exclusion than to exclude others. An Open Door colony under one's own sovereignty may be preferable to a highly protected colony under another's. In such a case, the value of possession is to be considered as a prevention of a loss which would have been caused by an exclusive economic regime imposed by another Power. . .

Even though a country has no trade with any colony, it may, nevertheless, share in the profits of colonial enterprises. Its trade with foreign countries may be increased as a result of their trade with colonies; and its investors may find more profitable employment for their capital both at home and abroad through the increased opportunities which result from the development of colonies even though none of their capital is invested directly in colonial territory. . .

Finally, presuming that special advantages do accrue, the residents of the metropolitan country, who may or may not benefit from the special advantages accruing from the possession of colonies, fall into three classes—investors, taxpayers, and wage-earners; one individual may appear in all three roles, and usually in two. The investor receives the benefit of the additional return on his investment, whether this be an investment in colonial government securities, in companies operating in the colony or in companies that make goods required by the colony. The labour force may receive higher wages, an advantage passed on to them by the diversion of this capital to more profitable uses than would otherwise be possible. Labour might conceivably benefit if the exodus of settlers reduced the labour supply sufficiently to cause a rise in wages. Lastly, the taxpayer may be affected in several ways. Direct subsidies to the colony for administration or defence will make him poorer. He will set off the increased taxation necessary to make these subsidies against the better terms he gets as a capitalist or a wage-earner. Thus it is conceivable that different sections of the country will be affected in different ways, and that the possession of a colony will be of benefit to some, but of harm to others. . .

According to the various underlying assumptions, the query 'Do colonies pay?' may therefore be answered in general terms; but one that will satisfy everyone is impossible, not only because of lack of factual data, but also because of the difficulty of analysing the behavior of a great number of independent variables. We may, however, in conclusion, set forth the various items of debit and credit which would have to be drawn up for the whole period of a colony's existence as a preliminary to answering this question. . .

Subject to the reservations noted above, the metropolitan country will credit the colony with:

1—The interest received by investors in the metropolitan country on capital invested in the colony. . .

2—The benefits accruing to consumers in the metropolitan country as the result of the cheaper imports which the relatively low cost of production in the colony may enable them to obtain. It must be remembered that under an international system approximating to free trade these benefits would also accrue to consumers in countries other than the metropolitan Power.

3—The benefits accruing to producers in the metropolitan country as the result of direct and indirect profits on their exports (including invisible exports) to the colony. Indirect profits will include the advantages to be gained through an increase in the size of the producers' total output by the enlargement of their market. Such benefits may be shared with other than metropolitan producers.

4—Both the government and individuals in the colony may make money payments to the government or individuals in the metropolitan country, for defence, administration, family remittances, and for charitable or other purposes.

On the other side of the account the metropolitan country will debit the colony with:

1—The losses of metropolitan investors on their investments in the colony.

2—Losses of traders and others doing business with the colony, whether as importers or exporters.

3—Subsidies, grants, and subventions,

directly or indirectly made by the government or the citizens of the metropolitan Power to the government or inhabitants of the colony. These would include the cost of defence and administration of the colony, grants made by individuals to medical, educational, and other services, and the costs of tariffs, and other preferences in favor of the colony.

4—Finally, the cost of acquisition, by purchase or other means, of the colony should be included. . .

## IV. The Military Value of Colonies

One of the main motives of nations for obtaining colonies is to increase their power and thus become more secure against attack, or perhaps better able to commit aggression. It was asserted by officials of the United States Government during and after World War II that this country should control the former Japanese possessions in the Pacific in order to maintain peace in the Far East. As the extract below shows, an empire may be a military liability as well as an asset. If a nation is already strong, an empire may well increase its strength by providing military bases, economic resources, and manpower. But if a nation is weak, then the task of maintaining overseas territories and providing for their protection can easily become an undue strain. Until Great Britain was weakened by World War I and World War II, her Empire contributed greatly to her world power position. At the present time, however, this is no longer true, as evidenced by the fact that important parts of the Empire have been given up.

(Report by a Study Group of the Royal Institute of International Affairs, *The Colonial Problem,* London, 1937, pp. 28-30. Reprinted by permission of the Royal Institute of International Affairs.)

In attempting to define the relation of colonies to military power certain considerations must be borne in mind. Firstly, the strategic advantages and the military responsibilities of colonial possessions are aspects of one and the same thing; insistence upon the advantages to be derived from the control of strategic points has tended to obscure the liabilities involved. The mobility of a fleet in other than home waters depends upon the certainty of free access to ports, dockyard assistance and bunkering facilities; but on the other hand, security for the metropolitan Power demands a certain concentration in home waters, and is diminished by commitments in distant waters involving a dispersal of strength.

Secondly the axiom that 'defence depends on foreign policy' applies to colonial as well as to home defence. A metropolitan Power possessing scattered colonies, if on the defensive, is faced with the task of trying to be strong everywhere, while, for its military advisers, colonial dominion increases the uncertainties in their already complicated calculations.

Thirdly, special colonial duties—policing, pacification, and frontier conflicts—require an army differing essentially from one designed to take the offensive on the continent of Europe. . .

Fourthly, the development of air power has in some cases increased, and in others diminished, the value of many strategic points. Although it is widely held that an air force is the most mobile and rapid striking force, it is as widely forgotten that it depends upon ground organization (the supply of spares included), which must be securely guarded, and to which the power concerned must have free access. Again, although the power of the fleet may still be paramount on the ocean, strategically it has been affected in narrow seas by newer weapons, the aeroplane and the submarine. . .

During the World War both France and Great Britain derived considerable assistance in man-power from colonial sources. French African troops served in France; Indian troops, though some were brought to France for a short time, made their substantial effort in the Middle East, in which Indian interests are necessarily involved. African troops fought in both East and West Africa. . .

The main sea communications which Great Britain endeavours to make secure are five: one to North Africa, two to the Far East, and two to the Pacific. Of these, the sea routes to North America and to the Pacific via the Horn are both open, and are but little affected by recent developments; while the route to the Pacific via Panama is enclosed only by the Caribbean-Panama sector, where its security is guaranteed by the traditional friendship between Great Britain and the United States. Present-day interest centers in the two remaining routes, to the Far East and Australia.

Part of the route to the Far East via Suez is enclosed; but, since the Indian Ocean is virtually a British sea, British anxiety is concerned with the Mediterranean and the Singapore-Australasian sectors. The advent of air power has most affected the Mediterranean. . .

Upon the maintenance of free communications in the Mediterranean depends also the second part of Great Britain's problem in that sea—the support of her influence in the Levant, essential to the safety of the Suez Canal, the air route to India, and the Kirkirk pipeline. Great Britain has always regarded the protection of the Suez Canal as a paramount duty. . .

The United States has to maintain free sea communications between her east and west coast. This means first of all the defence of the Panama Canal, secured by exclusive control granted by the Republic of Panama of a zone five miles wide on either side of the canal. The United States purchased the Virgin Islands from the Danish Government on account of their strategic importance, lying as they do on the route from Europe to the Panama Canal. The United States also maintains a navy yard at Guantanamo, Cuba. In the Pacific Ocean there are extensive naval works and a naval air station at Pearl Harbor, near Honolulu, and at other places on the island of Oahu, all of which lie outside the Treaty area. The United States has in fact a semicircle of outposts, from Dutch Harbor in Alaska to Manila in the Philippines. . .

## V. The Surplus Population Argument

One of the arguments of the imperialist is that colonies act as 'safety valves' for surplus population. It is possible to show that the population of Europe grew from 362 million in 1890 to 506 million in 1930, a period of rapid empire building. Yet it is impossible to show much migration into colonial areas during these four decades, as the extracts below indicate. Moreover, what constitutes 'population pressure' is not clear. It is notable that the non industrialized areas in China and India, which do not afford adequate living standards for their hundreds of millions of people, have complained little, while Germany, Italy, and Japan have declared repeatedly that they need more land, although industrialized and able to give their peoples far better standards of living so long as they remain at peace. There is a suggestion in this fact that the surplus-population argument has been used for propaganda purposes. Apparently it is not so much that population pressure leads to expansion. Rather certain peoples have been led to believe that they are suffering from population pressure and need to expand.

## A. *Colonies as Population Outlets*

(N. Peffer, 'The Fallacy of Conquest,' *International Conciliation*, No. 318, 1938. Reprinted by permission of the Carnegie Endowment for International Peace.)

Does any country really need expansion? What, concretely, is its condition if it does? And when it is in that condition, what, concretely, can it do?

Granted for the moment that certain countries have a larger population than they can feed out of their own resources. This is all that pressure of population means of course. The word 'overcrowded' in itself is almost meaningless in an age when men live in metropolitan centers and produce by machinery. No country organized on a machine-industry economy can be overcrowded in the literal sense. Not magnitude of population but plenitude of resources is determinant. Nor need it be granted that there is any country that cannot feed its people if industrialized; this is in fact subject to serious question. But let it be granted for the sake of argument. What can such a country do? Expand, is the obvious answer. How? When the formula is stripped of all its accretions of diplomatic, military, and journalistic verbiage, expansion can take only three forms: it can seize partly uninhabited lands to which to send its excess population; it can seize undeveloped territories as markets for exports; it can seize territories with stores of unexplored raw materials. . .

Take outlet for population first. Here the experience of Italy is eloquent. For fifty years—or almost since national unification—Italy has strained such resources as it has had in order to win an empire, ostensibly to relieve the pressure of population. It joined in the scramble for colonies in Africa after 1880, fought wars against Abyssinia (now Ethiopia) and Tripoli, and because it could not agree with England and France on the division of the spoils in Africa, entered into the combination of alliances that brought on the World War—and then, ironically, changed sides. In 1914, when the war to which it had committed itself broke out, there were in all the colonies which it had won in Africa some eight thousand Italians. There were more than that number within a radius of a quarter of a mile in Cherry Street, New York City. . .

Take the example of Germany. It was in order to win an empire and get a place in England's sun that Germany challenged British naval supremacy after 1900 and thus foredoomed the World War. And in 1914, at the outbreak of the war which had been brought on by the lust for colonies and in which Germany was to ruin itself, there were in all the German colonies in Africa—900,000 square miles in extent—about 22,000 Germans and in all the German colonies in other parts of the world just 2,000 more. There were more than that number of Germans between 80th and 90th Streets on Manhattan Island. There were twenty-five times that number in New York State. . .

The other stock example of presumed over-population is Japan. At the cost of some 300,000 men Japan won South Manchuria from Russia in 1905. . . But in 1930, twenty-five years after the acquisition of South Manchuria, only 200,000 Japanese had settled there—fewer than had been killed in the war to acquire it and one-third the annual increase in population. There were half as many

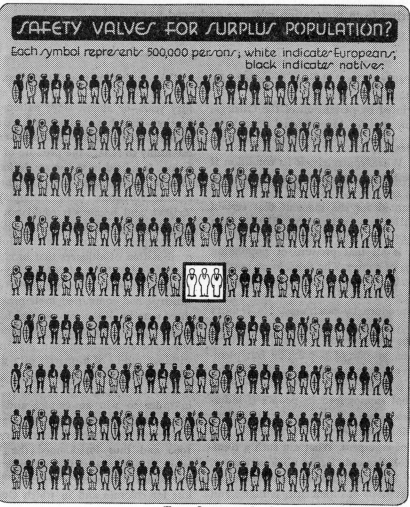

(From Langsam, *In Quest of Empire.* Reprinted by permission of the Foreign Policy Association.)

RATIO OF EUROPEAN WHITES IN TEN OVERSEAS POSSESSIONS

The areas represented are Algeria, French Morocco, Kenya, Nigeria, South West Africa, the Belgian Congo, Libya, Italian Somaliland, French Indo-China, and the Netherlands Indies. The actual figures are 1,383,000 whites in a total population of 131,000,000.

Japanese in California alone. But ostensibly it was pressure of population which compelled the Japanese to invade and seize all of Manchuria in 1931 at the risk of embroiling the country with Soviet Russia and the United States. . .

## VI. Humanitarian Motives

Intermingled with the more sordid motives there is usually a humanitarian urge in the business of empire-making. While it must be admitted that pious phrases are often a guise for selfish ambitions, with some people they express an honest desire to civilize 'backward' native populations. There may be a religious side to this motive, a belief that imperialism is a proper way to fulfil the injunction, 'Go ye into all the world and preach the gospel to every creature.' President William McKinley is quoted as stating after the Spanish-American War that 'there was nothing left for us to do but to take them all, and to educate the Filipinos, and uplift and civilize and Christianize them as our fellowmen for whom Christ also died.' This attitude was epitomized in 1899 by Rudyard Kipling in his poem, 'The White Man's Burden': *

> Take up the White Man's burden—
>    Send forth the best ye breed—
> Go bind your sons to exile
>    To serve your captives' need;
> To wait in heavy harness,
>    On fluttered fold and wild—
> Your new-caught, sullen peoples,
>    Half-devil and half-child.

It is true that imperialistic nations have brought better roads, better health, and schools, but often these good works are overshadowed by exploitation. In any case they are frequently accompanied by resentment among the peoples of dependent areas. In *Between Tears and Laughter* Lin Yutang asserted that the West had given China central heating, statistics, Diesel engines, high explosives, and innumerable gadgets, but that the Chinese people would prefer to have been left alone to be polite, drink tea, and look at the sunset. Colonial governments today continue to justify conquest abroad on the basis of a civilizing mission and point with pride to their accomplishments in dependent areas. Extract A below is an official Italian statement, made on 4 September 1935, justifying in part the conquest of Abyssinia. An assertion of British accomplishments in Africa follows in Extract B.

* 'The White Man's Burden' from *The Five Nations*, copyright 1903, 1931, by Rudyard Kipling. Reprinted by permission of Mrs. George Bambridge and Doubleday & Company, Inc.

## A. *Italy's Mission in Abyssinia*

(*Memorandum of the Italian Government on the Situation in Abyssinia,* submitted to the Council of the League of Nations, 4 September 1935, *Documents on International Affairs,* Royal Institute of International Affairs, 1935, vol. 2, p. 71. Reprinted by permission of the Royal Institute of International Affairs.)

The infringement of the Italo-Abyssinian treaties and the hostile attitude adopted by Abyssinia toward Italy are rendered all the more serious by the fact that Abyssinia today is in such a state of internal disorder and is so backward in her political, economic, and cultural structure as to make it impossible for that country to carry out, alone and unaided, that thorough reorganization which alone would enable her to cease from being a permanent danger to the neighboring Italian colonies. . .

These disorders have prevented a real strengthening of the Central Government and of the authority of the officials in the outlying districts, and have thus had a disastrous effect on the relations with the bordering colonies, which are unable to find in Abyssinia their natural outlet, and are deprived of the possibility of establishing peaceful trade relations and of co-operating with Abyssinia to secure progress along the path of civilization. The instability caused by the Emperor's change of policy, the exclusion of important chiefs who had a following of long date in some regions, their substitution by men of the Scioa, officials of the Central Government, who have taken the place of the traditional chiefs without being able to assert the central power in the outlying districts, are all circumstances which have contributed to make the internal situation in Abyssinia yet more unstable than it was in the time of the Negus Menelik.

Abyssinia, still largely medieval in its structure, with a very primitive administration vitiated by the special mentality of those who direct affairs at the centre and at the circumference, with a judicial organization no guarantee of impartiality, and with a special treaty regime for foreigners which has never been able to work in a satisfactory manner, with a financial system still patriarchal in character drawing no practical distinction between the budget of the state and the personal resources of the Negus, with a population to whom the advantages of education are unknown and which preserve barbarous customs and a very backward mentality, with an economic system based on slavery, with the almost total lack—the one exception being the Djibuti-Addis Ababa railway—of rapid means of communication with its outlying provinces, more especially those of the southeast and southwest, in a state of chronic disorder, is an anachronism when compared with the conditions of civilization and progress which all the other parts of Africa have for a long time past enjoyed. . .

The chronic disorder reigning in Abyssinia has for years past compelled the bordering powers to protect their interests by treaties and conventions regarding their relations with Abyssinia. . .

## B. *Britain's Claim of Accomplishments*

(*Africa Challenge,* The Story of the British in Tropical Africa, New York, 1945, pp. 43-51. Reprinted by permission of British Information Services.)

When the British came to Africa they found that, in districts which were not infested with tsetse fly, cattle could be kept. But although the people were under-nourished, very few of them ate meat or drank milk, and cattle were never used for ploughing. Instead, a man measured his wealth in terms of livestock. When he wanted to get married (and he might have several wives) he would have to give cattle to his wife's parents in exchange for their daughter, and the more sought-after the bride the more cattle her parents would demand. And so the British had first of all to prove to the Africans that their cattle had values hitherto unknown, then to show them how to breed better livestock and how to keep the animals healthy. . .

In a little town in the Mende country of Sierra Leone the town crier went on his rounds recently crying, 'Come to the Book Learning Place.' He did not shout, 'Come to School,' because his object was to interest adults who, although they could neither read nor write, would certainly not want to go to school with their children.

A great deal of careful planning lay behind the announcement which was part of a drive, started by three missionaries, to end illiteracy in a district where few of the people could read. First of all the missionaries went to see the local chief for they knew that without his influence they could do very little. They showed him simple books and charts which they had prepared and explained that they would need the help of everyone who could read in order to teach those who could not. The chief was enthusiastic and promised his support.

Government officials provided a grant of money and also the loan of a mobile movie van, one of a number which tour the countryside giving film shows with commentaries showing the people the importance of keeping their homes and villages clean, how to fight the malaria-carrying mosquito and so on. A film show was given in the town and attended by a large number of people. After the performance the chief described the plan to teach them all to read. They were very pleased, for Africans are intensely eager for learning, and so when the chief sent his town crier out the following day a large crowd soon collected. The first arrivals were immediately given a lesson. As soon as they had mastered it and before they were given a second, they were asked to give the first lesson to another batch of arrivals. By the end of the day a hundred people had started learning and some of them were making very good progress.

This experiment shows the kind of work which is being done among the older people few of whom had the advantage, which their children now enjoy, of going to school. It also explains the good results which are being achieved by co-operation between Government, missionaries and leaders of the people. To gain the support of the leaders is often more than half the battle as the following story which comes from Nigeria will show. . .

Some forty years ago a verse was written to commemorate a great discovery:

> know this little thing
> A Myriad men will save.
> O Death, where is thy sting?
> Thy victory, O Grave?

The author was a British Army doctor in the Indian Medical Service who for years had preferred art and writing to medicine and who, but for his father's insistence would never have become a doctor at all. His name was Ronald Ross and the 'little thing' of his verse was the discovery which he himself had made that malaria, the greatest single cause of sickness and death in Africa and the other tropical and subtropical regions of the world, is carried by a mosquito.

For hundreds of years it had been believed that malaria was caused by a poison given off by the soil of marshy ground—hence its name 'mal-aria' or 'bad air.' But in the 1880's this theory was exploded by the findings of several scientists, British, French and Russian. Their discoveries paved the way for Ross who, in 1895, started the momentous four years which were to solve the malaria problem. They were years of constant toil and anxiety, for Ross had to combine research with his work as a doctor, but at the end he was able to prove, first, that out of all the different species of mosquito the Anopheles is the carrier of human malaria and, secondly, that the malaria parasite is sucked up by the Anopheles from the blood of a person already infected with the disease and transmitted to healthy people when the infected mosquito bites them.

Ross did most of his work in India but it was in Sierra Leone in West Africa that he completed and verified his discovery. From then until his death he spent his time in research into the best methods of destroying the mosquito, a pertinacious enemy which can breed and multiply in stagnant water, in streams, pools, water tanks, even in a footprint which has collected rain water or a water-filled tin. When Ross laid down his work another British pioneer, Malcolm Watson, took it up and to him we owe the invention of a mixture of mineral oils which will kill the Anopheles even in fast-running streams but is harmless to man and beast.

The present war has seen big strides in preventive measures, invented by British and American scientists, to meet the acute shortage of quinine which occurred when the Japanese captured the Netherlands East Indies. With these and other weapons the scourge of malaria is being fought.

Weapons have also been forged to fight other diseases which threaten the lives of African men and cattle. Two British pioneers, David Bruce and Charles Swynnerton, fought the dangerous tsetse fly in much the same way as Ross and Watson fought the mosquito. . .

## VII. The British Commonwealth and Empire

Greatest of all the empires both in area and population is the British. Its numerous parts are most diverse in political status, as well as size, civilization, and ethnic background. This heterogeneity seems to give support to the oft-quoted statement that the empire was constructed 'in a prolonged fit of absence of mind.' Most advanced in status are the dominions, whose rights of self-government and independent action are quite as complete as those of Great Britain herself. These self-governing dominions together make up the Commonwealth of Nations, an organization for voluntary co-operation in trade, defense, and other matters of common interest. Southern Rhodesia, although somewhat less self-governing than other dominions, is technically included in the Commonwealth. Newfoundland was formerly classed as a dominion, but when in need of financial assistance gave up this position for a commission government under the authority of the British Parliament. In 1948 New-foundland voted to join the Canadian federation. There are, therefore, nine members of the British Commonwealth at present—Britain, Canada, Australia, New Zealand, South Africa, India, Pakistan, Ceylon, and Southern Rhodesia.

Britain's empire proper is composed of protectorates, protected states, and colonies. Then, too, there are the former mandates of the League of Nations or 'trust territories' as they are called under the United Nations system. Some of these are supervised by Britain, while others are administered by various dominions.

## A. *Dominion Status*

The dominions listed above have separate legislative bodies, separate cabinets, and separate courts. And, as provided in the Statute of Westminster (1931), no law passed by the dominion parliaments may be held invalid because it conflicts with acts of the British Parliament. On the other hand, the British Parliament may not enact a law applicable to a dominion without the latter's consent, and changes in the succession and titles of the crown may not be altered without the consent of the dominions. The king is represented in the dominions by governors-general, but these officials possess no political power, serving only as symbols of authority in much the same way that the king himself does in Great Britain. The dominions have their own courts, but in some cases appeals are allowed to the British Judicial Committee of the Privy Council. This right of appeal may be terminated by the dominion parliaments, however, as Canada in 1933 cut off appeal in criminal cases. The general equality of the status of the dominions to that of the mother country was expressed in the report of the Inter-Imperial Relations Committee in 1926, from which an extract is given below.

(Report of the Inter-Imperial Relations Committee, *Imperial Conference, 1926, Summary of Proceedings,* Cmd. 2768.)

The Committee are of opinion that nothing would be gained by attempting to lay down a Constitution for the British Empire. Its widely scattered parts have very different characteristics, very different histories, and are at very different stages of evolution; while, considered as a whole, it defies classification and bears no real resemblance to any other political organization which now exists or has ever yet been tried.

There is, however, one most important element in it which, from a strictly constitutional point of view, has now, as regards all vital matters, reached its full development—we refer to the group of self-governing communities composed of Great Britain and the Dominions. Their position and mutual relation may be readily defined. *They are autonomous Communities within the British Empire, equal in status, in no way subordinate one to another in any aspect of their domestic or external affairs, though united by a common allegiance to the Crown, and freely associated as members of the British Commonwealth of Nations.*

A foreigner endeavouring to understand the true character of the British Empire by the aid of this formula alone would be tempted to think that it was devised rather to make mutual interference impossible than to make mutual co-operation easy.

Such a criticism, however, completely ignores the historic situation. The rapid evolution of the Oversea Dominions during the last fifty years has involved many complicated adjustments of old political machinery to changing conditions. The tendency towards equality of status was both right and inevitable. Geographical and other conditions made this impossible of attainment by the way of federation. The only alternative was by the way of autonomy; and along this road it has been steadily sought. Every self-governing member of the Empire is now the master of its destiny. In fact, if not always in form, it is subject to no compulsion whatever. . .

## B. *India—The 1947 Independence Act*

British authority in India was first asserted in 1600, when the East India Company went there with power to govern and engage in trade; it did not come to an end until the British Parliament in 1947 enacted a law extending dominion status to the states of Pakistan and India. During this period of three and a half centuries India developed into a prize possession and offered many advantages in trade and investments to Englishmen. Many improvements were made during this long interval in the Government of India. The East India Company's authority, which had been reduced in 1776 and 1784, was completely terminated in 1857, and increasingly provisions were made for Indian participation, particularly after World War I. In spite of the material benefits brought by the British, Indian nationalism developed to the point that the issue of independence became pressing, and many conferences with Indian leaders were held by Britain during the 1930's and 1940's. One of the main obstacles to independence was the antagonism between religious groups, especially the Hindus and Moslems. On 3 June 1947, Prime Minister Clement Attlee announced his intention to introduce a bill in the House of Commons for the purpose of extending dominion status. A few weeks later the following law was passed.

(*Indian Information*, vol. 21, No. 213, 1947, pp. 119-24.)

. . . Be it enacted by the King's most Excellent Majesty, by and with the advice and consent of the Lords Spiritual and Temporal, and Commons, in this present Parliament assembled, and by the authority of the same, as follows:—

1. *The new Dominions.*—(1) As from the fifteenth day of August, nineteen hundred and forty-seven, two independent Dominions shall be set up in India, to be known respectively as India and Pakistan.

(2) The said Dominions are hereafter in this Act referred to as 'the new Dominions,' and the said fifteenth day of August is hereafter in this Act referred to as 'the appointed day.'

2. *Territories of the new Dominions.*— (1) Subject to the provisions of subsections (3) and (4) of this section, the territories of India shall be the territories under the sovereignty of His Majesty

which, immediately before the appointed day, were included in British India except the territories which, under subsection (2) of this section, are to be the territories of Pakistan. . .

6. *Legislation for the new Dominions.* —(1) The Legislature of each of the new Dominions shall have full power to make laws for that Dominion, including laws having extra-territorial operation.

(2) No law and no provision of any law made by the Legislature of either of the new Dominions shall be void or inoperative on the ground that it is repugnant to the law of England, or to the provisions of this or any existing or future Act of Parliament of the United Kingdom, or to any order, rule or regulation made under any such Act, and the powers of the Legislature of each Dominion include the power to repeal or amend any such Act, order, rule, or regulation in so far as it is part of the law of the Dominion.

(3) The Governor-General of each of the new Dominions shall have full power to assent in His Majesty's name to any law of the Legislature of that Dominion and so much of any Act as relates to the disallowance of laws by His Majesty or the reservation of laws for the signification of His Majesty's pleasure thereon or the suspension of the operation of laws until the signification of His Majesty's pleasure thereon shall not apply to laws of the Legislature of either of the new Dominions.

(4) No Act of Parliament of the United Kingdom passed on or after the appointed day shall extend, or be deemed to extend, to either of the new Dominions as part of the law of that Dominion unless it is extended thereto by a law of the Legislature of the Dominion.

(5) No Order in Council made on or after the appointed day under any Act passed before the appointed day, and no order, rule, or other instrument made on or after the appointed day under any such Act by any United Kingdom Minister or other authority, shall extend, or be deemed to extend, to either of the new Dominions as part of the law of that Dominion.

(6) The power referred to in subsection (1) of this section extends to the making of laws limiting for the future the powers of the Legislature of the Dominion.

7. *Consequences of the setting up of the new Dominions.*—(1) As from the appointed day—

(a) His Majesty's Government in the United Kingdom have no responsibility as respects the government of any of the territories which, immediately before that day, were included in British India;

(b) the suzerainty of His Majesty over the Indian States lapses, and with it, all treaties and agreements in force at the date of the passing of this Act between His Majesty and the rulers of Indian States, all functions exercisable by His Majesty at that date with respect to Indian States, all obligations of His Majesty existing at that date towards Indian States or the rulers thereof, and all powers, rights, authority, or jurisdiction exercisable by His Majesty at that date in or in relation to Indian States by treaty, grant, usage, sufferance, or otherwise; and

(c) there lapse also any treaties or agreements in force at the date of the passing of this Act between His Majesty and any persons having authority in the tribal areas, any obligations of His Majesty existing at that date to any such persons or with respect to the tribal areas, and all powers, rights, authority, or jurisdiction exercisable at that date by His Majesty in or in relation to the tribal areas by treaty, grant, usage, sufferance, or otherwise; . . .

## C. British Colonial Aims

British aims, policies, and methods of government in the colonies are described below.

(*Towards Self-Government in the Colonies,* New York, 1947, pp. 5-9, 57. Reprinted by permission of British Information Services.)

In the Colonial Empire, which stretches over the tropics from the West Indies across Africa to the islands of the Pacific, live some 63 million people in more than 50 different territories. Only a small proportion of these people are of European stock; the rest are colored people, two-thirds of them Africans and most of the remaining third Asiatics. Though 43 million inhabitants of British Africa are all African, they spring from widely differing stocks, speak many different tongues, and are at all sorts of different levels of culture and intelligence. Nigeria alone numbers 20 millions. There the vast Moslem emirates of the north contrast sharply with the pagan kingdoms of the south, while there is little in common between tribes of nomads driving their cattle from one pasture to another and African officials, lawyers and doctors educated in the European tradition. In Nigeria, with its great population, there is an immense variety of tribes, cultures, languages, and religions. There is the primitive animist, the Mohammedan Emir, the Christian lawyer with a European education; and self-government, if it is to bring real freedom, must depend on a reconciliation of these varying interests which in its turn can come about only through economic and educational development. In Kenya, the problem is complicated by the existence of a white settler community and of an Indian community whose immigration was largely Government-sponsored and to whose efforts the opening up and

development of the country (by which the Africans have benefited) is largely due. Here self-government must strike a balance between the white settler, the Indian settler, and the different African communities.

In Jamaica, the original constitution gave wide powers, but until the nineteenth century these were confined to one section of the population, namely, the white settlers. Emancipation and education of the Negro population altered the whole situation. After many changes, there is now a constitution based on universal suffrage.

These are only three examples. But they show that there can be no hard and fast rule, no uniformity of method, no simultaneous flowering of self-government in such varied conditions. 'We have no cut and dried pattern,' said a former Secretary of State for the Colonies, Lord Cranborne, in 1942: 'We have adopted and adapted existing systems, changing them readily as the need arose and experience taught.' This flexibility and elasticity has long been a characteristic of British constitutional methods. . .

Until recent years, Britain was chiefly concerned with providing the Dependencies with justice and security and promoting their progress towards self-government. Since the 1920's, however, it has been increasingly recognized that political advance is unreal unless it is reinforced by social and economic development. As so many of the peoples of the Colonial Empire are backward or primitive, their chances as citizens of self-governing communities are slight unless they are relieved of the incubus of disease and poverty and are adequately educated, and unless the economic resources of their countries are properly organized and the communications necessary for a healthy trade and effective government are well developed. In every area Britain is faced in varying degrees with the gigantic problem of raising the standard of living of the people, and the challenge has been accepted. It is not within the scope of this pamphlet to describe the schemes for social and economic improvement which are being put into practice nor the plans which are being made for the future, but they must not be forgotten.

In spite of the variety of the British Dependencies, some general classifications can be made. Most of the older Dependencies are known as Colonies and are directly governed under the system known as Crown Colony Government—a system capable of expansion all the way up to complete self-government. Many of the Dependencies, however, particularly in Africa, are described as Protectorates; and still others, again, are Protected States. In both these types central government operates through a system of indirect rule; that is to say, it governs through the existing native administrations and aims at developing and expanding these existing systems so that the native peoples acquire increasing responsibility. Malta and Jamaica are examples of Crown Colonies; Uganda and Nyasaland are examples of Protectorates. In a number of areas the original trading settlement became a Colony while the rest of the territory is a Protectorate; for example, the Gold Coast includes a Colony and a Protectorate. In such territories the aim is to develop the political systems in both areas towards a finally integrated form of self-government.

There are certain legal differences in the status of Colonies and Protectorates. Thus while a Colony is British territory under the Crown, in a Protectorate the Crown exercises authority without annexing the territory. In Protected States authority is vested in the sovereign of each State, and not in the Crown which derives its functions from treaty agreements conferring certain powers and duties upon it. For administrative purposes, however, the general framework is very similar.

The common denominator of all these Dependencies is the Governor, appointed by the Secretary of State for the Colonies in London, and directly responsible to him. The Secretary of State, in his turn, is responsible to the British public through its elected representatives in Parliament. The Governor in some cases rules unassisted; or he may have an Executive Council only; or he may have both an Executive and a Legislative Council; and the legislative body may consist of one or two Houses. These are the broad variations. Development of responsible government is being brought about by extending the vote, by increasing the number of elected members in the Legislature and finally by admitting to the executive body elected members drawn from the Legislature.

The various stages through which the authority of the people can develop are sometimes likened to the different rungs of a ladder. Between the top and the bottom there is scope for many intermediate steps, but their broad stages are these:

On the lowest rung stand those Dependencies which are administered by a Governor alone whose authority is supreme, subject to the approval of the Secretary of State. This is an exceptional form of government.

Next come the Dependencies where the Governor, exercising all legislative and executive functions, is assisted by a nominated council composed of the chief European officers—the Colonial Secretary, the Attorney-General, the Treasurer—and certain other officials or members of the public. In these Dependencies, although the Governor can veto the demands of the members of his council, they are empowered to appeal to the Secretary of State if they so desire.

A step higher and we can see the makings of a regular constitution. Here the Governor with his nominated Executive Council, which he is required to consult on all save the most urgent matters, has the additional assistance of a Legislative Council, a law-making, tax-raising body. The Legislative Council at first consists entirely of nominated official members, but as soon as the people are politically ready one or more of them is appointed to serve on it, and the Council is later expanded to include elected members. Gradually the elected element is increased until the elected members are in a majority, first over the nominated unofficial members, and then over the nominated unofficial and the official members combined.

Another step and we arrive at representative government. This often takes the form of a Legislative Assembly, entirely elected somewhat on the lines of the British House of Commons, and a nominated Legislative Council as an Upper House. These two bodies together form the Legislature. The Executive Council is still appointed by the Crown on the advice of the Governor, but the latter begins to nominate to it certain members of the Assembly. At this stage the elected representatives of the people, who form the Lower House, control taxation and have at the least a very large voice in all legislative and executive matters. In some cases, such as the Colonies of Bermuda, the Bahamas and Barbados, the Legislature, comprising the nominated Legislative Council and the elected House of Assembly, has the final voice in matters of legislation and taxation, although the Governor possesses the power of veto, which has not in fact been used in those Colonies for very many

years. Although, therefore, it may be said that in such Colonies the ultimate responsibility rests with the Governor, and through him with the Secretary of State, he does not in fact possess the ultimate power which normally accompanies responsibility, since in the vital fields of legislation and finance he has in the last resort only a negative voice.

At the top of the ladder, but below the status of a Dominion, are the Dependencies that have achieved responsible government. This means that the Executive Council is transformed into a Cabinet or Board of Ministers representing the majority party of a fully developed parliament, and guides and advises the Governor on practically every aspect of internal policy affecting the territory. This is the essential feature of parliamentary democracy as practised in Britain. Responsibility, formerly vested in the Governor, is now assumed by the Ministers who are directly answerable to the people.

Southern Rhodesia has had responsible government since 1923, and is therefore not strictly part of the Colonial Empire. It has its own Cabinet of Ministers who are responsible to a freely elected legislature. Britain still retains control over external affairs and to some extent over legislation affecting the large native population. Ceylon has had a form of responsible government since 1931, and in 1946 acquired virtually complete control over her own internal affairs. Malta, which was promised responsible government as soon as possible after the war, is at present discussing with the British Government the details of her new constitution. Jamaica now has a bicameral legislature and five of the ten members of the Executive Council are elected by the House of Assembly, itself elected by universal franchise. In several of the other West Indian Dependencies, in East and West Africa, in Fiji, and in the Seychelles there were advances during the war, and many others have taken place since the war ended. . .

'A uniform rate of progress in all Colonies is impossible. They contain a large variety of peoples at various stages of development, so that there is no magic formula by which they can be brought in regular procession to self-government,' said Viscount Hall, when Secretary of State for the Colonies in June, 1946. 'The keystone of our colonial policy for improving the wealth and well-being of our Colonial peoples,' he continued, 'is, in my view, co-ordination; and steady progress along several lines of development, all of which interact one on the other, with the administration at the Colonial Office and the Colonial Governments, each making their contribution in research, planning, men, money and materials. Without great improvement in basic economic conditions, few of the Colonies can be expected to show substantial social or political progress. Improved social services can make a contribution to greater efficiency and productivity, and in the Colonies the field of advance which will be opened up by better education is immense. Even political development of itself may react upon the social and economic welfare of a whole community, by releasing potentialities for self-reliance and self-help. . . If we can succeed, by patient industry, in providing the Colonies with more liberty, higher standards of health and better education, and with larger opportunities for creating their own wealth, then we shall have carried out our trust, and the expanding prosperity and happiness of the 60 million of our Colonial people will be assured.' . . .

## VIII. The Trusteeship System

The trusteeship system of the United Nations is based upon the same principle as that which underlay the mandate system. There are differences of detail between the two, however, and chief among them are the following:

(1) There has been some amendment of the list of areas to which the new system applies (see Article 77 of Charter);

(2) The A, B, and C types of areas used under the mandate system have given way to the idea of more individualized agreements (Article 81);

(3) Strategic areas may have special treatment under the trusteeship plan (Article 83);

(4) The Trusteeship Council is not composed in the same way as was the Mandates Commission (Article 86);

(5) The General Assembly of the United Nations is the final responsible authority (except in the case of strategic areas) instead of the Council, as under the League of Nations (Article 87);

(6) The Charter makes it possible, at times indicated by the administering authority, to send representatives into the trust territories, whereas there was no such provision in the mandate system (Article 87-c).

Members of the United Nations are not required to convert their present dependencies into trust territories, but they may do so if they wish. For areas not so converted the members agree under Articles 73 and 74 to respect a list of principles, designed to promote the welfare of the native peoples. The provisions of the Charter relating to non-self-governing dependencies and to the trusteeship system, contained in Articles 73-91, may be found in Chapter 3 of this book.

## A. *The Mandate or Trusteeship Principle*

The essence of the mandate or trusteeship principle was well stated in Article 22 of the Covenant of the League of Nations, as follows:

> To those colonies and territories which as a consequence of the late war have ceased to be under the sovereignty of the States which formerly governed them and which are inhabited by peoples not yet able to stand by themselves under the strenuous conditions of the modern world there should be applied the principle that the well-being and development of such peoples form a sacred trust of civilization and that securities for the performance of this trust should be embodied in this Covenant. The best method of giving practical effect to this principle is that the tutelage of such peoples should be entrusted to advanced nations who, by reason of their resources, their experience or their geographical position, can best undertake this responsibility, and who are willing to accept it, and that this tutelage should be exercised by them as mandatories on behalf of the League. . .

The development of this principle is described in the extract below.

(*The Mandate System*, Geneva, 1945, League of Nations Publications VI.A., pp. 7-17.)

Though the mandates system was an innovation in the fields of international law and of colonial policy and though it owed its creation mainly to the need for disposing of a pressing political problem, it is also the fact that, underlying this institution, are ideas which had for a long time been taking shape in the minds of idealists, statesmen and experts in colonial matters and in international law and which had been disseminated by philanthropic and progressive circles in different countries. Some of these ideas had in fact already found expression, though in somewhat indefinite form, in international conventions.

At the outset of the period of modern colonisation (in the 16th and 17th centuries), colonisers concerned themselves almost solely with the exploitation of the conquered areas for their own benefit and that of the mother-country. Though sometimes religious motives were alleged, nothing was as a rule undertaken in this direction beyond attempts to effect a rapid and superficial conversion of the natives, and if these failed the latter were very often exposed to the worst kind of treatment or even to extermination. International law, which began to develop at this period, was held to apply only as between Christian States and therefore afforded no protection whatsoever to peoples dwelling outside the sphere of European civilisation. Neither as individuals nor as communities could the natives possess any rights, but their conquerors acquired rights over them. Thus they were entirely dependent upon the humanitarian sentiments of the colonisers and these as a rule proved a very dubious safeguard. The well-being or material and moral needs of the natives were scarcely considered.

Gradually, however, humanitarian, political or economic considerations brought about a reaction against this state of affairs. A keener sense of moral responsibility for the welfare of native races began to develop among colonisers. Towards the end of the 18th century, and still more at the beginning of the 19th, theologians, philosophers and politicians of advanced ideas raised their voices against abuses such as slavery and advocated fairer treatment for the native inhabitants of colonial territories. At the same time a truer appreciation of the economic potentialities of such territories brought about a realisation that a policy of good treatment of the natives could not be otherwise than beneficial to the interests of the colonizers. The importance, from the point of view of the rational development of colonies, of having at hand a supply of native labour in good physical and moral condition was realised. During the French Revolution, the Law of the 16th Pluviose of the Year II abolished Negro slavery in the French colonies. In England and elsewhere, philanthropic societies were founded with a view to the suppression of the slave trade and the protection of native populations. This movement led —from about 1830 onwards—to a series of legislative measures directed against the slave trade. The status of the native began to improve; he was no longer a mere chattel in law and a possession to be exploited. Similarly, colonial practice began to be more scrupulous in its attitude towards native political entities; it became more and more usual to conclude treaties or agreements with the chiefs of tribes or of indigenous States, and, in the matter of terminology, the appearance at this period of various forms of 'protectorate' was significant.

At the period when the European Powers were all engaged in staking out claims in Central Africa (that is to say, from about 1880 onwards), humanitarian ideas were already in vogue. Alongside the principal aims pursued by this policy of colonial expansion, considerations of this kind were definitely observable in two international conventions concluded towards the end of the century. In these two conventions we already find in embryo some of the principles which, a generation later, were more precisely and effectively enunciated in the mandates system. These principles embraced not only those relating to the welfare of the natives, but also the principle of economic equality between all members of the international community.

According to its preamble, the *General Act of the Conference of Berlin,* signed on *February 26th,* 1885, pursued the following aims—which are incidentally enumerated in a significant order: (1) 'in a spirit of good and mutual accord, to regulate the conditions most favourable to the development of trade and civilisation in certain regions of Africa, and to assure to all nations the advantages of free navigation on the two chief rivers of Africa flowing into the Atlantic Ocean'; (2) 'to obviate the misunderstanding and disputes which might in future arise from new acts of occupation on the coast of Africa'; and, finally, (3) the *'furthering'* of *'the moral and material well-being of the native populations'* . . .

Meanwhile, colonial doctrine became more and more imbued with the idea of *tutelage* and trusteeship—a moral responsibility towards mankind for the treatment of the natives. Accordingly it was recognised, in theory and occasionally in practice, that these new principles implied a potential right on the part of native communities or colonial possessions to acquire autonomy or independence—a right which would become effective when they reached a sufficient degree of maturity.

Thus, in 1898, the United States recognised the right of Cuba to her independence and, after four years of temporary occupation, they withdrew their forces from the island. In 1899, the American Senate announced the intention of the United States to establish in the Philippines 'a government suitable to the wants and conditions of the inhabitants of the said islands and to prepare them for local self-government. . .' The President of the United States, in a message dated December 3rd, 1900, described the American possession of the Philippines as an 'unsought trust which should be unselfishly discharged'; he referred to the Filipinos as 'the wards of the nation' and to the task of the United States as 'an obligation as guardian' . . .

Furthermore, the mandatory idea made its appearance in the international sphere in a number of isolated cases in which the Powers entrusted one of their members with a specific task—sometimes of limited duration. Thus, in 1815, Great Britain took over the protection of the Ionian Islands, under a sort of mandate conferred upon her by Russia, Prussia and Austria at the Conference of Paris. In 1860, France intervened in Lebanon in order to protect the Christian population of that country (the Maronites), in virtue of a mandate from the Great Powers. A somewhat peculiar system was provided for in the case of Crete by the 'Provisional Regulations' adopted on December 18th, 1897: there was to be autonomy under the personal suzerainty of the Sultan of Turkey, the executive power was to be entrusted to a provisional Governor 'in virtue of a delegation from the Great Powers'; this Governor was to transmit every quarter to the representatives of the Great Powers in Constantinople a report on the administration of the island. At the time of the first crisis in connection with Morocco, the United States suggested that France and Spain should be given a mandate to supply officers for the instruction and command of the Moroccan forces and to maintain equality of com-

mercial treatment and the principle of the Open Door. The General Act of the Conference of Algeciras, signed on April 7th, 1906, adopted this solution as far as the organisation of the police is concerned, adding a clause to the effect that an inspectorate-general of the police should be established and entrusted to a senior officer of the Swiss Army. Lastly, mention should be made of the 'mandates' of a special kind conferred by the British Government on certain of the Dominions for the administration of various territories inhabited by backward races. In 1887, Australia was entrusted by the British Crown with the administration of the Protectorate of British New Guinea (known later as the Papua Territory). Similarly, the South Africa Act of September 20th, 1909 (Article 151), provided for the transfer to the Union of South Africa of the administration of certain adjoining territories, subject to a series of provisions drawn up in the interests of the natives. A schedule annexed to this Act contains clauses regarding the land system, traffic in intoxicating liquor, native customs, the employment of the revenue of the territory, etc.

It will thus be seen that the notions of *tutelage*, of *trusteeship*, and even of a *mandate* in respect of the native populations were not unknown prior to 1919. Equality of conditions in the economic sphere had also already been recognised in principle as regards certain parts of Africa. The main elements, therefore, of the mandates system existed not only in theory, but had even to a limited extent been put into practice in a few cases. . .

On taking up the question of the fate of the German colonies and of the territories of the Ottoman Empire inhabited by non-Turkish populations, the Peace Conference, in 1919, found itself confronted with a peculiarly complex problem. A medley of factors of different kinds had to be taken into account: the actual situation resulting from the war, the claims of Allied countries and the agreements reached between them, the interests of the inhabitants of the territories in question, the trends of public opinion, the principles formulated by the Governments which were to serve as criteria for the general peace settlement and, finally, the differing degrees of civilisation which had been attained by the peoples inhabiting these territories and which rendered a uniform solution impossible.

The German colonies had been occupied during the war by the forces of the Allied countries and some of the latter, with the support of their public opinion, had manifested an intention to annex one or other of the colonies in question (in particular those situated in the Pacific), adducing as a reason either the sacrifices made during the war, or motives of national security, or again humanitarian considerations. Certain official circles were, however, less inclined to favour an extension of the national colonial domain. There was, however, general agreement that the German colonies could not be allowed to revert to their former sovereignty. With regard to those territories of the former Ottoman Empire the fate of which had to be settled, they too had been occupied by the Allied armies. Subject to certain reservations and without any precise definition of frontiers, negotiations conducted in 1915 between British representatives and the Emir of Mecca had envisaged the independence of the Arab countries. On the other hand, a Franco-British agreement concluded in May 1916 had contemplated a special regime for Palestine and the Holy Places. Finally, in the Balfour Declaration of November 2nd, 1917, the British Government had undertaken to 'view with favour the establishment in Palestine of a national home for the Jewish people,' without prejudice to the 'civil and religious rights of existing non-Jewish communities in Palestine.' This Declaration had been approved by the American, French and Italian Governments.

The principle that the peace settlement should not be accompanied by any annexation and that it should be based on the right of nations to self-determination had been proclaimed towards the end of the war by the leaders of the Russian Revolution and also found expression in the declarations of Allied statesmen. The principle of 'non-annexation,' however, envisaged only the negative aspect of the problem, while the principle of self-determination could scarcely be applied automatically to peoples which had not yet attained an adequate degree of political maturity, and still less to populations devoid of any real national consciousness. In respect of such peoples, therefore, these principles had to be adapted to meet different requirements. . .

In the plan for a League of Nations published by General Smuts in December 1918, on the eve of the Conference of Peace, we find for the first time the broad outlines of an international mandates system. The author described in twenty-one points, each accompanied by a brief commentary, the main characteristics of what, in his view, should be the future international organisation. The first nine points related to the fate of countries which had belonged to the European or Near-Eastern Empires which had collapsed. In respect of these territories, General Smuts proposed that the League should be regarded as 'the reversionary in the most general sense and as clothed with the right of ultimate disposal in accordance with the fundamental principles. Reversion to the League of Nations should be substituted for any policy of national annexation.' The government of each of these countries should be established in accordance with the principle of self-determination. Nevertheless, the conditions prevailing in these territories varied considerably from one country to another and for some of them —General Smuts continues—'it will probably be found that they are as yet deficient in the qualities of Statehood and that, whereas they are perhaps capable of internal autonomy, they will in one degree or another require the guiding hand of some external authority to steady their administration. . .'

One question, however, at once arises: 'How is the League to provide this authority or administration? It will itself be a conference consisting of representatives of States. Any authority or administration directly exercised by it will therefore be of a joint international character.' The author goes on to indicate *the weak points of an international administration:* 'Now, joint international administration, in so far as it has been applied to territories or peoples, has been wanting wherever it has been tried. It has worked fairly well in international business arrangements of a limited scope, such as postal arrangements, the Danube Commission and similar cases. But in those few cases where it has been tried in respect of peoples or territories it has not been a success. The administering personnel taken from different nations do not work smoothly or loyally together; the inhabitants of the territory administered are either confused or, if they are sufficiently developed, make use of these differences by playing one set of nationals off against the other. In any case the result is paralysis tempered by intrigue. It may be safely asserted that, if the League of Nations attempts too soon to administer any people or territory directly through an international personnel it will run a very serious risk of discrediting itself. . . It will have to train its officials taken from various nationalities to work loyally together irrespective of their national interests; it will have to do these and many other things before it could successfully undertake a task requiring fundamental unity of aims, methods and spirit such as the administration of an undeveloped or partly developed people. . . The only successful administration of undeveloped or subject peoples has been carried on by States with long experience for the purpose and staffs whose training and singleness of mind fit them for so difficult and special a task. . . That is to say, where an autonomous people or territory requires a measure of administrative assistance, advice or control, the League should as a rule meet the case not by direct appointment of international officials but by nominating a particular State to act for and on behalf of it in the matter, so that, subject to the supervision and ultimate control of the League, the appointment of the necessary officials and the carrying on of the necessary administration should be done by this mandatory State.'

Nevertheless—General Smuts points out —'the delegation of certain powers to the mandatory State must not be looked upon as in any way impairing the ultimate authority and control of the League. . . For this purpose it is important that, in each such case of mandate, the League should issue a special Act or Charter clearly setting forth the policy which the mandatory will have to follow in that territory. . .'

## B. *Trusteeship Agreements*

The trusteeship system was set up by the United Nations General Assembly at the second half of its first session. Eight trusteeship agreements were approved after considerable debate on the subjects of monopolies, 'integral part,' military activities and 'states directly concerned.' A Trusteeship Council of ten members was selected. It was expected that agreements for other areas would be submitted later. The extract below outlines the trusteeship system and discusses problems presented in the formulation of the trusteeship agreements.

(E. H. Armstrong and W. I. Caro, 'The Inauguration of the Trusteeship System of the United Nations,' *Department of State Bulletin*, vol. XVI, No. 403, 1947, pp. 511-12, 516-20.)

The international trusteeship system established by the Charter of the United Nations at the San Francisco Conference of 1945 provides for the administration and supervision of such territories as may be placed thereunder by subsequent individual agreements.

## OBJECTIVES

Article 76 of the Charter states that the basic objectives of the trusteeship system shall be:

(a) the furtherance of international peace and security;

(b) the promotion of the political, economic, social, and educational advancement of the inhabitants of the trust territories, and their progressive development towards self-government or independence;

(c) the encouragement of respect for human rights and for fundamental freedoms for all without distinction as to race, sex, language, or religion; and

(d) the ensuring of equal treatment in social, economic, and commercial matters for all members of the United Nations, and also equal treatment for the latter in the administration of justice.

The Charter further provides (article 77) that the trusteeship system should apply to such territories in the following three categories as might be placed thereunder by means of trusteeship agreements:

'(a) territories now held under mandate;

'(b) territories which may be detached from enemy states as a result of the Second World War; and

'(c) territories voluntarily placed under the system by states responsible for their administration. . .'

The Trusteeship Council, operating under the authority of the General Assembly, is established to assist in carrying out the functions of the United Nations with regard to trusteeship agreements for all non-strategic areas (articles 85, 86). The Trusteeship Council is to consist of:

(a) those members administering trust territories;

(b) such of the permanent members of the Security Council as are not administering trust territories; and

(c) as many other members elected for three-year terms by the General Assembly as may be necessary to ensure that the total number of members of the Trusteeship Council should be equally divided between those which administer trust territories and those which do not.

The Trusteeship Council, under the authority of the General Assembly, may (article 87):

(a) consider reports submitted by the administering authority;

(b) accept and examine petitions;

(c) provide for periodic visits to the respective trust territories; and

(d) take these and other actions in conformity with the terms of the trusteeship agreements. . .

The General Assembly referred the eight draft trusteeship agreements which it received to its Fourth Committee, which in turn appointed a sub-committee of 17 member nations to consider the agreements and the 229 proposed amendments. The consideration of the trusteeship proposals involved questions both of the content of the agreements themselves and of the procedure by which the agreements were to be drawn up and approved.

## MONOPOLIES

The initial trusteeship drafts put forward by France, the United Kingdom, and Belgium for the 'B' mandates in Africa authorized the administering authority to establish private monopolies under conditions of proper public control when this was in the interests of the economic advancement of the inhabitants of the trust territory. Under the provisions of the mandates it was possible for the Mandatory Powers to organize essential public works and services and to create monopolies of a purely fiscal character. There was no general authority, however, to create private monopolies. The United States Government did not challenge the premise that, in certain special circumstances, a private monopoly could be in the interests of the economic advancement of the inhabitants of the territory. However, the United States took the position that a definitive step such as the granting of a private monopoly, involving considerations both as to its possible effect on the inhabitants of the territory and on the equal-treatment provisions of the Charter, should be open to consideration by the Trusteeship Council or an appropriate United Nations agency at a stage where the recommendations of such a body might be effective. At the General Assembly in New York, the United States Delegation proposed a specific amendment to the trusteeship agreements in question which incorporated this idea.

Although this United States proposal was defeated in the Trusteeship Subcom-

mittee, the detailed discussion of the question resulted in significant alterations in the original monopoly clauses proposed by the Mandatory Powers and in interpretative declarations by these powers. The Delegations of the United Kingdom and Belgium included in the trusteeship agreements a provision to ensure that any private monopoly contracts would be granted without discrimination on grounds of nationality against members of the United Nations or their nationals. The French Delegation stated that under French law private monopolies were not permitted at all in the trust territories which it would administer. Moreover, the United Kingdom and Belgian Delegations made the following declarations which form a part of the rapporteur's report to the General Assembly on the trusteeship agreements:

'(a) The Governments of Belgium and the United Kingdom have no intention of using the grant of private monopolies in Trust Territories as a normal instrument of policy;

'(b) Such private monopolies would be granted only when this was essential in order to enable a particular type of desirable economic development to be undertaken in the interest of the inhabitants;

'(c) In those special cases where such private monopolies were granted they would be granted for limited periods, and would be promptly reported to the Trusteeship Council.'

### 'INTEGRAL PART'

With the exception of the draft trusteeship agreements for Tanganyïka and New Guinea, all the draft agreements submitted to the General Assembly for approval contained a provision empowering the administering authority to administer the trust territory as an 'integral part' of its territory. The New Guinea draft used the expression 'as if it were an integral part.' The Tanganyika draft had no such provision. It was pointed out by the states submitting the draft trusteeship agreements that the phrase 'integral part' was contained in the mandate agreements and that its continuance in the trusteeship agreements would have no new significance. They further stated that the phrase carried no implication of sovereignty and that it was proposed solely for administrative convenience. Nevertheless, certain delegations regarded the use of the expression 'integral part' as contrary to the spirit of the trusteeship system and felt that it revealed 'annexationist tendencies.' The Soviet Union and India proposed the deletion of the phrase from each of the trusteeship agreements in which it was used. The Trusteeship Subcommittee recommended to New Zealand, whose draft for Western Samoa was considered first, that the phrase be deleted. Similar recommendations were made by Committee 4 with regard to the other trusteeship drafts which used the phrase. The New Zealand Government accepted the recommendation, but the other Mandatory Powers found themselves unable to agree to delete the phrase from their drafts and made to the Fourth Committee formal statements of the reasons underlying their refusal. Thus, in the eight agreements finally approved by the General Assembly the phrase 'integral part' appears in all of the agreements except those for Tanganyika and Western Samoa.

The Soviet Delegation carried its opposition to the phrase 'integral part' to the floor of the General Assembly. Before the final vote of the General Assembly approving the terms of trusteeship, the Soviet Delegation proposed a resolution advocating rejection of the trusteeship drafts partly on the grounds that they still contained the phrase 'integral part.' This resolution was rejected by a vote of 34 to 6 with 11 abstentions. . .

## MILITARY ESTABLISHMENTS

The powers of administering authorities with respect to the establishment of bases and the use of armed forces in trust territories emerged as one of the most serious issues confronting the General Assembly in its consideration of the eight draft trusteeship agreements.

All eight of the draft trusteeship agreements contained similar military clauses entitling the administering authority to establish bases and to station armed forces in the trust territory. The debate in the General Assembly was, therefore, a general one, based on Soviet, Indian, and Chinese amendments proposed to article X of the New Zealand agreement, article 5 (c) of the three British agreements, article 5 of the Belgian agreement, and article 4 (b) of the French agreements.

The position taken by these delegations opposing the military clauses was that article 84 of the Charter does not empower the administering authority, in the interest of international peace and security, to establish military bases or station armed forces in a trust territory. Such powers, it was contended, would be an extension of article 84 under which administering authorities were restricted to the use of 'volunteer forces, facilities, and assistance,' and further restricted by their obligations toward the Security Council. They asserted that the use of volunteer forces, facilities, and assistance would be possible only with the agreement of the Security Council. If the administering authority found it necessary to establish bases and employ forces in a trust territory the territory would, thereby, become a strategic area; its administration and the approval of the trusteeship agreement would therefore fall within the jurisdiction of the Security Council under articles 82 and 83 of the Charter. It was also contended that obligations undertaken toward the Security

Council would have to be governed by article 43 of the Charter and that no bases could be established in trust territories, or troops employed, until the special agreements, negotiated on the initiative of the Security Council under article 43, had been concluded. In this connection it was pointed out that the terms of the mandates did not permit fortification of the mandated territories.

The Mandatory Powers, supported by the United States, Canada, the Netherlands, and Uruguay, held that the Soviet, Indian, and Chinese proposed amendments were unacceptable and that article 84 made it not only the right but the duty of an administering authority to ensure that the trust territory play its part in the maintenance of international peace and security. This duty, it was pointed out, was inserted in the Charter deliberately for the benefit of the inhabitants of the trust territories. They should not, in the future, be left unprotected as they had been under the mandates system and must be encouraged to play their part in the system of international peace and security. Among the means by which this could be accomplished might be the use of volunteer forces, facilities, and assistance from the trust territories, in accordance with articles 84 and 43 of the Charter. However, the administering authority would still have the specific duty to ensure the territory's participation in the maintenance of international peace and security, notwithstanding any delay in the conclusion of the special agreements contemplated in article 43. Since the administering authority has this specific obligation, it has a corresponding right to the means of discharging it. The Mandatory Powers were unanimous in their view that the proposed military clauses were consistent with the Charter and that the establishment of military bases would have to be left to the discretion of the administering authority.

After lengthy debate of the military clauses of the trusteeship agreements, both the Trusteeship Subcommittee and Committee 4 sustained the original language of the draft trusteeship proposals. . .

## THE PROCEDURAL ISSUE: 'STATES DIRECTLY CONCERNED'

The language of article 79 of the Charter led to the principal procedural issue involved in drawing up and approving the trusteeship agreements. Article 79 provides, in part, that 'The terms of trusteeship for each territory to be placed under the trusteeship system . . . shall be agreed upon by the states directly concerned, including the mandatory power in the case of territories held under mandate by a Member of the United Nations. . .' The importance of the 'states directly concerned' in this procedural conception is readily apparent. Although this matter was clearly of less importance with respect to the operation of the trusteeship system than the terms of the trusteeship agreements themselves, it was an important hurdle which had to be surmounted if chapters XII and XIII of the Charter were to be given effect and the Trusteeship Council brought into operation. . .

In the subcommittee's consideration of the draft trusteeship agreements the question of 'states directly concerned' was raised owing to the fact that the preambles of the draft agreements stated that the provisions of article 79 had been complied with. Certain delegations, including principally the Soviet Delegation, contended that the Charter provisions had not been fulfilled, and called for an attempt to define the 'states directly concerned.' At the request of the Chairman of the subcommittee the Delegates from the Soviet Union and the United States undertook consultations in an attempt to find an agreed solution to the problem. Following the announcement that these consultations had been unsuccessful the subcommittee, on the initiative of the United States Delegation, approved the following proposal regarding 'states directly concerned':

'Approval of any terms of Trusteeship by this session of the General Assembly should be on the following understanding with respect to 'states directly concerned':

'All Members of the United Nations have had an opportunity to present their views with reference to the terms of Trusteeship now proposed to the General Assembly for approval. There has, however, been no specification by the General Assembly of 'states directly concerned' in relation to the proposed Trust Territories. Accordingly, the General Assembly in approving the terms of Trusteeship does not prejudge the question of what states are or are not 'directly concerned' within the meaning of article 79. It recognizes that no state has waived or prejudiced its right hereafter to claim to be such a 'state directly concerned' in relation to approval of subsequently proposed Trusteeship agreements and any alteration or amendment of those now approved, and that the procedure to be followed in the future with reference to such matters may be subject to later determination.

This statement was approved by an overwhelming majority of the full Trusteeship Committee of the General Assembly and constitutes, therefore, the understanding on which the Assembly approved the eight trusteeship agreements. . .

The territories thus placed under the trusteeship system, with their administering authorities, are as follows:

| TRUST TERRITORY | ADMINISTERING AUTHORITY |
|---|---|
| Cameroons (British) | United Kingdom |
| Cameroons (French) | France |
| New Guinea | Australia |
| Ruanda-Urundi | Belgium |
| Tanganyika | United Kingdom |
| Togoland (British) | United Kingdom |
| Togoland (French) | France |
| Western Samoa | New Zealand |

## C. United States Trusteeship for the Pacific Islands

Following is the text of the trusteeship agreement for the former Japanese-mandated islands, as submitted to the Security Council of the United Nations.

(Background Summary, Non-Self Governing Territories and the Trusteeship System, Office of Public Affairs, Department of State, 11 February 1947.)

### PREAMBLE

WHEREAS Article 75 of the Charter of the United Nations provides for the establishment of an international trusteeship system for the administration and supervision of such territories as may be placed thereunder by subsequent agreements; and

WHEREAS under Article 77 of the said Charter the trusteeship system may be applied to territories now held under mandate; and

WHEREAS on December 17, 1920, the Council of the League of Nations confirmed a mandate for the former German islands north of the equator to Japan, to be administered in accordance with Article 22 of the Covenant of the League of Nations; and

WHEREAS Japan, as a result of the Second World War, has ceased to exercise any authority in these islands;

Now, THEREFORE, the Security Council of the United Nations, having satisfied itself that the relevant articles of the Charter have been complied with, hereby resolves to approve the following terms of trusteeship for the Pacific Islands formerly under mandate to Japan.

## ARTICLE 1

The Territory of the Pacific Islands, consisting of the islands formerly held by Japan under mandate in accordance with Article 22 of the Covenant of the League of Nations, is hereby designated as a strategic area and placed under the trusteeship system established in the Charter of the United Nations. The Territory of the Pacific Islands is hereinafter referred to as the trust territory.

## ARTICLE 2

The United States of America is designated as the administering authority of the trust territory.

## ARTICLE 3

The administering authority shall have full powers of administration, legislation, and jurisdiction over the territory subject to the provisions of this agreement as an integral part of the United States, and may apply to the trust territory, subject to any modifications which the administering authority may consider desirable, such of the laws of the United States as it may deem appropriate to local conditions and requirements.

## ARTICLE 4

The administering authority, in discharging the obligations of trusteeship in the trust territory, shall act in accordance with the Charter of the United Nations, and the provisions of this agreement, and shall, as specified in Article 83 (2) of the Charter, apply the objectives of the international trusteeship system, as set forth in Article 76 of the Charter, to the people of the trust territory.

## ARTICLE 5

In discharging its obligations under Article 76 (a) and Article 84, of the Charter, the administering authority shall ensure that the trust territory shall play its part, in accordance with the Charter of the United Nations, in the maintenance of international peace and security. To this end the administering authority shall be entitled:

(1) to establish naval, military and air bases and to erect fortifications in the trust territory;

(2) to station and employ armed forces in the territory; and

(3) to make use of volunteer forces, facilities and assistance from the trust territory in carrying out the obligations towards the Security Council undertaken in this regard by the administering authority, as well as for the local defense and the maintenance of law and order within the trust territory.

## ARTICLE 6

In discharging its obligations under Article 76 (b) of the Charter, the administering authority shall:

(1) foster the development of such political institutions as are suited to the trust territory and shall promote the development of the inhabitants of the trust territory toward self-government, and to this end shall give to the inhabitants of the trust territory a progressively increasing share in the administrative services in the territory; shall develop their participation in local government; shall give due recognition to the customs of the inhabitants in providing a system of law for the territory; and shall take other appropriate measures toward these ends;

(2) promote the economic advancement and self-sufficiency of the inhabitants and to this end shall regulate the use of natural resources; encourage the development of fisheries, agriculture, and indus-

tries; protect the inhabitants against the loss of their lands and resources; and improve the means of transportation and communication;

(3) promote the social advancement of the inhabitants, and to this end shall protect the rights and fundamental freedoms of all elements of the population without

to pursue higher education, including training on the professional level.

ARTICLE 7

In discharging its obligations under Article 76 (c), of the Charter, the administering authority, subject only to the requirements of public order and security,

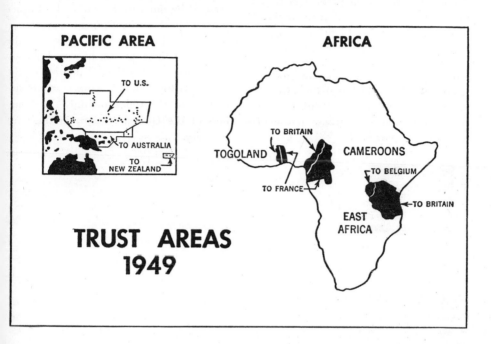

discrimination; protect the health of the inhabitants; control the traffic in arms and ammunition, opium and other dangerous drugs, and alcohol and other spiritous beverages; and institute such other regulations as may be necessary to protect the inhabitants against social abuses; and

(4) promote the educational advancement of the inhabitants, and to this end shall take steps toward the establishment of a general system of elementary education; facilitate the vocational and cultural advancement of the population; and shall encourage qualified students

shall guarantee to the inhabitants of the trust territory freedom of speech, of the press, and of assembly; freedom of conscience, of worship, and of religious teaching; and freedom of migration and movement.

ARTICLE 8

1. In discharging its obligations under Article 76 (d) of the Charter, as defined by Article 83 (2) of the Charter, the administering authority, subject to the requirements of security, and the obligation to promote the advancement of the inhabitants, shall accord to nationals of each Member of the United Nations and

to companies and associations organized in conformity with the laws of such Member, treatment in the trust territory no less favorable than that accorded therein to nationals, companies and associations of any other United Nation, except the administering authority.

2. The administering authority shall ensure equal treatment to the Members of the United Nations and their nationals in the administration of justice.

3. Nothing in this Article shall be so construed as to accord traffic rights to aircraft flying into and out of the trust territory. Such rights shall be subject to agreement between the administering authority and the state whose nationality such aircraft possesses.

4. The administering authority may negotiate and conclude commercial and other treaties and agreements with Members of the United Nations and other states, designed to attain for the inhabitants of the trust territory treatment by the Members of the United Nations and other states no less favorable than that granted by them to the nationals of other states. The Security Council may recommend, or invite other organs of the United Nations to consider and recommend, what rights the inhabitants of the trust territory should acquire in consideration of the rights obtained by Members of the United Nations in the trust territory. . .

# 12

# THE PROBLEM OF WAR

WAR is power politics in its ultimate form, as General Karl von Clause-witz said, a 'continuation of politics by other means.' It is resorted to for the purpose of obtaining or keeping by force something which cannot be obtained or kept by peaceful methods.

By means of war many changes have been brought to nations and mankind generally. Through war the thirteen American colonies gained freedom from England, and by the same revolutionary process the twenty Latin American republics threw off the rule of Spain and Portugal. China was opened to the West by the Opium War in 1840-42. It was war that broke up the old Austro-Hungarian Empire and brought several new small states in its place. War gave the Balkan countries freedom from Turkey and later shifted their boundaries about. It built and later brought to ruin the empire of Fascist Italy, as it destroyed and later reconstructed Poland. Within fifty years war transferred Alsace-Lorraine from France to Germany and back again.

Some of its most far-reaching results are never planned. It was war more than anything else that produced the system of nation states. The hatreds engendered by war have contributed materially to the nationalisms that play such an important part in contemporary international relations. World War I made room for communism in Russia and, ultimately, played a part in bringing about the severe world-wide economic depression of the 'thirties. Music, literature, and the other arts have been inspired by the conditions of war. And technological developments, including the recent release of atomic power, have been stimulated by the exigencies of war.

In spite of all this, war is essentially destructive. Where it has brought some gain, the cost has been high, and in recent wars the cost has mounted higher and higher. For instance, the number of deaths per 1000 in Great Britain caused by war was 15 in the seventeenth century and 48 in the first half of the twentieth century. Many hundreds of billions of dollars were spent by the nations that took part in World War II, and it left the United States with a debt of $270,000,000,000.

It is not surprising that so destructive a force has provoked wide and searching speculation among thoughtful people. Several points of view, not always mutually exclusive, have resulted from this thinking. To some, war has seemed a useful method by which a nation's strength is made secure and its people are enabled to fulfil their mission in the world. At the other extreme are those who concentrate more on the means than the end and, as pacifists, take the view that war is useless and has no place in a Christian world. Between these views is the attitude that only 'just wars' are admissible. War for aggrandizement of any kind would thus be ruled out. Many reformers, on the other hand, stress the substitution of agencies of international co-operation in place of war, and some the elimination of the causes of war or the denunciation of war by international law. Those who are not so optimistic advocate that, as long as war must be tolerated, it should be regulated by international law so that its excesses may be prevented and the welfare of innocent people protected. Several points of view toward war are dealt with in this chapter. Reference should also be made to Chapters 2 and 3 above for materials on the attempt to renounce war or bring it under regulation.

## I. WAR IN HISTORY

The following tables show the place war has occupied in selected periods of history since 1800. The types of wars are designated by B (balance of power), C (civil war), D (defensive war, in the sense of a war to defend modern civilization against an alien culture), and I (imperial war, for expansion). Data for other periods would show approximately the same frequency of war.

(Quincy Wright, *A Study of War*, 1942, vol. 1, Tables 37, 38, 41. Reprinted by permission of the University of Chicago Press.)

### LIST OF WARS

#### 1800-1825

Tripoli-U.S.A. (1801-05)—D
Haytian Revolt (1802-03)—C
1st Mahratta War (1802-03)—I
Russo-Persian War (1804-1813)—I
Napoleonic Wars (1803-1815)—B
  Third Coalition (1805)
  Franco Prussian (1806-07)
  Peninsular War (1807-14)
  Anglo-Danish (1807-14)
  Franco-Austrian (1809)
  Russian Expedition (1812-13)
  War of Liberation (1813-14)
  Hundred Days' War (1815)
Russo-Turkish (1806-12)—B
Russo-Swedish (1808-09)—B
Latin American Revolt (1810-24)—C
War of 1812 (1812-14)—B

Austria-Naples (1815)—B
Algiers-U.S.A. (1815)—D
2nd Mahratta War (1817-18)—I
Spanish Civil War (1821-23)—C
Greek Revolt (1821-30)—C
Haiti-Santo Domingo (1823)—B
1st Central American (1823)—B
Burmese War (1824-26)—I
La Plata War (1825-28)—B

#### 1825-1850

Spanish-Portuguese (1826-27)—B
Russia-Persian (1826-28)—I
Russo-Turkish (1828-1829)—B
Belgian Revolt (1830-1933)—C
Algerian Conquest (1830-47)—I
Polish Insurrection (1830-31)—C
2nd Central American (1831-45)—B
Carlist Revolt (1833-47)—C
Egyptian Revolt (1831-33)—C
Khivian Conquest (1839-42)—I
Portuguese Revolution (1831-1834)—C
Peru-Bolivia (1835-42)—B
Texan Revolt (1835-36)—C

Chili-Argentine (1836)—B
1st Afghan (1838-42)—I
2nd La Plata War (1839-42)—B
Egyptian War (1839-41)—I
1st Opium (1840-42)—I
France-Morocco (1844)—I
Mexico-U.S.A. (1846-48)—B
Denmark-Germany (1848-51)—B
Austria-Sardinia (1848-49)—B
Hungarian Insurrection (1848-49)—C

1900-1941

Boxer Expedition (1900-01)—I
Venezuelan War (1902-03)—B
Russo-Japanese War (1904-05)—B
Central American War (1906-07)—B
Mexican Revolution (1910-20)—C
Italo-Turkish War (1911-12)—I

1st Balkan War (1912-13)—B
2nd Balkan War (1913)—B
World War I (1914-20)—B
Chinese Civil Wars (1916-36)—C
Irish Rebellion (1916-22)—C
Russian Revolution (1917-20)—B
Russo-Polish War (1919-20)—B
3rd Afghan War (1919)—I
Vilna War (1920-27)—B
Greco-Turkish War (1921-24)—B
Riffian War (1921-25)—C
Chaco War (1928-35)—B
Manchurian Hostilities (1931-33)—B
Ethiopian War (1935-36)—I
Spanish Revolution (1936-39)—C
Chino-Japanese War (1937-45)—B
World War II (1939-45)—B
Russia-Finnish War (1939-40)—B

## II. CAUSES OF WAR

There is no simple explanation for war. It has many causes which operate with unequal force in different situations. The causes given in Extract A below were the findings of the Conference on the Cause and Cure of War held in Washington in 1925.

### A. *A List of Causes*

(*Report of the Conference on the Cause and Cure of War*, 1925, pp. 354-5.)

#### PSYCHOLOGICAL

1. Fear: (a) feeling of national insecurity; (b) fear of invasion; (c) fear of loss of property; (d) fear of change
2. Suspicion
3. Greed
4. Lust for power
5. Hate
6. Revenge
7. Jealousy
8. Envy

#### ECONOMIC

1. Aggressive imperialism: (a) territorial; (b) economic

2. Economic rivalries for: (a) markets; (b) energy resources; (c) essential raw materials
3. Government protection of private interests abroad without reference to the general welfare
4. Disregard of rights of backward peoples
5. Population pressure: (a) inequalities of access to resources; (b) customs barriers; (c) migration barriers
6. Profits in war

#### POLITICAL

1. Principle of balance of power
2. Secret treaties
3. Unjust treaties
4. Violation of treaties

5. Disregard of rights of minorities

6. Organization of the state for war

7. Ineffective or obstructive political machinery

SOCIAL AND CONTRIBUTORY

1. Exaggerated nationalism

2. Competitive armaments

3. Religious and racial antagonisms

4. General apathy, indifference and ignorance

5. War psychology created through various agencies, e.g., (a) the press; (b) motion pictures; (c) text-books; (d) home influences

6. Social inequalities

7. Social sanctions of war

8. Lack of spiritual ideals

## B. *Opinions on the Causes*

The extract below explains the opinions of scientists, historians, and practical politicians on the causes of war.

(Quincy Wright, *A Study of War*, 1942, vol. II, pp. 727-8, 731-8. Reprinted by permission of The University of Chicago Press.)

The phrase 'causes of war' has been used in many senses. Writers have declared the cause of World War I to have been the Russian or the German mobilization; the Austrian ultimatum; the Sarajevo assassination; the aims and ambitions of the Kaiser, Poincaré, Izvolsky, Berchtold, or someone else; the desire of France to recover Alsace-Lorraine or of Austria to dominate the Balkans; the European system of alliances; the activities of the munition-makers, the international bankers, or the diplomats; the lack of an adequate European political order; armament rivalries; colonial rivalries; commercial policies; the sentiment of nationality; the concept of sovereignty; the struggle for existence; the tendency of nations to expand; the unequal distribution of population, of resources, or of planes of living; the law of diminishing returns; the value of war as an instrument of national solidarity or as an instrument of national policy; ethnocentrism or group egotism; the failure of the human spirit; and many others.

To some a cause of war is an event, condition, act, or personality involved only in a particular war; to others it is a general proposition applicable to many wars. To some it is a class of human motives, ideals, or values; to others it is a class of impersonal forces, conditions, processes, patterns, or relations. To some it is the entrance or injection of a disturbing factor into a stable situation; to others it is the lack of essential conditions of stability in the situation itself or the human failure to realize potentialities. These differences of opinion reflect different meanings of the word 'cause.' The three sentences, respectively, contrast causes of war in the historic and scientific senses, in the practical and scientific senses, and in the historic and practical senses. . .

a) *Scientific causes of war.*—Scientists, in searching for the causes of phenomena, assume that the universal and the particular are aspects of one reality. They attempt to classify, combine, or analyze particular events into general concepts or ideas which represent measurable, controllable, repeatable, and observable phenomena capable of being treated as variables or constants in a formula.

While scientists realize that there are events in any field of study which have not yet been included in classes which can be precisely defined or measured, they are reluctant to believe that any factors are permanently 'vague' and 'imponderable'—a belief frequently held by practical men, historians, and poets. In dealing with war, scientists prefer concepts such as military forces, public opinion, attitudes, population, and international trade, which have been measured, even though crudely, or concepts such as jurisdiction, arbitration, war, aggression, and right, which have a precise meaning in a body of law, rather than such concepts as personal influence, civilizing mission, imperialism, accidental events, and social potentialities, which have neither of these characteristics. They prefer concepts which represent series of events that appear continuously or in regular cycles or oscillations in history, so that interpolation or extrapolation is possible where data are lacking. They prefer concepts which represent classes of facts that are abundant in the records or in the contemporary world, so that the properties of these classes can be verified by the use of historical sources or observation.

The scientifically minded have attempted to describe the normal functioning of the forces, interests, controls, and motives involved in international relations and to formulate abstract propositions relating, respectively, to the balance of power, to international law, to international organization, and to public opinion. While they have sometimes included war as a periodic recurrence in such normal functioning, they have usually attributed war to the high degree of unmeasurability, uncontrollability, incompleteness, or uncertainty of the factors which they have studied. Thus they have attributed war (1) to the difficulty of maintaining stable equilibrium among the uncertain and fluctuating political and military forces within the state system; (2) to the inadequacy of its sources and sanctions continually to keep international law an effective analysis of the changing interests of states and the changing values of humanity; (3) to the difficulty of so organizing political power that it can maintain internal order in a society not in relation to other societies external to itself; and (4) to the difficulty of making peace a more important symbol in world public opinion than particular symbols which may locally, temporarily, or generally favor war. In short, scientific investigators, giving due consideration to both the historic inertia and the inventive genius of mankind, have tended to attribute war to immaturities in social knowledge and control, as one might attribute epidemics to insufficient medical knowledge or to inadequate public health services.

b) *Historical causes of war.*—Historians assume that the future is a development of the past which includes, however, forward-looking intentions and aspirations. They attempt to classify events into ideas which represent commonly observed processes of change and development. Because of the common experience of small incidents releasing stored forces—the match and the fuse—they frequently distinguish the occasion from the causes of war. Because people ordinarily think they are familiar with biological evolution, with psychological and sociological processes, with economic, political, and religious interests, historians have customarily classified the causes of war under such headings.

This method may be illustrated by the causes of the Franco-Prussian War set forth in Ploetz's *Manual of Universal History.* These are divided into 'immediate causes,' 'special causes,' and 'general causes.' The first were said to be certain events which shortly preceded the war, including the election of the prince of Hohenzollern to the throne of Spain, the French demand that the Prussian king should never again permit the candidacy of the prince for the Spanish crown, and the Ems telegram from Bismarck announcing the king's refusal. The special causes were said to be the internal troubles of the French government, the controversy concerning French compensation for the Prussian aggrandizement of 1866, and the news of new German infantry weapons threatening the superiority of the French chassepot. The general causes were stated to be the French idea of natural frontiers as including the left bank of the Rhine and the long struggle of the German nation for unification, together with the French anxiety over it.

Historians have thus sought to demonstrate causes by drawing from a detailed knowledge of the antecedents of a particular war, events, circumstances, and conditions which can be related to the war by practical, political, and juristic commonplaces about human motives, impulses, and intentions. When they have written of the causes of war in a more general way, they have meant simply a classification of the causes of the particular wars in a given period of history. Thus certain of the causes of the Franco-Prussian War have been described by such words as 'aggressive policies,' 'changes in military techniques,' 'domestic difficulties,' 'unsettled controversies,' 'dynastic claims,' 'aspirations for national unification,' 'historic rivalries,' and 'insulting communications.' Even broader generalizations have been made classifying the causes of war in the Western world as political, juristic, idealistic, and psychological.

When generalization has reached this stage, the result is not unlike the scientific approach, for such words as 'an ideal,' 'a psychological attitude,' 'a policy,' or 'a law' represent concepts which, though limited by the historian to a historic epoch, are universals which may be manifested in varying degrees in all times and places. They are, in fact, variables susceptible, in theory, to mathematical treatment, however difficult it may be practically to measure their variations.

c) *Practical causes of war.*—Practical politicians, publicists, and jurists assume that changes result from free wills operating in an environment. They attempt to classify events according to the motives and purposes from which they seem to proceed. Their assumptions have thus resembled those of the historians, though they have formulated their problems toward practical ends and have often excluded events and impersonal forces which the historian frequently considers. Because men like to rationalize their actions, publicists have often distinguished the pretexts from the causes of war. Because they recognize that no free will ever really acts without antecedents, and therefore the origin of a series of causal events has to be determined arbitrarily, they have distinguished proximate from remote causes. While they have sometimes attributed wars to the failure of society to adopt particular reforms or to modify certain conditions, they have usually distinguished causes attributable to a responsible person from impersonal conditions and potential reforms. In the same way physicians more frequently attribute an illness to a germ rather than to the susceptibility of the patient because of a run-down condition or to his failure to take preventive or remedial precautions.

Practical men have, then, usually thought of war as a manifestation of human nature with its complex of ambitions, desires, purposes, animosities, aspirations, and irrationalities. They have insisted that the degree of consciousness or responsibility to be attributed to such manifestations is an important factor in devising measures for dealing with the problem. Classification of human motives from this point of view is familiar in law and economics. Publicists have often distinguished necessary, customary, rational and capricious acts in the causation of war. They suggest that wars arise in the following situations: (1) Men and governments find themselves in situations where they must fight or cease to exist, and so they fight from necessity. (2) Men and governments have a custom of fighting in the presence of certain stimulae, and so in appropriate situations they fight. (3) Men or governments want something— wealth, power, social solidarity—and, if the device of war is known to them and other means have failed, they use war as a means to get what they want. (4) Men and governments feel like fighting because they are pugnacious, bored, the victims of frustrations or complexes, and accordingly they fight spontaneously for relief or relaxation. . .

## III. Human Nature and War

It is often said that wars will not cease so long as human nature is what it is. In other words, biologically man requires war. Although this view is shared by countless people, the most reliable authorities are inclined to deny its validity. Admitting that war gives expression to such basic human impulses as acquisitiveness, revenge, destructiveness, and fear, they deny that war is the only means or a necessary means of giving vent to such drives. They point out that blood vengeance was based on such impulses as revenge and love, but that it has been virtually abolished as the processes of law have taken its place, without in any way changing human nature. Some views on this subject are given below.

### A. *Fear (Prior to World War II)*

(J. C. Smuts, 'The Present Outlook,' *International Conciliation*, No. 308, March, 1935, pp. 65-7. Reprinted by permission of the Carnegie Endowment for International Peace.)

Looking at the European situation today, as distinct from the wider world situation (to which I shall refer later), I am deeply impressed by the fact that two underlying forces are today creating and shaping policies—the fear complex and the inferiority complex. Both are dangerous complexes, the symptoms of disease and not of healthy growth, and unless they are treated on wise lines they may in the long run produce very serious consequences for the public mind and life of the world. It may seem a humiliating concession to make, but it appears to be a fact that fear is today the real driving force in our European relations. Fear, the meanest of human motives, is today the master of us all. The victors of the Great War, so far from feeling secure in their victory, are in fact obsessed with this almost neurotic fear. And the vanquished are reacting in the obvious and inevitable way by refusing to accept their enforced inferiority and their position as second-class nations in the comity of civilization. The victors are actuated not by confidence but by the fear of the defeated; the defeated are determined to reconquer their lost equality with the victors. The mental reactions seem in fact, to be reversing the roles created by the Great War. It is all a topsy-turvy and almost absurd state of affairs. But it is this mental topsy-turvydom which is today driving Europe forward on the road to chaos. In these obsessions reason is in abeyance, the finer human instincts are paralyzed, and a wrong twist is being given to our future development as a well-ordered continent. Every urgent question becomes insoluble in this atmosphere of distortion. Disarmament has almost suffered shipwreck when every solid reason points to its necessity; and international cooperation is endangered where every common European interest calls imperatively for it.

If Europe is ever to get back to the right road again, it seems to me necessary that the nations, both victors and vanquished, should be cured of their Freudian obsessions, should recover their commonsense and sanity, and should once more see things in their right and normal relations. There is no super-psychoanalyst to do this, but it is at least necessary to diagnose the disease, to recognize that it is a disease, and not a normal healthy condition. Once Europeans admit to themselves that they are perhaps a little mad, the cure would come of itself. A sense of humor, of good-humor, and a little laughter at themselves will do the rest. 'Know thyself' was the wise oracle to Socrates; 'Know thyself' is the word to be spoken today to Europe in its temporary obsessions and aberrations. There is no doubt that the spell will pass, but what irreparable mischief is being done while it is on! Let statesmen but be-

come the courageous doctors to their sick peoples and it will soon pass.

One of the symptoms of this fear complex is the war talk which is now so common. It is represented that we are on the brink of another war, that war is waiting just round the corner. This war talk is creating a war atmosphere and is more likely to lead to war than anything else. . .

The remedy for this fear complex is the Freudian way of dragging it out from its hidden depths, bringing it into the open and exposing it to the light of day. And this is exactly the method of the League of Nations. The League may not be a satisfactory source of security, it may be wanting in that element of sanctions which many consider so necessary. But at any rate it is an open forum for discussion among the nations, it is a round table for the statesmen around which they can ventilate and debate their grievances and view-points. The 'Open Diplomacy' for which Woodrow Wilson so ardently pleaded is enshrined in the Covenant and is today the settled and accepted method of international intercourse in the League. The League was designed to be first and foremost the Round Table of the nations, and at that table and in open discussion the secret fear complex can be treated and in the end cured along truly human and scientific lines. . .

## B. *Must Men Fight?*

(S. M. Duvall, *War and Human Nature*, Public Affairs Pamphlet No. 125, New York, pp. 5-11, 14-15. Reprinted by permission of the Public Affairs Committee, Inc., 32 E. 38th St., N. Y.)

We have often heard the statement: 'It is futile to attempt to abolish war. Men always have fought. They always will fight, because it is human nature to fight.'

The last part of the statement is true. It is human nature to fight, just as it is human nature to eat with a fork, go to ball games, drive automobiles, and play parchesi. But human nature is not merely something we are born with. It is also affected by what we have learned. It is natural for some people to be warlike, cruel, and treacherous, just as it is natural for some people to speak English or

Spanish. It is natural, not because they were born that way, but because they have learned to be like that.

A thousand years ago the Scandinavians (Norsemen) were the most cruel, treacherous, and warlike people in Europe. Today they are among the most peaceable people of the world. Five hundred years ago the most cruel and warlike people were the Swiss. Today the reverse is true. What has happened? Biologically they are essentially the same as were their ancestors. But their human nature has been changed as a result of what we call a 'conditioning process.' What was once natural is so no longer. Anyone who thinks that 'human nature cannot be changed' should just look around him and see how different many Americans are from their ancestors from other lands. Two of the staunchest supporters of democracy in America, Willkie and Eisenhower, were of German ancestry. They were not born any different from many in Germany who 'heiled Hitler.' The *Nisei* are essentially like the Americans, not like the Japanese. During the past year we have witnessed amazing changes in the nature of the Japanese people themselves. These formerly treacherous and vicious enemies may one day be among the most peaceable and democratic people in the world. As some 2,400 psychologists declared almost unanimously, 'War is not born in men; it is built into men. No race, nation, or social group is inevitably warlike.'

One word of caution should be added here. Human nature is usually not greatly affected by mere talk. We will not make the Germans democratic by 'teaching' (telling) them and their children that democracy is a grand thing. Human nature is learned in the process of living with people. In life, whatever gets us what we want tends to become 'natural.' If we satisfy ourselves best by pushing ahead and grabbing things away from other people, if cruelty and viciousness are reward-ing, they become 'natural.' If, on the other hand, we get more satisfactions out of peaceable, honest behavior, these traits become 'natural.' Character traits, good or bad, are natural, but they are not inborn. The nature and results of the experiences of life determine what is natural for any people.

Some years ago Dr. Ruth Benedict made an intensive study of the Zuñi Indians. She found that some of the characteristics which we Americans think are natural to all men, such as ambition and the desire to get ahead, were almost absent. We may say, 'That is because they are Indians. White men are naturally different.' But they are not. A similar study was made of the Hutterite religious communities. These people are white and racially like ourselves. They live in simple, agricultural communities. They care little about the attractions of city life and the gadgets that we strive so hard to get. To them, the most important thing in life is to live peaceably and harmoniously. They do not desire to 'get ahead' or to dominate. Incidentally, they have no police and practically no crime. Wrongdoers are controlled almost entirely by the pressures of public opinion. It would be too much to say that by controlling the experiences of life we can make human nature what we will. But we could, by proper and intelligent control, make peace as natural as war.

In answering this question we must first distinguish between fighting behavior and the will to fight. The girl who helps make tanks in a factory may be fighting in her behavior far more effectively than most men in uniform. Yet in her feelings she may not be fighting at all. In her mind she is merely doing what she did when she worked in the same factory before the war making tractors. In either case she is only doing what she is paid to do, and for essentially the same reasons. The same may be true of the professional soldier.

He may not in any way have wanted the war or caused it to come. He was just in the army when the war broke out. He fought, perhaps with great skill and effectiveness, because it was his job and he took pride in doing it well. Other men may fight for the same reason that they went to school when they were children. The law requires it. Many people 'fight' for essentially the same reasons that they engage in peacetime activities, because they have to, or because it is just their job. Obviously, then, the real problem is not fighting behavior but fighting feelings. Our real question is, not 'Why do people fight?' but 'Why do people want wars or results that they can get only through wars?'

### THE WILL TO WAR

Some wars of the past, such as tribal raids and the squabbles of kings over thrones and territories, can be easily explained. Somebody had something that somebody else wanted and thought he could get. So they fought. Often the only people seriously involved were the small armies who did the actual fighting, and those few who happened to live where the fighting was going on. Most of the people were not much affected, except in the taxes which they had to pay. We of today face quite a different problem— that of total war. Wars now affect everyone. They must be supported by everyone. Unless the will to war, or at least the acceptance of war, were widespread among the masses of the people, modern wars could not be conducted. We have now the problem of explaining why the rank and file of the people either want to fight, or are at least willing to support war. In a defensive war the problem is not difficult. When a nation is attacked, as the Americans were at Pearl Harbor, they will fight back. The really difficult problem is with the psychology of aggression. Why is it that whole popula-

tions sometimes either (1) seek wars with other peoples who do not in any serious way threaten them, or (2) place in power and vigorously support leaders who are pledged to aggressive policies which they know must result in war?

At this point it would be easy if we could give a simple economic explanation. But, as we have seen, it is not the 'have not' nations, but the 'middle class' nations who have proved the aggressors. Furthermore, within any nation it is not the poor who demand war. It is the malcontents, those who are psychologically disturbed within themselves, who are the war-makers. People are most warlike and aggressive when (1) the social and economic relationships of life have been disrupted so that people feel bewildered, confused, uncertain, and insecure; and when (2) people are frustrated.

Scientists have learned much about human beings by a study of lower animals, such as guinea pigs, dogs, and rats. This knowledge has not been limited to such matters as dietetics. We have learned much also about psychology. One significant experiment was that of producing neurosis, a 'nervous breakdown,' experimentally in a rat. The rat is put in a cage which is so arranged that, when he paws at a certain place, a door opens and he can get food. The rat quickly gets the idea and soon is happily able to get what he wants. Then the scientists play a trick on him. They rearrange the cage so that when he paws at the accustomed place he gets an electric shock instead of food. This changed situation the rat just cannot follow. First he gets mad and struggles all the harder, and gets shocked more and more. Then he becomes baffled, bewildered, and confused. Usually he just cannot 'take it.' As a result he develops some kind of mental disorder. Often he becomes sulky, morose, and finally just gives up and quits.

Human beings often run up against

situations that are just as baffling for them. Consider, for example, the experience of the Germans with war. For about a hundred years they had gotten what they wanted largely by fighting with other nations. Through war they won their independence from Napoleon. War brought them territories wrested from Denmark, Austria, and France. Through war Germany became a strong, united nation. War and military might made Germany powerful and respected among the nations of the world. Then, after a century of success, the situation was reversed. The war that began in 1914 brought Germany, not further gains, but loss. Instead of more territory, it resulted in less, including the humiliating division of Germany into two parts by the Polish Corridor. Instead of greater power, it brought defeat and weakness. Instead of making Germany respected and feared, it made Germany despised and scorned. On the home front, events were equally baffling. For many hundreds of years the Germans, like the rest of us, had been able to exchange their money for goods. Runaway inflation made that no longer possible. Everything seemed turned around. Policies and behavior that before had brought rich rewards now brought punishment. The Germans responded just as any group of either humans or animals would have responded under comparable circumstances. They felt helpless, baffled, and bewildered.

Human beings differ from the rat, however, in one important respect. They understand that bad conditions can be changed. Apparently it never occurs to the rat in the cage that he might gain control of the situation and fix things more to his liking. Not so with humans. Like the rat, they may continue to long for the 'good old days.' But, unlike the rat, they often come to the faith that the situations that baffle them can be changed. Sometimes they even believe that the old

situation can be restored. In Germany these natural and understandable longings were effectively exploited by an unusually skillful and unscrupulous leader. He persuaded the people that if he were given power, he would make things even better than they had been. At first Hitler seemed able to deliver. As soon as people came to believe in him they felt better. Despair changed to hope. People who used to shuffle and slink about began to march, not only with their feet but with their hearts. Germany took over much territory and became a power to be respected, at little cost. The masses did not endorse Hitler just because they were hungry. On the contrary they cheerfully accepted his program of 'guns instead of butter.'

Why did they cooperate gladly in his brutalities and even his aggressive, unprovoked attacks upon peaceable neighbors? Not because they were born cruel or vindictive. The Germans supported Hitler because their experiences seemed to prove that this was the best way to get what they wanted. In the final showdown they did not go to war because of any 'fighting instinct,' or because they are 'naturally' more warlike than anybody else. They fought because they felt insecure within themselves. No amount of territory and resources could make them peaceable. Hence the inevitable failure of appeasement. Economic considerations helped to bring on the war, yes. But these were the disruption of economic stability, not poverty and the lack of goods. The Germans fought to re-establish an order which they could understand. Those who would bring about world peace must provide a stability that confused people can understand.

Closely related to bewilderment is frustration. By frustration we mean here the unhappy feelings we have when we seem unable to get what we want very much. It depends more upon the way we look at things than upon what the situation actually is. Frustration arises not out of our *needs* but out of our *demands*. We may have far more than we need. But if we feel that we should have the world with a fence around it, we will feel frustrated no matter how much we have. On the other hand, if we feel that we have everything we have a right to expect, we may not be frustrated even if we starve. For many centuries the peasants of Europe were destitute while their lords lived in relative luxury. They rarely rebelled. Why? Because peasants did not expect to live like lords. They did not even feel that they could greatly improve their condition. As peasants they expected to live in extreme poverty, even to the point of starvation.

On the other hand, those who have most may feel terribly frustrated. The Count who feels that he should be a Duke, the Duke who feels that he should be a King, the King who feels that he should be an Emperor, the Emperor who feels that he should rule the world may feel terribly frustrated. They may therefore be ready to wage war whenever they feel that it will get them what they want. Frustration does not depend upon much or little. Only when people have come to feel that something more and better is possible, does frustration set in. . .

Frustrated people tend to blame their troubles on somebody else. They know that somehow they are being held back. Usually they do not know that the difficulty is really with their own inner conflicts. So naturally they blame others and feel hostile and resentful. This resentment is the soil in which grows the will to war. So long as the resentments are directed against individuals, they are not a menace to world peace. But they can be directed almost anywhere. Thus, where one man would have blamed his troubles on his mother-in-law, another on his boss, and a third on his rheumatism, a clever spellbinder may come along. He is able to persuade all three to blame their difficulties on the Jews, the Versailles Treaty, the British, the Communists, or anybody else.

The possibility of using frustrations to build up the will to war depends first of all on the amount and degree of frustration. People who are well adjusted and happy do not respond to tirades against others. Secondly, the will to war depends upon how the frustrations are focused. If enough people are sufficiently frustrated and if they can be persuaded to blame things upon some one group, the result may be war. But it depends on what people feel frustrated about. If the people care most about such things as musical and educational attainments, as the keeping of international agreements and leadership in world peace, frustration will make for peace rather than for war. But what if the really important matters are military success, economic supremacy, and the domination of other people? Then frustrations of a serious nature may arise from a failure to lord it over other people. When people seek goals which can be secured only by despoiling and repressing others, their frustrations will almost certainly lead to the will to war.

## C. *The Biological Aspects of War*

(Aldous Huxley, *An Encyclopedia of Pacifism,* London, 1937, pp. 7-8. Reprinted by permission of Harper & Brothers.)

War is often described as a Law of Nature. This is not true. Among the lower animals war is unknown. True there are carnivores which prey upon animals; but their activities are no more warlike than are the activities of fishermen or butchers. Moreover, the existence of carnivores should not blind us to the fact that there is at least as much co-operation in nature as strife.

Individuals of the same species often fight together; but these fights are seldom pushed to a finish; the conquered is rarely killed or even permanently hurt. Such duels waged in the heat of passion, under the stress of hunger or sexual impulse, are quite unlike war, which is mass murder, scientifically prepared in cold blood.

In nature, it is only among the social insects, such as the ants and termites, that we meet anything resembling war. And even here the resemblance is only superficial. Insect wars are conducted by members of one species against members of other species. Man is the only creature to organize mass murder of his own species.

It is often declared that war is inevitable, since man is descended from pugnacious ancestors, akin to the gorilla. This is probably not the case. Most zoologists are more of the opinion that man's ancestor was not a gorilla-like ape, but a gentle, sensitive creature, something like a tarsier. In any case, the gifts which brought man his extraordinary biological success were not ruthlessness and brute strength (plenty of animals are much stronger and fiercer than he is) but co-operation, intelligence, wondering curiosity and sensitiveness.

Another biological argument often invoked in defense of war is the following: war is civilization's equivalent of natural selection; it acts as nature's pruning-hook, ensuring the survival of the fittest. This is obviously untrue. War tends to kill off the young and healthy and to spare the unhealthy and those who are too old to beget children. In the second place, there is no reason to suppose that warlike peoples are superior to unwarlike peoples. Even if the violent were to survive (and war is not as likely to kill them off as to ensure the persistence of their stock), this would not necessarily mean the survival of the most satisfactory type of human beings; nor, conversely, are the most valuable necessarily the strongest. In so far as war is an agent of selection it selects dysgenically, ensuring the survival, not of the more desirable, but of the less desirable human traits. . .

## IV. Exponents of War

The view that war is a positive good is less commonly held today than formerly. In an Essay on the True Greatness of States, Francis Bacon (1561-1626) held that war provides the state with wholesome exercise, as work and play do for the individual. A century earlier, Niccolò Machiavelli (1469-1527), giving advice to an imaginary prince, used other arguments in support of war, as extract A brings out. Extract B is a still more recent argument for war.

### A. *Machiavelli on War*

(Niccolò Machiavelli, *The Prince*, translated by Luigi Ricci, revised by E. R. P. Vincent, Chap. xiv. London, 1935. Reprinted by permission of Oxford University Press.)

A prince should therefore have no other aim or thought, nor take up any other thing for his study, but war and its organisation and discipline, for that is the only art that is necessary to one who commands, and it is of such virtue that it not only maintains those who are born princes, but often enables men of private fortune to attain to that rank. And one sees, on the other hand, that when princes think more of luxury than of arms, they lose their state. The chief cause of the loss of states, is the contempt of this art, and the way to acquire them is to be well versed in the same.

Francesco Sforza, through being well armed, became, from private status, Duke of Milan; his sons, through wishing to avoid the fatigue and hardship of war, from dukes became private persons. For among other evils caused by being disarmed, it renders you contemptible; which is one of those disgraceful things which a prince must guard against, as will be explained later. Because there is no comparison whatever between an armed and a disarmed man, it is not reasonable to suppose that one who is armed will obey willingly one who is unarmed; or that any unarmed man will remain safe among armed servants. For one being disdainful and the other suspicious, it is not possible for them to act well together. And therefore a prince who is ignorant of military matters, besides the other misfortunes already mentioned, cannot be esteemed by his soldiers, nor have confidence in them.

He ought, therefore, never to let his thoughts stray from the exercise of war; and in peace he ought to practise it more than in war, which he can do in two ways: by action and by study. . .

## B. *Von Bernhardi's Views*

General Friedrich von Bernhardi (1849-1930) was one of the prominent German militarists before World War I. He wrote the following passage on the subject of war in 1912.

(F. von Bernhardi, *Germany and the Next War*, translated by A. H. Powles, London, 1914, pp. 17-8, 41. Reprinted by permission of Edward Arnold & Company.)

This desire for peace has rendered most civilized nations anaemic, and marks a decay of spirit and political courage such as has often been shown by a race of Epigoni. 'It has always been,' H. von Treitschke tells us, 'the weary, spiritless, and exhausted ages which have played with the dream of perpetual peace.'

Everyone will, within certain limits, admit that the endeavours to diminish the dangers of war and to mitigate the sufferings which war entails are justifiable. It is an incontestable fact that war temporarily disturbs industrial life, interrupts quiet economic development, brings widespread misery with it, and emphasizes the primitive brutality of man. It is therefore a most desirable consummation if wars for trivial reasons should be rendered impossible, and if efforts are made to restrict the evils which follow necessarily in the train of war, so far as is compatible with the essential nature of war. All that the Hague Peace Congress has accomplished in this limited sphere deserves, like every permissible humanization of war, universal acknowledgment. But it is quite another matter if the object is to abolish war entirely and to deny its necessary place in historical development.

This aspiration is directly antagonistic to the great universal laws which rule all life. War is a biological necessity of the first importance, a regulative element in the life of mankind which cannot be dispensed with, since without it an unhealthy development will follow, which excludes every advancement of the race, and therefore all real civilization. 'War is the father of all things.' The sages of antiquity long before Darwin recognized this.

The struggle for existence is, in the life of Nature, the basis of all healthy development. All existing things show themselves to be the result of contesting forces. So in the life of man the struggle is not merely the destructive but the life-giving principle. 'To supplant or to be supplanted is the essence of life,' says Goethe, and the strong life gains the upper hand. The law of the stronger holds good everywhere. Those forms survive which are able to procure themselves the most favourable conditions of life, and to assert themselves in the universal economy of Nature. The weaker succumb. . .

Wherever we open the pages of history we find proofs of the fact that wars, begun at the right moment with manly resolution, have effected the happiest results, both politically and socially. A feeble policy has always worked harm, since the statesman lacked the requisite firmness to take the risk of a necessary war, since he tried by diplomatic tact to adjust the differences of irreconcilable foes, and deceived himself as to the gravity of the situation and the real importance of the matter. Our own recent history in its vicissitudes supplies us with the most striking examples of this. . .

## V. THE THEORY OF JUST WARS

Admitting that war is evil, there are those who uphold it in specific situations on the ground that the cause involved is a just one. The doctrine has been upheld for centuries by certain philosophers and legalists, and especially by Churchmen. The extract below was written by a seventeenth-century writer on international law.

(S. Pufendorf, *De Jure Naturae et Gentium*, vol. II, translation of the edition of 1688 by C. H. Oldfather and W. A. Oldfather, Oxford, 1934, pp. 1292-3. Reprinted with permission of the Carnegie Endowment for International Peace, Division of International Law.)

. . . Now it is one of the first principles of natural law that no one unjustly do another hurt or damage, as well as that men should perform for each other the duties of humanity, and show especial zeal to fulfil the matters upon which they have entered into particular agreements. When men observe these duties in their relations one with another, it is called peace, which is a state most highly agreeable to human nature and fitted to preserve it, the creation and preservation of which constitute one of the chief reasons for the law of nature being placed in the hearts of men. . .

Despite all this war is lawful and sometimes even necessary for men, when another with evil interest threatens me with injury or without what is my due. For under such circumstances my care for my own safety gives me the power to maintain and defend myself and mine by any means at my disposal, even to the injury of my assailant, or, as Ulysses says in Dictys Cretenois, Bk. II (XXI): 'To extort by force a right which cannot be secured by friendly means.' Here belongs the statement of Maximus of Tyre, *Dissertations*, XIV (XXIV.II.e.): 'Consequently to the just war appears a necessity, to the unjust a voluntary act. . .' A further consideration lies in the fact that nature has not only instilled in the minds of men a bitter sense of injuries, so that they avoid in every way being harassed by the injuries of others, but has also given his body for its protection such agility and strength of hands that he may not be forced to bear them in patience. And yet nature permits war, on the condition that he who wages it shall have as his end the establishment of peace. . .

The causes of just wars may be reduced to the following heads: To preserve and protect ourselves and our possessions against others who attempt to injure us, or take from us or destroy what we have; to assert our claim to whatever others may owe us by a perfect right, when they refuse to perform it for us of their own accord; and, finally, to obtain reparation for losses which we have suffered by injuries, and to extort from him who did the injury guarantees that he will not offend in the future. As a result of these causes we have the division of just wars into offensive and defensive, of which we consider the latter to be those in which we defend and strive to retain what is

ours, the former those by which we extort debts which are denied us, and to seek guarantees for the future. . .

But in general the causes of war, and of offensive wars in particular, should be clear and leave no room for doubt. For time and again doubts arise on this point, either from ignorance of fact, when it is not clearly established whether a thing was done or not, or what was the purpose of the doing, or from an obscure comparison of strict right with the law of charity, or from an uncertain balancing of the advantages which are likely to follow upon the declaration or avoidance of war. Therefore, in the matter before us, neither should we rashly advance any vague claim, nor, on the other hand, fly at once to arms; but we should by all means try one of the three courses in order to prevent the affair from breaking out into open war, to wit, either a conference between the parties concerned or by their representation; or an appeal to arbitrators; or, finally, the use of the lot. . .

## VI. Pacifism

The word 'pacifist' is not always used with the same meaning. To some people it refers only to a person who wants and strives for peace among nations, even though under some conditions he will fight in self-defense. A narrower and probably a more accurate meaning refers to one who will not fight under any condition, the type of a person who is a conscientious objector in war and who very likely rejects violence in every form. Some pacifists base their position on religious tenets; others on secular grounds, arguing that war does not pay, or that it is not humanitarian.

### A. *Jonathan Dymond on War*

The position of the Quakers on war was well stated by Jonathan Dymond, a minister of the gospel, in a book first published in 1823. His book was a thorough exposition of the position of the English pacifists of his day. Admitting that there is something in war that 'glitters and allures,' he nevertheless held that no Christian under any circumstance can fight.

(Jonathan Dymond, *An Inquiry into the Accordancy of War with the Principles of Christianity,* Philadelphia, I. Ashmead and Co., 1834, pp. 102-3.)

The positions, then, which we have endeavored to establish, are these:—

I. That the general character of Christianity is wholly incongruous with war, and that its general duties are incompatible with it.

II. That some of the express precepts and declarations of Jesus Christ virtually forbid it.

III. That His practice is not reconcilable with the supposition of its lawfulness.

IV. That the precepts and practice of the apostles correspond with those of our Lord.

V. That the primitive Christians believed that Christ had forbidden war; and that some of them suffered death in affirmation of this belief.

VI. That God has declared in prophecy, that it is His will that war should eventually be eradicated from the earth: and this eradication will be effected by Christianity, by the influence of its present principles.

VII. That those who have refused to engage in war, in consequence of their belief in its inconsistency with Christianity, have found that Providence has protected them.

Now we think that the establishment of any considerable number of these positions is sufficient for our agreement. The establishment of the whole, forms a body of evidence, to which I am not able to believe that an inquirer, to whom the subject was new, would be able to withhold his assent. But since such an inquirer cannot be found, I would invite the reader to lay prepossession aside, to suppose himself to have now first hand of battles and slaughter, and dispassionately to examine whether the evidence in favour of peace be not very great, and whether the objections to it bear any proportion to the evidence itself. But whatever may be the determination upon this question, surely it is reasonable to try the experiment whether security cannot be maintained without slaughter. Whatever be the reasons for war, it is certain it produces enormous mischief. Even waving the obligation of Christianity, we have to choose between evils that are certain, and evils that are doubtful, between the actual endurance of a great calamity, and the possibility of a less. It certainly cannot be proved that peace would not be the best policy; and since we know that the present system is bad, it were reasonable and wise to try whether the other is not better. . .

## B. *The Early Church*

The early Church was pacifist, as the extract below shows. Later, however, churchmen came to approve of wars for 'just causes.'

(Aldous Huxley, *What Are You Going To Do About It?* New York, pp. 16-7. Reprinted by permission of the author.)

'The Church does not condemn war,' says an orthodox heckler. 'Why am I expected to be more pacifist than the bishops?'

The Church does not condemn war; but Jesus did condemn it. Moreover the

Christians who lived during the first three centuries of our era not only believed that Jesus had condemned war, but themselves repeated the condemnation in more specific terms. Here it is possible to give only the briefest summary of the historical evidence. . .

Among the Early Fathers, Justin Martyr and Tatian in the second century,

Tertullian, Origen, Cyprian, and Hippolytus in the third, Arnobius, Eusebius, and Lactantius in the fourth, all regarded war as an organized iniquity. Here are a few characteristic quotations from their writings on the subject.

The first two are from the *Divinae Institutiones* of Lactantius. 'When God prohibits killing, He not only forbids us to commit brigandage, which is not allowed even by the public laws; but He warns us that not even those things which are regarded as legal among men are to be done. And so it will not be lawful for a just man to serve as a soldier. . .

'How can he be just who injures, hates, despoils, kills? And those who strive to be of advantage to their own country (in war) do all these things. . .'

In the Canons of Hippolytus we read that a soldier who professes Christianity is to be excluded from the sacrament, until such time as he has done penance for the blood he has shed.

In the early part of the fourth century Christianity became the official religion of the Roman Empire. The Cross was used as a military standard and the pious Constantine had the nails with which Christ had been crucified converted into a helmet for himself and bits for his war-horse. The act was profoundly symbolical. In the words of Dean Milman, 'the meek and peaceful Jesus had become a God of Battle.'

The new political situation soon found reflection in Christian theory. Already in the middle years of the fourth century, Athanasius, the father of orthodoxy, is saying that 'to destroy opponents in war is lawful and worthy of praise.' St. Ambrose thirty years later and St. Augustine at the beginning of the fifth century respect and elaborate this argument. . .

Modern Christians have used a number of arguments to justify their complete disregard of the precepts of Jesus in regard to war. Of the two most commonly employed, the first is the argument which asserts that Jesus meant his followers to accept the 'spirit' of his teachings, without being bound by the 'letter.' In other words he meant them to ignore his words completely and go on behaving, in all the practical details of life, as though they had never been uttered. . .

The second argument is that Jesus meant his ethical system to apply only to relations obtaining between persons, not to those obtaining between nations. . .

## C. *A Contemporary Christian View*

(Harry Emerson Fosdick, 'A Christian Conscience About War,' sermon delivered in Geneva, Switzerland, 13 September 1925. Reprinted by permission of the author.)

One ought to read with awe these words spoken nearly two thousand years ago and only now beginning to seem obviously true. Reliance on violence is suicidal, said Jesus. 'All they that take the sword shall perish with the sword.'

When the Master said that, it could not possibly have seemed to be true. Then it seemed evident that those who took the sword and knew how to use it could rule the world. Reliance on violence did not seem suicidal but necessary, salutary, and rich in its rewards. In these words of Jesus we have one of those surprising insights where, far ahead of the event, a seer perceives an obscure truth which only long afterward will emerge clear, unmistakable, imperative, so that all men must believe it. . .

Today my plea is simple and direct. Of all the people on earth who ought to take in earnest this unforeseeable confirmation of the Master's insight, Christians come first. This question of war and its denial of the method and spirit of Jesus is peculiarly their business. . .

Two generations ago one of our great statesmen, Charles Sumner, said, 'Not that I love country less, but Humanity more, do I now and here plead the cause of a higher and truer patriotism. I cannot forget that we are men by a more sacred bond than we are citizens—that we are children of a common Father more than we are Americans. . .'

The first Christians saw this. 'The early Church,' says a recent writer, 'was the first peace society.' Then came Christianity's growing power—the days when Christians, no longer outcast, were stronger than their adversaries, until at last the imperial household of Constantine himself accepted Christianity. Then

Christianity, joined with state, forgot its earlier attitudes, bowed to the necessities of imperial action, became sponsor for war, blesser of war, cause of war, fighter of war. Since then the Church has come down through history too often trying to carry the Cross of Jesus in one hand and a dripping sword in the other, until now when Christians look out upon the consequence of it all, this abysmal disgrace of Christendom making mockery of the Gospel, the conviction arises that we would better go back to our first traditions, our early purity, and see whether those first disciples of the Lord were not nearer right than we have been.

We cannot reconcile Jesus Christ and war—that is the essence of the matter. That is the challenge which today should stir the conscience of Christendom. . .

## D. *Gandhi's Satyagraha*

(Mohandas K. Gandhi, *Young India*, 2nd ed., New York, 1924, pp. 11-12, 260. Reprinted by permission of The Viking Press, Inc.)

For the past thirty years I have been preaching and practicing Satyagraha. The principles of Satyagraha, as I know it today, constitute a gradual evolution.

Satyagraha differs from Passive Resistance as the North Pole from the South. The latter has been conceived as a weapon of the weak and does not exclude the use of physical force or violence for the purpose of gaining one's end, whereas the former has been conceived as a weapon of the strongest and excludes the use of violence in any shape or form.

The term Satyagraha was coined by me in South Africa to express the force that the Indians there used for full eight years and it was coined in order to distinguish it from the movement then going on in the United Kingdom and South

Africa under the name of Passive Resistance.

Its root meaning is holding on to Truth, hence Truth-force. I have also called it Love-force or Soul-force. In the application of Satyagraha I discovered in the early stages that pursuit of Truth did not admit of violence being inflicted on one's opponent but that he must be weaned from error by patience and sympathy. . .

But, on the political field the struggle on behalf of the people most consists in opposing error in the shape of unjust laws. When you have failed to bring the error home to the law-giver by way of petitions and the like, the only remedy open to you, if you do not wish to submit to error, is to compel him by physical force to yield to you or by suffering in your own person by inviting the penalty for the breach of the law. Hence Satyagraha largely appears to the public as

Civil Disobedience. It is civil in the sense that it is not criminal. . .

I do believe that, where there is only a choice between cowardice and violence, I would advise violence. Thus when my eldest son asked me what he should have done had he been present when I was almost fatally assaulted in 1908, whether he should have run away and seen me killed or whether he should have used his physical force which he could and wanted to use, and defended me, I told him that it was his duty to defend me even by using violence. Hence it was that I took part in the Boer War, the so-called Zulu rebellion and the late War. Hence also do I advocate training in arms for those who believe in the method of violence. I would rather have India resort to arms in order to defend her honour than that she should in a cowardly manner become or remain a helpless witness to her own dishonour.

But I believe that non-violence is infinitely superior to violence, forgiveness is more manly than punishment. . .

## VII. THE SOVIET PHILOSOPHY OF WAR

(D. Feodotoff White, 'The Soviet Philosophy of War,' *Political Science Quarterly*, vol. 51, September 1936, pp. 323-9. Reprinted by permission of the Political Science Quarterly.)

Strange as it may seem, until very recently there were no systematic authoritative works giving the Marxist viewpoint on war. In Marxist literature one often meets references to the rich heritage of ideas on war bequeathed by the major prophets of Communism—Marx, Engels and Lenin. However, the Great Soviet Encyclopedia, published in 1928, blandly admits that what Engels said, worth knowing, about war is contained in a few pages of the second part of *Anti-Dühring*, and that Marx scattered observations on war in some of his historical works. The subject index to the complete edition of Lenin's works, printed by the Soviet State Publishing Concern, discloses practically the same picture. This naturally leaves a wide field to the lesser fathers of the Soviet church for the wielding of their croziers in the inquisitions held on the heresiarchs and apostates of Marxian socialism.

However, in so far as the basic definition of war as a social phenomenon is concerned, there is no real divergence of opinion between the ardent followers of the party line of today and the anathematized Trotzky. They all agree that good old General von Clausewitz, bourgeois idealist as he was, hit the nail on the head by defining war as a continuation of state policy by other means. The Marxist Fathers adopted this dictum of the Prussian militarist and, according to Lenin, have always considered the view expressed by the author of *Vom Kriege* a basis for the study of the significance of any war. This was amplified, in line with the philosophy of historic materialism, to mean that war between states is the continuation of the struggle between their respective ruling classes. 'Policy' is of course understood by the Marxists in a sense very different from that of Clausewitz. They define policy as concentrated economics, and also as the struggle between the classes.

There is no sentiment whatsoever in the Soviet attitude toward war. Soviet thinkers are thoroughly hard-bitten in their views on war, as they are on most important practical problems, reserving their sentiment only for the socialist 'kingdom come.' Some of them think that St. Augustine's definition of war as *magna latrocinia* is somewhat too narrow; they agree with him, however, to the extent of claiming that wars are conducted for material reasons, which constitute, according to Lenin's terminology, 'the objective content' of hostilities.

The wars of our days, according to the Communist theory, will be of several kinds: on one hand there will be imperialistic wars, aimed at the acquisition of areas productive of raw materials; on the other hand, the Soviets are firmly convinced that another armed intervention of capitalistic countries in the affairs of the U.S.S.R. is likely to occur. The latter form of war will be interwoven with civil wars. Revolutionary wars will result from the revolutionary situation which will be created by the involving of the masses of the people in another armed struggle on a large scale.

The Communists foresee also another category of wars: struggles for freedom on the part of the oppressed peoples of Asia, Africa and elsewhere, where one race is kept in subjection by another. They believe, however, that such wars have a tendency to evolve into revolutionary wars of the proletariat. From the Soviet viewpoint, class feeling and class aspirations of the bourgeoisie of India and China now overshadow national aspirations for independence from foreign oppressors to such an extent that in the future the struggle for national independence of the oppressed races can take place only under the leadership of the proletariat and will assume the character of revolutionary class wars. The divergence between the Chinese Nationalists of Nanking and the Soviet government undoubtedly helped towards the crystallization of that theory.

The Soviet sociologists do not except wars for liberation from their general principle that material reasons are the underlying cause of any war; in other words, that the struggle for political independence is only an expression of aspirations for a greater share in the material resources of the country.

Communists do not agree with the extreme view that wars will continue as long as men live on earth. They are firmly convinced, however, that wars will cease only with the complete downfall of the capitalist system and the final victory of the proletariat. Wars will cease then, because class struggle, the chief reason for wars, will disappear with the formation of a classless society throughout the world. In other words, if you want to see the end of wars, wish for a world revolution and the abolition of private property in means of production.

Neither Marx nor Engels was ever pacifistically inclined in the field of foreign or internal politics. The author of *Das Kapital* foresaw that '*on the event of any complete reconstruction of society the last word of social science will be: war or death, a death struggle or annihilation. Such is the irrefutable situation.*' The traditional school of historians, who give a large place to war in their histories, will be surprised to know that in so doing they have the approval of the Soviet philosophers of war. According to the latter, any large war brings with it changes in the economic as well as the social structure of society and becomes a point of departure for a new line of historical development. War, they admit, expedites the unfolding of processes which already were developing under the surface at a much slower rate.

Marx, the founder of modern Communism, called war the midwife helping the birth of a new society from the loins of the old order. Soviet theoreticians think that, under these circumstances, war has a positive useful function to perform in tearing down senile institutions and forms of human relations, which are impeding the development of the living forces of humanity. They believe that war accelerates the growth of the revolutionary forces and advances the advent of the revolution. This view presents a rather striking contrast to the much-repeated dictum that war is often an opiate for internal troubles. . .

Lenin thought that socialists could not oppose war in general. He considered that civil wars of the proletariat against the bourgeoisie were inevitable, and he envisaged the possibility of a war waged by a socialist country against bourgeois or reactionary countries. He stated that there was not a grain of Marxism in a program of disarmament and opposed to this the program of arming the proletariat in order to conquer and to expropriate the bourgeoisie. He maintained that the proletariat cannot disarm until it accomplishes its historical mission, after disarming the bourgeoisie. 'We never said,' writes Lenin, 'that the socialist republic can exist without an armed force. . .'

It is only fair to say here that while the Communists are not at all pacifist in principle and admit that revolutionary wars and wars for national liberation should be regarded as desirable phenomena and not an evil at all, they do not make any attempt to idealize war nor are they unaware that war acts as a negative selective process, weeding out the best elements of a nation.

Their viewpoint is very aptly expressed by one of the younger generation of the Russian Communists, a pioneer in the study of war from the sociological angle, B. I. Gorev: 'A knife is an instrument of crime in the hands of a robber and a tool of healing and liberation in the hands of a surgeon.'

This statement raises the question as to who is a 'robber' and who a 'surgeon' in so far as wars are concerned. Lenin gives a very definite answer to that query. He says that if the real meaning of the war consists in the overthrowing of a foreign domination, this war should be considered a 'progressive' war in so far as the oppressed nationality is concerned. In case of a war between Morocco and France, India and Great Britain, etc., Morocco and India would have 'justice' on their side, and the wars could be considered 'defensive' in the case of these countries, entirely regardless of who was the first aggressor. On the other hand, wars between imperialistic nations, whatever the excuse for hostilities, are always robber wars. The present actual head of the Soviet Army, M. P. Tukhachevskii, amplifies this thought by saying that a war of the proletarian Soviet state against an imperialistic state would be a 'just' and 'defensive' war.

Thus the problem is solved in a very simple, and from the Communist viewpoint, a quite logical way. The capitalistic countries will always be in the wrong—should they be attacked by the 'oppressed' nations or should Soviet Russia declare war on them; justice will be on the side of the attackers and not of the attacked. . .

One could sum up the Soviet theory of war as follows: a great war between Western nations would expedite the latent social processes and would hasten the unavoidable world revolution and the consequent establishment of the dictatorship of the proletariat on a world scale. As all wars between capitalistic states are 'robber' wars according to the Marxian-Leninist theory, it does not matter who is the aggressor or who the victim of the aggression. All that interests the Soviet thinkers is the question of the evolution of such a war between capitalist countries into civil wars or into wars of liberation of the oppressed colonial races against their imperialistic oppressors. They recommend that the Communists in their revolutionary work should use every effort to change imperialistic wars into civil wars, that they should develop the persistent policy of a single front of the proletarian masses. The discrepancy between the theory and the present practice of the Soviets as to the maintenance of international peace is quite obvious. . .

## VIII. The Regulation of War

Since war persists in spite of all preventive measures, the view is often expressed that it should be regulated by law so as to eradicate its most inhumane features. Hugo Grotius, the Dutch writer who did so much to establish international law, was a strong advocate of the regulation of war. Writing in 1625, he stated his case in the book *War and Peace,* a portion of which is given below. Grotius was one of the supporters of 'just wars.' Since his day the international law of war has been greatly developed. There are laws dealing with blockade, contraband, the treatment of prisoners, postal correspondence in war, and a host of other subjects. It is well known that the law has not been well obeyed. The strain upon it in such wars as World War I and World War II was tremendous.

### A. *A Statement by Grotius*

(Hugo Grotius, *De Jure Belli ac Pacis,* translated by F. W. Kelsey, 1925, pp. 18-19. Reprinted by permission of the Carnegie Endowment for International Peace, Division of International Law.)

Least of all should it be admitted which some people imagine, that in war all laws are in abeyance. On the contrary war ought not to be undertaken except for the enforcement of rights; when once undertaken, it should be carried on only within the bounds of law and good faith. Demosthenes well said that war is directed against those who cannot be held in check by judicial processes. For judgments are efficacious against those who feel that they are too weak to resist; against those who are equally strong, or think they are, wars are undertaken. But in order that wars may be justified, they must be carried on with not less scrupulousness than judicial processes are wont to be.

Let the laws be silent, then, in the midst of arms, but only the laws of the state, those that the courts are concerned with, that are adapted only to a state of peace; not those other laws, which are of perpetual validity and suited to all times. It was exceedingly well said by Dio of Prusa, that between enemies written laws, that is, laws of particular states are not in force, but that unwritten laws are in force, that is those which nature prescribes, or the agreement of nations has established. This is set forth by the ancient formula of the Romans, 'I think that those things ought to be sought by means of a war that is blameless and righteous.'

The ancient Romans, as Varro noted, were slow in undertaking war, and permitted themselves no licence in that matter, because they held the view that a war ought not to be waged except when free from reproach. Camillus said that wars should be carried on justly no less than bravely; Scipio Africanus, that the Roman people commenced and ended wars justly. In another passage you may read: 'War has its laws no less than peace. . .'

## B. *The Laws of War and the Atomic Bomb*

As this extract shows, the regulation of war by law has always been difficult. Can the use of the atomic bomb be outlawed? The author of the extract gives an opinion on this subject. For further references to this problem see Chapter 3 above.

(E. C. Stowell, 'The Laws of War and the Atomic Bomb,' *The American Journal of International Law*, vol. 39, 1945, pp. 784-6. Reprinted by permission of the *American Journal of International Law*.)

The invention and use of the atomic bomb should clarify our theories relative to the application of the principles governing the laws of war. In the case of a great world war, when the role of the few neutral nations is comparatively insignificant, the very nature of the conflict seems to deny the existence of any supreme or overruling law. Nevertheless, even in such a war the contesting group of states do acknowledge and more or less faithfully observe military treaties and agreements. In general also states having recourse to war have observed the convention signed in time of peace by which they agreed to give a previous notice of their intention to attack. The Japanese treachery in this regard is an exception to the modern practice of the civilized world. The states have also observed, save for retaliatory measures, the conventions concluded in anticipation of war regulating the laws of war and the treatment of prisoners.

When we examine the sanction of these rules, we find that it lies in the fact that such observance is in the interest of all concerned. Any temporary or incidental advantage to be gained by a disregard of these rules, it is recognized, would be overweighed by the deterioration of the conflict into pure savagery. In other words the laws of war are observed because generally speaking and by and large they help to protect the interests of both parties and promote the efficiency of military operations. Whenever any of the laws of war have been found to be a definite and permanent obstacle to the achievement of the objectives of war the sanction of common interest and the reason for the continuance of the rule have disappeared and the rule has not long been observed. In some cases such a rule does survive for a certain period because public sentiment supports it, and it would not be effective fighting to conduct military operations in defiance of this opinion. This opposition of public opinion to the effective application of the rational principles of the laws of war is especially felt in this era, when all governments are swayed and largely controlled by popular sentiment. This aberration and interference with the rational application of the laws of war may disappear when democracies have learned to rely more largely upon the scientifically derived views of their competent experts. In the meantime military commanders, in order to secure necessary governmental support, must take popular sentiment into account. This they must do even when they may understand that the popular views interfere with the effective prosecution of military operations and are of a nature to retard the achievement of the aims for which the war has been undertaken.

There is at present widespread popular support for two irrational and erroneous ideas in regard to the conduct of war. The first of these is the false notion that war is in the nature of a fair fight, in which the contestants should employ only the recognized weapons of warfare. Whenever a nation has discovered or employed a new weapon or means of attack, it has been regarded by the opponent as an unfair and treacherous act, and this irrational and sentimental attitude will be found to be shared by a certain proportion of the citizens of the innovating nation. So it was when firearms were first introduced, and more recently chivalrous naval commanders condemned the use of red-hot or chained cannon shot. Nevertheless the true principle that any means is legitimate that will conduce to effective fighting has always prevailed in the end to surmount popular outcry and validate the use of each new weapon. Yet an outburst of latent popular sentiment against any new weapon seems even today as likely to occur as ever. Time was perhaps when the fair man-to-man fight principle had social value for the survival of the most effective tribal groups. In any event this ideal must now be regarded as obsolete and a counsel of ignorance. The fallacious sentiment that war is like a fair fight must be considered to be an inhibiting dogma that retards the efficiency of military operations.

The second irrational and sentimental popular opinion relates to the inviolability or immunity of civilians from the effects of military operations. Formerly it was contrary to the dictates of military efficiency to molest or interfere with civilians over and above the exaction of the necessary requisitions and contributions to meet military needs. In actual practice it was found that the best results could be obtained for the troops by paying for these requisitions. Accordingly the obligation to pay or give a receipt was recognized by the Hague Convention as a rule of warfare. Similar considerations explain the practice and, within the limits of military necessity, the obligation not to interfere with the normal administration of occupied territory.

The conditions of modern warfare have, however, greatly weakened, if they have not entirely destroyed, the rational significance of this rule. Formerly a nation was defeated and forced to yield when its relatively small armed forces in the field were overcome. But today the whole nation is in arms and the victory is won by breaking the will of the whole nation to continue the fight. Hence it has become logical to bring pressure to bear on the civilian population in order that they may induce the government to yield. In the case of a totalitarian government, which has such complete control as to make it possible to disregard civilian influence and popular opposition, the enemy may have no choice but to direct operations against the whole nation until the government is forced to yield either from national collapse or in the interest of national survival. Another consideration subjects the civilians indirectly or incidentally to the dire effects of warfare, namely the fact that practically every phase of national activity contributes to the support and success of modern war. When traffic and industrial centers are bombed, it serves a very direct and important military purpose. The incidental civilian loss and suffering is also of military advantage in that it weakens the enemy's morale. This advantage may be somewhat counterbalanced by the sentimental humanitarian objections referred to above. When each of the contestants may expect to derive the same advantage from an exemption, it would be a case of wanton destruction and needless cruelty not to enter into a self-denying agreement or to observe in common practice a mutually advantageous rule.

The fact that poison gas was not used to any extent in Europe during World War II may have been due to the recognition of such common advantage, or it may have been that a possible allied advantage was foregone in deference to allied sentimental considerations of humanity. Under modern conditions of warfare the ancient rule forbidding the use of poison and the conventions condemning poison gas have become irrational and are likely to prove a trap for the more humane nations. Now that Great Britain and the United States have the greatest naval and commercial fleets it might be in the general interest of humanity to proscribe the construction and use of submarines. For submarines could only be of real importance in a world war, and in such a war surface naval and air-forces would suffice for the conduct of hostilities, without the submarine's destruction of seaborne commerce, so disastrous for post-war recovery. But this elimination of submarines would require the agreement of the three other members of the Big Five. It remains to be seen whether international coöperation has advanced so far that they will be willing to forego the development of this weapon which tends to minimize the advantage of a power that controls the surface and the air. In view of their probable answer it is doubtful if the proposal will even be made.

Now comes the atom bomb to force a more fundamental searching of the nature of warfare and the legitimate means for the pursuit of military objectives. In view of the frightful efficiency of the bomb and the consequent indiscriminate destruction of civilian life and property, it has aroused a considerable popular opposition. At the same time our military and governmental authorities have given it their support on the ground that it hastens the defeat of the enemy with a consequent saving of the lives of Allied soldiers. The argument might well be made that the bomb had the effect of saving more civilian Japanese lives than it took, and that it saved as well the lives of countless Japanese soldiers. Furthermore it may have saved the very national existence of Japan. It may have been a blessing in disguise to the Japanese nation: the Divine Wind that saved Japan from national hara-kiri.

When the pros and cons are summed up and all the arguments heard, it will be found that, pending a more perfect world organization and union shown to be capable of preventing wars, the laws of war cannot rule out any means effective to secure the ends of war. Nevertheless, when both parties derive an equal advantage from the recognition of a certain exemption or immunity, it will ordinarily be observed. This salutary principle rests upon the common interest of all states and of all humanity to avoid even in war any unnecessary waste or cruelty. . .

PART THREE

WORLD ECONOMICS AND SOCIAL PROBLEMS

# 13

# Technology in the Atomic Era

Before the Industrial Revolution international relationships were simple. Nations traded and monarchs were in constant touch with each other, but in total amount the contacts among the peoples of different countries were few and insignificant compared with those of today. The technological developments of the past century and a half have brought this change. Nowadays transactions of all kinds across boundary lines are countless and commonplace. The personal possessions of an ordinary American include a long list of household goods and gadgets bought in whole or in part from abroad. His telephone contains cobalt from the Belgian Congo, tungsten from China, nickel from Canada, and many materials from a score of other countries. The food he eats was produced in many parts of the world—coffee in Central or South America, tea in the Far East, bananas in the tropics, sugar in the West Indies or the Philippines. A person who lives in a country that, like England, does not produce a great variety of food, is so dependent on foreign sources that when an enemy in war cuts off the supply, he will be threatened with starvation.

These increased contacts between peoples brought by the Industrial Revolution are apparent in many other areas of activity. It is not uncommon in normal times for a million Americans to tour Europe during the summer months. Thousands of Americans enter Canada daily, most of them on temporary missions. The owner of a radio may tune in and hear broadcasts from all corners of the earth. By cablegram, telephone, telegram, and radio it is possible for anyone to send messages thousands of miles more quickly and safely than our ancestors once sent them to a neighboring village.

These increased contacts between nations have revolutionized international relations. They have added item upon item to the subjects requiring diplomatic attention. They have brought new means of understanding, as well as new sources of friction. They have provided new opportunities for cooperation and new opportunities for rivalry. They have placed prosperity and depression on a world-wide basis. In short, the new technology has given the world instruments that may be used either to advance or retard the welfare of mankind. Among them atomic energy is unique in its capacity for both constructive and destructive feats.

To date the implications of the new technology have not been taken into

327

account as they should have been in the actual conduct of international affairs. Nationalistic ambitions have prevented the greater world unity in political and economic matters which is demanded by modern production, the airplane, radio, and atomic energy. While present-day methods of production and distribution call for a world market, politicians acting in response to popular thinking have continued the old-time trade barriers. Although the destructive capacity of modern war weapons calls for world unity and an end to all warfare, diplomats are powerless to bring these changes as long as thinking remains nationalistic. The unbalance between the world's technology and the world's politics has never been more striking.

Because the new technology calls for a world order which is still beyond reach, it is necessary to try to solve by diplomatic processes the problems brought by the railroad, the airplane, radio, and atomic energy. Airplanes and railway trains cannot be used to advantage if they are obliged to stop at national frontiers. On the other hand, radio messages cannot be effectively prevented from passing over boundary lines. If frontiers cannot be obliterated, as technology has steadfastly demanded, then agreements must be made by nations to minimize the handicaps that they involve. Consequently there are treaties dealing with civil aviation, the radio, and railway traffic. The Security Council of the United Nations established an Atomic Energy Commission in 1945 to negotiate an international agreement on atomic energy. Some of the problems brought by modern technology to international relations are discussed in this chapter; others are dealt with in the remainder of Part Three.

## I. SCIENCE AND MAN

(Francis Bacon, *Novum Organum*, 1620.)

If, before the discovery of cannon, one had described its effects in the following manner: 'There is a new invention, by which walls and the greatest bulwarks can be shaken and overthrown from a considerable distance,' it is improbable that any imagination or fancy would have hit upon a fiery blast expanding and developing itself so suddenly and violently, because none would have seen an instance at all resembling it, except perhaps in earthquakes or thunder, which they would have immediately rejected as the great operations of nature, not to be imitated by man.

The human mind is so awkward and ill regulated in the career of invention, that it is at first diffident, and then despises itself. For it appears at first incredible that it should so long have escaped man's research. All of which affords good reason for the hope that a vast mass of inventions yet remains, which may be deduced not only from the investigation of new modes of operation, but also from transferring, comparing, and applying those already known, by the method of what we have termed literate experience.

Let men only consider: if they would apply only a small portion of the infinite expenditure of talent, time and fortune now given to matters and studies of far inferior importance and value, to sound and solid learning, it would be sufficient to overcome every difficulty.

## II. TRANSPORTATION AND COMMUNICATION

Even when travel and transport depended on horse-drawn vehicles and sailboats, boundary lines were nuisances; today with easy, quick, and cheap transportation by rail, steamship, and airplane the artificial obstructions set up at national frontiers are well-nigh disastrous. Much has been done by treaty to minimize these hardships. The League of Nations set up a special organization on communication and transit to promote the negotiation of such agreements. As a result of its work nineteen conventions had been concluded by 1938 dealing with such subjects as road traffic signals, freedom of transit, maritime ports, railways, and waterways of international concern. To continue this work the United Nations has set up a special commission on the subject under the Economic and Social Council.

### A. *Some Effects of Technology*

(S. W. Boggs, 'Mapping Some of the Effects of Science and Technology on Human Relations,' *Department of State Bulletin*, vol. xii, No. 294, 1945, pp. 183-8.)

The earth has changed but little since Man appeared, but the geography of human relationships has been transformed in a few decades. Because science knows no frontiers, scientists perhaps tend to overlook the remarkably uneven geographic distribution of the effects of their work.

The popular picture of a rapidly shrinking globe, based on the reduction of time required in circumnavigating the earth, is inaccurate and unfortunate. The world has not shrunk as if two thousand million microscopic ants had been banished from a pumpkin to live on a cherry. For the individual and for all types of corporate society, the range of activity and experience and the resources at the command of the individual and society have expanded astronomically. But the effects are distributed very unequally over the earth's surface; the geographic distribution is shifting rapidly and will apparently continue to undergo great changes. The present picture therefore gives no

adequate concept of what the future will be like. It is as if the outlines of continents were picture frames within which appeared ever-changing motion pictures, like montage effects in the cinema newsreels.

Little has been done by geographers and others to map these phenomena. Any maps that might be devised to portray them would be as definitely dated as the constantly changing political maps of the world. A chronological series of such maps, however, would constitute a slow-motion study and, perhaps, would reveal or clarify important historical trends. Intelligent men instead of struggling warily against the tide of history—now more like a cataclysmic tidal wave—might adapt themselves to making use of its power.

It would not be necessary to go back much farther than 1790 or 1800 for perspective. Tool steel and machine tools, which date from about 1770, began to make possible the utilization of scientific discoveries. The period is likewise significant because of the birth in the Americas of an infant republic and the spread in Europe of the ideas of the French Revolution; while in China that period coincides with about the maximum ex-

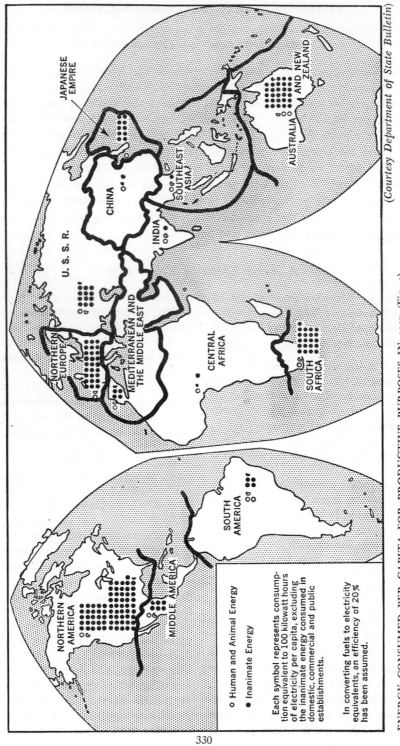

ENERGY CONSUMED PER CAPITA FOR PRODUCTIVE PURPOSES IN 1937 (Fig. 1)

(Courtesy Department of State Bulletin)

○ Human and Animal Energy
● Inanimate Energy

Each symbol represents consumption equivalent to 100 kilowatt hours of electricity per capita, excluding the inanimate energy consumed in domestic, commercial and public establishments.

In converting fuels to electricity equivalents, an efficiency of 20% has been assumed.

tent of the Manchu empire. Maps are advantageous for the presentation of data of this character because they show graphically the location and extent of change, and they cannot evade areas and subject-matter as dexterously as text can. . .

diversity in levels of living is largely due to differences in the quantities of energy consumed per capita for productive purposes. The map (fig. 1) reflects the situation in 1937. The changes within the last quarter century have been great, and

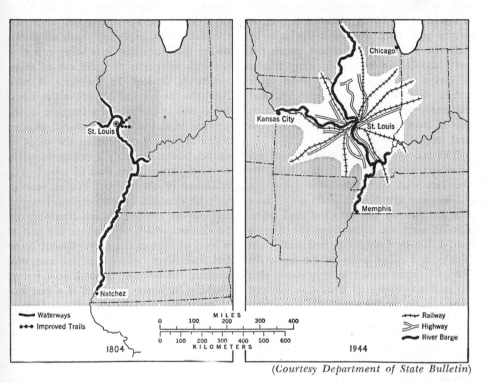

(Courtesy Department of State Bulletin)

EQUAL-COST DISTANCES FROM ST. LOUIS, MO., 1804 AND 1944 (Fig. 2)

In 1700 the distribution of available energy was practically uniform over the land surface of the globe, since man depended chiefly upon his own muscles, domestic animals, or slaves. But the multiplication of physical energy utilized by mankind, which is basic to all technological development, has resulted in an extremely uneven distribution of power utilized today. A lump of coal weighing about one pound now performs about as much work as a hard-working man in an eight-hour day; and one miner can mine several tons of coal a day. The present

they may be as great or even greater in the next 25 years.

Technological changes resulting in economical mass production and revolutionary developments in transportation and communication have produced two significant and closely related results: (1) Man's relation to his local environment has been radically altered; and (2) human relations have been transformed on a global scale. Men can go farther, bring more back home, utilize more raw materials, and do much more with what they get than even the scientifically minded and far-seeing Benjamin Franklin and Thomas Jefferson could imagine.

Available transportation maps usually show only the principal facilities. Little attempt has hitherto been made to show the significant differences in cost per ton-mile of freight movement. On a map centered at St. Louis, Missouri (fig. 2), as of the year 1804, equal-cost distances by different means of transport present a very simple pattern—with long fingers following the rivers, six or seven times longer downstream than upstream, and extremely slender because of the high cost of land transport in terms of human and animal effort.

The relative efficiency of land and sea transport prior to 1800 is illustrated by the fact that coal had been mined in Wales since Elizabethan times only where the sea actually cut into the coal fields. Cardiff, only six miles from the nearest coal fields by land, imported coal from Tenby and other ports to the west. An official customs report in 1775 stated that no coal was exported from Cardiff, 'nor ever can be, its distance from the water rendering it too expensive for any such sale.' Such are the hazards of prophecy in a world of changing technology. Indeed, as a supplement to navigable rivers, canals provided the only cheap inland transport, when they could be dug by the simple means then available.

On the map centered on St. Louis today the contrast with 1804 reveals great expansion in all directions, notably where railroads and motor roads rival the more efficient river transport. River rates, however, have been artificially raised to a certain percentage of railroad rates, so that the down-river distance for a given cost is now less than it was nearly a century and a half ago. . .

However great may be future changes in world maps showing the distribution of populations, transportation, and communication facilities, exploitation of min-

erals, and the like, the pattern appears to be already well developed. The abstract pattern of relationship possibilities, moreover, is not likely to change so much as it has already changed within the last century. In at least one direction the ultimate has already been attained. Communication is instantaneous, with the speed of light, and may reach all points of the globe at once; it is being extended through television and the use of many electronic devices. In the days of both Nebuchadnezzar and Napoleon the fastest travel was at the rate of a fraction of one percent of the velocity of sound, whereas today it rapidly approaches the speed of sound, but presumably it can never attain a speed many times that of sound. The efficiency of the railroad might conceivably be doubled or quadrupled, but presumably no method of land transport can be devised which will reduce the cost to a level of that of the most efficient ocean freighter. One factory machine may now perform the labor of 10,000 human beings working by hand, but even if a new machine is invented which will produce as much as one hundred machines do now, the order of change will be less than that which has already occurred. The wizardry of chemistry already unites rare materials from the ends of the earth so that men who produce tungsten in Kiangsi Province, China, are closer as economic neighbors in normal times to Pittsburgh, the Ruhr, and the British Midlands than to communities in China one hundred miles distant.

Scientists will doubtless produce marvels far beyond our present conceptions. Their insatiable curiosity is now penetrating fields of invisible and astonishing forces; they operate without fear and in a spirit of humility before fact which enables them to discard outworn hypotheses and to learn new ways very rapidly. The changes to come in many regions hitherto referred to as 'backward' may greatly exceed those already manifest in areas in which changes have been greatest in recent decades. The maps of human activi-

ties and relations will doubtless pass through rapid metamorphoses in the near future.

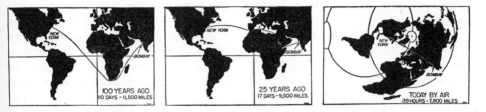

NEW YORK TO BOMBAY

## B. *Freeing International Travel*

Artificial obstacles to free international travel in the form of passports and frontier formalities are commonly set up by states. The League of Nations held several conferences on the subject, and the Economic and Social Council of the United Nations is continuing negotiations. The nature of the problem is discussed below.

('Freeing International Travel,' *United Nations Weekly Bulletin*, Vol. II, No. 12, 1 April 1947, pp. 330-3.)

International travel a generation ago was simple and leisurely paced. A traveller required a few minutes to buy a steamer ticket and possibly two weeks to cross the Atlantic. A business man who wanted to journey from one European capital city to another simply got aboard a train and went.

Today it takes barely a day to cross the Atlantic by plane. But the mandatory passport formalities preliminary to starting the journey may require weeks or even months. A flight between two national capitals may take only an hour, but the business man planning it may

need to begin passport negotiations two weeks before he leaves.

These hindrances to travel, which, in their modern form, developed at the time of the first World War and were intensified and increased during the second, have reached a point where they are 'both absurd and pernicious,' in the words of a report recently submitted to the Secretary-General by the International Chamber of Commerce. A large number of other organizations, both national and international, as well as manufacturers, airlines, railroads, shipping companies, travel agencies, and other groups and individuals interested in foreign commerce, have been working actively since the end of the war to secure a simplification of passport formalities as soon as possible. . .

Passports are of rather recent origin. It is an ironic coincidence that, before 1914, the international traveller could, with a few exceptions, move about freely without passport or visa, but that stifling formalities and restrictions began to grow at the same time that air transport increased the physical possibilities of very rapid travel.

In late Roman times and during the Middle Ages the passport, or the equivalent of it, was a document which helped rather than hindered travel. It authorized ambassadors, couriers, and important merchants to be provided with rooms at inns, fresh horses at relay stations, and armed guards. The passport was not an essential to travel, but it was a considerable convenience.

Following Europe's sixteenth- and seventeenth-century religious wars, the passport seems to have acquired its modern and vexing aspect when states began to use it as a means of excluding the great number of displaced persons who wandered over the continent. The rise of nationalism, industry, trade, and the middle class all contributed both to a tremendous increase in international commerce and travel on the one hand, and to the imposition of rules and formalities to regulate and control commerce and travel on the other.

In 1793, the Committee of Public Safety of the French Republic, in a defensive action directed at most of Europe's governments with which France was at war, instituted a comprehensive set of passport regulations. Restrictions similar to those were thereupon, again defensively, adopted by other continental powers. At the turn of the century, only Great Britain and the Scandinavian countries had failed to adopt extreme passport formalities.

The tide turned, however, early in the eighteen hundreds. Political liberalism was on the rise in Europe, and the railroads and telegraph stimulated international travel. By 1860, passport formalities were either abolished or generally disregarded in England, France, Germany, Italy, the Netherlands, Belgium, and Spain. The rules obtained strictly only in countries that were policed or that had not achieved liberal government, such as Austria-Hungary, the Balkans, Russia, Persia, and the Ottoman Empire. The severity of the czarist Russian laws was so pronounced that, in 1911, the United States abrogated a treaty with Russia because of them.

But outside Europe and the Near East the passport was almost unknown. The United States regarded a passport merely as a kind of letter of recommendation. Japan, which began to admit foreigners first in 1858, eliminated passports in 1899. Latin American countries had, for the greater part, policies of complete freedom.

The first World War changed the situation. A maze of documents and formalities suddenly came into being, seriously hampering international passenger movements even between friendly nations.

In 1920 the first gesture toward reform occurred—a Conference on Passports, Customs Formalities and Through Tickets, convened at Paris by the League of Nations, at which a series of recommendations designed to clear up the confusion was made. Thirty governments, replying to a subsequent inquiry by the League's Secretary-General, indicated that most of them had given effect, or were planning to give effect to the recommendations. Among the recommendations were the establishments of an identical 'international type' of passport, the principle that any fees charged should be non-fiscal and non-discriminatory, the limitation of visa requirements, and the abolition of the examination of registered luggage in transit. A second Passport Conference, at Geneva in 1926, further emphasized the need for these measures and advocated further reforms, including the regularization and simplification of control at frontiers, particularly in the case of journeys by train.

Matters never returned to the pre-1914 state, however. Little more was accomplished than the abolition by bi-lateral agreements of the visa requirement between a number of countries, and the simplification of formalities for obtaining passports. The second World War not only reimposed the old restrictions but brought additional ones, increasing the number and complexity of documents and formalities required for passenger travel. At the same time, the new factor of international air transport, with its special sensitivity to delay, has emphasized the need for simplification.

Simplification has, however, been very slow in coming. There are only a very few cheerful evidences of reform since the end of the war. Great Britain has recently made bi-lateral agreements, mutually abolishing visas, with Belgium, Luxembourg, France (including Algeria), and Norway. Five Central American countries are negotiating a five-way agreement for eliminating passports across their various frontiers.

In the above-mentioned survey of present conditions and of recommendations undertaken by the Secretariat as a preparatory memorandum to the Meeting of Experts to Prepare for a World Conference on Passports and Frontier Formalities, it is observed that the great variety of documentation required by travellers across national frontiers, includes passports (with entrance, transit, or even exit visas), health, smallpox, and police certificates, letters of recommendation, and landing cards. Some neighboring countries reciprocally dispense with the passport requirement for entrance, but as a rule these require some other form of identification of proof of nationality, such as tourist cards or birth certificates.

'The burden imposed by the number and variety of documents required,' the report states, 'is heightened by the variation in their form, by the variation in and frequent limitation of the duration and extent of their validity; by fees which are often fiscal; and by the formalities which attend the issuance of the documents.'

One of the more extreme proposals of the League's 1920 conference had general abolition of passports as its goal. By 1926, however, such a hope apparently was considered vain, and the conference of that year limited itself to recommending the facilitation of international passage by agreements between two or more states. The International Conference of National Tourist Organizations recommended last October that visa and passport simplification, in general terms, be effected at the earliest possible moment, and the International Chamber of Commerce recommended last June that facilities at least equal to those proposed in 1920 and 1926 be granted. . .

With regard to the visa (a word which, it is revealing to note, has been current in its present sense only since 1858, according to the *Oxford Dictionary*), most proposals noted in the memorandum call for complete abolition of what is clearly regarded in general as a nuisance. At the mildest, PICAO recommends that visa requirements be waived for non-immigrants and that the travel card it proposed be accepted in lieu both of travel-identity and of visa requirements.

It is proposed by PICAO that all Member states which require vaccination certificates should honor the international certificate of inoculation and vaccination of the International Sanitary Convention for Aerial Navigation of 1933 (amended in 1944). . .

## III. The Radio

To most of us the radio is only a source of enjoyment, but to statesmen it has presented many difficult problems. National legislatures have enacted volumes of laws to deal with the licensing of radio stations, wave lengths, and broadcasting policies. Internationally the radio has been the subject of both bilateral and multilateral negotiation and agreement. The use of the radio to assist ships at sea, the allocation of wave lengths, propaganda, and the promotion of understanding among nations have been the principal topics of negotiation. The extracts below deal with certain aspects of these subjects.

### A. *The Telecommunications Convention* (1931)

On 12 December 1901, wireless conquered the Atlantic Ocean, and two years later the first international radio conference was held in Berlin. The rules agreed upon in 1903, which are still in effect, require coastal stations to exchange telegrams with ship stations without regard to the system employed, provide that rates be divided on a 50-50 basis, that distress (SOS) calls have priority, that services be organized to avoid interference with other stations, and that the military and naval services are exempt from the provisions of the regulations except in regard to distress calls and interference. The Telecommunications Convention concluded in 1931 created a permanent Telecommunications Union, which, along with other activities, deals with wave lengths. In Europe the total number of wave lengths is slightly over a hundred in the medium wave band, while the long wave band provides space for only about twelve stations. Because the number of transmitters exceeds this supply of wave lengths it is necessary to share the ether. The first conference to deal with wave lengths was held in Washington in 1927. The distribution of wave lengths was revised at Madrid in 1932, and still later at Cairo in 1938. A conference at Montreux in 1939 confined itself to European wave lengths. Special attention may be called to the system of conferences set up within the International Telecommunications Union, whose constitution follows.

(*U.S. Treaty Series* 867.)

ARTICLE 1

*Constitution of the Union*

1. The countries, parties to the present Convention, form the International Telecommunication Union which shall replace the Telegraph Union and which shall be governed by the following provisions.

2. The terms used in this Convention are defined in the annex to the present document.

ARTICLE 2

*Regulations*

1. The provisions of the present Convention shall be completed by the following Regulations:

the Telegraph Regulations,
the Telephone Regulations,

the Radio Regulations (General Regulations and Additional Regulations), which shall bind only the contracting governments which have undertaken to apply them, and solely as regards governments which have taken the same obligation. . .

## ARTICLE 17

### Bureau of the Union

1. A central office, called the Bureau of the International Telecommunication Union, shall function under the conditions stated hereinafter:

2. (1) In addition to the work and operations provided for by the various other articles of the Convention and of the Regulations, the Bureau of the Union shall be charged with:

(a) work preparatory to and following conferences, in which it shall be represented in an advisory capacity;

(b) providing, in cooperation with the organizing administration involved, the secretariat of conferences of the Union, as well as, when so requested or when so provided for by the Regulations annexed to the present Convention, the secretariat of meetings of committees appointed by the Union or placed under the auspices of the latter;

(c) issuing such publications as will be found generally useful between two conferences.

(2) On the basis of the documents put at its disposal and of the information which it may gather, it shall publish periodically a journal of information and documentation concerning telecommunications.

(3) It must also, at all times, hold itself at the disposal of the contracting governments to furnish them with such opinions and information as they may need on questions concerning international telecommunications, and which it is in a better position to have or to obtain than these governments.

(4) It shall prepare an annual report on its activities, which shall be communicated to all members of the Union. The operating account shall be submitted, for examination and approval, to the plenipotentiary or administrative conferences provided for in article 18 of the present Convention.

. . .

## II–CONFERENCES

## ARTICLE 18

### Conferences of Plenipotentiaries and Administrative Conferences

1. The provisions of the present Convention shall be subject to revision by conferences of plenipotentiaries of the contracting governments.

2. Revision of the Convention shall be undertaken when it has been so decided by a preceding conference of plenipotentiaries, or when at least twenty contracting governments have so stated their desire to the government of the country in which the Bureau of the Union is located.

3. The provisions of the Regulations annexed to this Convention shall be subject to revision by administrative conferences of delegates from the contracting governments which have approved the Regulations to be revised, each conference itself determining the place and time for the following meeting.

4. Each administrative conference may permit the participation, in an advisory capacity, of private operating agencies recognized by the respective contracting governments. . .

## IV—SPECIAL PROVISIONS FOR RADIO

### ARTICLE 34

#### Intercommunication

1. Stations carrying on radio communications in the mobile service shall be bound, within the scope of their normal operation, to exchange radio communications with one another irrespective of the radio system they have adopted.

2. In order not to hinder scientific progress, however, the provisions of the preceding paragraph shall not prevent the use of a radio system incapable of communicating with other systems provided that this inability is due to the specific nature of the system and that it is not the result of devices adopted solely for the purpose of preventing intercommunication.

### ARTICLE 35

#### Interferences

1. All stations, regardless of their purpose, must, so far as possible, be established and operated in such a manner as not to interfere with the radio services or communications of either the other contracting governments, or the private operating agencies recognized by these contracting governments and of other duly authorized operating agencies which carry on radio-communication service.

2. Each contracting government which does not operate the radio facilities itself undertakes to require the private operating agencies recognized by it and the other operating agencies duly authorized for this purpose, to observe the provisions of 1 above.

### ARTICLE 36

#### Distress Calls and Messages

Stations participating in the mobile service shall be obliged to accept, with absolute priority, distress calls and messages regardless of their origin, to reply in the same manner to such messages, and immediately to take such action in regard thereto as they may require. . .

### ARTICLE 39

#### Installations of National Defense Services

The contracting governments retain their full freedom in regard to radio installations not covered by article 9 and, particularly, the military stations of land, maritime, or air forces. . .

## B. *The Political Use of Radio*

Radio broadcasts penetrate national frontiers and, unlike the printed word, reach millions of people who cannot read. For this reason the power of the radio as a propaganda weapon can scarcely be overestimated. Some broadcasts are directed at the home front and are intended to develop loyalty and unity, while others are for foreign consumption—to advance an ideology, to instill a feeling of distrust on the part of the listener toward his government, or to create good will toward the broadcasting state. The extract below describes these activities.

(Background Summary, *International Broadcasting,* Department of State, February 1947, pp. 1-8.)

Fifty-six nations, including the United States, today are beaming more than 4,000 hours of international short wave broad casting per week. These programs are designed to further national policy. At the same time, international broadcasting can make a tremendous contribution to understanding among people. Through the fair exchange of ideas and the spread of truthful, objective news people of varying creeds and ideologies can be brought closer in a world of rapidly shrinking frontiers. A brief examination of radio itself in its modern surroundings emphasizes its value to nations which use it for international purposes.

Scarcely more than a decade ago, international voice broadcasting was virtually unknown. Today broadcasts extend to the farthest hemispheres and can be heard by millions of persons of different races and nationalities. Radio is the only way in which one country can communicate directly and instantaneously with people in other countries. It is the only way of reaching large areas of the world blacked out by local censorship. It hurdles the barrier of illiteracy. It penetrates areas which have no access to or are denied other channels of information. It is not hampered by barriers to the flow of printed or pictorial matter. Restrictions on foreign exchange, paper or film shortages, cartel or tariff hurdles do not affect international broadcasting. Finally, the effect of the radio is personal and thus has an advantage over the printed word.

International voice broadcasting, like domestic broadcasting, aims at the largest possible audience. International voice broadcasting, however, may be considered successful if it reaches those persons abroad who exercise influence over public opinion and government decisions. Only an adequate signal and a sufficient number of receiving sets are needed to ensure the success of international radio. . .

## BRITISH BROADCASTING SYSTEM

The British Broadcasting Corporation, which is licensed by and controlled by the government, was broadcasting 616 hours and 35 minutes on 31 transmitters to foreign points per week during September, 1946. BBC short wave broadcasts to as many as 12 different places at the same time.

From its beginning in 1932, impartiality and objectivity have been the announced keynotes of BBC broadcasts throughout the world. This is brought out in a statement of British broadcasting policy presented to Parliament in July 1946 by the Postmaster General. It said: 'As far as the content of the Overseas service is concerned, the Government considers that great care should be taken to ensure the complete objectivity of the news bulletins which will form the kernel of all Overseas Broadcasting. The Corporation's reputation for telling the truth must be maintained and the treatment of an item in an Overseas bulletin must not differ in any material respect from its treatment in current news bulletins for domestic listeners.'

BBC programs to Europe in wartime served the dual purpose of refuting German propaganda and being a news source for underground newspapers. After the liberation of France, George Bidault, later to become President, said to BBC, 'It is partly, indeed largely, thanks to you, dear familiar voices, that our minds stayed free while our limbs were bound.'

Today BBC still performs an important and influential service in Europe. It broadcasts a total of 43 hours per day in 23 languages to Europe, impressing Europeans with what the British are doing at home. There is every indication that the British do not intend to allow their peacetime service to Europe to lag far behind their wartime broadcasts. . .

Broadcasting in 46 languages, BBC has been very active in other parts of the globe, too. Today it beams nine hours and 30 minutes per day to Latin American countries in Spanish and Portuguese. About three hours are beamed to the Far East in the following languages: Japanese, English, French, Malayan, Siamese, Burmese and Dutch and Kyoyu. To India it beams three hours and 15 minutes; four hours and 45 minutes to the Near and Middle East and five hours and 30 minutes to Africa. Its North American broadcasts total 14 hours and 15 minutes per day. In addition, BBC maintains a Pacific Service for Australia and New Zealand totalling four hours per day. For any who still are not contacted by BBC through any of these programs, there is a multi-direction antennae service known as the General Overseas Service which beams about 20 hours per day all around the globe. BBC recently inaugurated Russian-language broadcasts to the Soviet Union. . .

RADIO AUSTRALIA

The Commonwealth countries also maintain their own overseas radio services. 'Radio Australia,' for example, is operated by the Short Wave Division of the Commonwealth Department of Information in Melbourne. The short wave transmitters in Perth and Brisbane are heard well in most parts of the world, particularly in the United States.

In Australia there is a belief that short wave broadcasting might promote the products of the country. The following is from a recent issue of the *Australian Army Educational Journal,* 'Salt,' as quoted in the Radio News magazine, October, 1946: 'When it comes to advertisement of the goods we can and will produce, "Radio Australia" will be a big trade booster. What the commercial stations do for the local market can be done by "Radio Australia" for the world market. . .'

RADIO MOSCOW

In the Soviet Union, radio broadcasting is regarded as an ideal instrument for disseminating Soviet ideology. Andrei Vyshinsky, Deputy Commissar for Foreign Affairs, said it is 'a most important instrument of propaganda and agitation, . . . of Communist education of the people, . . . of enlightenment in the very highest sense of the word.'

International short wave broadcasts showed phenomenal growth in the Soviet Union during the war. Since then, it has been cut back in volume, but still remains an important means for the spread of Soviet views throughout the world. In May, 1944, the peak of Soviet international broadcasting, 90 hours and 44 minutes of short wave broadcasting were beamed daily in 37 languages through 15 short wave transmitters. By contrast, the USSR today broadcasts 42 hours and 10 minutes daily in 30 languages through 18 short wave transmitters. However, some countries which during the war were contacted only by international broadcasting now can be reached by other means. . .

Centralized control of the content of radio broadcasts, both internal and international, is assured by the administrative control over local radio committees by the All-Union Committee for Radio Broadcasting and Radio Communications. The Communist Party controls all propaganda activities. The nature of these activities is determined by the Central Committee of the Communist Party, in particular by its Politburo. The policies laid down by the Politburo are implemented by the Party's Chief Administration of Propaganda and Agitation. . .

A *New York Times* survey in April, 1946, showed the extent of Soviet influence by international broadcasting. This survey, made by *New York Times* Correspondents in principal European countries, showed that Communist propaganda is 'almost everywhere the most active and the most effective. Britain and United States are a bad second and third, with France an also-ran. . .'

## C. *The* 1936 *Convention*

The following agreement on the political use of the radio was negotiated under the auspices of the League of Nations and signed on 25 September 1936. It came into effect on 2 April 1938, but its provisions have not been carefully observed.

*(Bulletin of the League of Nations, Teaching,* No. 3, December 1936, pp. 173-4.)

### ARTICLE 1

The High Contracting Parties mutually undertake to prohibit and, if occasion arises, to stop without delay the broadcasting within their respective territories of any transmission which to the detriment of good international understanding is of such a character as to incite the population of any territory to acts incompatible with the internal order or the security of a territory of a High Contracting Party.

### ARTICLE 2

The High Contracting Parties mutually undertake to ensure that transmissions from stations within their respective territories shall not constitute an incitement either to war against another High Contracting Party or to acts likely to lead thereto.

### ARTICLE 3

The High Contracting Parties mutually undertake to prohibit and, if occasion arises, to stop without delay within their respective territories any transmission likely to harm good international understanding by statements the incorrectness of which is or ought to be known to the persons responsible for the broadcast.

They further mutually undertake to ensure that any transmission likely to harm good international understanding by incorrect statements shall be rectified at the earliest possible moment by the most effective means, even if the incorrectness has become apparent only after broadcast has taken place.

### ARTICLE 4

The High Contracting Parties mutually undertake to ensure, especially in time of crisis, that stations within their respective territories shall broadcast information concerning international relations the accuracy of which shall have been verified—and that by all means within their power—by the persons responsible for broadcasting the information.

### ARTICLE 5

Each of the High Contracting Parties undertakes to place at the disposal of the other High Contracting Parties, should they so request, any information that, in his opinion, is of such a character as to facilitate the broadcasting, by the various broadcasting services, of items calculated to promote a better knowledge of the civilization and the conditions of life of his own country as well as of the essential features of the development of his relations with peoples and of his contribution to the organisation of peace.

### ARTICLE 6

In order to give full effect to the obligations assumed under the preceding Articles, the High Contracting Parties mutually undertake to issue, for the guidance of governmental broadcasting services, appropriate instructions and regulations, and to secure their application by these services.

With the same end in view, the High Contracting Parties mutually undertake to include appropriate clauses for the guidance of any autonomous broadcasting organisations, either in the constitutive charter of a national institution, or in the conditions imposed upon a concessionary company, or in the rules applicable to other private concerns, and to take the necessary measures to ensure the application of these clauses. . .

### D. *The* 1936 *Inter-American Resolution on Radio*

*(International Conferences of American States,* First Supplement, 1933-39. A Collection of Conventions, Recommendations, Resolutions, etc., pp. 149-50. Reprinted by permission of the Carnegie Endowment for International Peace.)

Convinced that for the Moral Disarmament of peoples it is necessary to promote the 'stablishment of certain standards, in addition to those set forth in the Convention in force, concerning the use of radio-broadcasting in the interests of Peace,

The Inter-American Conference for the Maintenance of Peace

*Resolves:*

1. To recommend that the Governments of America, in so far as their respective internal legislation may permit, shall endeavor to encourage, in radio-broadcasting, the inclusion of themes relative to the benefits of peace and the peaceful settlement of international controversies, the scientific, intellectual, and material progress of Nations, and the promotion of a spirit of mutual understanding and moral disarmament of peoples;

2. To recommend that the Governments endeavor to avoid any radiobroadcasting, originating in any of the American Republics, or re-transmitted from some other source, by a radio station within its territory, that may disturb the peaceful relations between peoples, or wound national sensibilities of listeners in another country. . .

### IV. WORLD AVIATION

The airplane was invented only a few decades ago, but its use, both in peace and war, has become a vital concern of many nations. To date no effective control over its bombing activities has been established, although repeated efforts have been made in international law to confine its activities to military objectives. For its peacetime control there are many bilateral agreements, and three important multilateral treaties have been negotiated— the Paris Convention (1919), the Havana Convention (1929), and the Chicago Convention (1944). It was in recognition of the fact that civil aviation would be greatly expanded after World War II that the Chicago Conference was called to formulate a new agreement. This meeting was attended by the delegates of fifty-four states—all of the world with the exception of Russia, Argentina, and the enemy states. After some five weeks of deliberation in which several conflicting points of view were conciliated, an agreement was reached and a provisional organization set up. Subsequently, in March 1947, the permanent International Civil Aviation Organization came into being.

According to the Chicago agreement, a portion of which is given below, there is an Assembly in which each state will have an equal vote. This body may adopt amendments to the Convention by a two-thirds vote, and it selects a Council of twenty-one members. The Council elects its own president, who is a salaried official pledged to show no national favoritism. The Council is authorized to collect and distribute information on international air traffic—routes established and planned, subsidies, tariffs, airports, and the like. In addition it may, on request, investigate situations presenting obstacles to air navigation. A state may ask the Council to construct and administer its airport facilities.

### A. *The International Civil Aviation Convention*

#### PREAMBLE

WHEREAS the future development of international civil aviation can greatly help to create and preserve friendship and understanding among the nations and peoples of the world, yet its abuse can become a threat to the general security; and

WHEREAS it is desirable to avoid friction and to promote that cooperation between nations and peoples upon which the peace of the world depends;

THEREFORE, the undersigned governments having agreed on certain principles and arrangements in order that international civil aviation may be developed in a safe and orderly manner and that international air transport services may be established on the basis of equality of opportunity and operated soundly and economically;

Have accordingly concluded this Convention to that end.

. . .

#### PART II—THE INTERNATIONAL CIVIL AVIATION ORGANIZATION

#### VII—THE ORGANIZATION

ARTICLE 43—NAME AND COMPOSITION

An organization to be named the International Civil Aviation Organization is formed by the Convention. It is made up of an Assembly, a Council, and such other bodies as may be necessary.

ARTICLE 44—OBJECTIVES

The aims and objectives of the Organization are to develop the principles and techniques of international air navigation and to foster the planning and development of international air transport so as to:

(a) Insure the safe and orderly growth of international civil aviation throughout the world;

(b) Encourage the arts of aircraft design and operation for peaceful purposes;

(c) Encourage the development of airways, airports, and air navigation facilities for international civil aviation;

(d) Meet the needs of the peoples of the world for safe, regular, efficient and economical air transport;

(e) Prevent economic waste caused by unreasonable competition;

(f) Insure that the rights of contracting States are fully respected and that every contracting State has a fair opportunity to operate international airlines;

(g) Avoid discrimination between contracting States;

(h) Promote safety of flight in international air navigation;

(i) Promote generally the development of all aspects of international civil aeronautics.

. . .

## XIII—OTHER INTERNATIONAL ARRANGEMENTS

### ARTICLE 64—SECURITY ARRANGEMENTS

The Organization may, with respect to air matters within its competence directly affecting world security, by vote of the Assembly enter into appropriate arrangements with any general organization set up by the nations of the world to preserve peace.

### ARTICLE 65—ARRANGEMENTS WITH OTHER INTERNATIONAL BODIES

The Council, on behalf of the Organization, may enter into agreements with other international bodies for the maintenance of common services and for common arrangements concerning personnel and, with the approval of the Assembly, may enter into such other arrangements as may facilitate the work of the Organization.

### ARTICLE 66—FUNCTIONS RELATING TO OTHER AGREEMENTS

(a) The Organization shall also carry out the functions placed upon it by the International Air Services Transit Agreement and by the International Air Transport Agreement drawn up at Chicago on 7 December 1944 in accordance with the terms and conditions therein set forth.

(b) Members of the Assembly and the Council who have not accepted the International Air Services Transit Agreement or the International Air Transport Agreement drawn up at Chicago on 7 December 1944 shall not have the right to vote on any questions referred to the Assembly or Council under the provisions of the relevant Agreement.

## B. *The Bermuda Plan*

On 25 July 1946, the United States Government announced its intention to withdraw from the Chicago Agreement. Six months earlier an agreement had been signed at Bermuda by the representatives of the United States and Great Britain embodying a new air policy. The plan is a compromise between the points of view expressed by the United States and Great Britain at the Chicago Conference. It grants transit privileges and landing rights for non-traffic purposes on routes anywhere, subject to the Chicago provisions (freedoms one and two). Commercial privileges of entry and departure to discharge and pick up traffic are granted (freedoms three, four, and five), but only at designated ports and routes. It is necessary to have government approval for rates charged. Selected articles from the Bermuda agreement are given below.

*(Treaties and Other International Act Series*, 1507. Air Service Agreement between the United States and the United Kingdom, signed on 11 February 1946.)

## ARTICLE 1

Each Contracting Party grants to the other Contracting Party rights to the extent described in the Annex to this Agreement for the purpose of the establishment of air services described therein or as amended in accordance with Section IV of the Annex (hereinafter referred to as 'the agreed services').

## ARTICLE 2

(1) The agreed services may be inaugurated immediately or at a later date at the option of the Contracting Party to whom the rights are granted, but not before (a) the Contracting Party to whom the rights have been granted has designated an air carrier or carriers for the specified route or routes, and (b) the Contracting Party granting the rights has given the appropriate operating permission to the air carrier or carriers concerned [which, subject to the provisions of paragraph (2) of this Article and of Article 6, it shall do without undue delay].

(2) The designated air carrier or carriers may be required to satisfy the aeronautical authorities of the Contracting Party granting the rights that it or they is or are qualified to fulfil the conditions prescribed by or under the laws and regulations normally applied by those authorities to the operations of commercial air carriers.

(3) In areas of military occupation, or in areas affected thereby, such inauguration will continue to be subject, where necessary, to the approval of the competent military authorities.

## ARTICLE 3

(1) The charges which either of the Contracting Parties may impose, or permit to be imposed, on the designated air carrier or carriers of the other Contracting Party for the use of airports and other facilities shall not be higher than would be paid for the use of such airports and facilities by its national aircraft engaged in similar international air services.

(2) Fuel, lubricating oils and spare parts introduced into, or taken on board aircraft in, the territory of one Contracting Party by, or on behalf of, a designated air carrier of the other Contracting Party and intended solely for use by the aircraft of such carrier shall be accorded, with respect to customs duties, inspection fees or other charges imposed by the former Contracting Party, treatment not less favourable than that granted to national air carriers engaged in international air services or such carriers of the most favoured nation.

(3) Supplies of fuel, lubricating oils, spare parts, regular equipment and aircraft stores retained on board aircraft of a designated air carrier of one Contracting Party shall be exempt in the territory of the other Contracting Party from customs duties, inspection fees or similar duties or charges, even though such supplies be used by such aircraft on flights within that territory.

## ARTICLE 4

Certificates of airworthiness, certificates of competency and licenses issued or rendered valid by one Contracting Party and still in force shall be recognised as valid by the other Contracting Party for the purpose of operation of the agreed services. Each Contracting Party reserves the right, however, to refuse to recognise for the purpose of flight above its own territory, certificates of competency and licenses granted to its own nationals by another state.

## ARTICLE 5

(1) The laws and regulations of one Contracting Party relating to entry into or departure from its territory of aircraft engaged in international air navigation or to the operation and navigation of such aircraft while within its territory shall apply to aircraft of the designated air carrier or carriers of the other Contracting Party.

(2) The laws and regulations of one Contracting Party relating to the entry into or departure from its territory of passengers, crew, or cargo of aircraft (such as regulations relating to entry, clearance, immigration, passports, customs and quarantine) shall be applicable to the passengers, crew or cargo of the aircraft of the designated air carrier or carriers of the other Contracting Party while in the territory of the first Contracting Party.

## ARTICLE 6

Each Contracting Party reserves the right to withhold or revoke the exercise of the rights specified in the Annex to this Agreement by a carrier designated by the other Contracting Party in the event that it is not satisfied that substantial ownership and effective control of such carrier are vested in nationals of either Contracting Party, or in case of failure by that carrier to comply with the laws and regulations referred to in Article 5 hereof, or otherwise to fulfil the conditions under which the rights are granted in accordance with this Agreement and its Annex.

. . .

## C. *Aviation and World Politics*

(Quincy Wright, 'Aviation and World Politics,' *Air Affairs*, Vol. 1, No. 1, 1946, pp. 100-108. Reprinted by permission of *Air Affairs*.)

The airplane was invented and first flown in 1903. In forty-three years the trend of development has been regular and continuous for most indices with some temporary aberrations resulting from two world wars. Among these indices the following may be mentioned.

(1) The number of airplanes in the world has increased from one to a maximum of over a quarter of a million at the end of World War II. This number has diminished since hostilities ceased and possibly this maximum will not again be reached for a decade unless a new threat of war becomes serious. The number of non-military planes is, however, continually and rapidly increasing.

(2) The average size of planes has increased from less than half a ton to more than ten tons. While this average will probably decrease as the proportion of 'personal' and 'feeder' types of aircraft becomes greater, the size of transport and bombing planes will continue to increase.

(3) The average speed of planes has increased from thirty to over two hundred miles per hour, of military planes to almost four hundred miles per hour. The average speed will undoubtedly continue to increase.

(4) The safety of transport planes has increased from fatalities of twenty-seven to fatalities of under two per hundred million passenger-miles of travel. Even greater safety may be expected.

(5) The number of passengers carried in the United States increased from none to a present rate of six million per year. Further increases may be expected.

(6) The number of passenger-miles flown on regular routes in the United States has increased from none to four billion a year. Further increases can be anticipated.

(7) The cost of passenger travel has decreased from twelve cents to less than five cents per mile. Further decreases are expected.

(8) The quantity of mail and express carried has increased from nothing to 100 million ton-miles a year. Further increases are to be anticipated.

(9) The length of commercially feasible hops has increased from nothing to over three thousand miles.

(10) The number of types of planes has increased from one to hundreds specialized for peace and war. Non-military planes are specialized for speed, safety, water and ground landing, long and short hops, commercial use and personal use. Military planes specialized for transport, bombing, attack, reconnaissance, and water, ground, and carrier landing have proliferated in many types. The helicopter and other types for slow speed landing in limited space are in process of development, as are types for greater speeds, higher flights and longer flights.

(11) The number of regular operative routes has increased from none to a world network. Further routes are being continually opened.

(12) The number of airports in the world has increased from none to thousands. A large program of further airports is planned in the United States and in other countries.

(13) The equipment of airports and airways has improved with the development of means for providing accurate weather information, radio beacons, radar control, and other facilities for minimizing the influence of weather or regularity of schedules, and particularly safety of landing.

(14) The schedules of commercial planes have increased in regularity, reliability and frequency.

(15) The number of nations participating in the production of planes, the organization of airlines, and the licensing of pilots and routes has increased though the major commercial business is still conducted by companies or governments of less than a dozen states.

(16) Civil aviation has tended to be controlled by national governments in domestic commerce through government operation or regulation, and in international commerce through government owned or controlled 'chosen instruments.'

(17) While military aviation has predominated in number of planes used, the relative importance of civil aviation has tended to increase.

(18) As a military arm, aviation has tended to increase in relative importance as compared with armies and navies. . .

(19) The military characteristics of the airplane in performing its independent mission have developed steadily in all the elements which contribute to an efficient weapon, mobility, striking power, protection and holding power. Speeds of the bomber have increased to 400 miles per hour. Striking power has increased from comparative equality in man-hours cost and man-hours destroyed (characteristic of nearly all weapons of the past) to a ratio of 1 to 50 (1 to 6 for damage of strategic importance) for bombers with chemical explosives in the raids over Germany and Japan in 1945 and to a ratio 10 to 100 times greater with the atom bomb at Hiroshima and Nagasaki. A ratio many times greater is in prospect as the cost of atomic weapons decreases. Protection has increased not only through armor and machine guns, radar and observation bubbles but also through increased speed. Holding power has increased through the development of airborne troops and through the massive striking power of the

atom bomb, destroying all opposition over large areas.

(20) Use of the air arm in war has tremendously increased the power of the offensive compared with that of the defensive, particularly since the invention of the atom bomb greatly augmented the plane's striking power. This increase can be measured by the ratio of the cost of the weapon to its destructiveness in terms of man-hours, which with the atom bomb borne by airplane or rocket may rise to an order of a thousand man-hours of life and property destroyed to one man-hour expended in constructing and operating the weapon. The increase of offensive power can also be indicated by considering the influence of the extremes of mobility and striking power now possible through use of the plane. Mobility and protection are in general inversely related because protection, such as armor, interferes with mobility. But when mobility surpasses a certain threshold, it becomes invulnerable without special protection as did the Germans' V-2 weapon. Striking power and holding power are also usually inversely related, because high striking power ordinarily exhausts its ammunition and must retire unless a line of transport is maintained. When, however, striking power surpasses a certain threshold, it becomes invincible because it has destroyed all opposition. When the mobility and striking power of a weapon pass these thresholds, the offensive power of the weapon approaches the absolute. There is no defense except the fear of reprisal and even that defense may diminish as the power of the weapon becomes so great that the first attack by the aggressor may destroy its enemies' capacity to retaliate. In such circumstances the advantage of the initiative becomes tremendous. The war of surprise and pounce supersedes the war of momentum, of maneuver, and of attrition. . .

(21) Aviation has greatly increased the area over which government can exercise effective power to maintain order and justice. Estimates have been made of the average size of empires under different conditions in world history. These estimates made without knowledge of the atom bomb indicated that land forces alone could never have been adequate to implement world government. Sea power at its rate of advance might have been adequate for this purpose in some eight hundred years. Air power, however, had advanced so rapidly that it might be sufficient by 1950. Detailed studies have suggested that by a suitable distribution of bases and the organization of a relatively small policing force of reconnaissance, combat and bombing planes, international government could today prevent aggression and maintain justice and order throughout the world. The problem of world order has ceased to be primarily technical and has become almost entirely political.

In summary, the trend of the airplane has been toward increasing efficiency and increasing use as an instrument of transport, of communication, of commerce, of cultural diffusion, and of offensive war. This trend has progressively reduced technical and strategic distances in the world. It has diffused techniques and cultures, tending to reduce the differences of civilization throughout the world. It has increased the vulnerability of peoples everywhere to attack and has reduced the value of distance or geographic barriers as defenses against military attack, cultural penetration, or economic competition. It has created the technical possibility of a world police force capable of preventing aggression.

## CONDITION OF WORLD POLITICS

What has been the condition of world politics in this period?

(1) War has been more frequent, widespread, and destructive than in any pe-

riod of similar length, at least since the seventeenth century and probably in all human history.

(2) Centers of major military and political power have decreased in number and these centers have tended to exercise influence over the smaller states in their regions, thus augmenting the differential between the few 'great powers' and the other states.

(3) The balance of power has become less stable, international law has been less observed, and confidence in peace and order has declined.

(4) The governments of national states have tended to become more centralized and to plan economy and control opinion more completely and efficiently than ever before.

(5) War and preparation for war have tended to absorb a larger proportion of the population and the economic activities of the country than ever before.

(6) Persecutions and massacres under public authority or public tolerance have occurred with a barbarity and on a scale unprecedented in human history.

(7) International organization in the technical, economic, humanitarian and political fields has been more generally accepted, more comprehensive, and more active than ever before.

(8) International legislative treaties have been more abundant, more comprehensive, and more generally ratified than ever before.

(9) Institutions and procedures of international adjudication, conciliation, consultation, and inquiry have been accepted and used more widely than ever before.

(10) Declarations by governments, individually and collectively, have professed greater devotion to universal peace, to international justice, to human welfare, and to human rights than ever before.

These conditions, so obvious as to require no elaboration, manifest the extreme and conflicting developments, on the one hand, of government policies and actions supported by national sentiments oblivious to consideration of humanity, liberty, justice, and peace in the pursuit of national security, sovereignty and power. On the other hand, they manifest sentiments expressing the determination of all nations to promote the welfare and liberty of mankind, to pursue international peace and justice, and to develop a stable and orderly community of nations. There has been no general trend but two contradictory tendencies. Barbarities in the service of national power and expressions of allegiance to the most universal ideals have occurred simultaneously. . .

The airplane has been a powerful influence in the crisis of opinion, of world politics, and of civilization through which the world is struggling. Gunpowder, the printing press, and the mariner's compass steadily developed in efficiency and use during the fifteenth and sixteenth centuries, creating conditions to which medieval feudalism, ecclesiasticism, and cosmogony found it continually more difficult to adjust themselves. The diversities of opinion which resulted led to the chaotic politics and savage wars of the Renaissance and the Reformation. From these wars emerged the modern political order with the national state, international trade, and ideas of a universal family of nations.

Similarly today the airplane, the radio, and the atom bomb, steadily progressing in efficiency and use, are creating conditions to which the nationalism, the territorial sovereignty, and the power equilibrium of modern civilization find it difficult to adjust. Fortunately modern civilization has also developed ideas of humanism, liberalism, toleration, and scientific method better adapted to these new conditions. Emphatic and inconsistent opinions, however, have arisen, and have again produced chaotic world politics and bloody wars. From experience with these wars men as rational and social animals, but always inhibited by their varying loyalties from the past, are trying to create, select, and develop common ideas, beliefs, and institutions under which they can live in the age of the airplane, the Hertzian wave, and the nuclear fission. Can men reconcile their opinions as men and their opinions as citizens of the state by subordinating both to their opinions as citizens of the world? That is the problem which aviation has presented to world politics.

### V. TECHNOLOGY AND WAR

Dr. Harold C. Urey, a recipient of the Nobel Prize in chemistry, delivered an address on 21 October 1945, to commemorate the birthdate of Alfred Nobel. The following extract is from that address.

(H. C. Urey, 'The Atom and Humanity,' *International Conciliation,* No. 416, December 1945, pp. 790-95. Reprinted by permission of the Carnegie Endowment for International Peace.)

Alfred Nobel, whose birthday we celebrate today, was the inventor of dynamite and of smokeless propellent powders. At the same time that he engaged in this scientific research he was very much interested in bringing lasting peace to the world. In a conversation with one of his friends he remarked that his explosives would bring peace more quickly than peace societies. After some fifty years we now realize that Nobel was wrong in his conclusion, and we find that the peace societies were also unsuccessful. Today we are faced with far more powerful explosives than any that Nobel dreamed of, and we are still discussing wars and means of bringing peace to this planet. It is my purpose to discuss the relationship of this newest weapon, the atomic bomb, to the problem of world peace. May I say that this discussion has no relationship to any atomic bomb legislation or any diplomatic moves of the United States Government. It is intended to bring the urgency of the problem before you and to discuss some long-time views to enduring peace.

First of all I wish to show that the progress of every weapon that has been invented by man, proceeds through the stages of crude invention to successful improvements, and the development of counter-measures against it. The position of weapons of this kind, as we know them today, is that they are in use by major combatants, that they produce a great deal of destruction in modern war, and that no completely decisive defense against them has ever been secured. Only when a weapon is completely superseded by a more effective one does it disappear from war. Following this line of argument, we may expect that our atomic bombs will be obsolete only when more terrible weapons have been developed.

Machine guns were invented in the seventeenth century. They were relatively ineffective until the first World War when they were firing six hundred or seven hundred rounds per minute, and accounted for many casualties. During the second World War machine guns of many varieties were mounted on planes, tanks, ships, and other mobile mounts. Fighter planes carried as many as eight machine guns, and the large bombers were fully armed to take care of attack from any direction. The principle has been applied to larger caliber weapons, and these have had automatic aiming devices of great efficiency attached to them. No decisive counter-defense against the machine gun other than armor has been found, and there is no indication that any government in the world thinks that it does not need machine guns in modern war.

A submarine sunk the *Housatonic* at Charleston during our Civil War. Submarines were steadily improved. In the 1890's they had reached a size of about two hundred tons. In the first world war they began with six hundred to eight hundred tons and rose in size to about two thousand tons. In this last world war they very nearly won the battle of the Atlantic. Many counter-measures against the submarine were devised, and were found to be more expensive than the submarines which they fought. We won the battle of the Atlantic and the submarine was temporarily out. At the present time the talk is of larger submarines, and it is believed that they can be built.

The airplane was developed in the first years of this century. During the first World War it was used for scouting, and before the end of the war carried a machine gun. At the beginning of World War II the plane had evolved into the complicated machine of metal with engines of high power using high grade gasolines as fuels and carrying many machine guns and modern size bombs. Before the end of the war they evolved into enormous machines carrying many tons of bombs and machine guns to defend them. They finally were powered with jet-propelled engines and carried rockets to attack other airplanes and other objectives. They destroyed the cities of Germany and Japan and damaged cities of England, Russia, China, and Poland. No decisive defense against the airplane is known. Many intercepting devices have been developed, and they do prevent the plane from exerting its full effect. Only

superior air power was effective. Each combatant threw in every ounce of effort to manufacture more and better planes, bigger and more numerous bombs and more clever mechanisms to guide them and to detect them. And the victory came to the combatant with the greater industrial capacity. This victory came only after all combatants, with the exception of the United States, had been very seriously damaged by this weapon of modern war. In the future we may expect larger and faster military planes, and all cities of the world can be expected to crumble under the loads even of ordinary bombs which such planes will carry. Some will be intercepted, but some will get through any defenses that we are likely to devise.

I could repeat this story with tanks, plane carriers, high-caliber guns, and many other weapons great and small. Any abolition of a weapon is due to the invention of something still more effective in destructive power.

We might further mention some new weapons which were developed in this war. The V-1 or the so-called buzz bomb, caused some damage, but was rather easily intercepted because of its low speed. The V-2 was in a very different category. At the beginning of the war rockets were essentially toys, but at the end of the war this rocket travelled two hundred miles and rose nearly a hundred miles above the earth and arrived at a velocity above that of sound so that it could not be heard before it arrived. It seems that this weapon can be further improved and probably can be aimed from still greater distances and guided by radio control. It can be expected that it will follow the same course as others which we know.

Finally there is the most spectacular weapon of all—namely, the atomic bomb. This weapon stopped the war and probably saved the lives of many Allied soldiers. It also presents the people of the world with their most momentous problem. Briefly, it destroyed two cities of Japan. Four square miles of Hiroshima were utterly destroyed, and the area of devastation in the case of Nagasaki was even greater—approximately ten square miles. The total area of the city was not destroyed because of its narrow shape. The energy liberated was approximately equivalent to that released in the explosion of twenty thousand tons of TNT. These two bombs were the second and third of this type to be exploded, and the third one was definitely an improvement on the second.

In regard to the future development of this weapon, we can confidently expect that it will follow the course of other military weapons which I have discussed briefly above. We can hardly think that the atomic bomb is as primitive as the early machine guns, submarines, and airplanes at this stage, but that great improvements are possible seems a certainty. One can be quite sure that the ingenuity of man will make possible the manufacture of such bombs on a large scale.

Due to secrecy maintained in the development of this bomb, the attacks on the Japanese cities came as a complete surprise to the enemy. A single plane carried each bomb over its target. No attempt at interception by the enemy was encountered, so that bombing conditions were favorable as compared with what they would have been had the enemy expected an attack. The light construction of Japanese cities undoubtedly contributed to the vast destruction effected. It is hardly to be expected that steel structures would crumple so easily, though photographs of some of the industrial plants showed masses of twisted steel in the burned-out plants. In a modern city the destruction might not be so complete, but there is no doubt that the destruction would be vast and would probably set fires which would completely destroy modern buildings.

This weapon at its initial trial represents an advance over existing weapons beyond that secured by any other weapon ever devised, and considering the sort of weapons already mentioned this is indeed a remarkable statement. This weapon poses one of the most serious problems ever faced in the history of man, and beside it most other problems fade into insignificance. I am amazed that anyone can take our present day strikes, reconversion, transporting the soldiers home from abroad, and other current problems, very seriously. They will all be solved some way, and their solution, whatever it may be, will not affect any of us very greatly. But atomic bombs are a different matter entirely.

Let us consider the problem of a war of atomic bombs. X years from now we shall have a stock pile of these weapons and will have unprecedented power in our hands. If only no other countries have them we shall feel very safe and secure. Of course, the citizens of any other country in the world will feel the same way. Thus the British will feel safe if Britain has these bombs and no other country has them; the Russians will feel safe if they have them and no other country does, and so with the people of other countries. But if all of the countries of the world have them none of us will feel safe. On the contrary, we shall live in constant fear of sudden and violent death. A world of vast fear and apprehension will be our lot and that of our children. Whereas Hitler thought he could win his aggressive war in months, these weapons will encourage future aggressors to attempt the conquest of the world in a few days.

I have already mentioned what we may expect in regard to the future development of bombs, based upon the past experience with military weapons. It is unnecessary for me or you to have any special information in regard to future plans for atomic bombs to draw this conclusion. But even if no improvement in the bomb were possible, what we have learned from the newspaper accounts of the bombs already exploded, shows that they are bad enough. If one bomb will devastate an area of ten square miles, a thousand bombs of this kind if properly placed would devastate ten thousand square miles. The area of New York City covers a densely populated area of about three hundred square miles. From this it is easy to calculate that these one thousand bombs, if properly placed, would destroy thirty-three cities of the size of New York.

And what is there to prevent our assuming that with sufficient effort ten thousand bombs cannot be secured? It is wrong to assume that these weapons cannot be made in large numbers as a result of future improvements in known processes.

During World War I, a strip of country across northern France and Belgium was laid waste. In World War II the cities of Germany and Japan were almost totally destroyed, as were some of those of Russia and Poland. Extensive damage was done to the cities of England. Without considering the contribution that atomic bombs may make to the destruction of cities in future wars, is it not reasonable to expect that much more damage will be done in World War III? Is it not probable that the cities in the United States would also suffer? If atomic bombs are used in the next war it seems certain that all the principal cities of the world, including those of the United States, will be utterly destroyed, and their inhabitants killed. Perhaps some will disagree with this statement, but perhaps we can settle on half of them being destroyed, or a third, but does this make any difference in our considerations? Let us accept the fact that an atomic bomb war is bound to be much more destructive than this last war; that it is bound to extend to all of the industrial countries of the world.

We can expect that counter-measures will be devised, just as they have been in other cases. Some of these counter-measures will interfere with the delivery of the bombs. We can also expect that counter-measures to the counter-measures will be developed, and more effective methods for the delivery of bombs will be devised. It may be possible to interfere with the delivery of the bombs, but then some new device will be found by someone which will then make their delivery possible. What I wish to say is that we cannot expect that a defense will be devised which is so effective that neither the United States nor any other country will decide that it is useless to manufacture such bombs. It will again be the case of dog eat dog, and much effective indiscriminate biting will result in the process. Let us then set aside the assumption that a decisive defense will be secured. Such an assumption would be contrary to experience and would be the most foolish of wishful thinking. . .

## VI. Atomic Power

The most significant technological development of World War II was the discovery of atomic energy. It has already revolutionized warfare and its peacetime uses will be many and important. The implications of this new source of power to international relations are hard to overestimate. The utilization of atomic energy for the promotion of the health and welfare of people everywhere rather than for the manufacture of bombs is an imperative that can be realized only by international action. This new-found source of energy brings a new element into the field of power politics, a very disturbing element which adds immeasurably to the strength of nations able to produce it, so that the balancing of power has become more difficult. Although experience with atomic warfare is very limited, the world has learned enough about it to realize that it must in some way be prevented. All in all atomic energy gives new and strong arguments to the proponents of the one world principle. In the meantime, while the world must remain divided, the only way to control atomic energy is by agreement. The Security Council of the United Nations, working through a special Atomic Energy Commission, has been trying to devise a satisfactory system of control.

## A. *President Truman's Announcement—6 August* 1945

('Atomic Energy and American Policy,' *International Conciliation,* No. 416, December 1945, pp. 760-64. Reprinted by permission of the Carnegie Endowment for International Peace.)

Sixteen hours ago an American airplane dropped one bomb on Hiroshima, an important Japanese Army base. That bomb had more power than 20,000 tons of TNT. It had more than two thousand times the blast power of the British 'Grand Slam' which is the largest bomb ever yet used in the history of warfare.

The Japanese began the war from the air at Pearl Harbor. They have been repaid manyfold. And the end is not yet. With this bomb we have now added a new and revolutionary increase in destruction to supplement the growing power of our armed forces. In their present form these bombs are now in production and even more powerful forms are in development.

It is an atomic bomb. It is a harnessing of the basic power of the universe. The force from which the sun draws its powers has been loosed against those who brought war to the Far East.

Before 1939, it was the accepted belief of scientists that it was theoretically possible to release atomic energy. But no one knew any practical method of doing it. By 1942, however, we knew that the Germans were working feverishly to find a way to add atomic energy to the other engines of war with which they hoped to enslave the world. But they failed. We may be grateful to Providence that the Germans got the V-1's and the V-2's late and in limited quantities and even more grateful that they did not get the atomic bomb at all.

The battle of the laboratories held fateful risks for us as well as the battles of the air, land, and sea, and we have now won the battle of the laboratories as we have won the other battles.

Beginning in 1940, before Pearl Harbor, scientific knowledge useful in war was pooled between the United States and Great Britain, and many priceless helps to our victories have come from that arrangement. Under that general policy the research on the atomic bomb was begun. With American and British scientists working together, we entered the race of discovery against the Germans.

The United States had available a large number of scientists of distinction in the many needed areas of knowledge. It had the tremendous industrial and financial resources necessary for the project and they could be devoted to it without undue impairment of other vital war work. In the United States the laboratory work and the production plants, on which a substantial start had already been made, would be out of reach of enemy bombing, while at the time Britain was exposed to constant air attack and was still threatened with the possibility of invasion.

For these reasons Prime Minister Churchill and President Roosevelt agreed that it was wise to carry on the project here. We now have two great plants and many lesser works devoted to the production of atomic power. Employment during peak construction numbered 125,000, and over 65,000 individuals are even now engaged in operating the plants. Many have worked there for two and a half years. Few know what they have been producing. They see great quantities of material going in and they see nothing coming out of these plants, for the physical size of the explosive charge is exceedingly small. We have spent two billion dollars on the greatest scientific gamble in history—and won.

But the greatest marvel is not the size of the enterprise, its secrecy, or its cost, but the achievement of scientific brains in putting together infinitely complex pieces of knowledge held by many men in different fields of science into a workable plan. And hardly less marvelous has been the capacity of industry to design, and of labor to operate, the machines and methods to do things never done before so that the brain child of many minds came forth in physical shape and performed as it was supposed to do.

Both science and industry worked under the direction of the United States Army, which achieved a unique success in managing so diverse a problem in the advancement of knowledge in an amazingly short time. It is doubtful if such another combination could be got together in the world. What has been done is the greatest achievement of organized science in history. It was done under high pressure and without failure.

We are now prepared to obliterate more rapidly and completely every productive enterprise the Japanese have above ground in any city. We shall destroy their docks, their factories and their communications. Let there be no mistake; we shall completely destroy Japan's power to make war.

It was to spare the Japanese people from utter destruction that the ultimatum of July 26 was issued at Potsdam. Their leaders promptly rejected that ultimatum. If they do not now accept our terms they may expect a rain of ruin from the air, the like of which has never been seen on this earth. Behind this air attack will follow sea and land forces in such numbers and power as they have not yet seen and with the fighting skill of which they are already well aware.

The Secretary of War, who has kept in personal touch with all phases of the project, will immediately make public a statement giving further details.

His statement will give facts concerning the sites at Oak Ridge, near Knoxville, Tennessee, and at Richland, near Pasco, Washington, and an installation near Santa Fé, New Mexico. Although the workers at the sites have been making materials to be used in producing the greatest destructive force in history they have not themselves been in danger beyond that of many other occupations, for the utmost care has been taken for their safety.

The fact that we can release atomic energy ushers in a new era in man's understanding of nature's forces. Atomic energy may, in the future, supplement the power that now comes from coal, oil and falling water, but at present it cannot be produced on a basis to compete with them commercially. Before that comes there must be a long period of intensive research.

It has never been the habit of the scientists of this country or the policy of this Government to withhold from the world scientific knowledge. Normally, therefore, everything about the work with atomic energy would be made public.

But under present circumstances it is not intended to divulge the terminal processes of production or all the military applications, pending further examination of possible methods of protecting us and the rest of the world from the danger of sudden destruction.

I shall recommend that the Congress of the United States consider promptly the establishment of an appropriate commission to control the production and use of atomic power within the United States. I shall give further consideration and make further recommendations to the Congress as to how atomic power can become a powerful and forceful influence toward the maintenance of world peace.

## B. *United States Proposal*

The following is from an address delivered by Bernard M. Baruch, American representative on the Atomic Energy Commission of the United Nations, on 14 June 1946. He proposed an International Authority with extensive powers over all activities relating to atomic energy.

(United States Atomic Energy Proposals, *The United States and the United Nations,* Report Series No. 2, Department of State Publications, No. 2560.)

. . .

I now submit the following measures as representing the fundamental features of a plan which would give effect to certain of the conclusions which I have epitomized.

1. GENERAL. The Authority should set up a thorough plan for control of the field of atomic energy, through various forms of ownership, dominion, licenses, operation, inspection, research, and management by competent personnel. After this is provided for, there should be as little interference as may be with the economic plans and the present private, corporate, and state relationships in the several countries involved.

2. RAW MATERIALS. The Authority should have as one of its earliest purposes to obtain and maintain complete and accurate information on world supplies of uranium and thorium and to bring them under its dominion. The precise pattern of control for various types of deposits of such materials will have to depend upon the geological, mining, refining, and economic facts involved in different situations.

The Authority should conduct continuous surveys so that it will have the most complete knowledge of the world geology of uranium and thorium. Only after all current information on world sources of uranium and thorium is known to us all can equitable plans be made for their production, refining, and distribution.

3. PRIMARY PRODUCTION PLANTS. The Authority should exercise complete managerial control of the production of fissionable materials. This means that it should control and operate all plants producing fissionable materials in dangerous quantities and must own and control the product of these plants.

4. ATOMIC EXPLOSIVES. The Authority should be given sole and exclusive right to conduct research in the field of atomic explosives. Research activities in the field of atomic explosives are essential in or-

der that the Authority may keep in the forefront of knowledge in the field of atomic energy and fulfil the objective of preventing illicit manufacture of bombs. Only by maintaining its position as the best-informed agency will the Authority be able to determine the line between intrinsically dangerous and non-dangerous activities.

5. STRATEGIC DISTRIBUTION OF ACTIVITIES AND MATERIALS. The activities entrusted exclusively to the Authority because they are intrinsically dangerous to security should be distributed throughout the world. Similarly, stockpiles of raw materials and fissionable materials should not be centralized.

6. NON-DANGEROUS ACTIVITIES. A function of the Authority should be promotion of the peacetime benefits of atomic energy.

Atomic research (except in explosives), the use of research reactors, the production of radioactive tracers by means of non-dangerous reactors, the use of such tracers, and to some extent the production of power should be open to nations and their citizens under reasonable licensing arrangements from the Authority. Denatured materials, whose use we know also requires suitable safeguards, should be furnished for such purposes by the Authority under lease or other arrangement. Denaturing seems to have been overestimated by the public as a safety measure.

7. DEFINITION OF DANGEROUS AND NON-DANGEROUS ACTIVITIES. Although a reasonable dividing line can be drawn between dangerous and non-dangerous activities, it is not hard and fast. Provision should, therefore, be made to assure constant reexamination of the questions and to permit revision of the dividing line as changing conditions and new discoveries may require.

8. OPERATIONS OF DANGEROUS ACTIVITIES. Any plant dealing with uranium or thorium after it once reaches the potential of dangerous use must be not only subject to the most rigorous and competent inspection by the Authority, but its actual operation shall be under the management, supervision, and control of the Authority.

9. INSPECTION. By assigning intrinsically dangerous activities exclusively to the Authority, the difficulties of inspection are reduced. If the Authority is the only agency which may lawfully conduct dangerous activities, then visible operation by others than the Authority will constitute an unambiguous danger signal. Inspection will also occur in connection with the licensing functions of the Authority.

10. FREEDOM OF ACCESS. Adequate ingress and egress for all qualified representatives of the Authority must be assured. Many of the inspection activities of the Authority should grow out of, and be incidental to, its other functions. Important measures of inspection will be associated with the tight control of raw materials, for this is a keystone of the plan. The continuing activities of prospecting, survey, and research in relation to raw materials will be designed not only to serve the affirmative development functions of the Authority but also to assure that no surreptitious operations are conducted in the raw-materials field by nations or their citizens.

11. PERSONNEL. The personnel of the Authority should be recruited on a basis of proved competence but also so far as possible on an international basis.

12. PROGRESS BY STAGES. A primary step in the creation of the system of control is the setting forth, in comprehensive terms, of the functions, responsibilities, powers, and limitations of the Authority. Once a charter for the Authority has been adopted, the Authority and the system of control for which it will be responsible will require time to become fully organ-

ized and effective. The plan of control will, therefore, have to come into effect in successive stages. These should be specifically fixed in the charter or means should be otherwise set forth in the charter for transitions from one stage to another, as contemplated in the resolution of the United Nations Assembly which created this Commission.

13. DISCLOSURES. In the deliberations of the United Nations Commission on Atomic Energy, the United States is prepared to make available the information essential to a reasonable understanding of the proposals which it advocates. Further disclosures must be dependent, in the interests of all, upon the effective ratification of the treaty. When the Authority is actually created, the United States will join the other nations in making available the further information essential to that organization for the performance of its functions. As the successive stages of international control are reached, the United States will be prepared to yield, to the extent required by each stage, national control of activities in this field to the Authority.

14. INTERNATIONAL CONTROL. There will be questions about the extent of control to be allowed to national bodies, when the Authority is established. Purely national authorities for control and development of atomic energy should to the extent necessary for the effective operation of the Authority be subordinate to it. This is neither an endorsement nor a disapproval of the creation of national authorities. The Commission should evolve a clear demarcation of the scope of duties and responsibilities of such national authorities.

## C. *The Russian Point of View*

The Russian project for the control of atomic energy differs sharply from that of the United States. Russia has asked first for a convention outlawing atomic warfare, and second for the creation of committees on the exchange of scientific information and on the prevention of the use of atomic energy to the detriment of mankind. Extracts from the Russian plan follow.

*(Official Record of the United Nations Atomic Energy Commission, 19 June 1946, pp. 23-30.)*

### ARTICLE 1

The high contracting parties solemnly declare that they are unanimously resolved to prohibit the production and employment of weapons based on the use of atomic energy, and for this purpose assume the following obligations:

(a) not to use atomic weapons in any circumstances whatsoever;

(b) to prohibit the production and storing of weapons based on the use of atomic energy;

(c) to destroy, within a period of three months from the day of the entry into force of the present convention, all stocks of atomic energy weapons whether in a finished or unfinished condition.

### ARTICLE 2

The high contracting parties declare that any violation of Article 1 of the present convention is a most serious international crime against humanity.

### ARTICLE 3

The high contracting parties shall, within a period of six months from the day of the entry into force of the present convention, pass legislation providing severe penalties for violators of the statutes of the present convention.

## ARTICLE 4

The present convention shall be of indefinite duration.

## ARTICLE 5

The present convention shall be open for the adhesion of any State whether a Member or nonmember of the United Nations.

## ARTICLE 6

The present convention shall come into force after its approval by the Security Council and after the ratification and delivery of ratification documents to the Secretary-General for safekeeping by one half of the signatory States, including all the Member States of the United Nations named in Article 23 of the Charter of the Organization.

## ARTICLE 7

After the entry into force of the present convention it shall be binding on all States whether Members or nonmembers of the United Nations.

## ARTICLE 8

The present convention, of which the Russian, Chinese, French, English, and Spanish texts shall be authentic, is drawn up in one copy and shall be kept in the archives of the Secretary-General of the United Nations. The Secretary-General shall communicate certified copies to all the parties to the convention.

[*The text of the second proposal follows.*]

## CONCERNING THE ORGANIZATION OF THE WORK OF THE ATOMIC ENERGY COMMISSION

In accordance with the resolution of the General Assembly of 24 January, 1946, regarding the establishment of a commission to deal with problems raised by the discovery of atomic energy and other related matters, and in particular with Article 5 of the said resolution relating to the terms of reference of the Commission, the Soviet delegation deems it necessary to propose the following plan of organization of the work of the Commission for the initial stage of its activity.

### I. ESTABLISHMENT OF COMMITTEES OF THE COMMISSION

In pursuance of the aim indicated in the resolution of the General Assembly 'to proceed with the utmost dispatch and inquire into all phases of the problems,' it appears to be necessary to set up two committees which as auxiliary organs of the Commission would insure a thorough examination of the problem of atomic energy and the elaboration of recommendations, which the Commission must make in fulfilment of the resolution of the General Assembly and other organs of the United Nations.

It is proposed that the following committees should be set up:

*Committee for the Exchange of Scientific Information*

This committee shall be set up for the purpose of carrying out the aims indicated in point (a) of item 5 of the resolution of the General Assembly of 24 January, 1946.

The tasks of the committee shall include the elaboration of recommendations concerning practical measures for organizing the exchange of information:

(1) concerning the contents of scientific discoveries connected with the splitting of the atomic nucleus and other discoveries connected with obtaining and using atomic energy;
(2) concerning the technology and the organization of technological proc-

esses for obtaining and using atomic energy;

(3) concerning the organization and methods of industrial production of atomic energy and the use of this energy;

(4) concerning the forms, sources, and locations of the raw materials necessary for obtaining atomic energy.

*Committee for the Prevention of the Use of Atomic Energy to the Detriment of Mankind*

This committee shall be set up to carry out the aims set forth in points (b), (c) and (d) of item 5 of the resolution of the General Assembly.

The task of the committee shall be to elaborate recommendations:

(1) concerning the drafting of an international convention for outlawing weapons based on the use of atomic energy and prohibiting the production and use of such weapons and all other similar kinds of weapons capable of being used for mass destruction;

(2) concerning the quest for and establishment of measures to prohibit the production of weapons based on the use of atomic energy and to prevent the use of atomic weapons and all other main kinds of weapons capable of being used for mass destruction;

(3) concerning the measures, systems, and organization of control over the use of atomic energy and over the observance of the terms of the above-mentioned international convention for the outlawing of atomic weapons;

(4) concerning the elaboration of a system of sanctions to be applied against the unlawful use of atomic energy. . . .

## D. *Russian Criticism of the United States Plan*

The following extract is from a speech by Andrei Gromyko, Soviet delegate, before the Security Council on 5 March 1947.

(Text from *The New York Times,* 6 March 1947.)

. . .

Strict regulation of powers and duties of a control organ should exclude the unlimited access for inspection purposes to all equipment and operations, an access which is now provided for in the report of the Atomic Energy Commission, and should also exclude granting to inspection the right to shut down plants, to interfere with normal mining and milling operations and granting it the right of giving so-called licenses, that is, the permission to conduct definite activities on definite conditions, etc. Regulation of the activities of the control organs will exclude similar actions, which are described in such detail in the so-called first report on safeguards, contained in the report of the Atomic Energy Commission.

In reality to grant to the control organ unlimited rights and possession and management of the atomic establishments, cannot be looked upon as anything but an attempt by the United States to secure for itself world monopoly in the field of atomic energy. This tendency has found its expression in the proposals submitted by the representative of the United States on the Atomic Energy Commission and later laid down as the basis of the report of the Atomic Energy Commission. . .

The adoption of such proposals, as well as the plan of the atomic energy control as a whole, submitted some time ago by the representative of the United States is in contradiction with the basic economic and national interests of other States, for this plan is directed against their economic independence. It is directed against the independence of other States. The situation is not altered by the fact that such a proposal even finds support.

I have already had an opportunity to state the point of view of the Soviet delegation on the question of principle of unanimity of the five powers—permanent members of the Security Council, in connection with the discussion of the questions of the atomic energy control. The Soviet delegation considers that it will be impossible to reach an agreement on this question as long as the unacceptable proposal on the question of the so-called 'veto' is defended, since such a proposal is in contradiction with the principles of the United Nations.

I have also pointed out that there seems to be no difference of opinion among us on the question of the necessity of punishing violators, and there was not any on this subject. All agree that certain sanction measures should be applied against violators, if their guilt is proved. There is a divergence of opinions as to who . . . should take decisions on sanctions. Should such decisions be taken in accordance with the basic principles of the

United Nations or in violation of these principles?

The Soviet delegation considers that such decisions should be taken in strict conformity with the basic principles of our organization and should be taken by the organ which is charged with the primary responsibility for the maintenance of peace, that is, by the Security Council. The principle of unanimity of the five powers as such is not an obstacle to the effective control of atomic energy, no matter how someone tries to prove the opposite.

It is sometimes said that the proposals on the 'veto' question, contained in the American plan, did not touch the principle of unanimity of the five powers as such. Attempts are being made to prove this by the argument that the states themselves, according to the convention, should give up this right. Besides, it is pointed out that after an appropriate convention is concluded nobody should have the right of 'veto,' which might hinder the realization of this convention.

The same question remains as to whether the decisions on sanctions, after the conclusion of an appropriate convention, are to be taken by the Security Council, in which the principle of unanimity operates or by the control organ in which nobody will have the right of 'veto.' That is why the American proposals, in fact, affect the general question of the principle of unanimity in the Security Council. . .

## E. *Recommendations of the Atomic Energy Commission*

On 31 December 1946, the Atomic Energy Commission submitted a report to the Security Council. After setting forth its findings to date the Commission made several recommendations. Some of its findings, together with the recommendations, are given below. They conform closely to the American proposals submitted by Mr. Bernard Baruch.

('First Report of the Atomic Energy Commission,' *Department of State Bulletin,* Vol. XVI, No. 394, 19 January 1947, pp. 110-12.)

. . .

1. That scientifically, technologically, and practically, it is feasible,

(a) to extend among 'all nations the exchange of basic scientific information' on atomic energy 'for peaceful ends,'

(b) to control 'atomic energy to the extent necessary to ensure its use only for peaceful purposes,'

(c) to accomplish 'the elimination from national armaments of atomic weapons,' and

(d) to provide 'effective safeguards by way of inspection and other means to protect complying states against the hazards of violations and evasions.'

2. That effective control of atomic energy depends upon effective control of the production and use of uranium, thorium, and their fissionable derivatives. Appropriate mechanisms of control to prevent their unauthorized diversion or clandestine production and use and to reduce the dangers of seizure—including one or more of the following types of safeguards: accounting, inspection, supervision, management, and licensing—must be applied through the various stages of the processes from the time the uranium and thorium ores are severed from the ground to the time they become nuclear fuel and are used. (Cf. 'Findings on the Safeguards to Ensure the Use of Atomic Energy Only for Peaceful Purposes,' Part II B of this report.) Ownership by the international control agency of mines and of ores still in the ground is not to be regarded as mandatory.

3. That whether the ultimate nuclear fuel be destined for peaceful or destructive uses, the productive processes are identical and inseparable up to a very advanced state of manufacture. Thus, the control of atomic energy to ensure its use for peaceful purposes, the elimination of atomic weapons from national armaments, and the provision of effective safeguards to protect complying States against the hazards of violations and evasions must be accomplished through a single unified international system of control and inspection designed to carry out all of these related purposes.

4. That the development and use of atomic energy are not essentially matters of domestic concern of the individual nations, but rather have predominantly international implications and repercussions.

5. That an effective system for the control of atomic energy must be international, and must be established by an enforceable multilateral treaty or convention which in turn must be administered and operated by an international organ or agency within the United Nations, possessing adequate powers and properly organized, staffed, and equipped for the purpose.

Only by such an international system of control and inspection can the development and use of atomic energy be freed from nationalistic rivalries with consequent risks to the safety of all peoples. Only by such a system can the benefits of widespread exchange of scientific knowledge and of the peaceful uses of atomic energy be assured. Only such a system of control and inspection would merit and enjoy the confidence of the people of all nations.

6. That international agreement to outlaw the national production, possession, and use of atomic weapons is an essential part of any such international system of control and inspection. An international treaty or convention to this effect, if standing alone, would fail

(a) 'to ensure' the use of atomic energy 'only for peaceful purposes,' and

(b) to provide 'for effective safeguards by way of inspection and other means to protect complying States against the hazards of violations and evasions,' and thus would fail to meet the requirements of the terms of reference of the Commission. To be effective, such agreement must be embodied in a treaty or convention providing for a comprehensive international system of control and inspection and including guarantees and safeguards adequate to ensure the carrying out of the terms of the treaty or convention and 'to protect complying States against the hazards of violations and evasions.'

Based upon the findings of the Commission set forth in Part II of this report, the Commission makes the following recommendations to the Security Council with respect to certain of the matters covered by the terms of reference of the Commission, which recommendations are interdependent and not severable, embodying the fundamental principles and indicating the basic organizational mechanisms necessary to attain the objectives set forth in Part II C, General Findings, paragraph 1 (a)-(d) above.

1. There should be a strong and comprehensive international system of control and inspection aimed at attaining the objectives set forth in the Commission's terms of reference.

2. Such an international system of control and inspection should be established and its scope and functions defined by a treaty or convention in which all of the nations Members of the United Nations should be entitled to participate on fair and equitable terms.

The international system of control and inspection should become operative only when those Members of the United Nations necessary to assure its success by signing and ratifying the treaty or convention have bound themselves to accept and support it.

Consideration should be given to the matter of participation by non-Members of the United Nations.

3. The treaty or convention should include, among others, provisions

(a) Establishing, in the United Nations, an international control agency possessing powers and charged with responsibility necessary and appropriate for the prompt and effective discharge of the duties imposed upon it by the terms of the treaty or convention. Its rights, powers, and responsibilities, as well as its relations to the several organs of the United Nations, should be clearly established and defined by the treaty or convention. Such powers should be sufficiently broad and flexible to enable the international control agency to deal with new developments that may hereafter arise in the field of atomic energy. The treaty shall provide that the rule of unanimity of the permanent Members, which in certain circumstances exists in the Security Council, shall have no relation to the work of the international control agency. No government shall possess any right of veto over the fulfilment by the international control agency of the obligations imposed upon it by the treaty nor shall any government have the power, through the exercise of any right of veto or otherwise, to obstruct the course of control or inspection.

The international control agency shall promote among all nations the exchange of basic scientific information on atomic energy for peaceful ends, and shall be responsible for preventing the use of atomic energy for destructive purposes, and for the control of atomic energy to the extent necessary to ensure its use only for peaceful purposes.

The international control agency should have positive research and developmental responsibilities in order to remain in the forefront of atomic knowledge so as to render the international control agency more effective in promoting the beneficial uses of atomic energy and in eliminating its destructive ones. The exclusive right to carry on atomic research for destructive purposes should be vested in the international control agency.

Research in nuclear physics having a direct bearing on the use of atomic energy should be subject to appropriate safeguards established by the international control agency in accordance with the treaty or convention. Such safeguards should not interfere with the prosecution of pure scientific research, or the publication of its results, provided no dangerous use or purpose is involved.

Decisions of the international control agency pursuant to the powers conferred upon it by the treaty or convention should govern the operations of national agencies for atomic energy. In carrying out its prescribed functions, however, the international control agency should interfere as little as necessary with the operations of national agencies for atomic energy, or with the economic plans and the private, corporate, and State relationships in the several countries.

(b) Affording the duly accredited representatives of the international control agency unimpeded rights of ingress, egress, and access for the performance of their inspections and other duties into, from and within the territory of every participating nation, unhindered by national or local authorities.

(c) Prohibiting the manufacture, possession, and use of atomic weapons by all nations parties thereto and by all persons under their jurisdiction.

(d) Providing for the disposal of any existing stocks of atomic weapons and for the proper use of nuclear fuel adaptable for use in weapons.

(e) Specifying the means and methods of determining violations of its terms, setting forth such violations as shall constitute international crimes, and establishing the nature of the measures of enforcement and punishment to be imposed upon persons and upon nations guilty of violating the terms of the treaty or convention.

The judicial or other processes for determination of violations of the treaty or convention, and of punishments therefor, should be swift and certain. Serious violations of the treaty shall be reported immediately by the international control agency to the nations parties to the treaty, to the General Assembly and to the Security Council. Once the violations constituting international crimes have been defined and the measures of enforcement and punishment therefor agreed to in the treaty or convention, there shall be no legal right, by veto or otherwise, whereby a willful violator of the terms of the treaty or convention shall be protected from the consequences of violation of its terms.

The enforcement and punishment provisions of the treaty or convention would be ineffectual if, in any such situations, they could be rendered nugatory by the veto of a State which had voluntarily signed the treaty.

4. In consideration of the problem of violation of the terms of the treaty or convention, it should also be borne in mind that a violation might be of so grave a character as to give rise to the inherent right of self-defense recognized in Article 51 of the Charter of the United Nations.

5. The treaty or convention should embrace the entire programme for putting the international system of control and inspection into effect and should provide a schedule for the completion of the transitional process over a period of time, step by step, in an orderly and agreed sequence leading to the full and effective

establishment of international control of atomic energy. In order that the transition may be accomplished as rapidly as possible and with safety and equity to all, this Commission should supervise the transitional process, as prescribed in the treaty or convention, and should be empowered to determine when a particular stage or stages have been completed and subsequent ones are to commence.

# 14

# TRADE AND THE WORLD ECONOMY

MUCH of the subject matter of international relations is economic in character. Tariffs, most-favored-nations clauses, quotas, loans, cartels, civil aviation, raw materials, and currency are all world problems now. Ill will has been provoked by the protective tariff policy of the United States, by the British imperial preference system of 1932, by high-pressured Nazi trade agreements, and by currency manipulation on the part of many nations during the 1930's. Complaints have been made by Germany, Italy, and Japan that the world's supply of raw materials is badly distributed and that they have not had their fair share.

Most efforts to eliminate economic strife between nations have been aimed directly at the economic strife itself without trying to eradicate the struggle for power which often lies back of economic differences. These efforts are inspired by the fact that 'prosperity, like peace, is indivisible,' as Professor Eugene Staley has said, so that no nation can maintain a strong economy while others suffer from poverty and depression. It has been argued, too, that a reduction of economic strife will lead to a greater feeling of security and a consequent diminution of power politics. The more general economic basis of power politics was dealt with in Part Two. Here it is important to inquire—how far is it possible to carry economic co-operation in a world beset by the contest for power?

Followers of the free-trade theory, derived from the writings of Adam Smith, Richard Cobden, and John Bright—the latter two of the Manchester School of Economics in England—have insisted that international economic rivalry could be lessened, if not completely forestalled, by general acceptance among states of the policies they advocated. Since World War I, free trade has been accepted far more in theory than in fact by many of the most powerful national states. The trend toward planned economy in many parts of the world, accelerated to new heights by World War II, has led even further away from the practice of free trade. The United States, no less than other countries, has found it difficult to avoid using tariffs and other restrictive trade practices, but more recently this country has become the foremost proponent of freer international trade.

The League of Nations, through its Economic and Financial Organization, also worked persistently in this direction and succeeded in removing many

366

minor obstacles in world trade channels. The League was able to remove unnecessary formalities in customs administration and aided in freeing restrictions on the use of ports and waterways of international concern. It also arranged loans to destitute countries, but was unable to get at the heart of the problem, the real barriers to trade. Moreover, the World Economic Conference of 1933 called by the League to halt economic strife proved a complete failure. The most effective prewar action to diminish trade barriers was the tariff reduction program advanced by the United States after 1934. The effort of Secretary of State Cordell Hull, proponent of tariff reduction through reciprocal trade agreements, has also been continued in the postwar period.

The experience of the inter-war years, including the great depression and the resort to autarchy or economic nationalism in many areas of the world, made certain that economic problems would be given high priority in planning for peace after World War II. The devastation wrought by the war itself also forced economic problems to the forefront. To rebuild the devastated areas a temporary agency, the United Nations Rehabilitation and Relief Agency, was set to work. Two major lines of approach to postwar economic problems are dealt with in the extracts below. One is an examination of several new organizations designed to facilitate trade on a long-term basis and bring a measure of planning to bear on the more general problems of the world economy. The other relates to the co-operative efforts undertaken by the countries of western Europe to hasten their economic recovery at the suggestion of the United States and with large-scale financial backing from this country.

Among the new world bodies dealing with economic affairs, none may ultimately prove more valuable than the Economic and Social Council of the United Nations. Further explanation of this Council will be found in Chapter 15. The other international agencies for economic co-operation dealt with below include the International Trade Organization, the International Bank and the International Monetary Fund.

## I. FREE TRADE

The theory of free trade is generally accepted by economists, although it is not widely embodied in the practice of nations. Its advantages were first fully elaborated by Adam Smith in 1776 in his famous book *The Wealth of Nations*. Extract A below is taken from this work. This theory was further championed by Richard Cobden and John Bright of the Manchester School of Economists and held a prominent place in British thinking during the last half of the nineteenth century. Cobden and Bright, believing that war arose from economic causes, advocated free trade in order to achieve peace. Extract B following is a short statement by Cobden which develops this view.

## A. *Adam Smith on Free Trade*

(Adam Smith, *The Wealth of Nations,* edited by J. E. T. Rogers, Oxford, at the Clarendon Press, 1880, pp. 25-6, 31, 35-6, 38.)

By restraining, either by high duties, or by absolute prohibitions, the importation of such goods from foreign countries as can be produced at home, the monopoly of the home market is more or less secured to the domestic industry employed in producing them. Thus the prohibition of importing either live cattle or salt provisions from foreign countries secures to the graziers of Great Britain the monopoly of the home market for butcher's meat. The high duties upon the importation of corn which in times of moderate plenty amount to a prohibition, give a like advantage to the growers of that commodity. The prohibition of the importation of foreign woollens is equally favourable to the woollen manufactures. The silk manufacture, though altogether employed upon foreign materials, has lately obtained the same advantage. The linen manufacture has not yet obtained it, but is making great strides towards it. Many other sorts of manufacturers have, in the same manner, obtained in Great Britain, either altogether, or very nearly a monopoly against their countrymen. The variety of goods of which the importation into Great Britain is prohibited, either absolutely, or under certain circumstances, greatly exceeds what can easily be suspected by those who are not well acquainted with the laws of the customs.

That this monopoly of the home market frequently gives great encouragement to that particular species of industry which enjoys it, and frequently turns towards that employment a greater share of both the labour and stock of the society than would otherwise have gone to

it, cannot be doubted. But whether it tends either to increase the general industry of the society, or to give it the most advantageous direction, is not, perhaps, altogether so evident.

The general industry of the society never can exceed what the capital of the society can employ. As the number of workmen that can be kept in employment by any particular person must bear a certain proportion to his capital, so the number of those that can be continually employed by all the members of a great society, must bear a certain proportion to the whole capital of that society, and never can exceed that proportion. No regulation of commerce can increase the quantity of industry in any society beyond what its capital can maintain. It can only divert a part of it into a direction into which it might not otherwise have gone; and it is by no means certain that this artificial direction is likely to be more advantageous to the society than that into which it would have gone of its own accord.

Every individual is continually exerting himself to find out the most advantageous employment for whatever capital he can demand. It is his own advantage, indeed, and not that of the society, which he has in view. But the study of his own advantage naturally or rather necessarily, leads him to prefer that employment which is most advantageous to the society. . .

To give the monopoly of the home market to the produce of domestic industry, in any particular art or manufacture, is in some measure to direct private people in what manner they ought to employ their capitals, and must, in almost all cases be either a useless or hurtful regulation. If the produce of domestic can be brought there as cheap as that of foreign industry, the regulation is evidently useless. If it cannot, it must generally be hurtful. It is the maxim of every prudent master of a family, never to attempt to make at home what it will cost him more to make than to buy. The tailor does not attempt to make his own shoes, but buys them of the shoemaker. The shoemaker does not attempt to make his own clothes, but employs a tailor. . .

What is prudence in the conduct of every private family, can scarce be folly in that of a great kingdom. If a foreign country can supply us with a commodity cheaper than we ourselves can make it, better buy it of them with some part of the produce of our own industry, employed in a way in which we have some natural advantage. . .

The natural advantages which one country has over another in producing particular commodities are sometimes so great, that it is acknowledged by all the world to be in vain to struggle with them. By means of glasses, hot-beds, and hot-walls, very good grapes can be raised in Scotland, and very good wine too can be made of them at about thirty times the expense for which at least equally good wine can be brought from foreign countries. Would it be a reasonable law to prohibit the importation of all foreign wines, merely to encourage the making of claret and burgundy in Scotland? . . .

There seem, however, to be two cases in which it will generally be advantageous to lay some burden on foreign for the encouragement of domestic industry.

The first is, when some particular industry is necessary for the defence of the country. The defence of Great Britain, for example, depends very much upon the number of its sailors and shipping. The Act of Navigation, therefore, very properly endeavors to give the sailors and shipping of Great Britain the monopoly of the trade of their own country, in some cases by absolute prohibitions, and in others by heavy burdens upon the shipping of foreign countries. . .

The second case, in which it will generally be advantageous to lay some burden upon foreign for the encouragement of domestic industry, is, when some tax is imposed at home upon the produce of the latter. In this case, it seems reasonable that an equal tax should be imposed upon the like produce of the former. This would not give the monopoly of the home market to domestic industry, nor turn towards a particular employment a greater share of the stock and labour of the country than what would naturally go to it. . .

## B. *Free Trade and Peace*

(Speech, 28 September 1843, *Speeches by Richard Cobden,* London, 1870, p. 79.)

Free Trade! What is it? Why, breaking down the barriers that separate nations; those barriers, behind which nestle the feelings of pride, revenge, hatred, and jealousy, which every now and then burst their bounds, and deluge whole countries with blood; those feelings which nourish the poison of war and conquest, which assert that without conquest we can have no trade, which foster that lust for conquest and dominion which sends forth your warrior chiefs to scatter devastation through other lands, and then calls them back that they may be enthroned securely in your passions, but only to harass and oppress you at home.

## II. Economic Co-operation and Peace

At the outset of World War II, it was generally recognized that a far more earnest effort to achieve world-wide economic co-operation needed to be made after the war than had been undertaken following World War I. The 'economic anarchy' of the intervening period was too close to forget, and so were the futile efforts of the separate states to place their economies on a stable basis. Few competent observers doubted that the economic distress of the pre-war decades had contributed heavily to the cause of war. Debate still continues, however, on the question whether international economic co-operation can precede the achievement of world political security. This issue is discussed in Extract A below. It is followed in Extract B by a fuller review of the essential economic requirements which must be met if peace is to endure.

### A. *Economic or Political Peace?*

(F. D. Graham, 'Economics and Peace,' Chapter iv, in Craig *et al., The Second Chance*, pp. 115-26. Copyright 1944 by Princeton University Press.)

The famous dictum of Clausewitz, that war is but the continuation of a national policy hitherto pursued by other means, assumes that national policy is essentially invidious and that the interest of any one nation can be served only at the expense of others. To Clausewitz the state was essentially a fighting agency, inevitably predatory toward its neighbors, and the only important question was as to the means by which the predation should be carried on. Changing conditions might make it expedient to filch rather than rob, to use guile rather than force, to supplant frank and brutal violence by chicane, but the end was eternally the same—the exploitation and eventual destruction of rival states to the aggrandizement of one's own. War, in the broad sense of the term, was the natural, the persistent, the inevitable, relationship between states. The role of the statesman, therefore, was merely to choose the most effective means for its prosecution. Such international business as was carried on, in the interval between military conflicts, was merely a milder form of war, partly a substitute and partly a preparation for imminent military conflict. All other states were regarded as alien or hostile to one's own; their gain was your loss and their loss was your gain. The national objective in international transactions was to overreach, to deceive, and to exploit. . .

No one can understand the international aspects of Mercantilism, in the period from the beginning of the sixteenth to near the end of the eighteenth century, unless he looks on Mercantilism as essentially a political rather than an economic phenomenon. It is true, particularly in the later phases, that Mercantilism was perversely pressed on nations in the belief that economic progress was thereby promoted. In essence, however, Mercantilism had a purely political motivation. Its rationale was the rationale of war. Militarily weak states got no shrift unless they could play on the jealousies that the strong felt for one another. Special, non-reciprocal, favors were exacted from the weak states by the various strong powers and, at the same time, the weak states were conjured to cancel such favors to others. In this embarrassing position, and in a regime of international anarchy, their survival, if possible at all, was a matter of lucky accident. The Great Powers, with some vicissitudes, grew greater, and the small powers disappeared. . .

The leaders in the free trade movement in England had been ardent proponents of peace, and they thought that free trade would bring peace in its train. They mistook symptoms for causes and put the cart before the horse. Restraints on trade are rather the reflection than the cause of a warlike attitude, and their elimination is much more a result of a peaceful disposition than a prerequisite thereof. Though protection was nowhere, except in Britain, completely discarded, there had been no disposition to resort to discrimination between foreigners so long as the world remained free of the prospect of imminent international violence. But when, in the 'sixties and 'seventies of the last century, a new era of aggressive and illiberal empire-building was inaugurated, the results were as immediately apparent in the commercial as in the more purely political world. It is the great tragedy of our times that, after a peaceful spirit had been brought into international relations and the noncoercive ideals of economics had begun to sway the minds of men, the world did not proceed from strength to strength, in the conquest of war, but was overwhelmed in a resurgence of the wave of the past and not only reverted to, but exaggerated, all the invidious practices of Mercantilism in the apparent belief that theft rather than thrift is the road to wealth. The free traders in England had expected, and welcomed, the full independence of the various sectors of the British Empire. The parvenu empires were, therefore, not the result of any menace, but solely of national egotism.

The leader in the reversion to the bad old ways was Germany. In reviving the whole array of Mercantilistic practices, including unprovoked assaults on other nations, the Germans have argued that they were doing nothing that other states had not done before them. This is true but irrelevant. To accept the argument as a valid excuse for predatory conduct would be to put an end to all progress toward a better world. . .

The lesson of the last century clearly is that we cannot get peace through liberal economic policies but that we may get liberal economic policies through peace. Given international peace, there is every reason to believe that the mutual advantage to be obtained from commerce will progressively level existing barriers to trade. *But peace must come first.* If there is no peace or prospect of peace the only sane policy for any nation richly endowed with natural resources indispensable to war is to deprive potential enemies of access to them. This being so, we must make the approach to world peace in the political rather than in the economic sphere. As the political prospect improves, the possibility of liberal economic measures will increase, and we may then go on from peace to prosperity. A temporarily more prosperous world would not necessarily be peaceful but a peaceful world would surely promote prosperity. . .

## B. *The Economic Bases of Peace*

(E. Staley, 'The Economic Organization of Peace,' *Preliminary Report and Monographs,* Commission to Study the Organization of Peace, 1941, pp. 185-93. Reprinted by permission of the Commission.)

What are the essential economic conditions that must be met in the post-war world if the next peace is to be durable? Three things, this memorandum will suggest, are fundamental. First, there must be assurance of access to the world's markets and materials through peaceful exchange; that is, there must be economic alternatives to conquest. Second, there must be reasonable economic stability, for the disastrous booms and depressions which bring so much personal suffering also imperil the peace between nations. Third, there must be a coordinated program of progressive economic development, not merely because this will make rising living standards possible for the peoples of the world.

ECONOMIC ALTERNATIVES TO CONQUEST

Conquest as a means of increasing the economic opportunities of the peoples who engage in it is more likely than not to be a snare and delusion in the modern world. The people of Italy are worse off economically because they have Ethiopia. Japan's venture in China is not likely to improve the lot of the average Japanese citizen. Even if Germany should be victorious and should emerge from this war with complete control of Europe, and with a choice selection of overseas colonies, it is still questionable whether the ordinary German man or woman, paying taxes for the last war, supporting armies to defend the new conquest, preparing for still further battles, will have gained in his standard of living over what he might have enjoyed by peaceful trade. Modern military efforts are terrifically costly in terms of living standards, both before, during, and after the war. But even though conquest is a false road to economic opportunity, it may be tried if other roads seem to be blocked.

Even at the risk of appearing to lend support to misleading slogans like 'the haves versus the have-nots,' which are used by the propagandists of aggressor governments in ways that cannot stand critical examination, we must make this important point clear. Modern peoples cannot use their productive abilities to the best advantage if they are shut up within their own boundaries by regulations of their own governments or of other governments which drastically restrict access to the outside world. The industrial system of producing wealth demands large markets for standardized products and wide sources of supplies for important raw materials. Some national units in the world are so large that the market is wide enough and the raw material sources varied enough within their own boundaries to enable them to be fairly independent, if an emergency were to make that necessary. The United States, the Soviet Union, and the British Empire (as one entity) might be put in this class. Even these great areas, while they *could* get along under an industrial system with only their own resources, are much better off when they also have access to the markets and resources of the rest of the world. Thus, they can produce a surplus of their best specialties (cotton, wheat, tobacco, machinery, automobiles, electrical goods, et cetera, in the United States) and export them, using the purchasing power so obtained abroad to buy and import other things that are not so well produced within the country, e.g. coffee, tin, hand-made articles, fashion goods.

For all the other industrial countries of the world, however, and for countries not now industrialized where the people hope to raise their living standards by adopting modern techniques, this matter of access to the markets and the resources of the rest of the world is much more vital. All these countries must be able to sell and buy in the outside world, or else they must renounce much of modern production technology and depend on cruder, more primitive, less specialized ways of making a living—ways that certainly could not support at their accustomed levels of consumption anywhere near the present populations of such countries as Switzerland, Belgium, Japan, Germany, and Denmark. For the largest political units in the world, access by trade and investment to the different resources of other parts of the world is a great advantage; for the small and middle sized countries a certain amount of uninterrupted exchange is almost a matter of life and death.

One point must be seen clearly, because it is so often overlooked by advocates of economic isolation in America. If the large, well-endowed, political units, like the United States, build economic walls around themselves and decide to go in for self-sufficiency or even for a minimum of foreign trade, they are not merely renouncing the advantages of trade for themselves. *They are renouncing trade for other peoples, too.* The big country, giving up opportunities for two-way trade that it may be led to regard as unimportant, is depriving the small or middle-sized country of a necessity. . .

Are there peaceful alternatives which will enable energetic people to expand economically without having to extend the boundaries of their political sovereignty and without detracting from the economic opportunities of other people?

The answer is yes. The people in one country may benefit from the economic resources of the rest of the world if they have opportunity for exchange of goods, opportunity for borrowing or lending capital against future repayment, and opportunity for interchange of technical knowledge. An important characteristic of these three types of economic relations between peoples in different regions or different countries is that the benefit can be mutual. Trade, investment, and interchange of technical knowledge, if reasonably well organized, do not achieve a gain for one country at the expense of others, but enable all to be more productive and to increase their living standards beyond what they could achieve in isolation.

A word must be said about 'access to raw materials.' In large part the struggle for control over resources of raw materials is a struggle for military power. To satisfy the claims of those who want to be in a more effective position to wage war is certainly not the way to attain durable peace. On the other hand, there are certain legitimate claims bound up in the phrase 'access to raw materials.' In time of peace, every modern nation needs a steady flow of many different materials and foodstuffs; it can legitimately claim that it should not be penalized because it does not happen to have all the varieties it needs under its own flag. Have the countries with sovereignty over important raw material supplies withheld them from the so-called 'have-not' countries? The answer to this is, for the most part, no, not directly. (We are speaking now, of course, of peacetime conditions.) To be sure, there are many raw material restriction schemes—like the restrictions on cotton and wheat planting in the United States—but these have mainly been efforts to aid depressed producers and have not seriously impeded the 'access' of importing countries to raw material supplies. Cases of discrimination have been very few, so that by and large it is true to say that Germans and Japanese and Danes and Swedes have been able to buy American cotton or wheat or oil as cheaply as Americans, and they have been able to buy rubber or tin or nickel produced in the British Empire as cheaply as any Englishman. Indeed, discrimination has as often as not been against the home consumer, as when American agricultural price-raising measures have led to the 'dumping' of surpluses abroad. Furthermore, from the economic point of view (speaking of welfare economics, not war preparation) it was a misfortune to be too much of a raw material 'have' during the depression, for the raw material countries suffered more immediately and more severely than any others from the fall in prices. One so-called 'have-not' country (Japan) was able to stage a rapid recovery from the depression and even to embark on a boom while other lands were still in a slump, partly for the very reason that it did not produce its own raw materials and was able to import them at bargain prices. England's recovery also was aided by the cheapness of raw materials imported from abroad.

What reality there is behind the complaint about 'access to raw materials' in time of peace does not arise out of restrictions on raw materials as such. What really impedes access to raw materials is inability of potential purchasers of raw materials to sell enough of their own goods abroad in order to get the purchasing power that they need. In other words, it is the blocking of channels of trade in general, by tariffs, quotas, and all sorts of other import barriers, plus instability of world currency systems and the general sickness of trade in a depression that makes it difficult for countries which need raw materials to buy them. Trade has to be a two-way street. Impediments to a country's exports lower its ability to import (and vice versa). Thus, the general throttling of world commerce in recent years has made it hard for all countries to buy the things that they want. The other side of the lack of 'access to raw materials' which we hear so much about is an equal lack of 'access to finished goods' on the part of raw material producers who are unable to sell their commodities profitably. . .

## ECONOMIC STABILITY

A second condition of durable peace is reasonable economic stability. 'Stability' does not mean rigidity or lack of change and progress, but maintenance of balance among the shifting elements of the economic environment in such a way that changes can be fairly smooth. A wild boom, followed by a grim depression, throws millions out of jobs, disappoints the hopes of middle-class enterprises and investors, and creates a mental atmosphere of frustration. Under such conditions irrational political movements seize hold of the public mind and offer relief by projecting the people's troubles upon social enemies, real or imagined. Internally, the Jews, the Catholics, the Free Masons, the bankers, the 'reds,' are likely to be blamed. Externally, responsibility for the evils of the day may be projected onto foreign enemies, a humiliating treaty, loss of colonies, or military weakness. Nations, being composed of individual human beings, may be driven into something like a mass psychosis when reality becomes too hard to bear. Armament expenditures offer themselves as a remedy for economic troubles, and aggressive outward thrusts may appeal to political leaders as means of allaying popular discontent.

Violent economic fluctuations make peace insecure in still another way. In time of depression, when business men cannot market their goods and workers lose their jobs, the pressure on every national legislature to increase barriers against imports is irresistible. 'Keep the home market for home producers' is the universal slogan. Even the forty-eight United States of America, though forbidden by the federal constitution to interfere with inter-State commerce, find ingenious ways to erect trade barriers, especially in time of depression. Internationally, protectionism runs riot. Furthermore, emergency measures of many kinds —currency devaluations, exchange controls, quotas, NRA (National Recovery Act) regulations—add to the effective height of the economic walls around national boundaries. Thus, violent economic instability leads directly to measures which more than ever make economic opportunity seem to depend on political possession of territory—violating the first of the essential economic conditions of peace already discussed. . .

## ECONOMIC DEVELOPMENT

A third economic essential of durable peace is progressive economic development. There is an enormous amount of work still to be done in improving the productive equipment of the world, not only in the 'backward' countries but even in the most advanced industrial regions If this task can be properly organized in the postwar period, then all other economic adjustments, domestic and international, will be much easier to make. Large-scale construction, involving the expenditure of great sums in productive investments, will be necessary if we are to have an expanding world economy, and, practically speaking, it is only in a period of expansion that there will be

any chance of making real progress in the reduction of barriers to trade between nations or in the loosening of restrictions that hamper the internal economies of nations. Experience shows that in a contracting economy defensive, restrictionist, and nationalistic measures are likely to carry the day. Furthermore, large-scale construction plans, to be carried forward at a steady rate in the post-war period under the general leadership of governments, with ample provision for increasing the rate of publicly-stimulated investment when depression threatens, will be an indispensable part of any successful policy for maintaining world economic stability. Governmental leadership (which does not mean governmental execution of all projects) and international coordination will be necessary in order that there may be enough conscious planning and control over the rate of new investments to avoid sudden spurts and sudden cessations of activity like that which uncontrolled private investment produced in the late twenties.

Economic development through worldwide, coordinated construction plans, would, of course, justify itself in the long run by its effect in raising living standards. Only a few parts of the world are really well equipped, according to modern standards, for the daily battle against the niggardliness of nature, and even in such a well-equipped country as the United States many things still need to be done. All over the world there are tools to be made and installed, roads to be built, swamps to be drained, rivers to be controlled, waterfalls to be harnessed. It is probably in concerted efforts to do this job that the peoples of the world stand the best chance of finding what William James called 'a moral equivalent of war.'

III. Restrictions on Trade

Soon after World War II the United States Government formulated a list of proposals designed to promote freer international trade. The extract below is taken from a publication of the Department of State written in support of those proposals. It outlines the existing types of trade restrictions, both governmental and private, from which release is sought.

('New Horizons for World Trade,' *Commercial Policy Series,* No. 90, 1946, Department of State Publication 2591, pp. 3-9.)

1. Tariffs and Preferences

The restrictions imposed by governments on foreign trade take many forms.

Among the simplest are *customs duties* or *tariffs,* which are simply money payments exacted for the right to bring goods into the country.

Most countries have tariffs, and in most tariff systems the rates vary from article to article, depending on the extent it is desired to protect some local industry from foreign competition or to secure tax revenue. In the United States, for instance, coffee and bananas, which do not grow in our climate, both come into the country without any tariff—they are on the 'free list'—while wool and copper are both subject to rather heavy duties.

There is no magic formula for fixing the 'correct' tariff on articles in general or on any single article. The formula sometimes suggested—that tariffs should be high enough to protect any domestic producer from competition with goods produced at a lower cost in foreign countries—would simply stop all trade, barring smuggling. The only reasons for importing anything are that it cannot be obtained at home, that it is available in better quality or larger quantity abroad than at home, or that it can be bought more cheaply from abroad than at home. Nevertheless, in fixing the tariff rate for each commodity, differences of cost cannot be overlooked, together with other factors bearing on the demand for the supply of the commodity. The best expert judgment available must be applied to the problem. The whole national interest must be borne in mind, including the common interest in the expansion of trade and production.

It seems to be agreed that many tariff rates in many countries are too high. They tend to reduce the total level of world trade to the disadvantage of all nations. Many of the tariffs now in force came into existence during the depression and are a part of the economic conflict that dominated the 1930's. These high tariffs are not a good basis for the post-war economic revival that all nations want and which depends in large measure upon a general expansion in world trade.

The United States recognized early in the 1930's that its own tariff structure was reducing world trade and was too high for our own self-interest. Accordingly, since 1934, the United States has been embarked upon a program of tariff reduction by international agreement under the Reciprocal Trade Agreements Act.

Under this Act our own and foreign tariff rates are acted on selectively, item by item, by an orderly procedure of negotiation. Hearings are held on the commodities selected for consideration, and reductions in our rates are made after due consideration of all interests in return for concessions in other rates made by the other country. Every person in the United States with a special interest in the tariff placed on any commodity is given an opportunity to express his views. Many agreements have been made under the Act since 1934, and a considerable volume of trade in both directions has been stimulated without damage to any important American producing interest. . .

A more complicated form of regulating imports is the *tariff preference*. This means that the country that has tariff preferences has a low tariff rate, or none at all, on imports from certain places, and a higher rate on the same kind of imports from other places. We have such arrangements now with Cuba and will have with the Philippines after they have been independent for some years. The British countries have a more extensive system of imperial preference among themselves under the agreements made at Ottawa in 1932.

The effect of preferential tariffs is of course to channel trade between the parties to the preference arrangement to the exclusion, more or less, of outside countries. Whether it is more or less depends on how wide the margin is between the preferential and the regular rate. But whether the margin of preference is wide or narrow, outside countries are likely to regard it as a discrimination against them. Therefore, the Proposals suggest that the tariff negotiations to which they look forward should be directed to arrangements not only 'for the substantial reduction of tariffs' but also 'for the elimination of tariff preferences.'

Obviously, the extent to which countries maintaining tariff preferences will go in eliminating them will depend on the extent to which countries maintaining simple tariffs or other forms of trade control will go in the reduction of their own forms of armor.

## 2. Quotas, Embargoes, and Licensing Systems

Tariffs and preferences reduce the amount of goods which move in international trade by making the movement more expensive than it would otherwise be. Quotas reduce the amount directly by limiting the amount which may be imported or exported in a given period. Embargoes forbid import or export entirely.

When amounts are limited and more is offered than the limitation permits, obviously someone has to determine which of the goods offered will be permitted to enter or leave the country. Quota limitations are therefore often accompanied by licensing systems, under which officials of the government applying the quota select the transactions which are to be permitted and try to administer such systems fairly but often find it impossible to administer them to the satisfaction of all traders. They necessarily delay and complicate transactions and are the frequent cause of charges of favoritism and unfairness. If trade is to grow it is important that they be limited to really necessary cases and that fair rules for their administration be agreed to and be made known to traders.

It is impossible to outlaw the use of quotas and licensing systems altogether. No one would want to see unrestricted private trade in munitions or in dangerous drugs. Furthermore, when particular commodities are so scarce that they must be rationed to domestic consumers, no government can permit their unrestricted export. And when, in a particular country, foreign currency is scarce, the government has to make sure that the supply that is available is not wasted upon luxuries. For these and other reasons quota regulations both on imports and exports, and the licensing systems that go with them, will continue to exist. . .

### 3. SUBSIDIES

Many governments pay subsidies to stimulate the production of particular commodities, to sustain particular industries regarded as essential, or to stimulate exports of things that are produced in surplus.

During the war, for instance, the United States paid subsidies to bring highcost lead and copper mines into production and fixed 'support prices' to ensure supplies of various farm products. Under existing legislation, some of these support prices are guaranteed for two years after the war's end. At the end of the war export subsidies on cotton were resumed, in order to move part of the surplus to foreign markets. Under a wool plan recently recommended by the President, the Government would buy the domestic wool clip at fixed support prices, and resell the wool to mills at lower prices, competitive with foreign wool.

Other governments pay subsidies for a variety of reasons, though generally not on the scale which has been true in the United States in recent years. In general, subsidies seem to be a better way than tariffs or quotas to sustain those industries, regarded as essential, which could not survive unrestricted competition from abroad. Tariffs or quotas in such cases tend to restrict consumption by raising prices to all consumers; subsidies do not. The costs of special aid given industries of such national importance properly fall on taxpayers instead of on consumers. Also, since subsidies are visible and require appropriations of money from the treasury they are not so likely as tariffs to be continued after the need for them is over. The public can see what it is getting for its money. . .

### 4. EXCHANGE CONTROL

One of the most effective ways of controlling foreign trade is by manipulation of exchange rates or control of foreign exchange transactions. Traders have to deal in money, and governments which control their citizens' purchases and sales of foreign money have it largely within their power to control their foreign purchases and sales of goods. . .

### 5. STATE TRADING

The provisions so far outlined are for regulations imposed by governments on private traders. They obviously do not meet the case where governments conduct their foreign trade themselves.

There are two sorts of situations. In fully socialist countries, like the Soviet Union, all foreign trade is the monopoly of organs of the government. In other situations, like the old French tobacco monopoly, or the newer British arrangement for the public purchase of raw cotton, a government agency is the only authorized buyer or seller of some particular commodity. It is important to reach agreement on fair rules for the relations between both sorts of public traders and private enterprise abroad. . .

### 6. PRIVATE COMBINES

Trade may also be restricted by business interests in order to obtain the unfair advantage of monopoly.

In many lines this has not happened, but in others, as experience discloses, firms have banded together to restrain competition by fixing common selling prices, by dividing the world into exclusive markets, by curtailing production, by suppressing technology and invention, by excluding their rivals from particular fields, and by boycotting outsiders. These practices destroy fair competition and fair trade, damage new businesses and small businesses, and levy an unjust toll upon consumers. Upon occasion, they may be even more destructive of world trade than are restrictions imposed by governments.

Goods can surmount a tariff if they pay the duty; they can enter despite a quota if they are within it. But when a private agreement divides the markets of the world among the members of a cartel, none of those goods can move between the zones while the contract is in force. Clearly, if trade is to increase as a result of the lightening of government restrictions, the governments concerned must make sure that it is not restrained by private combinations. . .

## IV. Cartels and Commodity Agreements

Much objection has been raised to the restrictive effects of cartels on free international trade. In the form of agreements between independent business firms in various countries, these cartels are intended to increase profits by restrictions upon output or sales on the part of participating companies, by the allocation of market territories, price fixing, or patent and process exchange arrangements. Commodity agreements, on the other hand, are made by governments at the instigation, in most cases, of private business. Although they have dealt with the production and marketing of important products such as wheat, sugar, rubber, coffee, and tin, they have not been attacked as much as cartels. While both are restrictive of trade, the commodity agreements are publicized and are more concerned with the public interest than are cartels.

### A. *An Official American Statement*

(William Clayton, 'Private Barriers to International Trade,' a statement to a special committee of the Senate by the Assistant Secretary of State, *Department of State Bulletin*, vol. xii, No. 308, 1945, pp. 933-6.)

. . . A cartel is a kind of treaty of alliance between economic rivals. Cartels arise from a desire to avoid competition, which tends to lower prices, reduce profit margins, threaten the existence of high-cost producers, and diminish established capital values. The cartel may not completely eliminate rivalry, but it does suppress certain forms of rivalry, chiefly those which result in price competition. Individual firms may continue to seek their own expansion and preferment, but typically do so through striving for larger relative production quotas, control over patents and technological superiority, and through securing political support for extending their respective spheres of influence and control.

In their attempts to maintain or increase profits, cartels engage in a variety of practices. The most frequent of these practices are the partitioning of exclusive fields of industrial activity (e.g. the Standard Oil–I.G.Farben 'division of fields agreement' of 1929); division of markets through agreement to allocate trade territory (e.g. Dupont-Imperial Chemical Industries agreement for sharing world markets); allocation of production or export quotas through agreement to set absolute or relative limits on amounts of goods produced, sold, or exported (a standard device of the International Tin Cartel); restrictions upon new productive capacity (characteristic of the cartel arrangements among nitrogen producers); and fixing of prices and terms of sale (well illustrated by the International Aluminum Cartel).

These devices may be implemented by some form of direct agreement, by the terms of patent-licensing contracts, or by stock participations and joint control of subsidiary firms.

Cartels have enjoyed, moreover, some degree of government protection or support. Sometimes, indeed, government assistance seems to have been an essential requisite to the formation and continued existence or effectiveness of international cartel agreements. Both the tin and the rubber cartels belong in this category. Tacit government assent was given, furthermore, to master agreements of a cartel character made in the inter-war period among the top manufacturing associations of Germany and France and of Germany and England, followed after the outbreak of the present war by a similar agreement involving associations in England and France.

To avoid having to disclose their dealings to government inquiry and to escape prosecution in the country of operation, 'parent' companies have frequently sought to be domiciled under the protecting laws of countries in which regulation is lax and surveillance slight. Thus the efforts of a single country to control restrictive trade practices by an international combine may, in the absence of intergovernmental cooperation, be severely handicapped.

Cartelization of an industry typically results in reduced output, higher selling prices, higher profit margins, reduced employment, protection of highcost producer members, and more stable prices for cartel members.

In the international field, cartels impose by private treaty artificial barriers to international trade which give rise to international frictions and disputes, disturb the course of multilateral trade, and restrict opportunities for additional investment. By reserving the markets of colonies and mandates to producers situated in the imperial country, cartels also constitute a form of trade discrimination. For these reasons cartel practices are in conflict with measures to liberalize international trade policy.

International cartels also affect the balance of trade and the balance of payments of the various countries which are concerned either as buyers or as sellers of cartelized products. This influence is exercised through both price and quota allocation policies, and is most significant in a few cases in which a national economy rests heavily upon the exportation of one or two commodities. For example, on the one hand, Bolivia depends to a considerable extent upon tin exports for foreign exchange and public revenue. The maintenance of the tin cartel is therefore a matter of national interest to Bolivians. On the other hand, cartels in the chemical and other industries aggravate Bolivia's balance-of-trade difficulties by maintaining high prices upon imported commodities and by preventing so far as possible the development of manufacture in Latin America. . .

The political effects of cartels are subject to heated controversy, but four points at any rate seem beyond dispute. First, cartels necessarily imply the organization of producers, and organized groups exercise more political influence than unorganized groups. Hence cartels necessarily strengthen the political position of cartelized business as against unorganized business and the rest of the community. Second, the national interest is frequently asserted to be, and sometimes actually is, significantly involved in the success of a national group in an international cartel. Governments find themselves, therefore, under pressure to come to the support of their own business groups. Third, cartel policy often runs contrary to the policy of a national state, and under such circumstances may, in some cases, even circumvent or nullify national policies. Fourth, when an aggressive government undertakes political and industrial penetration of other countries, cartels often afford a convenient means.

This is what cartels do. What do we propose to do about them?

The cartel problem has been the subject of intensive study by a number of government agencies, through the mechanism of the Executive Committee on Economic Foreign Policy. I shall attempt to summarize briefly the major features of the cartel program which have emerged from this lengthy and exhaustive investigation.

Uncoordinated national action is not wholly satisfactory in meeting the problems raised by international cartels. The trade of every nation is affected by the operation of some international cartels which are beyond the reach of the laws of that nation. The United States, for example, has an important import interest in a number of commodities the production and sale of which are controlled by international cartels which are immune to prosecution under our antitrust laws.

Many Latin American countries and others as well are wholly at the mercy of international cartels in broad fields of business activity.

Moreover, the ability of cartel participants to choose a domicile which is especially favorable to the conduct of cartel activities means that other countries are seriously limited in their efforts to protect their own interests. Cartels which foresee difficulties in one jurisdiction are able to move to another whose laws protect the secrecy of business records and offer other facilities for the efficient conduct of cartel affairs.

Lastly, nations which are forced by the operations of foreign cartels to pay excessive prices for their imports are likely to be tempted to retaliate by encouraging the cartelization of industries in which they have an export interest. In this, as in so many other fields, uncoordinated national policies tend to multiply evils without really solving the underlying problems.

Accordingly, it has become clear to us that the international coordination of national policies is the most desirable means of meeting the problems raised by international cartels. . .

## B. *The Inter-American Coffee Agreement*

The coffee agreement given below is an example of international commodity agreements. Signed in 1940 by the main coffee-producing countries of Latin America and the United States, it was intended to stabilize the market by assuring a proportion of both the United States and the world-wide market for coffee to the various producers. As the agreement brings out, an element of flexibility in quotas is provided by the authority given to the Board to make adjustments where necessary.

*(U.S. Treaty Series,* 979.)

The Governments of Brazil, Colombia, Costa Rica, Cuba, the Dominican Republic, Ecuador, El Salvador, Guatemala, Haiti, Honduras, Mexico, Nicaragua, Peru, the United States of America, and Venezuela, Considering that in view of the unbalanced situation in the international trade in coffee affecting the economy of the Western Hemisphere, it is necessary and desirable to take steps to promote the orderly marketing of coffee, with a view to assuring terms of trade equitable for both producers and consumers by adjusting the supply to demand,

Have accordingly agreed as follows:

## ARTICLE 1

In order to allocate equitably the market of the United States of America for coffee among the various coffee-producing countries, the following quotas are adopted as basic annual quotas for the exportation of coffee to the United States of America from the other countries participating in this agreement:

| PRODUCING COUNTRY | BAGS OF 60 KILOGRAMS NET, OF EQUIVALENT QUANTITIES |
|---|---|
| Brazil | 9,300,000 |
| Colombia | 3,150,000 |
| Costa Rica | 200,000 |
| Cuba | 80,000 |
| Dominican Republic | 120,000 |
| Ecuador | 150,000 |
| El Salvador | 600,000 |
| Guatemala | 535,000 |
| Haiti | 275,000 |
| Honduras | 20,000 |
| Mexico | 475,000 |
| Nicaragua | 195,000 |
| Peru | 25,000 |
| Venezuela | 420,000 |
| Total | 15,545,000 |

For the control of the quotas for the United States market, the official import statistics compiled by the United States Department of Commerce shall be used.

## ARTICLE 2

The following quotas have been adopted as basic annual quotas for the exportation of coffee to the market outside the United States from the other countries participating in the Agreement:

| PRODUCING COUNTRY | BAGS OF 60 KILOGRAMS NET, OF EQUIVALENT QUANTITIES |
|---|---|
| Brazil | 7,813,000 |
| Colombia | 1,079,000 |
| Costa Rica | 242,000 |
| Cuba | 62,000 |
| Dominican Republic | 138,000 |
| Ecuador | 89,000 |
| El Salvador | 527,000 |
| Guatemala | 312,000 |
| Haiti | 327,000 |
| Honduras | 21,000 |
| Mexico | 239,000 |
| Nicaragua | 114,000 |
| Peru | 43,000 |
| Venezuela | 606,000 |
| Total | 11,612,000 |

## ARTICLE 3

The Inter-American Coffee Board provided for in Article IX of this Agreement shall have the authority to increase or decrease the quotas for the United States market in order to adjust supplies to estimated requirements. No such increase or decrease shall be made oftener than once every six months nor shall any change at any one time exceed 5 percent of the basic quotas specified in Article I. The total increase or decrease in the first quota year shall not exceed 5 percent of such basic quotas. Any increase or decrease in the quotas shall remain in effect until superseded by a new change in quotas, and the quotas for any quota year shall be calculated by applying to the basic quotas the weighted average of the changes made by the Board during the same year. Except as provided in Articles IV, V and VII, the percentage of each of the participating countries in the total quantity of coffee which these countries may export to the United States market shall be maintained unchanged.

The Board shall also have the authority to increase or decrease the export quotas for the market outside the United States to the extent that it deems necessary to adjust supplies to estimated requirements, maintaining unchanged the percentage of each of the participating countries in the total quantity of coffee to be exported to that market, except as provided in Articles IV, V, and VII. Nevertheless, the Board shall not have the authority to distribute these quotas among determined countries or regions of the market outside the United States.

## ARTICLE 4

Each producing country participating in this Agreement undertakes to limit its coffee exports to the United States of America during each quota year, to its respective export quota.

In the event that, due to unforeseen circumstances, a country's total exports of coffee to the United States of America exceed in any quota year its export quota for the United States market, that quota for the following year shall be decreased by the amount of the excess. . .

## ARTICLE 5

In view of the possibility of changes in the demand for coffee of a particular origin in the market outside the United States, the Board is empowered, by a two-thirds vote, to transfer, on the request of any participating country, a part of that country's quota for the United States market to its quota for the market outside the United States in order to bring about a better balance between supply and demand in special types of coffee. . .

## ARTICLE 9

The present Agreement shall be under the administration of a Board, which shall be known as the 'Inter-American Coffee Board,' and which shall be composed of delegates representing the Governments of the participating countries.

Each Government shall appoint a delegate to the Board upon approval of the Agreement. In the absence of the delegate of any participating country, his Government shall appoint an alternate who shall act in place of the delegate. Subsequent appointments shall be communicated by the respective Governments to the Chairman of the Board.

The Board shall elect from among its members a Chairman and a Vice Chairman who shall hold office for such period as it may determine.

The seat of the Board shall be in Washington, D. C.

## ARTICLE 10

The Board shall have the following powers and duties in addition to those specifically set forth in other Articles of this Agreement:

(a) The general administration of the present Agreement;

(b) To appoint any employees that it may consider necessary and determine their powers, duties, compensation and duration of employment;

(c) To appoint an Executive Committee and such other permanent or temporary committees as it considers advisable, and to determine their functions and duties;

(d) To approve an annual budget of expenses and fix the amount to be contributed by each participating Government, in accordance with the principles laid down in Article XIII;

(e) To seek such information as it may deem necessary to the proper operation and administration of this Agreement; and to publish such information as it may consider desirable;

(f) To make an annual report covering all of its activities and any other matters of interest in connection with this Agreement at the end of each quota year. This report shall be transmitted to each of the participating Governments. . .

ARTICLE 15

The votes to be exercised by the delegates of the participating Governments shall be as follows:

| | |
|---|---|
| Brazil | 9 |
| Colombia | 3 |
| Costa Rica | 1 |
| Cuba | 1 |
| Dominican Republic | 1 |

| | |
|---|---|
| Ecuador | 1 |
| El Salvador | 1 |
| Guatemala | 1 |
| Haiti | 1 |
| Honduras | 1 |
| Mexico | 1 |
| Nicaragua | 1 |
| Peru | 1 |
| United States of America | 12 |
| Venezuela | 1 |
| Total | 36 |

## V. THE INTERNATIONAL TRADE ORGANIZATION

In December 1945 the United States published its *Proposals for the Expansion of World Trade and Employment,* suggesting the creation of an International Trade Organization. This was expanded into a *Suggested Charter* in September 1946. Meeting successively at London, Lake Success, and Geneva, a Preparatory Commission of eighteen members set up by the United Nations incorporated several changes into the American draft. A United Nations Conference on Trade and Employment, meeting in Havana, Cuba, from 21 November 1947 to 24 March 1948, put the Charter in final form. The main objective of the I.T.O. is to raise living standards throughout the world. It proposes to do this by expanding international trade on a multilateral and non-discriminatory basis, by fostering production and employment, and by encouraging the economic development of backward areas. Extracts from an official summary of the charter prepared by the United Nations Department of Public Information are given below.

(Text from *The New York Times,* 25 March 1948.)

### I—PURPOSE AND OBJECTIVES

The first Chapter (Article 1) states in broad terms the purpose and objectives of the Charter and of the ITO. The purpose is defined by reference to Article 55 of the Charter of the United Nations. The objectives are listed as:

(a) To assure a large and steadily growing volume of real income and effective demand, to increase the production, consumption, and exchange of goods, and so to contribute to a balanced and expanding world economy.

(b) To promote industrial and general economic development, particularly of those countries which are still in the early stages of industrial development, and to encourage the international flow of capital for productive investment.

(c) To further the enjoyment by all countries, on equal terms, of access to the markets, products and productive facilities which are needed for their economic prosperity and development.

(d) To promote on a reciprocal and mutually advantageous basis the reduction of tariffs and other barriers to trade and the elimination of discriminatory treatment in international commerce.

(e) To enable countries, by increasing the opportunities for their trade and economic development, to abstain from measures which would disrupt world commerce, reduce productive employment or retard economic progress.

(f) To facilitate the solution of problems relating to international trade in the fields of employment, economic development, commercial policy, business practices and commodity policy.

## II—EMPLOYMENT AND ECONOMIC ACTIVITY

### (ARTICLES 2 TO 7)

Chapter 2 declares that the avoidance of unemployment and underemployment is not of domestic concern alone but is also a necessary condition for the realization of the general objectives of the Charter, including the expansion of international trade, and for the well-being of all other countries.

Under Article 3 (Maintenance of Domestic Employment) each member will take action to achieve and maintain full and productive employment and a large and steadily growing demand within its own territory through measures appropriate to its political, economic and social institutions. Members will seek to avoid measures creating balance-of-payments difficulties for other countries. Where persistent maladjustment in a member's balance of payments leads to balance-of-payments difficulties for other members, which would handicap them in maintaining full employment without resort to trade restrictions, the member is to make its full contribution and appropriate action is to be taken by the other members concerned to correct the situation. Such action should expand rather than contract international trade.

Article 6 (Safeguards for Members Subject to External Inflationary or Deflationary Pressure) recognizes that members may need to take action to safeguard their economies against inflationary or deflationary pressure from abroad. In the case of deflationary pressure special consideration is to be given to the effect on any member of a serious or abrupt decline in the effective demand of the other countries. Article 7 (Fair Labor Standards) calls on members to do whatever is appropriate and feasible to eliminate substandard conditions of labor, and refers in this connection to cooperation with the International Labor Organization.

## IV—COMMERCIAL POLICY

### (ARTICLES 16 TO 45)

SECTION A. *Tariffs, Preferences, and Internal Taxation and Regulation*

Under Article 16, members agree to give most-favored-nation treatment to other members in all matters respecting customs duties, charges on imports and exports or on transfer of payments for imports and exports, and importing and exporting rules and formalities. Existing preferential systems are allowed to remain, subject to the commitment, under Article 17, which obliges members to undertake negotiations directed to a substantial reduction of tariffs and to the elimination of preferences on a reciprocal and mutually advantageous basis. Existing preference margins are not to be increased. Rules are laid down for conducting such negotiations.

If a member is found to have failed to negotiate in good faith, the ITO may authorize the withholding of benefits under the most-favored-nation clause. Successful conclusion of negotiations will have the effect of bringing members into the group of contracting parties to the General Agreement on Tariffs and Trade.

Article 18 provides that internal taxes and trade regulations are in general not to be more severe upon products imported from other members than upon domestic products. One of the exceptions (Article 19) permits, subject to certain conditions, the use of screen quotas to protect national film industries. . .

## V—RESTRICTIVE BUSINESS PRACTICES

### (ARTICLES 46 TO 54)

Members are obligated to take action against restrictive business practices in international trade wherever they are contrary to the principles of the Charter. A procedure is laid down for the ITO to investigate complaints concerning the effects of such practices as price-fixing, territorial exclusion, discrimination, production quotas, technological restrictions, misuse of patents, trade-marks, and copyrights. The powers of the ITO will be limited mainly to instructing the offending member to correct the abuse and to publication of the facts.

As regards services such as transportation, insurance, and the commercial services of banks, the ITO will have only restricted authority for dealing with complaints of harmful practices. If direct negotiations between members are unsuccessful, the ITO will refer such complaints to the appropriate international agency, where one exists. In other cases, the ITO may be asked to make recommendations.

## VI—INTERGOVERNMENTAL COMMODITY AGREEMENTS

### (ARTICLES 55 TO 70)

Recognizing the special difficulties affecting primary commodities, Chapter 6 lays down the objectives of intergovernmental commodity agreements, the procedures for conducting study groups and for holding commodity conferences, the general principles which are to govern commodity agreements and the types of agreements which may be concluded. The ITO is to be concerned with all types of agreements, including 'expansionist' agreements intended to enlarge world production and consumption of a commodity. But the ITO is specially concerned in laying down rules to cover 'control' types of agreements, which may have harmful restrictive effects on trade.

Members are obligated to enter into new control type agreements only through Charter procedures. If, however, there is unreasonable delay, interested countries may proceed by direct negotiation.

Commodity-control agreements are to be entered into only when there is a burdensome surplus or widespread unemployment, which could not be corrected by normal market forces alone. . .

## VII—THE INTERNATIONAL TRADE ORGANIZATION

### (ARTICLES 71 TO 91)

Chapter 7 sets out the structure and functions of the ITO (except for settlement of differences).

SECTION A—(Articles 71 to 73) lays down the conditions of membership and provides for the admission of separate customs territories and United Nations Trust Territories under certain conditions. Article 69 lists the main functions of the ITO, in addition to those functions specified in other Chapters. The structure of the ITO is to comprise a Conference, an Executive Board and such Commissions as the ITO may establish. There is to be a Director General and staff.

SECTION B—(Articles 74 to 77) details the composition, sessions, procedure, officers, powers and duties of the Conference. Each member will have one vote in the Conference.

SECTION C—(Articles 78 to 81) details the composition and powers of the Executive Board. The board will consist of eighteen members, to be selected partly as representing members and customs unions of chief economic importance, and partly by a two-thirds majority vote. Each member of the board will have one vote.

SECTION D—(Articles 82 and 83) gives the Conference powers to set up Commissions.

SECTION E—(Articles 84 and 85) lays down regulations covering the Director General and the staff. . .

## VI. THE GENEVA TRADE AGREEMENT

Delegates of seventeen nations met at Geneva in 1947 to approve the charter of the I.T.O. and to negotiate trade agreements. The United States took part in this conference and became a party to a General Agreement on Tariffs and Trade that lowers tariff barriers for twenty-three countries. The extract below explains this development.

### A. *General Nature of the Agreement*

(Department of State Press Release. No. 860. 29 October 1947.)

The Department of State announced today that the delegations to the International Trade Conference at Geneva have completed their negotiations and will sign the Final Act of the Conference tomorrow morning. This Act authenticates the text of a General Agreement on Tariffs and Trade among twenty-three countries, belonging to sixteen customs areas, which carried on three-quarters of the world's trade before the war. The agreement covers more than 45,000 items and accounts for two-thirds of the trade among the countries in the group. It thus represents the most comprehensive action ever undertaken for the reduction of barriers to trade.

The countries participating in the negotiations leading to the agreement were Australia, the Belgium-Netherlands-Luxembourg Customs Union, Brazil, Canada, Chile, China, Cuba, Czechoslovakia, France, India and Pakistan, the customs union of Lebanon and Syria, New Zealand, Norway, the Union of South Africa, the United Kingdom, together with Burma, Ceylon, and Southern Rhodesia, and the United States.

The agreement brings to a successful conclusion six months of continuous sessions at Geneva preceded by more than a year of intensive preparation both here and abroad. It incorporates the results of negotiations that were carried on simultaneously between one hundred and six pairs of countries. The United States was a party to fifteen of these negotiations. Under the terms of the agreement, the concessions granted, not only in these cases but in the other ninety-one negotiations, will be extended, as a matter of right, to the United States.

The negotiations leading to the agreement were conducted on a selective, product-by-product basis. Action on individual products included substantial reductions in duties on some products, the binding of low rates of duty on others, and the binding of free entry on still others. Preferences affecting a large part of our trade with countries in the British Commonwealth have been substantially reduced and preferences on a long list of products which we export to the various countries of the Commonwealth have been eliminated. Under the terms of the agreement, no new preferences can be created and no existing preferences can be increased.

The concessions on tariffs and preferences contained in the agreement are safeguarded by general provisions that are designed to prevent participating countries from nullifying such concessions by resorting to other forms of restriction or discrimination. These provisions cover restrictive methods of customs administration, discriminatory internal taxes and regulations, import quota systems and exchange controls, and the operations of state trading enterprises. They require the general application of the principle of most-favored-nation treatment in international trade.

Concessions made by the United States in these negotiations are within the limits prescribed by Congress in the Reciprocal Trade Agreements Act, and all of the concessions contained in the agreement are subject to a provision required by American procedure under that Act. If, through unforeseen developments, a particular tariff reduction should increase imports so sharply as to cause or threaten serious injury to domestic producers, the country granting the reduction may suspend its operation in whole or in part. Other countries may then withdraw equivalent concessions so that the balance of the agreement may be restored. . .

## B. *Excerpts from State Department Report*

The following extract from a report by the Department of State shows some concessions made by the United States in the Geneva trade agreement.

(*The New York Times*, 18 November 1947.)

Some of the principal items on which the United States made concessions were summarized as follows:

### CONDENSED AND EVAPORATED MILK (INCLUDING SKIMMED MILK)

Par. 708(a) (Tariff Act of 1930)—Under the new trade agreement the tariff rate on unsweetened condensed milk (evaporated) in airtight containers (case goods) was reduced from 1.8 cents per pound to 1 cent per pound, from 2.75 cents per pound on sweetened condensed milk in airtight containers (case goods) to 1.75 cents per pound, and from 2.53 cents per pound on all other condensed and evaporated milk, i.e., in bulk, to 1.5 cents per pound.

### DRIED MILK AND CREAM, INCLUDING DRIED SKIM MILK AND BUTTERMILK

Par. 708(b) (Tariff Act of 1930)—In the new trade agreement the tariff rate for dried whole milk was reduced from 6½ cents per pound to 3.1 cents per pound, that for dried cream from 12⅓ cents per pound to 6.2 cents, and that for dried skimmed milk from 3 cents to 1.5 cents per pound. The rate of 1.5 cents per pound for dried buttermilk was bound in the present agreement.

### CHEDDAR CHEESE

Par. 710 (Tariff Act of 1930)—In the new agreement the duty is reduced from 4 cents per pound but not less than 25 per cent ad valorem to 3½ cents per pound but not less than 17½ per cent ad valorem on cheddar not further processed than by division into pieces.

The domestic production of cheddar cheese has been increasing for many years and reached a peak in 1945 of 878,000,000 pounds; production in 1946 amounted to 806,000,000 pounds.

Imports were not in significant volume before the war and became even smaller during the emergency. In 1946 dutiable imports amounted to only 20,000 pounds.

Exports, which are normally less than 2,000,000 pounds a year, increased to 158,000,000 pounds in 1943, due to wartime demands; in 1946 exports amounted to 82,000,000 pounds.

### FROZEN AND DRIED EGG PRODUCTS

Par. 713 (Tariff Act of 1930)—Under the new trade agreement the rate on dried egg products will be reduced from 27 to 17 cents per pound and on frozen egg products from 11 to 7 cents per pound.

### EDIBLE GELATIN VALUED AT LESS THAN 40 CENTS PER POUND

Par. 41 (Tariff Act of 1930)—In the new trade agreement the compound duty on edible gelatin has been reduced from 12 per cent plus 2½ cents per pound to 10 per cent plus 2½ cents per pound. . .

### METAL-WORKING MACHINERY

Par. 372 (Tariff Act of 1930)—This group covers practically all machinery used in producing any semi-finished materials, articles, or machines made of metal.

All of these machines, with three exceptions, were dutiable at 30 per cent under the act of 1930. This rate was reduced in the new agreement to 15 per cent. The exceptions are: (1) Gear-cutting or hobbing machines; (2) punches, shear, or bar cutters, the duty of which has now been reduced from 40 to 20 per cent; and (3) jig borers, the duty on which remains at the 15 per cent rate established in the agreement with Switzerland in 1936.

### TEXTILE MACHINERY

Par. 372 (Tariff Act of 1930)—The new rates range from 10 per cent to 40 per cent ad valorem, compared with the previous rates of 20 to 40 per cent.

The second most important group of textile equipment imported in 1946 was circular knitting machines and flat knitting machines. In this group the rate of duty on circular machines was reduced from 20 per cent to 15 per cent.

## VII. INTERNATIONAL INVESTMENTS

Investments by individuals abroad take several forms. First, bonds may be issued by the public authorities of a country on a national, state, or local basis. For example, an investor in Chicago may buy bonds issued by the city of Vera Cruz, Mexico. Second, a person may invest in the stocks or bonds of a foreign corporation. Thus an Englishman may purchase shares of General Electric stock. Finally, there are investments made by individuals and companies to develop concessions granted them abroad. The Standard Oil Company may invest in an oil concession granted to it by Venezuela. Several aspects of these international transactions are treated in the extracts that follow.

### A. *Advantages and Problems*

International investments often cause serious diplomatic problems, particularly when untoward developments—revolution, discriminatory taxes, socialization programs, or anti-foreign movements—in a weak or backward country place foreign capital in jeopardy. Generally, they are highly beneficial both to the lender and the borrower. Below is an extract on the subject taken from the report of a Special Joint Committee of the League of Nations, communicated to members of the League in 1946.

('Conditions of Private Foreign Investment,' *Report by the Special Joint Committee,* League of Nations, C.14, M.14,
1946, II A. pp. 11-12, 17-18.)

### Private Foreign Investment and the Economic System

Private foreign investment will thrive
if there is national and international political security, price stability, exchange
convertibility and freedom of trade. Conversely, sound foreign investment contributes to the creation and maintenance
of these conditions.

Private investment abroad opens business opportunities to the capital-exporting
countries, assists in the expansion of their
exports and imports and promotes employment. These benefits are, however,
conditional on the degree to which countries receiving foreign capital are capable
of meeting their external financial obligations. This in turn depends not only
on the capacity of capital-importing countries to export, but also on the willingness of capital-exporting countries to receive imports under a system of multilateral trade. For such trade to flourish, it
is moreover essential that governments
prevent unfair commercial practices such
as dumping, or undue restriction of production and distribution.

An inflow of resources and skills from
abroad enables the recipient country to
develop its productive capacity, to di-
versify and stabilize its economy, to improve its general standard of living and
to increase its exports and imports with
greater rapidity and less cost than if it
were to rely exclusively on its own savings and technical experience. To constitute an enduring contribution to eco
nomic and social advancement, private
foreign investment should be mutually
advantageous to both capital-importing
and capital-exporting countries.

The responsibility for establishing and
safeguarding the conditions conducive to
private foreign investment falls largely
on governments. Governmental action
may take the form of domestic legislation
or administrative measures. It may also
involve the conclusion of agreements with
other governments and participation in
the activities of international institutions to maintain peace, to stabilize exchanges and prices, to expand trade, and
to raise standards of living. Under a system of private enterprise, however, the
conditions conducive to foreign investment, and therefore the extent and outcome of such investment, must also depend on the judgment, initiative and behaviour of the business community as a
whole and, particularly, of those who invest abroad or obtain foreign capital. . .

Legality, equity and good faith should
be cardinal in the treatment of foreign
investment by all countries. But the individual attitude of each capital-importing
country will be determined largely by the
special interests of the country and by the
stage and direction of its social and economic development.

It is a natural concern of any self-
governing country to preserve its national
integrity and to keep the direction of
governmental policy free from foreign
control and interference, subject always
to treaty obligations and international
law. No country will long suffer the presence of any foreign interest which tends
to obstruct or distort governmental action
or which exercises an uncontrolled and
preponderant influence over the national
economy.

Foreign enterprises and investors will,
no doubt, appreciate the interest they
have in complying in letter and in spirit
with the domestic laws of the country in
which they do business and in seeking
no illegal favour or undue advantage
from public officials. Having regard to
their special position, they will see to it

that nothing they do will be considered as an interference in the conduct of national affairs. It goes without saying that foreign enterprises and investors should not induce domestic interests to conclude contracts which they know to be detri-

engaged in primary production should seek, whenever possible, to develop processing and complementary industries. If foreign enterprises established in a country follow a consistent policy of reinvesting part of their profits in the country,

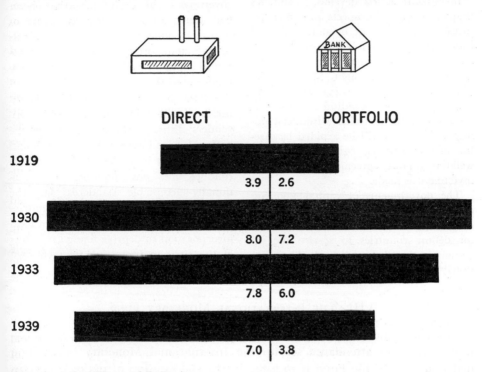

**Figures are in Billions of Dollars**

PRIVATE AMERICAN INVESTMENTS ABROAD

mental to the other party or impossible to fill.

Foreign investors can only expect to receive fair treatment that assures the security and remuneration of their investment if it is a contribution to the economic development and social welfare of the country. In the long run it will be to the advantage of all if investors place their funds in undertakings which not only assure a direct return, but which also further a balanced and properly diversified economic development. Concerns

this policy is likely to prove beneficial to all parties concerned.

Whenever feasible, foreign enterprises will be well advised to encourage early participation of domestic interest in their business by facilitating, for instance, the purchase of some of their equities and securities by residents of the country. The association between foreign and domestic interests should be not merely formal, but effective and *bona fide*. Harmony may be promoted if foreign enterprises engage local executives and technicians to the greatest possible extent, train local employees and workers and, above all, apply decent standards of remuneration and conditions of work and living, taking into account the prevailing levels in similar branches of activity in the country.

Investment in less developed countries frequently offers prospects of larger returns than investment in more advanced countries. The fundamental rules of business, however, always require caution, responsibility and foresight. Many of the disappointments that occur are due to ignorance of local conditions, laws, customs and national traits. Misunderstandings and failures will be avoided by careful market surveys, cost estimates and well-thought-out agreements before the investment is made.

The governments of capital-exporting countries must make it possible through the various channels of multilateral trade for debtor countries to service the investments they have received. Their nationals should be prepared to leave their capital abroad for long periods and to make reasonable arrangements for accommodation in periods of crisis.

By conducting their diplomatic relations in a manner which dispels any fear of political or economic imperialism, the governments of capital-exporting countries can contribute to the avoidance of restrictive policies against their nationals in capital-importing countries. To protect the person and the interests of nationals abroad is a recognized function of the state, but this responsibility should not be fulfilled in a manner which engenders distrust in countries where the nationals have interests. In no case should a state protect its nationals abroad whose conduct does not conform to internationally acceptable standards. On the other hand, capital-importing countries should not invoke the technicality of local incorporation to deprive foreign investors of the right to protection by their own governments. . .

## VIII. THE INTERNATIONAL MONETARY FUND

At a conference held in 1944 at Bretton Woods, New Hampshire, the forty-four nations in attendance set up the International Monetary Fund. The main purpose of the Fund is to assist in the stabilization of national currencies. Each member is expected (1) to define its currency in terms of gold, (2) to keep its currency within 1 per cent of its determined value, (3) not to restrict current transactions in its currency, and (4) to make no important change in the value of its currency without consulting the other members of the Fund. To assist in the accomplishment of these objectives, a Fund is made available—a pool of currencies and gold, into which each member has paid a fixed quota, with a larger amount of currency than gold. There are available in the Fund, therefore, dollars, pounds, belgas, pesos, and other currencies, as well as gold to purchase currency, that can be used in an emergency to keep a member nation's money sound. The stability sought would improve the conditions of trade and help eliminate the economic warfare which characterized the years preceding World War II when nations manipulated their currencies constantly in order to have a quick advantage in trade.

(Text of The Bretton Woods Agreement, *International Conciliation*, No. 413, 1945, pp. 563-605. Reprinted by permission of the Carnegie Endowment for International Peace.)

## INTRODUCTORY ARTICLE

The International Monetary Fund is established and shall operate in accordance with the following provisions:

## ARTICLE I—PURPOSES

The purposes of the International Monetary Fund are:

(i) To promote international monetary cooperation through a permanent institution which provides the machinery for consultation and collaboration on international monetary problems.

(ii) To facilitate the expansion and balanced growth of international trade, and to contribute thereby to the promotion and maintenance of high levels of employment and real income and to the development of the productive resources of all members as primary objectives of economic policy.

(iii) To promote exchange stability, to maintain orderly exchange arrangements among members, and to avoid competitive exchange depreciation.

(iv) To assist in the establishment of a multilateral system of payments in respect of current transactions between members and in the elimination of foreign exchange restrictions which hamper the growth of world trade.

(v) To give confidence to members by making the Fund's resources available to them under adequate safeguards, thus providing them with opportunity to correct maladjustments in their balance of payments

without resorting to measures destructive of national or international prosperity.

(vi) In accordance with the above, to shorten the duration and lessen the degree of disequilibrium in the international balances of payments of members.

The Fund shall be guided in all its decisions by the purposes set forth in this Article.

## ARTICLE II—MEMBERSHIP

SECTION 1. *Original members*—The original members of the Fund shall be those of the countries represented at the United Nations Monetary and Financial Conference whose governments accept membership before the date specified in Article xx, Section 2 (*e*).

SEC. 2. *Other members*—Membership shall be open to the governments of other countries at such times and in accordance with such terms as may be prescribed by the Fund.

## ARTICLE III—QUOTAS AND SUBSCRIPTIONS

SECTION 1. *Quotas*—Each member shall be assigned a quota. The quotas of the members represented at the United Nations Monetary and Financial Conference which accept membership before the date specified in Article xx, Section 2 (*e*), shall be those set forth in Schedule A. The quotas of other members shall be determined by the Fund.

SEC. 2. *Adjustment of quotas*—The Fund shall at intervals of five years review, and if it deems it appropriate propose an adjustment of, the quotas of the members. It may also, if it thinks fit, consider at any other time the adjustment of any particular quota at the request of the member concerned. A four-fifths majority of the total voting power shall be required for any change in quotas and no quota shall be changed without the consent of the member concerned.

SEC. 3. *Subscriptions: Time, place, and form of payment*—(a) The subscription of each member shall be equal to its quota and shall be paid in full to the Fund at the appropriate depository on or before the date when the member becomes eligible under Article xx, Section 4 (c) or (d), to buy currencies from the Fund.

(b) Each member shall pay in gold, as a minimum, the smaller of

(i) twenty-five per cent of its quota; or
(ii) ten per cent of its net official holdings of gold and United States dollars as at the date when the Fund notifies members under Article xx, Section 4 (a) that it will shortly be in a position to begin exchange transactions.

Each member shall furnish to the Fund the data necessary to determine its net official holdings of gold and United States dollars.

(c) Each member shall pay the balance of its quota in its own currency. . .

SEC. 5. *Substitution of securities for currency*—The Fund shall accept from any member in place of any part of the member's currency which in the judgment of the Fund is not needed for its operations, notes or similar obligations issued by the member or the depository designated by the member under Article xiii, Section 2, which shall be nonnegotiable, noninterest-bearing and payable at their par value on demand by crediting the account of the Fund in the designated depository. This Section shall apply not only to currency subscribed by members but also to any currency otherwise due to, or acquired by, the Fund.

## ARTICLE IV—PAR VALUES OF CURRENCIES

SECTION 1. *Expression of par values*—(a) The par value of the currency of each member shall be expressed in terms of gold as a common denominator or in terms of the United States dollar of the weight and fineness in effect on July 1, 1944.

(b) All computations relating to currencies of members for the purpose of applying the provisions of this Agreement shall be on the basis of their par values.

SEC. 2. *Gold purchases based on par values*—The Fund shall prescribe a margin above and below par value for transactions in gold by members, and no member shall buy gold at a price above par value plus the prescribed margin, or sell gold at a price below par value minus the prescribed margin.

SEC. 3. *Foreign exchange dealings based on parity*—The maximum and the minimum rates for exchange transactions between the currencies of members taking place within their territories shall not differ from parity,

(i) in the case of spot exchange transactions, by more than one per cent; and
(ii) in the case of other exchange transactions, by a margin which exceeds the margin for spot exchange transactions by more than the Fund considers reasonable.

SEC. 4. *Obligations regarding exchange stability*—(a) Each member undertakes to collaborate with the Fund to promote exchange stability, to maintain orderly exchange arrangements with other members, and to avoid competitive exchange alterations.

(b) Each member undertakes, through appropriate measures consistent with this Agreement, to permit within its territories exchange transactions between its currency and the currencies of other members only within the limits prescribed under Section 3 of this Article. A member whose monetary authorities, for the settlement of international transactions, in fact freely buy and sell gold within the limits prescribed by the Fund under

Section 2 of this Article shall be deemed to be fulfilling this undertaking.

SEC. 5. *Changes in par values*—(*a*) A member shall not propose a change in the par value of its currency except to correct a fundamental disequilibrium.

(*b*) A change in the par value of a member's currency may be made only on the proposal of the member and only after consultation with the Fund.

(*c*) When a change is proposed, the Fund shall first take into account the changes, if any, which have already taken place in the initial par value of the member's currency as determined under Article xx, Section 4. If the proposed change, together with all previous changes, whether increases or decreases,

(i) does not exceed ten per cent of the initial par value, the Fund shall raise no objection;

(ii) does not exceed a further ten per cent of the initial par value, the Fund may either concur or object, but shall declare its attitude within seventy-two hours if the member so requests;

(iii) is not within (i) or (ii) above, the Fund may either concur or object, but shall be entitled to a longer period in which to declare its attitude.

(*d*) Uniform changes in par values made under Section 7 of this Article shall not be taken into account in determining whether a proposed change falls within (i), (ii), or (iii) of (*c*) above.

(*e*) A member may change the par value of its currency without the concurrence of the Fund if the change does not affect the international transactions of members of the Fund.

(*f*) The Fund shall concur in a proposed change which is within the terms of (*c*) (ii) or (*c*) (iii) above if it is satisfied that the change is necessary to correct a fundamental disequilibrium. In particular, provided it is so satisfied, it shall not object to a proposed change because of the domestic social or political policies of the member proposing the change.

## IX. The International Bank

In addition to the establishment of the International Monetary Fund, the Bretton Woods Conference of 1944 set up an International Bank. The Bank was intended not only to finance postwar reconstruction but, as Lord Keynes, the chief of the British delegation, said, 'to develop the resources and productive capacity of the world, with special attention to the less developed countries.' To accomplish these purposes the Bank will be permanently available to loan money and to facilitate the international flow of capital that will be needed for the development of the world's resources. Excerpts from the text of the agreement follow.

(The Bretton Woods Agreement, *International Conciliation*, No. 413, 1945, pp. 606-35. Reprinted by permission of the Carnegie Endowment for International Peace.)

### INTRODUCTORY ARTICLE

The International Bank for Reconstruction and Development is established and shall operate in accordance with the following provisions:

### ARTICLE 1—PURPOSES

The purposes of the Bank are:

(i) To assist in the reconstruction and development of territories of members by facilitating the investment of capital for productive purposes, including the restoration of economies destroyed or disrupted by war, the reconversion of productive facilities to peacetime needs and the encouragement of the development of productive facilities and resources in less developed countries.

(ii) To promote private foreign investment by means of guarantees or participations in loans and other investments made by private investors; and when private capital is not available on reasonable terms, to supplement private investment by providing, on suitable conditions, finance for productive purposes out of its own capital, funds raised by it and its other resources.

(iii) To promote the long-range balanced growth of international trade and the maintenance of equilibrium in balances of payments by encouraging international investment for the development of the productive resources of members, thereby assisting in raising productivity, the standard of living and conditions of labor in their territories.

(iv) To arrange the loans made or guaranteed by it in relation to international loans through other channels so that the more useful and urgent projects, large and small alike, will be dealt with first.

(v) To conduct its operations with due regard to the effect of international investment on business conditions in the territories of members and, in the immediate postwar years, to assist in bringing about a smooth transition from a wartime to a peacetime economy.

The Bank shall be guided in all its decisions by the purposes set forth above.

ARTICLE 2—MEMBERSHIP IN AND CAPITAL OF THE BANK

SECTION 1. *Membership*—(a) The original members of the Bank shall be those members of the International Monetary Fund which accept membership in the Bank before the date specified in Article XI, Section 2 (e).

(b) Membership shall be open to other members of the Fund, at such times and in accordance with such terms as may be prescribed by the Bank.

SEC. 2. *Authorized capital*—(a) The authorized capital stock of the Bank shall be $10,000,000,000, in terms of United States dollars of the weight and fineness in effect on July 1, 1944. The capital stock shall be divided into 100,000 shares having a par value of $100,000 each, which shall be available for subscription only by members.

(b) The capital stock may be increased when the Bank deems it advisable by a three-fourths majority of the total voting power.

SEC. 3. *Subscription of shares*—(a) Each member shall subscribe shares of the capital stock of the Bank. The minimum number of shares to be subscribed by the original members shall be those set forth in Schedule A. The minimum number of shares to be subscribed by other members shall be determined by the Bank, which shall reserve a sufficient portion of its capital stock for subscription by such members.

(b) The Bank shall prescribe rules laying down the conditions under which members may subscribe shares of the authorized capital stock of the Bank in addition to their minimum subscriptions.

(c) If the authorized capital stock of the Bank is increased, each member shall have a reasonable opportunity to subscribe, under such conditions as the Bank shall decide, a proportion of the increase of stock equivalent to the proportion which its stock theretofore subscribed bears to the total capital stock of the Bank, but no member shall be obligated to subscribe any part of the increased capital.

SEC. 4. *Issue price of shares*—Shares included in the minimum subscriptions of original members shall be issued at par. Other shares shall be issued at par unless the Bank by a majority of the total voting power decides in special circumstances to issue them on other terms.

SEC. 5. *Division and calls of subscribed capital*—The subscription of each member shall be divided into two parts as follows:

(i) twenty per cent shall be paid or subject to call under Section 7 (i) of this Article as needed by the Bank for its operations;
(ii) the remaining eighty per cent shall be subject to call by the Bank only when required to meet obligations of the Bank created under Article IV, Sections 1 (a) (ii) and (iii).

Calls on unpaid subscriptions shall be uniform on all shares.

SEC. 6. *Limitation on Liability*—Liability on shares shall be limited to the unpaid portion of the issue price of the shares.

SEC. 7. *Method of payment of subscriptions for shares*—Payment of subscriptions for shares shall be made in gold or United States dollars and in the currencies of the members as follows:

(i) under Section 5 (i) of this Article, two per cent of the price of each share shall be payable in gold or United States dollars, and, when calls are made, the remaining eighteen per cent shall be paid in the currency of the member;
(ii) when a call is made under Section 5 (ii) of this Article, payment may be made at the option of the member either in gold, in United States dol-

lars or in the currency required to discharge the obligations of the Bank for the purpose for which the call is made;
(iii) when a member makes payments in any currency under (i) and (ii) above, such payments shall be made in amounts equal in value to the member's liability under the call. This liability shall be a proportionate part of the subscribed capital stock of the Bank as authorized and defined in Section 2 of this Article. . .

ARTICLE 3—GENERAL PROVISIONS RELATING TO LOANS AND GUARANTEES

SECTION 1. *Use of resources*—(a) The resources and the facilities of the Bank shall be used exclusively for the benefit of members with equitable consideration to projects for development and projects for reconstruction alike.

(b) For the purpose of facilitating the restoration and reconstruction of the economy of members whose metropolitan territories have suffered great devastation from enemy occupation or hostilities, the Bank, in determining the conditions and terms of loans made to such members, shall pay special regard to lightening the financial burden and expediting the completion of such restoration and reconstruction.

SEC. 2. *Dealings between members and the Bank*—Each member shall deal with the Bank only through its Treasury, central bank, stabilization fund or other similar fiscal agency, and the Bank shall deal with members only by or through the same agencies.

SEC. 3. *Limitations on guarantees and borrowings of the Bank*—The total amount outstanding of guarantees, participations in loans and direct loans made by the Bank shall not be increased at any time, if by such increase the total would exceed one hundred per cent of the unimpaired subscribed capital, reserves and surplus of the Bank.

SEC. 4. *Conditions on which the Bank may guarantee or make loans*—The Bank may guarantee, participate in, or make loans to any member or any political subdivision thereof and any business, industrial, and agricultural enterprise in the territories of a member, subject to the following conditions:

(i) When the member in whose territories the project is located is not itself the borrower, the member or the central bank or some comparable agency of the member which is acceptable to the Bank, fully guarantees the repayment of the principal and the payment of interest and other charges on the loan.

(ii) The Bank is satisfied that in the prevailing market conditions the borrower would be unable otherwise to obtain the loan under conditions which in the opinion of the Bank are reasonable for the borrower.

(iii) A competent committee, as provided for in Article v, Section 7, has submitted a written report recommending the project after a careful study of the merits of the proposal.

(iv) In the opinion of the Bank the rate of interest and other charges are reasonable and such rate, charges and the schedule for repayment of principal are appropriate to the project.

(v) In making or guaranteeing a loan, the Bank shall pay due regard to the prospects that the borrower, and, if the borrower is not a member, that the guarantor, will be in position to meet its obligations under the loan; and the Bank shall act prudently in the interests both of the particular member in whose territories the

project is located and of the members as a whole.

(vi) In guaranteeing a loan made by other investors, the Bank receives suitable compensation for its risk.

(vii) Loans made or guaranteed by the Bank shall, except in special circumstances, be for the purpose of specific projects of reconstruction or development.

ARTICLE 5—ORGANIZATION AND MANAGEMENT

SECTION 1. *Stucture of the Bank*—The Bank shall have a Board of Governors, Executive Directors, a President and such other officers and staff to perform such duties as the Bank may determine.

SEC. 2. *Board of Governors*—(a) All the powers of the Bank shall be vested in the Board of Governors consisting of one governor and one alternate appointed by each member in such manner as it may determine. Each governor and each alternate shall serve for five years, subject to the pleasure of the member appointing him, and may be reappointed. No alternate may vote except in the absence of his principal. The Board shall select one of the governors as Chairman.

(b) The Board of Governors may delegate to the Executive Directors authority to exercise any powers of the Board, except the power to:

(i) Admit new members and determine the conditions of their admission;

(ii) Increase or decrease the capital stock;

(iii) Suspend a member;

(iv) Decide appeals from interpretations of this Agreement given by the Executive Directors;

(v) Make arrangements to cooperate with other international organizations (other than informal arrangements of a temporary and administrative character);

(vi) Decide to suspend permanently the operations of the Bank and to distribute its assets;

(vii) Determine the distribution of the net income of the Bank.

· · ·

SEC. 3. *Voting*—(a) Each member shall have two hundred fifty votes plus one additional vote for each share of stock held.

(b) Except as otherwise specifically provided, all matters before the Bank shall be decided by a majority of the votes cast.

SEC. 4. *Executive Directors*—(a) The Executive Directors shall be responsible for the conduct of the general operations of the Bank, and for this purpose, shall exercise all the powers delegated to them by the Board of Governors.

(b) There shall be twelve Executive Directors, who need not be governors, and of whom:

(i) five shall be appointed, one by each of the five members having the largest number of shares;

(ii) seven shall be elected according to Schedule B by all the Governors other than those appointed by the five members referred to in (i) above.

· · ·

SEC. 5. *President and staff*—(a) The Executive Directors shall select a President who shall not be a governor or an executive director or an alternate for either. The President shall be Chairman of the Executive Directors, but shall have no vote except a deciding vote in case of an equal division. He may participate in meetings of the Board of Governors, but shall not vote at such meetings. The President shall cease to hold office when the Executive Directors so decide.

(b) The President shall be chief of the operating staff of the Bank and shall conduct, under the direction of the Executive Directors, the ordinary business of the Bank. Subject to the general control of the Executive Directors, he shall be responsible for the organization, appointment and dismissal of the officers and staff.

(c) The President, officers and staff of the Bank, in the discharge of their offices, owe their duty entirely to the Bank and to no other authority. Each member of the Bank shall respect the international character of this duty and shall refrain from all attempts to influence any of them in the discharge of their duties.

(d) In appointing the officers and staff the President shall, subject to the paramount importance of securing the highest standards of efficiency and of technical competence, pay due regard to the importance of recruiting personnel on as wide a geographical basis as possible.

SEC. 6. *Advisory Council*—(a) There shall be an Advisory Council of not less than seven persons selected by the Board of Governors including representatives of banking, commercial, industrial, labor, and agricultural interests, and with as wide a national representation as possible. In those fields where specialized international organizations exist, the members of the Council representative of those fields shall be selected in agreement with such organizations. The Council shall advise the Bank on matters of general policy. The Council shall meet annually and on such other occasions as the Bank may request.

(b) Councillors shall serve for two years and may be reappointed. They shall be paid their reasonable expenses incurred on behalf of the Bank.

SEC. 7. *Loan committees*—The committees required to report on loans under Article III, Section 4, shall be appointed by the Bank. Each such committee shall include an expert selected by the governor representing the member in whose territories the project is located and one or more members of the technical staff of the Bank.

· · ·

## X. The Marshall Plan

At the end of World War II Europe was so exhausted economically that recovery seemed impossible without more help than was available from existing relief and reconstruction agencies. In the meantime free government in Western Europe was in jeopardy as poverty and hunger remained unchecked. To meet this condition Secretary of State Marshall suggested on 5 June 1947 that European countries devise a program of reconstruction and indicated that the United States would be willing to assist financially in the fulfilment of the program. On 12 July, sixteen countries of Europe met at Paris and drafted a report, a portion of which is given below. Table II indicates the estimated amount of the assistance needed from the United States and other American nations. To administer the program the Economic Cooperation Administration (E.C.A.) was set up. By mid-1949 it became apparent that steady progress was under way in the achievement of European recovery.

(*Committee of European Economic Cooperation,* General Report, vol. 1, Department of State Publication No. 2930, September 1947.)

23. In this critical situation, the participating countries and Western Germany have examined their prospective requirements and resources over the next four years and have in common formulated a recovery programme. The various countries handle their economic affairs by diverse means; some work to a long-term plan, and others follow relatively unrestricted private enterprise. The means of carrying out this programme will therefore vary from country to country, but each will be able fully to play its part in the programme, and all are determined to do so.

24. The recovery programme is based upon four points:—

(i) A strong production effort by each of the participating countries, especially in agriculture, fuel and power, transport, and the modernisation of equipment.

(ii) The creation and maintenance of *internal financial stability* as an essential condition for securing the full use of Europe's productive and financial resources.

(iii) The development of economic *co-operation* between the participating countries.

(iv) A solution of the problem of the participating countries' *deficit with the American Continent* particularly by exports.

25. The production expansion which is envisaged by 1951 is similar in general scale to that achieved by the United States in the mobilisation years 1940 to 1944. It calls for an unprecedented peace-time effort of work by the whole population of all the participating countries. It is the maximum self-help which each country can accomplish; it will restore agricultural production to the pre-war level, and it will carry with it a significant expansion of mining and manufacturing production beyond the levels which were ruling in 1938.

26. The production programme provides for mutual help between the participating countries over a wide field, and for a number of practical steps for specific action, such as the International Power Project. In addition broader pro-

posals are made for the reduction of trade barriers and the removal of financial obstacles to intra-European trade.

27. The creation of internal financial stability in certain countries is necessary in order to get their entire productive and distributive systems into effective operation, and in order to secure the full use of internal and external financial resources. While the necessary economic

from normal sources in Eastern Europe and South-East Asia increases the urgency of the need for supplies from the American Continent. The financial counterpart of the unbalanced flow of goods and services from the American Continent is the dollar deficit of the participating countries.

29. The European recovery programme cannot get fully under way until the im-

Table 11. *Deficit with the American Continent of the Participating Countries (Including Their Dependent Territories) and Western Germany* 1948–51
($000 millions)

|  | 1948 | 1949 | 1950 | 1951 | Total |
|---|---|---|---|---|---|
| U.S.A. | 5.64 | 4.27 | 3.28 | 2.62 | 15.81 |
| Rest of American continent | 1.94 | 1.82 | 1.30 | 0.91 | 5.97 |
|  | 7.58 | 6.09 | 4.58 | 3.53 | 21.78 |
| Deficit of dependent territories | 0.46 | 0.26 | 0.07 | 0.13 [a] | 0.66 |
| Total | 8.04 | 6.35 | 4.65 | 3.40 | 22.44 |

[a] Surplus.

and financial reforms can be initiated without external assistance, such assistance will be required to make them fully effective.

28. In order to carry out their production effort, and after making full allowance for the supplies which they can obtain from each other, the participating countries need food, raw materials, fuel, and capital equipment from overseas. There are two difficulties to be overcome: the inadequate supplies of certain key commodities available in the world, and the lack of means of paying for them. In this report, it is estimated that available supplies to the participating countries, assuming complete achievement of their agricultural programmes, will be insufficient to permit even the restoration of the pre-war standard of food consumption by the end of 1951. Moreover, in the immediate future, the lack of supplies

mediate dollar problem is solved. Failure to solve it would destroy the basis of production and internal confidence in Europe; a descending spiral of production and consumption would become inevitable. Immediate and fully adequate aid in 1948 is therefore necessary as a first step for the fulfilment of the programme of production, stabilization and co-operation. If the initial stages of the programme can be successfully accomplished, a momentum will be created that will ease the task in the following years.

30. The productive effort which is generated in 1948 can be sustained and developed further only if the participating countries can obtain and pay for the necessary supplies from overseas. There will still be a large deficit in the following years. The purpose of the European recovery programme is to reduce this deficit as fast as possible. There will be

some deficit in 1951; the participating countries have always depended on dollar earnings from the rest of the world to meet their deficit with the American Continent, and will do so in the future. By the end of 1951, given reasonably favourable external conditions, the deficit should be of dimensions which will be manageable through normal means without special aid.

31. This is a fundamental problem which cannot be solved quickly. The effects of the war, which are so clearly illustrated by the lack of balance in the world's trading pattern, cannot be cured in a few months. But the participating countries are confident that in four years considerable and decisive progress can be made to overcome them. This recovery programme can break the back of the problem. But continuing constructive action by the European countries and by the rest of the world will be needed in order to keep the trading position balanced and to prevent the re-appearance of the international maladjustment which is the root of Europe's present difficulties.

32. In order to ensure that the recovery programme is carried out, the sixteen participating countries pledge themselves to join together, and invite other European countries to join with them, in working to this end. This pledge is undertaken by each country with respect to its own national programme, but it also takes into account similar pledges made by the other participating countries. In particular, each country undertakes to use all its efforts:—

(i) to develop its production to reach the targets, especially for food and coal;

(ii) to make the fullest and most effective use of its existing productive capacity and all available manpower;

(iii) to modernise its equipment and transport, so that labour becomes more productive, conditions of work are improved, and standards of living of all peoples of Europe are raised;

(iv) to apply all necessary measures leading to the rapid achievement of internal financial monetary and economic stability while maintaining in each country a high level of employment;

(v) to co-operate with one another and with like-minded countries in all possible steps to reduce the tariffs and other barriers to the expansion of trade both between themselves and with the rest of the world, in accordance with the principles of the draft Charter for an International Trade Organisation;

(vi) to remove progressively the obstacles to the free movement of persons within Europe;

(vii) to organise together the means by which common resources can be developed in partnership.

By these means and provided the necessary supplies can be obtained from overseas, European recovery can be achieved.

. . .

# 15

# SOCIAL PROBLEMS

A HUNDRED years ago there was little public recognition of social problems. Some few countries had undertaken poor relief, generally on a local basis, but society went little further in recognition of its responsibility. As the industrial revolution continued to change the pattern of life, the individual's need for protection against the hazards of work and the crowded conditions of cities became apparent. Nations began to enact social legislation and to take a constructive interest in the health and welfare of the masses.

With the introduction of still better methods of production, transportation, and communication, national treatment of an increasing number of social problems became as inadequate as local treatment had been a century earlier. With travel between nations easy and frequent, it became impossible for one nation alone to combat disease and prevent epidemics. International action was necessary. Modern methods of transportation enabled traffickers in opium to smuggle their wares into areas where opium production and consumption were forbidden by national law. If one nation legislated against opium production while its neighbor did not, the former had little chance of keeping the commodity from its people. As the white-slave traffic became international in scope, its eradication, too, required the co-operative effort of nations. At the same time many humanitarian projects came to the fore which were beyond the resources that any one nation might be expected to provide, such as the care of refugees and displaced peoples, whose total numbers were brought by World War II to unprecedented figures. Even where action of an international nature has not been necessary or possible, much benefit has derived from the discussion by international bodies of such problems as child welfare and social insurance, and from adoption of resolutions to encourage more effective national action.

A great deal has been done within the framework of the Pan American Union to advance the cause of social internationalism. There have been special conferences on selected subjects, and the agenda of the general conferences have contained item after item with distinct social implications. Some of the results are included in this chapter.

The League of Nations maintained a Health Organization, an Advisory Committee on Opium, and an Advisory Committee on Social Questions. With the assistance of these agencies special conferences were called and some important conventions were drafted. Well known among these conventions are those dealing with traffic in women and children, traffic in obscene publications, traffic in opium, slavery, and a relief union (to offer aid to victims of earthquakes and other disasters). The United Nations has organized under the Economic and Social Council a number of special agencies and commissions to continue the work so well advanced by the League.

## I. THE ECONOMIC AND SOCIAL COUNCIL

The Charter of the United Nations sets up an Economic and Social Council to promote '(a) higher standards of living, full employment, and conditions of economic and social progress and development; (b) solutions of international economic, health, and related problems; and international cultural and educational cooperation; and (c) universal respect for, and observance of, human rights and fundamental freedoms for all, without distinction as to race, sex, language, or religion.'

This Council, consisting of eighteen members selected by the General Assembly of the United Nations, is empowered to make studies relating to economic, social, cultural, educational, and health matters. It may make recommendations regarding social and economic questions to the Assembly and call international conferences to deal with special problems. Thus the Economic and Social Council places the United Nations in a strong position to carry forward the work of the League of Nations in this field.

Not all of the specialized bodies related in an organizational sense to the Economic and Social Council are dealt with in this chapter. Some of them, such as the International Labor Organization, the International Monetary Fund and Bank, are given greater prominence elsewhere. The United Nations Charter provisions—Articles 61-72—relating to the Economic and Social Council may be found in Chapter 3. Extract A below is drawn from the Report to the President, made by Edward R. Stettinius, Jr., at that time Secretary of State and Chairman of the United States Delegation at the San Francisco Conference.

## A. *An American Statement on the Economic and Social Council*

(*Report of the Chairman of the United States Delegation to the President*, 26 June 1945, Department of State Publication No. 2349, Conference Series 71, pp. 109-10.)

The battle of peace has to be fought on two fronts. The first is the security front where victory spells freedom from fear. The second is the economic and social front where victory means freedom from want. Only victory on both fronts can assure the world of an enduring peace.

In the next twenty-five years the development of the economic and social foundations of peace will be of paramount importance. If the United Nations cooperate effectively toward an expanding world economy, better living conditions for all men and women, and closer understanding among peoples, they will have gone far toward eliminating in advance the causes of another world war a generation hence. If they fail, there will be instead widespread depressions and economic warfare which would fatally undermine the world organization. No provisions that can be written into the Charter will enable the Security Council to make the world secure from war if men and women have no security in their homes and in their jobs. . .

The stake of the United States in the prompt and successful performance of this task is at least as great as that of any other nation. We cannot provide jobs . . . and maintain prosperity for ourselves unless the economy of the rest of the world is restored to health. Continuing poverty and despair abroad can only lead to mass unemployment in our own country. From the long-range point of view we cannot hope to maintain our comparative wealth unless there is effective international cooperation in the development of trade and higher standards of living throughout the world.

It is equally evident that the promotion of respect for human rights and freedoms, and closer cooperation in fighting ignorance and disease and in the exchange among nations of scientific knowledge and of information about each other are as necessary to peace as an expanding world economy.

Modern communications have brought the peoples of the world into closer contact with each other, and have made mutual understanding not merely desirable but indispensable to the maintenance of good neighborliness. Unless the peoples of the world learn to comprehend that, in spite of diversities in attitudes and outlook, they are bound together by common interests and common aspirations, the peace of the world will rest on uncertain foundations.

Similarly the struggle against disease and pestilence is a matter of international concern. In the age of aviation disease travels faster than ever, and becomes a threat to the highly developed countries with their vast centers of communication even more than to remote and undeveloped regions of the world. Nor is it enough to fight dread epidemics. Preventive medicine, mental hygiene, improved standards of nutrition, and better health in general are essential to the well-being of nations. They mean higher productivity, enlarged markets, and a general well-being which makes for peace.

Finally, no sure foundation of lasting peace and security can be laid which does not rest on the voluntary association of free peoples. Only so far as the rights and dignity of all men are respected and protected, only so far as men have free access to information, assurance of free speech and free assembly, freedom from discrimination on grounds of race, sex, language, or religion, and other fundamental rights and freedoms, will men insist upon the right to live at peace, to compose such differences as they may have by peaceful methods, and to be guided by reason and goodwill rather than driven by prejudice and resentment. . .

Unlike the Security Council, the Economic and Social Council was not to have any coercive powers. The Proposals recognized that in social and economic matters an international organization could aid in the solution of economic and social problems but could not interfere with the functions and powers of sovereign states. It could not command performance by individual member nations; it should not reach into the domestic affairs of Members. Its tools and procedures are those of study, discussion, report, and recommendation. These are the voluntary means of a free and voluntary association of nations. . .

# STRUCTURE OF THE ECONOMIC AND SOCIAL COUNCIL

AT THE CONCLUSION OF ITS THIRD SESSION OCTOBER 1946

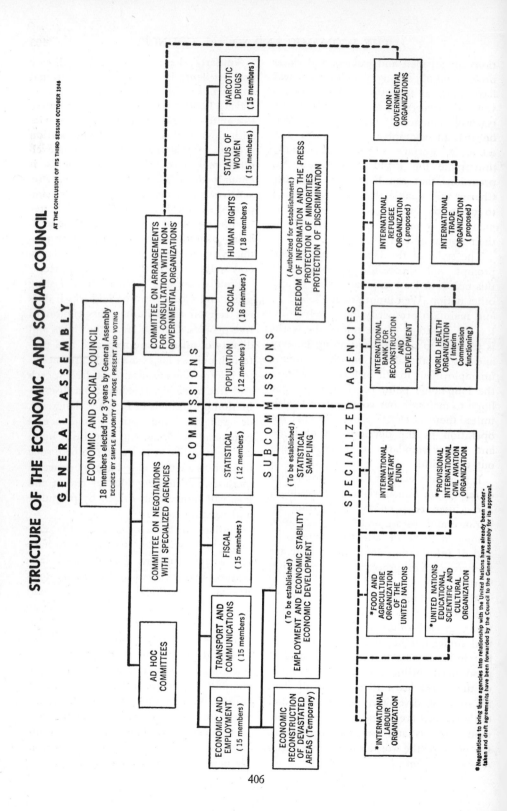

## B. *The Social Commission*

A temporary Social Commission under the Economic and Social Council recommended the creation of a permanent Social Commission. Its duties are defined below.

(Report of the Temporary Social Committee, *Journal of the Economic and Social Council.* First Year, No. 25, 13 June 1946, pp. 362-4.)

The Social Commission would be responsible in the first place for advising the Economic and Social Council on the development of general social policy and on the formulation of social principles which would constitute a frame of reference for the work of specialized agencies and commissions in the social field. Moreover, such principles would serve as statements of the aims and aspirations of the governments of the United Nations, bound together under the Charter in a common purpose to advance toward higher standards of living and social progress and development.

(b) *To aid in co-ordinating activities in the social field.*

In pursuing the objective social policy it is essential that all the resources available to the United Nations be fully utilized and adequately correlated. To aid the Economic and Social Council in achieving this objective would constitute the second major function of the permanent Social Commission. One of the ways in which the Commission could be of service would be to maintain a current record of all projects and activities of the specialized agencies, commissions, or other bodies working under or in relation to the Economic and Social Council. In this way full information concerning all projects would be available for the use of each organization in planning and carrying out its programme. Information and ad-

vice would be given to the Economic and Social Council concerning any re-alignments of functions or means of co-ordination of efforts that might be deemed advisable, including liaison relationship, joint committees, cross-representation, and other methods.

(c) *To keep the Economic and Social Council informed concerning the extent to which social policy is applied.*

The Social Commission would have a third function of obtaining from specialized agencies and United Nations commissions information available to them concerning progress made by Member Governments in the practical application of social policies formulated and recommended through the means earlier described, and making such information available to the Economic and Social Council where information in particular fields does not fall within the jurisdiction of any organization or where it is desirable to obtain a general picture of conditions that cannot be filled in through separate enquiries in particular fields, information would be obtained directly from various countries, in accordance with plans worked out in consultation with organizations in special fields.

(d) *To consider and advise on political measures that may be needed.*

The Social Commission would be charged with responsibility for considering measures that may need to be undertaken by international agencies or suggested to governments, for the purpose of the application or further developments of social policy. The results of its study would form the basis of advice to the Economic and Social Council or, through the Council, to other appropriate bodies or to Member Governments. . .

The members should be chosen from all Members of the United Nations, on such a basis as to secure wide geographic representation. It was agreed that all members should be selected because of expert knowledge, and that the Commission would profit from participation of both Government officials and persons who do not hold public office. It is recommended that the majority (the number suggested is thirteen) should be representatives of and appointed by governments of countries chosen for membership by the Economic and Social Council, it being understood that such representatives may be either government officials or persons who do not hold public office, and that five members should be non-governmental members appointed in their personal capacity by the Council on nomination of governments.

The permanent Social Commission will be concerned with many subjects. It should call in regularly to attend its sessions, representatives of specialized agencies. Moreover, it should be authorized to obtain the assistance of experts on special subjects when necessary. Reciprocal representation should be arranged with other commissions in the social and economic fields, and suitable arrangements should be made for the participation in the work of the Commission of representatives of non-governmental organizations and especially the World Federation of Trade Unions, in accordance with general principles laid down by the Economic and Social Council. The same provisions should apply to subcommissions. . .

## C. *The International Children's Emergency Fund*

Children were the most tragic victims of the last war and its aftermath. To improve their lot in war-devastated areas the United Nations has created an International Children's Emergency Fund.

(J. J. Charnow, 'The International Children's Emergency Fund,' Department of State Publication 2787; also *Department of State Bulletin*, 16 March 1947.)

The establishment of the International Children's Emergency Fund last December by the United Nations General Assembly constitutes a highly significant development in the international social field. Structurally, it illustrates the flexibility of the Charter in allowing for the development of new organizational forms to meet emerging needs in the social field. Functionally, it establishes the role of the United Nations beyond that of information, research, and advisory services to what the Temporary Social Commission in its report last June called 'practical help' in promoting solutions of international social problems.

In its report recommending the establishment of an International Children's Emergency Fund, the Third Committee of the General Assembly pointed out:

'The children of Europe and China were not only deprived of food for several cruel years, but lived in a constant state of terror, witnesses of the massacre of civilians and of the horrors of scientific warfare, and exposed to the progressive lowering of standards of social conduct. The urgent problem facing the United Nations is how to ensure the survival of these children. Millions of adults have emerged from the war less fit to meet the grave problems of the day than in 1939.

The hope of the world rests in the coming generations. . . Undernourishment and nutritional and social diseases are rampant among children and adolescents. Infant mortality has doubled or trebled in many areas. Millions of orphans are being cared for under the most deplorable conditions; crippled children in untold thousands are left with the scantiest care or no care at all. . .'

The International Children's Emergency Fund is based upon the fundamental concept that primary responsibility for child-welfare programs lies with the national governments. Within each country the responsibility for child welfare rests with the appropriate governmental authorities, voluntary agencies, and individual citizens. The purpose of the International Children's Emergency Fund is conceived of as being essentially one of providing sufficient supplementary assistance, where needed, to make national programs of child welfare a reality.

Assistance from the Fund may be used for extremely broad purposes by governments. The resolution states only that the resources of the Fund are to be used 'for the benefit' of children and adolescents and 'to assist in their rehabilitation' and 'for child health purposes generally.'

Despite the broad purposes possible under the Fund, discussions at the UNRRA Council, in the General Assembly, and in the Executive Board of the Fund make clear that certain child-welfare problems, because of their urgency, will have immediate call upon the resources of the Fund. The most urgent problem is that of securing for children at least the minimum nutritional supplement necessary to stave off the worst ravages of malnutrition. The Third Committee in its report to the General Assembly pointed out:

'Tragically enough, the home production from which the bulk of the food must come is manifestly insufficient. . . A desirable objective for each government is to ensure one square meal a day to children that can be easily reached; i.e., those in schools and institutions and the children of families receiving social security assistance. A meal of 700 calories a day would cost $20.00 per year per child. As indicated above, much of the food would come from home production, the proportion of the $20.00 that must be imported from overseas sources varying, from country to country, from one-fifth, to one-third, one-half, or even more. Unless the overseas supplies are secured, it is idle to expect the rising generation to build on a sound foundation the world of tomorrow.'

In addition to food, cod-liver oil and medical supplies are greatly needed. Lack of clothing and shoes in some countries constitute almost as serious a threat to child health as lack of food.

The second urgent problem which has been emphasized is the necessity of aiding in the reestablishment of children's institutions and services destroyed by the war as a matter of prime importance in the rehabilitation of homeless and suffering children.

A third urgent problem which received emphasis is the need for facilities to train the personnel necessary in implementing national programs. Encouragement of the training of personnel for child-health and child-welfare work is an essential part of a children's program in view of the serious personnel shortages resulting from the war. . .

## II. THE PROBLEM OF HEALTH

Recognizing that health is an international problem, the League of Nations set up a special Health Organization. This organization was a center for international co-operation in health matters throughout the League's existence, giving support to the efforts of national governments in many ways. The main parts of the organization were a General Advisory Health Council, a Health Committee, and a Secretariat. An Eastern Bureau was maintained at Singapore, where serious epidemics (plague, cholera, and smallpox) are prevalent, and a Center for Research on Leprosy was set up at Rio de Janeiro. Because the accomplishments of the League Health Organization were so substantial, the United Nations in 1946 set up a World Health Organization (W.H.O.), whose constitution is given in extract B, to continue the work.

## A. *An International Problem*

(William Benton, 'A New Instrument of United States Foreign Policy,' *Department of State Bulletin,* vol. xv, No. 380, 1946, pp. 671-4.)

Geography, language differences, and political boundaries have never been barriers to the free flow of bacteria. Bacteria affect and strike the rich and the publishers, along with the poor and the readers. Illness, suffering, and death throughout history have been remarkably disrespectful of national sovereignty. They have not distinguished among the Argentines, the Portuguese, and the Greeks—or the nurses, the physicians, and the board of trustees.

Those who care for the stricken have always been leaders among world internationalists.

I am very happy, therefore, to attend this international dinner of the American Hospital Association. It is especially fitting at this time that your association should make this an international dinner and turn its attention outwards across national boundaries. Efforts of private groups, such as your association, to increase the flow of knowledge and skills across national frontiers contribute greatly to the kind of understanding we must have in this desperately troubled world. . .

Great doctors have always freely shared their ideas, their discoveries, and their skills. There has never been any national monopoly or national exploitation of medical knowledge. As a result, millions of people living in the world today have been given additional decades of life expectancy.

America has learned most of what she knows from other countries in medicine, as in other sciences. There is no one nation which can claim even a large proportion of the great medical discoveries. But America through its citizens has been a leader in furthering international co-operation in medicine and in public health.

Today our medical and other scientific and technical experts are in demand on all continents.

During the 13 months I have been associated with the Department of State, I have had the privilege of serving as chairman of a unique governmental body known as the Interdepartmental Committee on Scientific and Cultural Co-operation. This Committee coordinates the international activities of 12 Government agencies, representing 42 separate bureaus. It is through this Committee that Government projects of scientific and cultural cooperation abroad are integrated with United States foreign policy. It is through this Committee, for example, that a project of the Public Health Service for training nurses in Liberia would be cleared with the State Department, or through which a request from the Liberian Government, say for a malaria survey, would be passed on to the Public Health Service.

. . . by helping other people to improve their health and way of life we create conditions favorable to the development of freedom and democracy, and this is the surest and most direct way to work against war. By lending technicians and specialists we help to raise living standards in countries where technology has not been developed as rapidly as in the United States. By advising on agricultural techniques, by improving nutritional standards, by reducing disease, we are attacking low living standards at their source. By advising on electric-power development, mining techniques, and transportation we are creating the means by which other peoples can better help themselves.

## B. *The World Health Organization*

At a conference held in New York City from 19 June to 22 July 1946, a constitution was approved for the World Health Organization. Its structure resembles those of the other specialized agencies of the United Nations. Like them, it is under the general supervision of the Economic and Social Council. General policies within the organization are formulated by the Health Assembly, composed of delegates from all of the members. There is an Executive Board of eighteen, elected by the Assembly to carry into effect its decisions and policies, and to perform other assigned tasks. A permanent Secretariat, headed by a Director-General, provides technical and other assistance needed by the organization for the accomplishment of its work. The extract below from the constitution of the W.H.O. brings out the objectives of the organization.

(Constitution of the W.H.O., *Department of State Bulletin*, vol. xv, No. 370, 1946, pp. 211-19.)

The States parties to this Constitution declare, in conformity with the Charter of the United Nations, that the following principles are basic to the happiness, harmonious relations and security of all peoples:

Health is a state of complete physical, mental and social well-being and not merely the absence of disease or infirmity.

The enjoyment of the highest attainable standard of health is one of the fundamental rights of every human being without distinction of race, religion, political belief, economic or social condition.

The health of all peoples is fundamental to the attainment of peace and security and is dependent upon the fullest co-operation of individuals and States.

The achievement of any State in the promotion and protection of health is of value to all.

Unequal development in different countries in the promotion of health and control of disease, especially communicable disease, is a common danger.

Healthy development of the child is of basic importance; the ability to live harmoniously in a changing total environment is essential to such development.

The extension to all peoples of the benefits of medical, psychological and related knowledge is essential to the fullest attainment of health.

Informed opinion and active co-operation on the part of the public are of the utmost importance in the improvement of the health of the people.

Governments have a responsibility for the health of their peoples which can be fulfilled only by the provision of adequate health and social measures.

Accepting these principles, and for the purpose of co-operation among themselves and with others to promote and protect the health of all peoples, THE CONTRACTING PARTIES agree to the present Constitution and hereby establish the World Health Organization as a specialized agency of the United Nations.

## I—OBJECTIVE

### ARTICLE 1

The objective of the World Health Organization (hereinafter called the Organization) shall be the attainment by all peoples of the highest possible level of health.

## II—FUNCTIONS

### ARTICLE 2

In order to achieve its objective, the functions of the Organization shall be:

(*a*) to act as the directing and co-ordinating authority on international health work;

(*b*) to establish and maintain effective collaboration with the United Nations, specialized agencies, governmental health administrations, professional groups and such other organizations as may be deemed appropriate;

(*c*) to assist governments, upon request, in strengthening health services;

(*d*) to furnish appropriate technical assistance and, in emergencies, necessary aid upon the request or acceptance of governments;

(*e*) to provide or assist in providing, upon the request of the United Nations, health services and facilities to special groups, such as the peoples of trust territories;

(*f*) to establish and maintain such administrative and technical services as may be required, including epidemiological and statistical services;

(*g*) to stimulate and advance work to eradicate epidemic, endemic, and other diseases;

(*h*) to promote, in co-operation with other specialized agencies where necessary, the prevention of accidental injuries;

(*i*) to promote, in co-operation with other specialized agencies where necessary, the improvement of nutrition, housing, sanitation, recreation, economic or working conditions and other aspects of environmental hygiene;

(*j*) to promote co-operation among scientific and professional groups which contribute to the advancement of health;

(*k*) to propose conventions, agreements and regulations, and make recommendations with respect to international health matters and to perform such duties as may be assigned thereby to the Organization and are consistent with its objective;

(*l*) to promote maternal and child health and welfare and to foster the ability to live harmoniously in a changing total environment;

(*m*) to foster activities in the field of mental health, especially those affecting the harmony of human relations;

(*n*) to promote and conduct research in the field of health;

(*o*) to promote improved standards of teaching and training in health, medical and related professions;

(*p*) to study and report on, in co-operation with other specialized agencies where necessary, administrative and social techniques affecting public health and medical care from preventive and curative points of view, including hospital services and social security;

(*q*) to provide information, counsel and assistance in the field of health;

(*r*) to assist in developing an informed public opinion among all peoples on matters of health;

(*s*) to establish and revise as necessary international nomenclatures of diseases, of causes of death and of public health practices;

(*t*) to standardize diagnostic procedures as necessary;

(*u*) to develop, establish and promote international standards with respect to food, biological, pharmaceutical and similar products;

(*v*) generally to take all necessary action to attain the objective of the Organization.

## III—MEMBERSHIP AND ASSOCIATE MEMBERSHIP

### ARTICLE 3

Membership in the Organization shall be open to all States.

### ARTICLE 4

Members of the United Nations may become Members of the Organization by signing or otherwise accepting this Constitution in accordance with the provisions of Chapter XIX and in accordance with their constitutional processes.

### ARTICLE 5

The States whose governments have been invited to send observers to the International Health Conference held in New York, 1946, may become Members by signing or otherwise accepting this Constitution in accordance with the provisions of Chapter XIX and in accordance with their constitutional processes provided that such signature or acceptance shall be completed before the first session of the Health Assembly.

### ARTICLE 6

Subject to the conditions of any agreement between the United Nations and the Organization, approved pursuant to Chapter XVI, States which do not become Members in accordance with Articles 4 and 5 may apply to become Members and shall be admitted as Members when their application has been approved by a simple majority vote of the Health Assembly. . .

## IV—ORGANS

### ARTICLE 9

The work of the Organization shall be carried out by:

(*a*) The World Health Assembly (hereinafter called the Health Assembly);

(*b*) The Executive Board (hereinafter called the Board);

(*c*) The Secretariat.

## V—THE WORLD HEALTH ASSEMBLY

### ARTICLE 10

The Health Assembly shall be composed of delegates representing Members.

### ARTICLE 11

Each Member shall be represented by not more than three delegates, one of whom shall be designated by the Member as chief delegate. These delegates should be chosen from among persons most qualified by their technical competence in the field of health, preferably representing the national health administration of the Member.

### ARTICLE 12

Alternates and advisers may accompany delegates.

### ARTICLE 13

The Health Assembly shall meet in regular annual session and in such special sessions as may be necessary. Special sessions shall be convened at the request of the Board or of a majority of the members.

. . .

## ARTICLE 18

The functions of the Health Assembly shall be:

(a) to determine the policies of the Organization;

(b) to name the Members entitled to designate a person to serve on the Board;

(c) to appoint the Director-General;

(d) to review and approve reports and activities of the Board and of the Director-General and to instruct the Board in regard to matters upon which action, study, investigation or report may be considered desirable;

(e) to establish such committees as may be considered necessary for the work of the Organization;

(f) to supervise the financial policies of the Organization and to review and approve the budget;

(g) to instruct the Board and the Director-General to bring to the attention of Members and of international organizations, governmental or non-governmental, any matter with regard to health which the Health Assembly may consider appropriate;

(h) to invite any organization, international or national, governmental or non-governmental, which has responsibilities related to those of the Organization, to appoint representatives to participate, without right of vote, in its meetings or in those of the committees and conferences convened under its authority, on conditions prescribed by the Health Assembly; but in the case of national organizations, invitations shall be issued only with the consent of the government concerned;

(i) to consider recommendations bearing on health made by the General Assembly, the Economic and Social Council, the Security Council or Trusteeship Council of the United Nations, and to report to them on the steps taken by the Organization to give effect to such recommendations;

(j) to report to the Economic and Social Council in accordance with any agreement between the Organization and the United Nations;

(k) to promote and conduct research in the field of health by the personnel of the Organization, by the establishment of its own institutions or by co-operation with official or non-official institutions of any Member with the consent of its government;

(l) to establish such other institutions as it may consider desirable;

(m) to take any other appropriate action to further the objective of the Organization.

## ARTICLE 19

The Health Assembly shall have authority to adopt conventions or agreements with respect to any matter within the competence of the Organization. A two-thirds vote of the Health Assembly shall be required for the adoption of such conventions or agreements which shall come into force for each Member when accepted by it in accordance with its constitutional processes.

## ARTICLE 20

Each Member undertakes that it will, within eighteen months after the adoption by the Health Assembly of a convention or agreement, take action relative to the acceptance of such convention or agreement. Each Member shall notify the Director-General of the action taken and if it does not accept such convention or agreement within the time limit, it will furnish a statement of the reasons for non-acceptance. In case of acceptance, each Member agrees to make an annual report to the Director-General in accordance with Chapter XIV.

### ARTICLE 21

The Health Assembly shall have authority to adopt regulations concerning:

(*a*) sanitary and quarantine requirements and other procedures designed to prevent the international spread of disease;

(*b*) nomenclatures with respect to diseases, causes of death and public health practices;

(*c*) standards with respect to diagnostic procedures for international use;

(*d*) standards with respect to the safety, purity and potency of biological, pharmaceutical and similar products moving in international commerce;

(*e*) advertising and labelling of biological, pharmaceutical and similar products moving in international commerce.

. . .

## VI—THE EXECUTIVE BOARD

### ARTICLE 24

The Board shall consist of eighteen persons designated by as many Members. The Health Assembly, taking into account an equitable geographical distribution, shall elect the Members entitled to designate a person to serve on the Board. Each of these Members should appoint to the Board a person technically qualified in the field of health, who may be accompanied by alternates and advisers.

### ARTICLE 25

The Members shall be elected for three years and may be re-elected; provided that of the Members elected at the first session of the Health Assembly, the terms of six Members shall be for one year and the terms of six Members shall be for two years, as determined by lot.

### ARTICLE 26

The Board shall meet at least twice a year and shall determine the place of each meeting.

### ARTICLE 27

The Board shall elect its Chairman from among its Members and shall adopt its rules of procedure.

### ARTICLE 28

The functions of the Board shall be:

(*a*) to give effect to the decisions and policies of the Health Assembly;

(*b*) to act as the executive organ of the Health Assembly;

(*c*) to perform any other functions entrusted to it by the Health Assembly;

(*d*) to advise the Health Assembly on questions referred to it by that body and on matters assigned to the Organization by conventions, agreements and regulations;

(*e*) to submit advice or proposals to the Health Assembly on its own initiative;

(*f*) to prepare the agenda of meetings of the Health Assembly;

(*g*) to submit to the Health Assembly for consideration and approval a general programme of work covering a specific period;

(*h*) to study all questions within its competence;

(*i*) to take emergency measures within the functions and financial resources of the Organization to deal with events requiring immediate action. In particular it may authorize the Director-General to take the necessary steps to combat epidemics, to participate in the organization of health relief to victims of a calamity and to undertake studies and research the urgency of which has been drawn to the attention of the Board by any Member or by the Director-General.

### ARTICLE 29

The Board shall exercise on behalf of the whole Health Assembly the powers delegated to it by that body.

## VII—THE SECRETARIAT

### ARTICLE 30

The Secretariat shall comprise the Director-General and such technical and administrative staff as the Organization may require.

### ARTICLE 31

The Director-General shall be appointed by the Health Assembly on the nomination of the Board on such terms as the Health Assembly may determine. The Director-General, subject to the authority of the Board, shall be the chief technical and administrative officer of the Organization.

. . .

## C. *World Health Organization Program*

The International Health Conference, which met in New York during the summer of 1946, established an Interim Commission to prepare the program of W.H.O. Some of the conclusions reached at the Commission's sessions in January and February 1948, are given below.

(H. van Z. Hyde, 'World Health Organization,' *Department of State Bulletin,* vol. xviii, No. 457, 1948, pp. 432-4, 437-8.)

The major task of the Interim Commission has been to lay the groundwork for the WHO. This planning is certain to shape the course of the WHO for many years to come. Although the program proposed by the Interim Commission will be modified in many ways by the World Health Assembly, it can be expected that the basic principles incorporated in it will remain as the determinants of WHO policy in its formative years.

It is important to examine, in a general way, the plans which have been formulated, in an attempt to preview the organization that is emerging and the factors giving it shape.

In developing program proposals, the Interim Commission has been conscious of the broad scope of the WHO constitution, which aims at the improvement of the physical, mental, and social health of all peoples. It has been conscious, as well, of the time range of this task, which indeed stretches into infinity. . .

In November 1947 the Commission, after careful deliberation, assigned top priority to certain fields of activity and intensified its planning activities in these fields. The disease problems thus chosen for emphasis have certain common characteristics, namely, high world attack rates, involving many millions of persons annually; increased incidence directly resulting from war; and methods of control not widely exploited. In addition to giving high priority to these diseases, the Commission recognized the paramount importance to the world of the development of healthy successor generations by the application of new techniques in maternal and child hygiene.

The disease entities singled out, on the above basis, for emphasis are malaria, tuberculosis, and the group of venereal diseases, with special reference to syphilis. It will be well to examine separately the reasons behind this selection.

## MALARIA

At first sight malaria would perhaps appear to be a disease of regional concern in the tropical and semitropical zones. Quite otherwise, it is today of prime importance to the entire world. In a time of acute world food shortage, it attacks some 300 million persons annually, killing some 3 million of them. For the most part these victims are the workers in the great agricultural areas of the world. The tremendous impact of malaria in these areas is felt in more favorable, nonmalarious climes in the deprivation of food and is evidenced by the effects of malnutrition. The debilitating effect of chronic and recurrent malaria reduces markedly the productivity of essential manpower. It suppresses the alertness of mind and body needed for the application of modern agricultural science in areas which remain backward in a forward-looking age. This situation persists even though malaria can be controlled even to the point of eradication by methods whose effectiveness has been proved in every continent. Today, with the advent of new tools of control, such as the dramatically effective DDT, malaria is more than ever susceptible of complete eradication.

What is required is the extension of knowledge and provision of leadership to affected areas. In Greece, for example, where, through the centuries, malaria has annually attacked 1 to 3 millions of a population of 7.5 millions, the disease has been reduced to a minor problem— by Greeks—under the leadership of a handful of experts sent into the country by UNRRA and maintained there now by the Interim Commission. As a further example of accomplishment in this field by a small outlay of funds—coupled with a large outlay of expertness—one can cite the wartime experience of Egypt with malaria. In 1944, upper Egypt was invaded by *Anopheles gambiae,* the most vicious vector of malaria. Tens of thousands of deaths resulted. In 1945, in one season, this mosquito was completely eradicated throughout Egypt—by Egyptians—with 'know-how' supplied by three or four experts of the Rockefeller Foundation. Malarious countries can themselves conquer malaria with incentive and technical assistance supplied on an international basis.

FAO, as well as WHO, has recognized the significance of malaria in retarding full agricultural productivity. FAO knows that it is handicapped in attaining its objectives so long as populations are held back physically and mentally by this disease. It has sought the aid and advice of the Interim Commission in this matter. In the FAO schemes for development of irrigation projects in malarious zones, such as the Middle East, there stands a threat of increasing the incidence of malaria unless plans are drawn and carried out with attention to mosquito control at each step.

The Interim Commission has seen in malaria a truly world problem toward the solution of which the WHO can make a major contribution by the rapid extension and application of existing technical knowledge.

## TUBERCULOSIS

Tuberculosis is, of course, one of the great enemies of mankind. During the war, deaths from this disease increased almost everywhere as a result of crowding, malnutrition, and the intimate association of open cases of the disease with the general population due to the breakdown of control measures. Indeed, during 1944 and 1945, the death rates in Europe reached most alarming heights, in many places doubling the prewar rate. Since that time there has been a deceptive reduction in current tuberculosis death rates, due to the fact that many of those persons who would normally have survived to swell the present death rate died earlier than would have been their expected lot. The rate of infection, however, remains high, as revealed by mass X-ray and tuberculin surveys, threatening a progressive increase in death rates during ensuing years. Important steps can be taken to ward off this increase and reduce, progressively, the rate of infection. Long-established methods of control, which have proved highly effective where they have been well developed, require extension and strengthening. The essence of these control measures is the finding and isolation of contagious cases.

There is, however, a relatively new tool, which only of late has won wide acceptance. The Scandinavian and other countries, including France, Canada, and the United States, have produced convincing evidence of the effectiveness, in the control of tuberculosis, of the use of a vaccine known as BCG (Bacillus Calmette-Guerin) which was developed in France almost three decades ago. It remains now to determine the exact place of BCG, in relation to other control measures, in the over-all control of tuberculosis. It is quite fully agreed however that BCG has a vital role to play in the international control of tuberculosis. It is the tool that offers hope of immediate benefit, while the world attempts to build the economic foundations which are essential to the control of tuberculosis by older, more orthodox control measures. These latter measures depend upon a sound economic structure which makes available to all proper food, clothing, housing, medical care, and hospitalization. Internationally, the final conquest of tuberculosis is in the hands of the United Nations itself and those of its specialized agencies concerned with world economic health. Tuberculosis is a disease that can be suppressed by a planned attack. The low death rate of 32 per 100,000 in Denmark, as contrasted with rates of 200 to 400 per 100,000 in several other areas of Europe, is a direct result of such attack. . .

### Absorption of Pre-existing Health Agencies

Certain rather extensive routine operating functions of the Interim Commission have been derived directly from the health organizations of the League of Nations and the International Office of Public Health in Paris, both of which have been or are being absorbed by the Interim Commission on behalf of the WHO. These functions have the solidity of international acceptance over a period of years. They perhaps lack the glamour of novelty but constitute a firm base for the new organization. These functions include the following:

The routine exchange of information between nations on the occurrence of pestilential disease, such as cholera, plague, smallpox, and typhus;

The administration of the international sanitary conventions;

The delineation of yellow-fever zones and approval of yellow-fever vaccines;

The revision of international sanitary convention procedures;

The development and maintenance of international standard preparations;

The preparation of monographs on drugs in the development of an international pharmacopoeia;

The analysis and presentation of statistical material regarding the occurrence of infectious diseases; and

The publication of bulletins, journals, fasciculi, and international lists covering scientific, legal, and statistical matters important to international control of disease and improvement of health.

## III. Displaced Persons

Between World War I and World War II the problem of refugees was so pressing that the League of Nations found it advisable to provide relief for them. Under the agreement for the exchange of minorities between Turkey and Greece concluded at Lausanne in 1923, more than a million people were obliged to change their homeland. Large numbers of Jews and Germans became refugees after Hitler came to power in Germany. It was during and after World War II that the problem of displaced persons became most acute, as the extract below shows. Because of the inability of the separate governments to act effectively, international action became necessary. At first the work was undertaken by the League High Commissioner for Refugees, the Intergovernmental Committee on Refugees, the United Nations Relief and Rehabilitation Administration, and a number of private agencies. At the first session of the General Assembly of the United Nations measures were instituted to create the International Refugee Organization (I.R.O.). The constitution of the I.R.O. was approved late in 1946, but, pending ratification, the work of repatriation was done by an Interim Committee. By the summer of 1949 all but about 225,000 of Europe's displaced persons had been repatriated. On 7 July 1949 the General Council of I.R.O. recommended that after 30 June 1950 the I.R.O. cease to exist. Intended to be a temporary agency to deal with a specific problem, this recommendation indicated that the problem was virtually solved. In accordance with the recommendation the I.R.O. will be disbanded on the date mentioned.

## A. *The Problem*

(*Refugees and Displaced Persons,* Prepared by the Office of Public Affairs, Department of State, August 1946.)

At the outbreak of World War II there were over a million refugees. As a result of the political changes emerging from the First World War, these refugees lived in uncertain civil status in various parts of Europe and the Near East. The majority were White Russians in France, Germany, and Austria and Armenians in Syria and Lebanon. Other thousands of White Russians were resident in China and Manchuria.

This number is small compared with the number of persons uprooted during World War II which brought the greatest problem of refugees and displaced persons ever encountered.

### Dislocation inside Germany

The principal dislocation was within Germany.

By early 1945 the total number of displaced persons within Germany of German race was estimated at from 21,000,000 to 30,000,000. The displacement was caused by many factors—the dispersal of industry within Germany, the bombing of the larger urban centers, the transfer of racial Germans into Germany (particularly from the Eastern European countries), and the substantial dislocations of the German populations during the final stages of the war.

Added to this displacement of Germans there were over 8,500,000 United Nations nationals most of whom had been forced into the German Reich as laborers, together with hundreds of thousands of prisoners of war, many of whom had been compelled to join the ranks of laborers contrary to the provisions of the Geneva Convention.

### PERSECUTION OF RACIAL VICTIMS

The Nazi pattern of persecution of racial victims, including deportations to concentration camps, initiated in Germany and Austria was applied with increasing violence in every country in Europe occupied during the war by the Germans. Out of a total of about six and a half million European Jews, about one and a quarter million European Jews survived the war.

### DISLOCATION IN ASIA AND AFRICA

The war dislocated populations elsewhere than in Europe. Some 20,000,000 Chinese were forced to flee from their usual habitations and take up residence elsewhere. At the end of the war there were approximately 12,000,000 refugees and displaced persons in Japan. About 2,000,000 of these were Koreans. The vast majority of the balance were Japanese displaced by bombing or moved from their homes to work as laborers in war-expanded industries.

These were the largest movements. However, practically no country in Europe and Asia was without internal displacement, while some European refugees found shelter during the war in Africa, India and the Western Hemisphere.

### NAZI POLICY OF RACIAL PURISM

In pursuit of the policy of racial purism, the Nazis transferred some 600,-000 racial Germans constituting German minorities in other countries to Germany and Western Poland after its incorporation into the Reich.

The first movement was that of the 'Balts' of German ancestry into the Reich. During the latter stages of the war German ethnic groups, such as those in the Black Sea areas of Russia, entered Germany ahead of the retreating Axis armies. Since the Axis defeat the transfer into Germany of the Sudeten Germans from Czechoslovakia, and German minority groups from Poland, Hungary and Yugoslavia has been under way.

### REPATRIATION BY MILITARY AUTHORITIES

*Germany.* The military authorities in Western Germany found at the end of the war in May, 1945 the problem of refugees and displaced persons was one of the most urgent with which they were faced. Refugees totalling six and one half million were discovered in the three zones. Repatriation by every conceivable means—railway, motor truck, airplane and on foot—reduced this number to slightly over a million by July, 1946. The return of Germans to their prewar homes in Germany has also reduced the internal displacement in Germany. . .

*Austria and Italy.* Repatriation problems in Austria and Italy are like those in Germany, but on a smaller scale. In July, 1946, over 150,000 displaced persons remained in Austria and Italy, of whom about half were United Nations nationals.

### THE NON-REPATRIABLES

The majority of the displaced persons who are now in Germany, Austria and Italy are expecting to constitute the 'hard core' of non-repatriables who are unable or unwilling for various reasons, chiefly political, to return to their countries of origin. These non-repatriables will become the concern of the International

Refugee Organization, the new refugee body to be established under the auspices of the United Nations.

The displaced persons remaining in Germany, Austria and Italy are for the most part Poles, Yugoslavs, Ukranians and Balts. In July, 1946 in the total group of about a million there were estimated to be over 100,000 Jewish refugees in Germany and Austria—over half of these of Polish nationality, the remainder stateless or of uncertain nationality. There has been an ever-increasing flow of Jews from Eastern European countries, chiefly Poland, into the United States zones of Germany and Austria and into Italy since the end of the war. . .

. . . At the first session of the General Assembly of the United Nations in January, 1946, it was recognized that the problem of refugees and displaced persons was international in scope. In order to provide a single international body which could handle adequately all phases of the problem presented by refugees and displaced persons, a special committee comprised of the representatives of 20 of the United Nations was established by the Economic and Social Council and convened in London on April 8, 1946.

The IRO will face the problem of returning the remaining displaced persons to a normal mode of life. Further repatriation will absorb some. Some will be absorbed in the area where they are found. Others will be established in adjacent countries. Palestine may offer a solution for some of the Jewish refugees. The remainder need to be resettled in various countries. The International Refugee Organization is intended to continue operations so long as a refugee problem exists, coordinating the activities of governmental bodies and of private voluntary agencies (of whom there are 31 in the United States alone) engaged in different types of services for refugees.

## B. *The International Refugee Organization*

The extract from the constitution of the I.R.O., given below, was adopted by the General Assembly of the United Nations on 15 December 1946. As previously stated, the organization will be disbanded in 1950.

(General Assembly, First Session, Text of Debates, 15 January 1947, Journal No. 75, Supplement A-64, Add. 1, pp. 860-66.)

### PREAMBLE

The Governments accepting this Constitution,

*Recognizing:* That genuine refugees and displaced persons constitute an urgent problem which is international in scope and character;

That as regards displaced persons, the main task to be performed is to encourage and assist in every way possible their early return to their country of origin;

That genuine refugees and displaced persons should be assisted by international action, either to return to their countries of nationality or former habitual residence, or to find new homes elsewhere, under the conditions provided for in this Constitution; or in the case of Spanish Republicans, to establish themselves temporarily in order to enable them to return to Spain when the present Falangist regime is succeeded by a democratic regime;

That re-settlement and re-establishment of refugees and displaced persons be contemplated only in cases indicated clearly in the Constitution;

That genuine refugees and displaced persons, until such time as their repatriation or re-settlement and re-establishment is effectively completed, should be protected in their rights and legitimate interests, should receive care and assistance and, as far as possible, should be put to useful employment in order to avoid the evil and anti-social consequences of continued idleness; and

That the expenses of repatriation to the extent practicable should be charged to Germany and Japan for persons displaced by those Powers from countries occupied by them:

*Have agreed:* For the accomplishment of the foregoing purposes in the shortest possible time, to establish and do hereby establish, a non-permanent organization to be called the International Refugee Organization, a specialized agency to be brought into relationship with the United Nations, and accordingly

*Have accepted the following articles:*

. . .

### ARTICLE 2—FUNCTIONS AND POWERS

1. The functions of the Organization to be carried out in accordance with the purposes and the principles of the Charter of the United Nations, shall be: the repatriation; the identification, registration and classification; the care and assistance; the legal and political protection; the transport; and the re-settlement and re-establishment, in countries able and willing to receive them, of persons who are the concern of the Organization under the provisions of Annex I. . .

### ARTICLE 4—MEMBERSHIP

1. Membership in the Organization is open to Members of the United Nations. Membership is also open to any other peace-loving States, not members of the United Nations, upon recommendation of the Executive Committee, by a two-thirds majority vote of Members of the General Council present and voting, subject to the conditions of the agreement between the Organization and the United Nations approved pursuant to Article 3 of this Constitution.

2. Subject to the provisions of paragraph 1 of this article, the members of the Organization shall be those States whose duly authorized representatives sign this Constitution without reservation as to subsequent acceptance, and those States which deposit with the Secretary-General of the United Nations their instruments of acceptance after their duly authorized representatives have signed this Constitution with such reservation. . .

### ARTICLE 5—Organs

There are established as the principal organs of the Organization: a General Council, an Executive Committee and a Secretariat.

### ARTICLE 6—THE GENERAL COUNCIL

1. The ultimate policy-making body of the Organization shall be the General Council in which each member shall have one representative and such alternates and advisers as may be necessary. Each member shall have one vote in the General Council.

2. The General Council shall be convened in regular session not less than once a year by the Executive Committee provided, however, that for three years after the Organization comes into being the General Council shall be convened in regular session not less than twice a year. . .

### ARTICLE 7—EXECUTIVE COMMITTEE

1. The Executive Committee shall perform such functions as may be necessary to give effect to the policies of the General Council, and may make, between sessions of the General Council, policy decisions of an emergency nature which it shall pass on to the Director-General,

who shall be guided thereby, and shall report to the Executive Committee on the action which he has taken thereon. These decisions shall be subject to reconsideration by the General Council.

2. The Executive Committee of the General Council shall consist of the representatives of nine members of the Organization. Each member of the Executive Committee shall be elected for a two-year term by the General Council at a regular session of the Council. . .

### ARTICLE 8—ADMINISTRATION

1. The chief administrative officer of the Organization shall be the Director-General. He shall be responsible to the General Council and the Executive Committee and shall carry out the administrative and executive functions of the Organization in accordance with the decisions of the General Council and the Executive Committee, and shall report on the action taken thereon.

2. The Director-General shall be nominated by the Executive Committee and appointed by the General Council. If no person acceptable to the General Council is nominated by the Executive Committee, the General Council may proceed to appoint a person who has not been nominated by the Committee. When a vacancy occurs in the office of the Director-General the Executive Committee may appoint an Acting Director-General to assume all the duties and functions of the office until a Director-General can be appointed by the General Council. . .

## IV. NARCOTIC CONTROL

The international problem relating to narcotics is the prevention of abuses. It is admitted that opium and other dangerous drugs have a legitimate medicinal utility which should be protected, but in the past they have been widely used by addicts who have injured themselves and society. Traffickers have obtained the drugs by illicit means and made them available to their luckless victims. The main opium-producing centers of the world are in Afghanistan, India, China, Iran, Mexico, Russia, Turkey, Yugoslavia, Korea, Bulgaria, and Japan, although there are a few other countries that produce opium in small quantities. The policies of these countries vary considerably, some having legislation forbidding production (China and Mexico), some restricting production (Russia), and others allowing production both for domestic use and export (Afghanistan and Turkey). Since 1912 efforts have been made to control the trade in opium, as one of the extracts below shows. The League of Nations was very active in connection with the drug trade, and that work is being expanded by the United Nations, which has set up a special commission on narcotics under the Economic and Social Council.

### A. *Past Control Efforts*

P. M. Burnett, 'International Bodies for Narcotic Control,' *Department of State Bulletin,* vol. XIII, No. 329, 1945, pp. 570-72.)

The Hague convention of 1912 represented the first formal step into the field of international narcotic-drug control. The convention provided that the par-

424     SOCIAL PROBLEMS

ticipating states should institute certain measures for controlling drugs within their own territories and it laid down a number of general principles which remain as the foundation of all subsequent work in this field. The convention was brought into force in 1915 by a few countries which, having deposited their instruments of ratification, signed a protocol to bring the convention into effect. With respect to a large number of countries, the convention came into force only by virtue of the fact that ratification of the Treaty of Versailles (art. 295) or of certain other treaties of peace concluded at the end of World War I was 'deemed in all respects equivalent' to ratification of the convention.

Under article 23 (c) of the Covenant of the League of Nations, the members of the League agreed to 'entrust the League with the general supervision over the execution of agreements with regard to . . . the traffic in opium and other dangerous drugs.'

The First Assembly of the League created the Advisory Committee on the Traffic in Opium and Other Dangerous Drugs to secure the fullest possible cooperation between the various countries in regard to narcotics control and to assist and advise the Council in dealing with any questions relating thereto.

The Geneva convention of 1925 strengthened the Hague convention and instituted further control over the international trade in narcotics by establishing a system of import certificates and export authorizations and by entrusting supervision over such trade to the Permanent Central Opium Board, the composition and functions of which were set forth in the convention.

The convention for Limiting the Manufacture and Regulating the Distribution of Narcotic Drugs (Geneva, 1931) advanced the area of control by limiting the world manufacture of narcotic drugs

to the world's medical and scientific needs and by limiting in each country the accumulation of stocks of such drugs. In both cases, the limitation was to be accomplished by means of a system of government estimates of annual drug requirements which should be examined by an international Supervisory Body provided for in the convention and which should thereafter be binding upon the estimating governments.

The Convention for the Suppression of the Illicit Traffic in Dangerous Drugs (Geneva, 1936) aimed at the standardization of penalties for illicit trafficking and at the international extradition of those guilty of drug offenses. This instrument came into force only in October 1939, as between 10 states. Since that time it has become effective with respect to 3 additional states.

Taken together, these conventions form an interdependent system that has steadily increased the effectiveness of international control over narcotic drugs.

The Hague convention of 1912 was in force (July 1945) with respect to some 60 states, not including the following: Argentina, Ethiopia, Iran, Lithuania, and the Union of Soviet Socialist Republics.

The Geneva convention of 1925 had been ratified or adhered to (July 1945) by some 54 states, which did not include the following: Afghanistan, Albania, Argentina, China, Ethiopia, Guatemala, Iceland, Iran, Liberia, Mexico, Nicaragua, Panama, Peru, Saudi Arabia, and the United States of America.

The limitation convention of 1931 had been ratified or adhered to (July 1945) by 64 states, which did not include the following: Argentina, Bolivia, Ethiopia, Iceland, Liberia, and Yugoslavia.

The 1936 convention had been ratified or adhered to (July 1945) by Belgium, Brazil, Canada, China, Colombia (ratification approved but not deposited), Egypt

France, Greece, Guatemala, Haiti, India, Rumania, and Turkey.

The Supervisory Body has as its primary responsibility the examination of the estimates that are submitted each year to the Permanent Central Opium Board by each government that is a party to the limitation convention of 1931. These are estimates of the annual requirements for medical and scientific needs within the territory of the government concerned, together with the quantity required for the establishment and maintenance of government stocks. If countries or territories to which the 1931 convention does not apply do not furnish estimates, the Supervisory Body, so far as possible, makes the estimates. The purpose of the examination by the Supervisory Body is to insure, so far as possible, against any overestimation that would swell the totals beyond the world's legitimate requirements and thereby permit an excess of production that would tend to find its way into the illicit traffic. The Supervisory Body may request from the governments further information; it may amend estimates, however, only with the consent of the governments concerned. Its suggestions to governments have generally been accepted, and it has a final power, when it circulates the estimates, of adding its own observations and comments upon the figures submitted. The quantities thus established become the basis for the upper limit of the quantities that may be manufactured annually in the several countries. The Supervisory Body publishes an annual statement entitled 'Estimated World Requirements of Dangerous Drugs.'

The Permanent Central Opium Board receives from the governments that are parties to the Geneva convention of 1925 statistical returns relating to the production, manufacture, consumption, stocks, import, and export of the raw materials or narcotic drugs covered by the convention. Under article 24 of the convention, the Board 'shall continuously watch the course of the international trade,' with a view to discovering whether 'excessive quantities of any substance covered by the present Convention are accumulating in any country,' or whether 'there is a danger of that country becoming a centre of the illicit traffic.' If the Board finds that either of these situations is developing, it may set in motion a procedure laid down in article 24, which includes asking for explanations, reporting these explanations to the parties to the convention . . . and recommending to the parties a temporary cessation of exports of narcotic substances to the country in question. Under article 14 of the limitation convention of 1931, the Board watches the exports to and imports from the several countries, including those not parties to the convention, and, if it finds that any country has obtained or will obtain through international trade quantities of drugs sufficient to exceed its estimates, the Board then immediately notifies the parties to the convention, which are thereupon bound not to authorize any new exports to the country in question. . .

The Advisory Committee on the Traffic in Opium and Other Dangerous Drugs, established by the Assembly in 1920, has from the outset materially influenced the shaping of policy, either through the undertaking or initiation of studies or through the guidance of preparations for new conventions. It has also supervised the general application of the drug conventions, especially through the standardization of governmental reporting.

Both the Assembly and Council of the League of Nations have important functions in the system of international narcotic control, which are derived from the terms of article 23 (c) of the Covenant. The functions of the Assembly include the making of decisions or recommendations relating to the work of the Advisory Committee on the Traffic in Opium and Other Dangerous Drugs and, through its budgetary powers, the providing for the financial support of the various drug bodies. The Council, like the Assembly, exercises a general and political supervision over the opium work of the League, but it also has certain executive functions. The Council requests the Advisory Committee to undertake studies, prepare international conventions, and make recommendations. The reports of the Committee and those of the Permanent Central Opium Board are submitted to the Council. Since the Advisory Committee is an organ advisory to the Council, all decisions taken by the Committee require the approval of the Council. The Council also has certain specific powers under the 1925 convention: Appointment of the members of the Permanent Central Opium Board; the taking of remedial measures under article 24; and the making of certain formal notifications. . .

## B. *The United Nations Commission on Narcotic Drugs*

On 18 February 1946, the Economic and Social Council created a Commission on Narcotic Drugs. Its functions, in the main, are similar to those of the Opium Advisory Committee of the League of Nations. With only eleven members, the Commission is smaller than the League committee, which had twenty-four. The following resolution establishing the United Nations Commission indicates the principal duties of the agency.

(G. A. Morlock, 'International Control of Dangerous Drugs,' *Department of State Bulletin,* vol. xv, No. 385, 1946, p. 886.)

1. The Economic and Social Council, in order to provide machinery whereby full effect may be given to the international conventions relating to narcotic drugs, and to provide for continuous review of and progress in the international control of such drugs, establishes a Commission on Narcotic Drugs.

2. The Commission shall:

(*a*) assist the Council in exercising such powers of supervision over the application of international conventions and agreements dealing with narcotic drugs as may be assumed by or conferred on the Council;

(*b*) carry out such functions entrusted to the League of Nations Advisory Committee on Traffic in Opium and other Dangerous Drugs by the international conventions on narcotic drugs as the Council may find necessary to assume and continue;

(*c*) advise the Council on all matters pertaining to the control of narcotic drugs, and prepare such draft international conventions as may be necessary;

(*d*) consider what changes may be required in the existing machinery for the international control of narcotic drugs and submit proposals thereon to the Council;

(*e*) perform such other functions relating to narcotic drugs as the Council may direct.

3. The Commission may make recommendations to the Council concerning any subcommission which it considers should be established.

4. The Commission shall be composed of fifteen Members of the United Nations which are important producing or manufacturing countries or countries in which illicit traffic in narcotic drugs constitutes a serious social problem. The term of of

fice of members is three years. They are eligible for reappointment.

5. The Commission is authorized by the Council to appoint in a consultative capacity, and without the right to vote, representatives of bodies created under the terms of international conventions on narcotic drugs.

6. The Council requests the following Governments to designate one representative each to constitute the Commission: Canada, China, Egypt, France, India, Iran, Mexico, Netherlands, Peru, Poland, Turkey, United Kingdom, United States of America, Union of Soviet Socialist Republics, and Yugoslavia.

## V. Social Principles of the Inter-american System

The following resolution was adopted by the Inter-American Conference on Problems of War and Peace, held in Mexico City early in 1945. It constitutes a Declaration of Social Principles of the Inter-American system.

### A. *Declaration of Principles*

(*Report of the Delegation of the United States to the Inter-American Conference on Problems of War and Peace,* Department of State Publications, 1945, pp. 129-33.)

*Whereas:*

One of the essential objectives of the future international organization is that of obtaining international cooperation in the solution of social problems, directed toward the improvement of the material conditions of the working classes of all countries;

Many of the principles adopted at the different International Labor Conferences have not yet been approved by the public authorities of all the American countries, and, consequently, it would be desirable if such standards of the rights of labor were effectively incorporated in the life of the peoples of this Continent, and if the adoption thereof were considered as a matter of public interest;

In order to seek the solution of problems arising from risks inherent in the loss of wages for reasons beyond the control of the worker, integrated programs of social security are necessary, which

should include measures for industrial safety and an adequate system of compensation, or be closely related to such measures;

To fulfill its aim the minimum wage must be flexible, in order that its remunerative capacity may protect and increase the purchasing power of the worker, in harmony and equilibrium with the changing conditions of time and place,

The Inter-American Conference on Problems of War and Peace

*Declares:*

1. That it recognizes and proclaims that man must be the center of interest of all efforts of peoples and governments.

2. That the failure of any nation to adopt just and humane labor conditions is an obstacle in the path of other nations that desire to comply with that indispensable principle.

3. That the family, as a social unit, is a fundamental institution, for whose moral stability, economic improvement, and social welfare the State should take the necessary measures.

4. That poverty, malnutrition, sickness and ignorance are lamentable and transitory conditions of human life, and that the American nations will undertake to

combat them energetically and decisively.

5. That the conditions of poverty, infirmity, and lack of culture, under which a part of the populations of the Latin American countries has lived because of adverse factors, must be overcome or solved for the rehabilitation of the American community. To attain such an end, the sincere and firm collaboration of all countries of the Continent is indispensable, particularly those that have attained higher levels of economic and financial capacity.

6. That, from a general point of view, the State should supervise and aid social and economic initiative, encouraging private action to cooperate for the realization of these purposes. Since education, public health, and social assistance and welfare are effective means for achievement of a rise in the standard of living, the attention of all the American nations will be focused upon these services.

7. That the American nations consider access to articles essential to life, such as adequate food, healthful housing and clothing, to be a service that must be stimulated by the governments, and also carried on in a supplementary way whenever private activity does not succeed in meeting the fundamental needs of the peoples and whenever the laws and economic policy of each country permit.

8. That the American nations agree that labor conditions with respect to remuneration, hours and conditions of work must be attended to with special care and, in any event, in such a manner that the well-being and prerogatives essential to human dignity are guaranteed.

9. That the nations of the Continent are determined that they will in this way encourage the vital, economic, moral and social rehabilitation of the American peoples, evaluating them as human beings, increasing their capacity to work and broadening their consuming power, in order that they may enjoy a life that is better, happier, and more useful to humanity.

10. That it is further recognized that, although the outlays social welfare services require represent a charge on the economy of the countries, they will result in effective improvement of labor output, economic production, and living standards in general.

11. That the American nations reiterate the necessity for ratifying the principles adopted at the various International Labor Conferences and express their desire that these standards of social right, inspired by lofty considerations of humanity and justice, will be incorporated in the legislation of all the nations of the Continent.

*Recommends:*

1. The adoption in all the American Republics, as a matter of international public interest, of social legislation protecting the working population and furnishing guarantees and rights, on a scale not lower than that indicated in the conventions and recommendations of the International Labor Organization, at least on the following matters:

a) Fixing of a minimum living wage, calculated on the basis of the living conditions peculiar to the geography and economy of each American country; maximum daily working hours; night work; work of women; work of minors; and recompense for rest periods;

b) Adoption of laws or appropriate agreements putting into effect standards protecting the worker against the different risks that should be covered in accordance with the principles of welfare, assistance and social security, approved by the International Labor Conferences and by the Inter-American Conference on Social Security;

c) Provision by the State of welfare and assistance services with respect to preventive and curative medicine, housing of workers, protection of mother and child, and nutrition; adoption of legislation establishing adequate means of hygiene, and industrial safety, and prevention of occupational risks;

d) Protection of maternity and organization of hospital and maternity services for the benefit of workers and their families;

e) Establishment of an adequate system of compensation and insurance at the expense of the employer for occupational risks, directed, among other considerations, to the rehabilitation of workers in case of partial disability;

f) Promotion and broadening of social security to cover sickness, old age, disability, death, maternity, and unemployment, in accordance with the social, economic and geographic conditions in each nation and in conformity with universal principles in respect to these subjects;

g) Recognition of the right of workers to organize, to bargain collectively, and to strike.

2. That the Governments of the American Republics incorporate in their legislation principles that establish:

a) That the minimum wage the worker ought to have shall be that which is considered sufficient, according to the conditions of each region, to meet the normal living requirements of the worker, and of his education and honest pleasures, considering him as head of the family;

b) That the minimum wage should be sufficiently flexible to be adapted to rising prices, in order that the remunerative capacity of the wage may protect and increase the purchasing power of the worker in harmony and equilibrium with the changing conditions of time and region, as well as with greater efficiency in production and resulting decrease in costs per unit.

3. That all the American Republics support the Permanent Inter-American Committee on Social Security created by the Inter-American Conference on Social Security of Santiago de Chile in September 1942, and that they appoint the members of the said Committee.

4. That an interchange of information and technical services be facilitated for the development and administration of social security programs.

5. That through the Permanent Inter-American Committee on Social Security studies be made of methods of cooperation in building hospitals, providing sanitary equipment and all materials necessary for the development of a program for adequate medical care, and for training doctors, dentists, nurses and other personnel necessary for such a program.

6. That the standard of living of workers be raised by promoting the development of public instruction, making primary education and the campaign against illiteracy obligatory and free, and endeavoring to extend the benefits of free instruction to the higher branches, including vocational education and rural education, in accordance with the possibilities of each State and with the aim of affording equality of opportunity to all American citizens.

7. That the policy of investment of social security funds intended to guarantee long-term obligations be directed in accordance with plans for the development of the national economies and the provision of a higher level of employment, such investments being governed by considerations of social utility.

8. That if the laws and economic policy of each country permit, policies of investment of social security reserves should take chiefly into account the desirability of forming companies controlled by such social security agencies and intended for the production of sanitary articles, food and clothing, at the same time bearing in mind the minimum return required by capitalization of the social security funds

and the development of the national economies.

9. That in order to combat unemployment the American Governments promote the development of public works and low-cost housing programs, either with their own resources or, if necessary, through Inter-American economic and technical cooperation.

10. That, independently of the foregoing recommendations, the Inter-American Juridical Committee be entrusted with the preparation of an 'Inter-American Charter of Social Guarantees,' collaborating with the International Labor Office and taking into account the agreements and recommendations of the latter and the social legislation of the American countries. The charter shall be submitted for consideration and approved by the Ninth International Conference of American States to be held at Bogota.

(Approved at the plenary session of 7 March 1945)

## B. *Child Welfare in the American Republics*

In 1924 the Pan-American Child Welfare Institute was established with permanent headquarters at Montevideo. The constitution of the organization, from which an extract is given below, indicates its purposes and methods.

(General Resolution adopted at the Pan American Child Welfare Congress, 1924. *Senate Documents,* 69th Congress, 2nd Session, Miscellaneous, vol. 1, pp. 2-4.)

### DEFINITION

For the purpose of complete and permanent collaboration dedicated to the mutual knowledge of efforts in behalf of childhood the subscribing countries of America decide to create a common institution with the name of International Institute of America for the Protection of Children.

The seat of this institution will be Montevideo.

The institute will be a center for study, for documentation, for conference and propaganda in America of everything pertaining to the child.

### PURPOSE

To favor the periodic convocation of Pan American Child Congresses.

In order to fulfill its purpose it should—

(a) Collect and publish the laws, regulations, and other documents which concern the protection of children, the official reports concerning the interpretation and execution of these laws and regulations with the corresponding studies.

(b) To record in every form the organizations and institutions, public and private, pertaining to children which exist in each country, particularly their form and organization.

(c) To collect the published works and magazines in the various countries on the protection of children as well as the reports and opinions relative to the different child organizations and institutions.

(d) To keep statistics, demographic charts, and general conclusions on the various questions which concern the protection of the child specially from sickness and from death.

(e) To advise, inform, give facts to the authorities and institutions concerning questions in its cognizance.

(f) To be a center of studies and of documentation for institutions and persons who wish to or who must produce reports or works on questions pertaining to the child.

### MANAGEMENT

This institute shall be presided over by an international council and a director.

(a) *International council.*—This council shall function permanently in Montevideo and will be of honorary character.

It shall be constituted of a delegate or representative from each adhering country named by the respective government and of those who may join later.

A president, a vice president, and a secretary shall be appointed from among them every two years.

It will be assembled in ordinary session at least once every year and in extraordinary session at the request of three of its members or of the director.

In ordinary session the council shall report on the progress of the institute, shall hear the annual report of the director, and shall draw up the budget for the following year.

(b) The director of the institute will be named by the international council by a simple majority of all its members. His term will be unlimited until the council decides otherwise. . .

# 16

# LABOR AND AGRICULTURE

FARMERS and industrial workers, the two largest of the economic groups, have interests that draw them inevitably into the current of international politics. World-shaking events such as wars and depressions hit all hard, but none harder than these two groups. World War I brought high prices to farmers in the United States, but within a few years a devastating deflation set in, and when the depression of the early 1930's gained full momentum, farm prices fell so low that many farmers lost their farms through foreclosures. At the same time millions of people were without sufficient food. The farmer fails when world conditions are depressed and prospers when general conditions are prosperous because he is a part of a single world economic unit. He is not self-sufficient, and he must sell his surplus crops abroad. Labor and the other groups of society are in the same dependent position.

When war comes, labor and agriculture feel the pinch in ways other than economic. Millions from their ranks are drafted and heavy loads fall upon the shoulders of those who remain at home. Agricultural machinery is manufactured in smaller quantity and is difficult or impossible to obtain. Under the emergency of war production, labor is obliged to work longer hours and under less satisfactory working conditions, with the right to strike—where it exists at all—temporarily in abeyance.

Besides experiencing the ups and downs of the world community to which they belong, both agriculture and labor have in still other ways projected themselves into the realm of world politics. Agriculture is closely related to the world's health, its productivity affecting the dietary standards of people everywhere. It is related, too, to transportation and refrigeration, as its products are carried to the consumer. Then the farmer is always anxious to have the advantages of scientific advances and new methods that have been made available to agriculture in other countries. Some idea of the international aspects of agriculture may be gained from the agenda of the Third Inter American Conference of Agriculture, held at Caracas, Venezuela, in 1945, which included such items as agricultural credit, postwar crop adjustments, foodstuffs, raw materials, markets, transportation, migration, and agricultural statistics. There are now two important permanent organizations operating in the field of agriculture: the Inter-American Institute of Agriculture and the Food and Agricultural Organization of the United Nations (F.A.O.).

Several years ago three hundred youth leaders, representing nearly a million unemployed young people, went to Geneva with petitions to submit to the International Labor Conference. Their spokesman said, 'Give us work or we must go to war.' This was a pointed statement of the fact that there is a close relation between the conditions of labor and international peace. Wide unemployment provides the breeding ground for the social unrest that is so likely to lead to dictatorships and aggressions. The preamble of the Constitution of the International Labor Organization puts the situation very well in the statement that 'peace can be established only if it is based upon social justice.'

Great improvement in the conditions of labor—hours of work, safety measures, and wages—has been achieved by national legislation in many countries. For years, it has been realized, however, that there is much to be gained by international action. Because labor costs are an important item of production, producers in any one country are reluctant to make concessions to their employees that will place them at a disadvantage over their competitors in other countries. Simultaneous adoption of labor legislation is for this reason a wise course of procedure, for the disadvantages to employers in different countries are then equalized.

Labor has shown its interest in international affairs in many ways, but none more important than in its contribution to the movement that led to the creation of the International Labor Organization at Paris in 1919. This organization was intended to place labor legislation on an international basis, and the I.L.O. has in fact worked actively for nearly three decades toward this end. It outlived World War II and is now continuing its work.

## I. Labor in World Affairs

Realizing as it does the importance of peace and prosperity to its welfare, labor takes a lively interest in international relations. Indicative of this interest are the two extracts that follow. Extract A includes two resolutions adopted at the A. F. of L. Convention in 1946, and Extract B is a statement made by Secretary of State George C. Marshall to the National Convention of the C.I.O. in 1947.

### A. *The A. F. of L. and International Co-operation*

(*Report of Proceedings of 65th Convention,* American Federation of Labor, pp. 533, 540.)

UNITED NATIONS SECURITY COUNCIL

*Resolution No.* 96—By Delegates John P. Redmond, George T. Slocum, and George J. Richardson, International Association of Fire Fighters.

WHEREAS, The delegates to the 65th convention of the American Federation of Labor feel that a third World War is inevitable unless positive action is taken at once. The United Nations Organization is at present inadequate and the major powers of the world have not reached agreement on vital issues that could prevent another war. Recent scientific developments make another war too horrible to contemplate and may set back immeasurably the progress of the human race. If courageous and effective action is taken now to strengthen the United Nations Organization, we believe that such a world-wide catastrophe can be prevented, therefore, be it

RESOLVED, That the American Federation of Labor in convention assembled in Chicago urgently recommend the immediate strengthening of the United Nations Organization by the adoption of three amendments to the United Nations Charter to provide for:

1. Reorganization of the United Nations Security Council and the World Court to give fair representation to all nations and to decide by majority vote all matters involving aggression, preparation for aggression. There must be no veto to protect aggressors.

2. Delegation to the Security Council of the powers to suppress aggression and control heavy and scientific weapons. The powers to be delegated should be strictly limited and well defined and these powers must be interpreted by the World Court. Aggression should be defined as an attack with weapons of violence by a sovereign state or its citizens against the territory of another sovereign state, or the production of specified weapons of violence by any sovereign state beyond quotas set by the Security Council, or by refusal to permit inspection by duly authorized representatives of the Security Council.

3. Establishment of a strong International Police Force. Such a force must be established to impartially support the powers of the Security Council.

The details of these amendments and the methods of procedure under them should be in accordance with the Quota Force Plan, and be it further

RESOLVED, That we urge the acceptance of the proposal of Mr. Bernard M. Baruch, United States Representative on the United Nations Atomic Energy Commission, for the creation of an International Atomic Development Authority. We further urge the incorporation of that proposal into the Quota Force Plan, and be it further

RESOLVED, That until such time as the above measures, or similar ones, go into effect, we urge the maintenance of the armed forces of the United States at levels recommended by the Chief of Staff, United States Army and the Chief of Naval Operations, United States Navy.

Your committee recommends that this resolution be referred to the Executive Council for study and action.

The recommendation of the committee was unanimously adopted.

## FOREIGN POLICY

*Resolution No.* 121—By Delegate Nicolas Nogueras Rivera, Puerto Rico Free Federation of Workingmen.

WHEREAS, The effective and glorious intervention of the United States in the last war placed our nation in a leading position in creating the instrumentality for a permanent peace and for the international economic adjustments, and

WHEREAS, American organized labor was the fundamental factor which made possible the victorious termination of the war, and

WHEREAS, The course of events shows that American organized labor should take an active part in building up world security through democratic principles and ideals, and

WHEREAS, This objective cannot be reached unless American organized labor is sincerely and solidly united behind a common foreign policy, therefore, be it

RESOLVED, That the 65th convention of

the American Federation of Labor assembled in Chicago, Ill., instruct and empower its Executive Council to invite the outstanding leaders of the Congress of Industrial Organizations and Independent Unions to a round-table conference to consider the advisability of working out a plan to carry on a common foreign policy of American organized labor as the best cooperation that could be given to the nation in its efforts to create world peace and social-economic stability.

Your committee recommends non-concurrence with the resolution.

The recommendation of the committee was unanimously adopted.

## B. *Labor and Foreign Policy*

(George C. Marshall, Address of 15 October 1947, *Department of State Bulletin*, vol. XVII, No. 434, 1947, pp. 826-7.)

This is my first opportunity as Secretary of State to discuss our foreign policy before a special gathering of American labor. You have an important part to play in the determination of that foreign policy and especially in making it effective.

Everyone agrees, I think, that labor plays a vital part in the functioning of the modern state. If labor can be confused or embittered, if labor can be made to lose faith in the community of which it forms a part, then the core of any national society is threatened. The enemies of democracy know this, and it explains the efforts they make to undermine the confidence of the labor element in the stability of our institutions and the soundness of our traditions.

I am confident of American labor's reaction to efforts made to disrupt the structure of our society in the domestic field. But the problems of foreign relations are in their very nature remote from the American scene and are more easily distorted. For this reason I wish to outline certain of the fundamental considerations which I believe are important to an understanding of the American position today.

There is a danger that the individual man, whose well-being is the chief concern of all democratic policies, foreign or domestic, is being lost sight of in the welter of ideological generalities and slogans which fill the air. Generalities are frequently accepted as gospel truth without even a superficial examination of the validity of their basic tenets. Often they are intended to obscure the basic issue which, as I see it today, is simply whether or not men are to be left free to organize their social, political, and economic existence in accordance with their desires, or whether they are to have their lives arranged and dictated for them by small groups of men who have arrogated to themselves this arbitrary power.

This issue is as old as recorded history. But in the world today it has assumed more menacing proportions than ever before. The great enemy of democracy has always been the concentration of arbitrary power in a few hands.

The particular theory used as a justification for the suppression and eventual elimination of civil liberties varies with the times. All such theories, however, contain within themselves the greatest of all historical fallacies—that in human affairs the end justifies the means.

I do not have to point out to this convention that the rights of labor and the hope and possibility of further gains for labor are absolutely dependent upon the preservation of civil liberties. The issue is not one of political labels, but whether or not civil liberties, the right of criticism, and the right of recall of individuals elected to governmental responsibility remain intact. No section of the American population has a more vital stake in the preservation of free institutions in the world than has American labor. For among the first victims of any dictatorial regime, and notably of the police state, is the right of labor to organize itself for the protection of its interests.

It is rather trite to say that the world is now a small place, but that is a fact, and what happens in distant places affects our affairs and our lives inevitably, often very quickly, and sometimes most seriously. The present situation in Europe is definitely of the last-mentioned character. . .

The productivity of American farms and factories is of tremendous concern to the entire world. For that and other reasons we occupy a very special position in the world, which carries with it a heavy responsibility which cannot be avoided, even if we might wish to do so. Therefore we must face the facts. The United States stands in the midst of a highly critical world period. The situation involves dangers which affect every American alike. It would be a great folly to assume that we can stand aloof or that we can straddle the issue. A very distinguished American recently stated that 'No private program and no public policy, in any sector of our national life can now escape from the compelling fact that if it is not framed with reference to the world it is framed with perfect futility.' What endangers the United States endangers all of us—labor, industry and agriculture alike. . .

## II. The International Labor Organization

The following extract is from the Constitution of the International Labor Organization as amended after World War II.

(International Labor Conferences, 29th Session, 1946. Constitutional Question Part 1, pp. 106-37.)

### SECTION I

### ORGANIZATION OF LABOUR

Whereas universal and lasting peace can be established only if it is based upon social justice;

And whereas conditions of labour exist involving such injustice, hardship and privation to large numbers of people as to produce unrest so great that the peace and harmony of the world are imperiled; and an improvement of those conditions is urgently required; as, for example, by the regulation of the hours of work, including the establishment of a maximum working day and week, the regulation of the labour supply, the prevention of un-employment, the provision of an adequate living wage, the protection of the worker against sickness, disease and injury arising out of his employment, the protection of children, young persons and women, provision for old age and injury, protection of the interests of workers when employed in countries other than their own, recognition of the principle of freedom of association, the organization of vocational and technical education and other measures;

Whereas also the failure of any nation to adopt humane conditions of labour is an obstacle in the way of other nations which desire to improve the conditions in their own countries;

The HIGH CONTRACTING PARTIES, moved by sentiments of justice and humanity as well as by the desire to secure the permanent peace of the world, agree to the following Constitution of the International Labour Organization.

## I—ORGANIZATION

### ARTICLE 1

1. A permanent organization is hereby established for the promotion of the objects set forth in the Preamble to this Constitution, and in the Declaration concerning the aims and purposes of the International Labour Organization adopted at Philadelphia on 10 May 1944, the text of which is annexed to this Constitution.

2. The Members of the International Labour Organization shall be the States which were Members of the Organization on 1 November 1945, and such other States as may become Members in pursuance of the provisions of paragraphs 3 and 4 of this article.

3. Any original Member of the United Nations and any State admitted to membership of the United Nations by a decision of the General Assembly in accordance with the provisions of the Charter may become a Member of the International Labour Organization by communicating to the Director of the International Labour Office its formal acceptance of the obligations of the Constitution of the International Labour Organization.

4. The General Conference of the International Labour Organization may also admit Members to the Organization by a vote concurred in by two-thirds of the delegates attending the session, including two-thirds of the Government delegates present and voting. Such admission shall take effect on the communication to the Director of the International Labour Office by the Government of the new Member of its formal acceptance of the obligations of the Constitution of the Organization.

5. No Member of the International Labour Organization may withdraw from the Organization without giving notice of its intention so to do to the Director of the International Labour Office. Such notice shall take effect two years after the date of its reception by the Director, subject to the Member having at that time fulfilled all financial obligations arising out of its membership. When a Member has ratified any international labour Convention, such withdrawal shall not affect the continued validity for the period provided for in the Convention of all obligations arising thereunder or relating thereto.

6. In the event of any State having ceased to be a Member of the Organization, its readmission to membership shall be governed by the provisions of paragraph 3 or paragraph 4 of this article as the case may be.

### ARTICLE 2

The permanent Organization shall consist of—

(a) a General Conference of representatives of the Members;

(b) a Governing Body composed as described in Article 7; and

(c) an International Labour Office controlled by the Governing Body.

### ARTICLE 3

1. The meetings of the General Conference of representatives of the Members shall be held from time to time as occasion may require, at least once in every year. It shall be composed of four representatives of each of the Members, of whom two shall be Government delegates and the two others shall be delegates representing respectively the employers and the work-people of each of the Members.

2. Each delegate may be accompanied by advisers, who shall not exceed two in number for each item on the agenda of

the meeting. When questions specially affecting women are to be considered by the Conference, one at least of the advisers should be a woman.

2A. Each Member which is responsible for the international relations of non-metropolitan territories may appoint as additional advisers to each of its delegates:

(a) persons nominated by it as representatives of territories referred to in paragraph 3 (a) of Article 35; and

(b) persons nominated by it to advise its delegates in regard to matters concerning non-self-governing territories.

3. The Members undertake to nominate non-Government delegates and advisers chosen in agreement with the industrial organizations, if such organizations exist, which are most representative of employers or work-people, as the case may be, in their respective countries.

4. Advisers shall not speak except on a request made by the delegate whom they accompany and by the special authorization of the President of the Conference, and may not vote.

5. A delegate may by notice in writing addressed to the President appoint one of his advisers to act as his deputy, and the adviser, while so acting, shall be allowed to speak and vote.

6. The names of the delegates and their advisers will be communicated to the International Labour Office by the Government of each of the Members.

7. The credentials of delegates and their advisers shall be subject to scrutiny by the Conference, which may, by two thirds of the votes cast by the delegates present, refuse to admit any delegate or adviser whom it deems not to have been nominated in accordance with this article.

## ARTICLE 4

1. Every delegate shall be entitled to vote individually on all matters which are taken into consideration by the Conference.

2. If one of the Members fails to nominate one of the non-Government delegates whom it is entitled to nominate, the other non-Government delegate shall be allowed to sit and speak at the Conference, but not to vote.

3. If in accordance with Article 3 the Conference refuses admission to a delegate of one of the Members, the provisions of the present article shall apply as if that delegate had not been nominated.

## ARTICLE 5

The meetings of the Conference shall, subject to any decisions which may have been taken by the Conference itself at a previous meeting, be held at such place as may be decided by the Governing Body.

## ARTICLE 6

Any change in the seat of the International Labour Office shall be decided by the Conference by a two-thirds majority of the votes cast by the delegates present.

## ARTICLE 7

1. The Governing Body shall consist of thirty-two persons:

Sixteen representing Governments,
Eight representing the Employers, and
Eight representing the Workers.

2. Of the sixteen persons representing Governments, eight shall be appointed by the Members of chief industrial importance, and eight shall be appointed by the Members selected for that purpose by the Government delegates to the Conference, excluding the delegates of the eight Members mentioned above.

3. The Governing Body shall as occasion requires determine which are the Members of the Organization of chief industrial importance and shall make rules to ensure that all questions relating to the selection of the Members of chief

industrial importance are impartially considered by a committee before being decided by the Governing Body.

4. The persons representing the Employers and the persons representing the Workers shall be elected respectively by the Employers' delegates and the Workers' delegates to the Conference.

5. The period of office of the Governing Body shall be three years. If for any reason the Governing Body elections do not take place on the expiry of this period, the Governing Body shall remain in office until such elections are held.

6. The method of filling vacancies and of appointing substitutes and other similar questions may be decided by the Governing Body subject to the approval of the Conference.

7. The Governing Body shall, from time to time, elect from its number a Chairman and two Vice-Chairmen, of whom one shall be a person representing a Government, one a person representing the Employers, and one a person representing the Workers.

8. The Governing Body shall regulate its own procedure and shall fix its own times of meeting. A special meeting shall be held if a written request to that effect is made by at least twelve of the representatives on the Governing Body.

## ARTICLE 8

1. There shall be a Director of the International Labour Office, who shall be appointed by the Governing Body, and, subject to the instructions of the Governing Body, shall be responsible for the efficient conduct of the International Labour Office and for such other duties as may be assigned to him.

2. The Director or his deputy shall attend all meetings of the Governing Body.

## ARTICLE 9

1. The staff of the International Labour Office shall be appointed by the Director under regulations approved by the Governing Body.

2. So far as is possible with due regard to the efficiency of the work of the Office the Director shall select persons of different nationalities.

3. A certain number of these persons shall be women.

4. The responsibilities of the Director and the staff shall be exclusively international in character. In the performance of their duties, the Director and the staff shall not seek or receive instructions from any Government or from any other authority external to the Organization. They shall refrain from any action which might reflect on their position as international officials responsible only to the Organization.

5. Each Member of the Organization undertakes to respect the exclusively international character of the responsibilities of the Director and the staff and not to seek to influence them in the discharge of their responsibilities.

. . .

## ARTICLE 18

1. When the Conference has decided on the adoption of proposals with regard to an item in the agenda, it will rest with the Conference to determine whether these proposals should take the form: (a) of an international Convention, or (b) of a recommendation to meet circumstances where the subject, or an aspect of it, dealt with is not considered suitable or appropriate at that time for a Convention.

2. In either case a majority of two-thirds of the votes cast by the delegates present shall be necessary on the final vote for the adoption of the Convention or Recommendation, as the case may be, by the Conference.

3. In framing any Convention or Recommendation of general application the Conference shall have due regard to those countries in which climatic conditions,

the imperfect development of industrial organisation, or other special circumstances make the industrial conditions substantially different and shall suggest the modifications, if any, which it considers may be required to meet the case of such countries.

4. Two copies of the Convention or Recommendation shall be authenticated by the signature of the President of the Conference and the Director. Of these copies one shall be deposited in the archives of the International Labour Office and the other with the Secretary-General of the United Nations. The Director will communicate a certified copy of the Convention or Recommendation to each of the Members.

5. In the case of a Convention—

(a) the Convention will be communicated to all Members for ratification;

(b) each of the Members undertakes that it will, within the period of one year at most from the closing of the session of the Conference, or if it is impossible owing to exceptional circumstances to do so within the period of one year, then at the earliest practicable moment and in no case later than eighteen months from the closing of the session of the Conference, bring the Convention before the authority or authorities within whose competence the matter lies, for the enactment of legislation or other action;

(c) members shall inform the Director of the International Labour Office of the measures taken in accordance with this article to bring the Convention before the said competent authority or authorities, with particulars of the authority or authorities regarded as competent, and of the action taken by them;

(d) if the Member obtains the consent of the authority or authorities within whose competence the matter lies it will communicate the formal ratification of the Convention to the Director and will

take such action as may be necessary to make effective the provisions of such Convention;

(e) if the Member does not obtain the consent of the authority or authorities within whose competence the matter lies, no further obligation shall rest upon the Member except that it shall report to the Director of the International Labour Office, at appropriate intervals as requested by the Governing Body, the position of its law and practice in regard to the matters dealt with in the Convention and showing the extent to which effect has been given, or is proposed to be given, to any of the provisions of the Convention by legislation, administrative action, collective agreements or otherwise and stating the difficulties which prevent or delay the ratification of such Convention.

6. In the case of a Recommendation—

(a) the Recommendation will be communicated to all Members for their consideration with a view to effect being given to it by national legislation or otherwise;

(b) each of the Members undertakes that it will, within a period of one year at most from the closing of the session of the Conference, or if it is impossible owing to exceptional circumstances to do so within the period of one year, then at the earliest practicable moment and in no case later than eighteen months after the closing of the Conference, submit the Recommendation to the authority or authorities within whose competence the matter lies for the enactment of legislation or other action;

(c) the Members will inform the Director of the International Labour Office of the measures taken in accordance with this article to bring the Recommendation before the said competent authority or authorities with particulars of the authority or authorities regarded as competent, and of the action taken by them;

(d) apart from bringing the Recommendation before the said competent authority or authorities, no further obligation shall rest upon the Members, except that they will report to the Director of the International Labour Office, at appropriate intervals as requested by the Governing Body, the position of the law and practice in their country in regard to the matters dealt with in the Recommendation and showing the extent to which effect has been given, or is proposed to be given, to the provisions of the Recommendation and such modifications of these provisions as have been found or may be found necessary to make in adopting or applying them.

7. In no case shall the adoption of any Convention or Recommendation by the Conference, or the ratification of any Convention by any Member, be deemed to affect any law, award, custom, or agreement which ensures more favourable conditions to the workers concerned than those provided for in the Convention or Recommendation.

8. If on a Recommendation no legislative or other action is taken to make a Recommendation effective, or if the draft Convention fails to obtain the consent of the authority or authorities within whose competence the matter lies, no further obligation shall rest upon the Member.

9. In the case of a federal State, the power of which to enter into Conventions on labour matters is subject to limitations, it shall be in the discretion of that Government to treat a draft Convention to which such limitations apply as a Recommendation only, and the provisions of this article with respect to Recommendations shall apply in such case. . .

## A. *Aims and Purposes of the International Labor Organization*

The following declaration was drafted at an International Labor Conference in 1944. It gives the long-range outlook of the I.L.O.

(*Department of State Bulletin,* vol. xi, 1944.)

The text of the proposed Declaration concerning the aims and purposes of the International Labour Organization submitted by the Special Drafting Committee follows:

The General Conference of the International Labour Organization, meeting in its Twenty-sixth Session in Philadelphia, hereby adopts, this day of May in the year nineteen hundred and forty-four, the present Declaration of the aims and purposes of the International Labour Organization and of the principles which should inspire the policy of its Members.

### I

The Conference reaffirms the fundamental principles on which the Organization is based and, in particular, that:

(a) labour is not a commodity;

(b) freedom of expression and of association are essential to sustained progress;

(c) poverty anywhere constitutes a danger to prosperity everywhere;

(d) the war against want requires to be carried on with unrelenting vigour within each nation, and by continuous and concerted international effort in which the representatives of workers and employers, enjoying equal status with those of Governments, join with them in free discussion and democratic decision with a view to the promotion of the common welfare.

### II

Believing that experience has fully demonstrated the truth of the statement in the Preamble to the Constitution of the International Labour Organization that lasting peace can be established only if it is based on social justice, the conference affirms that:

(a) all human beings, irrespective of race, creed or sex, have the right to pursue both their material well-being and their spiritual development in conditions of freedom and dignity, of economic security and equal opportunity;

(b) The attainment of the conditions in which this shall be possible must constitute the central aim of national and international policy;

(c) all national and international policies and measures, in particular those of an economic and financial character, should be judged in this light and accepted only in so far as they may be held to promote and not to hinder the achievement of this fundamental objective;

(d) It is a responsibility of the International Labour Organization to examine and consider all international economic and financial policies and measures in the light of this fundamental objective;

(e) in discharging the tasks entrusted to it the International Labour Organization, having considered all relevant economic and financial factors, may include in its decisions and recommendations any provisions which it considers appropriate.

(c) the provision, as a means to the attainment of this end and under adequate guarantees for all concerned, of facilities for training, and the transfer of labour, including migration for employment and settlement;

(d) policies in regard to wages and earnings, hours and other conditions of work calculated to ensure a just share of the fruits of progress to all, and a minimum living wage to all employed and in need of such protection;

(e) the effective recognition of the right of collective bargaining, the cooperation of management and labor in the continuous improvement of productive efficiency, and the collaboration of workers and employers in the preparation and application of social and economic measures;

(f) the extension of social security measures to provide a basic income to all in need of such protection and comprehensive medical care;

(g) adequate protection for the life and health of workers in all occupations;

(h) provision for child welfare and maternity protection;

(i) the provision of adequate nutrition, housing, and facilities for recreation and culture;

(j) the assurance of equality of educational and vocational opportunity.

## III

The Conference recognizes the solemn obligation of the International Labour Organization to further among the nations of the world programmes which will achieve:

(a) full employment and the raising of standards of living;

(b) the employment of workers in the occupations in which they can have the satisfaction of giving the fullest measure of their skill and attainments and make their greatest contribution to the common well-being;

## IV

Confident that the fuller and broader utilization of the world's productive resources necessary for the achievement of the objectives set forth in this Declaration can be secured by effective international and national action, including measures to expand production and consumption, to avoid severe economic fluctuations, to promote the economic and social advancement of the less developed regions of the world, to assure greater stability in world prices of primary products, and to promote a high and steady volume of international trade, the Conference pledges the full cooperation of the International Labour Organization with such international bodies as may be entrusted with a share of the responsibility for this great task and for the promotion of the health, education and well-being of all peoples.

V

The Conference affirms that the principles set forth in this Declaration are fully applicable to all peoples everywhere and that, while the manner of their application must be determined with due regard to the stage of social and economic development reached by each people, their progressive application to peoples who are still dependent, as well as to those who have already achieved self-government, is a matter of concern to the whole civilized world.

## III. The Food and Agriculture Organization

Representatives of the United Nations met at Hot Springs, Virginia, from 18 May to 3 June 1943, to deal with the agricultural side of the problem of freedom from want. An interim commission was set up to function until a permanent organization could be established. In October 1945, a conference at Quebec adopted the constitution of the F.A.O. As explained by Dean Acheson, then Assistant Secretary of State, the organization will serve not only as 'a forum for problems of mutual interest,' but also as a means of 'pooling the best knowledge and experience of all countries in the fields of nutrition, agricultural production and marketing, and in the efficient utilization of the land, forest, and fishery resources of the world.' In 1946 the F.A.O. took over the work of the International Institute of Agriculture, which had been in operation since 1905. The following extract is taken from the constitution of the F.A.O.

### PREAMBLE

The Nations accepting this Constitution, being determined to promote the common welfare by furthering separate and collective action on their part for the purposes of:

raising levels of nutrition and standards of living of the peoples under their respective jurisdictions,

securing improvements in the efficiency of the production and distribution of all food and agricultural products,

bettering the condition of rural populations, and thus contributing toward an expanding world economy,

hereby establish the Food and Agriculture Organization of the United Nations, hereinafter referred to as the 'Organization,' through which the Members will report to one another on the measures taken and the progress achieved in the fields of action set forth above.

### Article 1—Functions of the Organization

1. The Organization shall collect, analyze, interpret, and disseminate information relating to nutrition, food and agriculture.

2. The Organization shall promote and, where appropriate, shall recommend national and international action with respect to

(a) scientific, technological, social, and

economic research relating to nutrition, food and agriculture;

(b) the improvement of education and administration relating to nutrition, food and agriculture, and the spread of public knowledge of nutritional and agricultural science and practice;

(c) the conservation of natural resources and the adoption of improved methods of agricultural production;

(d) the improvement of the processing, marketing, and distribution of food and agricultural products;

(e) the adoption of policies for the provision of adequate agricultural credit, national and international;

(f) the adoption of international policies with respect to agricultural commodity arrangements.

3. It shall also be the function of the Organization

(a) to furnish such technical assistance as governments may request;

(b) to organize, in cooperation with the governments concerned, such missions as may be needed to assist them to fulfill the obligations arising from their acceptance of the recommendations of the United Nations Conference on Food and Agriculture; and

(c) generally to take all necessary and appropriate action to implement the purposes of the Organization as set forth in the Preamble.

### ARTICLE 2—MEMBERSHIP

1. The original Members of the Organization shall be such of the nations specified in Annex I as accept this Constitution in accordance with the provisions of Article XXI.

2. Additional Members may be admitted to the Organization by a vote concurred in by a two-thirds majority of all the members of the Conference and upon acceptance of this Constitution as in force at the time of admission.

### ARTICLE 3—THE CONFERENCE

1. There shall be a Conference of the Organization in which each Member nation shall be represented by one member.

2. Each Member nation may appoint an alternate, associates, and advisers to its member of the Conference. The Conference may make rules concerning the participation of alternates, associates, and advisers in its proceedings, but any such participation shall be without the right to vote except in the case of an alternate or associate participating in the place of a member.

3. No member of the Conference may represent more than one Member nation.

4. Each Member nation shall have only one vote.

5. The Conference may invite any public international organization which has responsibilities related to those of the Organization to appoint a representative who shall participate in its meetings on the conditions prescribed by the Conference. No such representative shall have the right to vote.

6. The Conference shall elect its own officers, regulate its own procedure, and make rules governing the convocation of sessions and the determination of agenda.

7. Except as otherwise expressly provided in this Constitution or by rules made by the Conference, all matters shall be decided by the Conference by a simple majority of the votes cast.

### ARTICLE 4—FUNCTIONS OF THE CONFERENCE

1. The Conference shall determine the policy and approve the budget of the Organization and shall exercise the other powers conferred upon it by this Constitution.

2. The Conference may by a two-thirds

majority of the votes cast make recommendations concerning questions relating to food and agriculture to be submitted to Member nations for consideration with a view to implementation by national action.

3. The Conference may by a two-thirds

prior to consideration by the Conference of proposed recommendations and conventions; and

(b) proper consultation with governments in regard to relations between the Organization and national institutions or private persons.

# FOOD AND AGRICULTURE ORGANIZATION

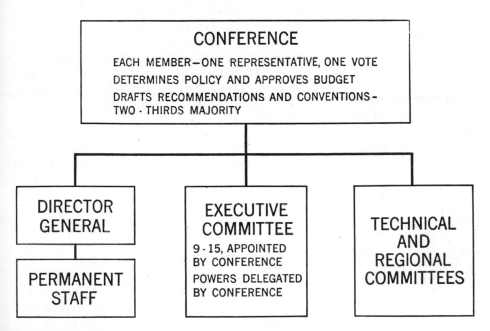

## CONFERENCE
EACH MEMBER—ONE REPRESENTATIVE, ONE VOTE
DETERMINES POLICY AND APPROVES BUDGET
DRAFTS RECOMMENDATIONS AND CONVENTIONS—
TWO - THIRDS MAJORITY

## DIRECTOR GENERAL
## PERMANENT STAFF

## EXECUTIVE COMMITTEE
9 - 15, APPOINTED BY CONFERENCE
POWERS DELEGATED BY CONFERENCE

## TECHNICAL AND REGIONAL COMMITTEES

majority of the votes cast submit conventions concerning questions relating to food and agriculture to Member nations for consideration with a view to their acceptance by the appropriate constitutional procedure.

4. The Conference shall make rules laying down the procedure to be followed to secure:

(a) proper consultation with governments and adequate technical preparation

5. The Conference may make recommendations to any public international organization regarding any matter pertaining to the purpose of the Organization.

6. The Conference may by a two-thirds majority of the votes cast agree to discharge any other functions consistent with the purposes of the Organization which may be assigned to it by governments or provided for by any arrange-

ment between the Organization and any other public international organization.

## ARTICLE 5—THE EXECUTIVE COMMITTEE

1. The Conference shall appoint an Executive Committee consisting of not less than nine or more than fifteen members or alternate or associate members of the Conference or their advisers who are qualified by administrative experience or other special qualifications to contribute to the attainment of the purpose of the Organization. There shall be not more than one member from any Member nation. The tenure and other conditions of office of the members of the Executive Committee shall be subject to rules to be made by the Conference.

2. Subject to the provisions of paragraph 1 of this Article, the Conference shall have regard in appointing the Executive Committee to the desirability that its membership should reflect as varied as possible an experience of different types of economy in relation to food and agriculture.

3. The Conference may delegate to the Executive Committee such powers as it may determine, with the exception of the powers set forth in paragraph 2 of Article II, Article IV, paragraph 1 of Article VII, Article XIII, and Article XX of this Constitution.

4. The members of the Executive Committee shall exercise the powers delegated to them by the Conference on behalf of the whole Conference and not as representatives of their respective governments.

5. The Executive Committee shall appoint its own officers and, subject to any decisions of the Conference, shall regulate its own procedure.

## ARTICLE 6—OTHER COMMITTEES AND CONFERENCES

1. The Conference may establish technical and regional standing committees and may appoint committees to study and report on any matter pertaining to the purpose of the Organization.

2. The Conference may convene general, technical, regional, or other special conferences and may provide for the representation at such conferences, in such manner as it may determine, of national and international bodies concerned with nutrition, food and agriculture.

## ARTICLE 7—THE DIRECTOR-GENERAL

1. There shall be a Director-General of the Organization who shall be appointed by the Conference by such procedure and on such terms as it may determine.

2. Subject to the general supervision of the Conference and its Executive Committee, the Director-General shall have full power and authority to direct the work of the Organization.

3. The Director-General or a representative designated by him shall participate, without the right to vote, in all meetings of the Conference and of its Executive Committee and shall formulate for consideration by the Conference and the Executive Committee proposals for appropriate action in regard to matters coming before them.

## ARTICLE 8—STAFF

1. The staff of the Organization shall be appointed by the Director-General in accordance with such procedure as may be determined by rules made by the Conference. . .

## ARTICLE 19—WITHDRAWAL

Any Member nation may give notice of withdrawal from the Organization at any time after the expiration of four years from the date of its acceptance of this Constitution. Such notice shall take effect one year after the date of its communication to the Director-General of the Organization subject to the Member nation's having at that time paid its annual contribution for each year of its membership including the financial year following the date of such notice.

ARTICLE 20—AMENDMENT OF CONSTITU-
TION

1. Amendments to this Constitution involving new obligations for Member nations shall require the approval of the Conference by a vote concurred in by a two-thirds majority of all the members of the Conference and shall take effect on acceptance by two-thirds of the Member nations for each Member nation accepting the amendment and thereafter for each remaining Member nation on acceptance by it.

2. Other amendments shall take effect on adoption by the Conference by a vote concurred in by a two-thirds majority of all the members of the Conference. . .

## A. *Program of the Food and Agriculture Organization*

At the Copenhagen Conference of the F.A.O., held in September 1946, a Preparatory Commission was set up to prepare concrete recommendations and proposals for international action. The extract below, taken from the report of the Commission, indicates some of the problems and objectives of the F.A.O.

(*Report of the F.A.O. Preparatory Commission on World Food Problems*, 1947. Published by the F.A.O., pp. 6-10.)

. . . The World Food Survey has shown that more than half the population of the world is normally malnourished and has a diet equivalent to less than 2250 calories daily at a retail level. Even in the most favorably situated countries at least a third of the population had, prior to the war, an inadequate diet, particularly when judged by mineral and vitamin requirements. The first task to be considered is what steps can be taken to increase the supply of food for improving the nutrition of such malnourished countries and groups.

In the more advanced countries, the major problem is to improve the quality of the food supply by increasing the proportion of protective foods in the diet and to achieve a better distribution so as to ensure that vulnerable groups obtain the particular foods they need. In the less developed countries, the whole volume of the food supply has to be substantially increased—especially the protective foods, but in many cases the energy foods too.

This is a gigantic task which involves a large increase in the agricultural output of those countries, and, where food imports may be needed, a large increase in the volume of appropriate exports in order to obtain the necessary foreign exchange. In this chapter we deal with the agricultural and nutritional aspects of these tasks. The general economic development and industrialization which will be necessary is dealt with in Chapter III [of this report].

The World Food Survey indicates that in the less developed countries, in order to reach intermediate nutritional targets with a calorie intake of some 2,600 calories per head daily, by 1960 the food supply would need to be increased by 90 percent above prewar (of which 55 percent would be accounted for by improvement in the diet, and 35 percent by population growth since the period 1935-39). By 1970 the food supply would need to be 110 percent above prewar. Whether or not such a doubling of food supply is practicable by this date, i.e., within less than twenty-five years, it is clear that, especially in the less developed countries, only an agricultural revolution can bring reality to this objective.

In some less developed areas farming is still in the primitive stage and completely unmechanized. The production revolution which has characterized twentieth-century agriculture in some advanced countries is precluded in the poorer countries by such factors as smallness of holdings, unimproved varieties of crops and livestock, archaic or ill-adapted systems of land tenure and rural organization, lack of capital, poor health, inadequate farm implements, and excessive density of rural populations. In many of these countries 'one farm family manages to produce only enough to feed itself and half another family,' whereas in some advanced countries 'one farm family feeds itself and four other families at a comparatively high nutritional level.' The output of food per man is ten times greater in the latter than in the former countries.

The excellent research done in many poorer countries demonstrates that modern science and its application is not a monopoly of advanced countries. In experimental herds in India the annual yield of milk per cow has in twenty years been raised from the national average of 1,500 pounds to 6,000 pounds. This change has been brought about very largely by improved feeding and by the selection of the better animals available from the native stock. In Java the improved sugarcane variety P.O.J. 2878 has increased potential yields per unit of area by 50 percent. Varieties of rice which can on ordinary farms yield two or three times as much as the commonly used types have been bred by plant geneticists. These are examples of what can be done for livestock and plants. Besides this, research is making increasingly available knowledge, methods, and techniques which will enable areas to be brought into use that were hitherto too unfavorable for settlement and food production. The applica-

tion of these findings could bring very large additional areas of land into production in Asia, Africa, and South America.

The Commission therefore wishes to reemphasize the importance which the Quebec and Copenhagen Conferences placed on the need for research and its practical application to agricultural production. But it is also convinced that (a) education, (b) rural development programs, and (c) industrialization are equally essential if the peoples of less developed areas are, in the twentieth century, substantially to enjoy better standards of diet, health, and living. Better education is needed to enable farm people and consumers to reap, on their farms and in their homes, the fruits of modern science and technology. Rural development programs including such measures as revised systems of land tenure and land utilization, the extension of cultivation to suitable unused land by large-scale irrigation projects and similar public works, the improvement of roads and communications, and the expansion or modernization of processing and marketing facilities must, as stressed at Quebec and Copenhagen, also be an integral part of the drive for more and better food. Industrialization, which is discussed in Chapter III [of this report], is needed not only to draw excess population from the land, raise productivity and the general standard of living, but also to manufacture fertilizers, agricultural chemicals, machinery, and general farm requirements to supplement other imports needed to expand farm production.

It is thus apparent, especially in the less developed areas where the greater part of the population depends directly on the land, not only that the several parts of each national agricultural development program should be closely integrated, but also that the farm program must itself be an integral part of a dynamic and progressive policy embracing the whole national economy. India and other countries have already formulated comprehensive programs of this type with five- and ten-year objectives, and we commend this approach to other governments faced with comparable problems.

While FAO and other international agencies such as the Economic and Social Council and the International Bank for Reconstruction and Development can, on request, help governments with such programs and policies, the responsibility for their initiation and execution clearly lies with the governments of individual member nations. They alone can provide both the driving force and the direction. Accordingly, in this chapter we consider (a) how national governments can place themselves in a better position to expand food production and develop nutrition programs, (b) how FAO can help governments to help themselves in formulating and carrying out such policies, and (c) what steps are necessary at the international level to co-ordinate the national food and agricultural programs which many nations are already making or which we hope may emerge as a result of our recommendations.

## ACTIVITIES OF NATIONAL GOVERNMENTS

It is clear from the foregoing that the first task of governments, especially in the nutritionally disadvantaged countries, is to frame over-all programs for the expansion of essential agricultural production. Many such governments are confronted with a very numerous agricultural population occupying extremely small farms and lacking equipment, capital, and technical knowledge. Programs have to be framed in practical terms to meet the needs of these people.

They should include first and foremost the provision of education and information so that the people can understand and co-operate in the various projects for technical improvement. They should include instruction in the production of nutritive foodstuffs and essential protective foods for the farm families themselves. Such programs would also make provision for better quality seeds, certain useful pesticides, fertilizers for raising the quality and in some cases the quantity of farm livestock, and for suitable handtools and other farm implements. . .

### FOREIGN EXPERIENCE

Nations have much to gain from developing scientific, technical, and other contacts with foreign countries. Improvement of agriculture can often be speeded by sending missions abroad to study particular methods and practices. Research workers, technical officers, and administrators can widen their experience by foreign study. Many countries have also found it advantageous to send agricultural attachés or other agricultural officers to countries of special significance to them. Further expansion of this system of agricultural attachés might be helpful to many other countries. In these various ways the countries embarking on development programs can discover valuable means of self-help. The actual arrangements will normally be made by the countries themselves. But FAO should keep itself informed of what is being done and may in some cases be able to provide services as a clearinghouse of information regarding facilities for such foreign visits and training. . .

### FAO NATIONAL COMMITTEES

In order that governments may co-operate effectively with FAO, we recommend as a matter of urgency the setting up of National FAO Committees where such do not already exist. These Committees serve as a link between their country and FAO. While certain matters such as proposals involving national commitments should normally be communicated by FAO to governments through foreign ministries, matters concerning agricultural and nutritional policies should be communicated through the FAO National Committee unless otherwise provided. Arrangements should also be made by which communications on routine matters can take place directly between the unit in FAO and the proper corresponding unit in the national government.

It is also important that each member nation supply promptly to FAO copies of all significant current reports and publications relating to food and agriculture. If FAO is to serve nations effectively, the nations in turn must answer promptly and fully requests from FAO for information. In addition to agreeing on channels for communication, the government of each member nation should see that appropriate measures are taken to ensure prompt replies to such requests. . .

In view of the importance we attach to education, extension, and advisory services, we suggest that FAO establish a unit or units staffed with experts well qualified to aid individual countries in this field. We further suggest that FAO as soon as possible collect and make available information on educational methods which have been found most effective in various kinds of countries.

In order that FAO effectively assist the personnel interchanges which we have recommended under 'National Activities,' and since such aid involves knowledge of regions where conditions are most comparable to those of a given country, we recommend that FAO should build up a central index of the types of farming regions of member countries, together with a central subject index of institutions and professional workers, in order to facilitate contact between member nations with similar agricultural economies and problems. We further recommend that FAO should act as a clearinghouse in these matters and should prepare a list of scholarships, fellowships, and personnel exchange opportunities in the various countries. . .

## B. *United States Proposals on the Constitution of the Food and Agriculture Organization*

On 23 April 1946, the United States Government submitted the following proposed amendments to the constitution of the Food and Agriculture Organization. The principal objective of the proposal was to substitute a Council of government representatives in place of the Executive Committee. The proposal was adopted and is now in force.

(Food and Agriculture Organization, *Department of State Publication* No. 2826.)

### ARTICLE 5—THE COUNCIL

1. It is proposed that Article 5 be amended to read as follows:

The Conference shall elect a Council of the Food and Agriculture Organization consisting of representatives of eighteen Member nations of the Organization. The tenure and other conditions of office of the members of the Council shall be subject to rules to be made by the Conference.

The Conference may delegate to the Council such powers as it may determine, with the exception of powers set forth in paragraph 2 of Article 2, Article 4, paragraph 1 of Article 7, Article 13 and Article 20 of the Constitution.

The Council shall appoint its Chairman and other officers and, subject to any decisions of the Conference, shall adopt its own rules of procedure.

. . .

ARTICLE 7—THE DIRECTOR-GENERAL

2. It is proposed that Article 7, paragraphs 2 and 3, be amended to read as follows:

Subject to the general supervision of the Conference and the Council, the Director-General shall have full power and authority to direct the work of the Organization.

The Director-General or a representative designated by him shall participate, without the right to vote, in all meetings of the Conference and of the Council and shall formulate for consideration by the Conference and the Council proposals for appropriate action in regard to matters coming before them.

The United States Government proposal to amend Article 5 of the FAO Constitution and to make necessary consequential amendment in Article 7 would result in transforming the Executive Committee of FAO from a body composed of persons selected in an individual capacity to a body known as the *Council of the Food and Agriculture Organization*— (FAO), composed of representatives of Member governments. . .

ORGANIZATION AND FUNCTIONS OF THE
COUNCIL OF FAO

It is proposed that the Council of FAO be composed of representatives of 18 Member nations of FAO. Details concerning the Council's organization, meetings, terms of office, provision for the attendance of observers, and similar matters should be governed by rules to be made by the Conference, along lines indicated in Paragraphs 251-256 of the Preparatory Commission Report. The Director-General should be entitled to attend all sessions of the Council, without vote. He would also be requested to supply the necessary secretarial assistance to the Council, both during and between sessions, from the Organization's staff. It is the view of this Government that the Council should be an integral part of the Organization, and should not be permitted to become a separate entity within the FAO. This was the clear intention of the Commission as this Government understood it at the time. This Government pointed out informally to the Secretariat that Paragraph 256.2 of the Report appears to be inaccurately drafted on this point.

It is proposed that the Council exercise such powers and perform such functions as the Conference may delegate to it. These would include the present functions of the Executive Committee which are concerned with the entire program of FAO in the field of food and agricultural policy. This Government is studying the various alternatives for continuing the functions of Financial Control now exercised by the Executive Committee, and will include recommendations on this matter in proposed draft amendments to the Financial Regulations.

This Government considers that the recommendation of the FAO Preparatory Commission for an annual intergovernmental review and consultation on national agricultural and nutrition programs is an important one and should be adopted by the Conference. One of the major tasks of the Council would then be to assist the Director-General to prepare the report and agenda for the annual consultations. To do this, the Council would need to review and where appropriate make recommendations concerning technical developments in agriculture, nutrition, forestry, and fisheries; national and international programs and policies in food and agriculture; international trade problems affecting food and agriculture, including agricultural commodity problems; general economic development especially in relation to agricultural and nutrition policies; and methods by which the Organization may carry out its obligations in these fields.

It is proposed that the functions of the Director-General remain as they now are except that his responsibilities will undoubtedly increase because of the enlarged activities which the Council may develop.

The United States Government will submit to the Conference draft amendments to the Rules of Procedure and Financial Regulations, which will embody the above suggestions.

. . .

REASONS FOR PROPOSED RECOMMENDATIONS

The United States Government recommends that the Executive Committee be reconstituted as a Council of 18 Member governments for the following reasons:

1. As recommendations of international organizations depend on Member governments for their implementation, such recommendations should express not only desirable goals but goals practically attainable. Experience in many fields has demonstrated that governments are most likely to implement by national action those international recommendations which they themselves, or a representative body composed of governments, have had a hand in shaping. This is a major reason why the United States Government favors the establishment of a Council of government representatives.

2. While all Member governments participate annually in the formulation of recommendations which constitute FAO policy, events and conditions change and require constant survey, review, and possible further recommendation. A body exercising powers delegated by the Conference, and acting on its behalf, should reflect as closely as possible the Conference itself. Rules to be made by the Conference can provide for the selection of members of the Council in such a way that they will reflect in balanced fashion the interests of all the Members of the Conference.

3. The proposed Council of FAO should be attended regularly by representatives of all Member governments elected to serve upon it. It has been demonstrated that, for unavoidable and often unexpected reasons, individuals selected to serve in their personal capacity on the Executive Committee have been unable to attend meetings regularly. Under a system of personal selection, there cannot consistently be a provision for selection of a successor in case of sudden vacancy. On the other hand, a Member nation elected to the Council could always insure the attendance of a representative at meetings of the Council.

4. It is felt that experts serving in an individual capacity on a body such as the Executive Committee, which has policy functions of a non-technical character, are placed in an anomalous situation. They often must consider their government's official views on important policy matters, yet they have neither official responsibility to their governments, nor the benefit of official instructions from their governments. It is felt that the proposed change will help to remedy this situation. . .

IV. THE INTER-AMERICAN INSTITUTE OF AGRICULTURAL SCIENCES

A permanent organization of the twenty-one American republics was established in 1944 to deal with agriculture. Its purpose is to 'encourage and advance the development of agricultural sciences' through research, teaching, and extension activities. The text of the Convention setting up the organization is given below.

(Inter-American Institute of Agricultural Sciences, *U.S. Treaty Series,* No. 987.)

The Governments of the American Republics, desiring to promote the advancement of the agricultural sciences and related arts and sciences; and wishing to give practical effect to the resolution approved by the Eighth American Scientific Congress held in Washington in 1940, recommending the establishment of an Inter-American Institute of Tropical Agriculture, have agreed to conclude a Convention in order to recognize the permanent status of the Inter-American Institute of Agricultural Sciences, hereinafter referred to as 'the Institute,' on the basis of the following Articles:

### ARTICLE 1

The Contracting States hereby recognize the permanent status of the Inter-American Institute of Agricultural Sciences, incorporated under the laws of the District of Columbia, United States of America, on June 18, 1942; and they agree to recognize the Institute as a legal entity in accordance with their own legislation. The Institute shall have all the rights, benefits, assets, lands and other property to which it was or may be entitled as a corporation, and shall assume all the obligations and contracts for which it became responsible as a corporation.

The executive headquarters of the Institute shall be located in Washington, D. C. The principal field headquarters of the Institute shall be located in Turrialba, Costa Rica. Regional offices of the Institute may be maintained throughout the American Republics.

## PURPOSES

### ARTICLE 2

The purposes of the Institute are to encourage and advance the development of agricultural sciences in the American Republics through research, teaching and extension activities in the theory and practice of agriculture and related arts and sciences.

In furtherance of these purposes the Institute may, subject to the laws of the several countries, exercise the following powers: To develop, finance and operate similar establishments and installations in one or more of the American Republics; to give assistance in the establishment and maintenance of organizations having similar purposes in the said Republics; to purchase, sell, lease, improve, or operate any property in the American Republics, in accordance with the purposes of the Institute; to collaborate with the Government of any American Republic, or with any other organization or entity, and to give assistance to the same; to receive contributions and donations of money or property, both real and personal; to enter into and carry out contracts and agreements; to raise or acquire and, in any manner, dispose of all agricultural commodities and products thereof essential for experimental or research purposes; and to carry on any other business or activity appropriate to the foregoing purposes.

## THE BOARD OF DIRECTORS

### ARTICLE 3

The representatives of the twenty-one American Republics on the Governing

Board of the Pan American Union shall serve as members of the Institute, and shall be considered as members of the Board of Directors thereof. In the event that any member is unable to attend a meeting of the Board of Directors the said member or his government may designate an alternate for that purpose. The decisions of the Board shall be adopted by a majority vote of its members, which majority vote shall include the votes of a majority of the members representing Contracting States. The Board shall have, among others, the following functions:

To elect the Director of the Institute and to approve the appointment of the Secretary made by the Director.

To remove both the Director and the Secretary.

To determine the compensation of the Director and the Secretary.

To supervise the activities of the Director, who shall be responsible for carrying out all orders and resolutions of said Board.

To appoint and define the duties and compensation of an administrative committee consisting of not more than eight persons, of whom one shall be the Director of the Institute *ex officio*. The members of this administrative committee need not be members of the Board of Directors.

To approve the budget for the administration of the Institute to be submitted annually by the Director.

To fix the annual quotas of the Institute.

The Board shall receive an annual report from the Director upon the activities of the Institute as well as upon its general condition and financial status.

## OFFICERS

### ARTICLE 4

The Institute shall have a Director and a Secretary. The Director shall be elected by the Board of Directors in plenary session for a term of six years; he may be reelected one or more times. The first term of the Director under the provisions of this Convention shall begin as of the day on which this Convention enters into force.

The Secretary shall be appointed by the Director with the approval of the Board of Directors of the Institute and shall be directly responsible to the Director.

The Director and the Secretary shall hold office until their respective successors shall be chosen and shall qualify; but they may be removed by vote of the majority of the members of the Institute.

## THE DIRECTOR

### ARTICLE 5

1. The Director under the supervision of the Board of Directors shall have ample and full powers to direct the activities of the Institute; and he shall be responsible for carrying out all orders and resolutions of said Board.

2. The Director under the supervision of the Board of Directors shall be the legal representative of the Institute; and he may legalize, with the seal of the Institute, all contracts, conveyances and other instruments which require such legalization and which in his opinion are necessary and advantageous to the operation of the Institute. In addition, he shall be authorized to take any other step necessary to validate such instruments as may be required or permitted by law. The Director may grant powers to others for all those acts which he cannot perform personally.

3. The Director, under the supervision of the Board of Directors of the Institute, shall have the power to appoint, remove, and determine the compensation of employees.

4. The Director shall prepare the budget of the Institute for each fiscal year, and submit it to the Board of Directors at least two months before the annual meeting at which it will be considered for approval.

5. The Director shall submit an annual report to the Board of Directors of the Institute two months before the annual meeting, setting forth the work of the Institute during the year and its general condition and financial status, and he shall submit to the approval of the said Board the budget and the plans for the following year.

## THE SECRETARY

### ARTICLE 6

The Secretary shall keep the minutes and records of the Institute, shall exercise all prerogatives and carry out all administrative duties assigned to him by the Director.

## TECHNICAL ADVISORY COUNCIL

### ARTICLE 7

Provision is made for the establishment of a Technical Advisory Council, as follows:

1. Each of the Contracting States may appoint an agricultural expert to be its representative in the Technical Advisory Council of the Institute. This Council shall cooperate with the Director on agricultural matters of a technical nature. The appointment of each representative shall be officially notified to the Secretary of the Institute. The members of the Council shall serve for a period of five years at the will of their respective governments, and may be reappointed one or more times.

2. The Technical Advisory Council shall meet at least once a year, under the chairmanship of the Director of the Institute, at such place as the activities of the Institute may require. The Director may call special meetings of the Council on his own initiative, whenever the best interests of the Institute may require. Notice with respect to any meeting shall be given at least two months in advance and shall state the purpose or purposes of the proposed meeting. A majority of the members of the Council shall constitute a quorum.

3. No member of the Technical Advisory Council, as such, shall receive from the Institute any pecuniary compensation for his services, although the Institute may defray traveling expenses of the members of the Council to the annual meeting.

## FISCAL AGENT

### ARTICLE 8

The Pan American Union shall act as fiscal agent for and on behalf of the Institute, and as such shall receive and disburse the funds of the Institute.

## MAINTENANCE OF THE INSTITUTE

### ARTICLE 9

The income of the Institute for its maintenance and operation shall consist of annual quotas paid by the Contracting States, as well as of legacies, donations and contributions which the Institute may accept. Such funds and contributions shall be used only for purposes in keeping with the character of the Institute.

. . .

PART FOUR

THE INDIVIDUAL AND THE WORLD OF IDEAS

## Human Rights and Minority Rights

Not until the twentieth century has the individual figured prominently in international affairs. Even yet his interests abroad are represented and safeguarded principally by the state of which he is a national. If his person or property abroad is injured and redress is not granted by the local authorities, his government will, if it sees fit, intervene to get an adjustment in his favor. If he trades abroad it is as a national of a state and in accordance with the law as set forth by his state, by the foreign state, or by treaty. If he travels in alien lands, again it is as a national of a state. The subjects of international law are states, and it is principally as the national of a state that the individual derives rights and duties under the law.

During the last few decades the individual has taken on a new importance in the political relations of nations, if not in legal matters. On the one hand he has been subjected to persecution on a large scale, particularly in countries with dictators. Millions of Jews have been slaughtered and other minority groups—national and religious—have been mistreated. Political minorities too have been liquidated on a large scale in Russia and Germany and to a less extent in other dictatorships. On the other hand, ironical as it may seem, while all of this persecution has been going on, the individual has been wooed as never before by governments anxious to have the support of public thinking. Never before in history have nations engaged in propaganda activities on such a scale as today.

These developments point to the need for international action of some kind to protect the individual, his life, and his freedom to think as he will, from the aggressive actions of states. How to insure the basic human freedoms, especially man's right to use his mind freely, is one of the crucial issues of the contemporary world.

In the chapters that follow the halting efforts to deal with these problems at the international level are discussed. In this chapter the attempts that have been made to protect minority groups are reviewed, including the work of the United Nations Commission on Human Rights and the recent Assembly action on genocide—a new term defined as the crime of mass slaughter of entire racial or cultural groups. Ethical and religious aspects of international relations are treated in Chapter 18. The final chapter has to do with problems of education, opinion, propaganda, and the free flow of information in world affairs. Reference should also be made to Chapter 5, where attention is given to the individual's status in international law and to the individual responsibility of war criminals.

## I. THE FOUR FREEDOMS

President Franklin D. Roosevelt's idea of the 'Four Freedoms' was most clearly set forth in his message to Congress on the State of the Union, delivered on 6 January 1941. This concept will always rank high among the historic statements on liberty. Roosevelt recognized that basic human freedoms must become world-wide in application.

(Franklin D. Roosevelt, *Message to Congress on the State of the Union*, 6 January 1941.)

. . . In the future days, which we seek to make secure, we look forward to a world founded upon four essential human freedoms.

The first is freedom of speech and expression—everywhere in the world.

The second is freedom of every person to worship God in his own way—everywhere in the world.

The third is freedom from want—which, translated into world terms, means economic understandings which will secure to every nation a healthy peacetime life for its inhabitants—everywhere in the world.

The fourth is freedom from fear—which, translated into world terms, means a world-wide reduction of armaments to such a point and in such a thorough fashion that no nation will be in a position to commit an act of physical aggression against any neighbor—anywhere in the world.

That is no vision of a distant millennium. It is a definite basis for a kind of world attainable in our time and gen-

eration. That kind of world is the very antithesis of the so-called new order of tyranny which the dictators seek to create with the crash of a bomb.

To that new order we oppose the greater conception—the moral order. A good society is able to face schemes of world domination and foreign revolutions alike without fear.

Since the beginning of our American history we have been engaged in change—in a perpetual peaceful revolution—a revolution which goes on steadily, quietly adjusting itself to changing conditions—without the concentration camp or the quick-lime in the ditch. The world order which we seek is the cooperation of free countries, working together in a friendly civilized society.

This nation has placed its destiny in the hands and heads and hearts of its millions of free men and women; and its faith in freedom under the guidance of God. Freedom means the supremacy of human rights everywhere. Our support goes to those who struggle to gain those rights or keep them. Our strength is in our unity of purpose.

To that high concept there can be no end save victory.

## II. THE UNITED NATIONS AND HUMAN RIGHTS

The Charter of the United Nations pledges the member governments 'to take joint and separate action in co-operation with the Organization' for the promotion of 'universal respect for, and observance of, human rights and fundamental freedoms for all without distinction as to race, sex, language, or religion.' But the Charter confers on the United Nations no power to enforce the observance of human rights. It did, however, specify that a Commission on Human Rights be established by the Economic and Social Council. The work of this Commission has progressed to the point that an International Declaration of Human Rights has been adopted by the General Assembly. The following Extracts A, B, C, and D trace the developments toward this end.

## A. *Recommendations on a Bill of Rights*

The nuclear Commission on Human Rights recommended in May 1946 that an international bill of rights should be adopted, but it advised against haste in drafting one. Some of its recommendations follow.

(*Journal of the Economic and Social Council,* No. 14, 24 May 1946.)

### DOCUMENTATION

The Commission recommends that:

1. The Economic and Social Council should instruct the Secretariat:

(a) to compile a yearbook, the first edition of which should contain all declarations and bills on human rights now in force in the various countries.

(b) to collect and publish information on the activities of the General Assembly, the Economic and Social Council, the Security Council, the Hague Court, the Commission on Human Rights, and all other organs of the United Nations dealing with human rights and fundamental freedoms; to include information on the Nuremberg and Tokyo trials which might be important in the field of human rights; to include also a survey of the developments of human rights, as well as plans and declarations by specialized agencies and non-governmental national and international organizations;

2. The Economic and Social Council might suggest to the Member Nations to establish information groups or local human rights committees within their countries who would transmit, periodically, information to the Commission on Human Rights on the observance of human rights in their countries, both in their legal systems and their jurisdictional and administrative practice.

### DRAFT DECLARATIONS

The Commission recommends that:

1. The full Commission should draft an international bill of rights as soon as possible. The nuclear Commission should proceed with the preparations for such a bill. The draft of the international bill of rights, as completed by the full Commission should be circulated among the United Nations governments for their suggestions; . . .

### HUMAN RIGHTS IN INTERNATIONAL TREATIES

The Commission recommends that:

Without waiting for an international bill of rights to be written, the general principle should be accepted that provisions for basic human rights be included in international treaties, particularly peace treaties, that similar provisions be accepted by all States, Members of the United Nations, and by States seeking admission to the United Nations.

PROVISIONS FOR IMPLEMENTATION

The Commission recommends that:

1. It shall be considered that the purpose of the United Nations with regard to the promotion and observance of human rights, as defined in the Charter of the United Nations, could only be fulfilled if provisions were made for the implementation of the observance of human rights and of an international bill of rights; . . .

## B. *The Commission on Human Rights*

The Economic and Social Council adopted the following resolution on 21 June 1946, setting up a permanent Commission on Human Rights, as recommended by the nuclear Commission.

(*Journal of the Economic and Social Council,* No. 29, 13 July 1946.)

### 1. FUNCTIONS

The functions of the Commission on Human Rights shall be those set forth in the terms of reference of the Commission, approved by the Economic and Social Council in its resolution of 16 February 1946, with the addition to paragraph 2 of that resolution of a new sub-paragraph (e) as follows:

(e) any other matter concerning human rights not covered by items (a), (b), (c), and (d).

### 2. COMPOSITION

(a) The Commission on Human Rights shall consist of one representative from each of eighteen members of the United Nations selected by the Council.

(b) With a view to securing a balanced representation in the various fields covered by the Commission, the Secretary-General shall consult with the governments so selected before the representatives are finally nominated by these governments and confirmed by the Council.

(c) Except for the initial period, the term of office shall be for three years. For the initial period, one-third of the members shall serve for two years, one-third for three years, and one-third for four years, the term of each member to be determined by lot.

(d) Retiring members shall be eligible for re-election.

(e) In the event that a member of the Commission is unable to serve for the full three-year term, the vacancy thus arising shall be filled by a representative designated by the Member Government, subject to the provisions of paragraph (b) above.

### DOCUMENTATION

The Secretary-General is requested to make arrangements for:

(a) the compilation and publication of a year-book on law and usage relating to human rights, the first edition of which should include all declarations and bills on human rights now in force in the various countries;

(b) the collection and publication of information on the activities concerning human rights of all organs of the United Nations;

(c) the collection and publication of information concerning human rights arising from trials of war criminals, quislings, and traitors, and in particular from the Nuremberg and Tokyo trials;

(d) the preparation and publication of a survey of the development of human rights;

(e) the collection and publication of plans and declarations on human rights by specialized agencies and non-governmental national and international organizations. . .

### 5. INFORMATION GROUPS

Members of the United Nations are invited to consider the desirability of establishing information groups or local human rights committees within their respective countries to collaborate with them in furthering the work of the Commission on Human Rights.

### 6. HUMAN RIGHTS IN INTERNATIONAL TREATIES

Pending the adoption of an international bill of rights, the general principle shall be accepted that international treaties involving basic human rights, including to the fullest extent practicable treaties of peace, shall conform to the fundamental standards relative to such rights set forth in the Charter. . .

### 8. SUB-COMMISSION ON FREEDOM OF INFORMATION AND OF THE PRESS

(a) The Commission on Human Rights is empowered to establish a Sub-Commission on Freedom of Information and of the Press.

(b) The function of the Sub-Commission shall be, in the first instance, to examine what rights, obligations, and practices should be included in the concept of freedom of information, and to report to the Commission on Human Rights on any issues that may arise from such examination.

### 9. SUB-COMMISSION ON PROTECTION OF MINORITIES

(a) The Commission on Human Rights is empowered to establish a Sub-Commission on the Protection of Minorities.

(b) Unless the Commission otherwise decides, the function of the Sub-Commission shall be, in the first instance, to examine what provisions should be adopted in the definition of the principles which are to be applied in the field of protection of minorities, and to deal with the urgent problems in this field by making recommendations to the Commission.

### 10. SUB-COMMISSION ON THE PREVENTION OF DISCRIMINATION

(a) The Commission on Human Rights is empowered to establish a Sub-Commission on the prevention of discrimination on the grounds of race, sex, language, or religion. . .

## C. *Progress Report on Human Rights*

The following article by a member of the Department of State describes the action taken by the United Nations Commission on Human Rights in its first two years of service. The importance of the Declaration of Rights is taken up, and the author also discusses the Covenant of Human Rights which has been proposed as a method of implementing the Declaration.

(J. P. Hendrick, 'Progress Report on Human Rights,' *Department of State Bulletin*, vol. XIX, No. 475, 1948, pp. 159-64.)

The United Nations Commission on Human Rights has completed its second year of service, devoted for the most part to planning for and working on the project of an international bill of human rights.

An international bill of human rights could consist of a statement of general principles, such as the American Declaration of Independence or the French Declaration of the Rights and Duties of Man. On the other hand it could take the form of a document having legally binding force—an international equivalent of the United States Bill of Rights. The Commission on Human Rights decided at its second session in Geneva that both a statement of principles and a treaty were necessary; it defined the term 'international bill of human rights' as including both a declaration (i.e. statement of principles), and a covenant (i.e. treaty) as well as measures of implementation. It produced a draft declaration and a draft covenant, and examined (but neither approved nor disapproved) the report of a working group on implementation.

The substantive work of the Commission at its third session (May 24 to June 18, 1948) was the completion of a declaration, the question of implementation being considered briefly. The Commission's Drafting Committee, which met from May 3 to May 21, 1948, considered the covenant on human rights as well as doing preliminary work on the declaration. This article will deal with the progress made in the preparation of an international bill of human rights at these two sessions.

Definitive work on a covenant and measures of implementation must await the fourth session of the Commission to be held early in 1949.

## INTERNATIONAL DECLARATION OF HUMAN RIGHTS

There has at no time been serious controversy among Commission members over the general content of the declaration. It has been agreed that the declaration should specify, first, fundamental *civil rights,* known to countries such as the United States for one hundred and fifty or more years; and, second, *social and economic rights,* which have been recognized as a development of the twentieth century. There had, however, until the third session of the Commission, been no very general agreement on two salient

points concerning the declaration: length and effect.

### 'A SHORT AND CONCISE' DECLARATION

The first draft of the declaration was an outline prepared by the United Nations Secretariat, consisting of 48 articles. Though the Geneva draft was reduced to 33 articles, it was recognized that even this was perhaps overlong. The United States and China in successive sessions pressed for a document which would be drastically shortened. . .

### EFFECT OF THE DECLARATION

At the risk of over-simplification, it can be said that three theories have been considered as to the effect of the declaration:

1. The declaration imposes an immediate obligation upon all member states to bring their laws into conformity with its provisions.

2. The declaration imposes no obligation of any sort.

3. The declaration represents a common standard of achievement for all peoples and all nations and may thus be considered to impose a moral, but not a legal, obligation to strive progressively to secure universal and effective recognition and observance of the rights and freedoms therein set forth.

The first of these theories rests on the assumption that the United Nations Charter, particularly in articles 55 and 56, sets forth an obligation in treaty form to observe human rights and that the declaration, as an 'extension' of the Charter, defines these rights.

The second theory rests upon a far more strict construction of the Charter and constant reliance upon its domestic jurisdiction clause.

The third theory is based upon what is considered a fair interpretation of action appropriate to be taken under the Charter. It is in no way intended to derogate from the domestic jurisdiction clause of the Charter, although its proponents freely admit that a covenant, as distinguished from a declaration, is a necessary element in the program and that a covenant would bring up for scrutiny matters which have heretofore been considered domestic.

It is the third of these theories which has now been adopted by the Commission. It finds expression in the preamble to the declaration, reciting that 'Member states have pledged themselves to achieve, in cooperation with the Organization, the promotion of universal respect for and observance of human rights and fundamental freedoms,' and proclaiming the declaration as a 'common standard of achievement for all peoples and all nations, to the end that every individual and every organ of society, keeping this declaration constantly in mind, shall strive by teaching and education to promote respect for these rights and freedoms and by progressive measures, national and international, to secure their universal and effective recognition and observance.' It finds expression also in the introduction to the articles dealing with social and economic rights: 'Everyone as a member of society . . . is entitled to the realization, through national effort and international cooperation, and in accordance with the organization and resources of each State, of the economic, social and cultural rights set out below.' Finally, the theory finds expression in article 26 which states that 'Everyone is entitled to a good social and international order in which the rights and freedoms set out in this Declaration can be fully realized.'

A necessary consequence of the adoption of this theory has been the abandonment of language contained in the Geneva draft purporting to place an immediate legislative obligation with respect to certain articles. Such language is now reserved for use in the covenant. A further consequence has been the defeat of proposals that violations of the declaration should be punished by law.

DECLARATION: PRESENT STATUS

The Commission on Human Rights has accordingly approved a declaration which is short and concise; its effect is clearly stated, and its meaning is obvious. This accomplishment of major proportions is a tribute to the leadership of the Commission's Chairman, Mrs. Franklin D. Roosevelt.

The declaration remains to be approved by the Economic and Social Council and thereafter by the General Assembly in order to attain its full stature in the field of human rights.

## THE COVENANT OF HUMAN RIGHTS AND MEASURES OF IMPLEMENTATION

The Human Rights Drafting Committee started its second session with consideration of the covenant on human rights. At the time it appeared possible that both the Committee and the Commission would be able to develop definitive drafts of both covenant and declaration, and reach a conclusion as to what should be done with respect to implementation. However, despite extraordinary efforts and a seriousness of purpose which was not questioned, the problems proved to be too difficult, and too diffuse, for solution in the time allotted. The Commission did not consider the covenant at its third session. It preferred to do a thorough job on one document—the declaration—rather than a superficial job on two.

### COVENANT—SUBSTANTIVE PROBLEMS

As drafted by the Commission at its Geneva session, the covenant included most of the basic civil rights set forth in the declaration. Notable exceptions were the right to marriage, the right to property, the right to participate in government, and freedom from searches and seizures. The Geneva covenant included none of the social and economic rights. At the outset of the second session of the Drafting Committee, a proposal was made by the Australian member to include in the covenant virtually all the rights enumerated in the declaration. What the result would have been had this proposal been voted upon article by article is a matter of conjecture; in fact, the proposal was voted upon *en bloc,* and defeated. The result was that the substance of the covenant as passed upon by the Drafting Committee remained for the most part unchanged from the Geneva draft.

### COVENANT—PROCEDURAL PROBLEMS

At the second session a difference of opinion had developed with respect to the manner in which limitations on rights should be expressed in the covenant. On one hand it was thought that the covenant should state the rights and at the same time state in detail all limitations on the rights; on the other hand, that the covenant should contain one over-all statement of limitations, roughly analogous to that contained in the declaration. The proponents of the first theory urged that there was no object in having a covenant which each adherent state could construe in accordance with its own wishes and that this was the inevitable result of an over-all clause so broad that anyone could 'drive a team of horses through it.' The proponents of the over-all clause urged that it was impossible to codify the exceptions to general rules already existing in the law except by employing very broad language and that it was equally impossible to foresee in detail what new exceptions it might be necessary to formulate.

An example in point was freedom of information. Certain limitations have been generally acknowledged by most countries as necessary with respect to this right, although practices have varied considerably. Yet the enumeration in the covenant of limitations on the right of freedom of information, started with six and has been progressively increased to 25, with proponents of the over-all clause stating that there are more to come. These limitations failed to take into account new limitations which might be required in connection with television or other unforeseen techniques. Discussion of the problem was continued throughout the Conference on Freedom of Information and the second session of the Human Rights Drafting Committee. The report of the Drafting Committee leaves the problem unresolved.

Nevertheless there are grounds for hope that a solution can be found. The differences between the two opinions have been exaggerated. Both have in fact been in favor of a general clause. The proponents of detailed limitations would, however, limit its application to cases of 'war or other public emergency' and would require a report of its application in each case to the Secretary-General of the United Nations. A substantial number of the articles in the covenant as approved by the Drafting Committee contain provisions which are in effect as broad, or almost as broad, as a general over-all limitation clause. Finally, the pressure for achieving agreement on this procedural question, which threatens the very existence of the covenant, should be so great as to force a solution.

A further point of particular interest to the United States is a provision that the covenant shall make allowance for the problems of federal states. In the case of the United States, for example, the covenant would bind the Federal Government, but not necessarily bind the 48 State governments. This provision, modeled after the pattern established by the International Labor Organization, was adopted in the Geneva draft of the covenant and was not changed in the third session of the Commission.

One other procedural question has been of particular importance to the United States Delegation. In the United States not all treaties are self-executing, since certain treaties require implementing legislation. In countries such as the United Kingdom, legislation is necessary in order to establish the ratified treaty as part of domestic law. The members of the Drafting Committee were sympathetic with the view that time should be given to bring legislation, to the extent necessary, in accord with provisions of the covenant. The covenant accordingly contains wording tentatively designed to make it clear that so far as domestic enforcement is concerned it may require enabling legislation.

## IMPLEMENTATION

The three leading theories as to what should be done in the event of a violation of the covenant may be summarized.

According to the Australian theory, any violation of the covenant should be considered by a new, six-member, international court of human rights whose decisions shall be complied with by covenanting states. Individual complaints as well as complaints by states should be dealt with.

Violations, according to the French theory, should be considered by a Commission empowered to make recommendations to parties concerned. Individual complaints as well as complaints by states should be dealt with.

According to the China-United States theory, violations not settled by direct negotiation should be referred to a committee empowered to make a recommendation to the state or states concerned. Complaints are to be limited, for the time being, to those made by states.

Although it would be impossible to draw any conclusions from the brief debate on the subject at the Commission's third session, it may be noted that the China-United States proposal was specifically supported by more members of the Commission than any other proposal on implementation. Certain points in connection with the China-United States proposal may be of special interest. Of these the most widely discussed was the question of petitions.

## PETITIONS

The covenant is directed primarily at insuring the rights of the individual. The following argument may be made in favor of allowing individuals to bring their cases to the attention of the committee or court which is to consider violations of the covenant: A state cannot be relied upon to bring up cases arising within its own borders; and reliance on other states to take the initiative in such matters, in the absence of an inspection procedure (which would surely prove unacceptable in many countries), would mean that serious violations might never come to light. A precedent was established for consideration of individual petitions in connection with minorities problems by the League of Nations, and according to some evidence at least the procedure was successful. A fundamental basis of effective democratic government is recognition of the right of individual appeal; among the significant contributions made by the United States to the philosophy of government has been the concept that sovereignty is lodged in the people, which thereby permits individual access to federal courts and does not limit cases to those brought by states which, like corporations, 'have no souls.'

In contrast to this argument, if the covenant is to attain widespread adherence, it is essential that its provisions should not interfere unduly with the domestic jurisdiction of member states. The theory of the covenant in itself is revolutionary: an undertaking by international treaty to insure certain rights which have traditionally been regarded as being solely of national concern. A sufficient impetus has been created in the Commission for the completion of a covenant, on the basis of a sincere desire to avoid catastrophes such as those launched by Hitler in his persecution of the Jews, and to improve the standards of international human rights in a field which appears to many to be more important than the ever expanding field of science. But this impetus may be lost if the initial program is too ambitious. To allow an individual to appeal from a decision of his country's court of last resort is a serious step; yet this might be the consequence of recognizing the right of individual petition.

### THE INTERNATIONAL COURT OF JUSTICE

The China-United States proposal recognizes that certain cases arising under the covenant may be considered by the International Court of Justice. Compulsory jurisdiction, however, is not expressly provided.

### COMMITTEE TO CONSIDER COMPLAINTS

The China-United States proposal provides for 'the appointment of a Committee by Covenanting States . . .' which is in contradistinction to the French proposal, providing for an eleven-member special commission, to be appointed by a 'two-thirds majority of the General Assembly of the United Nations with due consideration of equitable geographical distribution.' The theory of the China-United States proposal is that countries which do not agree to assume the burdens of the covenant should not, without the consent of ratifying states, be concerned with its implementation.

### PROGRAM FOR THE FUTURE

The Commission on Human Rights did not express an opinion on whether the declaration should be approved at once, or whether its expression as a formal document of the General Assembly should be postponed until the time that a covenant could be submitted simultaneously for ratification. This is a problem which must be considered by the Economic and Social Council, and by the General Assembly.

Although unanimous approval of the declaration was secured (with abstentions on the part of the four eastern European members), it is clear that agreement on a legally binding covenant involves even greater problems than those posed, and now solved, in connection with the declaration. Even assuming, as it must be assumed, that the procedural aspects of the covenant will be taken care of to the satisfaction of a substantial majority, the question of which substantive rights are to be included in the covenant and also the question to what extent they are to be included are matters of almost infinite complexity; and the further question of implementation is perhaps even more difficult.

If it is decided to proceed along the line of attracting within a reasonable time as many ratifications of the covenant as possible, it will be necessary to limit the covenant to a small number of fundamental rights, such as freedom from slavery, and limit implementation to machinery of a rather sketchy nature. Such a covenant, starting in effect on the principle of the lowest common denominator, could of course be followed by other covenants covering other rights and further expansion of the implementation machinery.

An alternative procedure would be to aim at once for a comprehensive covenant, with full implementation. Such a document would presumably be ratified only by a relatively small number of states at the outset, and the all-important question would be whether this exclusive 'club' could successfully attract new members.

Still another method of operation would be to invite 'like-minded' member states to enter into covenants covering the rights in which they were particularly interested, with the possibility of several covenants entered into by different groups, all having the same primary purpose: the progressive promotion throughout the world of respect for human rights.

Whatever procedure is adopted, one thing is clear. The Commission of Human Rights is not content to see a declaration of general principles approved and consider its task done. It is the view of the Commission, that 'the completion of a Covenant, containing measures of implementation is essential.'

Those members of the United Nations who were chiefly responsible for the insertion of no less than seven references to human rights in the Charter, and for the creation of the Commission on Human Rights, have assumed a heavy burden, which has not yet been discharged.

## D. *Declaration of Human Rights*

On 10 December 1948 the General Assembly of the United Nations approved the Universal Declaration of Human Rights, the text of which follows.

(*The New York Times,* 7 December 1948.)

### PREAMBLE

*Whereas,* recognition of the inherent dignity and of the equal and inalienable rights of all members of the human family is the foundation of freedom, justice and peace in the world; and

*Whereas,* disregard and contempt for human rights have resulted in barbarous acts which have outraged the conscience of mankind, and the advent of a world in which human beings shall enjoy freedom of speech and belief and freedom from fear and want has been proclaimed as the highest aspiration of the common people; and

*Whereas,* it is essential if man is not to be compelled to have recourse as a last resort to rebellion against tyranny and oppression that human rights should be protected by the rule of law; and

*Whereas,* it is essential to promote the development of friendly relations between nations; and

*Whereas,* the peoples of the United Nations have in the Charter reaffirmed their faith in fundamental human rights, in the dignity and worth of the human person and in the equal rights of men and women, and determined to promote social progress and better standards of life in larger freedom; and

*Whereas,* the member states have pledged themselves to achieve, in cooperation with the United Nations, the promotion of universal respect for and observance of human rights and fundamental freedoms; and

*Whereas,* a common understanding of these rights and freedoms is of the greatest importance for the full realization of this pledge,

Now, therefore,

*The General Assembly proclaims* this Declaration of Human Rights as a common standard of achievement for all peoples and all nations, to the end that every individual and every organ of society, keeping this Declaration constantly in mind, shall strive by teaching and education to promote respect for these rights and freedoms and by progressive measures, national and international, to secure their universal and effective recognition and observance, both among the peoples of member states themselves and among the peoples of territories under their jurisdiction.

### ARTICLE 1

All human beings are born free and equal, in dignity and rights. They are endowed with reason and conscience, and should act towards one another in a spirit of brotherhood.

### ARTICLE 2

Everyone is entitled to all the rights and freedoms set forth in this Declaration, without distinction of any kind, such as race, color, sex, language, religion, political or other opinion, national or social origin, property, birth or other status.

### ARTICLE 3

The rights set forth in this Declaration apply equally to all inhabitants of trust and nonselfgoverning territories.

### ARTICLE 4

Everyone has the right to life, liberty and security of person.

### ARTICLE 5

No one shall be held in slavery or servitude; slavery and the slave trade shall be prohibited in all their forms.

### ARTICLE 6

No one shall be subjected to torture or to cruel, inhuman or degrading treatment or punishment.

### ARTICLE 7

Everyone has the right to recognition everywhere as a person before the law.

### ARTICLE 8

All are equal before the law and are entitled without any discrimination to equal protection of the law. All are entitled to equal protection against any discrimination in violation of this Declaration and against any incitement to such discrimination.

### ARTICLE 9

Everyone has the right to an effective remedy by the competent national tribunals for acts violating the fundamental rights granted him by the Constitution or by law.

### ARTICLE 10

No one shall be subjected to arbitrary arrest, detention or exile.

### ARTICLE 11

Everyone is entitled in full equality to a fair and public hearing by an independent and impartial tribunal, in the determination of his rights and obligations and of any criminal charge against him.

### ARTICLE 12

1. Everyone charged with a penal offence has the right to be presumed innocent until proved guilty according to law in a public trial at which he has had all the guarantees necessary for his defence.

2. No one shall be held guilty of any penal offence on account of any act or omission which did not constitute a penal offence, under national or international law, at the time when it was committed. Nor shall a heavier penalty be imposed than the one that was applicable at the time the penal offence was committed.

### ARTICLE 13

No one shall be subjected to arbitrary interference with his private family, home or correspondence, nor to attacks upon his honor and reputation. Everyone has the right to the protection of the law against such interference or attacks.

## ARTICLE 14

1. Everyone has the right to freedom of movement and residence within the borders of each state.

2. Everyone has the right to leave any country, including his own, and to return to his country.

## ARTICLE 15

1. Everyone has the right to seek and to enjoy in other countries asylum from persecution.

2. This right may not be invoked in the case of prosecutions genuinely arising from non-political crimes or from acts contrary to the purposes and principles of the United Nations.

## ARTICLE 16

1. Everyone has the right to a nationality.

2. No one shall be arbitrarily deprived of his nationality nor denied the right to change his nationality.

## ARTICLE 17

1. Men and women of full age, without any limitation due to race, nationality or religion, have the right to marry and to found a family. They are entitled to equal rights as to marriage, during marriage and at its dissolution.

2. Marriage shall be entered into only with the free and full consent of the intending spouses.

3. The family is the natural and fundamental group unit of society and is entitled to protection by society and the state.

## ARTICLE 18

1. Everyone has the right to own property alone as well as in association with others.

2. No one shall be arbitrarily deprived of his property.

## ARTICLE 19

Everyone has the right to freedom of thought, conscience and religion; this right includes freedom to change his religion or belief, and freedom, either alone or in community with others and in public or private, to manifest his religion or belief in teaching, practice, worship and observance.

## ARTICLE 20

Everyone has the right to freedom of opinion and expression; this right includes freedom to hold opinions without interference and to seek, receive and impart information and ideas through any media and regardless of frontiers.

## ARTICLE 21

1. Everyone has the right to freedom of peaceful assembly and association.

2. No one may be compelled to belong to an association.

## ARTICLE 22

1. Everyone has the right to take part in the Government of his country, directly or through freely chosen representatives.

2. Everyone has the right of equal access to public service in his country.

3. The will of the people shall be the basis of the authority of Government; this will shall be expressed in periodic and genuine elections which shall be by universal and equal suffrage and shall be held by secret vote or by equivalent free voting procedures.

## ARTICLE 23

Everyone, as a member of society, has the right to social security and is entitled to the realization, through national effort and international cooperation and in accordance with the organization and resources of each state, of the economic, social and cultural rights indispensable for his dignity and the free development of his personality.

## ARTICLE 24

1. Everyone has the right to work, to free choice of employment, to just and favorable conditions of work and to protection against unemployment.

2. Everyone, without any discrimination, has the right to equal pay for equal work.

3. Everyone who works has the right to just and favorable remuneration, insuring for himself and his family an existence worthy of human dignity, and supplemented, if necessary, by other means of social protection.

4. Everyone has the right to form and to join trade unions for the protection of his interests.

## ARTICLE 25

Everyone has the right to rest and leisure, including reasonable limitation of working hours and periodic holidays with pay.

## ARTICLE 26

1. Everyone has the right to a standard of living adequate for the health and well-being of himself and of his family, including food, clothing, housing and medical care and necessary social services, and the right to security in the event of unemployment, sickness, disability, widowhood, old age or other lack of livelihood in circumstances beyond his control.

2. Motherhood and childhood are entitled to special care and assistance. All children, whether born in or out of wedlock, shall enjoy the same social protection.

## ARTICLE 27

1. Everyone has the right to education. Education shall be free, at least in the elementary and fundamental stages. Elementary education shall be compulsory. Technical and professional education shall be made generally available, and higher education shall be equally accessible to all on the basis of merit.

2. Education shall be directed to the full development of the human personality and to the strengthening of respect for human rights and fundamental freedoms, it shall promote understanding, tolerance and friendship among all nations, racial or religious groups, and shall further the activities of the United Nations for the maintenance of peace.

3. Parents have a prior right to choose the kind of education that shall be given to their children.

## ARTICLE 28

1. Everyone has the right freely to participate in the cultural life of the community, to enjoy the arts and to share in scientific advancement and its benefits.

2. Everyone has the right to the protection of the moral and material interests resulting from any scientific, literary or artistic production of which he is the author.

## ARTICLE 29

Everyone is entitled to a social and international order in which the rights and freedoms set forth in this Declaration can be fully realized.

## ARTICLE 30

1. Everyone has duties to the community in which alone the free and full development of his personality is possible.

2. In the exercise of his rights and freedoms, everyone shall be subject only to such limitations as are prescribed by law solely for the purpose of securing due recognition and respect for the rights and freedoms of others and of meeting the

just requirements of morality, public order and the general welfare in a democratic society.

3. These rights and freedoms may in no case be exercised contrary to the purposes and principles of the United Nations.

Nothing in this Declaration may be interpreted as implying for any states, groups or persons, any right to engage in any activity or to perform any act aimed at the destruction of any of the rights and freedoms prescribed herein.

## III. THE MINORITY PROBLEM

The rights of minorities are closely related to human rights considered on an individual basis. Were man's civil, social, and economic rights respected throughout the world, the minorities problem would not arise. In fact, they are not respected and consequently the minority problem has been growing more acute.

The present distribution of ethnic groups in Europe is a result of the early migrations during the early centuries after Christ. Today great areas are inhabited by several national groups living side by side. The expression 'Scratch a Russian and you find a Tartar' recalls the great invasion of Tartars into Russian territory. Most of the countries on the continent of Europe contain several sizable national groups, usually some one of them dominant and the others living as 'minority' peoples.

In the past the majority groups have often persecuted the minorities under them, trying to destroy their national, cultural, and religious identity. During the Middle Ages and in early modern times, when all Europe was under the Catholic Church, it was religious minorities that were persecuted. Since the rise of nationalism, however, it has been national minorities that have been obliged to knuckle under. The stronger nationalism has become and the more general, the more serious has the problem grown.

After World War I, the rights of minorities in the central European states, where the problem has been most acute, were defined in treaties and declarations, and a right of appeal to the League of Nations was provided where infringements of rights were alleged. Many cases were brought to the League and constructive help was given, but the problem still continued to complicate the relations of European nations. After Hitler came to power in Germany the Jews suffered the most severe persecution that Europe has known for centuries.

Some of the attempts to deal with the issue of minority persecution are reviewed below. The preliminary steps taken by the United Nations on racial persecution and genocide are set forth in Extracts A and B.

## A. *Assembly Resolution on Racial Persecution*

The following resolution was unanimously adopted by the General Assembly on 19 November 1946.

*(Journal of the United Nations, No. 46, 30 November 1946, p. 36.)*

The General Assembly of the United Nations declares that it is in the higher interests of humanity to put an immediate end to religious and so-called racial persecutions and discrimination, and calls on the Governments and responsible authorities to conform both to the letter and to the spirit of the Charter of the United Nations, and to take the most prompt and energetic steps to that end.

## B. *Convention Outlawing Genocide*

On 9 December 1948 the General Assembly of the United Nations adopted the following convention outlawing genocide.

*(The New York Times, 2 December 1948.)*

### CONVENTION ON PREVENTION AND PUNISHMENT OF THE CRIME OF GENOCIDE

*The Contracting Parties,*

*Having considered* the declaration made by the General Assembly of the United Nations in its Resolution 96 (I) dated 11 December 1946 that genocide is a crime under international law, contrary to the spirit and aims of the United Nations and condemned by the civilized world;

*Recognizing* that at all periods of history genocide has inflicted great losses on humanity; and

*Being convinced* that, in order to liberate mankind from such an odious scourge, international cooperation is required;

HEREBY AGREE as hereinafter provided:

#### ARTICLE 1

The contracting parties confirm that genocide, whether committed in time of peace or in time of war, is a crime under international law which they undertake to prevent and to punish.

#### ARTICLE 2

In the present convention genocide means any of the following acts committed with intent to destroy, in whole or in part, a national, ethnical, racial or religious group, as such:

(A) Killing members of the group;

(B) Causing serious bodily or mental harm to members of the group;

(C) Deliberately inflicting on the group conditions of life calculated to bring about its physical destruction in whole or in part;

(D) Imposing measures intended to prevent births within the group;

(E) Forcibly transferring children of the group to another group.

#### ARTICLE 3

The following acts shall be punishable:

(A) Genocide;

(B) Conspiracy to commit genocide;

(C) Direct and public incitement to commit genocide;

(D) Attempt to commit genocide;

(E) Complicity in genocide.

## ARTICLE 4

Persons committing genocide or any of the other acts enumerated in Article III shall be punished, whether they are constitutionally responsible rulers, public officials or private individuals.

## ARTICLE 5

The contracting parties undertake to enact, in accordance with their respective constitutions, the necessary legislation to give effect to the provisions of the present convention and, in particular, to provide effective penalties for persons guilty of genocide or any of the other acts enumerated in Article III.

## ARTICLE 6

Persons charged with genocide or any of the other acts enumerated in Article III shall be tried by a competent tribunal of the State in the territory of which the act was committed, or by such international penal tribunal as may have jurisdiction with respect to such contracting parties as shall have accepted the jurisdiction of such tribunal.

## ARTICLE 7

Genocide and the other acts enumerated in Article III shall not be considered as political crimes for the purpose of extradition.

The contracting parties pledge themselves in such cases to grant extradition in accordance with their laws and treaties in force.

## ARTICLE 8

Any contracting party may call upon the competent organs of the United Nations to take such action under the Charter of the United Nations as they consider appropriate for the prevention and suppression of acts of genocide or any of the other acts enumerated in Article III.

## ARTICLE 9

Disputes between the contracting parties relating to the interpretation, application or fulfillment of the present convention, including those relating to the responsibility of a State for genocide or any of the other acts enumerated in Article III, shall be submitted to the International Court of Justice at the request of any of the parties to the dispute.

## ARTICLE 10

The present convention, of which the Chinese, English, French, Russian and Spanish texts are equally authentic, shall bear the date of ——.

## ARTICLE 11

The present convention shall be open until 31 December, 1949, for signature on behalf of any member of the United Nations and of any nonmember State to which an invitation to sign has been addressed by the General Assembly.

The present convention shall be ratified, and the instruments of ratification shall be deposited with the Secretary-General of the United Nations.

After 1 January, 1950, the present convention may be acceded to on behalf of any member of the United Nations and of any nonmember State which has received an invitation as aforesaid.

Instruments of accession shall be deposited with the Secretary-General of the United Nations.

## ARTICLE 12

Any contracting party may at any time, by notification addressed to the Secretary-General of the United Nations, extend the application of the present convention to all or any of the territories for the conduct of whose foreign relations that contracting party is responsible.

## ARTICLE 13

On the day when the first twenty instruments of ratification have been deposited the Secretary-General shall draw up a procès-verbal and transmit a copy of it to each member of the United Nations and to each of the nonmember States contemplated in Article xi.

The present convention shall come into force on the ninetieth day following the date of deposit of the twentieth instrument of ratification or accession.

Any ratification or accession effected subsequent to the latter date shall become effective on the ninetieth day following the deposit of the instrument of ratification or accession.

## ARTICLE 14

The present convention shall remain in effect for a period of ten years dating from its coming into force.

It shall thereafter remain in force for successive periods of five years for such contracting parties as have not denounced it at least six months before the expiration of the current period.

Denunciation shall be effected by a written notification addressed to the Secretary-General of the United Nations.

## ARTICLE 15

If, as a result of denunciations, the number of parties to the present convention should become less than sixteen the convention shall cease to be in force as from the date on which the last of these denunciations shall become effective.

## ARTICLE 16

A request for the revision of the present convention may be made at any time by any contracting party by means of a notification in writing addressed to the Secretary-General.

The General Assembly shall decide upon the steps, if any, to be taken in respect of such request.

## ARTICLE 17

The Secretary-General of the United Nations shall notify all members of the United Nations and the nonmember States contemplated in Article xi of the following:

(A) Signatures, ratifications and accessions received with Article xi;

(B) Notifications received in accordance with Article xii;

(C) The date upon which the present convention comes into force in accordance with Article xiii;

(D) Denunciations received in accordance with Article xiv;

(E) The abrogation of the convention in accordance with Article xv;

(F) Notifications received in accordance with Article xvi.

## ARTICLE 18

The original of the present convention shall be deposited in the archives of the United Nations.

A certified copy of the convention shall be transmitted to all members of the United Nations and to the nonmember States contemplated in Article xi.

## ARTICLE 19

The present convention shall be registered by the Secretary-General of the United Nations on the date of its coming into force.

## IV. Minorities in the Soviet Union

There are many minorities in Russia. If the Ukrainians and White Russians are to be regarded as minorities, and in the strict sense they should be, they alone number over forty million. There are also Lithuanians, Letts, Estonians, Finns, Poles, Rumanians, Tartars, Kirghiz, Boskirs, Kalmuks, Germans, and many others. Before the Communist Revolution in 1917 these peoples were persecuted as part of a ruthless policy of Russification. A new policy of toleration was inaugurated by the Communists in 1917. A declaration of 15 November 1917 announced a policy of equality for all peoples and freedom for all who wished to dissociate themselves from the Union. A number of minority groups, including the Lithuanians, Letts, Estonians, and Ukrainians, announced their independence and set up separate states, but in 1922 Ukrainia came back into the Union, and in World War II the Baltic States were forcibly annexed. Today the minorities are free to use their own languages and to follow their own traditions. Many of them have set up autonomous republics, regions, or areas which govern themselves in local matters and are represented in the Council of Nationalities, a branch of the Supreme Council of the Union. All of them, however, are parts of the economic system of the Union. The extract below gives the declaration of 1917 on national minorities, and an article in the Russian Constitution of 1936.

### A. *Declaration of Rights of the People of Russia*

(*Declaration of the Rights of the People of Russia*, 15 November 1917, *International Conciliation*, No. 386, p. 11. Reprinted by permission of the Carnegie Endowment for International Peace.)

The October Revolution has started under the general banner of emancipation.

There remain the peoples (nationalities) in Russia. The Congress of Soviets has proclaimed in June of this year the right of Russia's nationalities for free self-determination.

The Second Congress of Soviets has confirmed more categorically and determined this inalienable right of the Russian nationalities.

The Council of the People's Commissars, executing the will of those Congresses, has decided to lay down as a foundation of its policy toward the problem of Russia's nationalities, the following principles:

1. The equality and sovereignty of Russia's nationalities;

2. The right of Russia's nationalities to free self-determination up to seceding and the organization of an independent State;

. . .

4. The free development of the national minorities and ethnographical groups located within the territory of Russia.

Signed, Lenin, the Chairman of the Council of the People's Commissars.

Stalin

The People's Commissar for the Nationalities' Affairs

## B. *Article 123 of the Russian Constitution*

(Constitution of the U.S.S.R., 1936, Co-operative Publishing Company, U.S.S.R.)

ARTICLE 123

The equality of the rights of citizens of the U.S.S.R., irrespective of their nationality or race, in all spheres of economic, state, cultural, social and political life, is an irrevocable law.

Any direct or indirect restriction of the rights of, or, conversely, the establishment of direct or indirect privileges for citizens on account of their race or nationality, as well as the advocacy of racial or national exclusiveness or hatred and contempt, is punishable by law.

## V. THE TRANSFER OF POPULATIONS

A somewhat ruthless method of trying to solve the minority problem is to expel minority groups from their homes and move them into the territory of the states to which they belong by nationality. This was a policy Nazi Germany pursued vigorously after 1939. On 6 October 1939, Hitler announced to the Reichstag that there would be a 'new order of ethnographical conditions, that is to say, a resettlement of nationalities in such a manner that the process will result in the obtaining of better dividing lines.' In conformity with this announcement several hundred thousand Germans were transferred to the Reich from Italy, the Baltic States, and from regions beyond the Carpathian Mountains. They were settled on land that Poles and Czechs were obliged to leave. After the German surrender, millions of Germans were forced to leave the Sudetenland, Silesia, East Prussia, and territories east of the Oder in order to resettle in Germany. These Germans were among the displaced populations who underwent great suffering in spite of the assistance provided by international agencies. In the extract that follows, Sarah Wambaugh, who has had much experience in handling minority problems, admits the great hardships involved in the compulsory transfers of large numbers of people, but believes that those hardships can be mitigated by international safeguards. Since the date of her article the Germans of East Prussia and the Sudetenland, to whom she refers, have been moved into Germany.

(S. Wambaugh, 'New Tools for Peaceful Settlement,' *The Annals of the American Academy of Political and Social Science,* vol. 240, July 1945, pp. 1-3. Reprinted by permission of *The Annals*.)

. . . To move any population or to cut any area and its people from the country to which they feel that they rightfully belong, inevitably offends the citizens of

the democracies, for the principle of self-determination lies at the very basis of our thinking. But in this stern world, where justice does not yet have force behind it, even those most devoted to the principle of self-determination, and I am surely one of them, must recognize that there is a higher right which should prevail—the right of organized society to take the measures which its members are agreed are necessary to maintain the peace for the welfare of the whole. In municipal law the state enjoys the right of eminent domain. Should not organized society possess in some degree the same resource? . . .

On the eastern side of Germany it is apparently decided, and I think wisely decided, that East Prussia shall be removed from the Sovereignty of the Reich and divided between Russia and Poland, even though the population, of some two million and over, is overwhelmingly German. There are, no doubt, some Lithuanians in the part to be absorbed, together with Lithuania, by the Soviet Union, but the number of Lithuanians is at best small, and surely there are no Russians. In the west of East Prussia there is an inconsiderable area which for three centuries before the First Partition was part of Poland, but under Prussian rule there have been few intellectuals left to keep alive Polish feeling. The vote for the Polish Party in the German Reichstag in 1912 was only 35 per cent of the total vote in this small area, and in the plebiscite in 1920 the vote for Poland was only a little over 7 per cent. The District of Allenstein, which forms the southeast part of East Prussia, was for many centuries under Polish suzerainty, but the rule was Prussian. Many still speak a Polish dialect, but except in the town of Allenstein they are Protestant, not Catholic, and so never suffered from Bismarck's *Kulturkampf.* Only 12 per cent of the voters in this area voted in 1912 for the Polish Party, and in the 1920 plebiscite the vote for Poland was very small indeed. It is true that the number might have been larger had the Red Army not been at that moment at the gates of Warsaw, but there can be no question that the great mass is German and there can be no prospect whatever that they will be loyal citizens of either Poland or Russia.

The only hope, then, of tranquil administration is to force the Germans to migrate and to replace them by Poles in the Polish part and Russians in the part to go to Russia. There will also be the Sudetendeutsch who will be forced to leave Czechoslovakia.

Forced migrations are a sorrowful part of our long human experience. Except for the Exodus, a migration which, even under divine guidance, took forty years for the survivors to reach Canaan, forced migrations are associated in our minds with some of the greatest cruelty and suffering visited by man on man. Hitler, with his merciless forced migration of millions of his victims under every condition of extreme cruelty planned with the deliberate intent that they should perish, has made it more possible for us today to contemplate the moving of a large number of Germans from East Prussia to the Reich. Yet, even though the Germans showed no pity for their victims, our Christian conscience demands that the moving be done as mercifully as possible, and with the intent that all shall survive.

Fortunately we know that the inevitable suffering can be largely mitigated by the international safeguards worked out by the League of Nations in the exchange and resettlement of minorities—Bulgarians and Greeks, and Greeks and Turks—shortly after the First World War under the Conventions of Neuilly and Lausanne.

In both cases the exchange was effected under mixed commissions on which the League appointed as its representatives men not from any of the great European powers but from small states far removed from the issue. To the Greco-Bulgarian Commission it appointed citizens of Belgium and New Zealand; to the Greco-Turkish Commission, citizens of Sweden, Spain, and Denmark, eventually replaced by others from Norway, Denmark, and Chile.

The two exchanges together affected about two million people. They proved so salutary for the relations between Greece and Bulgaria and Greece and Turkey, and the resettlement in Bulgaria and Greece, again with the aid of League commissions, so greatly benefited health, agriculture, and industry in both countries, that the tool may indeed prove to be a useful one for dealing with the problem of East Prussia. . .

# 18

# ETHICS AND RELIGION

IT HAS been said that international politics cannot be discussed from an ethical point of view. Everything, so the argument goes, is based on power, and where power reigns there is no room for ethical principles. God is on the side of the heaviest artillery, as Napoleon believed. Continuing the argument, its proponents say that there are no standards of morality that are generally accepted as applying to the conduct of states, as there are for individuals in society.

It must be admitted that nations are far more indifferent both to ethics and to religion in their conduct than are individuals. As Aldous Huxley puts it, 'In practice we have two systems of morality: one for the individual and another for communities.' And he goes on to say that behavior that in the individual is condemned may be commended when indulged in by the state. In the name of the state a man may steal, lie, and murder, and society will decorate him for what he has done; yet, if he does these things against a fellow member of his own society he will be prosecuted. Obviously this places the state in a very unrestrained position from a moral point of view.

Examples of state conduct in defiance of common ethical principles are by no means difficult to find. The history of imperialism is full of them. Powerful states have forced weak or backward peoples into submission; they have exploited them, duped them into one-sided agreements, dictated their economic patterns of life, and taken slaves from them. The frequency with which large and powerful nations take advantage of independent, small states is another case in point. The United States, in order to get the right to build the Panama Canal, took advantage of a revolution in Colombia and quickly recognized the new state of Panama, whose Government was willing to sign on the dotted line. The relations of the western powers with China afford many illustrations of indifference to moral principles. In 1840-42 Great Britain fought the Opium War with China and, while the right to ship opium into China was by no means the only cause of the war, it was one cause and after the war that right was confirmed. Some few decades later Chinese coolies were carried to the western countries for cheap labor under disgraceful conditions, many thousands of them dying on board the overloaded and germ-infested ships. Japan has browbeaten the Chinese time after time into new concessions of territory and economic privileges.

Conceding that states are not circumspect in their relations with each other, there is another side to the story that deserves attention. If morals are lax, there is nevertheless much moralizing. Governments appeal to the principles of right and justice constantly in their communications, and they pretend to have the utmost respect for moral principles. When he was Secretary of State, John Hay said that American foreign policy was based upon the golden rule. Governments coin phrases with moral content to apply to their policies; they speak of 'the freedom of the seas,' an 'open door,' a 'new order,' and a 'good neighbor policy.' Such fine phrases are often mere pretense, a guise for purely selfish motives. At times, there is the happy coincidence that a selfish policy is at the same time one highly beneficial to another, and in this case a high-sounding name for it is not a complete misfit. For instance, the open-door policy which Secretary Hay promoted for China was good for us and also for China.

Whether it is pretense or not, the point is that, in their diplomacy, appeals by governments to moral principles show that they prefer to be looked upon as doing the right thing and being fair and square. They want their own people to be convinced of the propriety of their conduct even more than they are concerned with the reaction of other nations, for their people have votes that count, at least in democracies. Here, however, is where propaganda enters to detract even more from the reality of moral standards, for by radio campaigns, moving pictures, clever speeches, and censored news, the people may be led to believe in the moral justification of their government's policy; whereas, if left alone, they would be severely critical. Propaganda enables a government to play power politics with popular support, as moral issues are twisted to promote rather than hinder what is done. By Nazi propaganda in the years from 1933 to 1945, the German people were led to believe that the aggressive policies of their government were actually just and right.

The cause of ethics in international affairs has also been retarded by popular attitudes toward the nation state, providing a loyalty that easily takes precedence over issues of right and wrong. When their collective welfare or security is at stake, a people incline to relegate moral principles into the background. The end appears to justify the means, and if the future of the state is at stake it is felt that there is nothing more important than self-preservation. When Germany violated the neutrality of Belgium in 1914, she admitted that her action was illegal, but justified it on the ground that it was a necessary means of self-defense.

Then, too, there are the usual obstacles to ethical conduct, faced by individuals as well as by nations, though less easily surmounted by the latter. Issues of right and wrong are rarely clean cut, and it is natural to give oneself the benefit of the doubt. Like individuals, nations are more concerned, as a rule, with the ethical conduct of others than with their own. The people of the United Nations were horrified when Germany used new weapons in World War II, the V-1 and V-2, but justified the American use of the atomic bomb in Japan on the ground that American lives would be saved and the war shortened.

The only generally accepted standard of international conduct at the present time is that provided by international law. Influenced as it was during its formative period by the law of nature, it had a distinctly moral quality until, more recently, the stress upon practice and positive sources has detracted from the importance of the law of nature. Now the law is formed more by what nations do than by abstract ideas of right and justice. This does not mean that international law has lost its moral strength, but rather that there is less emphasis now than formerly on ethics in the law. International law is still a standard of conduct, incomplete, it is true, and not always enforceable. As a standard it is almost never openly flouted. Nations wishing to violate it do not repudiate it, but try by interpretation to prove that the law is on their side.

Increasingly the churches have been interesting themselves in the ethics of international politics. There have been Papal pronouncements and there have been statements from church groups in many countries on international affairs. If religion is to apply in a practical way to living, it is consistent to apply it to the conduct of nations. Several of the extracts in this chapter show the interest and activities of church groups in international problems. Further evidence of that interest was provided by the meeting in Amsterdam of the World Council of Churches in 1948. This conference was attended by 450 delegates from all over the world and it devoted a great deal of its discussions to the problem of peace.

## I. Morality in International Politics

(E. H. Carr, *The Twenty Years' Crisis, 1919-1939*, London, 1940, pp. 194-9. Reprinted by permission of The Macmillan Company.)

Before we consider the moral assumptions which underlie current thinking about international affairs, we must take some account of current theories of international morality. For though it is the assumptions of the ordinary man, not the assumptions of the philosopher, which determine the accepted moral code and govern moral behaviour, the theories of philosophers also exercise an influence on the thought (and, less frequently, on the action) of the ordinary man, and cannot be left altogether out of the picture. Theories of international morality tend to fall into two categories. Realists—and, as we have seen, some who are not realists —hold that relations between states are governed solely by power and that morality plays no part in them. The opposite theory, propounded by most utopian writers, is that the same code of morality is applicable to individuals and to states.

The realist view that no ethical standards are applicable to relations between states can be traced from Machiavelli through Spinoza and Hobbes to Hegel, in whom it found its most finished and thorough-going expression. For Hegel, states are complete and morally self-sufficient entities; and relations between them express only the concordance or conflict of independent wills not united by any mutual obligation. The converse view that the same standard is applicable to individuals and to states was implicit in the original conception of the personification of the state and has found frequent expression not only in the writings of philosophers, but in the utterances of statesmen of utopian inclinations. 'The moral law was not written for men alone in their individual character,' said Bright in a speech on foreign policy in 1858, '. . . it was written as well for nations.' 'We are at the beginning of an age,' said Woodrow Wilson in his address to Congress on the declaration of war in 1917, 'in which it will be insisted that the same standards of conduct and of responsibility for wrong shall be observed among nations and their governments that are observed among the individual citizens of civilised states.' And when in July 1918 the faithful House tried his hand at the first draft of a League of Nations, Article 1 ran as follows:

The same standards of honour and ethics shall prevail internationally and in affairs of nations as in other matters. The agreement or promise of a power shall be inviolate.

No corresponding pronouncement was included in the Covenant. But Dr. Benes at one of the early Assemblies remarked that the League was *'ipso facto* an attempt to introduce into international relationships the principles and methods employed . . . in the mutual relations of private individuals.' In his famous Chicago speech of October 5, 1937, President Roosevelt declared that 'national morality is as vital as private morality.' But he did not specifically identify them.

Neither the realist view that no moral obligations are binding on states, nor the utopian view that states are subject to the same moral obligations as individuals, corresponds to the assumptions of the ordinary man about international morality.

Our task is now to examine these assumptions.

It is noteworthy that the attempt to deny the relevance of ethical standards to international relations has been made almost exclusively by the philosopher, not by the statesman or the man in the street. Some recognition of an obligation to our fellow-men as such seems implicit in our conception of civilisation; and the idea of certain obligations automatically incumbent on civilised men has given birth to the idea of similar (though not necessarily identical) obligations incumbent on civilised nations. A state which does not conform to certain standards of behaviour towards its own citizens and, more particularly, towards foreigners will be branded as 'uncivilised.' Some people would apply this epithet to the present German Reich. On the other hand, Herr Hitler in one of his speeches declined to conclude a pact with Lithuania 'because we cannot enter into political treaties with a state which disregards the most primitive laws of human society'; and he has frequently alleged the immorality of Bolshevism as a reason for excluding Soviet Russia from the family of nations. All agree that there is an international moral code binding on states. One of the most important and most clearly recognised items in this code is the obligation not to inflict *unnecessary* death or suffering on other human beings, i.e. death or suffering not necessary for the attainment of some higher purpose which is held, rightly or wrongly, to justify a derogation from the general obligation. This is the foundation of most of the rules of war, the earliest and most developed chapter of international law; and these rules have on the whole been observed in so far as they did not impede the effective conduct of military operations. A similar humanitarian motive has inspired international conventions for the protection of the 'backward races' or of national minorities, and for the relief of refugees.

The obligations so far mentioned have been obligations of the state to individuals. But the obligation of state to state is also clearly recognised. The number of synonyms current in international practice for what used to be called 'the comity of nations' shows the persistence of the belief that states are members of a community and have obligations as such. A new state on becoming, in virtue of recognition by other Powers, a member of the international community, is assumed to regard itself as automatically bound, without any express stipulation, by the accepted rules of international law and canons of international morality. As we have seen, the concept of internationalism has been so freely used in recent years for the purpose of justifying the ascendancy of the satisfied Powers that it has fallen into some disrepute with the dissatisfied Powers. But this natural reaction was not a denial of the existence of an international community so much as a protest against exclusion from the privileges of membership. The result of the Versailles Treaty, wrote Dr. Goebbels recently, was 'to expel Germany from the comity of powerful political countries,' and the function of National Socialism was to 'unite the people and once more lead it back to its rightful place in the comity of nations.' During Herr Hitler's visit to Rome in May 1938, Signor Mussolini declared that the common aim of Italy and Germany was 'to seek between them and with others a regime of international comity which may restore equally for all more effective guarantees of justice, security and peace.' Constant appeals are made by both these Powers to the injustice of the conditions imposed on them in the past and the justice of demands now made by them; and nobody who knows the countries in question will doubt that both leaders and people are sincerely and passionately concerned to justify their policy in the light of universal standards of international morality. . .

In particular, the theory that, since states have no moral obligations toward one another, treaties have no binding force, is not held even by those statesmen who exhibit least taste for international co-operation. Every state concludes treaties in the expectation that they will be observed; and states which violate treaties either deny that they have done so, or else defend the violation by argument designed to show that it was legally or morally justified. The Soviet Government in the first years of its existence openly violated not only treaties signed by previous Russian governments, but the treaty which it had itself signed at Brest-Litovsk, and propounded a philosophy which denied all international obligation and international morality. But it simultaneously concluded, and offered to conclude, other treaties with the manifest intention of observing them and expecting others to observe them. The German Government accompanied its violation of the Locarno Treaty in 1936 with an offer to enter into a fresh treaty. In neither case is it necessary to doubt the sincerity of the government concerned. Violation of treaties, even when frequently practised, is felt to be something exceptional requiring special justification. The general sense of obligation remains.

The view that the same ethical standard is applicable to the behaviour of states as to that of individuals is, however, just as far from current belief as the view that no standard at all applies to states. The fact is that most people, while believing that states ought to act morally, do not expect of them the same kind of moral behaviour which they expect of themselves and one another.

Many utopian thinkers have been so puzzled by this phenomenon that they have refused to recognise it. Others have sincerely confessed their bewilderment. 'Men's morals are paralysed when it comes to international conduct,' observes Professor Dewey; and Professor Zimmern detects 'a rooted prejudice against law and order in the international domain.' The discrepancy is less surprising than it appears at first sight. Casuists have long been familiar with the problem of in-compatibilities between personal, professional and commercial morality. International morality is another category with standards which are in part peculiar to itself. Some of the problems of state morality are common to the whole field of the morality of group persons. Others are peculiar to the state in virtue of its position as the supreme holder of political power. The analogy between the state and other group persons is therefore useful, but not decisive. . .

## II. CHAMBERLAIN ON HITLERIAN ETHICS

(Neville Chamberlain, Speech before the House of Commons, 12 October 1939, *International Conciliation*, No. 354, November 1939, p. 531. Reprinted by permission of the Carnegie Endowment for International Peace.)

On September 1 Herr Hitler violated the Polish frontier and invaded Poland, beating down by force of arms and machinery the resistance of the Polish nation and army.

As attested by neutral observers, Polish towns and villages were bombed and shelled into ruins and civilians were slaughtered wholesale in contravention, at any rate in the later stages, of all the undertakings of which Herr Hitler now speaks with pride as though he had fulfilled them.

It is after this wanton act of aggression, which has cost so many Polish and German lives sacrificed to satisfy his own insistence on the use of force, that the German Chancellor now puts forward his proposals.

If there existed any expectation that in these proposals would be included some attempt to make amends for this grievous crime against humanity, following so soon upon the violation of the rights of the Czecho-Slovak nation, it has been doomed to disappointment. The Polish State and its leaders are covered with abuse.

What the fate of that part of Poland which Herr Hitler described as the German sphere of interest is to be does not clearly emerge from his speech, but it is evident that he regards it as a matter for the consideration of Germany alone, to be settled solely in accordance with German interests.

The final shaping of this territory and the question of the restoration of a Polish State are, in Herr Hitler's view, problems which cannot be settled by war in the West, but exclusively by Russia on the one side and Germany on the other.

We must take it, then, that the proposals which the German Chancellor puts forward for the establishment of what he calls 'the certainty of European security' are to be based on recognition of his conquests and his right to do what he pleases with the conquered.

It would be impossible for Great Britain to accept any such basis without forfeiting her honor and abandoning her claim that international disputes should be settled by discussion and not by force.

The passages in the speech designed to give fresh assurances to Herr Hitler's neighbors I pass over, since they will know what value should be attached to them by reference to the similar assurances he has given in the past.

It would be easy to quote sentences from his speeches in 1935, 1936, and 1938, stating in the most definite terms his determination not to annex Austria or conclude an Anschluss with her, not to fall upon Czecho-Slovakia, and not to make any further territorial claims in Europe after the Sudetenland question had been settled in September, 1938.

Nor can we pass over Herr Hitler's radical departure from the long professed principles of his policy and creed, as instanced by the inclusion in the German Reich of many millions of Poles and Czechs, despite his repeated professions to the contrary, and by the pact with the Soviet Union, concluded after his repeated and violent denunciation of bolshevism.

This repeated disregard of his word and these sudden reversals of policy bring me to the fundamental difficulty in dealing with the wider proposals in the German Chancellor's speech. The plain truth is that, after our past experience, it is no longer possible to rely upon the unsupported word of the present German Government.
. . .

### III. INTERNATIONAL LAW AS A STANDARD OF CONDUCT

In its formative years, as we have said, international law was based in large part upon the law of nature or abstract principles of right and justice. The extract below, taken from a report of the Inter-American Juridical Committee, brings this out and shows that the more recent stress of international law on positive sources has weakened the moral force of the law.

('Preliminary Recommendations on Postwar Problems,' formulated by the Inter-American Juridical Committee, January 1942, *International Conciliation*, No. 387, February 1943, pp. 103-4, 119. Reprinted by permission of the Carnegie Endowment for International Peace.)

In the years preceding the war of 1914 the general theory of international law was based upon false premises. The early writers on international law, the Spanish theologians, Grotius and other authors, appear to have had a clear conception of the moral basis of international law, however far removed from moral standards the actual conduct of nations in those times may have been. They recognized the existence of a law of nature, representing the dictate of right reason and applicable to the relations of States. Later writers, such as Vattel in the eighteenth century, showed a tendency to adjust moral principles to the actual conduct of nations and to establish the theory that each nation was the judge of its own moral conduct. By the end of the nineteenth century there was a tendency on the part of many writers to adopt what was called a 'positive' attitude toward international law. These writers abandoned almost entirely the task of formulating moral standards by which the conduct of nations might be judged, and instead they adopted the pragmatic standard that the actual practice of nations, as expressed in usages and customs, constituted the only valid international law. The result was that the exponents of this mistaken theory came to determine the existence of rules of international law by the record of the conduct of nations, instead of judging the conduct of nations by the principles of law.

After the first World War the necessity

was seen of a new theory of international law, and the effort was made to assign to the new law the function not only of enforcing existing rules of conduct but of bringing the law itself into harmony with a higher standard of international justice and a better organized community of nations. Nevertheless the tendency still continued of asserting the priority of the will of the individual State over the fundamental principles of the moral law. . .

Nations must recognize in their mutual relations the priority of the moral law, which is the same for nations as for individuals; and they must make their conduct conform to the fundamental principles derived from that law.

Existing rules of positive law must not be regarded as fixing permanently the *status quo,* but rather as the necessary basis of international order and stability pending the adoption of rules more in accord with the new needs of the international community. . .

## IV. HEGEL'S IDEA OF STATE MORALITY

One of the principal exponents of the idea that the state is above morality was the German philosopher Georg Hegel (1770-1831). His doctrines have played an important part in German thinking during recent decades. The substance of these views are given below.

(Georg Hegel, *The Philosophy of Right,* London, 1896, paragraphs 258, 330-8. Reprinted by permission of George Bell and Sons.)

The state as a completed reality is the ethical whole and the actualization of freedom. The state is the spirit, which abides in the world and there realizes itself consciously; while in nature it is realized only as the other of itself or the sleeping spirit. Let man be aware of it or not, this essence realizes itself as an independent power, in which particular persons are only phases. The state is the march of God in the world. When thinking of the idea of the state, we must not have in our mind any particular state, or particular institution, but must rather contemplate the idea, this actual God, by itself. Although a state may be declared to violate right principles and to be defective in various ways, it always contains the essential moments of its existence, if, that is to say, it belongs to the full formed states of our own time. But as it is more easy to detect shortcomings than to grasp the positive meaning, one easily falls into the mistake of dwelling so much upon special aspects of the state as to overlook its inner organic being. The state is not a work of art. It is in the world, in the sphere of caprice, accident, and error. Evil behaviour can doubtless disfigure it in many ways, but the ugliest man, the criminal, the invalid, the cripple, are living men. The positive thing, the life, is present in spite of defects, and it is with this affirmative that we have here to deal.

A state is not a private person, but in itself a completely independent totality. Hence, the relation of states to one another is not merely that of morality and private right. It is often desired that states should be regarded from the standpoint of private right and morality. But the position of private persons is such that they have over them a law court, which realizes what is intrinsically right. A relation between states ought also to be intrinsically right, and in mundane affairs that which is intrinsically right ought to have power. But as against the state there is no power to decide what is intrinsically right and to realize this decision. Hence, we must here remain by the absolute command. States in their relation to one another are independent, and look upon the stipulations which they make one with another as provisional.

(333) International law, or the law which is universal, and is meant to hold absolutely good between states, is to be distinguished from the special content of positive treaties, and has at its basis the proposition that treaties, as they involve the mutual obligations of states, must be kept inviolate. But because the relation of states to one another has sovereignty as its principle, they are so far in a condition of nature one to the other. Their rights have reality in their particular wills. Accordingly the fundamental proposition of international law remains a good intention, while in the actual situation the relation established by the treaty is being continually shifted or abrogated.

There is no judge over states, at most only a referee or mediator, and even the mediatorial function is only an accidental thing, being due to particular wills. Kant's idea was that eternal peace should be secured by an alliance of states. This alliance should settle every dispute, make impossible the resort to arms for a decision, and be recognized by every state. This idea assumes that states are in accord, an agreement which, strengthened though it might be by moral, religious, and other considerations, nevertheless always rested on the private sovereign will, and was therefore liable to be disturbed by the element of contingency.

(334) Therefore, when the particular wills of states can come to no agreement, the controversy can be settled only by war. Owing to the wide field and the varied relations of the citizens of different states to one another, injuries oc-

cur easily and frequently. What of these injuries is to be viewed as a specific breach of a treaty or as a violation of formal recognition and honour remains from the nature of the case indefinite. A state may introduce its infinitude and honour into every one of its separate compartments. It is all the more tempted to make or seek some occasion for a display of irritability, if the individuality within it has been strengthened by long internal rest, and desires an outlet for its pent-up activity.

(337) The substantive weal of the state is its weal as a particular state in its definite interests and condition, its peculiar external circumstances, and its particular treaty obligations. Thus the government is a particular wisdom and not universal providence. So, too, its end in relation to other states, the principle justifying its wars and treaties, is not a general thought, such as philanthropy, but the actually wronged or threatened weal in its definite particularity.

At one time a lengthy discussion was held with regard to the opposition between morals and politics, and the demand was made that politics should be in accordance with morality. Here it may be remarked merely that the commonweal has quite another authority than the weal of the individual, and that the ethical substance of the state has directly its reality or right not in an abstract but in a concrete existence. This existence, and not one of the many general thoughts held to be moral commands, must be the principle of its conduct. The view that politics in this assumed opposition is presumptively in the wrong depends on a shallow notion both of morality and of the nature of the state in relation to morality. . .

## V. A Catholic Statement on States and Morality

(Preliminary Report Presented to the Catholic Association by its Committee on International Ethics, *International Ethics*, 1928, pp. 8-10. Reprinted by permission of the Catholic Association for International Peace.)

Against all theories which either expressly or by implication assert that the state is independent of the moral law we set forth the Catholic position that states, like individuals, are subject to the moral precepts of both nature and revelation.

When two or more individuals unite to form a private society, such as a business partnership or a benevolent association, they are obviously bound by the moral law in their corporate acts. A moral or corporate person is subject to ethical rules quite as definitely and extensively as a physical or natural person. To deny this principle would be to authorize men to exempt themselves from the moral law in large spheres of conduct through the simple device of a formal association. In their corporate capacity they could lawfully do that which is forbidden them as individuals. This would be especially convenient in economic relations. The business corporation and the trade union could do no wrong.

Since the state is a community of human beings it is as truly subject to the moral law as any private society. The fact that it is a necessary society does not affect its character as a moral person. Its acts are the acts of an organized group of human beings. Its international conduct affects other human beings. While its end is primarily the welfare of its own members, it must attain that end with due regard to the welfare of persons who are outside its jurisdiction, just as the acts of a family must be consistent with the

rights and claims of other families. Hence, the state is bound by the precepts of justice, charity, veracity and all the other moral rules which govern human relations.

To be sure, some provisions of the moral law do not apply to states in the same way as to individuals. When crime has been committed the state may deprive men of liberty, property and even life. The state has a right to wage war. On the other hand it may not subordinate itself or the welfare of its members to the interests of some other political community. Reservations and modifications of this sort, however, have to do with the manner not the fact of the subjection of the state to the moral law.

From another point of view the same truth emerges. Man is bound by the moral law in all the circumstances of life, whether individual, social or civil. Nothing in the nature of the human person, either individually or socially considered, can be adduced as a logical basis for the supposition that he becomes exempt from the moral law in his political or international relations. In the words of Chancellor Kent: 'States or bodies politic are to be considered as moral persons having a public will, capable and free to do right and wrong, inasmuch as they are collections of individuals, each of whom carries with him into the service of the community the same binding law of morality and religion which ought to control his conduct in private life.'

Finally, the welfare of the human race requires that states be governed by the moral law. Every international action of a state must be justified or condemned in the light of its effect upon the welfare of human beings. And the moral claims of all state groups are of equal intrinsic worth. Now, injury done by one state to another is injury done to human beings. Therefore, just as no state has a right to harm its own members, neither is it justified in causing damage to the members of other states.

## VI. THE UNITING FORCE IN RELIGION

To what extent is religion a unifying force in the world, breaking down separatism, and thus contributing to an enduring peace? An opinion on this subject, together with some developments along this line, are given below.

(W. P. Merrill, 'The World of Religion,' *Preliminary Report and Monographs,* Commission to Study the Organization of Peace, pp. 62-8. Reprinted by permission of the Commission.)

It is painfully obvious that something is needed to hold the world together. It becomes increasingly evident to the thoughtful that the only alternative to a warring world is an organized world. The keen mind of Kant saw that plainly 145 years ago. Yet the breakdown of the League of Nations provides indubitable proof that political organization is not sufficient. Something is needed that goes deeper than political policies and plans for international government.

There is an analogy in recent political life in the United States. One of the most decisive failures in the cultural history of this country is the attempt to solve the liquor problem by legal and political means. A constitutional amendment was adopted, laws were passed, police power used; and yet the cause failed. Why? Because, in too many parts of the country, popular sentiment was either opposed to the regime or lukewarm in support of it.

The breakdown of the League of Nations was largely due to the same cause. There was not a community of interest, understanding, and good will, to give force to the political organization. And the most admirable plan and program will fail under such conditions.

This fact was set forth strongly in a brilliant article in one of the numbers of the *North American Review* for 1938, by Professor José Ortega y Gasset. He contended that it is useless to trust treaties and pacts, or organizations in the interest of world order, or individual renunciation of war. There must come a body of attitudes, assumptions, understandings, accepted generally in the life of the world, practically authoritative in that life; in short we must have a world system or world community, very real, even if intangible, before institutions and laws and agreements can be effective and lasting. For, as he shows, laws, treaties, organizations, made in defiance of, or far in advance of, common public opinion, are foredoomed to failure. Here stands out one of the supremely vital tasks of our age,—the development of such a common mind and soul and understanding.

In this great task religion may and should play a leading part. And the Christian religion above all others should do its utmost to discharge this duty. . .

Our present world needs, in order to achieve a right and permanent organization of peace, some force to lift races and groups above nationalism, a superloyalty; and this must take form, not only in ideals, but in an actual brotherhood of men, based on common faith, hope, and generosity.

Religion can and should supply, or at least help greatly in supplying, this vital need.

Irresponsible and uncontrolled nationalism is the reef upon which the best-built ship of internationalism will be wrecked. Only a higher loyalty than that to a nation can clear this obstacle from the course of world development.

Now religion professes to have just such a possession, in its exaltation of God as supreme. Judaism gave to the world the first and greatest of commandments, 'Thou shalt love the Lord thy God with all thy heart and with all thy soul and with all thy strength and with all thy mind. . .'

We must not linger over the history of Christianity, the centuries during which church and empire lived together in harmony or conflict, but each of them a world unity. The Reformation split Christendom into fragments. National churches sprang up. The tendency was for each to cherish its peculiar relation with the national government. 'Established' churches arose, supported in part by the State. Some such still exist. It is peculiarly hard for them to keep the universal spirit and touch. For a considerable time Protestantism had but a feeble sense of World Christianity. Each nation had its church, each church its national connection.

During the recent past, however, Christianity has been regaining its consciousness of the universal quality of its faith and hope. Especially since the dawn of the present century has the movement toward unity, or 'ecumenicity' as it is being called, gained rapidly. There were forerunners, notably the great missionary movements, the Bible Societies, the Evangelical Alliance, and other efforts at large groupings, such as the Y.M.C.A. and the Y.W.C.A. But a new era may be dated from the great Missionary Conference of the Protestant Churches, at Edinburgh in 1910, from which eventually came the 'International Missionary Council,' and an impulse to other world movements. . .

In 1905 a movement to federate the Protestant churches in the United States began to take shape. It was necessary that it start in a small way and grow quietly. But under wise and enthusiastic leadership it has developed into an institution of real power and influence, the Federal Council of the Churches of Christ in America. It must speak and act cautiously, lest some of the cooperating bodies become alarmed or take offense. But it is increasingly effective and steadily grows toward wider inclusiveness and stronger influence. The very existence of such a Council, and the contacts it has established and maintained with churches in Europe, has considerable effect in the cause of Christian cooperation and union.

Early in the century leading churchmen in Great Britain and Germany became apprehensive as to the growing tension between the two nations. Together they planned exchange visits of leading ministers and laymen. In 1908, one hundred and thirty German churchmen, Lutheran, Reformed, Catholic, and others, visited Great Britain, and in the following year return visits to Germany were made by a similar group from Great Britain. Out of this grew the 'Churches' Council for Promoting Friendly Relations between Great Britain and Germany,' founded in 1909. Each national group began publishing a journal. The movement aroused no little public interest.

Early in 1914 a letter was sent out by the church leaders in Switzerland, calling attention of Christians everywhere to the alarming increase in armament, and urging that Christian leaders from all lands should confer on the matter.

These and other influences led to the holding of a 'peace conference' in the summer of 1914 at Constance, Germany. A new body, the Church Peace Union, had been created in the United States, and endowed by Mr. Andrew Carnegie. This organization helped materially in planning and financing the holding of the Conference.

The World Alliance managed to hold together during the difficult days of the war, arranging a conference in Switzerland in 1915, attended by British, Germans, Danes, Hollanders, and Swiss; and a general conference attended by representatives of thirteen nations at The Hague in 1919.

From that time on, the official church bodies in the leading nations began to take an ever-deepening interest in the integration of Christianity, and in the providing of means for more unified action and influence. These led to two important general conferences, one on 'Life and Work' held at Stockholm in 1925, the other on 'Faith and Order' at Lausanne in 1927. As the names indicate, one of these dealt with possible unity in creed and organization, the other with possible cooperation in practical life and service. The 'Life and Work' movement soon became the 'Universal Christian Council.' It carried on considerable relief work among the impoverished churches in central and eastern Europe, and brought churchmen of the various branches of Christianity into close affiliations. The Eastern Orthodox Churches joined in the two movements, thus bringing about a cooperation of practically all the major Christian church organizations, except the Roman Catholic, which did not see its way to cooperate officially. These two movements, 'Faith and Order' and 'Life and Work,' held conferences in the summer of 1937 at Oxford and Edinburgh, at which the two were merged in one body, now functioning as the 'World Council of Churches.' Thus, for the first time since the Reformation, Christians of all varieties, with the sole exception of the Roman Catholic Church, are working in real cooperation and unity.

. . .

Two important gatherings were held just before the outbreak of the present war. In December, 1938, under the auspices of the International Missionary Council, a conference was held at Madras, India, at which the Christian churches of Asia and Africa were more largely represented and more actively interested than in any previous gathering. In July-August, 1939, a Youth Conference was held at Amsterdam, the Netherlands, planned and carried out by joint action of the World Council of Churches and the World Alliance for International Friendship through the Churches. Some fifteen hundred delegates were present, representing seventy-three nations; more than 50 per cent of the delegates were under thirty years of age. There were large delegations not only from Europe and America, but from Asia and Africa. The proceedings of this conference, and the statements issuing from it, show the deep and enthusiastic interest taken by the young people of the churches in the problem of international organization and unity.

This is a hasty and inadequate summary, but it does show a wholesome growth of the Christian churches toward fuller unity and cooperation. It warrants the hope that the Christian churches, in full and hearty fellowship with their Jewish brethren, and eventually in closer, sympathetic relation with those of other faiths, may be of indispensable service in fostering a common and cooperative spirit, which may help to sustain good international relations.

Two facts or conclusions are evident:

1. Religion can be of very great and real help in providing that higher common loyalty which preconditions lasting international organization;

2. Religion is itself deeply affected by international discord, division, and lack of organized world life and government. . .

## VII. RELIGION AND INTERNATIONAL AFFAIRS

What contributions can religion make to the peaceful conduct of international relations? Some ideas on this subject are given in the following extract.

(Canon Cyril E. Hudson, 'The Church and International Affairs,' *International Affairs*, vol. XXIII, No. 1, 1947, pp. 1-10. Reprinted by permission of the Royal Institute of International Affairs.)

Political thought in the Middle Ages was dominated by the idea of Natural Law. Life in community, it was held, which is the life proper to man, the only kind of life congruous with his divinely-ordained status and nature, is impossible, since the Fall, without *dominium* and the exercise of authority of some men over others. That is the case for secular government. As early as the seventh century Saint Isidore of Seville had formulated a doctrine which was adopted, with slight modifications, by later writers and passed into the common stock of mediaeval political theory. The *ius gentium* is part of *ius naturale;* it is the common possession of 'all nations,' to whom it belongs, not in virtue of 'any (human) constitution,' but *instinctu naturae,* though it must be rationally comprehended. The conventions of this *ius gentium,* covering such matters as war captivity, reconciliation, treaties of peace, truces, the immunity of ambassadors and the prohibition of marriages with aliens, are immutable. They do not proceed from any State or human legislator. They emanate from God and are prior to and take precedence of, *ius civile* or positive law; and human laws are valid only when they conform to the principles of *ius naturale.*

To describe such a conception as this as a 'law' would seem to many, perhaps, a misnomer. It is law, of course, not in the sense of enactment or legislation, but in the Ciceronian sense of 'right reason in agreement with nature: of universal application, unchanging and everlasting' —what our own Richard Hooker called 'the law which human nature knoweth itself in reason universally bound thereto,' embracing 'all those things which men by the light of their natural understanding evidently know (or at leastwise may know) to be beseeming or unbeseeming, virtuous or vicious, good or evil for them to do.'. . .

But by the fourteenth century this conception had begun to be replaced: the new, 'national' kings—of England and France and Spain—so far from thinking of themselves as servants of the communities they ruled, were laying the foundations of the modern, omnicompetent, sovereign State. The Conciliar Movement, which Figgis called 'the watershed between the mediaeval and the modern world,' was an attempt to find some tolerable form of association between secular governments, highly conscious of their new-found power, and the Papacy. The mounting claims of the latter, from the days of Gregory VII onwards, were 'totalitarian' claims in the strict sense of that word, in that they recognized no social or individual activity as having any right to be exercised save under the aegis and control of the ecclesiastical hierarchy. These claims at length provoked a revolt —not always very self-conscious or articulate—of the secular impulses of man; and it can hardly be denied that the refusal of the Church to recognize the validity of this revolt (crystallized in the Conciliar Movement) facilitated the process which led, ultimately, to that assertion of the absolute autonomy and unrelatedness of every department of social life—including the political—which is characteristic of the modern world.

The failure of the Conciliar Movement led to the apotheosis of absolutism in both spheres: in the spiritual sphere, to ultramontanism; in the secular, to sovereign States acknowledging no political superior. And the Movement failed, not merely through the resistance of the Papacy, but because, as Professor Laski has observed, 'the ideas which were the foundation' upon which the advocates of conciliar reform relied—above all, reverence for Natural Law—'were already decaying in the secular world when men sought to transfer them to the ecclesiastical.'

I shall argue later that it is upon the conception of Natural Law that the Church today must base its concern with international affairs. But if the expression of that concern is to commend itself to the world, Christians must show a keener appreciation than they commonly do of both sides of the equation. They must have an understanding of the meaning of the phrase 'international affairs' at the present day which goes beyond a vague and general realization that these affairs are extremely complex. . .

The essential problem in international relations is commonly described as the moralization of power, and it is here that the Church is expected to 'come in.' What has happened, it is said, is that mankind's moral enthusiasm has failed to keep pace with its technical and scientific progress. (Cf. *Report on the Politics of Atomic Energy:* 'the heart of the problem' is to *accelerate* 'the humanising of our selfish and savage instincts' so as to make international organs effective before mankind has used atomic energy to destroy itself.) What is required is an ethical spurt: and what is the Church for, if not to inspire and to organize ethical

spurts? Sometimes it is suggested that a more intense concentration of human thought and energy on the advancement of scientific knowledge and research would of itself generate the moral dynamic required: thus, Professor J. B. S. Haldane assures us that, if science does not kill us, it will 'make us behave better.' But, more commonly, it is taken for granted that what is wanted is a greater determination, on the part of the common people and their leaders throughout the world, to make existing instruments for the peaceful solution of international disagreements *'work'*—chiefly of course the United Nations Organization. Mankind, in short, possesses the engines of peace, though they are capable of improvement, and it is for the Church to grease the wheels.

There are two comments to be made on this way of regarding the Church's task in relation to international affairs. It mistakes both the function of the Church and the nature of the international problem. In the first place the trouble with contemporary society is not so much moral as psychological. It is not that it does not want to be good, but that it is frustrated, at every turn, by an interior conflict: a conflict analogous to that described by Saint Paul, between two principles at work in the same personality—the principle in the 'members,' and the principle in the 'mind.' Modern society is suffering from a similar schizophrenia, which is most clearly discernible perhaps in the divorce between civilization's conscious moral aims and the unexamined and uncriticized assumptions which govern its economic activities; but discernible, also, in the general doubt and uncertainty as to the ends which the life of man in society ought to serve. 'Who,' asks Mannheim, 'is to plan the planners?' Time was, when Christian theology was thought of as *regina scientiarum*. We may argue as to whether the decline of that monarch's influence in the world of affairs is the consequence of abdication or of deposition. The fact remains that she is no longer recognized. Who or what is to take her place?

There is a fairly general awareness—witness the title of Jung's widely-read *Modern Man in Search of a Soul*—that, in some sense not very clearly understood, civilization has lost its 'soul.' What it would, it does not, since the deep, underlying energy to do it is absent, or is, at the least, seriously weakened. Merely moral exhortations, therefore, or appeals for more 'idealism,' or for the 'application of the principles of the Sermon on the Mount' to modern political and economic problems, are as useless as are adjurations to 'pull himself together' addressed to a neurotic patient. Our contemporary civilization is neurotic. In the new era that has dawned with the discovery of atomic energy, it faces an inescapable dilemma: the abolition of war, or, at the very least, in Mr. Churchill's words, 'measureless havoc upon the entire globe.' But civilization is impotent to solve the dilemma in the way suggested by every consideration of prudence, self-interest and morality, since it plainly lacks the psychological and spiritual resources for foregoing war as an instrument of power.

There is a temptation to the Church in this situation; the temptation to 'cash in' on the world's predicament: to forget her own complacency and lack of charity, her unconcern, over long centuries, with social evils that cried to heaven, her timorous subservience to the powers that be, her introverted absorption in matters of ecclesiastical machinery, her nervous anxiety in the face of threats to property and privilege, her supine acceptance of the awful 'scandal' of schism—to forget all this, and to point to civilization's resourcelessness with the threat, explicit or implied, Come back, Come in—*or else!*

This temptation to exploit the situation must be resisted. Yet the Church cannot deny her mission or betray her Master. The Gospel she is charged to proclaim is a Gospel, neither of good advice nor (save consequentially) of ethical idealism, but of deliverance, salvation, redemption. The Person of Christ, rather than His precepts, is its central and dynamic core: and the Church must proclaim it. It is from this perspective that the Church must observe and evaluate the historical process, including contemporary trends and movements in international affairs. Professor Whitehead once 'hazarded the prophecy that that religion will conquer which can render clear to popular understanding some eternal greatness incarnate in the passage of temporal fact.' All the modern substitutes for Christianity—religious in content, though not in form—try to do this, of course. But only Christianity, by virtue of its doctrine of sin, refuses to regard 'the passage of temporal fact' as itself redemptive: only Christianity sees that the essence of the political problem lies in the nature of man himself, which impels him to corrupt the very instruments and institutions which he devises for the ordering of his social life.

There is no possibility of the total elimination of power from human affairs. And all power tends to become power 'over.' It follows, therefore, that approximation towards *justice,* which is the fundamental condition of natural order, is to be measured by the degree in which power is subjected to law. In the biblical and Christian view, justice is the form in which love expresses itself in social organization: and from this follows orthodox, historic Christianity's 'high' view of the State, as an institution with its own specific and unique function to fulfil in the divine economy: the function, precisely, of creating an ordered framework within which men may be enabled to carry on the activities congenial to them, and develop their natural gregariousness in the fellowship of families, churches, professions, crafts and the like. 'The powers that be,' therefore, 'are ordained of God'; in the patristic formula, the State is a 'remedy against sin' though it is at the same time, from another point of view, the consequence of sin, and the punishment for sin. But the subordination of all other interests and associations to itself—which must be a continuous temptation in the Welfare State towards which we are moving—is a perversion of the political function.

But of course there are no States in which the ideal is fully embodied. If there were, international problems would still exist, no doubt, in plenty. But they would be different from, and less intractable than, those which face us today. We need not subscribe to the strict Marxist view, that the State is always and necessarily a weapon of oppression and exploitation in the hands of the economically dominant class, to recognize that in all historic States, and a fortiori in the relations between States, the subjugation of power to law in the interests of justice is very far from being attained. We may rightly believe, I think, that this process has been carried furthest in our own tradition. But the task of extending that tradition—with its emphasis on the supremacy of law, the sovereignty of Parliament and the value of freedom of discussion and criticism—to the international plane appears so formidable that many people (especially young people) are drawn to what Mr. Arthur Koestler calls the *Yogi* position. A recent writer, Mr. Alexander Miller, speaking of the contemporary social crisis, refers to 'the sense that events are out of hand, that our generation is in the grip of gigantic forces whose nature no man can understand and which are beyond the power of men or of democratic assemblies to control. The

future of society is being shaped by influences impersonal or daemonic, so that intelligent decision or democratic action is impossible or meaningless, and can have no constructive effect. This sense of overmastering "fate" is shattering in its effect on personal and group initiative. It takes the stuffing out of voluntary societies of all kinds, and creates in the majority a numbness of mind and soul, a sense of political helplessness and sheer frustration. They tend more and more to concentrate on their own personal future, on that narrow range of choices which are within their own personal control. They take exams, they fall in love, they marry, they try for a temporary niche of security . . . as a man on a sinking ship might shut himself in his 8 ft. by 8 ft. cabin to keep the illusion of safety for just five minutes more. This is not purely a war-time mood, and the end of the shooting war has left it relatively unaffected. It springs from the totality of social chaos which has been the lifelong experience of the present generation.'

But the policy of withdrawal is clearly a policy of despair: a surrender to the doctrine of Thrasymachus. Any democratic State which adopted it—as, for example, by unilateral disarmament in atomic weapons of warfare—would be proclaiming its belief in the inevitability of a World State, in the sense of a world tyranny exercised by the most ruthless of Great Powers, acting on the view that Machiavelli has said the last word in political ethics, and 'degrading national States to the level of local authorities without either the will or the means to fight each other.'

The only alternative to throwing up the sponge in despair is to persevere, in spite of difficulties which seem insuperable, in the task of creating an effective *community* out of the existing *congeries* of nations. And an essential precondition of this task would seem to be the recovery of that acceptance of Natural Law on which the existing *corpus* of International Law, tenuous as it is, is founded. It is important to remember what Natural Law essentially is. It is a doctrine, not of what ought to be, but of what is: a doctrine of the pattern and structure of man. It affirms that man is essentially a rational and moral being, responsible to the Transcendent Reality from whence he comes, and to which he goes: designed for life in obedience to God, and *therefore* for life in community with his fellows. It denies the doctrine that he is 'naturally' a predatory, lawless and hostile creature: when he behaves thus, on the contrary, he is rebelling against the nature of things: *sin is lawlessness.* . .

I have argued that an essential preliminary to the establishment of international relations upon a basis which shall not constitute a perpetual threat of war lies in the recovery, or discovery, of some agreed body of ideas about man and society. I am bound, in conclusion, to suggest that no such common *ethos,* divorced from its interpretation and fulfilment in revealed religion, is likely to be found. I have used words like 'law' and 'justice' and 'power' a good many times. But whence comes the *authority* and the *validity* of law? From Prince or Parliament? Is everything law that Parliament, or Stalin, or Hitler enacts? Can no law enacted by the State be unjust, as Hobbes affirmed? Or is there a higher and ultimate Law to which all human, positive law is related either by way of correspondence or of opposition? And can this view be maintained save on theological grounds? Justice, again: can we quarrel with the totalitarian doctrine that justice is what serves the State in the assertion of its power, or maintain the view that power must be conceived as a means to moral ends, and not as an end in itself, unless we believe that men

are 'naturally' brothers? And, in the last analysis, what ground is there for believing that, other than the conviction that God is their Father? And can that conviction be maintained save on the foundation of the Christian Faith? Mr. C. N. Cochrane, commenting upon similarities of terminology in the writings of Stoic and Christian writers—including phrases like 'the City of God,' 'the fatherhood of God and the brotherhood of man,' and 'the law of charity'—observes that 'such apparent analogies should occasion no surprise, since all they mean is that the Stoics agreed with the Christians in dreaming of a better world. The real point, however, is what ground of assurance they had for so doing.' Mr. Cochrane quotes a passage from Marcus Aurelius in which the emperor dwells 'with a pathetic insistence upon the right to believe in an orderly world, despite an accumulation of evidence which seemed to belie his faith'; and concludes: 'The religion of reason thus professed by Marcus has been hailed (by Renan) as "the absolute religion, that which issues from the simple fact of a high moral sense face to face with the universe." This religion has been declared "independent of race and country." "No revolution, no progress, no discovery could possibly upset it." In point of fact, it constitutes an audacious anthropomorphism, a kind of sky-writing, which projects upon the cosmos a merely human rationality and translates it into an account of nature and of God.'

It is possible that now, at the end of my paper, someone may be asking: Is that all? Does the writer suggest that the Church's only concern with international affairs is to give the Christian 'O.K.' to the doctrine of Natural Law? Is he telling us that civilization, in the desperate crisis in which it finds itself—with the nations which 'won the war' further from unity among themselves than they were in the moment of victory—can be talked into safety by the reiteration of philosophical platitudes?

I did not mean this. But then I do not believe that the world can 'save' itself, in any final sense, at all; and it is certainly no part of the Church's duty to suggest that it can. The doom which hangs over our civilization is the last and inevitable term of that banishment of God from human affairs which has characterized the (nominally Christian) Western world in recent centuries. For this apostasy the Church herself has been largely responsible; she is implicated in its consequences, and cannot dissociate herself from the humiliation and repentance which it demands, and of which she must seek to make the generality of men conscious. People ask, 'Why don't the Churches give a lead?' Sometimes this means, Why doesn't the Archbishop of Canterbury—or the Pope, or the British Council of Churches—say what I think they ought to say? Sometimes it means, Why can't they show us how to eat our cake and have it, how to run with the hare and hunt with the hounds, how to get us to the goal we have set ourselves without asking us to change our route? The Church cannot 'lead' thus. She must say that the only way out is the way back—to God: and that a civilization virtually founded upon the denial of His sovereign claim on its obedience must expect to incur His judgments and to vindicate His righteousness. . .

## VIII. A Church Program for Peace

The Federal Council of the Churches of Christ in America, through its Executive Committee, addressed itself to the critical international situation existing in 1948 and drafted the following program for peace. It was submitted to President Harry S. Truman and then publicized widely in the country at large. It stresses reliance on non-military measures for the preservation of peace.

('Program for Peace,' issued by the Federal Council of the Churches of Christ in America, text from *The New York Times*, 1 May 1948.)

Powerful forces have pushed mankind to the brink of an awful abyss. The first and urgent task is to check those forces. Therefore, we do not deal here with the long-range task of building peace, but with a short-range task of averting war without yielding sound democratic principles. We call upon our people immediately to change the present prevailing mood which makes for war. This will not remove the basic causes of the present tension, but it will provide an increased margin of safety.

I. Our people should not tolerate any complacency about war. War would engulf all in misery and would bring other consequences quite the opposite of our intentions.

II. Our people should combat a mood of hysteria or blind hatred.

III. Our people should reject fatalism about war. War is not inevitable. If it should come, it would be because of conditions that men could have changed.

IV. Our people should not rely on military strategy to meet Communist aggression. Such reliance is more apt to bring war than prevent it. There should be greater concentration on positive programs of an economic, social, political and moral character.

V. Our people should press for positive programs which have immediate possibilities for peace and justice. They could, for example, quickly move toward: a. Greater economic well-being throughout the world; b. Greater emphasis on increasing social welfare; c. Greater observance of human rights, to check terrorism; d. Greater use of processes of international conversation and negotiation.

VI. Our people ought, each one of them, to contribute to a change of mood so as to increase the chance of averting war without compromise of basic convictions.

VII. Our churches ought to testify with renewed vigor to God's righteous love for all men and the reality of the Christian world fellowship.

## I—No Complacency About War

Our people should not tolerate any complacency about war. War would engulf all in misery and would bring other consequences quite the opposite of our intentions.

Some have come to look upon 'a preventive war' as an acceptable means of settling the present international conflict. Such a state of mind we unqualifiedly condemn.

The last war ended with the dropping of two bombs which alone killed over 100,000 persons and shattered the lives of many more. New war would plunge the world into utter misery. Whatever the military result, there would be an intensification of the misery which makes men willing to exchange freedom for dictatorship.

Circumstances may at times make forcible resistance a lesser evil than surrender, but no man should be deluded into thinking that new war will achieve the ends for which he would profess to be fighting. . .

## IV—More Than Armed Force Needed

Our people should not rely primarily on military strategy to meet Communist aggression. Such reliance is more apt to bring war than prevent it. There should be greater concentration on positive programs of an economic, social, political and moral character.

In times of international crisis men tend to look to military measures as a means of salvation. That is happening in America now. Nearly a year ago Secretary Marshall put forward the statesmanlike idea of the European Recovery Plan. In many respects, however, our recent international policy seems to have been much dominated by military thinking. Such domination increases the risk of war.

In present conditions of international anarchy, where international law and international police power are lacking, national military strength is necessary, while we continually strive for the multilateral reduction and control of armaments through the United Nations. But the main defenses of what we treasure are to be found in nonmilitary measures which will change the conditions favoring the spread of despotism. To provide those defenses is not the task for military advisers.

Therefore, the American people, in conformity with the principle of democratic government, should not permit policy-making to pass predominantly into the hands of those who think primarily in military terms, as seems to be the case today.

Our people and Government should not feel satisfied with merely military measures but should diligently develop and carry through programs of an economic, social, political and moral character. Thus, the real security of the

United States and of the world may be safeguarded, and war may be averted.

## V—PEACE PROGRAM DETAILED

Our people should press for positive programs which have immediate possibilities for peace and justice. They could, for example, quickly move toward: a. Greater economic well-being throughout the world; b. Greater emphasis on increasing social welfare; c. Greater observance of human rights, to check terrorism; d. Greater use of processes of international conversation and negotiation.

We believe that the positive programs which we here propose by way of illustration flow directly from our Christian faith and its requirements for relations of mutual helpfulness and goodwill among men.

In urging at this time economic assistance to those in need, increased opportunity for human welfare, and greater observance of the rights and freedoms which are claimed by virtue of man's dignity in God's sight, we are setting forth tasks which should at all times command the support of our Christian people. We are convinced that both the inherent right of these steps and their direct bearing upon the present international crisis will commend them to all men of goodwill. . .

## VI—PRAYER AND ACTION ASKED

Our people ought, each one of them, to contribute to a change of mood so as to increase the chance of averting war without compromise of basic convictions.

This is a time for prayer. Also it is a time for action. Men of goodwill must promptly lay hold of the means at hand to increase the margin of safety against war. This is a task in which every one can play a constructive part.

. . .

## DUTY OF CHRISTIANS CITED

Our churches ought to testify with renewed vigor to God's righteous love for all men and the reality of the Christian world fellowship.

Christians have their own divine commission to proclaim the kingdom of God and His righteousness at home and abroad. God is a God of judgment as well as of mercy. In His sight all nations, including our own, and all men, including ourselves, have left undone those things which they ought to have done and done those things which they ought not to have done. We are called to recognize the just condemnation of His judgment but if we turn to Him in repentance and faith we shall avail ourselves of His mercy. We are called to be steadfast in prayer for all the peoples of the world that they may learn the things that belong to their peace; for our nation and our Government, that they may become willing to serve the purposes of God.

Our churches are part of a world-wide community of Christians. They have come into being as a universal fellowship in our own time through the work of the missionary movement and through the new discovery of the unity in Christ that binds Christians of many communions.

Let us always remember the great company of fellow Christians in Russia with whom we share a common faith that should transcend all the differences that make for conflict. Already in many places Christ has broken down the middle wall of partition in His Church, even where Christians have been divided by the enmities of war.

We find our ultimate hope for peace in the faith that God, through Christ, is seeking to draw all men to Himself and into fellowship with one another.

## IX. A Statement by British Church Leaders

The following statement, in the form of a letter, was addressed to *The Times* of London and published on 21 December 1940. Among the signatories were the Archbishop of Canterbury and the Archbishop of York from the Church of England, the chief representative of the Roman Catholic Church in England, and the Moderator of the Free Church Council.

('Foundations of Peace,' *International Conciliation*, No. 368, March 1941, pp. 189-90. Reprinted by permission of the Carnegie Endowment for International Peace.)

Sir,—The present evils in the world are due to the failure of nations and peoples to carry out the laws of God. No permanent peace is possible in Europe unless the principles of the Christian religion are made the foundation of national policy and of all social life. This involves regarding all nations as members of one family under the Fatherhood of God.

We accept the five points of Pope Pius XII as carrying out this principle:

1. The assurance to all nations of their right to life and independence. The will of one nation to live must never mean the sentence of death passed upon another. When this equality of rights has been destroyed, attacked, or threatened order demands that reparation shall be made, and the measure and extent of that reparation are determined, not by the sword nor by the arbitrary decision of self-interest, but by the rules of justice and reciprocal equity.

2. This requires that the nations be delivered from the slavery imposed upon them by the race for armaments and from the danger that material force, instead of serving to protect the right, may become an overbearing and tyrannical master. The order thus established requires a mutually agreed organic progressive disarmament, spiritual as well as material, and security for the effective implementing of such an agreement.

3. Some juridical institution which shall guarantee the loyal and faithful fulfilment of conditions agreed upon and which shall in case of recognized need revise and correct them.

4. The real needs and just demands of nations and populations and racial minorities to be adjusted as occasion may require, even where no strictly legal right can be established, and a foundation of mutual confidence to be thus laid, whereby many incentives to violent action will be removed.

5. The development among peoples and their rulers of that sense of deep and keen responsibility which weighs human statutes according to the sacred and inviolable standards of the laws of God. They must hunger and thirst after justice and be guided by that universal love which is the compendium and most general expression of the Christian ideal.

With these basic principles for the ordering of international life we would associate five standards by which economic situations and proposals may be tested:

1. Extreme inequality in wealth and possessions should be abolished;

2. Every child, regardless of race or class, should have equal opportunities of education, suitable for the development of his peculiar capacities;

3. The family as a social unit must be safeguarded;

4. The sense of a Divine vocation must be restored to man's daily work;

5. The resources of the earth should be used as God's gift to the whole human race, and used with due consideration for the needs of the present and future generations.

We are confident that the principles which we have enumerated would be accepted by rulers and statesmen throughout the British Commonwealth of Nations and would be regarded as the true basis on which a lasting peace could be established.

COSMO CANTUAR, Archbishop of Canterbury.

A. CARDINAL HINSLEY, Archbishop of Westminster.

WALTER H. ARMSTRONG, Moderator, Free Church Federal Council.

WILLIAM EBOR, Archbishop of York.

# 19

## Opinion, Education, and World Affairs

Although diplomacy is conducted by governments, it is the individual who gives direction and substance to the policies pursued, and it is he who, in the long run, gains or loses. Whether governments provide autarchy or trade, isolation or international co-operation, war or peace is ultimately decided by public thinking. As stated in the preamble to the United Nations Educational, Scientific and Cultural Organization (UNESCO), 'Wars begin in the minds of men,' and 'It is in the minds of men that the defenses of peace must be constructed.'

It is the considered opinion of authoritative students of the human mind that man is not inherently war-like. Most people are against war, but they are quite ineffectual and hopeless in their denunciation of it. While preferring peace, most people think in terms of war, indulge in racial and national prejudices, and seek advantages in territory, trade, and security that can be obtained only at the risk of war. They rationalize their own ambitions and policies without making an effort to understand those of other nations. In ignorance they often support policies that will not produce the results sought, as in protectionism, imperialism, and aggression.

The importance of public thinking was strikingly brought out by the actions of Europe's dictators both before and during World War II. Realizing that public support for their policies was needed, they did their utmost to control the formulation of opinion through propaganda and censorship. Even democracies resort to these techniques, especially under the stress of war.

One of the first men of modern history to comment on the power of ideas in international affairs was John Comenius (1592-1671), the Moravian pastor and teacher. Having witnessed the desolation of the Thirty Years' War, he advocated a 'universal rededication of minds,' an 'internal peace of minds inspired by a system of ideas and feelings.' He suggested a college where scholars from all lands might study for the promotion of mutual understanding.

Some years later Marc-Antoine Jullien (1775-1848) advocated a commission to undertake a comparative study of education in Europe with the purpose of promoting peace. Still later other men took up the project, but they were always too isolated and too much in advance of their fellows to gain support.

At the instigation of Mrs. Fannie Fern Andrews of Boston, preliminaries were undertaken in 1913 for the convocation of an international conference on education, but it was found necessary to postpone it, and shortly the beginning of the First World War permanently side-tracked it. After the War, the League of Nations, acting through the Institute of Intellectual Co-operation, took the first step toward placing education on an international basis. UNESCO is continuing this work along new and interesting lines.

It is the assumption of the UNESCO that an understanding by national groups of the aspirations, culture, and life of others will be constructive. When Charles Lamb once said that he hated a certain person, his listener remarked, 'Why, Charles, I didn't know that you knew him,' to which Lamb replied, 'Oh, I don't, I can't hate a man I know.' This incident was related by President Wilson in London when on his way to Paris for the purpose of organizing a League of Nations.

Much of the enthusiasm exhibited toward the study of nations and their relations to each other is often wasted in sentimentality and lacks the thoroughness and intellectual fearlessness which generally characterize education. The individual with such an approach was once referred to by Viscount Grey as having a 'head of feathers.' He went on to say, 'The emotional side is not going to do much good unless it has some foundation; it may even do mischief.'

It should be realized that only a beginning has been made in the field of international education. Today an international educational body with powers comparable to an American state board of education would be unthinkable. The nationalistic attitudes so prevalent would strongly oppose such an agency, and yet it may be noted that these are the very attitudes which an internationalized educational system would be expected to combat. Herein lies the problem.

## I. PUBLIC OPINION AND POWER

Ideas have power, and nations wishing to be powerful are aware of this fact. Governments frequently try to control public thinking, so that in time of emergency they can count on the general support of the people. The extract below brings out this fact.

(E. H. Carr, *The Twenty Years' Crisis,* 1919-1939, London, 1940, pp. 168-72. Reprinted by permission of The Macmillan Company.)

Power over opinion is the third form of power. The 'Jingoes' who sang 'We've got the ships, we've got the men, we've got the money too' had accurately diagnosed the three essential elements of po-litical power: armaments, man-power and economic power. But man-power is not reckoned by mere counting of heads. 'The Soldan of Egypt or the Emperor of Rome.' as Hume remarked, 'might drive his harmless subjects like brute beasts against their sentiments and inclinations. But he must at least have led his *mamelukes* or pretorian bands like men by their opinions.' Power over opinion is therefore not less essential for political purposes than military and economic power, and has always been closely associated with them. The art of persuasion has always been a necessary part of the equipment of a political leader. Rhetoric has a long and honoured record in the annals of statesmanship. But the popular view which regards propaganda as a distinctively modern weapon is, none the less, substantially correct.

The most obvious reason for the increasing prominence attached to power over opinion in recent times is the broadening of the basis of politics, which has vastly increased the number of those whose opinion is politically important. Until comparatively modern times, those whose opinion it was worth while to influence were few in number, united by close ties of interest and, generally speaking, highly educated; and the means of persuasion were correspondingly limited. 'Scientific exposition,' as Herr Hitler puts it, is for the intelligentsia. The modern weapon of propaganda is for the masses. Christianity seems to have been the first great movement in history with a mass appeal. Appropriately enough, it was the Catholic church which first understood and developed the potentialities of power over large masses of opinion. The Catholic church in the Middle Ages was—and has, within the limits of its power, remained—an institution for diffusing certain opinions and extirpating other opinions contrary to them: it created the first censorship and the first propaganda organisation. There is much point in the remark of a recent historian that the mediaeval church was the first totalitarian state. The Reformation was a movement which simultaneously deprived it, in several parts of Europe, of its power over opinion, of its wealth and of the authority which the military power of the Empire had conferred on it.

The problem of power over opinion in its modern mass form has been created by developments in economic and military technique—by the substitution of mass-production industries for individual craftsmanship and of the conscript citizen army for the volunteer professional force. . .

## II. FOREIGN POLICY AND THE DEMOCRATIC PROCESS

There is ample evidence that public opinion plays an important role in foreign policy in spite of the fact that elections are rarely decided on foreign issues. Officials in our Department of State have often admitted the influence upon them of letters, telegrams, and petitions. Secretary of State Cordell Hull remarked a few years ago that, 'Since the time when Thomas Jefferson insisted upon a "decent respect to the opinions of mankind," public opinion has controlled foreign policies in all democracies.' Public opinion is important in dictatorships, too, but there is the basic difference that dictators control public thinking far more than do democratic governments. The statement below was made by Francis H. Russell, Director of the Office of Public Affairs in the Department of State.

(F. H. Russell, 'Foreign Policy and the Democratic Process,' *Department of State Bulletin,* vol. XVII, No. 443, 1947, pp. 1253-5.)

The pattern of life that we know as democracy is the present product of centuries of trials and errors. History has been our cradle. It can be our guide—but it cannot be our limousine. Our way of life will survive in today's bitter ideological controversy only if it continues to provide better answers than any other system. Since democracy is engaged in a life or death competition—life or death, in all probability, not only for our way of life but for us as well—it is mere common prudence to check over from time to time the elements that make our system function and see that they are in a healthy state—such things as education, a constant flow of truthful information, widespread discussion, and a maximum development of the intellectual and moral resources of every person.

We shall need an adequate sense of responsibility on the part of those upon whom responsibility rests. In this country, for instance, our newspapers are not only responsible for purveying the news and for editorializing, but they are also responsible for performing, to a large extent, a function that in such a country as England rests in Parliament—the examining of the Executive Branch of the Government both to elicit information and to subject to careful scrutiny the soundness of the Government's policies. Obviously such a function must be carried out with an eye to the national welfare as well as to the headlines.

Another vital function of our democracy is carried on in a way that is not referred to in any constitution. That is the function of public discussion; not mere listening and absorption of facts but the sharp appraisal of views, the give and take of debate, and the arriving at a consensus. In earlier days it was done largely through town meetings that went on in every town and hamlet. Now it takes place to an increasing extent through chambers of commerce, labor groups, farm organizations, education and professional societies, women's clubs, foreign-affairs associations—organizations having all kinds of basic interests, all knowing that their interests are related in one degree or another to foreign-affairs developments.

The fact is that a little-noticed revolution in the way in which we do our national thinking is being carried out by the thousands of men and women throughout the country who, by their participation and work in organized groups, constitute a major force in developing and expressing a body of opinion on questions of foreign policy. The interest that gave rise to this movement became noticeably apparent during the first World War. It was stimulated to further growth by the debates over American participation in the League of Nations and by concern over the expansion of totalitarianism during the thirties. The recent war and its aftermath provided another impetus to this grass-roots concern with international affairs. Its recent growth is indicated by the fact that in 1946 the State Department received requests for liaison arrangements from 211 private organizations; a year later, the number had increased to 409. It is reflected, of course, in article 71 of the United Nations Charter.

A public-opinion poll indicates that about one out of every six or seven American adults belongs to an organization where world affairs are discussed. A similar survey indicates that persons having membership in such organizations are 50 percent more likely to be well informed about world affairs than are nonmembers.

At the same time, there has never been a period when the people who have the primary responsibility for formulating and executing our foreign policy have been as conscious as they are today of the need of an informed and understanding public opinion. . .

More and more, I think, we are coming to recognize that as we approach any substantial problem of foreign policy, there is bound to be a period when we must first ascertain what the questions are, a further period when we must make sure that we have all of the available facts, and a further period when we must balance alternatives and make sure that we are adopting the best answer. In a democracy answers cannot come instantaneously. Indeed, if they do, it may be a sign that the democratic process has not been vigorously at work.

Justice Holmes used to remark that there are some statements to which the only answer is, 'Well, I'll be damned.' There are also, in this world, some situations posing policy problems where any answer that can conceivably be advanced can be conclusively demonstrated to be wrong. There are occasions when it is quite simple to make out a strong case against a particular line of action, and all that can be said in its favor is that an even stronger case can be made against any other course. That is life in this imperfect world. It will do no good to be hysterical or morose about it. . .

For our part, in the State Department, in implementing this democratic process, we are making every effort to find and follow the path of full and frank information that leads between secrecy and public statements consisting only of predigested intellectual pabulum on the one hand and high-pressure propaganda on the other.

In our democracy there are three general ways in which the nongovernmental members of our body politic contribute to the strength and success of our foreign policy.

The first role of public opinion is to fix the limits within which our foreign policy must operate: either to support or weaken particular courses of action. Foreign policy in this country can never get very far ahead of or very far behind public opinion. If a particular policy receives public support it is likely to succeed. If it does not, in the long run it will be doomed to failure. In 1937 public opinion was not prepared to support even a quarantine foreign policy. Today it is apparent, from the way in which the Friendship Train has stirred public imagination, from public-opinion polls, from editorial and commentator opinion, that the public is increasingly aware of the kind of world we inhabit and of the implications of that world. . .

The second function which the public plays with respect to foreign policy is that of executing it. In normal times the day-to-day buying habits of the American people, for instance, have almost as much to do with our economic foreign relations as so-called 'policy decisions' in Washington. So does their buying restraint in times like these. Similarly with UNESCO. It is well and good to adopt a charter which says, 'It is in the minds of men that the defenses of peace must be constructed.' But the adoption of the charter accomplishes little if people do not aid in the educational reconstruction of war-devastated countries, make their personal opinion felt in their communities, take an active part in training for peace, join personally in adult education, and promote good will and understanding among the racial and religious groups in their communities.

The third function of the public is to provide the ferment of constructive thinking, to make sure that the fullest possible discussion is given to any particular subject, that all possible alternatives are carefully canvassed so that from this free enterprise of ideas the best will emerge into what we call public opinion. It is not too much to assert that the foreign policy of tomorrow will be the result of the studies and discussion that are going on today all over the country. We find ourselves today confronted with a problem of international policy which illustrates the essential role of this process. That is the question of how to prevent the destructive use of atomic energy. . .

## III. PROPAGANDA

Propaganda may be defined as a concerted effort to promote a doctrine or practice. The word has come to have a somewhat evil connotation, for the reason that propaganda has so often been used to support unworthy doctrines and practices, or because it has offered untruths and half-truths. Propaganda can be constructive, and much of it is. Good or bad, its influence on popular thinking in national and international politics has become tremendous in these days of inexpensive newspapers, movies, and radios. The extract below explains the development of propaganda and its importance.

(F. H. Carr, *Propaganda in International Politics*, Pamphlet on World Affairs, No. 16, 1939, pp. 4-20. Reprinted by permission of The Clarendon Press, Oxford.)

Propaganda in its modern form has been called into being by developments in economic and military technique—by the substitution of mass-production industries for individual craftsmanship and of the conscript citizen army for the volunteer professional force. Contemporary politics are vitally dependent on the opinion of large masses of more or less politically conscious people, of whom the most vocal, the most influential, and the most accessible to propaganda are those who live in and around great cities. The problem is one which no modern government ignores. In theory, the attitude adopted towards it by democracies and by totalitarian States is diametrically opposed. Democracies purport to follow mass opinion; totalitarian States set a standard and enforce conformity to it. In practice, the contrast is less clear-cut. Totalitarian governments, in determining their policy, profess to represent the will of the masses; and the profession is not wholly vain. Democracies, or the groups which control them, are not altogether innocent of the arts of moulding and directing mass opinion. Totalitarian propagandists, whether Marxist or Fascist, continually insist on the illusory character of the freedom of opinion enjoyed in democratic countries. There remains a solid substratum of difference between the attitude of democracies and totalitarian States towards mass opinion; and this difference may prove a decisive factor in times of crisis. But both agree in recognizing its paramount importance.

The same economic and social conditions, which have made mass opinion supremely important in politics, have also created instruments of unparalleled range and efficiency for moulding and directing it. The oldest, and still perhaps the most powerful, of these instruments is universal popular education. The State which provides the education necessarily determines its content. No State will allow its future citizens to imbibe in its schools teaching subversive of the principles on which it is based. In democracies, the child is taught to prize the liberties of democracy; in totalitarian States, to admire the strength and discipline of totalitarianism. In both, he is taught to respect the traditions and creeds and institutions of his own country, and to think it better than any other. The influence of this early unconscious moulding is difficult to exaggerate. During the War spontaneous belief in the righteousness of the national cause was most easily generated and most firmly maintained in those countries where universal education was of long standing. Every country in the world now recognizes the importance of education in moulding a united nation. Marx's dictum that 'the worker has no country' has ceased to be true since the worker has passed through national schools.

But when we speak of propaganda to-day, we think first and foremost of those other instruments whose use popular education has made possible: the radio, the film, and the popular press. These instruments of mass appeal have created propaganda in its modern form and have rendered inevitable a re-examination of our whole attitude towards power over opinion.

In the nineteenth century the philosophers of *laissez-faire* believed that opinion, like trade, should be free from all controls, and that this absolute freedom would be an infallible guarantee of the public welfare. If every opinion were given an equal chance to assert itself, the right one was bound to prevail.

The prejudice which the word 'propaganda' excites in many minds to-day is closely parallel to the prejudice against State control of industry and trade. Opinion, like trade and industry, should under the old liberal conception be allowed to flow in its own natural channels without artificial regulation.

This conception has broken down on the hard fact that in modern conditions opinion, like trade and industry, is not and cannot be exempt from artificial controls. The radio, the film, and the press share to the fullest extent the characteristic attribute of modern industry: mass-production, quasi-monopoly, and standardization are a condition of their economical and efficient working. Their management has, in the natural course of development become concentrated in fewer and fewer hands; and this concentration facilitates and makes inevitable the centralized control of opinion. The mass production of opinion is the corollary of the mass production of goods. Just as the nineteenth-century conception of political freedom was rendered illusory for large masses of the population by the growth and concentration of economic power, so the nineteenth-century conception of freedom of thought is being fundamentally modified by the development of these new and extremely powerful instruments of power over opinion. The issue is no longer whether men shall be politically free to express their opinions, but whether freedom of opinion has, for large masses of people, any meaning but subjection to the influence of innumerable forms of propaganda directed by vested interests of one kind or another. An interesting and revealing debate took place in the House of Commons on 7 December 1938 on the freedom of the press. The spokesman of the Liberal Opposition, who initiated the debate, argued for the freedom of the press on familiar nineteenth-century lines. The spokesman of the Labour Opposition, on the other hand, declared that the press had already lost its independence, being 'controlled by financiers, advertisers, and press magnates,' and wanted to 'make every newspaper in the country responsible for every item of news it prints and answerable to this House or some public authority.'

Though the government of the day is always liable in democratic countries to be attacked for any specific measures which it takes to control and influence the expression of opinion through the press, the radio, or the film, there is substantial agreement among all parties everywhere—at any rate in Europe—that such measures are in some cases necessary. No future government, either in Great Britain or elsewhere, will be able to allow these immensely powerful organs of opinion to operate at the unfettered discretion of private interests and without any form of official direction. Some control by the State, however discreetly veiled, over the instruments of propaganda has become unavoidable if the public good is to be served and if the community is to survive. In the totalitarian countries, radio, press, and film are State industries absolutely controlled by governments. In democratic countries, conditions vary, but are everywhere tending towards more and more centralized control. Immense corporations are called into existence, which are too powerful and too vital to the community to remain wholly independent of the machine of government, and which themselves find it convenient to accept voluntary collaboration with the State as an alternative to formal control by it. It is significant that what a distinguished historian has called 'the nationalization of thought' has proceeded everywhere *pari passu* with the nationalization of industry. Both are completest in Soviet Russia, and almost equally complete in the other totalitarian States. In democratic countries, both are achieved by indirect and partial methods which still leave a wide scope for individual initiative and for rivalry between conflicting interests and parties. The major problem in democratic countries is no longer whether the government should seek to influence opinion, but how to ensure that this power is exercised for recognizably national, and not for merely party, interests. War has inevitably led to the elaboration of far-reaching schemes for the controlling and moulding of opinion by the State, and thereby stimulated the nationalization of thought as well as of other aspects of national life.

The organized use of propaganda as a regular instrument of foreign policy is a modern development. Prior to 1914, cases occurred of the use of propaganda by governments in international relations. The press was freely used by Bismarck, Cavour, and other statesmen, though rather, perhaps, for the purpose of making pronouncements, or putting out feelers, to foreign governments than as a means of influencing public opinion at large. Co-operation between the missionary and the trader, and the support of both by military force, may be cited as a familiar nineteenth-century example of unofficial—and in part, no doubt, unconscious—association between propaganda and economic and military power in the interests of national expansion. But the field of propaganda was limited. The people who exploited it most intensively were the revolutionaries; and they have many claims to be regarded as the fathers of modern propaganda. Prior to 1914, any systematic resort to propaganda by governments would have been thought undignified and rather disreputable.

It did not take long for the belligerents of 1914-18 to realize that, as a recent writer has put it, 'psychological war must accompany economic war and military war.' It was a condition of success on the military and economic fronts that the 'morale' of one's own side should be maintained, and that of the other side sapped and destroyed. Propaganda was the instrument by which both these ends were pursued. Leaflets were dropped over the enemy lines inciting his troops to mutiny; and this procedure, like most new weapons of war, was at first denounced as being contrary to international law. In 1917 two British airmen captured by the Germans were sentenced to ten years' hard labour for dropping such leaflets in contravention of the laws of war. The sentences were remitted on a British threat of reprisals. During the latter part of the War the paper balloon was the instrument most commonly used on all sides for dropping propaganda over enemy lines. Such propaganda was explicitly sanctioned in The Hague rules of 1923 for the conduct of aerial warfare.

Throughout the War of 1914-18 the close interdependence between the three forms of power was constantly demonstrated. The success of propaganda on both sides, both at home and in neutral and enemy countries, rose and fell with the varying fortunes of the military and economic struggle. When at length the Allied blockade and Allied victories in the field crippled German resources, Allied propaganda became enormously effective and played a considerable part in the final collapse. The victory of 1918 was achieved by a skilful combination of military power, economic power, and propaganda.

Notwithstanding the general recognition of the importance of propaganda in the later stages of the War, it was still regarded by almost every one as a weapon specially appropriate to a period of hostilities. 'In the same way as I send shells into the enemy trenches, or as I discharge poison gas at him,' wrote the German general who was primarily responsible for dispatching Lenin and his party in the sealed train to Russia, 'I, as an enemy, have the right to use propaganda against him.' For General Hoffmann the use of propaganda in time of peace would apparently have been as unthinkable as the use of shells or poison gas. And this view was probably typical. The abolition of ministries and departments of propaganda at the end of the War was an automatic measure of demobilization whose necessity and desirability nobody questioned. Yet within twenty years of the Peace Treaties many governments were, in time of peace, already conducting propaganda with an intensity unsurpassed in the War period; and new official or semi-official agencies for the influencing of opinion at home and abroad were springing up in every country. This new development was rendered possible and inevitable by the popularization of international politics and by the growing efficiency of propaganda methods. Even in peace, propaganda seems likely for the future to be recognized as a regular instrument of foreign policy.

The initiative in introducing propaganda as a regular instrument of international relations must be credited to the Soviet Government. The causes of this were partly accidental. The Bolsheviks, when they seized power in Russia, found themselves desperately weak in the ordinary military and economic weapons of international conflict. Their principal strength lay in their influence over opinion in other countries; and it was therefore natural and necessary that they should exploit this weapon to the utmost. In early days they seriously believed in their ability to dissolve the German armies by the distribution of propaganda leaflets and by fraternization between the lines. Later, they counted on propaganda in Allied countries to paralyse Allied intervention against them in the civil war. Had not propaganda been supplemented by the creation of a well-disciplined Red Army, it might by itself have proved ineffective. But the importance of the role it played is sufficiently indicated by the fear of Bolshevik propaganda felt for many years afterwards, and not yet extinct in many European and Asiatic countries. Soviet Russia was the first modern State to establish, in the form of the Communist International, a large-scale permanent international propaganda organization. . .

Propaganda soon became so well recognized as a national political weapon that stipulations regarding its use were embodied in international agreements. Such stipulations were first introduced into agreements made with the Soviet Government for the purpose of limiting the activities of the Communist International. In the Anglo-Soviet Trade Agreement of March 1921—the first important agreement concluded by Soviet Russia with a Western Power—each party undertook to 'refrain from conducting outside its own borders any official propaganda direct or indirect against the institutions' of the other party. The British Government never accepted the Soviet plea that the Soviet Government had no responsibility for the activities of the Communist International; and complaints about Communist propaganda were a constantly disturbing factor in Anglo-Soviet relations. The British General Election of 1924 was enlivened by the issue of the alleged 'Zinoviev letter' (its authenticity was firmly denied by the Soviet authorities) which contained instructions to the British Communist Party regarding propaganda in Great Britain.

But relations with Soviet Russia were for many years thought of as an exceptional case. Outside Soviet Russia, the first recorded international agreement to abstain from hostile propaganda seems to have been one concluded in 1931 between the German and Polish broadcasting companies, which undertook to assure that 'the matter broadcast does not in any way offend the national sentiment of listeners who are nationals of the other contracting party.' Propaganda was first raised to the dignity of a universal issue when the Polish Government made proposals to the Disarmament Conference for a convention on 'moral disarmament.' To limit the propaganda weapon by a general convention proved as hopeless a task as to limit the military weapon, though an international agreement to refrain from the broadcasting of 'incitements to war' or other hostile propaganda was signed at Geneva by most of the surviving members of the League in September 1936. A bilateral agreement for terminating hostile propaganda was concluded between Germany and Poland in January 1934; and this agreement was successful for some five years in damming the flood of mutual recriminations on the subject of Danzig, the 'Corridor,' the German minority in Poland, and other contentious issues. In July 1936 an agreement was signed between Germany and Austria under which both countries were to 'refrain from all aggressive uses of the wireless, films, news services and the theatre. . .'

## IV. FREEDOM OF INFORMATION

Some barriers to the free flow of information between states, such as language and illiteracy, are inevitable at the present time. There are, however, others of a very different type set up by governments in order to control the thinking of the people. These legal-administrative barriers take on many forms. A number of governments insist that their newspapers get information only from domestic agencies, denying them the right to purchase from foreign news organizations. Unfair rates in international communication are often imposed to prevent news from crossing the frontier. Generally it is more difficult to get news out of a country than to import it. For many years reporters have complained of obstacles often placed in their way by foreign governments, so that access to the news sources is not available. Certain countries have not permitted foreign reporters to enter their territory at all except under exceptional circumstances and then under the continuous supervision of public officials. Censorship provides another common obstacle to the export of information. In some countries, foreign newspapers and magazines cannot be imported, and there have been situations in which governments have forbidden the people to listen to foreign broadcasts. In the last few years the western nations have complained a great deal about the difficulty of getting news from territory under Russian control. The whole subject has been under discussion within the United Nations, and it has been the policy of the United States to do all that it can to open up the channels of news.

At the United Nations Conference on Freedom of Information, held at Geneva, Switzerland, from 23 March to 21 April 1948, draft conventions were drawn up on the gathering and international transmission of news, on the right of correcting news reports, and on general principles of freedom of information. In addition the conference adopted numerous resolutions, some of general, others of technical, interest. Those reprinted in Extract A show the wide range of problems dealt with by the conference. That the subjects covered are of vital importance cannot be doubted but whether these resolutions can be effectively implemented is another matter. The Final Act of the Conference, including the draft conventions and resolutions, was referred to the Economic and Social Council for study. The Conference's Final Act was adopted by 30 votes to 1 (Poland) against, with 5 abstentions (Byelorussia, Czechoslovakia, Ukraine, U.S.S.R., and Yugoslavia). On freedom of information, as on human rights generally, the East-West cleavage is apparent from this voting tally.

## A. *Geneva Resolutions*

*(United Nations Conference on Freedom of Information,* Report of the United States Delegation with Related Documents, Department of State, Publication 3150.)

### RESOLUTION NO. 1 [FUNDAMENTAL PRINCIPLES]

*Whereas* Freedom of Information is a fundamental right of the people, and is the touchstone of all the freedoms to which the United Nations is dedicated, without which world peace cannot well be preserved; and

Freedom of information carries the right to gather, transmit, and disseminate news anywhere and everywhere without fetters; and

Freedom of information depends for its validity upon the availability to the people of a diversity of sources of news and of opinion; and

Freedom of information further depends upon the willingness of the press and other agencies of information to employ the privileges derived from the people without abuse, and to accept and comply with the obligations to seek the facts without prejudice and to spread knowledge without malicious intent; and

Freedom of information further depends upon the effective enforcement of recognized responsibilities,

The United Nations Conference on Freedom of Information

*Resolves,* therefore,

1. That everyone shall have the right to freedom of thought and expression:

this shall include freedom to hold opinions without interference; and to seek, receive and impart information and ideas by any means and regardless of frontiers;

2. That the right of news personnel to have the widest possible access to the sources of information, to travel unhampered in pursuit thereof, and to transmit copy without unreasonable or discriminatory limitations, should be guaranteed by action on the national and international plane;

3. That the exercise of these rights should be limited only by recognition of and respect for the rights of others, and the protection afforded by law to the freedom, welfare, and security of all;

4. That in order to prevent abuses of freedom of information, governments in so far as they are able should support measures which will help to improve the quality of information and to make a diversity of news and opinion available to the people;

5. That it is the moral obligation of the press and other agencies of information to seek the truth and report the facts, thereby contributing to the solution of the world's problems through the free interchange of information bearing on them, promoting respect for human rights and fundamental freedoms without discrimination, fostering understanding and co-operation between peoples, and helping maintain international peace and security;

6. That this moral obligation, under the spur of public opinion, can be advanced through organizations and associations of journalists and through individual news personnel;

7. That encouragement should be given to the establishment and to the functioning within the territory of a State of one or more non-official organizations of persons employed in the collection and dissemination of information to the public, and that such organization or organizations should encourage the fulfilment *inter alia* of the following obligations by all individuals or organizations engaged in the collection and dissemination of information:

(a) To report facts without prejudice and in their proper context and to make comments without malicious intent;

(b) To facilitate the solution of the economic, social and humanitarian problems of the world as a whole through the free interchange of information bearing on such problems;

(c) To help promote respect for human rights and fundamental freedoms without discrimination;

(d) To help maintain international peace and security;

(e) To counteract the spreading of intentionally false or distorted reports which promote hatred or prejudice against States, persons or groups of different race, language, religion or philosophical conviction;

8. That observance of the obligations of the press and other agencies of information, except those of a recognized legal nature, can also be effectively advanced by the people served by these instrumentalities, provided that news and opinion reach them through a diversity of sources and that the people have adequate means of obtaining and promoting a better performance from the press and other agencies of information.

RESOLUTION No. 2 [PROPAGANDA INCITING TO WAR AND FALSE REPORTING]

*Whereas* the peoples of the world have embodied in the United Nations their determination to protect mankind from the scourge of war and to prevent the recurrence of aggression from Nazi, Fascist, or any other source;

*Whereas* the attainment of a just and lasting peace depends in great degree upon the free flow of true and honest information to all peoples and upon the spirit of responsibility with which all personnel of the press and other agencies of information seek the truth and report the facts;

and *Whereas,* by inaccurate reports, by defective or distorted presentation and deliberate or malicious misinterpretation of facts in various parts of the world, peoples have been misled and their mutual understanding has been seriously endangered;

The United Nations Conference on Freedom of Information

*Endorses* the resolutions of the second General Assembly on propaganda which is either designed or likely to provoke or encourage any threat to the peace, breach of the peace, or act of aggression, and on the spreading of false and distorted reports;

*Declares* that all such propaganda and such reports:

(a) are contrary to the purposes of the United Nations as defined in the Charter;

(b) constitute a problem of the first importance calling for urgent corrective action on the national and international planes;

*Condemns* solemnly all propaganda either designed or likely to provoke or encourage any threat to the peace, breach of the peace, or act of aggression, and all distortion and falsification of news through whatever channels, private or governmental, since such activities can only promote misunderstanding and mistrust between the peoples of the world and thereby endanger the lasting peace which the United Nations is consecrated to maintain;

*Appeals* vigorously to the personnel of the press and other agencies of information of all the countries of the world, and to those responsible for their activities, to serve the aims of friendship, understanding and peace by accomplishing their task in a spirit of accuracy, fairness and responsibility;

*Expresses* its profound conviction that only organs of information in all countries of the world that are free to seek and to disseminate the truth, and thus to carry out their responsibility to the people, can greatly contribute to the counteracting of Nazi, Fascist or any other propaganda of aggression or of racial, national and religious discrimination and to the prevention of recurrence of Nazi, Fascist, or any other aggression;

And therefore *recommends* that all countries take within their respective territories the measures which they consider necessary to give effect to this Resolution.

. . .

RESOLUTION NO. 4 [RACIAL AND NATIONAL HATRED]

*Considering* that there are in some countries media of information which disseminate racial and national hatred,

The United Nations Conference on Freedom of Information

*Recommends* that the governments of such countries should:

(a) Encourage the widest possible dissemination of free information through a diversity of sources as the best safeguard against the creation of racial and national hatred and prejudice;

(b) Encourage, in consultation with organizations of journalists, suitable and effective non-legislative measures against the dissemination of such hatred and prejudice; and

(c) Take, within their constitutional limits, appropriate measures to encourage the dissemination of information promoting friendly relations between races and nations based upon the purposes and principles of the United Nations Charter.

RESOLUTION NO. 5 [FACILITATING MOVEMENT OF CORRESPONDENTS]

The United Nations Conference on Freedom of Information

*Resolves* that:

1. Governments should encourage the freest possible movement of foreign correspondents in the performance of their functions; and that

2. Governments should expedite in a manner consistent with their respective laws and procedures the administrative measures necessary for the entry, residence, movement and travel of foreign correspondents, together with their professional equipment, and should impose no special, discriminatory or unusual restrictions on such ingress or egress, or upon the transit through or residence in their territories of such correspondents.

. . .

### RESOLUTION NO. 12 [CENSORSHIP]

The United Nations Conference on Freedom of Information

*Resolves*

That governments should permit egress from their territory of all news material of foreign correspondents and foreign information agencies, whether of information or opinion, and whether visual or auditory, without censorship, editing or delay; provided that governments may make and enforce regulations relating directly to the maintenance of national military security; and

That such regulation should, however, be communicated to foreign correspondents and should apply equally to all foreign correspondents and foreign information agencies. . .

### RESOLUTION NO. 13 [CENSORSHIP]

*Strongly convinced* that Freedom of Information should be assured to everyone,

*Holding* that any form of censorship constitutes a curtailment of this freedom,

*Considering* that censorship deprives the information which it passes of its credibility and often gives information

from unspecified sources an unwarranted value;

The United Nations Conference on Freedom of Information

*Solemnly condemns* the use in peacetime of censorship which restricts or controls freedom of information, and

*Invites* governments to take the necessary steps to promote its progressive abolition;

*And considers* that

Nothing in this resolution shall, however, prevent governments from maintaining regulation of newsreels provided their release may only be prohibited on grounds of public morality.

. . .

### RESOLUTION NO. 39 [CONTINUING MACHINERY TO PROMOTE THE FREE FLOW OF INFORMATION]

*Considering*

That the work of the various Committees has shown the need to set up continuing international machinery to carry on the work undertaken by the Conference on Freedom of Information and, in particular, to study the problems involved in the application of the resolutions adopted by this Conference and the implementation of the draft conventions recommended by it,

*Considering*

That it is expedient, in order to avoid the multiplication of specialized agencies, to entrust this task to the Sub-Commission on Freedom of Information and of the Press,

The United Nations Conference on Freedom of Information

*Resolves*

1. That the Economic and Social Council be requested to continue the Sub-Commission on Freedom of Information and of the Press for a period of three years;

2. That the Sub-Commission's terms of

reference include the consideration of issues and problems involved in the dissemination of information by newspapers and news periodicals, radio broadcasts and newsreels;

3. That, to carry out these terms of reference, the Sub-Commission may:

(a) Study and report to the Economic and Social Council on:

(1) Political, economic and other barriers to the free flow of information;

(2) The extent to which freedom of information is accorded to the various peoples of the world;

(3) The adequacy of the news available to them;

(4) The development of high standards of professional conduct;

(5) The persistent dissemination of information which is false, distorted or otherwise injurious to the principles of the Charter of the United Nations;

(6) The operation of any inter-governmental agreements in the field of freedom of information;

(b) Receive for its own information communications from any legally constituted national or international press, information, broadcasting or newsreel enterprise or association relating to the items enumerated in paragraph 3 (a) above with a view to assisting it in the formulation of general principles and proposals in the field of freedom of information;

(c) Discharge with the approval of the General Assembly and the Economic and Social Council such other functions as may be entrusted to it by inter-governmental agreements on information; and

(d) Initiate studies and make recommendations to the Economic and Social Council concerning:

(1) The promotion of a wider degree of freedom of information and the reduction or elimination of obstacles thereto;

(2) The promotion of the dissemination of true information to counteract Nazi, Fascist or any other propaganda of aggression or of racial, national and religious discrimination;

(3) The conclusion or improvement of inter-governmental agreements in the field of freedom of information; and

(4) Measures to facilitate the work of foreign news personnel.

4. That the General Assembly be requested to make adequate funds available for the work of the Sub-Commission and in particular, funds for providing the Sub-Commission with the full-time expert staff, within the Secretariat of the United Nations, necessary for the discharge of its important functions.

## B. *Resolution of the Inter-American Conference*

The following resolution was adopted by the Inter-American Conference on Problems of War and Peace, held at Mexico City early in 1945.

(*Report of the Delegation of the United States to the Inter-American Conference on Problems of War and Peace,* Mexico City, 1945, pp. 99-100.)

*Whereas:*

The American Republics have repeatedly expressed their firm desire to assure a peace that will defend and protect the fundamental rights of man everywhere and permit all peoples to live free from the evils of tyranny, oppression, and slavery;

The progress of mankind depends on the supremacy of truth among men;

Truth is the enemy of tyranny, which cannot exist where truth prevails, so that those who would erect tyrannies are constrained to attempt its suppression or to raise barriers against it;

Freedom of expression of thought, oral and written, is an essential condition to the development of an active and vigilant public opinion throughout the world to guard against any attempt at aggression;

One of the most pernicious acts against humanity is the method employed by totalitarian governments in isolating their people from the influence of foreign information, depriving them of access to the truth about international affairs, as well as creating obstacles abroad to an exact knowledge of internal conditions in their countries;

It is one of the fundamental lessons of the present world war that there can be no freedom, peace, or security where men are not assured of free access to the truth through the various media of public information,

The Inter-American Conference on Problems of War and Peace

*Recommends:*

1. That the American Republics recognize their essential obligation to guarantee to their people, free and impartial access to sources of information.

2. That, having this guarantee in view,

they undertake, upon the conclusion of the war, the earliest possible abandonment of those measures of censorship, and of control over the services of press, motion picture and radio, which have been necessary in wartime to combat the subversive political tactics and espionage activities of the Axis states.

3. That the Governments of the American Republics take measures, individually and in cooperation with one another, to promote a free exchange of information among their peoples.

4. That the American Republics, having accepted the principle of free access to information for all, make every effort to the end that when a judicial order in the world is assured, there may be established the principle of free transmission and reception of information, oral or written, published in books or by the press, broadcast by radio or disseminated by any other means, under proper responsibility and without need of previous censorship, as is the case with private correspondence by letter, telegram, or any other means in time of peace.

(Approved at the plenary session of 7 March 1945)

## V. EDUCATION

In the past education everywhere has stressed national attitudes and has been much too indifferent to internationalism. The special stress of Nazi education upon a narrow and bigoted nationalism brought out strikingly the need for a more active international educational organization than the Institute of Intellectual Co-operation or the Inter-American Institute of Intellectual Co-operation which had been in operation before World War II.

### A. *Nazi Education*

(L. Fuller, 'Education in Germany under the National Socialist Regime,' *Department of State Bulletin,* vol. XI, No. 280, 1944, pp. 551-5.)

THE NAZI ATTITUDE TOWARD SCIENCE

National Socialist reforms in the field of higher learning can be understood only in the light of the Nazi attitude toward science and research—an attitude which springs inevitably from the ethnocentric nature of the premises underlying all National Socialist thinking. It attacks first the detachment of the scientist. 'Scientific objectivity,' asserts a German educational journal, 'is only one of the many errors of liberalism. . .'

Every science is necessarily conditioned by a racial-political awareness; each observer is bound, whether consciously or not, by the forces of his race, surroundings, people, and soil. The alleged objectivity of science is, in fact, only a reflection of the 'Bourgeois secular spirit' of the times. Science is no mere 'function of the intellect'; it cannot shut out will, faith, and passion. . .

It follows from the Nazi assumptions that science can have no autonomy—there can be no 'science for science's sake.' It must serve the German folk-movement. Its specialists must enroll in the joint enterprise, and learning must serve the great cultural and political tasks of the epoch. Only pragmatic and useful truths are of value. In the preamble of the law of March 16, 1937, for establishing a National Research Council, the mobilization of research in behalf of the Four Year Plan was justified on the grounds that, by necessity, 'scientific investigation has the task of reaching goals on which the existence of the whole nation depends.' The entire purpose of Nazi science was expressed most candidly by Professor Kahrstedt of Göttingen:

'We renounce international science. We renounce the international republic of learning. We renounce research for its own sake. We teach and learn medicine, not to increase the number of known microbes, but to keep the German people strong and healthy. We teach and learn history, not to say how things actually happened, but to instruct the German people from the past. We teach and learn

the sciences, not to discover abstract laws, but to sharpen the implements of the German people in their competition with other peoples.'

## NAZIFICATION OF THE UNIVERSITIES AND HIGHER SCHOOLS

*The Nazi View of Higher Learning.* The attitude of the Nazi regime toward Germany's world-famous universities and other institutions of higher learning was dictated by its conception of the role of education and science as outlined above. Despite the fact that the universities had remained distinctly reactionary under the Republic and had continued to recruit both student bodies and faculty personnel from upper-class conservative elements, Nazi educational leaders discovered ample grounds for attacking them. The university (in the words of student-Führer Dr. Schul) is 'in constant danger of degenerating into a purely intellectual institution, whereas its true function is that of a training center.'

There must be no dabbling in irrelevant knowledge; all research must contribute directly to the upbuilding of the nation. All work, even the most specialized, must rest upon the firm ground of a common *Weltanschauung*. So-called academic freedom was a sham since there could be no freedom to question truths historically conditioned by the imperatives of 'folkish' existence. The 'salon skepticism,' the 'pulpit nihilism' of teachers who felt no sense of responsibility to *Volk* and nation could no longer be tolerated. The aloofness of the universities from political life and the ivory-tower existence of the professor engrossed in his researches but indifferent to the vital needs of his students and of his nation were condemned.

The true function of the institution of advanced learning, training, and research in the National Socialist state was the furnishing of direction, leadership, and inspiration in the molding of those students best qualified for high responsibility. The German university had never enrolled more than an exceedingly small percentage of the eligible age group, which by the Nazis was reduced still further. The last remnants of individualism were swept away, bringing to an end the 'positivist cult of the intellect.' Student and professor alike were to be deemed public functionaries performing essential national tasks. Research was to become directed investigation determined by the demands of a totalitarian society. The university must become *völkisch*, rooted in the national soil, serving the most vital interests of the nation. . .

Three types of schools for the development of future leaders have been set up under the exclusive control of the party:

1. *The Adolf Hitler Schools.* These schools, established in 1937, are 10 in number and are designed to train selected boys from 12 to 18 who are recruited from the ranks of the Hitler Youth. Scholastic background is unimportant; leadership traits are considered the prime essential. Successful graduation is the key to entrance to a university or professional school or to posts in the army or state or party bureaucracy. 'Political orientation' is the essence of the course which centers around biological, racial, and 'folkish' science. World affairs are presented from the party standpoint. The instructors are specially trained party leaders who are devoid of any academic background or experience. Only a few hundred boys are admitted to these schools each year.

2. *The National Political Institutes of Education.* These are Nazified versions of the old Prussian cadet schools. They are 31 in number and concentrate on preparation of leaders in the armed formations of the party, Storm Troopers and Elite Guards, or in the Labor Service camps. Their program, according to *Das Reich,* April 27, 1941, 'is essentially centered around struggle and competition. Combat is the organ of selection in peace and war is the primary instrument of education in these institutions.' The curriculum emphasizes physical training supplemented by Nazi indoctrination. Entrance is based on the results of rigorous selective tests, and the unfit are rapidly weeded out. The term is eight years, after which time graduates may enter a university, the state police, or posts in the armed formations of the party. A large number of these institutes, some of which have operated since 1933, have been added since the outbreak of war in 1939.

3. *The Order Castles (Ordensburgen).* Four of these have been set up for the purpose of developing a super-elite from the most select graduates of the other leadership schools. Admission must be preceded by two years of military service, one year of labor service, and one to three years of activity in youth and party organizations. Students concentrate first on racial and ideological 'science,' second on physical training, and finally on political education accompanied by the development of physical and military skills. The culminating year at Marienburg in East Prussia emphasizes the medieval conquest of the East by the Teutonic Knights and the predestined right of the master race to living space in the East at the expense of the native Slavic population. . .

### B. *The Role of Intellectual Co-operation*

Below is a statement on the purposes and objectives of intellectual co-operation, made by Gonzague de Reynold, then chairman of the Swiss National Committee on Intellectual Co-operation.

(*Bulletin of the League of Nations, Teaching*, No. 4, 1937, pp. 13-16.)

I shall take as my starting-point, not the organisation—but the idea of intellectual co-operation. Can this idea exert an influence, can intellectual co-operation play a part in the contemporary world, in this world of disequilibrium and disharmony, in a Europe which has ceased to be homogeneous?

A disciple of Confucius once asked his master what would be his first action if he was made Emperor of China. Confucius replied: 'I should begin by fixing the meaning of words.' I shall therefore begin by fixing that of the word 'co-operation,' which, since 1922, we have continually used in our reports and speeches.

The word came into the French language through the door of theology. Its first meaning is that of the action or effect of divine grace on the soul of man in bringing about his own good. The 'co-operating grace' is that which is added to the human will and which follows it in order to help it. Reciprocally, man's will co-operates with 'grace' when it tries to deserve it and to keep it. Thus in the words 'co-operation' and 'co-operate' is found the idea of a co-ordinated action for a common good. 'Co-operation' is thus a stronger term than 'collaboration.' While the latter signifies simply that one shares with others in an agreed and limited task, 'co-operation' implies a closer agreement, a more sustained determination, a predisposition of the spirit and aspiration towards a common ideal.

When we talk of intellectual co-operation, this common ideal consists of spiritual values, civilisation in general, indeed peace itself. It requires of all those who make themselves its defenders and promoters a kind of vocation which simple collaboration does not require.

By this, I do not at all mean to say that, in order to co-operate, it is necessary to take our stand on an ideology like angels on a cloud. On the contrary, ideologies are the sworn enemies of all intellectual co-operation. Ideologies engender fanaticism which is a mental passion for the abstract. There is nothing which narrows and clouds the intelligence, nothing which weakens the meaning of life, so much as fanaticism. Fanaticism kills curiosity. But curiosity about what one does not know, about what one does not understand, about what one does not like is the essential condition of all intellectual co-operation. Without this prerequisite and sympathetic curiosity, the contemporary world remains incomprehensible, and all attempt to influence that world is doomed to failure.

The aim of intellectual co-operation is to bring men's minds into harmony: but it cannot require them to abdicate their intelligence.

Intellectual co-operation must not be a neutral place with a cloakroom at the entrance where one momentarily leaves one's convictions and personality behind. On the contrary, I think that intellectual co-operation is a place where agreement has been reached on the following fact: A whole great period of history is closed; we are in an intermediate period between a world which is dying and a world which is being born. During such periods everything is in a state of flux, the curve of general civilisation declines and peace is threatened. It is therefore more than ever necessary that the best minds should come together and should endeavor to maintain at least in themselves the idea of civilisation, order and peace. Their task is to link the old world to the new; to save the essential values of the old world, to help the values of the new world to find expression and practical application, and to see that they mutually enlighten and stimulate one another. This implies co-operation in producing synthesis and harmony. But it also implies minds which are different and which are curious of their very differences. . .

## C. Intellectual Co-operation in the Americas

The Sixth Inter-American Conference of 1928 provided that an Inter-American Congress of Rectors, Deans, and Educators should be held for the purpose of setting up organs of co-operation in intellectual matters. Early in 1930 the Congress convened at Havana, Cuba. A convention was signed creating the Inter-American Institute of Intellectual Co-operation and resolutions were adopted regarding the exchange between universities of professors, students, research workers, and cultural missions. Havana was designated as the seat of the Institute. The text of the convention on intellectual co-operation is given below.

*(Inter-American Congress of Rectors, Deans, and Educators in General,* Havana, Cuba, 20-23 February 1930, *Report of the Chairman of the Delegation of the United States of America,* pp. 118-22.)

### CONVENTION

(Inter-American Institute of Intellectual Cooperation)

The rectors, deans, and educators, acting as official representatives of the American republics invited to this congress, held in Habana, Republic of Cuba; after having exchanged their respective full powers, which were found to be in due form, and after the explanatory addresses and discussions which took place at the plenary session of February 23, 1930, submit *ad referendum* to their respective governments the convention entitled 'Inter-American Institute of Intellectual Cooperation.'

### ARTICLE 1

With a view to systematizing the factors tending to intellectual cooperation among the nations of the American Continent in sciences, arts, and letters, an Inter-American Institute of Intellectual Cooperation shall be established, in close relationship with the Governing Board of the Pan American Union.

The Institute shall be composed of a National Council for Intellectual Cooperation in each of the American republics, and an Inter-American Central Council of Intellectual Cooperation. The program of work proposed by the Institute, together with a report of its activities, shall be presented annually to the Governing Board of the Pan American Union; and a special report shall also be presented to the International American Conference.

### ARTICLE 2—THE NATIONAL COUNCILS

(a) *Organization.*—The Pan American Union will request the Secretariat or Department of Public Instruction of each of the American republics to invite the universities and other institutions of higher education, as well as the academies, associations (especially those of professors and students), institutes, museums, libraries, and other similar organizations devoted to the promotion of arts, letters, sciences, and professions, to appoint delegates to integrate the Inter-American National Council of Intellectual Cooperation, the purpose being to collaborate with the Inter-American Central Council and with the other National Councils in the study and solution of the problems of intellectual life in the Americas.

In those countries in which there is already a Committee of International Intellectual Cooperation, this committee may be utilized as an agency for cooperation with the Inter-American Institute of Intellectual Cooperation.

· · ·

The National Councils shall keep the Inter-American Central Council constantly informed regarding the progress of their work, and shall transmit to it annually a report summarizing the results of their activities.

(b) *Functions.*—The functions of the National Councils shall be:

1. (a) To formulate proposals as to the problems of intellectual life that require study, or projects whose execution calls for cooperative action, and to transmit these to the Inter-American Central Council; (b) to ascertain the opinion of national elements on such problems or projects as may be submitted to them by the Inter-American Central Council, and to form for the purpose any necessary committees.

2. (a) To collect appropriate data regarding the institutions concerned with education, science, arts, and letters in their respective countries, and regarding the facilities afforded by these institutions to foreign professors, students, and re-

search workers; and to transmit such data to the Inter-American Central Council; (b) to receive and disseminate similar information concerning other countries; (c) to promote actively the exchange of professors, students, research workers, and cultural missions among the American republics.

3. To promote in their respective countries the study of such subjects as shall contribute an understanding of the development and culture of the other American nations.

4. To endeavor to secure the adherence of their respective countries to international agreements and international programs of intellectual cooperation.

5. To encourage national institutions and associations to enter into close relations with similar organizations in other American republics, especially in such a way as will accord with whatever program of international action may be worked out by the Inter-American Institute.

6. To cooperate in carrying out such projects as may be committed to the Inter-American Institute by future international conferences of American states.

7. In general, to serve as an instrument of contact between the intellectual elements of their respective countries and those of the other American republics.

ARTICLE 3—THE INTER-AMERICAN CENTRAL COUNCIL

(a) *Organization.*—The Inter-American Central Council shall be composed of the delegates designated by the National Councils, on the basis of one delegate for each National Council. It shall also have the technical and clerical staff that may be necessary. In order to utilize the contacts that have already been formed by the Pan American Union in the realm of intellectual cooperation, and also in order to derive advantage from the library of the latter, its postal privileges, and its other important facilities, the Division of

Intellectual Cooperation of the Union shall cooperate with the Inter-American Central Council as long as may be required by the growth of the Institute.

The Inter-American Central Council shall transmit annually to the Governing Board of the Pan American Union the program of work proposed for the following year, and shall present a report of the work accomplished during the previous year. The report and the program shall also be transmitted annually to the National Councils.

(b) *Functions.*—The functions of the Inter-American Central Council shall be:

1. (a) To examine proposals received from the National Councils regarding problems of intellectual life that call for consideration, or projects whose execution requires cooperative action, and to transmit these to the Governing Board of the Pan American Union, with recommendations; (b) to advise the National Councils of any project that may be approved by the Governing Board.

2. To obtain and disseminate appropriate information concerning institutions of education, science, arts, and let-ters in the American republics, in order to encourage the establishment of closer relations among them.

3. To appoint, in cooperation with the National Councils, inter-American committees for the purpose of conducting special investigations, and to keep in touch with inter-American institutions or commissions of a scientific and cultural character, as well as with the International Institute of Intellectual Cooperation of the League of Nations.

4. To collaborate, by the aid of the National Councils, with the organizing committees of the Pan American Scientific Congresses in the preparation of their programs, in order that these congresses may serve as a forum for the discussion of intellectual problems; and to organize, in connection with the scientific or other congresses, special meetings of accredited delegates of the National Councils for the discussion of the work of the Inter-American Institute.

5. In general, to serve as a coordinating center for the work of the National Councils for Intellectual Cooperation.

(23 *February* 1930)

## D. *The Cinema*

The extract below was taken from a resolution adopted at the International Congress of Educational and Instructional Cinematography held in Rome during the month of April 1934. The meeting was held under the auspices of the Institute of Intellectual Co-operation.

(*Bulletin of the League of Nations, Teaching,* No. 1, 1934, pp. 144-5.)

*The Congress,*

Recognizes the great importance of the problems raised by the diffusion of films among peoples of different mentalities and cultures;

Considers, that it is essential to make provisions so that the films to be distributed in different countries or regions should not exert a pernicious influence in propagating from one country to another wrong appreciations of the characteristics of different civilizations;

Considers, on the other hand, that the task of the cinema, in the face of problems of this kind, must be the promotion of the development of the culture and the conservation of the traditions of the peoples concerned; at the same time, the cinema must favour intellectual exchanges between the various peoples, and further their mutual understanding; . . .

The Congress declares that the essential object of its work is to emphasise the influence of the cinema on the moral and intellectual formation of the peoples as well as on the development of a better understanding among them.

The Congress considers that this educational function of the cinema entails a heavy responsibility on the part of the authors, producers and exhibitors of films, and more generally on any authority, group or person responsible for the diffusion of films.

The Congress considers that an entirely free and unencumbered circulation, on the largest possible scale, of educational films from one country to another remains one of the best means to reach the goal of international amity and understanding. In this connection, the Congress considers that the censorship and customs as well as the administrative regulations must consequently be drafted in such a way as not to interfere with the application of this principle.

The Congress, however, considers that suitable censorship and administrative restrictions must be put into effect in order to prevent the diffusion, by unscrupulous producers and distributors, of films likely to arouse animosity between nations.

The Congress wishes most sincerely that the Governments take in the future all possible measures to encourage the diffusion of unbiased and impartial films, and put a check to the circulation of those showing prejudice and negligence in this respect.

In order to put this recommendation into effect, the Congress proposes to the International Educational Cinematographic Institute, and more especially to its Consultative and Technical Committee working jointly with the Intellectual Co-operation Organisation and its Paris Institute, the following measures:

1. To call the attention of the Governments to the international importance of cinema and its use as a means to further international understanding. . .

2. To promote 'gentlemen's agreements' between producers and also seek their collaboration in order to encourage the production of films conceived in a spirit of impartiality, and presenting a real intellectual value, and likely to contribute to international understanding with the International Educational Cinematographic Institute.

3. To gather and classify, by means of the national committees or institutes corresponding with the International Educational Cinematographic Institute already existing or to be founded, all the cinematographic documentation capable of illustrating the material and spiritual life of the different peoples.

. . .

## E. *The Teaching of History*

Under the supervision of the League of Nations Committee on Intellectual Co-operation the following declaration was written and signed at Geneva on 2 October 1937.

(*Bulletin of the League of Nations, Teaching*, No. 4, 1937, pp. 197-8.)

The undersigned plenipotentiaries in the name of their respective Governments:

Desirous of strengthening and developing the good relations uniting them with other countries;

Convinced that those relations will be further strengthened if the younger generation in every country is given a wider knowledge of the history of other nations;

Realising the necessity of obviating the dangers that may arise through the tendentious presentation of certain historical events in school textbooks:

Declare that they agree, each for its own part, upon the following principles:

1. It is desirable that the attention of the competent authorities in every country, and of authors of school textbooks, should be drawn to the expediency:

(a) Of assigning as large a place as possible to the history of other nations;

(b) Of giving prominence, in the teaching of world history, to facts calculated to bring about a realisation of the interdependence of nations.

2. It is desirable that every Government should endeavor to ascertain by what means, more especially in connection with the choice of schoolbooks, school-children may be put on their guard against all such allegations and interpretations as might arouse unjust prejudices against other nations.

. . .

## VI. The United Nations and Intellectual Co-operation

The opening phrases of the Constitution of UNESCO are but a paraphrase of Immanuel Kant's famous statement: 'It is a mistake to think that peace is a political problem; it is a moral problem.' The Preamble later states that peace must, if it is not to fail, be founded on the intellectual and moral solidarity of mankind. But only the most optimistic can expect UNESCO to supplant the United Nations Security Council and General Assembly in the near future as the organization best equipped to solve the many present-day political and security differences between nations. Just how and when understanding between the peoples of the world can be brought about defies the most scientific inquiry today. UNESCO has, among its other tasks, to attack this very basic problem. Its program for 1948, given in Extract B, shows that it is already trying to determine the conditions that will promote understanding between nations. The program for 1948 was adopted at the Conference held in Mexico City in December 1947. It embraces a wide variety of enterprises, too wide in the opinion of many of its critics. The Constitution in Extract A, immediately below, presents the aims of UNESCO and its organizational framework.

## A. *Constitution of the United Nations Educational, Scientific and Cultural Organization*

*The Governments of the States Parties to This Constitution on Behalf of Their Peoples Declare*

that since wars begin in the minds of men, it is in the minds of men that the defences of peace must be constructed;

that ignorance of each other's ways and lives has been a common cause, through-out the history of mankind, of that suspicion and mistrust between the peoples of the world through which their differences have all too often broken into war;

that the great and terrible war which has now ended was a war made possible by the denial of the democratic principles of the dignity, equality and mutual respect of men, and by the propagation, in their place, through ignorance and prejudice, of the doctrine of the inequality of men and races;

that the wide diffusion of culture, and the education of humanity for justice and liberty and peace are indispensable to the dignity of man and constitute a sacred duty which all the nations must fulfil in a spirit of mutual assistance and concern;

that a peace based exclusively upon the political and economic arrangements of governments would not be a peace which could secure the unanimous, lasting and sincere support of the peoples of the world, and that the peace must therefore be founded, if it is not to fail, upon the intellectual and moral solidarity of mankind.

*For These Reasons,*

the States parties to this Constitution, believing in full and equal opportunities for education for all, in the unrestricted pursuit of objective truth, and in the free exchange of ideas and knowledge, are agreed and determined to develop and to increase the means of communication between their peoples and to employ these means for the purposes of mutual understanding and a truer and more perfect knowledge of each other's lives;

*In Consequence Whereof*

they do hereby create the United Nations Educational, Scientific and Cultural Organisation for the purpose of advancing, through the educational and scientific and cultural relations of the peoples of the world, the objectives of international peace and of the common welfare of mankind for which the United Nations Organisation was established and which its Charter proclaims.

## Article 1—Purposes and Functions

1. The purpose of the Organisation is to contribute to peace and security by promoting collaboration among the nations through education, science and culture in order to further universal respect for justice, for the rule of law and for the human rights and fundamental freedoms which are affirmed for the peoples of the world, without distinction of race, sex, language or religion, by the Charter of the United Nations.

2. To realise this purpose the Organisation will:

(a) collaborate in the work of advancing the mutual knowledge and understanding of peoples, through all means of mass communication and to that end recommend such international agreements as may be necessary to promote the free flow of ideas by word and image;

(b) give fresh impulse to popular education and to the spread of culture;

by collaborating with Members, at their request, in the development of educational activities;

by instituting collaboration among the nations to advance the ideal of equality of educational opportunity without regard to race, sex or any distinctions, economic or social;

by suggesting educational methods best suited to prepare the children of the world for the responsibilities of freedom;

(c) maintain, increase and diffuse knowledge;

by assuring the conservation and protection of the world's inheritance of books, works of art and monuments of history and science, and recommending to the nations concerned the necessary international conventions;

by encouraging cooperation among the nations in all branches of intellectual activity, including the international exchange of persons active in the fields of education, science and culture and the exchange of publications, objects of artistic and scientific interest and other materials of information;

by initiating methods of international cooperation calculated to give the people of all countries access to the printed and published materials produced by any of them.

3. With a view to preserving the independence, integrity and fruitful diversity of the cultures and educational systems of the States Members of this Organisation, the Organisation is prohibited from intervening in matters which are essentially within their domestic jurisdiction.

## ARTICLE 2—MEMBERSHIP

1. Membership of the United Nations Organisation shall carry with it the right to membership of the United Nations Educational, Scientific and Cultural Organisation.

2. Subject to the conditions of the agreement between this Organisation and the United Nations Organisation, approved pursuant to Article x of this Constitution, States not members of the United Nations Organisation may be admitted to membership of the Organisation, upon recommendation of the Executive Board, by a two-thirds majority vote of the General Conference.

3. Members of the Organisation which are suspended from the exercise of the rights and privileges of membership of the United Nations Organisation shall, upon the request of the latter, be suspended from the rights and privileges of this Organisation.

4. Members of the Organisation which are expelled from the United Nations Organisation shall automatically cease to be members of this Organisation.

## ARTICLE 3—ORGANS

The Organisation shall include a General Conference, an Executive Board and a Secretariat.

## ARTICLE 4—THE GENERAL CONFERENCE

### A. Composition

1. The General Conference shall consist of the representatives of the States Members of the Organisation. The Government of each Member State shall appoint not more than five delegates, who shall be selected after consultation with the National Commission, if established, or with educational, scientific and cultural bodies.

### B. Functions

2. The General Conference shall determine the policies and the main lines of work of the Organisation. It shall take decisions on programmes drawn up by the Executive Board.

3. The General Conference shall, when it deems it desirable, summon international conferences on education, the sciences and humanities and the dissemination of knowledge.

4. The General Conference shall, in adopting proposals for submission to the Member States, distinguish between recommendations and international conventions submitted for their approval. In the former case a majority vote shall suffice; in the latter case a two-thirds majority shall be required. Each of the Member States shall submit recommendations or conventions to its competent authorities within a period of one year from the close of the session of the General Conference at which they were adopted.

5. The General Conference shall advise the United Nations Organisation on the educational, scientific and cultural aspects of matters of concern to the latter, in accordance with the terms and procedure agreed upon between the appropriate authorities of the two Organisations.

6. The General Conference shall receive and consider the reports submitted periodically by Member States as provided by Article VIII.

7. The General Conference shall elect the members of the Executive Board and, on the recommendation of the Board, shall appoint the Director-General.

## C. Voting

8. Each Member State shall have one vote in the General Conference. Decisions shall be made by a simple majority except in cases in which a two-thirds majority is required by the provisions of this Constitution. A majority shall be a majority of the Members present and voting.

## D. Procedure

9. The General Conference shall meet annually in ordinary session; it may meet in extraordinary session on the call of the Executive Board. At each session the location of its next session shall be designated by the General Conference and shall vary from year to year.

10. The General Conference shall, at each session, elect a President and other officers and adopt rules of procedure.

11. The General Conference shall set up special and technical committees and such other subordinate bodies as may be necessary for its purposes.

12. The General Conference shall cause arrangements to be made for public access to meetings, subject to such regulations as it shall prescribe.

## E. Observers

13. The General Conference, on the recommendation of the Executive Board

and by a two-thirds majority may, subject to its rules of procedure, invite as observers at specified sessions of the Conference or of its commissions representatives of international organisations, such as those referred to in Article XI, paragraph 4.

## ARTICLE 5—EXECUTIVE BOARD

### A. Composition

1. The Executive Board shall consist of eighteen members elected by the General Conference from among the delegates appointed by the Member States, together with the President of the Conference who shall sit *ex officio* in an advisory capacity.

2. In electing the members of the Executive Board the General Conference shall endeavour to include persons competent in the arts, the humanities, the sciences, education and the diffusion of ideas, and qualified by their experience and capacity to fulfil the administrative and executive duties of the Board. It shall also have regard to the diversity of cultures and a balanced geographical distribution. Not more than one national of any Member State shall serve on the Board at any one time, the President of the Conference excepted.

3. The elected members of the Executive Board shall serve for a term of three years, and shall be immediately eligible for a second term, but shall not serve consecutively for more than two terms. At the first election eighteen members shall be elected of whom one-third shall retire at the end of the first year and one-third at the end of the second year, the order of retirement being determined immediately after the election by the drawing of lots. Thereafter six members shall be elected each year.

4. In the event of the death or resignation of one of its members, the Execu-

tive Board shall appoint, from among the delegates of the Member State concerned, a substitute, who shall serve until the next session of the General Conference which shall elect a member for the remainder of the term.

### B. Functions

5. The Executive Board, acting under the authority of the General Conference, shall be responsible for the execution of the programme adopted by the Conference and shall prepare its agenda and programme of work.

6. The Executive Board shall recommend to the General Conference the admission of new Members to the Organisation.

7. Subject to decisions of the General Conference, the Executive Board shall adopt its own rules of procedure. It shall elect its officers from among its members.

8. The Executive Board shall meet in regular session at least twice a year and may meet in special session if convoked by the Chairman on his own initiative or upon the request of six members of the Board.

9. The Chairman of the Executive Board shall present to the General Conference, with or without comment, the annual report of the Director-General on the activities of the Organisation, which shall have been previously submitted to the Board.

10. The Executive Board shall make all necessary arrangements to consult the representatives of international organisations or qualified persons concerned with questions within its competence.

11. The members of the Executive Board shall exercise the powers delegated to them by the General Conference on behalf of the Conference as a whole and not as representatives of their respective Governments.

### ARTICLE 6—SECRETARIAT

1. The Secretariat shall consist of a Director-General and such staff as may be required.

2. The Director-General shall be nominated by the Executive Board and appointed by the General Conference for a period of six years, under such conditions as the Conference may approve, and shall be eligible for re-appointment. He shall be the chief administrative officer of the Organisation.

3. The Director-General, or a deputy designated by him, shall participate, without the right to vote, in all meetings of the General Conference, of the Executive Board, and of the committees of the Organisation. He shall formulate proposals for appropriate action by the Conference and the Board.

4. The Director-General shall appoint the staff of the Secretariat in accordance with staff regulations to be approved by the General Conference. Subject to the paramount consideration of securing the highest standards of integrity, efficiency and technical competence, appointment to the staff shall be on as wide a geographical basis as possible.

5. The responsibilities of the Director-General and of the staff shall be exclusively international in character. In the discharge of their duties they shall not seek or receive instructions from any government or from any authority external to the Organisation. They shall refrain from any action which might prejudice their position as international officials. Each State Member of the Organisation undertakes to respect the international character of the responsibilities of the Director-General and the staff, and not to seek to influence them in the discharge of their duties.

6. Nothing in this Article shall preclude the Organisation from entering

into special arrangements within the United Nations Organisation for common services and staff and for the interchange of personnel.

## ARTICLE 7—NATIONAL CO-OPERATING BODIES

1. Each Member State shall make such arrangements as suit its particular conditions for the purpose of associating its principal bodies interested in educational, scientific and cultural matters with the work of the Organisation, preferably by the formation of a National Commission broadly representative of the Government and such bodies.

2. National Commissions or national co-operating bodies, where they exist, shall act in an advisory capacity to their respective delegations to the General Conference and to their Governments in matters relating to the Organisation and shall function as agencies of liaison in all matters of interest to it.

3. The Organisation may, on the request of a Member State, delegate, either temporarily or permanently, a member of its Secretariat to serve on the National Commission of that State, in order to assist in the development of its work.

## ARTICLE 8—REPORTS BY MEMBER STATES

Each Member State shall report periodically to the Organisation, in a manner to be determined by the General Conference, on its laws, regulations and statistics relating to educational, scientific and cultural life and institutions, and on the action taken upon the recommendations and conventions referred to in Article IV, paragraph 4.

## ARTICLE 9—BUDGET

1. The budget shall be administered by the Organisation.

2. The General Conference shall approve and give final effect to the budget and to the apportionment of financial responsibility among the States Members of the Organisation subject to such arrangement with the United Nations as may be provided in the agreement to be entered into pursuant to Article x.

3. The Director-General, with the approval of the Executive Board, may receive gifts, bequests, and subventions directly from governments, public and private institutions, associations and private persons.

. . .

# B. *The Program of UNESCO*, 1948

(UNESCO at Mexico City, Final Report, published by the Department of State.)

## RECONSTRUCTION

The General Conference recommends that National Committees of non-governmental organizations for educational, scientific and cultural reconstruction be formed in all Member States to assist in rebuilding the means of learning and culture in war-devastated countries. . .

*Information on Needs and Campaign Aids*—The Director-General is instructed:

To advise both governmental and non-governmental contributors concerning priorities of need for books and other materials of the devastated countries.

To seek to obtain from donor organizations full reports upon their activities.

To provide on a larger scale than in 1947 services needed to make campaigns more effective, especially the preparation of selective analyses of the needs of the war-devastated countries, including the new Member States of UNESCO, and the production of materials suitable for national campaigns, particularly films and illustrated pamphlets.

*Work of Member States*—The General Conference recommends to Member States the urgent importance of arranging for duty-free entrance of contributed educational material.

*Emergency Action by UNESCO*—The Director-General is instructed to purchase and distribute, within the limits of allocated funds, books, educational material, scientific and technical equipment.

The Executive Board is instructed to advise the Director-General in the allocation of these supplies among war-devastated countries.

*Meeting Technical Needs*—In order to promote the implementation of the recommendations made in the first report of the Commission on Technical Needs, the Director-General is instructed:

To explore the possibility of launching an appeal to public and private bodies and individuals to contribute to a fund to help war-devastated countries to reconstruct their media of mass communication, and launch such an appeal if he is satisfied that it is likely to be successful. . .

#### COMMUNICATION

*Exchange of Persons*—The Director-General is instructed:

To request the co-operation of Member States in the preparation of reports on the activities of governmental and non-governmental organizations affecting the international movement of persons.

To collect, compile, analyse and publish this and other relevant material.

To administer in collaboration with national commissions or appropriate bodies in the Member States the fellowships already authorized out of UNESCO's 1947 funds, and in addition ten new fellowships (or the equivalent expenditure for travel grants) to be awarded in exceptional cases where UNESCO's purposes are clearly involved and where no other funds are available.

To study, in collaboration with the relevant organs of the UN, the barriers which impede the interchange of persons between and among nations and to take such measures as are appropriate and practicable to remove these barriers.

To study the possibility of encouraging the interchange of persons through bilateral or multilateral conventions among Member States.

*Mass Communications*—The Director-General is instructed:

To continue and expand the enquiry initiated in 1947 through the Commission on Technical Needs in Mass Communications in order to cover a number of countries in South and Central America, India, Burma, Malaya, Siam, Indonesia and some further countries in Europe; and to publish the reports of the Commission.

To collect and analyse on a continuing basis objective information on obstacles to the free flow of information. . .

*Radio*—In the development of the radio work of the Organization, the Director-General is instructed:

To co-operate in the operation of a United Nations world radio network if one is established, by accepting membership of the proposed Radio Board which will govern its programme policies and by participating in the programming of educational, scientific and cultural material for the Network, provided that in the early stages such participation must be of limited extent.

To re-examine the possibility and advisability of establishing a UNESCO World Radio Network if a United Nations network is not established. . .

*Films*—In the development of the film work of the production unit referred to above, the Director-General is instructed:

To promote the production of international series of films on the special achievements of a number of nations in the fields of education, science and culture, and the production of films on subjects of a multi-national character in the

fields of UNESCO's interest by co-operative action between groups of countries
concerned with each theme.

In the development of the work of the
production unit referred to above, the
Director-General is instructed to promote
the simultaneous presentation, by press,
film and radio groups in a number of
countries, of four major themes of world
significance within the field of UNESCO's
interests.

The Director-General is instructed to
encourage the creation of an International Institute of the Press and Information.

*Libraries*—The Director-General is instructed to negotiate with a European library school to conduct a summer school
for working librarians, in co-operation
with the International Federation of Library Associations, for discussion of outstanding problems of public library development; and to aid the conduct of
such a summer school by the provision of
staff, consultants or financial grants.

*Bibliographic Work*—The Director-
General is instructed:

As a basis for the co-ordination of bibliographic activities, to carry on a survey
of bibliographic services jointly with the
Library of Congress of the United States
and to seek the active co-operation of
other national libraries in the development of the survey. . .

*Books*—The Director-General is instructed to:

Explore all possible means of encouraging the inexpensive production of
books, periodicals, and teaching materials in the fields of UNESCO's interests.

Continue the exploration, and if possible begin the experimental application,
of an international book coupon scheme
or other devices to permit institutions and
individuals in 'soft' currency countries to
buy books and periodicals from 'hard'
currency countries.

*Publications*—UNESCO will in 1948 undertake the publication of a volume of
essays on the philosophical principles of
human rights produced as a result of the
philosophic consultation undertaken by
UNESCO in 1947. . .

### EDUCATION

The Director-General is urged to combine under a single administrative head
the activities of the Organization in Fundamental Education and other forms of
Education, for the purposes of mutual
strengthening of these related activities
and of closer co-ordination of educational
activities with all aspects of UNESCO's
program.

*Priority Projects*—In carrying out
UNESCO's program in Education, the
Director-General will give first and equal
priority in the educational program to the
proposals formulated at the Second Session of the General Conference respecting: (1) Fundamental Education; (2)
Adult Education; (3) Work with Universities; (4) Educational Seminars; (5) Enquiry into Education for International
Understanding in Primary and Secondary
Schools of Member States, including the
contests for young people; (6) Improvement of Textbooks and Teaching Materials; and, (7) Consultative Educational
Missions to such Member States as request them.

*Fundamental Education*—The Director-
General is instructed:

To encourage Member States to fulfill
the obligations of establishing a minimum Fundamental Education for all
their people, in conformity with the
spirit of Article 1, paragraph 2 (b) of
UNESCO's Constitution; among these
obligations would be the establishment,
within the shortest possible time of universal free and compulsory primary education and the essential minimum education for adults.

To regard as of primary importance
UNESCO's functions as a clearing house

of information on Fundamental Education. . .

*Adult Education*—The Director-General is instructed:

To collect and disseminate information on new techniques and methods in adult education, and in collaboration with adult education organizations, leaders and persons prominent in adult education, to produce materials on international affairs suitable for adaptation and extensive use by adult study groups. A Conference for leaders and workers in adult education for international understanding shall be convened when sufficient information is available, if possible in 1948.

*Work with Universities*—The Director-General is instructed to call together a meeting of representatives of universities:

To consider plans for the development of an international association of universities.

To consider the problem of equivalence of degrees utilizing data which has been requested by UNESCO in 1947 from international associations concerned.

To study the possibility of organizing in certain universities throughout the world, international departments consisting of scholars, professors, and educators from foreign countries.

*Educational Seminars*—The Director-General is instructed:

To arrange for the conduct, in 1948, of at least three Seminars in Education. Each shall be held in a different region but with all Member States invited to participate in all seminars. UNESCO should bear the administrative expenses and the cost of board and lodging of the participants. The Seminars should deal with selected aspects of the total range of education. Recommended topics are: (1) Education of teachers; (2) Education of pre-adolescent children; (3) Education through youth organizations; and (4) In collaboration with the United Nations,

education about the United Nations and its Specialized Agencies. . .

*Teaching of International Understanding in Schools*—The Director-General is instructed:

To confine the Enquiry on Education for International Understanding during 1948 to teaching regarding the United Nations and its Specialized Agencies, and to carry on this work in close cooperation with the United Nations and other Specialized Agencies.

To sponsor in 1948 two competitions for young persons in order to stimulate wide public interest in the work of UNESCO. . .

## CULTURAL INTERCHANGE

*Arts and Letters*—The Director-General is instructed to:

Continue to support by technical advice the creation of an International Theatre Institute, independent of UNESCO, and to provide a limited secretariat for it during its formative stage.

Make preliminary enquiries for the establishment of an International Music Institute and prepare proposals for furthering such a project for submission to the Third Session of the General Conference in 1948.

Extend the scope of the International Pool of Literature, for the supply to journals and reviews of published and unpublished material within UNESCO's sphere of interest.

*Reproductions in Art and Music*—The Director-General is instructed:

To secure from appropriate agencies in all Member States for international distribution lists of the available fine colour reproductions of works of art by their national artists.

To draw up, in collaboration with experts selected with the assistance of the International Council of Museums, a list of available high quality colour reproductions designed to illustrate the most important phases and movements in art. . .

*Translations of Great Books*—The Director-General is instructed, in continuation of the work of the Conference of Allied Ministers of Education, and in response to the invitation of the Economic and Social Council of the United Nations, to formulate a plan for the translation of classics, for submission to the Council by 1 June 1948. . .

### HUMAN AND SOCIAL RELATIONS

*Tensions Affecting International Understanding*—The Director-General is instructed to promote:

Enquiries into the distinctive character of the various national cultures, ideals, and legal systems, with the aim of stimulating the sympathy and respect of nations for each other's ideals and aspirations and the appreciation of national problems.

Enquiries into the conceptions which the people of one nation entertain of its own and of other nations.

Enquiries into modern techniques which have been developed in education, political science, philosophy and psychology for changing mental attitudes and for revealing the processes and forces involved when human minds are in conflict.

An enquiry into the influences throughout life which predispose towards international understanding on the one hand and aggressive nationalism on the other.

The preparation of a Source Book describing the work already under way in Member States in the study of tensions that arise from technological improvements and the resulting shift of populations. Before this is undertaken, information should be obtained about the intentions of the Economic and Social Council in this matter. . .

*Humanistic Aspects of Culture*—The Director-General is instructed to address to scholars and experts of the Member States of UNESCO a series of questions concerning the idea held by a country, or by a group within a country, of its own culture and the relations of that culture with other cultures, individually or as a whole. Also, to submit the results of this enquiry to a meeting of experts called by UNESCO to discuss them and to recommend the measures for dissemination to be taken subsequently.

*Methods in Political Science*—The Director-General is instructed to promote a study of the subject matter and problems treated by political scientists of various countries in recent research materials, the various types of approach and emphasis, the methods, techniques and terminology employed. . .

### NATURAL SCIENCES

*Field Science Co-operation Offices*—The Director-General is instructed to maintain Field Science Co-operation Offices in the Middle East, the Far East, and Latin America and to establish an Office in South Asia in 1948, as undertakings of the highest priority within the Natural Sciences program.

*Latin-American Conference*—The Director-General is instructed to convene a Panel of Experts in Latin America to advise UNESCO as to the best way in which the development of science in Latin America may be assisted in the future. . .

*High Altitude Stations*—The Director-General is instructed to convene a conference in Paris of expert delegates from Member States, appropriate international organizations and Specialized Agencies of the United Nations interested in the establishment and maintenance of high altitude stations for the study of the effects of high altitudes on life and of physical phenomena observable only at high altitudes, for the purpose of making recommendations to UNESCO and to the United Nations concerning international stations of this kind. . .